How Children Learn

AN EDUCATIONAL PSYCHOLOGY

How Children Learn

AN EDUCATIONAL PSYCHOLOGY

by Arden N. Frandsen

DEPARTMENT OF PSYCHOLOGY
UTAH STATE AGRICULTURAL COLLEGE

McGRAW-HILL BOOK COMPANY, INC.

NEW YORK   TORONTO   LONDON   1957

HOW CHILDREN LEARN: AN EDUCATIONAL PSYCHOLOGY

Library of Congress Catalog Card Number 56-11712

III

THE MAPLE PRESS COMPANY, YORK, PA.

To Julia
whose inspiring zest in learning and
creative interests should characterize
the development of all children

Editor's Introduction

One of the most serious charges that some professors of education are currently making against themselves is that they have been drifting away from their supporting sciences for thirty years. Instead of keeping in close touch with research workers in their supporting fields, informing them of educational problems that require basic scientific investigation, and submitting their research findings to the test of field practice, the professional educators have too often wandered into theoretical and methodological byways, as unhampered by scientific reality as were their educational forebears of the nineteenth century.

This drift is particularly embarrassing with respect to psychology, the primary supporting science of education. It is not easy to assess the blame for this situation, and it may not be very important to do so. It is enough to recognize that it exists and to seek a means of remedying it as promptly and effectively as possible.

Professor Frandsen has made a brilliant contribution to the improvement of this situation. He has written this book with the intent of helping students close the gap between education and its chief supporting science. He has developed an integrated theory of learning and applied it to the practical job of teaching children in a modern elementary school. He has done this difficult task well, marshaling theories with precision, presenting research data in direct and simple terms, and making educational applications with the easy confidence that comes only from fruitful experience in the schools.

The editor is convinced that this book is a landmark in education-textbook writing. He is proud to be associated with the author's achievement.

HAROLD BENJAMIN
*George Peabody College
for Teachers*

McGRAW-HILL SERIES IN EDUCATION
Harold Benjamin, *Consulting Editor*

Preface

This book applies the general principles of educational psychology specifically to the problems of understanding and teaching elementary school children. The accelerating production of scientific literature in child psychology and elementary education during the present century has made feasible an educational psychology directed especially to the elementary level. Indeed, as this book itself demonstrates, even a selective but comprehensive recognition of the accumulated pertinent literature is extensive enough to make up a separate volume. Moreover, by focusing attention mainly on elementary school children, educational psychology can be taught for more effective applications to teaching. Many of the specific experiments and school practices cited in support of the psychological principles discussed, since they are based mainly on observations of children, suggest directly specific and desirable teaching applications. Therefore, in writing this educational psychology especially for elementary teachers, the author has attempted to develop an organized and interrelated set of scientific principles which will have maximum practical value to teachers in their guidance of children's learning. To facilitate this purpose, the sequence of chapters is organized around the major functions of teaching.

These major functions are fivefold. First, the teacher needs to achieve a working concept of the aims of the elementary school. What are the objectives toward which elementary school children should strive? Having tentatively answered this question or having found an approach toward answering it, the teacher determines next the kinds of learning activities or curriculum experiences by which these objectives may best be attained. These two teaching functions are introduced and emphasized in Chapter 1; but they are developed, elaborated, and interrelated to other teaching functions in appropriate places throughout the book.

Since pupils attain educational objectives through their learning activities, the third major function of teaching is to provide the conditions for effective learning. This is the central function of teaching, and the psychological principles applied to it give the entire book a systematic and sustained organization. From a comprehensive study of learning theories an integrated theory of learning is developed in Chapter 2. From this theory of learning there are in turn derived seven essential conditions of effective learning. Each of the following seven chapters is devoted to citing the experimental literature in support of one of these conditions of learning and to suggesting applications of it to the teaching and guidance of children. The conditions considered in succession are sufficient maturity and an appropriate pattern of abilities; teacher-guidance of learning activities; the role of practice; trial and checking to confirm or revise concepts or skills (a central condition of learning); transfer of training; motivation of learning; and promoting confidence and avoiding emotional disturbances connected with learning. In concluding consideration of this teaching function, Chapter 10 applies the developed principles as an organized whole in analyzing illustrations of effective teaching. In Chapter 11 a theory of remembering and the principles for retaining worthwhile learnings are developed.

A fourth major function of teaching is the recognition of and provision for the marked individual differences among school children, both interindividual and intraindividual variations, which give each child a unique pattern of abilities. Chapter 12 develops concepts and procedures for appraising individual differences in abilities. Chapter 13 presents and evaluates a comprehensive school program for providing education suited to each child's unique pattern of abilities and needs.

Finally, having decided upon worthwhile and attainable goals for elementary school children, having selected and organized an appropriate curriculum, having created the conditions for effective learning, and having made adequate provisions for individual differences both in curriculum and methods of teaching, the teacher will need to evaluate periodically or continuously children's progress toward their developmental goals. Chapter 14 on Appraising School Achievement implements this fifth teaching function. It presents a variety of evaluation and measurement principles and techniques for diagnosing and appraising achievement of a comprehensive scope of elementary school objectives. These appraisal devices provide data for teacher and pupil guidance at every stage of learning. Thus they facilitate continuous pupil learning and indirectly contribute to every other teaching function.

Although child psychology and development concepts find extensive application throughout this book, it is intended for a course complementing rather than supplanting the course in child psychology and development which is becoming popular in elementary education. These courses in child psychology and in the educational psychology of elementary teaching should together provide effectively for the minimum contributions of psychology to the elementary teacher's training.

Although some concepts in the book, especially in the sections on learning, on psychological and educational experimentation, and on statistical interpretations of test scores, may challenge students, it is believed that sufficient care has been taken in the development of these concepts so that they can be managed by upper-division undergraduate students in elementary education. On the other hand, for teachers who have taken as undergraduates the usual general course in educational psychology, this book is sufficiently intensive in its treatment of topics to be suitable for graduate study in elementary education, either for campus or for in-service training courses.

As the numerous references listed at the ends of the chapters and cited or quoted in the text show, many writers and publishers have contributed to this book. For permission to use these rich sources of ideas I am very grateful. For their generous contributions of pictures to illustrate learning activities, I am happy to acknowledge my indebtedness to the Adams Elementary School in Logan, Utah; to the Central, Lincoln, and McKinley Elementary Schools in Box Elder County, Utah; to the Dilworth and Emerson Elementary Schools in Salt Lake City; to the teacher-training elementary schools at the University of Michigan, the University of Minnesota, the University of Utah, and the Utah State Agricultural College; to the McGraw-Hill Text-Film Department, and especially to the children in the pictures.

I appreciate especially my working relationship with the consulting editor, Dr. Harold Benjamin, whose constructive criticism and many specific suggestions have greatly improved my writing efforts. Finally, I express here my thanks to Miss Marilyn Cole for her especial care in typing the manuscript, to Mrs. Ida Marie Logan for her help in securing interlibrary loans, and to the Utah State Agricultural College for providing this valued assistance.

Acknowledgments to Publishers

From the more extensive lists in the bibliographies of publications merely cited or quoted only very briefly, I am pleased to express my appreciation for permissions to reproduce figures or longer quotations from the following sources: publications of the American Council on Education, the American Psychological Association, Appleton-Century-Crofts, Inc., California Test Bureau, The Dryden Press, Inc., Educational Test Bureau of Educational Publishers, Inc., The Free Press, Ginn & Company, Harcourt, Brace and Company, Inc., Harper & Brothers, D. C. Heath and Company, Houghton Mifflin Company, The Journal Press, Longmans, Green & Company, Inc., The Macmillan Company, McGraw-Hill Book Company, Inc., National

Council of Teachers of Mathematics, National Education Association of the United States, W. W. Norton & Company, The Odyssey Press, Inc., The Palmer Company Publishers, Prentice-Hall, Inc., The Psychological Corporation, Public School Publishing Company, Rinehart & Company, Inc., The Ronald Press Company, Russel Sage Foundation, W. B. Saunders Company, Science Research Associates, Scott, Foresman and Company, United States Government Printing Office, John Wiley & Sons, World Book Company; articles in *The Annals of the American Academy of Political and Social Sciences, American Journal of Mental Deficiency, American Journal of Orthopsychiatry, American Journal of Psychology, American Psychologist, The Arithmetic Teacher, British Journal of Psychology, Child Development, Childhood Education, Child Study, Education, Educational Leadership, Educational Outlook, Elementary School Journal, Harvard Educational Review, Journal of Abnormal and Social Psychology, Journal of Consulting Psychology, Journal of Counseling Psychology, Journal of Educational Psychology, Journal of Experimental Education, Journal of Experimental Psychology, Journal of Educational Research, Journal of General Psychology, Journal of Genetic Psychology, Journal of Personality, National Education Association Journal, The Nervous Child, Progressive Education, Psychological Review, Quarterly Journal of Speech, Research Quarterly of the American Association of Health, Physical Education, and Recreation, School and Society, The School Executive, The School Review, Training School Bulletin, Understanding the Child;* university publications of Cambridge University Press, University of Chicago Press, Iowa Child Welfare Research Station, University of the State of New York, Stanford University Press, Bureau of Publications of Teachers College, Yale University Press; and from yearbooks of the American Association of School Administrators, National Council of Teachers of Mathematics, and the National Society for the Study of Education. Specific acknowledgments both to the authors and publishers of these materials are made at appropriate places in the text, as parenthetical references keyed to the bibliographies.

ARDEN N. FRANDSEN

Contents

Chapter 1

Aims and Curriculum of the Elementary School

W HAT ARE the aims of elementary education? What should the pupils and teacher in an elementary classroom be doing? What general guides can they follow? These are broad philosophical questions which every teacher or prospective teacher of elementary school children needs to ask and to try to answer.

Sometimes teachers are confronted with narrowly conceived answers. A newspaper reporter who interviewed some of the merchants on "Main Street" for his answers mentioned only proficiency in reading, arithmetic, penmanship, and spelling—these potential employers especially wanted better spelling. It may often seem, however, that the elementary school is expected to accomplish too much for young children. Objectives which have been suggested are proficiency in the three R's, transmission of the social heritage, efficiency in problem solving, development of creative talents, self-realization, preparation for democratic living, development of well-adjusted personalities, and cultivation of ethical character.

Rousseau, on the other hand, while expecting "natural development" to produce happy, creative individuals, proposed a greatly restricted elementary school curriculum. As a philosopher, biased by his conflict with his own society, he suggested [20, p. 126]:

If you could be content to do nothing yourself, and could prevent anything being done by others; if you could bring up your pupil healthy and robust to the age of twelve years, without his being able to distinguish his right hand from his left, the eyes of his understanding would be open to reason at your first lesson; void of habit and prejudice, his passions would not operate against your endeavors, and he would become, under proper instructions, the wisest of men. It is thus, by attempting nothing in the beginning, you might produce a prodigy of education.

More thoroughly considered answers to our questions on the aims and curriculum of the elementary school come from many sources. They come from philosophers and psychologists, from statesmen and social scientists, from parents and educators, and, above all, from the children themselves. All these people have notions concerning the life values to be sought through education, and the wise teacher should consider them all.

General Aims of Education

Education is concerned both with the development of the individual and with the welfare of his society. For the individual, education should provide opportunities for maximum development of his talents and his potentialities for happiness. In doing this, it should "prepare every member to contribute to the fullest to the welfare of his society" [15]. In our democratic society [15, p. 11],

Each individual should have the kind and amount of education which will (a) make him most useful to himself and to others according to the principles of American democracy, (b) lead him to understand the principles and goals of our democratic way of life so that he may have a basis for his beliefs and loyalties, (c) help him to be an active and discerning participant in local, state, and national concerns so that this country may have exemplary leadership in its governmental affairs, (d) stimulate him to contribute all he can to the development and preservation of peaceful, cooperative, and equitable world relations, and (e) help him to recognize and understand the operation of natural laws in his environment.

In another joint formulation [16] of general educational objectives, which gives consideration to the individual in his society, four broad aims are defined: (1) The individual should achieve through education "self-realization," which includes development of an inquiring mind; skills for effective communication; knowledge for maintaining, protecting, and improving his health; satisfying intellectual, recreational, and aesthetic interests and skills; and responsible character. (2) The individual should achieve comfortable, effective, and happy social relationships in his family, with friends, and at work and play with others. He should develop respect for humanity in general. (3) He should attain economic efficiency by becoming an intelligent consumer and by preparing for efficient work performance in a field suited to his talents and interests and to the needs of his society. (4) He should develop civic responsibility, which involves a sense of social justice, understanding of one's society, participation as a citizen, tolerance, contributions to conservation, and devotion to the ideals of democracy.

In formulating these objectives it is apparent that the authors, as social scientists and philosophers, have considered the needs of society. Since human beings are, of course, social creatures and live only in society, their education needs to be adapted to the nature and needs of their society. But the formulation of aims should also be made with awareness of the nature of the child to be educated—his general capacity, his talents and other characteristics, his needs and interests, the sequential patterns of his development, and how he learns. Here the educational psychologist should make important contributions [21]. Parents and teachers, because of their intimate relationships with children and because of their direct responsibilities in teaching, are in the most strategic positions for translating general aims into specific criteria for the selection and guidance of curriculum activities. Every teacher, besides studying the aims already formulated and being formulated for the children he teaches, has an opportunity to make creative and constructive contributions to the continuous reformulation of such aims. It is important that parents also cooperate in this role, because they also provide curriculum experiences toward attaining the aims of the elementary school.

General Aims for Elementary School Children

Speaking for parents, Lee and Lee [14, p. 4] say that during the elementary school years we want our child:

To get along well in work and play with his playmates and with older people.
To be able to speak clearly and correctly.
To be able to start a job and keep at it until it is finished.
To be able to do his share, either of work or play.
To have wide interests in art, music, science, and the world around him.
To be fairly capable of locating what he wants to know.
To have control over some working tools such as being able to use numbers, dictionaries, and maps.
To be able to write clearly.
To be able to read well.
To have a wide outlook.
To have some understanding of the processes by which man lives on this world.
To be well and strong.
To be decent, etc.

Teachers and prospective teachers in courses in educational psychology usually accept this list as indicating worthwhile and attainable goals. These teachers have recognized, of course, that many of the goals are not attained completely during the elementary school years, but that significant progress toward them is made, the degree of progress varying widely among individual children. Teachers consider the list a useful general guide in selecting curriculum experiences and in directing learning activities. When encouraged to think about it constructively and critically, drawing upon both their study and experience, they have offered corrections, elaborations, and additions to it.

You will note that the list includes both traditional subject matter and more general child development goals. Proficiency in the school subjects, such as reading, writing, language, spelling, arithmetic, history, geography, science, arts, and crafts is recognized as needed both for self-realization and for effective living in our society. However, with "getting along well in work and play with his playmates and older people" listed first, the importance of sensitive, comfortable, responsible, and constructive social participation is also implied.

"Being able to start a job and keep at it until it is finished" may be generalized to imply a generally confident, habitual, and efficient problem-solving approach to tasks. This would include efficient habits of study and work, interest in learning how to learn, intellectual curiosity, constructive and critical thinking, tolerance of some frustration in problem solving, and confidence in and reliance on learning and problem solving as approaches to life problems.

In addition to recognizing the value of "wide *interests* in art, music, science, and the world about him," the teacher will also want to include encouragement of the development of *creative skills* in art, music, dancing, crafts, literature, and science. And besides the development of general interests and creative skills in these varied areas of knowledge, art, and science, he will suggest for each child the discovery and cultivation of his *special* interests and abilities.

He will want to make it explicit that "being well and strong" refers to both physical and emotional health.

He will recognize that "being decent," though perhaps implying only restraint, is intended to suggest the importance of training for love, trust, and ethical relations with other people—for positive, responsible, constructive, moral citizenship. In our society especially there should be an emphasis on appreciation of, understanding of, and effective and constructive participation in democratic ways of living.

Such statements of the general objectives of the elementary school, of which several different formulations can be found [9, pp. 4–13], provide general guidance to a teacher in planning curricula, specific units, and methods of teaching.

It is also helpful to reduce these general objectives to more specific goals of knowledge, understandings, skills, interests, attitudes, and habits for the various areas of the curriculum. This tremendous task, in which each teacher participates daily, has been done most thoroughly on a general level by a committee of elementary education and child development specialists, and an integrated report of their study has been published by Kearney [12].

Specific Elementary School Objectives

Kearney's report includes nearly 2,000 specific objectives contributed by 13 specialists in elementary education and child development and evaluated as appropriate by 10 successful classroom teachers and supervisors. Beside being guided by the general objectives of elementary education, these specialists tried especially to formulate objectives which are attainable and observable, and thus susceptible to measurement and evaluation.

To provide a frame for achieving an organized conception of these objectives, Kearney has classified them into nine curriculum areas [12, p. 40] in which children develop continuously throughout the school periods considered. The areas are: (1) physical development, health, and body care—including individual health, elementary aspects of public health, safety, physical education, grooming, and understanding of growth; (2) individual social and emotional development—including mental health, emotional stability, growth of personality, and self-understanding and -evaluation; (3) ethical behavior, standards, and values—including observance of moral and civil laws, observance of the customs and mores of the culture, and the development of such characteristics as sportsmanship, kindliness, and helpfulness; (4) social relations, a category which grows out of the two preceding, and "is devoted to the individual as a person in his personal-social relations with others, when he has to consider the needs, interests, motives, convictions, and ideals of others with whom he associates in home, community, and place of work"; (5) the social world, which considers the behavior of the child in relation to the broader social setting of community, state, and nation—and includes geography, civics, economics, government, and the traditional American way of life; (6) the natural environment, as revealed by the physical and biological sciences—which emphasize learning to think scientifically and the use of scientific methods both by scientists and for solving problems in everyday living; (7) aesthetic development—including both appreciation and expression in art, music, crafts, and other creative activities; (8) communication—including understanding and constructive uses of and skills in reading, writing, composition, correct usage, spelling, punctuation, speaking, and listening; and (9) quantitative relationships, which for the elementary school are mainly arithmetic—including understanding our number system and how it is widely used in solving quantitative problems in society, and development of problem-solving skills.

Within each of these broad and interrelated categories, objectives are further classified as indicative of four "types of behavioral change," including (A) knowledge and understandings, (B) skills and competencies, (C) attitudes and interests or motives, and (D) action patterns which "refer to broad generalized ways of behaving, such as ways of responding to problem situations through the union of intelligence with good working habits and scientific methods of thinking."

As an illustration of these specific objectives, those for "physical development, health, and body care" are adapted and abbreviated below [12, pp. 52–57]:

1. *Physical development, health, and body care*

A. Knowledge and understandings. For the primary period, the child learns the values of pure air, good food, proper exercise, clean hands, brushing the teeth, good health habits, adequate sleep, preventive medication. He understands how infections are spread. And he learns the need for safety practices in crossing streets, using fire, handling tools, strange animals, and using unknown contents of bottles.

For the intermediate period, in addition to continued attention to primary period goals, the child acquires understanding of the need for community sanitation and health safeguards, how to prevent fires, simple rules for preventing spread of infections, and means of preserving personal health. He acquires knowledge of individual differences in development, of the rapid growth in adolescence, and of games and recreation for his age. He learns about the food combinations for a wholesome meal, the basic principles of first aid, and how to handle home and school appliances safely.

B. Skills and competencies. For the primary period, the child acquires skills in play involving skipping, hopping on one foot, climbing, descending, jumping, jumping rope, suspending from a bar, running, performing stunts appropriate for his age, throwing and catching a softball, skipping to music in unison with others. He learns how to build boats and houses of blocks. He acquires skills in handling pencils, paint brushes, hammer, saw, screw driver, broom, mop, dust brush, dust cloth. He learns the skills appropriate to caring for hair, teeth, nails and skin and for dressing himself and eating without undue spilling. And he learns such safety skills as hanging on tight when climbing.

The added skills and competencies for the intermediate period are in social groups and games, folk dancing with figures and sets and a variety of rhythmic steps, and beginning skill in social dancing, both group and individual games, and popular sports. The child acquires the skills for personal grooming—combing and brushing hair, tying sashes and neckties, manicuring and so on. Girls acquire increasing motor coordination and dexterity in sewing and handling cooking utensils. Boys acquire skills in using hammer, saw, screw driver, plane, square, chisel, brace and bit. And both boys and girls acquire camp skills—making beds, building fires; craft skills—ceramics, metalwork, leatherwork, wood and soap carving; and hobby skills—airplane and boat models, erector sets, art kits.

C. Attitudes and interests. In the primary period, the child develops interest in his own growth and development, acceptance of his own physical and intellectual limitations, eagerness without fear in learning and trying out new games, and generalized eagerness to learn about his adjustment to life around him.

Further attitudes and interests for the intermediate period are approval of health and safety rules, enjoyment of active games, interest in and acceptance of bodily changes and sex development, desire to be clean and attractive, and eagerness to be creative.

D. Action patterns. For the primary period, the child acquires habits of washing hands before eating and after going to the toilet, of attending to personal cleanliness, of covering nose and mouth with handkerchief when sneezing or coughing, of keeping hands and objects out of mouth, of using only own towels, toothbrush, and other personal articles. He makes habitual engaging in active play, eating wholesome food, chewing it well, and accepting it in some variety, getting adequate sleep, resting when tired, and engaging in quiet activities after eating. He learns to avoid contact with other people when he or they have communicable diseases, to have no fear of doctor, dentist, or nurse. He shows concern for proper room temperature, good light, and safety conditions where playing or working. He learns safety practices with fire, tools, sharp objects, matches, traffic, bicycles, and public vehicles.

For the intermediate period, he acquires such additional action patterns as being responsible for health and safety of self and others at play and work, for persistence in practice to improve game and work skills, for participating in both active and sedentary recreation, and for eating some basic foods each day.

For general orientation the general aims are sufficient; but for guidance in day-to-day curriculum planning, such specific statements of objectives as the above are desirable. Perhaps before giving attention to the curriculum experiences for achieving them, Kearney's entire list [12] should be scanned.

Curriculum

Having achieved a working concept of the general and specific objectives of the elementary school, the teacher's next function is the provision of a curriculum through which the objectives can be attained. The curriculum includes all the learning experiences from which the desired understandings, skills, attitudes and interests, and action patterns are to be achieved. The content of such a curriculum is partially implied in the foregoing statement of aims, which includes both subject-matter and personal-and-social-development objectives.

Elementary School Subjects. The school subjects which became a part of the curriculum in the colonial period of American education and which have been expanded with its history are still justified by modern objectives. Both for self-realization and for his role in democratic society, the child needs effectiveness and enjoyment in communication activities, including reading, oral and written expression, listening, handwriting, and spelling. He needs arithmetic understanding and skills in computing and problem solving for many personal and social functions. To understand and to participate effectively in his social world, he needs organized concepts from history, geography, civics, sociology, economics, vocations, and biography—all of which contribute to the social studies of the elementary school curriculum. In order to understand his natural environment, he needs to know something of the physical and biological sciences, including nature study, plants, animals, the earth, astronomy, agriculture, industry, the achievements of science, and the scientific method of problem solving. Interests and creative expression in art, sculpture, crafts, music, literature, creative writing, and rhythm and varied recreational activities will contribute to both his aesthetic development and his effectiveness in several other life activities. Study of health, physical development, and body care are essential to self-realization and to effectiveness as a citizen.

Personal-Social Experiences. Several important objectives concerned with social and emotional development; the development of ethical behavior and ideals; the achievement of secure, effective, and happy social relations; and the development of self-understanding, feelings of personal worth, and self-confidence, are not directly related to specific subject-matter experiences. All the child's experiences, however, both in school subjects and in group-living experiences, contribute to these objectives. He achieves an adequate self-concept and self-understanding from provisions for discovery and development of his individual talents, interests, and creative abilities in a wide variety of activities and from living in an accepting, permissive, approving, and encouraging atmosphere. Social and ethical understandings, skills, and attitudes are developed by experiences in a school considered a "working democracy" [11], which provides in every subject and activity numerous opportunities for guided social experience.

As an illustration of such opportunities for improving group living, consider the effectiveness of a "simple organization through which [second grade children] handled many of their group problems" [6]. When a parent-teacher

FIG. 1–1. The school as a working democracy provides many social learning experiences. These children participate in a social control for their safety. (*Courtesy of Whittier School, Utah State Agricultural College.*)

conference prevented their teacher from supervising a playground period, the children were prevented by their own arguing from playing the game they had planned. In a discussion of their frustrating experience, however, they concluded that "they needed to clarify their own responsibilities on the playground so that they could actually play when they went outside. The situation was discussed and each understood his responsibility with regard to his own action as well as to the action of others" [6, p. 147]. In such group activities, children learn under guidance that sharing, contributing one's part in a team, taking individual responsibility, being a good sport, and similar social skills are both satisfying and effective patterns of social behavior.

Curriculum Principles

The potential range of curricular experiences, including both subject matter and living experiences in the school, home, and community, is so great that no actual curriculum can include them all. Selection is necessary. The experiences selected need to be arranged into good learning sequences. The different sub-

FIG. 1–2. A rich curriculum affords many opportunities for child leadership and cooperation. (*Courtesy of Lincoln School, Brigham City, Utah.*)

jects and living activities need to be organized for the most effective means of attaining educational objectives. The following principles are applied to these problems.

1. Transmitting the Cultural Heritage. Previous generations have evolved a large and tremendously useful body of knowledge for effective and satisfying living, including language, mathematics, science, art, and literature. The schools, by transmitting this rich and growing cultural heritage, enable each new generation "to ride on the shoulders of previous generations" and eventually to enrich the heritage for succeeding generations [15]. Some educational philosophers have believed that "a realistic knowledge of man's cultural heritage is the most reliable guide for future action" [3].

This cultural heritage is, of course, drawn upon for the school's subject matter; but it is too vast, complicated, and even contradictory for passing on as a whole [2]. It is also questionable whether the school curriculum should be patterned on its logical structure [17]; perhaps the irregular order of problems as they are met in everyday living should determine the structure of the curriculum rather than the logical classifications of knowledge.

While a problem-solving approach to life problems, in which the social heritage is turned to only for aid in their solutions, does perhaps result in better motivation and applications, there is still value in learning about the logical organization of knowledge. In a curriculum designed for meeting problems "encountered in everyday living, there will be times when it is desirable to study a subject-matter area as an *organized body of knowledge*" [17, p. 149]. Acquaintance with the organized classifications of knowledge in texts, encyclopedias, and libraries enables the child to "locate what he wants to know." It also makes more meaningful, and thus more easily learned and better remembered, what would otherwise be numerous isolated facts. But despite the value in acquaintance with the general structure of the classified bodies of knowledge, only a relatively small part of it can be taught to elementary school children. In making appropriate selections, several criteria are applied.

2. *Planning Curricula to Meet Changing Needs.* Each generation tends to emphasize in its elementary school curriculum what at the time seems important. In the colonial period (1647–1776) of our history, when religious motives were especially strong, the curriculum consisted of reading, writing, spelling, arithmetic, the catechism, prayers, and singing of hymns, plus severe moral and social discipline [17, pp. 8–9]. In the national period (1776–1876), inspired by such political ideals as were expressed in the Declaration of Independence, the universal development of intelligent and effective citizens became a dominant purpose of the schools. The curriculum then included reading, writing, spelling, grammar, arithmetic, physiology, hygiene, history, geography, agriculture, drawing, music, and good behavior [17, pp. 10–12]. In the period of expansion and reform (1876–1929), with its emphasis upon efficiency and economic interests, the curriculum was further expanded. It came to include reading, writing, spelling, usage, grammar, language, literature, arithmetic, physiology, hygiene, history, the Constitution of the United States, geography, music, art, handwork, manual training, homemaking, nature study, civics, citizenship, physical education, and good behavior [17, pp. 12–15]. Mastery of facts and skills was emphasized. From 1929 to the present there has been emphasis in the elementary school curriculum on democratic ideals, on developing a problem-solving approach to life and community problems, and on encouraging self-direction, self-discipline, freedom with responsibilities, and creative expression [17, pp. 15–19]. The curriculum at present is coming to reflect more closely the contemporary scientific, industrialized, and democratic features of our society.

Some of the contemporary social characteristics having implications for the curriculum are "(a) the dynamic nature of our society, (b) the interdependence of our society, (c) the changing status of the home, (d) problems confronting the consumer, (e) crime and delinquency, (f) the conservation of natural resources, and (g) the nation's health" [17, p. 99]. Subject matter is being reorganized, and emphasis is now more upon its functional use in solving life and community problems rather than upon mastery of facts. There are the language arts, social studies, science, arithmetic, arts and crafts, health, and physical education. The ideals of democracy are practiced in a "functional democracy." The three R's are learned by using them in meaningful situations, and the curriculum is being adapted to individual differences [17]. Because society is changing so rapidly, the specific facts and skills needed for the future cannot, it is assumed, be predicted; thus problem-solving and creative approaches are advocated as the best preparation both for the present and for meeting unforeseeable future problems.

3. *The Criterion of Social Utility.* Since the entire social heritage cannot be included, "Horn found a place in the curriculum for only those ideas, skills, and abilities which could be known to be of great social use because they were crucial, universal, and frequently encountered in life outside of the school" [3, p. 21]. In applying this criterion, surveys [18] were made of several activities of representative adults in the country. The frequencies of the different words they had occasion to spell in their letters and other writing were counted. Sales slips, home accounts, and vocational uses of arithmetic were examined to determine the universality and the relative frequency of adult uses of different arithmetic concepts and skills. Their popular reading was analyzed to determine their need for different social science concepts. These surveys have shown that if the curriculum were reduced to the minimum essentials, a relatively few concepts and skills which are used over and over would meet the needs of the great majority of the people.

For example, Wilson's review [24] of studies of adult uses of arithmetic shows that the universally and frequently used concepts and skills are very simple. Eighty-five per cent of them involve only the fundamental operations. The commonly used fractions ($\frac{1}{2}$, $\frac{1}{4}$, $\frac{3}{4}$, $\frac{1}{3}$, $\frac{3}{4}$, $\frac{1}{3}$, $\frac{2}{3}$, $\frac{1}{5}$, and $\frac{1}{8}$) cover 94 per cent of all the uses reported. In problems using measures, reductions are rare. Compound interest, proportion, insurance, plastering, masonry, bank discount "are almost negligible." And he reports "no problems involving taxes, investment, stocks, bonds, equation of payments, foreign exchange, apothecaries' weight, alligation, annual interest, compound and complex fractions, troy weight, or the metric system." In a study of the uses of decimals, he found approximately 75 to 85 per cent of industrial employees making no use of decimals, 5 to 20 per cent needing a reading knowledge of decimals, and only 2 to 7 per cent needing to make decimal computations [23]. Such studies suggest that high degrees of computational skill are required for only a few arithmetic processes. The range of understanding, however, should include a wide range of concepts. And those who need computational skills beyond the scope of the minimum essentials should secure them as a part of their vocational training.

As an illustration of curriculum determination on the basis of this criterion of social utility, there is presented in Table 1–1 a core vocabulary of spelling words compiled by Kyte and Neel [13, pp. 32–33].

This list is comprised of words which both children and adults have been found to need most frequently in their writing. The "adult words" were selected from Horn's *A Basic Writing Vocabulary*, which contains the 10,000 words most commonly used in adult writing [8]. Twenty-eight hundred of the most frequently used of these words account for 97.2 per cent of the words adults write [14, p. 386]. Rinsland's [19] "basic vocabulary of elementary school children," which includes the 14,571 different words used three or more times in 6,012,359 running words of children's writing for all elementary school grades, supplied the "children's words." Kyte and Neel note that 500 of the most frequently used of these words account for 82 per cent of the running words. The 501 spelling words in Table 1–1 should, therefore, have great social utility; mastery of it "should assure spelling proficiency in the case of a large per cent of the words written by adults and by children at various grade levels" [13].

This criterion of social utility is undoubtedly an important guide for developing a more useful curriculum, and it has resulted in the elimination of much useless and irrelevant content [18]. But as a sole criterion it would have limitations. The static curriculum based on "present adult activities" which it would produce would not meet the contemporary needs of a constantly changing society. Furthermore, the present practices of parents are not necessarily ideal models for their children. For example, adults might communicate more effectively and enjoyably if they used a greater variety of words in their writing. Again, current and quite universal diet practices are probably in need of improvement. Moreover, in order to develop thorough understanding and effective application of concepts, it may be desirable to teach some concepts infrequently used in life activities. For example, classroom experience with a wide range of fractions will probably result in deeper understanding and more effective use of the few fractions that are actually used frequently.

4. Selection, According to Children's Needs, and Interests. "Progressive education," as a modern movement in education, advocates a curriculum based on

Table 1-1. Social Utility
(Illustrated in a core vocabulary of 501 spelling words)

Type I. 315 words occurring in identical form among 500 most commonly used
words in adults' and in children's writing

a	call	from	kind	now	since	two
about	called	full	knew	of	six	under
after	came	gave	know	off	small	until
afternoon	can	get	large	old	so	up
again	can't	getting	last	on	some	upon
ago	car	girl	later	once	something	us
all	care	give	left	one	soon	use
almost	city	glad	let	only	sorry	used
along	class	go	letter	open	stay	very
also	close	going	life	or	still	want
always	cold	gone	like	other	such	wanted
am	come	good	little	our	summer	war
an	coming	got	long	out	Sunday	was
and	could	great	look	over	sure	way
another	country	guess	looking	paper	take	we
answer	cut	had	lot	part	tell	week
any	day	half	love	party	ten	weeks
anything	days	hand	made	people	than	well
are	dear	happy	make	place	thank	went
around	did	hard	making	play	that	were
as	didn't	has	man	please	the	what
ask	different	have	many	pretty	their	when
asked	dinner	having	may	put	them	where
at	do	he	me	quite	then	which
away	does	hear	men	read	there	while
back	doing	heard	might	ready	these	who
bad	done	help	money	received	they	why
be	don't	her	more	rest	thing	will
because	down	here	morning	right	things	winter
bed	each	high	most	room	think	wish
been	early	him	mother	run	this	with
before	end	his	Mr.	said	those	work
being	enough	home	Mrs.	same	thought	world
best	ever	hope	much	Saturday	three	would
better	every	house	must	saw	through	write
big	far	how	my	say	time	writing
book	few	I	name	school	to	wrote
books	find	if	near	second	today	year
both	fine	in	never	see	together	years
box	first	into	new	send	told	yes
boy	five	is	next	sent	too	yesterday
bring	for	it	nice	set	took	yet
but	found	its	night	she	town	you
buy	four	just	no	should	truly	your
by	friend	keen	not	show	try	yours

Table 1–1. Social Utility (*Continued.*)

Type II. 55 words occurring among the 300 most frequently used words in children's writing

aunt	candy	door	girls	milk	ride	teacher
baby	cat	eat	grade	Miss	Santa Claus	toys
ball	children	father	ground	o'clock	side	train
beautiful	Christmas	feet	head	oh	sister	tree
black	comes	fire	live	played	sometimes	trees
boys	daddy	fish	lived	playing	snow	water
brother	dog	food	looked	ran	started	white
brought	doll	fun	lots	red	story	

Type III. 21 words occurring in fourth 100 in children's writing and in second 500 of adults' writing

blue	dress	farm	goes	light	seen	store
couldn't	eyes	friends	hair	miss	spring	times
decided	family	game	land	picture	street	walk

Type IV. 39 words occurring in first 500 of adults' writing and in second 500 of children's writing and also in first 500 in one elementary-school grade

able	course	given	Monday	real	suppose	tomorrow
address	during	job	month	remember	surely	weather
against	even	leave	myself	several	taken	without
between	evening	letters	need	shall	talk	young
bill	everything	line	nothing	sincerely		
card	Friday	mail	own	state		

Type V. 27 words occurring in first 500 of adults' writing and in second 500 in at least one elementary-school grade

above	company	however	office	possible	receive	though
amount	cannot	interest	order	present	returned	written
believe	expect	matter	past	rather	seems	whether
business	feel	number	pay	really	sending	

Type VI. 45 words occurring in first 330 in adults' writing but not in first 1,000 in any elementary-school grade

account	check	enclosed	herewith	pleased	return	therefore
advise	copy	enclosing	information	pleasure	satisfactory	trust
appreciate	covering	fact	kindly	price	service	understand
attention	credit	favor	material	receipt	shipment	
balance	date	forward	necessary	regard	sir	
case	department	further	No.	regarding	stock	
certainly	desire	future	note	reply	thanking	

Source: G. C. Kyte and V. M. Neel, *Elem. Sch. J.*, 54: 32–33, 1953. Reprinted by permission of The University of Chicago Press.

children's needs and interests, in which concepts and skills from the social heritage are taught as children find need and use for them in carrying on constructive and creative activities in a rich and stimulating environment. Such a curriculum is thought to prepare individuals to function effectively in a changing society with an unpredictable future by enabling them to develop competence and confidence in problem solving [3]. It relies upon natural and intrinsic child motives. Thus learning is more efficient because it is more meaningful. Retention and applications to later life problems are more likely because concepts and skills have been learned for the purpose of making significant applications.

This view of the curriculum is based on the well-established assumption that the child is "active and creative" and that "he should have a part in initiating, planning, carrying out, and evaluating his [curriculum] experiences" [11, p. 210]. To assume that children are naturally intellectually active and creative and that their interests and needs should help to determine the curriculum does not, however, minimize the need for teacher-guidance and planning. Interests are not, as Jersild and Tasch [10] have shown, innate. The *capacity* for being highly and enjoyably motivated by interests is probably an innate characteristic, but interests are developed from children's experiences. "According to this conception, we will not simply utilize the interests a child happens to have acquired as a guide to what and how to teach" [10, p. 86]. As children, under teacher-guidance, explore and participate in activities in their environment, they develop interests and needs which are satisfied by understanding of subject matter, mastery of useful skills, and creative effort. Such preplanned sequences for the first six grades as the following have been found to enlist and expand children's interests [17, p. 145]:

    I. Home and school life.
    II. Community life.
    III. Adaptation to environmental forces of nature.
    IV. Adaptation of life to advancing physical frontiers.
    V. Effects of inventions and discoveries upon our living.
    VI. Effects of machine production upon our lives.

Within such centers of interest the problems are developed around the concrete living experiences of the children concerned. "Subject-matter becomes something one uses in the solution of everyday problems. One uses it to find out, to verify some point, to gather new information, to enjoy, and to appreciate something" [11, p. 334]. As the children develop needs for expressing understandings and appreciations, they use many creative media. "They may

Fig. 1–3. Following their interests, children read library sources, take excursions, and express themselves in art, writing, and crafts in their study of Indian arts. (*Courtesy of William M. Stewart School, University of Utah.*)

draw, paint, engage in dramatic play, express themselves through pantomime or impersonation, or with puppets or other dramatic forms; may develop rhythms, or dances, with music to be sung or played, or make a simple musical instrument; may model with clay, weave, cook, sew, build with blocks, and write stories or poems" [7, p. 1]. All these media may be used for creative expression in unified curriculum projects; and as children use them, they will find needs for teacher-guidance in improving skills in them. When such guidance is given in response to children's needs, it does not discourage "their willingness to experiment, to be independent, to express original ideas."

Similar needs for subject matter, skills, and creative problem solving are found as children meet problems of living in their "functional democracy." They want a baseball field, so they construct it. They have need for safety in crossing streets, so they participate in solving their traffic problem. They enjoy efficient and happy classroom activities, so they plan improved classroom arrangements and organization. They want to entertain their parents at Christmas time, so they plan and produce a program for them. And so on for innumerable problems of living.

Fig. 1–4. All the children of the school cooperate in planning and presenting a May Day program for their parents. (*Courtesy of Whittier School, Utah State Agricultural College.*)

Such a curriculum, organized around children's interests and needs, draws upon much of the traditional subject matter. But it emphasizes child purposes, problem solving, and creative effort as children meet the problems of their society.

5. Curriculum Resources in the Local Environment. Although most school activities are centered in the classroom, the curriculum is greatly enriched by extending it to include other activities within the school, home activities, and school activities in the community [1, 2, 4, 5, 6, 11].

Opportunities for attaining many of both the subject-matter and child development objectives are increased by experiences in the school library, the auditorium, the playground, the lunchroom and its kitchen, and other departments of some schools. Moreover, the special talents in art, music, dramatics, science, etc., of each teacher can on occasion be utilized to enrich the curricula of all classes in a school. By sharing the unique projects of each classroom through interclass visits or auditorium contributions, the children in each class can contribute toward enriching the curricula of all classes.

For certain objectives, the home supplies the major part of the curriculum, and parents play significant teaching roles [5]. For example, it is mainly at home that children should learn to eat good food, well served, happily and without worry. They should learn there to get enough rest, to avoid fatigue and over-stimulating activities, and to avoid spreading communicable diseases. They may learn about sharing home responsibilities, being responsible about spending money, and earning some. They may also learn emotional control in frustrating situations, healthy self-discipline, and how to enjoy hobbies and other recreations in free time.

Many concepts in science and social studies, social attitudes and habits, aesthetic interests, and so on, are learned from teacher-guided pupil excursions into the community—to a theater, a zoo, a park, a museum, a library, a farm, a factory, a power plant, a grocery store, a house in process of construction (to observe the roles of different workers), and so on for many others, the choices depending on the specific resources of each community. Some schools feel that this kind of curriculum enrichment is so important that school buses are maintained, not only for bringing children to school, but for taking them into the community and its environs for educative experiences.

6. *Adjusting the Curriculum to Child Maturity.* During the elementary school years children are growing and learning. They gradually become ready for effective participation at more advanced levels in the developmental sequences of learning activities. The good curriculum is adjusted to children's changing "stages" of maturity. Each year it provides rich, full, satisfying experiences suited to each child's particular pattern of abilities, interests, and needs [15]. To this problem of matching the curriculum to the maturity levels of the children the entire third chapter is devoted.

7. *The Principle of Transfer of Training.* Since this principle is also elaborated in a separate chapter, its significance for curriculum planning is only mentioned here. The principle refers to the application to new learning and problem solving of already acquired generalizations. Without such generalizing, children's learning could not progress stepladder fashion as it does. The more effectively learning sequences are organized for application of prior learning, the more efficient will be the learning. Thus, according to this criterion, a good curriculum should emphasize meanings, the interrelationship among concepts, and the inductive discovery and wide-scope applications of principles. Among these principles, perhaps the most valuable is learning how to learn and to solve problems effectively. Since the entire social heritage cannot be mastered and since future specific needs cannot be predicted accurately, perhaps "the most important obligation of all is to help children learn how to learn and develop a desire to continue learning" [15, p. 52]. If the child learns effective learning and problem-solving procedures by applying them to a

Fɪɢ. 1–5. For children at different levels of maturity and with varying patterns of abilities and interests a broad and varied curriculum is needed. (*Courtesy of Central School, Brigham City, Utah.*)

sampling of significant problems as he grows up, "he might then leave school with confidence that he knows how to learn other things as the necessity arises" [15, p. 52].

8. *Adapting the Curriculum to Individual Differences.* Each child is a unique individual. In every classroom children differ widely in mental maturity, in experience background, and in patterns of abilities and achievements. First grade children may range in mental maturity from mental ages of 4 to 9. As they advance through school, the differences increase. A fifth grade class may have a range of seven years in reading ability. Moreover, each child has a pattern of unevenly developed abilities. For example, a child of average intelligence may be below average in reading, at the average in arithmetic, and distinctly superior in art. Such diversities in individual children make necessary a curriculum of broad and varied activities, flexible enough to provide for the needs of each child. This curriculum principle emphasizes the need of striving "for a curriculum sufficiently broad and flexible to recognize and reward the great variety of combinations of aptitude and interest of its pupils, enabling them to learn what their peculiar strengths and weaknesses are and preparing

them to fit into our complex society with its multiplicity of demands for workers with varying aptitudes" [3, p. 365]. To the applications of this principle two later chapters are devoted.

Curriculum Organization

Paralleling the continuous reconsideration of the aims and curriculum resources for elementary education, educators have persistently striven, especially during the last quarter of the century [11] to find the most effective pattern of curriculum organization. Up to about 1930, the curriculum was mainly subject-centered. Then it became child-centered; and this concept evolved rapidly into the contemporary child-in-society emphasis [11]. From the thinking about curriculum organization four types have emerged: (1) the curriculum as a separate list of subjects which in themselves are not directly related either to the child's interests and needs or to society's problems; (2) correlations within the curriculum, such as combining the study of geography and history or of writing and spelling, which is a step toward integration; (3) fusion of subjects into broad fields, such as language arts (fusing reading, composition, writing, spelling, grammar, punctuation, oral speech, and listening), social studies (history, geography, civics, and the American way of life), science and health (or science and arithmetic, or health and physical education), and arts and crafts; and (4) the integrated, developmental-activity curriculum, which organizes units of learning around developed child interests in both his own activities and society's major functions [3, 17]. All four of these types, or combinations of them, are found in America's schools. Although a curriculum organization established by adequate research is still to be achieved [11], many contemporary leaders in curriculum planning favor some variation of the fourth type of curriculum organization [1, 4, 6, 11, 17].

In such a curriculum, learning and problem-solving "units" may grow out of a specific child need, as for a baseball field, or out of his developed interest in such constant social functions as: (1) protection and conservation of life, property, and natural resources; (2) production of goods and services and distribution of returns of production; (3) consumption of goods and services; (4) communication and transportation of goods and people; (5) recreation; (6) expression of aesthetic impulses; (7) expression of religious impulses; (8) education; (9) extension of freedom; (10) integration of the individual; or (11) exploration [17, p. 145]. For solutions to such problems, children draw upon the organized sources of knowledge from the social heritage and upon observation, exploration, and experimentation in their present environment.

Fig. 1–6. Developing in children an understanding of how their community is supplied with food involves planning, reading, excursions, arts and crafts, and cooperative problem solving. (*Courtesy of Emerson School, Salt Lake City and the Dairy Council, Utah.*)

Thus they find incentive for mastering the concepts, skills, and arts needed in executing such projects.

As examples of good units which teacher and pupils have planned and worked through together, the John Dewey Society suggests for grade 1 "Growing up in Grandview," "How our fathers help everyone," and "Where we get our food"; for grade 2 "Going places in Grandview" and "Where our food comes from"; for grade 3 "How we share our thoughts and ideas" and "The news goes to press"; for grade 4 "Let's explore our state" and "Our modern friends acquaint us with strangers"; for grade 5 "What the U.S. does for the world" and "From moccasins to air travel"; and for grade 6 "How people from earliest times to the present have helped us" and "How and why from wood to steel" [11, pp. 327–328]. Each of these units involves sustained study, observation, research, and creative expression over a four-to-six-week period.

As criteria for selecting and evaluating such unit activities, Beck, Cook, and Kearney [3, pp. 264–267] have proposed the following: (1) "A good unit should be broad enough to provide for various types of learning," for different media of study and expression, for varied levels of mental maturity, and for each child's unique pattern of interests and talents. (2) "A good unit should provide real purposes" and opportunities for mastering the skills of communication, arithmetic, and creative expression. (3) The "felt needs" arising out of study of the unit problems "should lead into several subject-matter fields." (4) A good unit should provide opportunities for learning and problem solving "compatible with each child's understanding, vocabulary, interests, abilities," and environmental resources. (5) "A good unit should provide a wide balance and variety of activities—dramatic, constructive, creative, research, experimental, and exploratory." (6) "A good unit should familiarize the group with the processes of selecting, planning, carrying out, and evaluating an experiment." (7) There should be continuity between the sequence of units and relations to other activities. "A good unit of work should stimulate children to acquire further information concerning the topic at hand and other related topics." (8) The reading material in the unit should be varied, abundant, and suited to each child's maturity. (9) Facts learned should lead to generalizations of wide-scope application. (10) "Throughout the unit, emphasis should be placed on problem-solving." (11) Teacher-guidance of each child's participation in the unit should be based on understanding the needs of his "whole personality"—"his culture, socio-economic background, nationality, color and religion, mental and physical health, place of residence, acceptance by his group, past fortunate and unfortunate experiences." In the light of this understanding, the teacher is concerned with each child's progress toward attainment of both subject-matter and child development objectives.

As a conclusion to this chapter on the aims and curriculum of the elementary school, let us look at an example of how such concepts can influence a teacher's guidance of children's learning activities.

A Teaching Unit on Nutrition

As the teacher of a fifth grade group of children, Mrs. F. followed generally a curriculum of subjects fused into broad fields, such as "language arts" and "science and health." But she was interested in taking the step toward the fourth type of curriculum organization—to the integrated, activity curriculum. She was, therefore, continuously alert to manifestations of interest and suitable opportunities for expanding any subject activity into a project which would integrate as much of the curriculum as possible and which would achieve important child development objectives as well. The study of nutrition as a phase of the science-and-health curriculum offered such an opportunity.

Fig. 1–7. Experimenting is fun; but for accurate results, careful handling of the animals, weighing, and recording are required. (*Courtesy of Whittier School, Utah State Agricultural College.*)

Using rats to demonstrate dramatically the health values of adequate nutrition promised to be both highly interesting for the children and rich in learning experiences for several phases of the total curriculum. Phases of the study of health, science, reading, language, arithmetic, and art could all be integrated into a problem-solving pattern by their inclusion in such a project. Mrs. F. therefore encouraged the children at the introduction to the study of nutrition to consider conducting a diet experiment with rats.

They read first a bulletin on an "outline of a rat demonstration to show the value of good diets" [22]. From this they learned that the rat's nutritional requirements are similar to the human's and that, because the rat's growth rate is so rapid—six weeks being equal to a year of human growth—the rat is especially suitable for such experimentation. They also learned how to select rats for an experiment, to prepare them for experimentation, to choose diets for different purposes, to care for them, to handle them skillfully, to provide necessary equipment, to observe weight, appearance, special symptoms, and behavior changes, and to record their results.

Because the diets of the children themselves often consisted of a combination of regular meals, snacks, and sweets, the children decided to make a comparison using two rats and two different diets, one "adequate" and the other "inadequate."

The adequate diet consisted of a basic mix (beans, 4 grams; potatoes, 10 grams, rolled oats, 5 grams; white flour, 25 grams; margarine, 5 grams; lard, 10 grams; sugar, 20 grams; salt, 1 gram; apples, 5 grams) plus dried milk and other foods required to make up a well-rounded diet. These additional foods are indicated in one of the children's written reports: "Reddie is being fed a good diet. He gets food from each of seven groups each day." [From the teacher's notes: "We checked a food wheel to see that our adequately fed rat had available items from each of seven basic food groups."] "We feed him meat, eggs, raw vegetables, raw fruit, dry milk."

The inadequate diet included the same basic mix as the "adequate" diet, plus snack-type foods. As noted in another child's corrected report: "We offered Blue Boy all he wanted each day of foods that we often use for snacks. We gave him chocolate candy, raisin bread, cup cakes, cookies, potato chips, pickles, nuts, and soda pop."

How the experiment was conducted is indicated in still another child's report: "About two weeks ago we got two rats. We named them Reddie and Blue Boy. Reddie got a very good diet and Blue Boy a snack diet. At first Blue Boy gained but started losing or staying even. After about three days he started to look smaller and his fur became rough and dirty looking. His face looked pinched and his eyes lost brightness. After about 8 days spots began to appear on his tail. These spots are a sign of bad health. Reddie gained and gained but after about 5 days we had a little trouble getting him home on Friday. We had to take him in a cab to Mrs. F.'s home. The cab turned and shook Reddie's cage a little and pinched his tail. He lost weight that week end but he recovered after a few days. After 12 days we put both Reddie and Blue Boy on a good diet and Blue Boy surprised everybody by coming to weigh more than Reddie. After 15 days we returned both Reddie and Blue Boy to the College."

Each child had his turn at mixing the food, feeding, watering, cleaning the cages, and weighing and handling the animals; and each recorded his observations. Their joint record is shown in Table 1–2. A graph showing the weight gains for each rat is shown in Figure 1–8.

The conclusions drawn from this experiment by the children are indicated in excerpts from the notes of the different children for oral reports to fourth and sixth grade classes at the end of 12 days: "Reddie grew each day. His fur is glossy. His muscles are firm and strong. His ears are a healthy pink. His eyes are bright. He is friendly and curious."

"Blue Boy gained weight the first day, but he lost weight the second. He curled up in a little ball and didn't seem hungry the third day. His fur became shaggy and his muscles flabby. He is restless. He does not like to be caught to be weighed. He seems to be hunting for something he isn't getting."

Table 1–2. Children's Record of Rat Diet Experiment
(Snack versus adequate diet)

Date	Weight, g		Description	
	R	BB	Reddie	Blue Boy
3/1/54	37	41	Healthy, lively, hungry	Same
3/2/54	43	46	Healthy, lively, hungry	Prefers potato chips to sweets
3/3/54	44	44	Healthy, lively, hungry	Not hungry, restless
3/4/54	49	44	Healthy, eager to be picked up	Not easy to weigh
3/5/54	50	45	Healthy, friendly	Hair wet-looking
3/6/54	51	45	Healthy, frisky	Sits rolled up in feeding bottle
3/7/54	53	45	Healthy, likes to get out of cage	Acts frightened
3/8/54	55	45	Healthy	Sick, watery eyes
3/9/54	59	45	Healthy, lively	Sick, watery eyes, sore tail, lesions on skin
3/10/54	64	44	Healthy, shining coat (so lively that he got his tail in the door; note loss in weight)	Skin and bones
3/11/54	60	45		
3/12/54	64	45	Not so hungry after his tail injury	Begins getting adequate diet today
3/13/54	64	55		Eats heartily
3/14/54	64	56		
3/15/54	65	65		Is still shabby-looking

Source: Whittier School, Utah State Agricultural College, 1954.

"In our science we are studying about foods. We are studying about foods which help us to grow and keep healthy. We have made a chart which pictures seven basic groups of foods. We need one of each of these groups each day. A rat grows and keeps well on foods which we need."

The interest and appreciation of the children in this project were indicated daily in their activities, by their desire to make special reports of their experience to the fourth and sixth grades, and in the "thank-you" letters written to the college personnel who lent the rats and supplied the food for the basic mix. One of the letters, which also illustrates another of the language activities, follows:

Whittier School
Logan, Utah
March 7, 1954

Dear Dr. Wilcox:

We wish to thank you for the food you were kind enough to lend us.

If you have time come and see our rats. I feel sorry for Blue Boy because he had to have the disadvantage to be the one who has a snak diet.

We are having a lot of fun though.

I hope you liked my letter.

Sincerely yours,
C.B.

During this project on nutrition, interest and attention were focused continuously on the central problem-solving features; but the varied activities

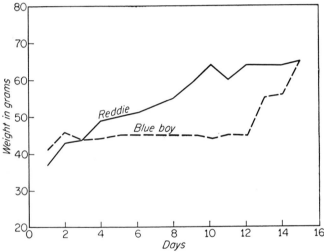

FIG. 1–8. Children chart gains in weight for "Reddie," the rat fed an adequate diet, and for "Blue Boy," the rat fed an inadequate diet, for 12 days. After the twelfth day both rats were fed an adequate diet until the end of the experiment. (*Courtesy of Whittier School, Utah State Agricultural College, 1954.*)

also made possible functional learning and applications of knowledge and skills from health, science, reading, language, arithmetic, and art. Study and reading of health references were involved, and generalizations developed were applied by the children to themselves. Teacher-parent conferences revealed some of these applications. For example, one child now refused candy just before dinnertime. The children learned a scientific approach to problems. The project also afforded considerable reading practice and developed new interests. When an article reporting the use of rats in a nutrition experiment appeared in the local newspaper, it was read and commented on by many of the children. In language there were record keeping, organization and formulation of reports, and letter writing. In arithmetic there were occasions for measuring, weighing, converting grams to pounds and ounces, chart making, and graphing. Art work included posters, bulletin-board arrangements, and making the chart of the seven basic foods.

In addition to the use of these concepts, special practice periods for improving skills in them were included. For example, when it proved difficult or unsatisfying to read a child's report because of his failure to capitalize and punctuate correctly, special language sessions for improvement of these skills were scheduled. One day Mrs. F. wrote on the chalkboard her report of some observations on the experiment, leaving out all capitalization and punctuation. Then the children and teacher corrected it together by adding the proper punctuation and capitalization, and from it they generalized the principles of capitalization and punctuation at this level. Following this general learning exercise, the children corrected their own similar reports, with Mrs. F. checking their efforts and helping them individually as needed. Both pupils and teacher were happy with both the project itself and their learning outcomes. It is also possible to evaluate such a project more systematically and according to trustworthy standards.

Using Kearney's *Elementary School Objectives* [12] as a check list, it appears that some intermediate-level specific objectives in every division were partially or completely attained. In regard to "Physical development, health, and body care," Mrs. F. decided that the children had acquired knowledge of "food combinations for a wholesome meal" and that habits of "eating wholesome food" had been strengthened. Within the category "Individual social and emotional development," the experience probably contributed to greater "interest and pride in physical growth and development, health and strength." The project also provided satisfying experiences in and therefore strengthened habits of "volunteering to assume responsibilities and to carry them out," both alone and as a member of a team or group. With respect to "Ethical behavior, standards, and values," through "acts of cooperation, sharing, responsibility, and in subordinating self-interest in working with others," ethical values were likely strengthened. In the area of "Social relations," the children increased their understanding of the need for "accepting their membership roles in the organized and unorganized groups of which they are a part" and improved their skills in "leadership of or cooperative membership of peer groups" and in being "courteous speakers or listeners." There was occasion for "sustained cooperation in a project" over more than two weeks.

Under the heading "The natural environment: biological and physical sciences," it is justifiable to check as objectives at least partially attained "further knowledge about growth and physiological processes"; understanding "that scientific progress is generally a cooperative enterprise"; skill in observing accurately and describing carefully the results of individual investigations, in measuring and reading to summarize data, in interpreting graphs, tables, and charts, and in "conducting simple scientific experiments"; increased "respect for good evidence and the nature of proof"; and habits of "seeking scientific answers to questions about physical health and growth, of keeping an open mind, of being willing to change opinions in the face of compelling evidence, of pursuing scientific interests, and of applying generalizations." As for "Aesthetic development," there was occasion to "use art work in connection with a study theme." Within the area of "Communication," knowledge gains included increased vocabulary of scientific, quantitative, and technical words, and the meaning of tables and graphs. Gains in skills included "presentation of reports, writing legibly, acquisition of a sentence sense, use of capitals to begin sentences and for proper names, uses of a period at the end of sentences, following orderly arrangement of ideas." Attitude gains included "interest in evaluating their communication skills in reading, writing, and speaking; enjoyment of listening as well as talking; and pleasure in gratifying intellectual curiosity." Within the category "Quantitative relations," there were gains in understanding of weight, skill in weighing, and constructing and reading graphs. In addition to attaining several important elementary school objectives, the project would also meet most of the criteria of a "good unit" [3].

Summary

Understanding of the aims of the elementary school and ability to participate in their continuous reformulation are among the most important responsibilities of the teacher. His conception of these aims is an important guide or frame of reference in carrying out every other teaching function—in developing the curriculum, in providing the essential conditions for learning and in guiding effective learning, in providing for individual differences, and in determining outcomes which need to be evaluated and measured. Teachers who have evaluated according to Kearney's list of objectives curriculum projects such as the one reported here on nutrition have mentioned five uses of such an analysis: (1) Since Kearney's list of objectives is so competently and thoroughly prepared, when a teacher finds that a good teaching project has been directed toward attainment of many of those objectives, she feels that something worthwhile has been accomplished and will be more confident in using adaptations of the project again. (2) By reading over the objectives at the beginning of a year and at intervals during the year, she can plan curriculum activities to accomplish more of these desirable objectives. (3) When children's interests in an activity are being considered as a basis for a curriculum project, its potential richness in useful learning experiences can be tested by using the list of objectives as a check list. (4) Studying a project or teaching activity from the point of view of the objectives to be attained, the teacher is alerted to more possibilities, and can arrange and guide the learning activities so as to achieve *more* useful results from the same project. (5) Checking a curriculum activity according to this comprehensive list of objectives indicates that usually multiple and varied outcomes are to be expected. Hence evaluation and appraisal of these outcomes will require varied appraisal devices. The list of objectives is a guide to what needs to be measured, and it contains some suggestions on how attainment of these multiple objectives can be evaluated.

Review and Applications

1. In regard to Lee and Lee's list of general objectives for the elementary school, what qualifications, elaborations, and additions can you suggest?

2. From a new or a recalled observation of an elementary class at work, and using Kearney's outline of specific objectives (or the entire list if the reference [12] is available to you), try to infer the objectives toward which the pupils and their teacher were striving.

3. Is "Johnny" failing to become as proficient as he otherwise might in reading, arithmetic, and writing because modern schools overemphasize such personal-social objectives as democratic ideals, problem solving, self-direction, self-discipline, freedom with responsibilities, creative expression, and healthy self-concepts? In thinking about this question, consider the eight curriculum principles discussed.

4. For a fourth grade child who "reads fairly well, but is able to spell only a few words and has no systematic approach to spelling," how could his teacher use the list in Table 1?

5. Evaluate the fifth grade unit on nutrition according to the eleven criteria of a good teaching unit.

References

1. Anderson, J. E.: "Changing emphasis in early childhood education," *Sch. Soc.*, 49: 1–9, 1939.
2. "Bases for selecting school programs," *Sch. Exec.*, 70: 61–74, 1951.

3. Beck, R. H., W. W. Cook, and N. C. Kearney: *Curriculum in the Modern Elementary School*, Prentice-Hall, Englewood Cliffs, N.J., 1953.

4. Bruner, H. B.: "Some requirements of the elementary school curriculum," *Teach. Coll. Rec.*, 39: 273–286, 1937–1938.

5. Committee on Emotional Stability of the Metropolitan School Study Council: *Parents as Teachers: A Guide for Parents of Elementary School Children.* Teachers College, Columbia University, Bureau of Publications, New York, 1947.

6. *Education for All American Children*, National Education Association and American Association of School Administrators, Educational Policies Commission, Washington, 1948.

7. Hill, Wilhelmina, Helen K. Mackintosh, and Arne Randall: *How Children Can Be Creative*, U.S. Department of Health, Education, and Welfare Bulletin 12, 1954.

8. Horn, E.: *A Basic Writing Vocabulary*, University of Iowa Monographs in Education, ser. 1, no. 4, 1926.

9. Hugget, A. J., and C. V. Millard: *Growth and Learning in the Elementary School*, Heath, Boston, 1946.

10. Jersild, A. T., and R. J. Tasch: *Children's Interests and What They Suggest for Education*, Teachers College, Columbia University, Bureau of Publications, New York, 1949.

11. John Dewey Society, H. G. Shane, ed.: *The American Elementary School*, Thirteenth Yearbook of the society, Harper, New York, 1953.

12. Kearney, N. C.: *Elementary School Objectives*, Russell Sage, New York, 1953.

13. Kyte, G. C., and V. M. Neel: "A core vocabulary of spelling words," *Elem. Sch. J.*, 54: 29–34, Copyright 1953 by the University of Chicago. Reprinted by permission of the University of Chicago Press.

14. Lee, J. M., and Doris M. Lee: *The Child and His Curriculum*, Appleton-Century-Crofts, New York, 1940.

15. National Education Association, American Association of School Administrators, Commission of American School Curriculum, *The American School Curriculum*, Thirty-first Yearbook of the association, Washington, 1953.

16. *The Purposes of Education in American Democracy*, National Education Association, Educational Policies Commission, Washington, 1938.

17. Ragan, W. B.: *Modern Elementary Curriculum*. Copyright 1953 by The Dryden Press, Inc., New York.

18. Reed, H. B.: *Psychology of Elementary School Subjects*, Ginn, Boston, 1938.

19. Rinsland, H. D.: *A Basic Vocabulary of Elementary School Children*, Macmillan, New York, 1945.

20. Rousseau, J. J.: *Emelius: Or a Treatise of Education*, vol. I, A. Donaldson, London and Edinburgh, 1773.

21. Washburne, C. (Chairman). *Child Development and the Curriculum*, 38th Yearbook of the Nat. Soc. Stud. Educ., Part I. Chicago: Distributed by the University of Chicago Press, 1939.

22. Wilcox, Ethelwyn B., and Margaret B. Merkley: *Outline of Rat Demonstration to Show the Value of Good Diets*, bulletin of the School of Home Economics, Utah State Agricultural College, Logan, 1954.

23. Wilson, G. M.: "Basic considerations for profitable research in arithmetic," *J. Educ. Res.*, 38: 119–123, 1944.

24. ———: "The social utility theory as applied to arithmetic, its research basis, and some of its implications," *J. Educ. Res.*, 41: 321–337, 1947–1948.

Chapter 2

Learning: An Integration of Theories

DESPITE THE fact that scientific appraisals reveal that today's children equal or exceed the scholastic attainments of their parents at the same ages [1], parents and the popular press often challenge teachers to justify their new methods of teaching. For example, observing the "rat tending" and other unusual individual and social activities of the children who participated in the diet experiment with Reddie and Blue Boy, a parent whose elementary school experiences had been restricted largely to teacher-directed drill might blame such "progressive" methods for his immature child's unfortunate deficiencies in reading, spelling, and arithmetic, or for his resistance in conforming to rigid parental discipline at home. One parent claims that the happiness of his young children is the product of their frustration-free lives; but a neighbor wonders if these children are being disciplined sufficiently to prepare them for the "harsher realities" he foresees for them as adults. Still another critic, the writer of a popular book, apparently thinks that in American schools phonics has been abandoned for the word method in teaching children to read; as a consequence, he challengingly asserts that the method of teaching reading is entirely wrong [11]. A defender of the current methods, however, who believes that phonics, rather than being abandoned, has become part of a more comprehensive approach, explains that a proper combination of the word method in the initial stages, the introduction of phonetic and other word-analysis techniques as children mature, and the emphasis throughout on reading for meaning develops the proficiency in reading characteristic of the great majority of American school children.

As a basis for meeting such challenges and for intelligent interpretation of such controversies, teachers need to understand the scientifically established theories and conditions of effective learning. Also, it is from understanding these theories and conditions of learning that creative teachers are able to invent new and more effective ways of teaching and child guidance.

In attaining the objectives of the elementary school, children acquire several different kinds of behavior patterns. These patterns include, as was noted in the preceding chapter, combinations of knowledge and understandings, skills and competencies, attitudes and interests, and habits and action patterns—with both intellectual and emotional components. Moreover, the curriculum content comprises study in several different areas, such as language, reading, arithmetic, social studies, natural science, and arts, and includes child development goals as well. As a general guide to teachers in creating conditions for effective learning of these different behavior patterns in all these curriculum areas, we shall attempt to formulate a comprehensive and practical outline of learning principles. In achieving this purpose, we shall be eclectic in our consideration of learning theories, but we shall try to achieve an integration rather than a collection of ideas. We shall strive to anchor our formulation securely to the pertinent observational facts and experiments in psychology and education.

Theories of Learning

In the attempts to understand and to control learning, three different approaches or schools of thought have evolved: the conditioned-response theory, of which one particular view has been systematically developed and comprehensively applied to practical learning situations by Guthrie [4, 5, 6]; the "trial-and-error" or "effect" theory of Thorndike, which for application to teaching has been given modern interpretations by both Thorndike [22] and Gates [2]; and the gestalt or "insight" theory, of which the applications have been elaborated by Hartman [8], Lewin [12], and Wheeler and Perkins [24]. Within these three approaches there are several particular theoretical formulations [10]. Most of the writers who have developed theories within any one of these general approaches have attempted to encompass all the pertinent facts known about learning within their systems of explanation, and with results which, I believe, would be considered at least logical. This is not surprising, because, as Guthrie has remarked, "Theories are not true or false, they are useful or less useful." It would appear, however, that each of the three general theories, because of its particular emphasis, is most adequate or useful for explaining a different phase of learning or learning situation. And since we are concerned here with developing a formulation of learning theory which will have maximum usefulness as a guide to teaching, we shall examine the theories from this point of view.

Differences in the learning situations to which the three learning approaches have been applied are illustrated diagrammatically in Figure 2–1.

In stating the principle of conditioning, Guthrie writes that "a combination of stimuli which has accompanied a movement will on its recurrence tend to be followed by that movement" [6, p. 23]. In diagramming this formulation, we may assume that (R_1) is a reaction which has occurred in response to the pattern of stimuli (S_1) and (S_2) or (S_3), (S_1) being already adequate (because of

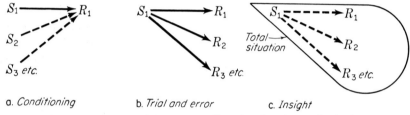

a. *Conditioning*   b. *Trial and error*   c. *Insight*

Fig. 2–1. Diagrams of three kinds of learning situations and behavior.

innate development or prior conditioning) to elicit (R_1). Next time this pattern of stimuli is presented or only a significant part of it—only (S_2) or (S_3), which originally were not adequate to elicit (R_1)—is presented, (R_1) will tend to recur. In this way a person may learn to make a given response to an extended range of stimuli.

In the trial-and-error situation, the individual is confronted with (S_1), to which he has no habitual or adequate response immediately available. By making several "provisional tries" [10, p. 335]—(R_1), (R_2), (R_3), etc.—he discovers from the effects of each trial a suitable response. The insight situation does not differ basically from the trial-and-error situation, except that the learner is often assumed to perceive or to conceptualize (correctly or incorrectly) the meaning of the total situation before acting. Mentally or vicariously he has anticipated the consequences of making (R_1), (R_2), or (R_3) to (S_1), and he chooses without overt trials what he assumes will be an adequate response in the situation. The insight explanation does not differ fundamentally from the trial-and-error explanation, because in the latter also it is assumed that each response is made in the light of at least partial and tentative insight. It is assumed that each provisional trial is guided by hypotheses about the expected outcomes, "to be confirmed or denied by its success or failure" [10, p. 336]. In the historical development of learning theories, however, it is the gestalt (or configural) psychologists who have emphasized the perceptual and cognitive (or meaning) aspects of learning.

To clarify further the contributions to explanations of learning of these three general theories, an example of how each explains a learning activity may be helpful.

Example of Conditioning. Peter, a child of three years, was taught by Dr. M. C. Jones [21, pp. 428–429] to make the same kind of pleasurable and emotionally confident response which he made to a friendly adult or a well-liked food also to a rabbit, which had previously elicited marked fear. The friendly adult and the food at lunchtime—(S_1) in the diagrammatic illustration of conditioning—already evoked a comfortable and pleasurable reaction; and when the rabbit—(S_2), which in this instance is the conditioned stimulus—was in successive trials moved closer to Peter so that it gradually became a significant part of the combination of stimuli leading to comfort and pleasure, it also came to elicit this reaction in place of fear. Peter could finally stroke the rabbit with one hand and eat with the other.

Many school situations are analogous to this example. When the first grade child enters school, because it is his first long absence from home and because the school is new and strange, he may feel timid. But if his teacher is warm, friendly, and reassuring, and does not press him too quickly into new or difficult activities, he responds to her with feelings of security and confidence; and very shortly this response to his teacher is extended to all school situations of which she has been a significant part. In general, the formula for teaching by conditioning, according to Guthrie, is: When a response has been elicited by a combination of stimuli (already adequate and to-be-conditioned stimuli) frequently enough to make the conditioned stimulus a significant part of the combination, then, if only a part of the combination (the conditioned stimulus), is represented, the response tends to recur [5, p. 26]. In Guthrie's treatment of conditioning, the only essential considered fundamental is that of contiguity (or nearness) between the conditioned stimulus and the desired response. And only one trial would be required for learning if in that trial the conditioned stimulus served as the significant stimulus in eliciting the conditioned response. But adventitious stimuli often interfere, and thus the usual need for several trials.

Example of Trial-and-error Learning. Trial-and-error learning is rather dramatically illustrated in a simple experiment reported by Miller and Dollard [15]. Under the bottom edge of the center book on the lower shelf of a

4-foot-long bookcase containing books of similar color and size a flat piece of candy is hidden. A six-year-old girl fond of this particular candy is brought into the room and told that a piece of candy is hidden under one of the books in the case, and that she may have it to eat if she is able to find it. As she searches, she is directed to return each book after looking under it. Motivated by her appetite for the candy and by the challenging, gamelike problem, she makes several goal-directed trials [15, pp. 14–16]:

First, she looks under a few books on the top shelf. Then she turns around. After a brief pause, she starts taking out the books on the lower shelf, one by one. When she has removed eight of these books without finding the candy, she temporarily leaves the books and starts looking under the magazines on the top shelf. Then she returns to look again on the top shelf under several of the books she has already picked up. After this, she turns toward the experimenter and asks, "Where is the candy?" After a pause, she pulls out a few more books on the bottom shelf, stops, sits down, and looks at the books for about half a minute, turns away from the bookcase, looks under a book on a nearby table, then returns and pulls out more books. Under the thirty-seventh book which she examines, she finds the piece of candy. Uttering an exclamation of delight, she picks it up and eats it. On this trial, it has taken her 200 seconds to find the candy.

She is sent out of the room, candy is hidden under the same book, and she is called back again for another trial. This time she goes directly to the lower shelf of books, taking out each book methodically. She does not stop to sit down, turn away, or ask the experimenter questions. Under the twelfth book she finds the candy. She has finished in 86 seconds.

On the third trial, she goes almost directly to the right place, finding the candy under the second book picked up. She has taken only 11 seconds.

On the following trial, the girl does not do so well. Either the previous spectacular success has been due partly to chance, or some uncontrolled factor has intervened. This time the girl begins at the far end of the shelf and examines 15 books before finding the candy. She has required 86 seconds.

Thereafter, her scores improve progressively until, on the ninth trial, she picks up the correct book immediately and secures the candy in three seconds. On the tenth trial, she again goes directly to the correct book and gets the candy in two seconds.

Her behavior has changed markedly. Instead of requiring 210 seconds and stopping, asking questions, turning away, looking under magazines, searching in other parts of the room, picking up wrong books, and making other useless responses, she now goes directly to the right book and gets the candy in two seconds. She has learned.

From Miller and Dollard's description of this child's learning behavior, we note that, as signs of learning progress, there were gradual though uneven reductions in the number of provisional trials and in the time required. It seems safe to infer also that the child's concept of the solution to the problem became clearer and more differentiated, and that she became more confident in her approach.

Often it is helpful to both the learner and his teacher to see a graphic portrayal of some phase of the progress made at each trial. Figure 2–2 demonstrates the progress of this child in terms of the number of books examined, showing an error score for each trial.

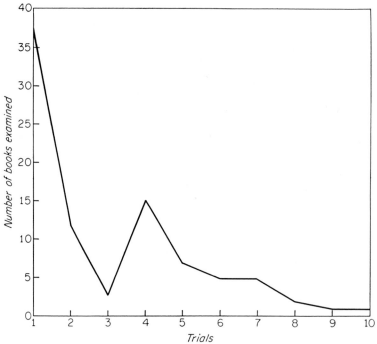

FIG. 2–2. Learning curve for six-year-old girl's trial-and-error efforts to find candy under a certain book in a bookcase. (*From Miller, N. E., and Dollard, J.: Social Learning and Imitation, Yale University Press, New Haven, Conn., 1941, p. 15.*)

For interpreting such examples of learning, Thorndike, over a period of a half century of experimenting and theorizing, has developed several principles, which constitute his trial-and-error, or "connectionist," theory of learning [2, 22]. (1) In this instance, the child, motivated by her desire for the candy and by the challenging task, is in a state of "readiness," or is mentally set by the directions for a certain kind of searching behavior. (2) A "multiple and varied attack" on the problem begins; she tries provisionally book after book and makes other explorations as well in her search for the candy. (3) According to the "law of effect," the responses followed by motive satisfaction are selected for continued use (learned), and those attended by dissatisfaction are eliminated. In this instance, the obviously unrewarding explorations are quickly eliminated, and eventually only the book covering the candy is picked up. (4) It is also assumed in the theory that with repeated "exercise" of the correct stimulus-response connections, and when accompanied by "belonging-ness," or motive satisfaction, these connections are strengthened. The learning curve shows that by the ninth trial the S-R connection between perception of the right book and picking it up has been so strengthened that there is no longer any competition from any other book or exploratory effort. (5) Two supplementary principles should be mentioned as being significant, especially from the point of view of teaching activities analogous to this one. First, the correct S-R connection would have been learned more readily if the significant stimulus had been more "identifiable"—if the correct book had been marked distinctively instead of resembling all the other books on the shelf. And second, if this six-year-old child had had readily "available" such a counting response as "seventh book from the left on the bottom shelf," she would have mastered the problem more quickly. (6) Another important aspect of the theory is the assumption that, on meeting other situations which have elements in common with this one, the child will respond by "analogy" with a pattern of behavior similar to that found successful in this searching problem. (7) Also, on sub-sequent occasions, we may expect that only a part of the total situation will be necessary to elicit this problem-solving approach; that is, "associative shift-ing" (shifting the response to fewer or even, at first, inadequate cues) will occur.

In the attempt to bring out all Thorndike's explanatory concepts of learning, the interpretation of this illustration has become somewhat strained. The central feature of this theory is the law of effect. Finding herself in a problem situation—(S_1) in (b) of the diagram presented earlier—the child tries out as responses (R_1), (R_2), (R_3), etc., and on the basis of the effects, she discovers an adequate mode of adjusting to this and to similar situations. In both the subject-matter and the child development aspects of the curriculum, much of the child's learning may be readily explained according to this general theory. The child will learn and use those responses which he perceives are correct and which he experiences as motive-satisfying. And it should be remarked in passing that rewarding desired behavior has been found much more effective than punishing undesired behavior in developing desirable behavior.

Example of Learning with Insight. Using the Obstacle Peg Test shown in Figure 2-3 with 74 two-to-six-year-old children, Harter [7] demonstrated both overt, trial-and-error learning and, in some of these children, insight learning. Confronted with the device pictured—an $8\frac{1}{4}$-inch-diameter grooved board containing within the grooved path three unremovable pegs with differently colored tops—each child is asked, "Slide the red ball [pointing to the red peg top] to the red hole in the center [pointing again]." Since the pegs are not removable, the task can be accomplished only by sliding the otherwise interfering yellow and green pegs out of the way into the grooves at 2, 3, 4, or 5.

Of the 74 children tested, 53 succeeded by overt, trial-and-error moves and 21 failed, within the five minutes allowed. That maturity is one factor determining success in this task is indicated by the fact that the successful group exceeded the failing group both in average chronological and in average mental age. But at this time our interest is especially in insight learning, the role of which in this solution-learning problem is suggested in two ways. (1) The successful group made fewer moves than did the failure group; apparently a better perception of the problem as a whole, or insight into it, made their moves surer. (2) Of the 50 children in the successful group who were given a second trial, "thirty-two made no trial-and-error moves"; the insight or understanding achieved on

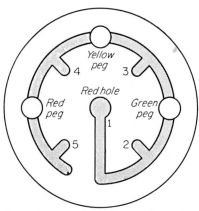

Fig. 2–3. Obstacle Peg Test, illustrating trial and error and insight learning: "Slide the red peg to the No. 1 hole." (*From Harter, G. L.: J. Genet. Psychol., 38: 362, 1930.*)

the first trial served as a sufficient cognitive guide for clearing the path and moving the red peg without error moves directly to the center hole.

According to gestalt, or insight, psychologists, the important changes constituting learning are perceptual and cognitive (or mental). Hartmann, in explaining this instance of learning, would probably say that the children in the Obstacle Peg Test situation, as a result of their goal-directed observation and thinking, progressed perceptually "from a relatively undifferentiated, homogeneous stage to a more elaborate and internally differentiated condition" [8, p. 202]. Insight was achieved in that "the point of the situation" was seen by a process of organizing or reorganizing perceptual patterns of the significant elements in the situation in relation to the goal. Lewin [12, pp. 224–229] would speak of these perceptual changes as changes in "cognitive structure." A "previously vague and unstructured area becomes cognitively structured and specific." According to his views, learning is a process of differentiating the relatively unstructured, and the "cognitive maps" or mental guides thus constructed and reconstructed become guides to more adequate action in problem situations. As a child first observes the Obstacle Peg Test, he probably perceives it as an undifferentiated pattern of pegs and grooves. But as he observes this vaguely structured situation, because he is goal-directed to slide the red peg to the center hole, he reorganizes his perception and concept of it. Mentally he differentiates the clear path from the side paths for the obstructing pegs; and guided by this specifically structured "cognitive map," he executes the pattern of moves required.

Much of the child's problem-solving learning in school can be thus explained. In application to motor skills, for example, Hartmann writes that the "heart of such learning lies in the vivid sensory perception of this structure (the configuration of action required in performance of the motor skill) and its essential reproduction in the pattern of movement of the body of the learner" [8, p. 188]. Similar analyses could be made of the process of identifying the meaning of words in reading, of understanding concepts in science and social studies, of problem solving in arithmetic, of achieving a satisfying result in creative art—indeed, for every aspect of the curriculum. With the modern emphasis on meaning, generalizing, and applying principles in school learning, this explanation of learning is favored.

Insight and Trial-and-error Learning. This analysis of learning by insight is not, as has already been mentioned, inconsistent with the trial-and-error explanation. In fact, the two views may be harmonized as one. In our particular integration of the two approaches to learning, however, the perceptual aspects, or, in Lewin's terminology, the changes in cognitive structure, predominate in what we shall call learning. Thorndike's law of effect, which in the trial-and-error theory accounts for the selection of right responses and the elimination of wrong responses, needs to be extended. In addition to motive satisfaction or dissatisfaction, the selection-and-elimination process is guided also by the learner's perception of the effects of each provisional trial. This perceptual factor is of crucial importance.

A Two-factor Theory of Learning

Having noted that so-called "trial-and-error" and "insight" learning are fundamentally similar, we are left with only two basic kinds of learning, which Mowrer [16, 18] has designated as (1) "conditioning," or stimulus substitution—(a) of Figure 2–1—and (2) "problem solving," or response substitution—(b) and (c) of Figure 2–1. According to Mowrer, habits, knowledge, understandings, language, motor skills—all voluntary behavior mediated by the central nervous system—are acquired by problem solving. Emotional learning, including love, anger, fear, anxiety, etc., and also secondary motives, interests, likes and dislikes, and attitudes are acquired by conditioning. In these emotional learnings the autonomic nervous system is important in mediating responses which are largely involuntary. In problem solving, the law of effect is an important explanatory principle; in conditioning, "contiguity," in agreement with Guthrie, is the only explanatory principle needed.

Tuttle [23] has expressed a similar view in saying that there are two kinds of learning: (1) "intellectual" learning—of skills, memorized facts, and reasoning; and (2) "affective" learning—of attitudes, drives to action, appreciations, interests, morals, tastes, and standards. These two kinds of learning may occur separately in sequence (conditioning leading to problem solving, or

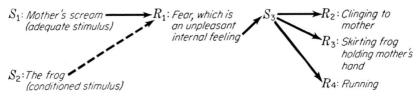

FIG. 2–4. Two-factor learning theory diagrammed: a conditioned fear response becomes internal stimulus (S_3) for varied responses (R_1), (R_2), and (R_3).

vice versa), but they also occur frequently in intertwined, simultaneous relationships.

How a six-year-old boy came to fear a frog, and the patterns of behavior he learned in dealing with it, illustrate conditioning and problem solving combined. As the child, who had theretofore exhibited only interest and curiosity about frogs, was about to cross a grass-covered irrigation ditch with his mother on the way to their car, a lively frog hopped out of the ditch. The mother, with a scream of terror, jumped back away from the frog; and the boy, in response to his mother's scream, also scampered back and clung to her. Then, resuming the approach to the car, the child, who had now, like the mother, been conditioned to fear the frog, met the problem by joining his mother in a path skirting widely around it, choosing to hold his mother's hand on the side away from the frog. When it was discovered that the child had forgotten his cap in the house they were leaving and must return for it, he this time reacted to his newly conditioned fear of the frog by running very quickly on the part of the path where the frog had appeared.

Figure 2–4 presents diagrammatically the two-factor-theory explanation [17] of this instance of learning. In the diagram, (S_1) is an adequate stimulus for eliciting fear in this child. In this instance, because the theretofore nonfrightening frog was a significant part of a combination of stimuli—(S_1) and (S_2)—eliciting fear, it also, even without the mother's demonstration of fear, became a conditioned stimulus for exciting fear in the child. This fear will presumably always occur in the boy as a response to frogs until a substitute response is learned. But the fear response is also a stimulus as an unpleasant internal condition. The child will attempt to allay it by varied problem-solving efforts. In this case, he responded first by clinging to his mother; second, by taking a path to avoid the frog and by holding his mother's hand; and third, by running quickly past the frog.

Definition of Learning. With this background for an eclectic approach to learning, we are now ready to attempt an integrated statement of what learning *is*—and, since we are primarily concerned with teaching, of the essential conditions for effective learning. Guided by both Melton [14, pp. 667–668] and Munn [19, p. 374], we may define learning as "a change in experience or behavior resulting from purposeful observation, overt activity, or thinking, and accompanied by motivational-emotional reactions, which results in more adequate satisfaction of the motivating conditions." In the meaning of the phrase "experience or behavior" we explicitly include perceptions, cognitions, overt actions, motivational-emotional feelings, and attitudes. In typical learning situations, such as learning to recognize the meaning of new words in reading, the child is changing in many ways. Vague visual-stimulus patterns are being differentiated into meaningful percepts. Cognitive structures which determine how new words and ideas shall be perceived are being organized. Verbal- and visual-action patterns are being differentiated and connected with the appropriate stimulus patterns. And important motivational-emotional attitudes are developing simultaneously. While he is learning to read by problem solving, the child is also acquiring interest and confidence in, or distaste for and anxiety about, the activity, depending on the conditioning aspects of the situation.

By saying in our definition of learning that the changes achieved result in more adequate satisfaction of motives, we imply an emphasis upon the motivational, purposive, and goal-directed nature of learning. Since both intellectual and emotional learnings are involved in typical instances of learning, we shall need, according to Mowrer, a theory which encompasses both problem solving and conditioning. This Mowrer's two-factor theory of learning accomplishes. But before we adapt it to an integrated formulation as a guide to teaching, we shall first describe the two aspects separately.

Problem-solving Learning. Descriptively, problem-solving learning involves the following phases: (1) A motivated person, who, upon meeting (2) a situation—(S_1) in (b) or (c) of Figure 2-1—to which he cannot adjust adequately on the basis of either innate behavior patterns or prior learning, (3) makes multiple, goal-directed, provisional tries. (4) Experiencing the effects of these trials, both perceptually and as motive satisfaction or dissatisfaction, he (5) selects ("differentiates" or "integrates"), often from several trials, a pattern of behavior which promises to meet the motivating conditions more adequately. (6) When this or a similar situation arises again, the more adequate pattern will recur more directly and with less attention and effort. The central feature in this learning behavior is the perceptual experience which results in changing the cognitive structure (or mental map) for reacting to the situation; and the persistence of this new cognitive structure constitutes the learning that has taken place. As illustrations of this concept, the child's trial-and-error search for candy and the solution by insight of the Obstacle Peg Test may be recalled.

As a further exercise in applying this pattern of analysis, we may consider how a five-year-old learns to articulate g correctly so that he pronounces gun as "gun" rather than as "dun." In a friendly, nonthreatening relationship with an adult (*conditioning confidence*), he may be made interested in saying "gun" just as the adult does (*motivation*). But he is at first unable to do so (*problem*). As leads to goal-directed trials, he may observe the adult's pronunciation more closely, or be guided by the adult's explanation and demonstration of where to place his tongue and lips and how to use his throat in saying "gun" (*teacher-guidance of goal-directed trials*). As he perceives that his own attempts are coming to resemble more closely the adult model or that they still deviate from it, he repeats with slight or with more radical modifications his attempts to articulate the word, and experiences more or less satisfaction of mastery and approval (*perception of effects* and *motive satisfaction*). Often, while his attention is on pronouncing the word, he fails to perceive the results of his trials. He can be helped in this respect by a mirror or sound recorder (*perception of effects*). Out of these repeated goal-directed trials, in which his perceptions of the effects of preceding trials become guides for performance in subsequent trials, he differentiates and integrates—both cognitively and as a motor pattern—a satisfying response for the situation (*pattern selection*). Finally, in addition to habitually pronouncing gun as "gun," he may now, even without special training, say "go" instead of "doe" (*transfer*).

A little reflection will reveal that much of the teacher-directed learning in the elementary school conforms to this pattern of analysis. As examples, the following may be mentioned: in *language*, improvement of articulation, correct usage, understanding of meanings of words and more complex verbal expressions, learning how to make a speech or write a composition, etc.; in *hand-*

writing, understanding of how letters are formed, improvement in legibility and speed, and improvement in such features as uniformity of slant and alignment, quality of line, and spacing; in *spelling*, learning how to learn to spell words, mastery of the 3,000 to 5,000 most needed words, learning how to use the dictionary, and recognition of the correctness or incorrectness of words spelled in writing; in *reading*, learning independent recognition of words, improvement in comprehension and speed of reading, vocabulary development, and learning how to adapt reading to a variety of purposes and uses; in *arithmetic*, learning the combinations, acquiring understanding of and skill in problem solving, and understanding the uses of arithmetic; in *science*, acquiring understanding of and skill in using concepts; in *art* and *music*, acquiring skills, knowledge, and understanding; in *health* and *physical education*, acquiring motor skills, knowledge, and understanding; and in *development of healthy personality*, *character*, and *social behavior*, understandings, knowledge, techniques, and skills. In all these activities, the learning is basically by trial and error or by problem solving.

Conditioning. In all the above-mentioned areas there are also important motivational-emotional components. These components, such as interests, appreciations, and attitudes, are learned by conditioning. That is, when reading, social studies, music, art, or other activities are made a part of a combination of stimuli already adequate for leading to satisfying uses, mastery, pleasure, approval, and other gratifications, then these subjects, or parts of them, also become effective as conditioned stimuli in arousing interest and appreciation. As Pressey has written, "An interest grows with tropical lushness in the warm sun of success and approval. It withers if not so nourished and stimulated, may even be blighted by only one devastating experience if instead of success and approval it meets ridicule or contempt and failure." [20, p. 156].

The motivational-emotional components in interests and appreciations, however, are not learned as isolated elements; what a person *does* to satisfy his interest or to escape anxiety or a feared object, he learns to do by problem solving, as was illustrated in the case of the child's fear of the frog, mentioned earlier. We are reminded again that, typically, learning by problem solving and by conditioning are going on simultaneously. Our formula for teaching interests, appreciations, and attitudes, since they involve motivational-emotional components, should therefore include, besides the principle of contiguity from conditioning, the principle of "effect" or motive satisfaction from problem-solving learning.

In general, then, to develop interest in a new activity, associate it with conditions which already lead to motive satisfactions, and arrange that the adaptive responses made in this situation be rewarding.

Deriving the Conditions for Effective Learning. In this essentially eclectic consideration of learning theories, an adaptation of Mowrer's two-factor theory has provided a basis for integrating traditional theories into a concept of learning comprehensive enough to cover both its intellectual and emotional aspects. From the conditioning theory an explanation of the learning of interests, emotions, and attitudes has been derived. Explanations of problem-solving learning have drawn from the trial-and-error theory the concepts of multiple provisional trials and of the role of motive satisfaction or dissatisfaction in selecting responses, and from the insight theory the concept of perception and cognition as guides to behavior. Restating a definition of learning based on this integrated theory, it may be said that learning results from reacting purposefully to environmental and self situations, and that learning involves a change or reorganization of an individual's perceptual, cognitive, and motivational-emotional structure which may be utilized as a guide to more adequate adjustments to the given situations and to related situations. As deductions from and elaborations of this theory and definition, we shall now formulate a practical outline of learning principles for application to teaching.

Essential Conditions for Effective Learning

For elementary school children to learn effectively to read, to understand arithmetic or social studies, to acquire appropriate social techniques, or to learn effectively in any of the areas previously outlined, at the same time acquiring confidence as learners and interests in many learning activities, the following conditions are considered essential: (1) sufficient mental maturity and an appropriate pattern of abilities; (2) teacher-guidance in focusing attention on (a) goal-directing hypotheses (mental sets leading to identification, discrimination, and differentiation of stimulus clues, and to tentative formulation of means-to-goal response patterns), (b) efficient modes of attack, and (c) adjustments in goals or standards to the progress of the learner; (3) practice which consists of provisional trials or hypothesis-guided self-activity oriented toward discovery, differentiation, and integration of more effective patterns of behavior; (4) perception of the effects of each trial, with provision for checking the correctness and adequacy of each and for revising subsequent efforts in the light of clear perception of the results of previous goal-directed attempts; (5) provision for transfer of training, which involves emphasis upon meanings, the inductive learning of principles, the interorganization and ex-

Fig. 2–5. Initial guidance on how to perform a skill is frequently accomplished by the teacher's explanations and demonstrations. (*Courtesy of Adams School, Logan, Utah.*)

pansion of these principles, and their useful application; (6) motivation, which arouses, sustains, directs, and determines the intensity of learning effort, and which in cooperation with perception of the effects defines and evaluates the consequences of provisional trials; and (7) freedom from anxiety and distorting attitudes which impair or prevent effective learning. How these conditions determine effectiveness of learning will first be illustrated by an example. This will be followed in subsequent chapters by experimental data supporting the validity of the principles and indicating further applications of them.

An Example: Learning Manuscript Writing. To illustrate the conditions of effective learning, we may apply them to a plan for teaching first grade children manuscript writing. Considerable research indicates that manuscript writing is well suited to the maturity level of primary grade children. Hildreth says that, in comparison to cursive writing, it is easier to learn, is adjusted to the growth tendencies of children, is immediately legible, and aids in learning to read and to spell [9]. Thus the first condition, that of "sufficient maturity and an appropriate pattern of abilities," is at least partially met. First grade children will differ, of course, in the patterns of their abilities, and some may have specific handicaps in perception or motor skills which make even manuscript writing difficult.

Teacher-guidance in focusing attention on goal-directing hypotheses implies teacher-guidance in how to write. This is usually provided by setting forth models to imitate and by demonstrations or explanations. Since there are usually several ways to perform a skill, not all equally efficient, the research on efficient modes of attack in learning the elementary school subjects should be consulted for suggestions. In this instance, Lewry, in an article on improving manuscript writing in the primary grades, supplies us with a good model [13]. Guided by the criteria of simplicity and of most frequent use in primary reading materials, he developed the system which is presented in Figure 2–6 and which we shall use as our model in this instance.

a b c d e f g h i j k l m n o p q r s t u v w x y z A B C D E F G H I J K L M N O P Q R S T U V W X Y Z

Order and direction of movement: a b c d e

Fig. 2–6. Letter models for teaching mode of attack in manuscript writing. (*From Lewry, M. E.: Elem. Sch. J., 47: 508–515, 1947. Reprinted by permission of the University of Chicago Press.*)

By presentation of this model on the blackboard or in a smaller model at each pupil's seat, by teacher-demonstration of how the letters are formed, and by some verbal explanation, the child is helped to discriminate and to comprehend the stimulus clues (the model) to which he is to react, and to conceive a mental guide (or cognitive structure or map) for making appropriate goal-directed responses.

The practice begins with writing content in which the child is interested and which is so restricted in length and difficulty as to ensure some degree of initial success.

Perhaps not just at the beginning, when too great complexity of goal might arouse anxiety, but as soon as some progress in forming the letters correctly has been made, attention is called to an efficient mode of attack in forming letters. Lewry marked letters with numbers and arrows, as shown in Figure 2–6, to indicate an efficient order and direction of movements in forming the letters. The teacher may guide pupils in acquiring this mode of attack by demonstrations and accompanying verbal explanations. As the pupils make progress in formation of letters and come to feel some confidence and comfort in using manuscript in "creative" writing, new goals and standards are introduced; otherwise plateaus in the progress curve would occur. These new goals, added periodically throughout the primary grades, should include learning to space more closely between letters within a word and to space more widely between words, greater uniformity of slant and alignment, even quality of line, and improvement in speed. Individual characteristics of style develop as variations from these essentials for legibility and efficiency.

If skill in manuscript writing is to be achieved, practice will, of course, be necessary. Both short, daily periods of systematic, teacher-guided practice and practice in writing in a variety of school activities should continue at least throughout the primary grades and may well be extended beyond this period [9]. But practice alone, though necessary for learning a skill, is not sufficient, as will be demonstrated later. For practice to be effective, there must also be continuous attention to goal-directing ideas—ways and techniques for improving. At least a part of each practice period should be used for actively discovering, differentiating, and integrating more effective writing techniques, rather than merely for passive repetitions of response patterns already achieved, which may be relatively good or poor. To manage practice efficiently, the teacher will need to consider such factors as length of each practice period and suitability of content from the points of view of interest, difficulty, and amount for each lesson. These factors will be elaborated in a later general discussion of the conditions for effective learning.

To provide for perception of the effects of each trial, the pupil, with the help of his teacher, will check, following each trial at achieving a manuscript-writing objective (or at least periodically during each practice period), to see whether his performance meets the standards of his model or goal. Has he confined himself to the simple circles, straight lines, and curves indicated in Figure 2–6, or has he used irregular ovals and unnecessary curves? Has his progression from left to right been inefficient, as in making the stem before the circle in writing *d*? Has he spaced properly between words, etc.? Perception of the effects of each trial makes possible corrections that lead to continuous improvement or confirm the already accomplished correct patterns. At first the teacher will need to help children individually so as to check the adequacy of their performances, but they should also be taught to check or "proofread" for themselves so that they may become independent in using this important condition for effective learning.

In learning manuscript writing, as in most learning activities, consideration of the provision for transfer of training multiplies the efficiency of each practice period. In learning to write the 26 lower-case letters, for example, it is conceivable that a pupil might see them as 26 different characters, each one consisting of several different features to be meticulously copied. But this would be a very wasteful procedure, because there are not 26 different formations; there are only three, as an inductive examination of the letters will reveal. All the letters consist of simple circles or part circles; straight lines— perpendicular or horizontal; and simple curves, as in *f* or *j*. At the outset, as a part of the teacher-guidance in goal-directing ideas, the teacher should show by demonstration and verbal explanation that all the letters are simply variations of circles, lines, and curves. Since these formations are already within the repertory of skills of primary grade children, the single letters also are familiar forms, not requiring meticulous copying. Other transfer advantages derive from practicing with words needed and therefore used in writing, and from practicing on words or letters which overcome specific difficulties for particular children.

In motivating children to practice handwriting, perhaps the best incentive is to provide for using the skill in writing one's name, in labeling various objects, and, eventually, in creative writing. It is also possible to arrange conditions so as to appeal to the child's desire for mastery, knowledge of progress, and teacher approval.

If the child feels generally secure at school, where he is away from home perhaps for the first time, if he is successful in his initial attempts, sees himself making satisfactory progress, finds opportunities to use his developing skills, and is approved by a warm, friendly teacher for his efforts, he is likely to be conditioned to respond to handwriting practice with interest and confidence. But if he is denied these satisfactions, if in his initial efforts he is perplexed, or experiences failure and criticism, he may become anxious and self-distrustful, and may need to avoid handwriting as an escape from an anxiety-provoking situation. Or, if he is expected to learn to "write," and regards manuscript as mere "printing," he may resist acquiring the skill.

An example of such interfering attitudes is the experience of a six-year-old child who went timidly away to the first grade with her confidence bolstered by the fact that she could already write her name. But during the "writing lesson," when the teacher wrote each child's name on the board in manuscript, she was disturbed to find that it was not written in the way she had learned to write it. Among other variations, *a* was written in Lewry's simple style, rather than in the more complicated form she had learned. This was so disturbing that she actually went to the board and with her hand erased the name as written by her teacher, saying that it was not her name. This, of course, would not be the time to help this child learn a simpler and more efficient way of manuscript writing. The need for supporting her confidence with the skill brought from home was more important at this particular time; later, when she had found security in her new relationships at school and confidence from her growing skills, she would be ready to change with satisfaction her way of writing.

Consideration of the need for developing and maintaining interest and confidence in school children reminds us that too much pressure too early to acquire efficient modes of attack, and too much conscientious checking of errors, may, rather than make learning more effective, impair learning efficiency. In making a beginning in manuscript writing, children should perhaps be left free for some time to use their crude achievements in writing activities. Eventually there will be many evidences of self-confidence and even questions from the children about how to improve some feature of their writing. These are the signs of readiness for accepting new standards and for substituting more effective modes of attack for less efficient ones.

Analyses similar to this analysis of manuscript teaching could be made for any school learning activity. If the teaching includes adequate consideration as to (1) maturity and abilities, (2) teacher-guidance in showing or in arranging conditions for self-discovery of how to accomplish learning goals efficiently, (3) practice, (4) perception of the effects of provisional trials, (5) provision for transfer, (6) motivation, and (7) freedom from anxiety and distorting attitudes, the conditions for effective learning will have been provided. Such analyses are useful in evaluating a new method of teaching. These conditions serve as guides in developing one's own methods of providing for effective teaching. In instances of failure to learn, one may very well investigate to determine which one or combination of these conditions is not being provided. And in striving for improvements in teaching, teachers may well consider ways of providing more adequately for these essential conditions of effective learning.

In this chapter, the reader has been expected to consider these conditions of effective learning as valid deductions from learning theory. In the next seven chapters, the supporting observational and experimental data for each condition will be presented. Further elaborations and applications will also be suggested.

Review and Applications

1. Why do teachers need to understand a comprehensive and practical theory of learning?

2. Explain, according to the conditioned-response model, how children may learn to feel secure, worthy, confident, and interested in their school activities and relationships.

3. Explain, according to the trial-and-error or problem-solving theory, how a child learns to identify words by reading from context, phonetic analysis, and other clues.

4. Cite examples of the role of insight or of cognitive "map making" in learning by problem solving.

5. From your observation of a well-taught learning activity, from reading about an example of effective teaching (perhaps in an issue of *The Arithmetic Teacher, Childhood Education, Elementary English,* or the *Elementary School Journal*), or from seeing a film on teaching, try to find applications of the seven conditions of effective learning.

References

1. Finch, F. H., and V. W. Gillenwater: "Reading achievement then and now," *Elem. Sch. J.,* 49: 446–454, 1948–1949.

2. Gates, A. I.: "Connectionism: Present concepts and interpretations." *The Psychology of Learning,* pp. 141–164. 41st Yearbook of the Nat. Soc. Stud. Educ., Part II. Chicago: Distributed by the University of Chicago Press, 1942.

3. Gurnee, H.: *Elements of Social Psychology,* Farrar & Rinehart, New York, 1936.

4. Guthrie, E. R.: "Conditioning: A theory of learning in terms of stimulus response and association." *The Psychology of Learning,* pp. 17–68. 41st Yearbook of the Nat. Soc. Stud. Educ., Part II. Chicago: Distributed by the University of Chicago Press, 1942.

5. ———: *The Psychology of Learning,* Harper, New York, 1935.

6. ———: *The Psychology of Learning,* rev. ed., Harper, New York, 1952.

7. Harter, G. L.: "Overt trial-and-error in problem solving of pre-school children," *J. Genet. Psychol.,* 38: 361–372, 1930.

8. Hartmann, G. W.: "The field theory of learning and its educational consequences." *The Psychology of Learning,* pp. 165–214. 41st Yearbook of the Nat. Soc. Stud. Educ., Part II, Chicago: Distributed by the University of Chicago Press, 1942.

9. Hildreth, Gertrude: "Should manuscript writing be continued in the upper grades?" *Elem. Sch. J.,* 44: 85–93, 1944.

10. Hilgard, E. R.: *Theories of Learning,* Appleton-Century-Crofts, New York, 1948. See also Second Edition, 1956.

11. "How Johnny reads" (editorial), *Time,* June 20, 1955, pp. 55–56.

12. Lewin, K.: "Field theory and learning." *The Psychology of Learning,* pp. 215–242.

41st Yearbook of the Nat. Soc. Stud. Educ., Part II. Chicago: Distributed by the University of Chicago Press, 1942.

13. Lewry, Marion E.: "Improving manuscript writing in primary grades," *Elem. Sch. J.*, 47: 508–515, copyright 1947 by the University of Chicago. Reprinted by permission of the University of Chicago Press.

14. Melton, A. W.: "Learning," in W. S. Monroe: *Encyclopedia of Educational Research*, Macmillan, New York, 1952.

15. Miller, N. E., and J. Dollard: *Social Learning and Imitation*, Yale University Press, New Haven, Conn., 1941.

16. Mowrer, O. H.: *Learning Theory and Personality Dynamics*. Ronald, New York, 1950.

17. ————: "Learning theory," *Rev. Educ. Res.*, 22: 475–495, 1952.

18. ————: "On the dual nature of learning—a re-interpretation of 'conditioning' and 'problem-solving,'" *Harv. Educ. Rev.*, 17: 102–148, 1947.

19. Munn, N. L.: "Learning in children," in L. Carmichael (ed.): *Manual of Child Psychology*, Wiley, New York, Copyright 1954.

20. Pressey, S. L., and F. P. Robinson: *Psychology & the New Education*, Harper, New York, 1944.

21. Ruch, F. L.: *Psychology and Life*, Scott, Foresman and Company, Chicago, Copyright, 1948.

22. Thorndike, E. L.: *Human Learning*, Appleton-Century-Crofts, New York, 1931.

23. Tuttle, H. S.: "Two kinds of learning," *J. Psychol.*, 22: 267–279, 1946.

24. Wheeler, R. H., and F. T. Perkins: *Principles of Mental Development*, Crowell, New York, 1932.

Chapter 3

Maturity
and Learning

TED, a child of eight about to complete a year in the second grade, illustrates an aggressive reaction to the frustration of being continually asked to try tasks beyond his mental maturity. His teacher, in cooperating with the school psychologist who was asked to assist her in understanding Ted, wrote about him:

In my several months with Ted, I find him a very difficult and unusual child. He does not understand how to get along with people at all. He is continuously doing things on the sly. Here are several annoying things he did in the room: (1) He tore the reading charts while I was out of the room. (2) He put the board chalk in the waste basket. (3) He scribbled all over my desk blotter. (4) He hits boys and girls at various times. His achievement in the class is far below the group. That is the picture I have of Ted.

Since such poor school achievement, social immaturity, and misbehavior in the classroom are sometimes associated with mental immaturity, the Stanford-Binet intelligence scale was used to determine Ted's intelligence. Though chronologically 8-1, Ted was found to have a mental age of 5-8, resulting in an IQ of 70. Besides a mental age still below the minimum for expectation of success with such academic activities as first grade reading, the individual test also revealed other school-achievement handicaps. Ted's language articulation was found immature: he said "stin" for skin, "nano" for banana, and so on for a large proportion of his vocabulary. He sometimes reacted impulsively, failing the maze test at year 6 because he didn't wait to hear the directions completely. Because of his self-distracting impulses and unconfident attitude, which disturbed his attention and concentration, he failed the memory test at year 5. Ted's poor school and social adjustments and the impairments of his problem-

54

solving ability are probably the consequences of being pressed to try many tasks beyond his maturity level.

Reactions to the frustration of failure are not always aggressive. Mary, who was in the fifth grade and was unable to read at all, except for recognition of a few "sight" words, protected herself from feelings of inadequacy by trying conscientiously to be very nice to people and by avoiding, whenever possible, situations in which her deficiency in reading would be detected. When her group joined the teacher at the reading table for oral reading, she sat quietly with them, watching them for a clue to turn the page in her book at the right time. When her group returned to their individual seats for silent reading, the school psychologist, interested in learning the level at which she could read, joined her at her desk and suggested that she read a little to him. But smiling up at him, she said, "Let's read silent." Next day, however, she brought a book to him to show him that she could read. That she had tried to memorize the selection was revealed, however, by the frequent mismatching of the words she "read" with those printed.

Mary's present mental age is 7-8, which is sufficient for expectation of success with first grade reading. But when she first began her attempts at reading during the first and second grades, her mental age then being only between 4 and 5, she was too immature for success. At that time, as a reaction to the frustration of attempting the impossible, she learned to avoid trying and to make up for her limitations by being especially nice. When she became mature enough for success with reading, the earlier-acquired habits and attitudes persisted to interfere with the confident, systematic problem-solving effort required in learning to read.

Alertness to the need for radical adjustments in the curriculum to match the slow rates of maturing of these two children would have aided in preventing their maladjustments. They can still be helped, however. Ted will still need, for almost another year, a prereading curriculum. Mary now needs individualized teaching in reading. Both need especially all the confidence-building experiences which can be planned and contrived for them. As a further condition of effective learning, the curriculum of every child needs to be suited to his level and rate of maturing and to his particular pattern of abilities.

If children undertake the mastery of such tasks as reading, riding a bicycle, or cooperative participation in a social studies project with sufficient maturity for initial success in them, several desirable outcomes will result. They will progress efficiently in their learning. Because of their satisfactions in these activities, they will probably become more interested in them. Also, because of their successes, they will become more self-confident as learners and problem solvers; and thus they will attack with greater effectiveness an ever-widening array of activities. On the other hand, if children are pressed to attempt learning tasks beyond their present maturation levels, they will be denied these achievements and health-promoting advantages, and several undesirable outcomes may ensue. Besides making no, or at most only painfully slow, progress, they are likely to lose interest in learning; to become, like Ted, rebellious and resistant to teacher-guidance, or overdependent on it; to come to feel inferior and even guilty; or to develop other defenses, such as Mary did against feeling "dumb" or inadequate, which interfere with effective use of their abilities at any level.

In teaching children as they progress through the grades or levels of the elementary school, it is important to recognize that they are also growing. Year by year they are increasing in size, changing in bodily proportions, and developing nervous systems which make possible more complex and effective learning and problem solving. Their gradual attainment of both subject-matter and child development (or social and personal development) objectives is a joint product of both their growing and their learning experiences. Their development is a product of maturation and environmental stimulation. And it is highly important, in providing the conditions for effective learning, that the learning tasks and activities be adjusted to each child's level of maturity and pattern of abilities.

General Patterns of Growth and Development

As a guide to teachers in adjusting the school curriculum to each child's level of maturity and pattern of abilities, thorough understanding of child psychology and development is desirable. There is presented here for the elementary school years only an outline of trends, including the physical, motor, social, intellectual, and school-accomplishment phases of child development. As the child matures, new abilities and capacities for learning emerge; and as he both matures and learns, his skills in all these phases of development gradually improve.

Physical Growth. The general trend of body growth is indicated in Figure 3–1, which shows average child growth in height from birth to maturity, and in Figure 3–2, which reveals the accompanying weight increments. Both the height and weight curves show especially rapid growth in infancy and in preadolescence. During the elementary school years, which cover the period from about age 5 or 6 through age 12, growth typically continues at a steady but slower pace. Perhaps a clearer and more meaningful concept of the general

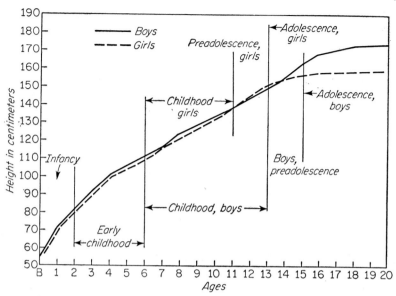

FIG. 3–1. Growth in height of boys and girls from birth to maturity. (*From Cole, L., and Morgan, J. B.: Psychology of Childhood and Adolescence, Rinehart, New York, 1947, p. 4. 1 cm = 0.4 inch.*)

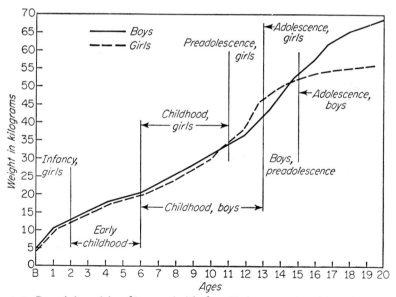

FIG. 3–2. Growth in weight of boys and girls from birth to maturity. (*From Cole, L., and Morgan, J. B.: Psychology of Childhood and Adolescence, Rinehart, New York, 1947, p. 5.*)

Fig. 3–3. Growth through the elementary school years, as indicated by the boy and girl of median height in each grade from kindergarten through sixth. First row, kindergarten through third; second row, fourth through sixth. (*Courtesy of Whittier School, Utah State Agricultural College.*)

growth which occurs during the elementary school period is suggested in Figure 3–3, which pictures the boy and girl of median height at each grade from kindergarten through sixth of one school. The corresponding ages are approximately from 5½ through 11½.

Five-year-old children, having attained a median height of 42 or 43 inches, have entered the childhood period of slower, steady growth, during which they grow, on the average, 2 to 3 inches a year. Typical six-year-old children are about 45 inches tall and have by now lost most of their baby contours. This change in bodily proportion has not, of course, dramatically occurred since age 5; it has been a gradual development since infancy. Continuing to grow 2 to 3 inches a year, the typical seven-year-old has a height of 47 or 48 inches. By age 8, the child is about halfway "up the stairs" in his general progress toward maturity. He is about 50 inches tall; and now, for the next year or two, boys may often be taller than girls. Bodily development is also continuing toward the mature form. At age 9, the median child is about 52 inches tall. He is longer-legged; and in bodily proportions he is definitely more mature. Because there are marked individual differences in rate of maturation, an occasional girl may have already begun the rapid growth spurt characteristic of preadolescence. Ten-year-olds, on the average, have attained a height of about 54 inches. And because so many girls have begun a more rapid rate of growth and thus have caught up with or surpassed the boys, the average heights of the sexes are again about equal.

By ages 11 and 12, most of the girls and an occasional boy will have entered the period of preadolescent growth, marked by variations in rate, in time of onset, and in unevenness. Following a plateau of little or no gain in size for a few months, children beginning the preadolescent growth spurt may gain in height, weight, or both, several times as much during a year as in a previous year. But since some children—especially boys— may continue to grow during ages 11 and 12 at the same slow, steady rate characteristic of childhood, this period is marked by great individual differences in size. Since girls typically mature earlier, they are often larger than boys—creating a difference which is noticeable in such activities as social dancing, which is sometimes begun in the elementary school. By 12 years of age, girls average about 58 inches and boys about 57 inches in height. It is in this period that children may become alarmed by a gain in weight of "as much as twenty pounds" [19]. And since at this time growth is also uneven, preadolescents often worry because they perceive themselves as disproportioned; as being either too large or too small; as having oversized feet, hands, or noses; or as being either overdeveloped or underdeveloped with respect to sexual characteristics.

Development of Motor Skills. Paralleling their growth in size, from ages 5 to 12 elementary school children also make steady and continuous gains in motor skills. Their progress in "hand" skills illustrates this general development. (The quotation marks are placed around "hand" because the patterns of hand movement are, of course, guided by perceptual cues and cognitive patterns.) Before age 6, children have abandoned scribbling for constructive, though imprecise, use of pencil, crayons, or paints. At four years, the typical child can copy a circle and a square. At six or seven years, he can copy forms of such complexity as a diamond. Making gradual improvements from six to twelve years, with general arm control preceding control of precise finger movements, the child reaches at twelve years almost adult precision in control of shoulder, arm, wrist, hand, and fingers in writing, drawing, and manipulation of musical instruments and of craft tools. As further illustrations of this general trend in development of motor skills, two examples of more precisely measured development are cited—one covering the primary period, and one for the intermediate school years.

As an indication of the gradual improvements in motor skills of primary grade children from ages 5 through 7, curves from Jenkins's data [20] are presented in Figure 3–4. Similar patterns of motor development, including consideration of the sex difference favoring the boys, who are also very slightly larger during these years, are shown by Jenkins for running, jumping, hopping, and accuracy of throwing.

Carpenter [8] has presented similar data showing progressive improvement from ages 6 to 9 in accuracy of hopping on a hopscotchlike pattern. In this instance, however, the sex difference favors the girls, an advantage which

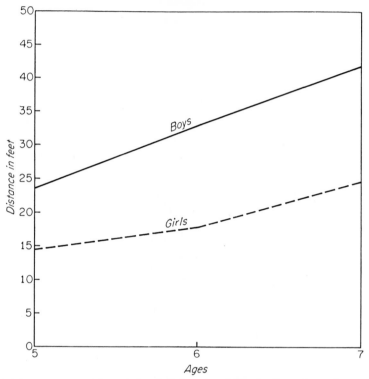

Fig. 3–4. Improvement with age in baseball-throwing ability for five-, six-, and seven-year-old boys and girls (50 in each age-sex group). (*Adapted from Jenkins, L. M.: A Comparative Study of Motor Achievement of Children Five, Six, and Seven Years of Age, Teachers College, Columbia University, New York, Bureau of Publications, 1930, p. 28.*)

Carpenter attributes to the greater amount of self-guided practice which girls have in this particular skill. Whether or not this hypothesis can be confirmed in this instance, it does suggest the general theory that development is a product of both maturation and learning.

Using 20 tests covering a variety of complex motor skills, Brace, in testing several hundred boys and girls of age 9 to 16, found with increasing age or maturity gradual increases in the number of these different tests passed by the children [4, p. 129].

Figure 3–5 shows that the emergence of abilities for these complex motor performances is especially marked from ages 9 to 12. In this instance, rather than showing increases in skill on a single test, the curve shows that with increasing age tests which were failed at younger ages can be mastered. This illustrates the earlier-mentioned concept that with increases in maturity new abilities emerge. The nature and variations in complexity of these 20 tests are

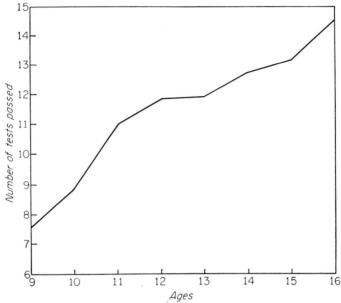

Fɪɢ. 3–5. Emergence of motor abilities over some elementary school years, as indicated by increasing number of Brace tests passed. (*From Brace, D. K.: Measuring Motor Ability: A Scale of Motor Ability Tests, A. S. Barnes, New York, 1930, p. 129.*)

suggested by items (10) to (13), from the middle range of difficulty [4, pp. 114–117]:

10. Hold the toes of either foot in the opposite hand. Jump up and jump the free foot over the foot that is held, without letting go.

11. Jump into the air and slap both heels with the hands behind the back.

12. Stand, kick the right foot up so that the toes come at least level with the shoulders. Do not fall down on the floor.

13. Stand on the left foot. Bend forward and place both hands on the floor. Raise the right leg and stretch it back. Touch the head to the floor, and regain the standing position without losing the balance.

More specific information on the motor skills characteristic of children as they develop from five to twelve years is supplied by Jenkins, Shacter, and

Bauer [19]. Five-year-old children, they note, have achieved moderately good body control and use it purposefully and fairly skillfully in running, jumping, skipping, free dancing, and climbing. Some of them are even learning to throw and catch a ball, to roller-skate, and to ride a small bicycle (at first, perhaps, with extra hind-wheel supports). Their large-muscle control is better than their control of hands and fingers, as required in drawing and writing.

While precise motor control is still not efficient, the typical six-year-old is making gains in running, jumping, climbing, hauling, managing wagons and scooters, and building with blocks and boards. Many of them can now ride a bicycle even without the hind-wheel supports. They are learning to paste, cut, paint, use crayon and pencil constructively, handle craft tools, skate, jump rope, and bat a ball.

By age 7, greater motor skill is being developed in both large and small muscles. Seven-year-olds have often learned to write in manuscript style, and they are more skillful in drawing and in manipulation of tools. They often like elaborating their skills in climbing, in turning somersaults, or in trapeze play such as "skinning the cat."

At age 8, the typical child has good control of both large and small muscles. Manuscript writing is now quite legible. The eight-year-old is often ready for cursive writing, though this may well be delayed in favor of using his manuscript skill in creative writing. His representative drawing of such things as a fire engine is nearly always recognizable. He can manipulate craft tools skillfully. His play, besides being more skillful from the point of view of motor control, is more organized. He likes to play baseball, soccer, football, and other games according to rules.

By age 9 children take pride in their motor and game skills, and practice them directly for improvement. In fact, there is danger that children may become discouraged in such activities as art when they fail to meet their own high standards. In the motor skills required in writing, drawing, manipulation of musical instruments and craft tools, and in weaving and sewing, nine-year-olds can exercise quite precise control.

Although development of many skills and the emergence of new abilities continue through adolescence, from ten to twelve years of age many of the hand skills approach adult maturity. By the sixth grade, many children write cursively as legibly as the average adult, although not as fast. They manipulate craft tools with definite skill. Special interests have often developed, and some children may draw, play a musical instrument, or construct puppets or model airplanes with mature skill. Boys are adept in playing such team games as basketball, football, and baseball. Girls are beginning to sew and cook skillfully, and may even begin 4-H competition in these activities. Both boys and girls are learning to execute skillful patterns in skating, dancing, and swimming.

Intellectual Development. The development of symbolic processes—including language, percepts, concepts, memory, imagination, and reasoning—is similar in some respects to the pattern of physical growth. Curves showing the growth of intelligence indicate relatively rapid growth in infancy and continuous development at a gradually slower rate until a plateau is reached at maturity. The spurt in physical growth during preadolescence, however, is apparently not matched by a similar spurt in intellectual growth. Some intelligence tests

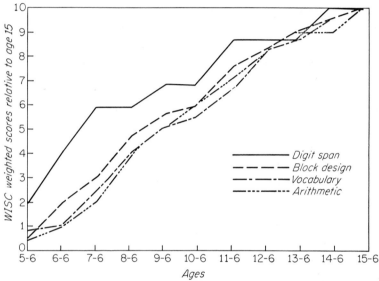

FIG. 3–6. Mental growth as reflected by four subtests of Wechsler's Intelligence Scale for Children. (*Adapted from Wechsler, D.: Child Develpm., 21: 47, 1951.*)

show continuous growth, although at a greatly decelerated rate, throughout adolescence. But on the very frequently used Stanford-Binet intelligence scale, maturity is usually reached at age 16.

Although most of us think of intelligence as a general capacity for learning and problem solving, psychologists have also found it useful to think of intelligence as comprised of several different abilities and mental processes. For these different mental processes the patterns of development may vary. To indicate both the general trend of mental growth during the elementary school years and also the patterns for different mental processes, curves of growth for four of the eleven tests from the Wechsler Intelligence Scale for Children are presented in Figure 3–6. These curves of mental growth show roughly the proportion[1] of fifteen-year maturity achieved at each age from $5\frac{1}{2}$ to $15\frac{1}{2}$. Reasoning with verbal, numerical, and spatial symbols develops at a steady though slightly decelerated rate from ages $5\frac{1}{2}$ to $15\frac{1}{2}$, as is indicated by the curves for vocabulary, arithmetic, and block designs (a task requiring analysis and copying of spatial patterns). The rate of mental growth is apparently faster for memory span for digits (verbal reproduction from auditory presentation of from two to eight digits), since by age $7\frac{1}{2}$ a level of maturity is reached that is not attained in the other three mental processes until about age $10\frac{1}{2}$.

As Jenkins, Shacter, and Bauer's observations [19] reveal, intellectual growth is also expressed in the emergence of and participation in a variety of specific activities. Compared to younger children, five-year-olds are much more goal-directed, constructive, and creative in their activities. With almost mature articulation (typically only about 10 per cent of their speech sounds being misarticulated), they use language in carrying on conversation and in expressing their ideas. By six years of age, in addition to fairly skillful use of language, the child begins to use other symbols. Some six-year-olds make progress in reading, in writing, in counting and other modes of dealing with quantities, and in creative activities with art media, sand, blocks, boards, and toys. At age seven, the typical child is still more goal-directed and self-critical in his acquisition of skills, including reading, drawing, construction, hopscotch, and other work and play activities. He wants to understand how such things as trains, airplanes, and cars work. He is beginning independent reading and enjoys fairy tales, myths, animal stories about real animals, and stories about other children. By eight years, intellectual and reading interests are being both extended and intensified. The eight-year-old may begin collections—of stones, bugs, stamps, or books he especially likes. The broadened and intensified intellectual interests of nine-year-olds are also suggested by their wider reading on such topics as science; study of community, state, nation, and other countries; biographies of heroes and great persons; and social and economic processes such as business, industry, shipping, farming, and mining. During the period from ten to twelve, differentiated interests, independent work methods, and ability for more constructive and critical reasoning in science and other intellectual areas develop. Children now enjoy such scientific activities as the diet experiment mentioned in Chapter 1. Many

---

[1] For $15\frac{1}{2}$-year-olds, the scores on all tests are converted to standard scores with a mean of 10 and a standard deviation of 3. The mean score at each age is interpreted relative to this standard. Thus the digit-span scores for ages $9\frac{1}{2}$ and $10\frac{1}{2}$, for example, are found to be one standard deviation below the mean of $15\frac{1}{2}$-year-olds.

of them are able to do library research and to write a well-organized and creative report on some special topic of interest.

Progress in School Achievement. The gradual growth in some specific aspects of school achievement has already been indicated in the above discussion of intellectual development. Since the progress toward specific school objectives over the primary and intermediate grades has been outlined in greater detail in Chapter 1, here it is perhaps desirable to indicate only the general trend of school accomplishment.

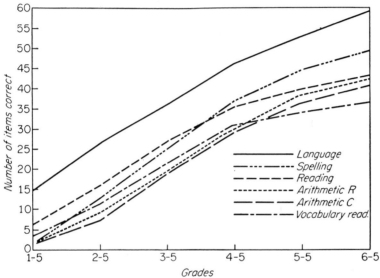

FIG. 3–7. Progress in accomplishment and maturity in the Stanford Achievement Test [Elementary Battery, Form J], as indicated by norms of raw scores. (These raw scores are not comparable between different tests.) (*World, Yonkers, N.Y., 1953.*)

The steady, gradual nature of school progress over the elementary grades, as measured by carefully prepared tests of school achievement, is shown in Figure 3–7. These curves, revealing gradual progress in language, spelling, reading, vocabulary, and arithmetic from grade 1 through grade 6, are similar to the patterns of physical, motor, and intellectual development. The progress reflected in the achievement curves is probably a product of physical and especially of intellectual maturation combined with learning experiences in these subjects. It should also be observed that the curves show only a segment of academic accomplishment. Informal growth in these subjects occurred before grade 1, and development will continue into junior and senior high school.

Fig. 3–8. Readiness for the first grade depends upon both maturation and the kinds of quantitative, verbal, social, and problem-solving experiences children enjoy in the kindergarten. (*Courtesy of McKinley School, Tremonton, Utah.*)

Social Development. Growth in size, in motor skills, in intellectual abilities, and in understanding and school accomplishments all contribute to the child's social development. As the child matures in these respects, he becomes more independent and plays his various roles more effectively, becoming both a participating and a contributing member of family, school, and other peer groups. Some of the changes which constitute his social development include (1) gradually more effective participation in groups of increasing size and complexity, (2) extension of social attachments from mother and family to peer friendships and to gang and other organized peer groups, (3) increasing responsiveness to social motives, (4) enriched self-understanding and differentiation of his role in various activities and interpersonal relationships, and (5) greater self-direction, with increasing responsibility, consideration, and love for other people [1].

The Vineland Social Maturity Scale [11], which lists in order of development 117 items indicative of social maturing, shows that by five years of age, 56 of these items have been achieved by the average child, including such items as "dressing self, except for tying" and "going about the neighborhood unassisted." By age 11 to 12, the child of average social maturity has accom-

FIG. 3–9. Five-year-olds recognize both themselves and others as distinct personalities, and they enjoy dramatic role-playing in cooperative relationships. (*Courtesy of William M. Stewart School, University of Utah.*)

plished 84 of these items and now "does simple creative work," "is left to care for self or others," and independently "enjoys books, newspapers, and magazines."

Five-year-olds, as compared with preschool children, are typically more independent, goal-directed, and social in their behavior. They have achieved considerable independence in self-care with respect to eating, dressing, and toilet. They like using building blocks, paints, toy trucks or fire engines, and miniature housekeeping equipment purposefully and constructively. In their dramatic role-playing, they take such parts as "Mother," "Father," or "Fireman." They participate, both competitively and cooperatively, in small-group activities. They are responsive to approval, are beginning to enjoy thinking of themselves as being right or good, and like the responsibility of being trusted with simple errands or tasks [19].

Except for some children who meet the experience partially in the kindergarten, the big developmental task for the six-year-old is leaving the familiar safety of home for a full day of meeting challenging, new activities and unfamiliar people at school. If he adjusts satisfactorily to school, he takes a great stride in social development [33]. He becomes more independent, responsible, confident, and self-directing at home, with his playmates, and at school. He acquires a more realistic concept of himself with respect to both his relative strengths and limitations. He extends his group contacts, participates more effectively in cooperative projects, and competes more aggressively. He learns to take frustration more readily, without crying. His role-playing is beginning to be somewhat differentiated, girls play house and boys play cowboys.

Continuing his growth toward social maturity, the seven-year-old is more self-assertive, competitive, and effective in cooperative efforts, and can also on occasion be sympathetic. Although he still needs and accepts guidance, he is striving for even more independence. He can bathe himself, brush his teeth, and dress himself, including tying shoelaces, and he likes to be given chores which he does well. He is more sensitive to the feelings and attitudes of others and to his own social role as well. He likes to do things right, to conform to rules, and to meet standards, and for his efforts he enjoys the approval of both adults and his peers. Although boys and girls still play group games together, their interests continue to diverge, and "best friends are almost always of the same sex" [19].

By age 8, further growth in independence, self-understanding, and social responsibility have occurred. Because of his better understanding of time and feelings of independence and responsibility, the eight-year-old adjusts himself better to schedules—time for meals, for school, for bed, and to events planned in terms of days or months. As encouragement in independence and responsibility, he needs an allowance. Peer social attachments, such as close friendships and membership in the gang or in other peer organizations, are being strengthened. In school projects, clubs, and afterschool organized activities and games he plays his role constructively, effectively, and with satisfaction. Interest in dramatic play continues, but it is more organized, as in putting on a play. Membership in and identification with his own sex group are now quite definite.

The nine-year-old is still more socially mature—more independent, responsible, self-directing, and morally concerned. He likes to be trusted with special responsibilities in school projects and family undertakings. He takes pride in his accomplishments and appreciates recognition for responsible role-taking. Friendships are needed, and membership in peer groups is important. The nine-year-old likes to conform to his group's standards in dress, speaking, and activities. Differentiation of membership and activities along sex lines continues to be strong. In their striving for social maturity, nine-year-olds still need parent- and teacher-support and -guidance; but guidance needs to be on a basis of reasoning and of democratic participation by both children and adults.

FIG. 3–10. Twelve-year-olds continue to enjoy dramatic role-taking, especially when the roles match their own maturing self-concepts and emerging boy-girl interests. (*Courtesy of McGraw-Hill Text-Film Department.*)

By ages 10 to 12, if children have experienced healthy development, they have achieved a sense of accomplishment. They feel confident in their social roles in their immediate community of school and home and confident of eventual effective participation in the wider community of their society, of which they are becoming increasingly aware. They are to a high degree independent in self-care, and they like sharing and carrying their responsibilities in home and school. They often perform responsible routine chores, and some may do part-time remunerative work after school or during summer vacation. Membership in their own sex groups is still important; but for some children boy-girl interests are developing.

As phases of the child's socialization, his developing self-concept, or self-definition, and his increasingly satisfying and complex peer relationships are significant both for his mental health and for his social effectiveness. By five years of age, the socially mature child recognizes himself and others as distinct individuals. He accepts his role in the family and immediate neighborhood, and in his roles relates himself cooperatively to parents, siblings, and small peer groups of neighborhood children. From ages 5 to 12, his peer relationships expand greatly in number and diversity of social patterns, require the learning *from his peers* of more complex "rules" and social skills, and become more important determinants of the child's behavior, satisfactions, and evaluation of himself. The twelve-year-old, although he still needs guidance, support, and encouragement from his parents, is becoming less dependent upon them and more dependent upon satisfying peer relationships. Children who develop, as they mature, the necessary patterns of abilities and who feel secure and confident in their relations with their parents usually learn with and from their peers the social skills and attitudes required for effective participation with them. Such children, because they meet the accomplishment, play, and friendship standards of their peer culture, are more likely to develop self-concepts characterized by feelings of competence, confidence, and personal worth.

Individual Variations and Patterns of Development. In the above discussion of the average or theoretically typical child, except for occasional hints at deviations from the norm, it might have been assumed that every child, as he grows up, demonstrates the same pattern of development. This, of course, would be a serious mistake. With every general aspect of development considered—size, motor skills, intellectual abilities, school achievement, and social development —intragroup differences at each age are much larger than the mean differences between different age groups.

For example, the average child beginning the fourth grade is 9½ years old and has a mental age of 9-6. But in nearly every fourth grade class some child is likely to have a mental age as low as 6-6, and some child is likely to have a mental age as high as 12-6. The bright 9½-year-old with the mental age of 12-6 is also very likely to be advanced in school achievement, and he has a better-than-average chance (though not a certainty) of being more socially mature than the average 9½-year-old. But in size, he may be large, average, or small. In the motor skills, important to good adjustment on the playground and in some school activities, he may likewise be highly skillful, average, or awkward. Similarly, the dull 9½-year-old with the mental age of only 6-6 may vary in his total pattern of development. He is likely to be very retarded in school achievement. Only at 9½ will his mental maturity be sufficient for expectation of success in reading at the first grade level. Probably because of the frustration he is likely to have experienced, he may be both socially immature and emotionally maladjusted. With wise and accepting parents and teachers, however, his social development may have been healthy. Like the brighter child, he has almost even chances of being tall, average, or short. In the motor skills important for playground status and success in some school activities, he also may excel, be adequate, or be as retarded, as in intellectual development. Even this picture of intraindividual variation portrays the real situation too simply.

Typically, children also vary within their developmental patterns of motor skills, of intellectual abilities, and of achievement in various school subjects. James, a ten-year-old about to complete the fourth grade, illustrates this concept. James is of average size, sturdily built and well proportioned. He plays baseball moderately well, rides his bicycle expertly, and skates awkwardly. His mental age is a little above the average for his chronological-age group, but he does better in the performance than in the verbal parts of the intelligence test. His arithmetic in school is "good." He does well in using the science and social studies information he gains from sources other than reading. He is alert and curious, and he reasons well. In reading and in spelling, however, James performs at about the beginning-of-the-second-grade level. Socially, he is independent in self-care (rides his bicycle over a mile to and from school) and gets along in work and play with other children (has some close friends and belongs to a gang). He is embarrassed, and sometimes cries when he tells his mother about it, when another child comments to him on his poor reading. And in his efforts in remedial reading, his biggest handicap is his lack of confidence.

Because every child is as unique an individual as James, the above presentation of developmental norms is not, of course, a guide for what to expect of every child at each age level. It is rather a set of criteria for appraising each child's pattern, sequence, and individual rate of development in these important areas.

Experimental Demonstrations of the Role of Maturation in Development

The observational and measurement data already presented confirm in a general way the hypothesis that a child's development is a product both of his growing and of his learning experiences. This hypothesis has also been explored for some phases of development by more precise, experimental procedures.

Age and Capacity for Learning. Dusenberry [13] found that the distance children can throw a ball is determined by both age and training. Fifty-six children ages 3 to 7 were equated into two groups on the basis of age, sex, and initial throwing score. Both groups were given pretests and end-tests, with an interval of three weeks between, but only one group was trained. The trained group, practicing twice a week over a period of three weeks, was given demonstrations, explanations, correction of faults, reminders to use good form, and verbal and candy rewards for their learning efforts. The directions were: "Stand behind this line and see how far you can throw the ball—like this."

The results for two different age groups within both the trained and the control (untrained) groups are graphed in Figure 3–11. The advantage of being 5 to 6 rather than 3 to 4 for this particular motor ability is shown both by

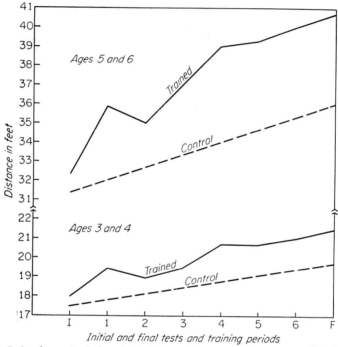

Fig. 3–11. Role of maturity in learning is indicated by average distances a ball is thrown by boys in trained and in control groups, age 3 to 4 and 5 to 6. (*From Dusenberry, L.: Res. Quart. Amer. Ass. Hlth. Phys. Educ. Recr., 23: 13, 1952.*)

the higher initial scores of the older children and by their much greater capacity to profit from training. However, that training also affects the development of this skill is indicated by the greater progress made by the trained group than by the control group, who merely matured (and possibly engaged in some incidental practice) for three weeks between the initial and final tests.

Both observation of children's learning of such complex skills as ball playing, skating, swimming, or writing and an experimental investigation of the hypothesis [25] indicates that for complex skills, training makes a relatively greater contribution to improvement than for simple skills. But for complex skills, neither uninstructed practice nor teacher-guided training can make up for limitations in maturity, as Hicks [17] and Garr [15] have shown. Hicks compared the results of control and uninstructed practice with two two-to-six-year-old groups learning to throw a ball more accurately at a moving target. Between the pretests and the end-tests, separated by eight weeks of undirected practice for the practice group, neither the control nor the practice group made significant gains. But since for Hicks's practice group, "in no case was a child given instruction in ways of improving his skill," Garr assumed that the failure to improve in this complex skill may have resulted from lack of teacher-guidance. He, therefore, compared the progress of a control group and a carefully instructed group of five-year-old children in the same target skill. Again, since neither group made significant progress, Garr was forced to the conclusion that in this complex skill five-year-olds are too immature to profit from even good instruction.

Age maturity plays a similar role in other phases of development. Beginning before the elementary school years and continuing throughout the elementary school period, it is apparent from observation that children improve in their ability to reason. Using children ages 5, 8, and 11, Ausubel and Schiff [2] found increases with age, especially from 8 to 11, in the ability to learn causal relationships, such as that the longer side of a teeter-totter from the fulcrum will fall when both sides are released from their supports.

This review points to the conclusion that general capacity for learning during childhood increases with age. Such a conclusion might tend to lead teachers to delay many learning activities. But sometimes, in the specific scientific investigations required to relate the curriculum to child development, we are surprised at the marked influences of early training. Jersild and Bienstock [23], for example, found that with special training in helping them to extend their range of singing tones, preschool children attained almost twice the range of their untrained peers. They reached a singing range equal to that of untrained eight-year-olds. Without training in such a skill, which improves to a certain extent from maturation and self-initiated activity alone, it is quite possible that children often fail to realize their potentialities. A similar discovery was made for improvement with early training in speech articulation. At entrance to kindergarten, average children misarticulate about 10 per cent of their speech sounds, and some children misarticulate a much greater proportion. Sommer [31] found that a group with 12 weeks of corrective training improved 57 per cent in speech articulation, while during this same time a control group improved only 28 per cent. Delay in training when it is needed or delay much beyond the stage when a child is ready for instruction may be as unfortunate for a child's development as premature training efforts [22].

Mental Age and Capacity for Learning. It has been shown above that, as children become older, new abilities emerge and their capacity for improving skills increases. For the academic or symbolic phases of the school curriculum, mental maturity is often a sharper index of capacity for learning and problem solving than age alone. Mental age is therefore regarded as a better sign of readiness for some new learning undertaking than chronological age. Foster

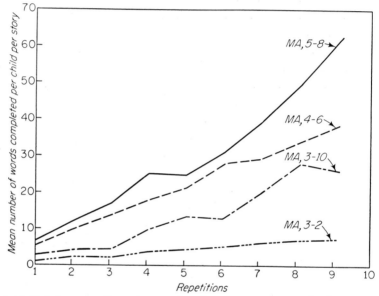

FIG. 3–12. Verbal memory for stories reread 10 times improves in maturing from mental age 2 to 4. (*From Foster, J. C.: J. Genet. Psychol., 35: 34, 1928.*)

[14] has shown that for preschool children, ability to memorize stories read to them improves from mental ages 3 to 5. Eight different stories, such as "The Dog and the Kitty Cats" were read and reread 10 times to 22 children ages 2-7 to 4-9. After the first reading, the experimenter paused at a certain definite place in each story and asked each child to complete the story as far as he could. The child was rewarded with approval for his successes, and the experimenter reread the uncompleted or incorrectly recalled parts. The averages in number of words completed per story per child for four mental age groups are presented in Figure 3–12.

The figure reveals that children with mental ages as low as 3-2 are mentally too immature to memorize these stories by the method employed. It also shows that increases in mental capacity from 3-10 to 5-8 are accompanied by improvements in capacity to master this problem.

Morphett and Washburne [29] have tried to answer, experimentally and in terms of mental age, the question "When should children begin to read?" After a semester of instruction of first grade children in reading, they determined the percentages at each half year of mental age from 5 to 8 who succeeded in reaching a certain standard of satisfactory reading achievement. Their results are graphed in Figure 3–13.

This maturation curve indicates that no child with a mental age as low as 5-0 succeeded in reading and that only an occasional child with a mental age

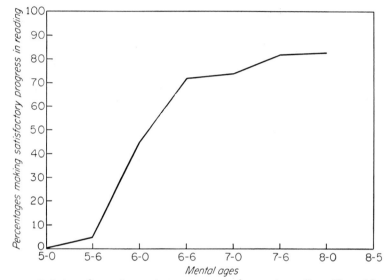

FIG. 3–13. Relation of mental maturity to success in first grade reading. (*From Morphett, M. V., and Washburne, C.: Elem. Sch. J., 31: 500, Copyright 1931. Reprinted by permission of the University of Chicago Press.*)

of 5-6 may be expected to succeed. Even at mental age 6-0, less than half the children succeeded. At mental age 6-6, however, over 70 per cent of the children made satisfactory progress. On the basis of these and similar data, a mental age of about 6½ is often accepted by teachers as the minimum for expectation of success with first grade reading as it is usually taught at present. Since, however, even at mental ages of 7 or 8 not every child succeeded in reading, it is apparent that other conditions of effective learning are also essential.

For children six years of age who enter the first grade with mental maturity below the minimum here found desirable, reading instruction needs to be delayed. In the meantime these children can be greatly aided in their preparation for reading by participation in a rich prereading program directed toward improvement of articulation, understanding, and expression in language; concrete understanding of their local environment; interest in hearing and telling stories and experiences; and building social skills and self-confidence. When reading is delayed for such mentally immature children, their eventual progress, it has been shown, is much more efficient [3].

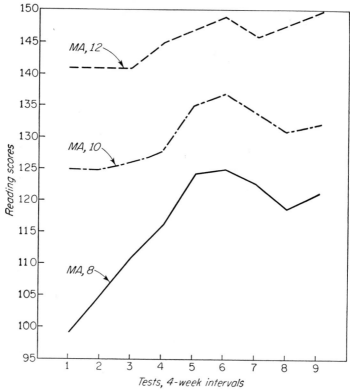

FIG. 3–14. Nine forms of Thorndike-McCall Reading Test, given at 4-week intervals to pupils at 3 MA levels, show reading levels related to mental maturity. (*From Brueckner, L. J.:* *"Techniques of diagnosis" in Educational Diagnosis, p. 138, 34th Yearbook of the Nat. Soc. Stud. Educ., Chicago, Distributed by the University of Chicago Press, 1935.*)

Besides being important in determining when reading may be begun successfully, mental age is also significantly related to the rate of progress in reading at later ages. This is indicated in Figure 3–14, which shows the differential levels of progress in reading made by children at mental ages 8, 10, and 12 [6].

These children began the reading instruction at three maturity levels related to their mental age; and, as is shown by their scores on nine different forms of the Thorndike-McCall Reading Test, administered at four-week intervals, they maintained these relative positions over a period of 36 weeks [6, p. 138]. Equal amounts of instruction evidently do not eliminate original heterogeneity. Although it is not apparent in Figure 3–14 as it is in Figure 3–12, equal, extended amounts of training in complex skills usually result in extending the range of individual differences. The apparently greater progress made by the eight-year mental age group suggests that in this instance the reading instruction is better suited to their maturity level than to that of the more mature children. It may also mean, however, that small score gains at the higher levels in this test may represent more actual reading progress than similar gains in score at the lower levels.

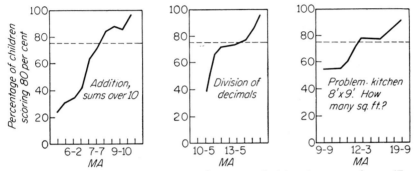

FIG. 3–15. Relation of achievement on specific aspects of arithmetic to mental age. (*From Washburne, C.: "The work of the Committee of Seven on grade-placement in arithmetic," Child Development and the Curriculum, pp. 303–307. 38th Yearbook of the Nat. Soc. Stud. Educ., Part I, Chicago, Distributed by the University of Chicago Press, 1939.*)

Determination of the minimum or optimum mental ages at which different concepts or skills can be mastered has been proposed as a general procedure for determining the proper grade placement of much of the elementary school content. Perhaps the most extensive investigation (300 school systems) employing this principle has been conducted by a committee of the National Society for the Study of Education headed by Washburne [35]. This committee arranged to have taught according to the then current methods many of the computational processes in arithmetic, each process to be taught over a range of three grade levels. Setting a minimum standard of 80 per cent accuracy to be attained by 75 per cent of the children, they determined for each concept or skill the percentage of children attaining this standard at various mental ages.

As examples of their numerous specific findings, the curves of achievement in relation to mental age for three concepts are presented in Figure 3–15.

Table 3–1. Tentative Recommendations of the Committee of Seven
(On placement of arithmetic concepts in relation to mental age)

Optimum MA	Arithmetic items
6–7	Informal activities with concrete numbers and space relations; addition sums under 10; begin easy subtraction.
7–8	Continue informal activities; comparisons of length, height, and width of objects, and recognition that one object is 2, 3, or 4 times as long, high, or wide as another; measure and draw lines inches long; learn inches in feet; read clock to even hour; learn both easy and hard addition facts, and easy subtraction facts.
8–9	Difficult subtraction facts (3-digit subtraction); easy multiplication (products under 20, and 5 × 5); simplest forms of square measure and comparisons of areas; learn minutes, hours, days as measures of time; learn to read calendar, and clock to quarter hour.
9–10	Column addition of digits 3 high and 3 wide; multiplication of products over 20; easy division facts (dividends under 20); meaning of $\frac{1}{2}$, $\frac{1}{3}$, $\frac{1}{4}$, $\frac{3}{4}$, etc., of whole objects; learn inches in yards; learn areas of rectangles.
10–11	Column addition 4 digits high and 4 wide; learn meaning of addition and subtraction of simple decimals; addition and subtraction of simple fractions and mixed numbers with like denominators; learn to read and make simple bar graphs; measure and draw lines in feet and inches to quarter inch; estimate and recognize lengths of cloth, distance between cities, height of buildings, etc.; subtraction and multiplication of feet and inches; master time precisely (to seconds, to leap years).
11–12	Mastery of all multiplication facts; multiplication with multipliers as high as 3 digits and multiplicands as high as 4 digits; division facts; short division (one-place divisor); long division; fractional and decimal equivalents; division and multiplication with decimals; learn square measure in feet or inches.
12–13	More difficult two-place-quotient division; fraction relations (3 objects is $\frac{1}{3}$ of 9 objects); multiplication and division of fractions; percentage; draw and measure lines to $\frac{1}{8}$ inch; calculate inches in fraction of a yard; measure distance on maps with scale of miles; measure and compare areas; discriminate squares, rectangles, triangles, trapezoids, etc.; time problems.

Source: C. Washburne (Chairman). *Child Development and the Curriculum*, pp. 309–314. 38th Yearbook of the Nat. Soc. Stud. Educ., Part I. Chicago: Distributed by the University of Chicago Press, 1939.

These curves show that, for a range of mental age somewhat below and above the optimum, with increasing mental maturity greater percentages of children meet the criterion of satisfactory learning. For addition sums over 10, the optimum mental age for mastery appears to be 8-2. For division of decimals, it is over 13-5. And for learning to solve area problems, the optimum mental age is about 12-3. Guided by such maturation-achievement curves, the committee recommended such mental age placements for arithmetic concepts and skills as are presented in Table 3–1.

Since the publication of such tables on the placement of topics in arithmetic, courses of study in arithmetic have been reevaluated; and in many revisions, topics have been shifted to more advanced grades. Johnson [24] has compared the achievement in arithmetic of children in grades 3 to 8 before and after a revision upward in harmony with the placement recommendations of the Committee of Seven. He reports a gain in achievement of 21 per cent following the revision.

The demonstration of a significant relationship between degree of mental maturity and capacity to master various concepts in arithmetic is a substantial contribution to the general maturation-learning concept. Undoubtedly arithmetic courses of study have benefited from revisions in the light of such findings. But such data are not an adequate guide for permanent grade placement. Already they are at least somewhat out of date. As new ways of improving teaching are discovered, different minimum and optimum mental age levels for mastery are needed. And besides mental maturity, such other criteria as child interests and needs and transfer-of-training principles should be considered in the placement of topics on grade levels and in the learning sequences of individual children.

Determining Readiness for Learning

Both casual observations of children's learning efforts and systematic experimental studies of the role of maturation in learning have demonstrated that sufficient maturity is an essential condition of effective learning. For the verbal and other symbolic phases of the school curriculum, sufficient *mental* maturity is an especially significant condition for satisfactory progress. But in considering the readiness of each child for effective participation in the school's widely varied curriculum activities, it is important to evaluate his entire pattern of abilities. Further attention to this phase of the problem is reserved for later chapters. In closing this chapter, however, it is appropriate to offer a summary answer to the practical-teaching question "How can a teacher tell when a child is ready for some learning undertaking; what are the signs of readiness?"

1. Age and Mental Age Norms. One very general guide to pupil readiness is, of course, knowledge of the average or typical behavior which observation and experimentation have shown may be expected at a given age or mental level. For this purpose, the trends described above of physical, motor, mental, and school accomplishments, and social development of children during the elementary school years are useful. Tentative age norms have been experimentally established for mastery of many motor skills, for the time when pitch range in singing can be extended, for early correction of immature articulation, and for many more such activities. Tentative mental age norms have been similarly established for beginning reading, for mental age placement of many computational topics in arithmetic, and for several other phases of the elementary school curriculum [34]. Although useful, such norms have limitations. As new methods of teaching and new curriculum content are developed, new norms need to be established. Also, the norms cannot be successfully applied to a grade group as a unit. For example, content suitable for age or mental age $9\frac{1}{2}$ will not be appropriate for every fourth grade pupil. The norms need to be adapted to the wide range of individual differences and variations in patterns of ability characteristic of the pupils in every class.

A good example of an adaptation of grade norms for use in such individualized instruction is that made by a fourth grade teacher in connection with his pupils' reading. Opposite each pupil's name in his roll, he listed the pupil's grade-equivalent score in reading as obtained from a recently administered reading test. In this particular class, scores ranged from grade equivalent 2 to 8. Then, using *The Winnetka Chart for Determining Grade Placement of Childrens' Books* [30], the teacher chose from the school library for each pupil a book which matched in difficulty his grade level in reading and which was also within the child's range of special interests, as determined by other means.

2. Developmental Sequences. Implicit in the above discussion of general developmental trends is the assumption that children follow similar developmental patterns or sequences, though not at the same rate. It is practical for teaching purposes to conceive of the gradual, progressive development in children of concepts and skills in language, reading, arithmetic, science, art, and so on in the elementary school curriculum as a succession of stages or steps. As each child takes these developmental steps—not at the same rate in different learning activities—the best answer to the question about his readiness for the next step is evidence that he is about to complete the previous step. Such an adjustment of each child's curriculum to his own learning pace is likely to augment his learning efficiency, as is illustrated in a study by Dubin [12] of development of graphic-representation ability in preschool children.

Monroe has classified preschool children's graphic representation into four stages: (1) unnamed scribble, (2) named scribble, (3) diagrammatic drawings, and (4) design and representation—the last typically appearing at about four to five years of age. Using two equated groups of preschool children engaged in drawing activities, Dubin adopted Monroe's classification for one group, directing each child's attention to features of the next developmental stage. For example, to a child in the "named-scribble" stage his teacher would say' "Tell me about your picture." If the child gave it a name, the teacher would continue, "Tell me more about it," or "What part is this?" and would finally point out, "If you look carefully, you can see that there are lots of parts to your picture, and altogether they make something nice." As a result of such pacing, the experimental group made significantly greater gains in graphic representation than did the control group.

As another example of the principle of developmental sequences in determining children's readiness for new learning activities, progress in reading comprehension may be analyzed into a developmental sequence of stages. The first step is comprised of the prereading activities of the kindergarten and the introductory part of the first grade, already outlined above. Taking the second step, the children learn to recognize some sight words. They recognize their names on their lockers and art compartments, the names of animals under their pictures on the wall, and some of the words the teacher uses to write their experiences on the chalkboard. In this stage, words are recognized usually only by their general contours and from the context or setting. "Rabbit," for example, has two "ears" in the middle, and "dog" is a small word. When enough sight words are recognized for effective use of context in simple sentences or paragraphs, the children take the third step; that of learning independent methods of identifying unfamiliar words. In connection with the context—a constantly employed technique—they learn to use also in identifying unfamiliar words word-form clues, phonetic analysis, and structural analysis. As the fourth step, when some initial understanding of these techniques has been acquired, children learn to use them skillfully, confidently, and in an efficient, hierarchical order for more rapid reading. By the time they have accomplished step 4, children are quite rapid and proficient in reading comprehension. They are now ready for the fifth step: that of learning techniques suited to different purposes— skimming, following a narrative for a general understanding, reading for organization of details, following directions, outlining, evaluating critically, and selecting or rejecting ideas for the purpose at hand.

In almost any grade some children will be found at most of these stages. In the third grade, for example, Joe may not be beyond the stage of recognizing words by their general contour. He is probably ready for the third stage—that of learning how to identify words independently. Jane, however, in the same grade, may already be using all the techniques of word identification rapidly and efficiently, even in relatively difficult material. She is, of course, ready to take the fifth step, not usually approached until the fifth grade level.

3. *Tests of Readiness Aptitudes.* Whether a child has attained the developmental norm considered necessary for some learning undertaking or whether he is ready for the next step in a learning sequence may sometimes be determined by readiness tests. An individual test of general mental maturity, standardized tests of readiness for beginning reading or arithmetic, and teacher-made tests of readiness for taking the next step in any learning sequence are all useful for this purpose. The general purpose in the construction and use of such readiness tests is to inventory the specific abilities which analysis reveals as desirable or necessary for mastering the next learning task.

For example, before a child is ready to progress from prereading activities to initial attempts to read, his oral-language comprehension and expression should at least equal the vocabulary level of the "experience reading" and primers in which he will begin to read. He should understand and speak easily in four- or five-word sentences. His experience and information background should include the concepts about which he will read and hear read to him. He should be able to make rather precise perceptual discriminations, differentiating both auditorily and visually between such sounds and visual symbols as "big" and "pig." His own articulation should not be distinctly immature. He should be able to learn from his experience—to understand and to remember, for example, the parts of a story read to him. And he needs sufficient social calm and self-confidence to be able to exert himself in problem solving with systematic effort and assurance.

As a gauge of some of these abilities, the Monroe *Reading Aptitude Tests* [28] include measures of language comprehension, expression in sentences, and articulation; tests of visual and auditory perception; and a motor test appraising ability to follow with a pencil patterns of dots and lines. The *Gates Reading Readiness Tests* [16] measure (1) the ability to grasp and execute directions, (2) familiarity with printed words and ability to discriminate between them ("Among the following, which two words are alike: 'hard, hand, head, hard?'"), (3) ability to learn new words (Among four words—keep, ship, sheep, sleep—the child recognizes the one word just previously presented for five seconds.), (4) auditory discrimination (The child marks the one among four pictures—of a flag, of a pig, of a man, and of a box—for which the name rhymes with "big."), and (5) ability to read the letters of the alphabet and the numbers from 0 to 9—an ability probably not directly significant, but which Gates has found correlates with first grade reading achievement. The *Metropolitan Readiness Tests* [18], intended to measure "total readiness" for the first grade, include tests of comprehension vocabulary; understanding of sentences; range of information; visual, perceptual discrimination of animals, objects, figures, letters, and words; and knowledge of numbers. They also include a copying test intended to measure visual perception and motor control, such as that required in learning to write.

In the hands of a skilled school psychologist, perhaps the Stanford-Binet individual intelligence test can be made to yield as much or more useful information about a child's readiness for reading in comparison with any other test. Besides determining mental age and IQ, this examination contributes information on problem-solving methods; indications of teachability, quality of social adjustment and emotional control; and appraisals of some of the specific aptitudes required in reading. This is illustrated in the report given below of the psychological examination of C.H., who in the preceding June was being considered for entrance in the fall into the first grade, though she would then still be one month short of meeting the usual chronological age requirements.

Results: CA, 5-7; MA, 6-10; IQ, 122; Percentile, 91

Level	\	\	Pattern	\	\	\	Years	Months
	1	2	3	4	5	6	Years	Months
VI	+	+	+	+	+	+	6	0
VII	+	+	−	−	−	+		6
VIII	+	+	−	−	−	−		4
IX	−	−	−	−	−	−		0
							6 −	10

The IQ of 122 classifies "C" as "superior" in general mental ability, at the 91st percentile of children of her age, according to Terman's norms. When school begins in September, C's mental age will probably be about 7 years, 2 months, which will probably place her in mental maturity a little above the average of first grade children, and above the minimum mental age set by Morphett and Washburne's experiment for satisfactory progress in first grade reading.

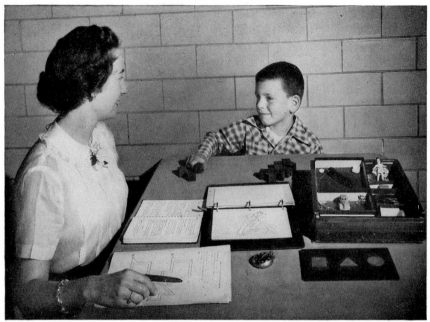

F𝐈𝐆. 3–16. Individual examinations of intelligence, in addition to yielding mental ages and IQs, reveal children's problem-solving methods, their zest in or fear of challenging tasks, their confidence or insecurity in social situations, and some specific proficiencies. (*Courtesy of Whittier School, Utah State Agricultural College.*)

Several other traits revealed in the testing are indicative of probable good adjustment to school. Her vocabulary is at the eight year level (Shown in the pattern, item VIII:1). Her articulation is mature. Her sentence structure and verbal formulations are excellent for a six year old. For example, "envelope" is defined as "Something you put a letter in," and "scorch" as "Something an iron does—it browns it if you get it on cloth." (The average sentence length of six year olds is five words.) And she is confident enough with a strange examiner to participate spontaneously in conversation with him. Her approach to problems indicates that she should be a good learner: she listens intently and grasps directions promptly, she persists in trying varied attacks on a problem, and she profits immediately from her learning experiences. For example, after the third trial (new digits each trial), she was able to repeat correctly five digits (item VII:6). And although she didn't succeed with copying the diamond (VII:3), she did make improvements in three successive trials. She is able to remember and to report the ideas of a story read to her as well as the average eight year old (VIII:2). Precise auditory perception is indicated by her promptness and accuracy in following directions. Adequate visual perceptual discrimination is suggested by her success in discriminating the one slightly different form from four similar identical forms in test VI:5. Her number concepts are also probably beyond the six year level, as she demonstrated by counting out blocks in *groups* rather than singly as is usual at this level (VI:4) She seems confident of her abilities, and her lack of timidity toward the examiner suggests that she would also likely be socially secure with her teacher and classmates. Despite all these signs of freedom from anxiety, however, she may feel in stress situations some insecurity, as was suggested by her occasional fingernail biting. Perhaps she needs help in coming to feel, both in her home and at school, that even without intense striving or distinctive achievement, she is thoroughly accepted, approved, and loved.

For use in addition to tests of intelligence and of specific reading-readiness aptitudes, Monroe has also developed the following informal inventory of questions as an aid to teachers in determining the reading readiness of their first grade pupils [27, p. 18]:

1. Does the child know and can he repeat nursery rhymes or poems?
2. Can he tell a little story from memory?
3. Does he enjoy listening to stories?
4. Does he give good attention during the story period?
5. Can he describe or talk about a picture using sentences containing four or more words?
6. Can he relate an experience he has had?
7. Can he repeat verbatim a sentence of six or eight words?
8. Can he discover and say the missing word in a rhyme he knows if one word is left out?
9. Can he classify pictures or objects? All the animals? All the toys? All the things we ride in?
10. Can he detect small differences in objects that look almost alike?
11. Can he tell the words that sound alike in a rhyme?
12. Does he speak without infantile mispronunciations?
13. Does he enjoy looking at picture books?
14. Does he handle books carefully?
15. Can he write or print his name?
16. Does he notice printed symbols and ask, "What does that say?"
17. Does he enter into games with other children?
18. Is he self-reliant?
19. Can he match printed words?
20. Does he have good motor control in skipping, hopping, drawing?
21. Does he work with a group without tension, anxiety, or self-consciousness?

Similar procedures are available or can be teacher-made for determining readiness for learning in other curriculum areas; moreover, they need not be confined to determining readiness for the initial stage in learning. Diagnostic readiness tests can be used effectively at the beginning of any step in a sequence of learning activities. Brueckner [7], for example, reports on some fifth grade pupils who, when they were about to begin the study of division with two-figure divisors, were given a test based on an analysis of the skills judged to be necessary for succeeding with long division. The test included (1) understanding of place value of three-digit numbers, (2) multiplication used in division in the form of quotient times divisor, (3) knowledge of difficult division combinations, (4) skill with one-figure divisors with dividends of two to four figures, (5) judging the correctness of quotients, (6) checking given quotient figures, (7) subtraction used in division, (8) mental multiplication of a two-figure by a one-figure number, and (9) comparing the product of a two-place number and a one-place number with a given number, that is, with the dividend.

Just as the reading-readiness-test scores indicate which children need more prereading instruction and which may expect to advance successfully with reading, this test of readiness for division with two-figure divisors shows which pupils need further instruction on a lower level and which may expect to take the next step successfully. For six fifth grade classes about to begin two-figure divisors in division, Brueckner found that the range of errors was from no to every item incorrect. And since the total score on the readiness test correlates .46[1] with that on the final achievement test, it is evident that mastery of these subprocesses measured in the readiness test is important for success with two-figure-divisor division. Therefore, this test revealed that many of the pupils needed remedial instruction on certain of these essential subprocesses before taking the next step.

Having prepared a readiness test which explored the experiential back-

---

[1] Coefficients of correlation are statistical indices of the precise degree to which two measures applied to the same population of individuals tend to vary together. Theoretically, the relationship between such pairs of measurements can range from −1.00 (indicative of perfect inverse relationship), through .00 (showing a purely random pairing of the measures), to +1.00 (indicative of perfect positive correspondence between pairs of measures throughout the population, from the lowest to the highest pair). Between these extremes, a correlation of .90 may be considered as indicating a "very high" relationship; .80 a "high" relationship; .70 a "fairly high" relationship; .60 a "definite" relationship; .50 a "rather definite" relationship; .40 "some" relationship; .30 a "low" relationship; .20 a "very low" relationship; and .10 a "practically negligible, almost random" correspondence between the pairs of measures. Between −1.00 and .00, the complementary negative correlations indicate corresponding degrees of inverse relationship.

For a graphic representation of such a relationship between pairs of measures, see the scatter diagram on p. 384 showing the relationship between measures of intelligence and school achievement for a population of 50 children. The coefficient of correlation computed from the 50 pairs of scores there tabulated is .63, which, according to the above interpretive labels, indicates a "definite" relationship between intelligence and school achievement for these children. Between the readiness and final achievement tests there is "some" relationship.

ground considered essential for learning addition and subtraction of fractions, Souder [32] found that a fifth grade group with whom the test was used to guide their instruction made better progress than an equated group who were taught without specific knowledge about their individual levels of readiness.

4. *Interests as Signs of Readiness.* Supplementing age or mental age norms and developmental sequences, manifestations of children's emerging interests are further signs of readiness for learning. The child who spontaneously chooses to occupy herself with picture books, who asks Mother to read to her the line under a picture, or who writes a sequence of letters of the alphabet and then asks, "What does it say?" is possibly ready to read. Similarly, a child who repeatedly tries to draw a robin "so it looks like it is really pulling a worm out of the lawn" is perhaps ready for some instruction in the technique of representing live action.

Both abilities and interests develop gradually; and some students of child psychology believe that, as new abilities emerge, children spontaneously express them in activities and find high satisfaction in doing so. In a child's development, writes Jersild, "as his capacities for doing, thinking, and feeling emerge in the process of growth he has an impulse to put them to use" [21, p. 24]. Thus it is thought that a child's interest in an activity may be indicative of his ability for effective participation in it. One support for such a hypothesis is the fact that interests are differentiated between levels of intelligence. Intellectually gifted children often learn to read without systematic instruction before entering school. And while eight-year-old children of average intelligence read from four to ten books a year, some intellectually superior children read as many as 150 books a year [26]. The parallel between intellectual and social development and development of reading interests—to take as an example only one phase of children's developing interests—also tends to support the hypothesis.

Reading interests develop gradually—from interest in simple to more complex events and plots; from preference for active to more symbolic activities; from egocentric to more social interests; from preference for fanciful to more realistic concepts of animals, things and people; and from playful to more responsible life roles [10, p. 35]. Five-year-olds like to have read to them jingles, nursery rhymes, and stories of talking animals. Simon and Schuster's *Little Golden Book of Fairy Tales* and Flack's *Angus and the Ducks* are favorites [37]. At primary school ages, children enjoy fairy tales, animal stories, nature stories of the fanciful type, and stories of children and familiar experiences. They enjoy surprise, humor in narration, and plot. Some of their favorites are *Little Black Sambo* and Disney's *Bambi* [37]. From about age 8 to 10, typical interests include animal stories of a realistic nature (Knight's *Lassie Come Home* being a favorite), adventure (such as *Robin Hood*), stories of children in home and school, and stories of children in other lands (as *Heidi* and *The Good Master*). Interests typical of children at ages 11 to 12 include stories of adventure, action, excitement, mystery, humor, and mischief. Children at these ages also are interested in information about their physical and social world, in inventions and other creative activities, in nature and science, in sportsmanship and bravery, and in stories of heroes and famous men (such as d'Aulaire's *Abraham Lincoln*). For girls at these ages, interest in romantic fiction is growing.

The gradual emergence of these interests is further indicated in a study by McGehee [26] of children's hobbies. Among fourth, fifth, and sixth grade children, reading history is selected as a hobby by 15, 19, and 22 per cent, respectively, of boys and by 14, 18, and 19 per cent, respectively, of girls. Novel reading is the hobby in these grades of 28, 39, and 40 per cent of boys and of 44, 49, and 50 per cent of girls.

As developmental trends, these typical interest sequences tend to support the hypothesis that emerging interests are indicative to some extent of maturing and of readiness for specific learning activities. Lack of spontaneous interest in some learning activity is not, however, a sure sign of immaturity. An expected interest may fail to develop for lack of experience or because of unfortunate experience. A current indifference to an activity may, following highly satisfying experiences in it, be transformed into an enthusiasm. It is also recognized that the above-described trends are general and limited in scope. Actually, "Children are characterized by wide and varied interests which lead them to choose a rich and varied assortment of books in many fields." [37, p. 277].

Manifestations of interests are supplementary cues to learning readiness. Like the developmental sequences presented as our second criterion of readiness, they are indicative of readiness for specific learning activities of *individual* children. As such, however, they are useful; and the teacher, in guiding children's learning activities, needs to be alert to their appearance. Children reveal their interests by their contributions to regular class activities and projects, by the things they bring to class for "sharing," by their choices of reading or other activities in free periods, and by self-initiated learning projects. They may also be discovered by teacher-pupil interviews, by asking children to rank in order of preference different activities in which they have been recently engaged, and by interest inventories [5], of which more need to be developed for younger children.

Review and Applications

1. What are the probable consequences to children of curricula (1) suited to their levels of mental maturity, (2) beyond their maturity, (3) below their abilities?

2. Characterize and compare the patterns of children's physical growth during childhood and preadolescence.

3. Cite examples showing that maturation of motor abilities consists of both increases in proficiency and the emergence of new abilities.

4. Explain how intellectual development may be considered a product of both maturation and learning.

5. In order to achieve as components of his developing self-concept senses of accomplishment, personal worth, confidence, being loved, and loving others, what kinds of social experiences does a child need with his parents, teachers, and peers? What are some obstacles to achieving such a self-concept?

6. From the data cited in your text and from other references, such as [34], summarize the findings on the relation of mental maturity to learning different subjects in the elementary school curriculum.

7. Cite examples applying (1) chronological and mental age norms, (2) developmental sequences, (3) readiness tests, and (4) interests in determining children's readiness for beginning or proceeding in learning reading, arithmetic, writing, or some other curriculum activity.

References

1. Anderson, J. E.: "The development of social behavior," *Amer. J. Sociol.*, 44: 839–857, 1939.
2. Ausubel, D. P., and H. M. Schiff: "The effect of incidental and experimentally induced experience in learning of relevant and irrelevant causal relations by children," *J. Genet. Psychol.*, 84: 109–123, 1954.
3. Boney, C. DeW.: "Shall beginning reading be delayed?" *Childh. Educ.*, 26: 168–172, 1949.
4. Brace, D. K.: *Measuring Motor Ability: A Scale of Motor Ability Tests*, A. S. Barnes, New York, 1930.
5. Brainard, F. J., and P. P. Brainard: *Specific Interest Inventory: Forms B and G*, Psychological Corporation, New York, 1932.
6. Brueckner, L. J.: "Techniques of diagnosis." *Educational Diagnosis*, pp. 131–153, 34th Yearbook of the Nat. Soc. Stud. Educ., Chicago: Distributed by the University of Chicago Press, 1935.
7. ————.: "The development of readiness tests in arithmetic," *J. Educ. Res.*, 34: 15–20, 1940–1941.
8. Carpenter, A.: "Tests of motor educability for the first three grades," *Child Develpm.*, 11: 293–299, 1940.

9. Cole, Luella, and J. B. Morgan: *Psychology of Childhood and Adolescence*, Rinehart, New York, 1947.

10. Davis, R. A., and H. E. Taylor: "Significance of research on interests for the classroom teacher," *Educ. Admin. Supervis.*, 29: 357–369, 1943.

11. Doll, E. A.: *Vineland Social Maturity Scale*, Psychological Corporation, New York, 1936.

12. Dubin, Elisabeth R.: "The effect of training on the tempo of development of graphic representation in pre-school children," *J. Exp. Educ.*, 15: 166–173, 1946.

13. Dusenberry, Lois: "A study of the effects of training in ball throwing by children ages three to seven," *Res. Quart. Amer. Ass. Hlth. Phys. Educ. Recr.*, 23: 9–14, 1952.

14. Foster, Josephine C.: "Verbal memory in the preschool child," *J. Genet. Psychol.*, 35: 26–44, 1928.

15. Garr, J. M.: "A study of the effects of systematic instruction upon a complex motor skill," unpublished master's thesis, Utah State Agricultural College Library, Logan, 1954.

16. Gates, A. I.: *Gates Reading Readiness Tests*, Bureau of Publications, Teachers College, Columbia University, New York, 1939.

17. Hicks, J. A.: "The acquisition of motor skill in young children: A study of the effects of practice in throwing at a moving target," *Child Develpm.*, 1–2: 90–105, 1930–1931.

18. Hildreth, Gertrude H., and N. L. Griffiths: *Metropolitan Readiness Tests*. World, Yonkers, N.Y., 1949.

19. Jenkins, Gladys G., Helen Shacter, and W. W. Bauer: *These Are Your Children*, expanded ed. Copyright, 1953, by Scott, Foresman and Company, Chicago, and used with their permission.

20. Jenkins, Lulu M.: *A Comparative Study of Motor Achievement of Children Five, Six, and Seven Years of Age*, Contributions to Education, no. 414, Teachers College, Columbia University, Bureau of Publications, New York, 1930.

21. Jersild, A. T.: *Child Psychology*, 4th ed., Copyright, 1954, by Prentice-Hall, Englewood Cliffs, N.J., and used with their permission.

22. ———: "Effects of delay on growth," *J. Nat. Educ. Ass.*, 37: 150–151, 1948.

23. ———, and S. F. Bienstock: "The influence of training on the vocal ability of three year old children," *Child Develpm.*, 2: 272–291, 1931.

24. Johnson, J. T.: "An evaluation of research on gradation in the field of arithmetic," *J. Educ. Res.*, 37: 161–173, 1943.

25. Mattson, Marion L.: "The relation between the complexity of the habit to be acquired and the form of the learning curve in young children," *Genet. Psychol. Monogr.*, 13: 299–398, 1933.

26. McGehee, W.: "Changes in interest with change in grade status of elementary school children," *J. Educ. Psychol.*, 32: 151–156, 1941.

27. Monroe, Marion: "Determining reading readiness," *Understand. Child*, 9: 15–19, 1940.

28. ———: *Reading Aptitude Tests*, primary form, Houghton Mifflin, Boston, 1935.

29. Morphett, Mabel V., and C. Washburne: "When should children begin to read?" *Elem. Sch. J.*, 31: 496–503, Copyright, 1931, by the University of Chicago. Reprinted by permission of the University of Chicago Press.

30. ———, W. Weedon, and C. Washburne: *The Winnetka Chart for Determining Grade Placement of Children's Books*, Winnetka Public Schools, Winnetka, Ill.

31. Sommer, A. T.: "The effect of group training upon the correction of articulatory defects in pre-school children," *Child Develpm.*, 3: 91–103, 1932.

32. Souder, H. C.: "The construction and evaluation of certain readiness tests in common fractions," *J. Educ. Res.*, 37: 127–134, 1943.

33. Stendler, Celia B., and N. Young: "The impact of beginning first grade upon socialization as reported by mothers," *Child Develpm.*, 21: 241–260, 1950.

34. Washburne, C. (Chairman): *Child Development and the Curriculum*, 38th Yearbook of the Nat. Soc. Stud. Educ., Part I, Chicago, Distributed by the University of Chicago Press, 1939.

35. Washburne, C.: "The work of the Committee of Seven on grade-placement in arithmetic." *Child Development and the Curriculum*, pp. 299–324. 38th Yearbook of the Nat. Soc. Stud. Educ., Part I, Chicago, Distributed by the University of Chicago Press, 1939.

36. Wechsler, D.: "Intellectual development and psychological maturity," *Child Develpm.*, 21: 45–50, 1950.

37. Witty, P., A. Coomer, and D. McBear: "Children's choices of favorite books: a study conducted in ten elementary schools," *J. Educ. Psychol.*, 37: 266–278, 1946.

Chapter 4

Teacher-guidance
of Learning
Activities

For SELF-REALIZATION of his potential talents and interests and to fulfill his roles effectively in society, the child has a tremendous amount of learning to do. His social heritage and the experiences of everyday living, however, are rich in opportunities for acquiring the knowledge, skills, attitudes, and action patterns he needs. To guide the child both in selecting what is worth learning and in becoming efficient as a learner, his society provides teachers. Since the role of the teacher in guiding children's learning is a very important condition of learning, teachers need to understand the principles of effective teacher-guidance.

Learning Is Always Goal-directed

However purposeless and random a child's learning efforts may sometimes appear, closer examination will usually reveal them to be purposeful and goal-directed. When a child meets in his reading a word he does not recognize, in his writing a word he cannot spell, or in his arithmetic a problem he cannot solve, he will probably exhibit multiple and varied responses. But his behavior will not be random; it will be highly purposeful. To solve such problems, the child will make goal-directed, provisional (hypothesis-testing) trials, guided by the motivating conditions and his cognitive organization of past experiences, and influenced by his current ongoing activity. "Whatever the exact organization of machinery may prove to be that accomplishes this marvelous result, it

92

involves taking into account many, many factors of past experience, weighing or evaluating them on the basis of the probability that a certain reaction to a certain set of circumstances will be a good bet (promise an expected good outcome) and then acting accordingly" [8, p. 39].

Sometimes, however, the problem-solving behavior of children does not appear to the teacher to be so carefully considered. Rimer, Wilson, and Knight [48], who asked children to "think out loud" as they solved arithmetic problems, observed several ineffective diversions from systematic problem solving. When uncertain of the correct procedure, children resorted to "peculiar ways." They sometimes decided which arithmetic processes to use on the basis of the size of the numbers; or they operated with all the numbers, both relevant and irrelevant; or they tried different processes, attempting to find one which would be approved by the teacher. Some of their "solutions" to the problem "Joseph rode on the merry-go-round 12 times. Each time cost him 3 cents. How much did he pay for all the rides?" illustrate their baffling confusion. One ten-year-old girl answered "36," explaining, "I multiplied because it said times." An eleven-year-old girl multiplied "because there is just two numbers." And still another child multiplied "because there wasn't enough numbers to add." These groping responses, springing from faulty and poorly organized concepts, show that the problem has been naively misconstrued, but the contingent use of "because" indicates that from the child's own point of view, they are purposeful, though highly tentative and provisional.

A superficial examination of the arithmetic examples collected from fourth grade children by Tilton [57] and here presented in Table 4–1 suggests also, at first sight, almost random problem-solving effort. But to infer from the

Table 4–1. Illustrations of Purposeful although Erroneous Arithmetic Problem Solving (By fourth grade children)

(a)	770	(b)	7	(c)	760
	−545		+14		−15
	235		12		655
(d)	32	(e)	84	(f)	46
	×49		×10		× 3
	88		80		201

Source: J. W. Tilton: *J. Educ. Psychol.*, 38: 83–88, 1947.

incorrect answers to these problems that the children's problem-solving efforts were sheer random guessing would be misleading. By some ingenuity in inferring, the erroneous hypotheses that led to the above results might be induced from careful inspection of the papers alone. As a phase of a diagnostic and remedial teaching program, however, each child was asked to think out loud as he attempted to solve a problem. From this experiment, the purposeful and goal-directed character of each child's efforts were made clear. In (*a*), the child said he took the smaller number from the larger, regardless of position; in (*b*), the single digits were added; in (*c*), the smaller digit was taken from the larger, and the odd digit 7 was paired with the 1 already used once; in (*d*), 9 was multiplied by 2, the 1 being carried and added to 4 and 3; in (*e*), the digits were paired vertically and each pair multiplied together; and in (*f*), the larger of the two digits was carried in the multiplication process. It was thus made apparent that the errors were not accidents; they resulted rather from application of faulty rules (hypotheses) and from failure to understand the meaning of numbers, especially as concerns the place value of digits. In (*b*), for example, had the child understood that the "1" in "14" has a value of 10 units, his sum would probably have been correct.

Hildreth [28] has pointed out one general approach to difficulties in problem solving which explains in part these and other kinds of error. When children meet problems beyond their ability or skill to solve, they tend to respond by simplifying the problems and their modes of attack. The errors and distortions in perception, word meanings, and reasoning thus introduced are not random; from the angle of the child's mental set, the solutions of the simplified problems are meaningful. Examples of this tendency are reading "organize" as "orange"; defining "muzzle," in the Stanford-Binet vocabulary list, by "Your arm is strong"; copying ovals as circles or diamonds as squares; and answering the question "Who discovered the North Pole?"—which the child could not do—by converting it into one he could answer: "Oh yes, who discovered America? Why, Columbus!"

Children Need Guidance

John [32], like Rimer, Wilson, and Knight and Tilton, has shown how baffling problem solving in arithmetic can be to children who lack a confident, systematic approach. By observing, questioning, and recording as 60 pupils in grades 4, 5, and 6 attempted to solve orally two-step problems, she noted a great variety of errors stemming from a faulty mode of attack, including faulty reasoning, use of wrong process, disregard of significant facts, using unrelated numbers and irrelevant facts, hesitation over method of solution, using an unnecessarily long process, confusion in method, irrational selection of method, combining unlike quantities, and other erroneous or inefficient methods.

Similarly, Bond and Fay [3] have shown that children who experience difficulty in learning to read often do so because of faulty goal-directing ideas and inefficient modes of attack. For 23 such children ages 8 to 13, they found, among other specific weaknesses, faulty word-recognition techniques (in 22 out of 23); phonetic analysis used to the exclusion of other methods of identifying unfamiliar words; poor habits, such as lip movements and inability to phrase; and reading which was too slow or too fast for the purpose. Besides these faulty modes of attack, they also found emotional disturbance, negative attitudes, fatigue and listlessness, immaturity of vocabulary, and speech defects interfering with progress in reading. These other factors remind us, of course,

FIG. 4–1. Appropriate teacher-guidance when needed, especially in the initial stages of learning, leads to more efficient and confident reading. (*Courtesy of Whittier School, Utah State Agricultural College.*)

that "sufficient maturity and appropriate patterns of abilities" and "freedom from anxiety and distorting attitudes" are also essential for effective learning.

An especially striking example of what may happen when children are not given adequate teacher-guidance in efficient modes of attack is provided by Cole, who has pointed out the awkward and ineffective techniques which left-handed children, for whom the instruction given to the right-handed child is sometimes not directly applicable, often hit upon in learning to write when left to their own devices, [9, pp. 443–447]. All these examples indicate a need for teacher-guidance in introducing a child to new problems and new phases of learning sequences. Indeed, it is at this point that a most important teaching role is played. As an example of teaching effective modes of attack, Cole's instruction in modes of attack in writing adapted to the left-handed child is offered. To avoid the strain and difficulty for the left-handed child in writing legibly, the following system is proposed:

1. The position of the paper should be such that the lower edge is at right angles to the arm being used—just the opposite of the position for the right-handed child.

2. The pencil or pen should be grasped at least an inch or an inch and a half from the point. This will avoid the child's covering or smearing with his fingers what he has just written.

3. The hand should slide along on the ends of the two smallest fingers, far enough below the line being written to miss the longest loops.

4. "Any slant between vertical and 45 degrees to the left of the base line is entirely satisfactory." The usual right slant from the base line would require of the left-handed child too great a proportion of push rather than pull movements, which are easier to execute without pricking the paper.

5. As a further aid, the point of the pen should have a rounded nib.

6. As with the right-handed pupil, either an arm movement or a wrist-and-hand movement may be used.

7. "The proportions of the letters are, of course, the same no matter what hand is used," except that the slant is reversed or vertical.

In this instance, the explicit teacher-guidance suggested is perhaps appropriate. But orienting a child to correct goal-directing ideas and efficient modes of attack need not always be done by directive teaching or by verbal explanations. Often, by provision of a suitable sequence of learning experiences and by development of a general set to search for principles and efficient modes of attack, a child can be helped to discover inductively for himself useful principles and modes of attack in solving problems. This is often better. Harlow has interpreted some of Katona's experiments to indicate that pupils who are taught to search for general solutions in a variety of problems are likely to do better than those given explicit, verbalized principles [23, 24]. This would not, of course, justify leaving children to themselves to find their own modes of attack in problem solving. As Reed has shown, even though learners may find their own principles and modes of attack, teacher-guidance which directs the learners to search for principles is an aid in learning [45].

Experiments on Teacher-guidance in Learning

Provided the child feels secure and confident in his modes of attack, learning takes place most readily in a stimulating environment which presents him continually with new and interesting learning opportunities. Feeling and seeing himself mastering and making progress in useful and interesting knowledge and skills increases his zest and skill for further learning. The pace, of course, can be so fast that the child comes to feel the insecurity of being continually on completely unfamiliar ground. But by relating the new to the familiar and with adequate teacher-guidance, he can progress efficiently and with confidence. Several experiments [10, 11, 12, 43, 55] have demonstrated the important role of teacher-guidance in effective learning.

Thompson [55] has attempted to determine experimentally the effects of different amounts of teacher-guidance on the attainment of educational objectives at the preschool level, using 19 four-year-old nursery school children divided into equated groups. Group A was given little teacher-guidance and Group B much teacher-guidance in direction of their activities. Both groups were measured before and again after eight months of teaching on objective and reliable observational scales of ascendance, social participation, leadership, constructiveness in reaction to the frustration of possible failure, and number of nervous habits.

With Group A, given little teacher-guidance, "the teacher made on her own initiative a minimum of contacts with the children, permitting them to work out their own plans for the school day and giving assistance to them only upon request." Group B was given information, more specific helps, more directive guidance—including more structuring suggestions ("You could look in some of these books and see how they [airplanes] are made.") and leading questions ("How can we fix it so that we can reach it?"), more overt friendly gestures, and in general more stimulation to the children's thinking.

On all the educational measures applied, the pretest–to–end-test gains favored the group given more teacher-guidance. They excelled in ascendant behavior, social participation, leadership, and constructiveness when faced with a possible failure, and they showed fewer nervous habits. On only the last measure was the difference too small to meet the criterion for statistical significance.

The role of teacher-guidance in effective learning is general. Even with adolescents and adults, who have had more experience with learning and have learned more about how to learn, teacher-guidance improves learning efficiency. Priebe and Burton [43], working with adolescents, found the use of slow-motion pictures, which added guidance by demonstrations to other teacher-guidance techniques, to result in faster progress and better achievement in the high jump than that made by a group not given this aid. And Craig [10], in training adults on verbal problems, found that teacher-guidance in directing their attention to principles resulted both in avoidance of more errors while learning and in greater transfer to similar situations.

The general importance of teacher-guidance is shown very clearly in an experiment by Davies on the effect of instruction upon the process of learning a complex motor skill [11]. Two matched groups of 20 college students each practiced archery for two 50-minute periods a week for three months, one group with tuition and the other group without any teacher-guidance. Tuition for the guided group included during each practice period demonstrations, analyses of procedures used, descriptions of correct process and methods of

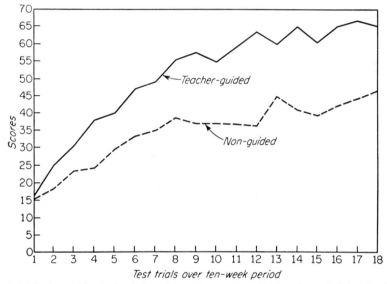

Fig. 4–2. Teacher-guidance aids in learning archery. (*From Davies, D. R.: J. Educ. Psychol.,* *36: 356, 1935.*)

work, direction of attention to more adequate modes of attack, suggestions on how to break up faulty techniques, and explanations leading to insights.

The superior progress made by the teacher-guided group is clearly revealed in Figure 4–2. Both groups started the practice with equal proficiency. But the guided group made better progress from the outset and maintained a steady and faster rate of progress throughout the learning period. The uninstructed group, besides showing slower initial progress, reached a plateau at the eighth session and continued with practically no progress for nearly half the entire period of training. From these data, Davies concludes that "apparently it takes teaching to prevent the learner from early falling into a set pattern far below his potentialities, yet bringing some measure of success."

FIG. 4–3. Children improve in singing, dancing, and rhythms through growth and self-teaching; but they become more proficient and have more fun with some teacher-guidance. (*Courtesy of Standard Oil Company of New Jersey.*)

In the light of these experimental demonstrations of the value of teacher-guidance as a condition of effective learning, it may be pertinent to comment further on two experiments mentioned in the previous chapter. Dusenberry [12], it will be recalled, found that the skill of five- and six-year-old children in throwing a ball was significantly improved (compared with a control group) by practice plus specific instruction on stance, use of an overhead movement in throwing, how to shift weight in body rotation, and how to release the ball. Hicks [26, 27], however, in attempting to teach three- to six-year-old children the even more complex motor skill of throwing a ball at a moving target, failed to get greater gains from the practice than from the control group. Neither group made any progress. But for Hicks's practice group, specific teacher-guidance was withheld: "In no case, however, were instructions given as to ways in which the child might improve his skill." Hicks's careful observational notes do, however, indicate a need for teacher-guidance in better modes of attack. Children often failed to wait for the target to reach the center of the running path; overhand throws were likely to be low; force was insufficient to carry the ball to the target, or it was too strong for good control; some did not take time to aim; grip of the ball was sometimes too tight and sometimes too loose; and there was failure to use self-criticism. "Children went on throwing in awkward unsuccessful ways, unable in this complex situation to eliminate errors" [27, p. 53]. It is quite possible that Hicks's subjects were too immature to learn this complex motor skill. But it is also very probable that the progress of more mature children in this skill could be affected significantly by teacher-guidance in correcting their errors and in suggesting more effective modes of attack.

Satisfaction with Inferior Modes of Attack

It was noted earlier that Davies's uninstructed archery subjects reached a plateau early in a series of practice sessions. They became satisfied with a moderate degree of skill and ceased to make appreciable further improvement. Brownell has also shown how satisfaction with "some measure of success" may divert the learner from acquiring more efficient modes of attack which could lead to even greater proficiency. His data show that, as third grade children practice addition combinations [7] and as fifth grade children practice multiplication combinations [4], they make progress in both accuracy and speed, attaining the usual norm standards. But individual diagnostic interviewing revealed that without teacher-guidance in acquiring efficient modes of attack, they tend to make "progress" in the use of inferior work methods. In adding, for example, rather than arriving at sums by confident, immediate recall, many children continue to add by counting and to arrive at solutions indirectly (for $3 + 4 = ?$, $3 + 3 = 6$ and $6 + 1 = 7$) and by uncertain guessing. In multiplication, they also continue to count ($3 \times 4 = 3, 6, 9, 12$), to recite the tables up to the desired product, to visualize ($4 \times 5 = 4 \times 5$ nickels $= 20\cent = 20$), to reverse factors ($6 \times 3 = 3 \times 6 =$), etc., rather than arriving at products directly, with understanding and confidence.

From results such as these, Brownell concludes that "learning consists of progressive reorganization of processes or procedures" [5] and that drill "makes little, if any, contribution to growth in quantitative thinking by supplying maturer ways of dealing with numbers." It tends "to maintain the use of whatever procedures they [children] have found satisfy their needs" [7]. In other words, unless teachers give guidance (explicitly or indirectly by arranging conditions for self-discovery) in learning effective modes of attack, children often find satisfaction in and make some gains with inefficient processes. An example from experience with diagnostic and remedial teaching, where work methods or modes of attack are highly important, will further illustrate this concept.

Modes of Attack in Diagnostic and Remedial Teaching. A twelve-year-old child in the sixth grade was referred to the author for help because she could not read well enough to keep up with the considerable reading required in her grade. Frequently poor reading is associated with low intelligence; but on the Stanford-Binet intelligence scale she earned a mental age of 14, which is about 1½ years beyond the average for her grade. Her scores on five reading tests are shown in Table 4–2.

Table 4–2. Grade, Age, and Accuracy Scores in Reading for Sixth Grade Girl Indicate Need for Remedial Teaching

Test	Grade	Age	Accuracy, per cent
Gray's oral reading paragraphs...............	3.4		
Gates, A (general impression)...............	3.1	8-7	75
Gates, B (predicting outcome)...............	3.1	8-7	75
Gates, C (directions).......................	3.8	9-4	100
Gates, D (details).........................	3.4	8-10	90

Source: A. N. Frandsen: *Ment. Hlth.*, (Utah Society for Mental Hygiene), 13: 5, 1946.

The general trend of scores in this table indicates that the child reads at about the third grade level, which is about three grades below her actual grade level. The causes of her difficulty, however, are not apparent in the pattern of scores, which are about equal for all five types of reading tested. But important clues were noted as the examiner observed her oral reading of Gray's paragraphs. She read slowly, and every unfamiliar word she came upon was recognized only upon sounding it out phonetically. Questioning her, however, revealed that she understood the word-identification devices of using the context of a word and of visual analysis. Upon first sight she did not, for example, recognize "blackberrying"; but when instructed to look for its main parts, she analyzed the word as "black-berry-ing," each part of which she recognized separately. She then synthesized the meaning of the whole word. Although she knew all three word-identification techniques, it was revealed upon further questioning that she habitually relied upon the phonetic device to the exclusion of the other two.

Children need to learn all these word-identification procedures, and there are occasions when any one or combination of them is effective and appropriate. To rely almost wholly upon the phonetic method would result in relatively slow reading for a sixth grade child. At this level, use of context cues, in the main, plus visual analysis would be much more appropriate to the speed needed for the extensive reading expected. Since our observational diagnosis indicated that insufficient speed of reading was probably the primary difficulty, the speed of the child's reading was measured. It was found to be only 45 words per minute. The median speed for sixth grade children is about 200 words per minute [46]. The remedy suggested, of course, is the cultivation of work methods or modes of attack which would make possible considerable improvement in speed of reading.

Since she was a very intelligent child, it was easy to explain to her what was thought to be making her a less efficient reader in the sixth grade than she could be. It was suggested to her that, whenever she had occasion to read, she keep in mind as the goal "Learn to comprehend more quickly." It was also explained that to comprehend a paragraph or sentence, it is not necessary even to look at every word. She was advised, when she came upon unfamiliar words, to "guess at their meanings" to complete the general meaning of the sentence, or to analyze them visually, as she had done for "blackberrying." Only as a last resort was she to sound out the words. Besides the application of this procedure to the reading assigned in her classes, she was given supervised practice in silent reading every other day on some interesting material at the third grade level of difficulty. The relatively low level of difficulty (third grade as indicated by the tests) was chosen to ensure initial success and progress toward attainment of her goal of faster reading. To ensure attention to meaning also, objective comprehension questions followed each reading exercise. The results of the first 10 days of practice of one-half hour every other day for five weeks are shown in Figure 4–4.

The excellent progress made in the short period covered in the graph indicates that when, following a diagnosis indicating a need for it, attention is given to the acquisition of more efficient modes of attack, rapid improvement may sometimes be expected. But why did remedial teaching become necessary? Very probably because, when this sixth grade girl began reading in the first grade, where reading is not easy even for a bright child, she found in a trial-and-discovery process that sounding out each word made reading possible. Since this procedure achieved her goal and in a measure satisfied her motives in reading activities, it was accepted, and became her habitual mode of attack in reading. This, of course, does not happen often; usually a child takes pleasure in attaining continuously higher and higher levels of proficiency. An insecure child is more likely to continue using beyond the need for it a relatively simple way of approaching problems which has been found workable, rather than venturing into new areas of learning. But this aspect of remedial teaching will be treated in a later chapter. Here it may suffice to remark that for this child, at some point in her reading progress prior to the sixth grade, attention to increasingly more adequate modes of attack should have led earlier to the prac-

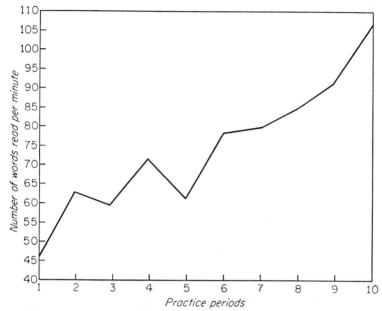

FIG. 4-4. Improvement in speed of reading from remedial teaching involves learning more efficient modes of attack. (*From Frandsen, A. N.: Mental Health (Utah Society for Mental Hygiene), 13, 6, 1946.*)

tice of reading ideas rather than words and to using context clues and visual analysis as well as phonetic methods in the identification of unfamiliar words.

General Principles of Teacher-guidance

This review has shown thus far that in the learning of both subject matter and healthy child development behavior patterns, children need teacher-guidance, and that the efficiency of their learning depends to an important extent upon the effectiveness of that teacher-guidance. It has also been indicated that in teaching children how to go about achieving an educational goal—how to use effective modes of attack in learning—several teaching procedures are appropriate. In teaching children how to identify unfamiliar words in reading, to solve problems in arithmetic, or to acquire a motor skill, the teacher may explain, demonstrate, correct pupils' provisional trials, or provide pupil self-

FIG. 4–5. This child finds her textbook an effective guide on how to write a letter. (*Courtesy of McGraw-Hill Text-Film Department.*)

discovery experiences through arrangement of learning sequences and leading questions. There are numerous variations of these general teacher-guidance techniques. For example, demonstrations may be supplemented by films and other visual aids. And the devices may be used singly or—often more effectively—in various combinations, as with demonstrations accompanied by verbal explanations.

In his role of giving guidance on modes of attack in learning, the teacher has two major purposes. He is interested in helping children to learn as efficiently as possible the subject matter or activity being pursued at the time. But he is also and even more concerned with helping children to develop independence and effectiveness as learners; that is, an important objective in teacher-guidance is helping children learn how to learn. How then can the teacher develop teacher-guidance procedures which will achieve these two important purposes? A survey of the literature of educational psychology for aids to teachers in developing effective teacher-guidance methods has yielded the following twelve principles.

1. Self-recitation. Gates's experiment on recitation as a factor in memorizing [16] was one of the first to show the greater efficiency of an active self-reciting mode of attack and attitude as compared with the more passive reading and rereading in memorizing. Among other learning tasks, children from grades 3 to 8 memorized short biographies, employing different amounts of time in self-recitation. One group spent the entire learning period in reading and rereading. Five other groups spent, respectively, the last 20, 40, 60, 80, and 90 per cent of the time allowed, in "self-recitation"—that is, in trying to recite the biography without reading from the copy, looking at it only when it was necessary to prompt themselves. The relative effectiveness of each amount of self-recitation was expressed as the percentage which the ideas recalled for

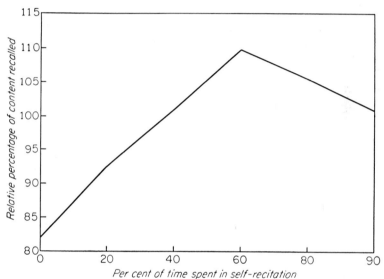

FIG. 4–6. Self-recitation facilitates memorizing. (*Adapted from Gates, A. I.: Arch. Psychol., 6(40): 41, 1917.*)

each condition was of the average number recalled for all conditions. These relative scores are presented in Figure 4–6.

As can be seen from this figure, when any fraction of the time is spent in self-recitation, it results in more effective memorizing than when all the time is spent in reading and rereading only. In this particular learning activity, it is advantageous to spend from 40 to 90 per cent of the time in self-recitation, the optimum proportion being 60 per cent. The optimum ratio between amounts of reading and recitation will, of course, vary with the nature of the material to be learned. The important principle, which can be applied generally, is that some amount of active self-recitation increases the efficiency of memorizing. For longer selections, the proportion of time spent in reading will probably need to be greater. Usually the amount of time spent in self-recitation will be fairly great. As soon as sufficient readings have been accomplished to grasp well the meaning of what is to be memorized, the learner should begin self-reciting, with checks for accuracy and with self-promptings as needed.

That active self-recitation is a general principle of learning has been shown in experimental applications of the concept to other kinds of learning. Forlano found that learning by self-reciting improved efficiency in spelling by 19 per cent, nonsense-syllable memorizing by 24 per cent, English vocabulary by 28 per cent, and arithmetic by 7 per cent [14]. In teaching beginners hand-writing, Hertzberg found that a copying method requiring the equivalent of active self-recitation resulted in 40 per cent greater gains than were made with four different tracing methods, in which the child's hand was guided passively in forming the letters by grooves, by sandpaper outlines, by finger models, and by transparent paper [25]. In understanding and remembering content read in such subjects as social studies, applications of the principle of self-recitation in the forms of outlining, summarizing, and reading to answer questions have proved effective [13, 17, 18, 19, 60].

There are many applications of this principle. One would be to teach reading as an active reasoning, problem-solving, or creative activity. As a specific device in reading to understand and to remember the content in social studies or science, children might be taught to convert topical headings in their texts into questions and to read to answer for themselves these questions. Another example would be to teach children to outline by making up a question-and-answer outline in their own words, rather than lifting phrases and sentences verbatim from their references. Broader and more comprehensive applications of the principle are individual pupil research, as in using diverse library sources for such topics as "The Country of My Ancestors," and active pupil participation in planning and carrying out unified projects, such as the diet experiment in connection with the study of health.

2. Goal-directing Ideas Made Explicit by Verbalization. Words are perhaps the human being's most effective tool for designating, describing, discriminating, differentiating, classifying, organizing, operating, and otherwise "managing" things and activities, both perceptually and symbolically. Telling how or explaining is the procedure used most often by teachers in guiding pupils' learning activities. It will not be surprising therefore to find it effective. Sometimes verbalization of a complex motor skill has been found to make the learning of it easier. The writer, for example, in trying to imitate a certain skating figure being executed by a more expert skater found it very difficult until his friend *explained* as well as demonstrated the pattern the writer was trying to

Fig. 4–7. Teacher-explanation, demonstrations, and their own self-discovery experiences aid these children in understanding and constructing crystal radio sets. (*Courtesy of Whittier School, Utah State Agricultural College.*)

learn. With a verbal clarification, or a sharper differentiation of the cognitive structure guiding the process, it was easier to execute the motor pattern. According to the theory of learning already outlined, verbalization should aid learning because it makes the goal-directing idea more explicit.

Hovland has reported an experiment done by Thompson [51, p. 629] which supports this principle. Five equated groups of children were given different kinds and varying amounts of guidance toward verbalization of a procedure for learning to assemble a mechanical puzzle. Differences in their performance proved that effective verbalization of the "steps" in solving the puzzle greatly facilitates the mastery of it. Children prevented from verbalizing by being required to count as they watched a silent demonstration of the solution required almost twice as many trials as children who silently watched the experimenter describe as well as demonstrate the procedure. Even higher proficiency in mastering the puzzle was achieved, however, when children themselves described the demonstration and were corrected when their descriptions were in error. In this most effective procedure, accurate verbalization of the process was combined with an active, self-reciting attack and with teacher-help in checking the effects of each provisional trial.

Two investigations with children have indicated that naming objects, compared to visual perception alone, helps children to remember them and to deal with them in multiple-choice problem-solving situations. Kurtz and Hovland [35] found that when elementary school children both encircled and named aloud each of 16 familiar objects, they remembered more of them a week later than a comparable group who had merely encircled them. Pyles [44], using six comparable groups of about 25 each of children ages 2 to 7, presented to them—in counterbalanced order, to control effects of practice—a three-part multiple-choice problem. The problem consisted of identifying under which of five differently nonsense-shaped molds a toy had been placed. At each trial the molds were rearranged, but the toy always was placed under the same mold. For condition A, the children were told, "One of these shapes has a toy under it; see if you can find which shape has the toy." For condition B, the directions were the same, except that, when the toy was found, the mold was given a name, such as "Mobie," and the child was directed to repeat the name. For condition C, the directions were similar to those for B, except that the names were of animals with which the children were already familiar (cat, dog, rabbit, bear, monkey).

The advantage of naming objects to be identified and remembered is indicated in Figure 4–8, which shows the trials required to master the three successively presented variations of this problem. That fewer trials were required at each presentation to identify the named than the unnamed object shows that teacher-guidance in naming the object to be discriminated, thus making it more explicitly recognizable, facilitates such learning.

The role of transfer in learning is indicated by two aspects of these results. First, the advantage of employing familiar names results from the use in this situation of already accomplished learning. And second, the gains from the first to the third presentations, using in each instance a different variation of the problem (the toy under a different mold) indicate transfer in learning how to learn.

3. Meaningful Approach. In teaching concepts or skills, procedures which emphasize meaning, understanding (or insight), and generalization of principles are superior, especially for long-range or permanent learning. It has already been noted in Chapter 2 that for children who achieved insight into the interrelated structure and parts of the Obstacle Peg Test, only one trial was required for building a "cognitive map." The map served as a guide for clearing the path and moving the red peg without error directly to the center hole.

Using children ages 5, 8, and 11, Ausubel and Schiff [1] found a correspondence between increases in age, especially from 8 to 11, and the ability to learn causal relations (such as that the longer side of a teeter-totter from the fulcrum will fall when both sides are released from their supports). And for the children better able to learn such principles (ages 8 and 11), a meaningful principle was more readily learned than an irrelevant sequence of events (predicting which end of the teeter-totter will fall when the only cue available is the arbitrary

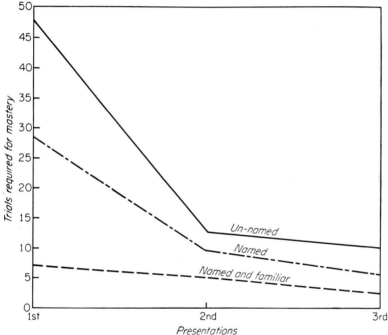

FIG. 4-8. Verbalization and transfer help in learning multiple-choice problems, such as "Find the hidden toy." (Children ages 2 to 7.) (*From Pyles, M. K.: Child Develpm., 3: 108–113, 1932.*)

arrangement that it will be the side with a red rather than a green block on it). In this instance, the meaningfulness of the relevant principle was probably the result of the generalizing and understanding which the older children had achieved from previous incidental experience with teeter-totters and other fulcrum objects.

Generally, emphasizing meaning in learning has two advantages: it utilizes the organized concepts or principles achieved from accumulated prior learnings, and it consolidates what would otherwise be numerous separate learnings into applications of a few unifying principles. This latter advantage was illustrated earlier in the passage on the teaching of manuscript writing, where it was noted that the 26 different letters of the alphabet are all comprised of simple circles, straight lines, and curved lines. This principle of meaning needs constant application in every phase of the elementary school curriculum. Recently it has been especially emphasized in the teaching of arithmetic [6, 37, 47, 49, 61, 62].

In analyzing meaning as applied to teaching arithmetic, Van Engen [59] finds that it has three elements: (1) an event or object, called the "referent"; (2) a symbol for the referent; and (3) an individual to interpret the symbol as referring to the referent. In arithmetic, the symbols which guide the child in operations with numbers are a system of interrelated ideas which the child needs to learn to comprehend gradually as a system [61]. Especially in beginning to deal with symbols as guides for operations, he will need ample concrete experience with the objects and events to which the symbols refer.

The advantage in drawing upon children's concrete-experience background is illustrated in an observation reported by Wheat [62, pp. 86–87]:

A fifth grade teacher in a preliminary test found that his pupils knew little about the relative sizes of the simple fractions [represented symbolically]. They made blunders in recognizing the largest of the three written representations, such as $\frac{1}{2}$, $\frac{2}{3}$, $\frac{1}{4}$, and the smallest of $\frac{2}{3}$, $\frac{2}{5}$, and $\frac{2}{2}$. However, when he began his instruction, he discovered at once that the concrete representations of the sizes of the common fractions, one-half of an apple, two-thirds of a circle and so on, were not unfamiliar to the pupils. Indeed when he gave the opportunity, most of the pupils were able to provide ample illustration from their own experiences, and gave clear evidence of the possession of the meanings of the fractions whose written representations had been confusing. The teacher found that he did not have to teach size at all at the outset, but rather the way of representing size [that is, the symbol for size]. He found the idea of size present, but it had to be recalled and concentrated upon. He therefore, by suggestion and otherwise, encouraged the recall of those experiences which served to bring to the fore the desired idea.

Brownell's report of an experiment [6] comparing two procedures in teaching third grade children subtraction indicates the value in understanding arithmetic as a system of interrelated ideas. In this instance the need for understanding the place values of numbers is especially illustrated. Two equated groups were taught to "borrow" in subtraction in such examples as $92 - 47$. One group, following the textbook, learned by a "mechanical procedure," without understanding the place values of numbers. "The other group learned to borrow on the basis of understanding. The latter were led to see that 92 can be changed, without loss of value, to $80 + 12$, so that the 7 of 47 can then be subtracted from the 12 (1's) and the 4 of 47 from the 8 (10's)." On final tests of similar problems and also on problems involving borrowing from both tens and hundreds (for example, 425 − 268), the children who had been taught meaningfully "outscored by a wide margin" those who had been taught "mechanically." When some forgetting of the skill occurred with temporary disuse, relearning was also better for the group taught meaningfully.

As an example of a unifying idea in arithmetic, it may be pointed out that in over a dozen different situations, the child, as he progresses in arithmetic, meets three kinds of problems—really three aspects of one principle: $N_1 = N_2 \times N_3$. Sometimes he needs to find part of a number ($\frac{1}{4}$ of 12 = ?). Again, he may need to find what part one number is of another (3 is what part of 12?). And third, he is sometimes required to find a number when a part of it is given (3 is $\frac{1}{4}$ of what number?) These three variations of the principle of a number being equal to the product of two factors occur and recur in fractions, decimals, percentages. The same principle is applied in interest, gain and loss, cost and selling price, insurance, measurement of areas, rate and distance problems, etc. If the general principle is recognized, it becomes a unifying idea which multiplies the efficiency of learning the numerous variations of it [62].

If arithmetic is taught meaningfully, the child's developing understanding of the number system provides satisfying and useful answers to such questions, which an otherwise perplexed "Tom" might ask, as "How come you move the decimal point over that many places?" "How come when you borrow one and add you get 12? One and two are only three," "How come you don't add the denominators like you add the numerators when you add fractions, and how's come you multiply them when you multiply fractions?" and "How come you invert and multiply the divisor when you divide fractions?" [49, p. 89]. The answers to these questions would not consist of a list of rules; they would derive from Tom's understanding of the number system as a whole.

Similar examples of the role of meaning in effective learning could be pointed out in other curriculum areas. Reading as a reasoning process emphasizes meaning. Using in identifying unfamiliar words the over-all context and in word analysis looking for meaning units and pronounceable parts rather than for single vowels and vowel-consonant combinations also stress meaning. Even in spelling, the building up of a background of generalizations is helpful. In the social studies and in science, projects with central, unifying ideas give helpful meaning to what would otherwise often be lists of relatively useless and difficult-to-remember facts. Hildreth believes that one of the advantages of teaching all the basic skills as a part of a unified "activity" program is that here the approach is more meaningful, "for the pupil actually is practicing the skill while working on genuine problems" [29].

4. *An Over-all View First.* One special way to emphasize meaning in learning is to take an overview at the outset of a learning activity. An integrated and unified approach to a problem as a whole is often more efficient than a piecemeal, part-by-part approach, especially in the initial stages of a learning undertaking. Referring again to the Obstacle Peg Test, it may be observed that some of the children achieved one-trial insight into this problem because they could perceive as a whole the organization and interrelations of its significant parts. There are many situations where a general understanding of the whole would make experiences with the parts more meaningful. One could perhaps explore a new city street by street; but having a map showing the relationship of each street to the whole would make each separate exploration more meaningful [36]. Again, in making a garden, an over-all plan aids in achieving a good arrangement.

Such initial over-all views have been found helpful in planning science and social studies units. The symbolic expression of an arithmetic problem as a guide to the operations to be performed likewise aids in seeing through the problem. In learning a motor skill, such as swimming, practice on the skill as a whole before separate practice on such aspects as kicking, arm movements, or breathing makes practice on these separate features more meaningful and effective.

As an experimental demonstration of the value of the overview, Hildreth's comparison of two approaches to puzzle solving may be cited [30]. Three jigsaw picture puzzles were presented to 100 children ages 7 to 10 who were subdivided into groups in one or the other of two ways. In the uninstructed condition of presentation, the picture puzzle to be assembled was presented without explanation or prior opportunity to see it. In the other procedure, a preliminary overview was given: As an aid in organizing the parts, the teacher, prior to the assembly task, showed the children the completed picture puzzle and named and pointed out its various features. In order to control practice effects and individual differences in ability, the 100 children were subdivided differently for the three different pictures (train, steam shovel, and ferryboat), and the order of presentation of the two procedures was varied. A comparison of the results of the two procedures revealed that "puzzle solving proved to be easier and quicker" when preceded by a preliminary overview. [30, p. 604]. The educational implication is that "school problem-solving will be more successful to the extent that the pupils can be given an overview of the whole, some knowledge of the central meaning of the problem, and some meaningful clues to aid solution" [30, p. 604].

5. *From the Simple to the Complex.* The well-known teaching rule of proceeding from the simple to the complex, from the familiar to the new, or from the concrete to the abstract, is often efficient as a mode of attack in learning. Experiencing a new principle first in a simple illustration which gives the idea facilitates finding solutions to similar problems in more complex settings. For example, a sixth grade child might be baffled by this problem: "A contractor building his own house was permitted to purchase his materials at wholesale prices, the total cost amounting to $13,294.25. The retail cost would have been $15,000. What proportion of the retail cost did he save by purchasing at wholesale prices?" He might succeed with the more complex problem, however, after several simpler problems like the following: "The school bought basketball suits which were quoted at $10 each but saved $2 per suit by paying cash. The saving was what proportion of the original price?" In symbolic formulation, both problems are, of course, similar:

$$\$15,000 - \$13,294.25 = n \times 15,000 \qquad \text{and} \qquad 2 = n \times 10$$

respectively. But by proceeding from the simple to the complex, the solutions would be easier.

A special variation of this principle is the development of abstract concepts inductively out of experience first with concrete objects and situations. Thiele illustrates this corollary in his suggestions for introducing number concepts in the primary grades by easy transitions from visual to abstract form, here adapted [53]:

(1) Concrete stage. Arrange and rearrange four actual chairs in a space on the floor. (2) Picture stage. Arrange and re-arrange pictured chairs thus: 4 hhhh into hh & hh, or h & hhh, or hhh & h. (3) Semi-concrete stage. Group and re-group 4 marks thus: //// into // & //, or / & ///, or /// & /. (4) Abstract number stage. Regroupings of 4 things can be expressed as 2 and 2, or 1 and 3, or 3 and 1.

Swenson, in discussing arithmetic for the primary grades, also emphasizes this principle [52, pp. 57–58]:

Children need to become familiar with preliminary concepts before they can be expected to deal successfully with later concepts which rest upon earlier ones. If each new idea can be presented so that the learner sees it as a clear and orderly extension of something he already knows and understands, he is saved the bewilderment and even panic which is so natural when one new and strange concept after another is forced upon him. [As an example,] Counting in progressively more mature ways should run right along with instruction in the four fundamental processes, providing for children one of the familiar and reassuring "knowns" which will make the new and previously "unknown" seem somewhat familiar and comfortable.

In this context, we may be reminded that proceeding from the simple to the complex is an effective mode of attack because it provides for two other conditions of effective learning: transfer and freedom from anxiety.

6. *Relevant Features Made Identifiable.* A teacher can often aid a pupil in his initial attempts to understand or to grasp the relationships among significant elements or features of a problem or complex situation by making significant stimulus cues identifiable [56]. Such devices as diagrams, charts, outlines, and models make the relevant cues or facts stand out from their otherwise embedding background. As a fairly superficial device for focusing pupil attention on the significant phases of division and multiplication as they are being introduced to pupils, Hall suggests the use of different colors of chalk for different elements in a process as the teacher demonstrates them on the blackboard [22]. The graphic-dependencies method of analyzing arithmetic problems, to be discussed below, is a better example of this principle.

7. *Persistence Balanced with Variability of Attack.* Necessary factors in the multiple approach to a problem include careful, thorough persistence balanced with variability of attack, open-mindedness and a search for different leads, and avoidance of both single-tracked persistence and perfunctoriness. Children often fail in learning to solve a problem because they either are not thorough enough or give up too quickly. The child who reports on his arithmetic paper that "$0.20 \div 0.05 = 0.04$" has not been thorough enough to check his answer against a reasonable estimate. Children also sometimes fail to try enough different approaches. W., in trying to read the sentence "It's no fun doing things all alone," persisted in reading the last word as "al-one," "all-one," or "al-own," and finally gave up because he couldn't make sense of it. He needed, of course, to give up his first approach to identifying "alone" and to try a different word-analysis pattern. For adults, Maier found that these three hints improved efficiency in problem solving [38, p. 147]:

(1) Locate a difficulty and try to overcome it. If you fail, get it completely out of your mind and seek an entirely different difficulty. (2) Do not be a creature of habit and stay in a rut. Keep your mind open for new meanings. (3) The solution-pattern appears suddenly. You cannot force it. Keep your mind open for new combinations and do not waste time on unsuccessful attempts.

In individual teaching situations such as the examples here mentioned, guidance both in being thorough and in trying different modes of approach to problem solving can be given.

8. *Appropriate Crutches.* The appropriate use of "crutches" sometimes makes learning more efficient in the initial stages without impairing efficiency in advanced stages of progress. Brownell, for example, found the use of a crutch in third grade learning of borrowing in subtraction resulted in better understanding and increased accuracy. In the initial stage of learning, when full attention to the fundamental process of borrowing in subtraction was required, actual writing out of the digits and marks in the problem, as at the right, helped the child to remember that the unit 1 had been increased to 11 by borrowing a 10 from the 6 tens, which was then reduced to 5 tens. When the crutch was no longer needed as a reminder, it was dropped. It was used again, however, when borrowing was once more required after a lapse in use of the skill, especially with difficult problems and when long division was learned [5].

$$\begin{array}{r} 5\ 1 \\ 8\ \not{6}\ 1 \\ -5\ 4\ 9 \\ \hline 3\ 1\ 2 \end{array}$$

From one point of view, writing down the successive partial divisor-quotient products and the partial remainder-dividend terms in long division, as compared to doing all the computations mentally, as in short division, might be considered a crutch. Both John [33] and Olander [42] found that a considerable majority of the children (about 3 to 1) in all grades who have been taught both forms choose to use the long-division form with both one-digit and two-digit divisors when left free to do so; and they were also found to be slightly more accurate with the long form. Emphasis in teacher-guidance on one form or the other, however, was found to be important in determining which form children use. Both John and Olander agree in recommending that the long-division form should be taught first and applied to examples with any number of digits. Later, when more skill and confidence with the division process have been developed, short division should be taught as a short cut, to be applied to problems with divisors of one digit or with two or three digits but ending in zero and with even and familiar multiples.

As a further example of both the principle of meaning and the use of a crutch at a stage of development where it is helpful, Grossnickle's discussion [21] of how to find the position of the decimal point in the quotient is instructive. There are three alternatives. (1) A caret may be inserted:

$$0.2\ _{\wedge}\overline{\big)5.0\ _{\wedge}}^{\textstyle 25.}$$

(2) The divisor may be converted to a whole number by multiplying both divisor and dividend by a power of 10:

$$0.2/\overline{5} = \frac{5}{0.2} = \frac{10 \times 5}{10 \times 0.2} = \frac{50}{2} = 2\overline{/50}^{25}$$

(3) The number of decimal places in the divisor may be subtracted from the number of decimal places in the dividend:

$$0.2\overline{/5.0}^{25}$$

Two criteria determine the choice of procedure: (1) The process should be meaningful and at an immature level be possible to visualize and objectify, so that a pupil can discover the essential steps in the process. (2) The mode of attack which meets this criterion may be used only temporarily as a stage in development toward a more mature procedure. At the immature level, alternative (2) above would be chosen because it is meaningful and can be visualized thus:

50 tenths contains 2 tenths 25 times. That is, 2 tenths can be subtracted from 50 tenths 25 times.

When the basic process is understood, the pupil is shifted to alternative (1)—the use of the caret—as a more efficient short cut. And finally, at the adult level of mastery, the answer is estimated without shifting the point by either multiplying or using the caret, on the basis of understanding the place values of the numbers (that is, that every unit contains 10 tenths):

$$0.2\overline{/\,5}^{25}$$

Other such crutches are double-lined writing paper for primary grade children to guide them in attaining the correct heights for different letters and strips of paper used as markers to help them keep their places in reading.

An objection to the use of crutches in teaching is that repetition of such immature procedures will make them fixed habits which will divert the learner from ever acquiring more mature and efficient procedures. But this objection, as we shall learn in the next chapter, assumes for repetition much too potent an influence on habit formation. It is not repetition so much as motive satisfaction which binds us to habits. So when a child is ready for a more mature procedure which is more satisfying because it is more efficient, he will, as Brownell has shown, give up the more practiced but less efficient procedure. In the mean-time, however, at a less mature stage of development, the crutch may have served a useful purpose by making learning more meaningful or otherwise easier. For children who prolong unnecessarily the use of crutches, the teacher might, in calling attention to the next stage of progress in mode of attack, motivate them to take the short cut of doing mentally what they have up to now been writing down as a crutch. Again it may be suggested that it is most likely to be the insecure child who is slow to abandon crutches for more effi-cient modes of attack.

9. Job Analyses of Learning Tasks. It is said that there is more than one way to skin a cat. And there are often available several different ways (not equally efficient) of performing each of the numerous learning tasks of the elementary school curriculum. For example, in adding the column of numbers at the right, pupils might learn to use any one of four modes of attack: (1) A pupil might add the column by counting either on his fingers or imaginary "points" on the figures themselves. (2) He might group tens, noting that $8 + 2 = 10, 7 + 3 = 10$, and $4 + 5 = 10 - 1$, the sum being $30 - 1$, or 29. Or (3) he might add directly down the column, mentally com-puting and saying to himself each cumulative sum; as, $8 + 7 = 15$, $15 + 2 = 17, 17 + 3 = 20, 20 + 4 = 24$, and $24 + 5 = 29$. And (4) he might add the digits directly, but by "thinking" only the succession of cumulative sums; as, 15, 17, 20, 24, 29. From the point of view of time-and-motion analysis, the fourth procedure is, of course, most efficient. The first is slow, the second often leads to inaccuracy from missing digits, and the third, although good, is unnecessarily repetitive. Teachers can often make such "job analyses" of learning tasks, which will lead to the selection of an efficient mode of attack. Pupils themselves, as a part of their training in learning how to learn efficiently, can profit from encouragement toward independent efforts at discovering the most efficient ways of performing tasks. For teachers, the literature on methods of teaching is replete with such analyses, two examples of which are cited here.

In a survey of methods of teaching subtraction, Wilson [65] has found a dozen different ways of handling such a problem as subtracting 17 from 73, in-cluding take away—borrowing—upward (7 from 13, 1 from 6), take away—borrowing—downward (13 take away 7, 6 take away 1), take away— equal additions—upward (7 from 13, 2 from 7), take away—equal additions—downward (13 take away 7, 7 take away 2), additive—borrowing—upward (7 and 6 are 13, 1 and 5 are 6), additive—borrowing—downward (13 are 7 and 6, 6 are 1 and 5), additive—equal additions—upward (7 and 6 are 13, 2 and 5 are 7), and additive—equal additions—downward (13 are 7 and 6, 7 are 2 and 5), plus four other infrequently used variations. Wilson's survey revealed the first mentioned procedure (take away—borrowing—upward) to be used much more frequently than any other procedure. And since experimental evaluations [45] have indicated no other method consistently superior to it,Wilson thinks that this method should be used universally to avoid confusing pupils as they pass from teacher to teacher.

In acquiring independence in identification or recognition of unfamiliar words, a variety of techniques are useful, including context, general word configuration, visual analysis of words into meaning or syllabic units—roots, prefixes and suffixes, parts of compound words, and syllables—and a functional and flexible use of phonetic analysis. For proficient reading, the child gradually needs to become adaptive and versatile in these techniques, using each or combinations of them in the particular situations in which they are most effective [15]. As a general approach in reading, however, a hierarchical pattern of these techniques is most efficient. In this hierarchy, meaningful context and general word configurations are the predominant guides to identifying new words; when these are not sufficient, visual analysis to the extent needed is employed; and, supplementing these techniques, variations of phonetic analysis are used as needed.

10. Explicit, Systematic Teacher-guidance. Implicit in the discussion of efficient modes of attack is the principle that pupils should learn how to learn and to perform efficiently. In achieving this objective, the amount of teacher-guidance considered desirable may vary. It may consist of detailed and explicit demonstrations and verbal explanations showing how to accomplish each learning task. Sometimes, however, the discovery of efficient procedures may be a joint pupil-teacher undertaking, the teacher participating by encouraging initiative, throwing out hints and suggestions, and correcting mistakes, the pupil by discovering to a greater extent from his own exploratory efforts efficient work methods. At the other end of this continuum, pupils may be encouraged to exercise great freedom and initiative in discovering for themselves effective problem-solving approaches. Perhaps for younger children, relatively more teacher-guidance will be needed; but as they mature, greater initiative should probably be encouraged. However, as the general tenor of this chapter suggests and as even strong advocates of learning skills in functional programs believe [29, pp. 16–22], some teacher-guidance will be helpful at every level of instruction. In support of explicit, systematic teacher-guidance, there are some specific experimental data.

Wilburn [64] taught first grade children by demonstration and explanation a systematic procedure of studying numbers, based on counting, comparing, and taking apart and putting together groups of objects, which they then employed effectively in their self-instruction. Bedell and Nelson found that systematic instruction in word-recognition procedures improved reading efficiency at the fourth, fifth, and sixth grade levels [2]. At the adult level, while practicing memorizing failed to improve memorizing efficiency, Woodrow [67] did find that systematic training in better methods of memorizing (learning by wholes, active self-recitation, use of rhythm, grouping, attention to meaning) greatly improved proficiency in memorizing.

Although the number of cases are too few to yield conclusive results, the experiment designed to evaluate most specifically the effectiveness of explicit, systematic guidance is that of Goodenough and Brian [20]. These experimenters subdivided 20 four-year-old children into three groups and, using three different guidance procedures, trained them all to toss rings onto a 6-inch peg 4 feet 10½ inches away. Group A, consisting of 10 children, "[was] given no instruction whatsoever as to manner of throwing, only the direction: 'This is a game where we try to throw rings over a post. You stand here on this base—be sure both feet are inside the base all the time—and I'll hand you the rings. Try to throw them on that part over there. Do you see what I mean? All right, go ahead.' " Group B, including 6 children, was given Group A's directions plus demonstration, explanation, and error correction, such as "Watch me, and I'll show you how," "Hold the rings here where they are fastened together and then try to throw them so they will go over the post," "Not quite so far next time," or "A little bit higher so it won't hit the post." But with this group, each child was allowed to work out and to use any method or methods he chose. Group C, comprised of 4 children, was given the same general directions as Group B. But unlike Group B, the children of Group C were required to adhere to a prescribed, constant method: " . . . to grasp the ring at the point of juncture, to hold it in a horizontal position, and after swinging the arm back and forth a few times, to pitch the ring forward and upward toward the post. The procedure was frequently illustrated and any departure from the established method was promptly corrected." These three guidance procedures were continued for 50 successive days, 20 trials being given per day. The median gains in the number of ringers achieved in the second 25 days as compared with the first 25 days were for Group A, 11.5; for Group B, 17.5; and for Group C, 20.5. Both Groups B and C, given some guidance, learned more effectively than Group A, which was given no guidance.

For these four-year-old children on this particular task, the experiment suggests a slight advantage in learning an explicit, systematic mode of approach.

Such an approach defines explicitly the task to be mastered, and thus practice can be directed toward proficiency in this defined skill, eliminating the wasteful procedures of discovering varied approaches or of practicing inefficient modes of attack. For some children, such a systematic approach is likely to be helpful because it increases their confidence in the undertaking. Such a child feels at the outset, "I know how to do it."

11. A Set to Learn from Self-guided Experience. Despite the greater *median* gains made by the children taught a systematic approach by Goodenough and Brian, it should be observed that some children in each group learned proficiency in ring tossing. In fact, intragroup differences in gains far exceeded intergroup median differences. This fact suggests that as a result of already accumulated learning experiences, these children had developed varied amounts of skill in how to learn. Therefore, even without teacher-guidance, some children taught themselves proficiency in this motor skill. Other children had learned so little about how to learn or for other reasons were so unable to profit from instruction that they failed to improve even with systematic teacher-guidance. These individual differences in proficiency in learning are illustrated in the learning curves presented in Figure 4–9 for child A_{10}, given no instruction, and for child C_2, given systematic instruction.

The detailed descriptions of each child's learning behavior help to account for the marked difference in progress which the learning curves for these two children reveal. Child A_{10}, without teacher-guidance, during the first week discovered for himself an effective mode of attack and "throughout the experimental period continued . . . with very little change in his general procedure." Child C_2, despite systematic teacher-guidance, gave the task "defective attention." First she was distracted by "an almost uncontrollable tendency to chatter on all sorts of subjects," and later she developed "a habit of watching the movements of her arm and hand instead of looking at the post."

Pyles's earlier-mentioned experiment [44] on verbalization as a factor in learning also contributed data on the phenomenon of learning from self-guided experience. It will be recalled that the group of children given names for the five nonsense-shaped molds required, on the average, fewer trials than the non-naming group, for discovering under which one a toy had been hidden. But in the group of children not given names for the molds, 13 resourceful children, without teacher-guidance, spontaneously named objects ("the cup," "Old Mother Shoe," "the slide," "the smoothed one"). In the first presentation of this series, these children, who on their own initiative adopted what experimentally was proved the most effective mode of attack, required only 11.9 trials to master it, while the group as a whole required 47.1 trials.

The principle in learning from self-guided experience is that, when one meets a new or baffling problem for which one's background of experience does not suggest immediately promising leads, it is often effective to try out something provisionally and to note the effect of such trials. One would try first to generalize from experience with related problems; but even when the

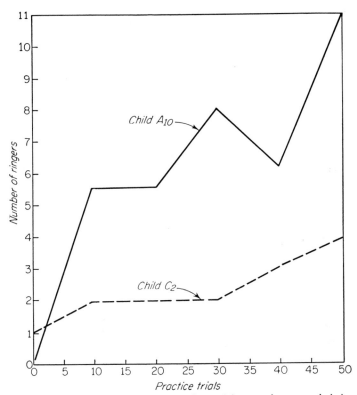

FIG. 4–9. Some self-taught children who have learned how to learn excel their teacher-guided classmates, as is illustrated by child A_{10}, given no guidance, and child C_2, given systematic teacher-guidance. (*From Goodenough, F. L., and Brian, D. R.: J. Exp. Psychol., 12: 127–155, 1929.*)

problem appears to be completely new, it is effective to try and then check an approach. In solving mechanical puzzles, for example, we have all discovered promising leads and often eventually succeeded just by trying out manipulations and noting what happened. The school child uses this principle to advantage when he makes repeated trials at getting a plausible result in an arithmetic problem, when he guesses at an unfamiliar word in reading and notes whether or not it makes sense in the context, or when, after several trials and partial erasing, he achieves the drawing he intended or finds satisfying.

Sometimes this discovery by a child of a mode of attack in learning is revealed in sharp detail. For example, in drawing a diamond as a part of the Stanford-Binet intelligence test, a six-year-old child in three trials made the improvements indicated in (*a*), (*b*), and (*c*). A five-year-old child, whose

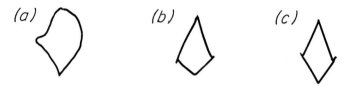

learning goal was to throw a tennis ball so as to hit a duck picture in the center of a four-foot-diameter moving target, for the first three trials stood with her back so close to the wall and exerted so little force that the ball always fell far short of the target. But just before the fourth trial she paused, apparently to consider the task more thoroughly, and herself devised a more effective procedure. Looking behind her, she noted that she stood so close to the wall that she could not bring her arm back far enough to get sufficient force in her throws. So she stepped away from the wall and nearer to the throwing mark on the floor before her and found that she was able to exert the force required to reach the target. In succeeding trials this self-discovered better procedure was continued.

As a more formal demonstration of the validity of the principle of learning how to learn from self-guided experience, data from Winch's early experiment on memorizing are adapted here [66]. Winch had 36 children, six of each age from 7 to 13 (omitting age 12), try to memorize from two verbal presentations as many as they could of different sets of 12 consonants (such as "y p j t, c t b s, h r g w"). After hearing each list twice, the children were requested to reproduce in writing as much of it as could be remembered. Ten lists were presented in each of five weekly practice periods. Since the lists were of approximately equal difficulty (each containing 12 randomly arranged consonants), improvements in later practice periods may be interpreted as improvement in memorizing proficiency. The results, showing an improvement in the average of all 36 children in number of consonants recalled at each succeeding practice session, are presented in Figure 4–10.

In response to questioning, some of the children revealed that their improved proficiency in memorizing resulted from discovering better ways of "how to set about the work." As examples of the self-discovered modes of attack, "s n r d" was memorized as "sin" and "red," "p n" was thought of as "pen," and "l q" was associated with "lick," etc.

Even without teacher-guidance, in response to repeated presentations of the same challenging task, many of these children learned more effective ways of memorizing consonants. However, without teacher-guidance, as has already been shown, children do not often learn the most efficient modes of attack. As has been noted, after acquiring a minimum measure of proficiency in some

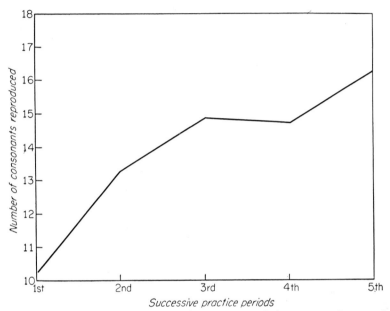

Fig. 4–10. That children learn how to learn is shown by their improvement in memorizing successive sets of different consonants, originally of equal difficulty. (*Adapted from Winch, W. H.: Brit. J. Psychol., 2: 52–57, 1906–1908.*)

process, they are not likely to develop further proficiency without teacher-guidance. Despite these limitations, however, learning how to learn from self-guided experience is so important as an objective that every possible opportunity should be utilized to encourage and reward children's independent learning efforts.

12. *Teacher-guidance of Pupils' Self-discovery Experiences.* Everything that pupils need to learn cannot be discovered by them on their own. Often it is appropriate for the teacher to tell how, to explain, and to demonstrate. But pupils can learn many things from their own self-discovery experiences. Because such learning experiences, besides giving mastery of specific concepts and skills, probably yield also such highly important values as independence, thrilling

motivation, ingenuity, resourcefulness, and confidence, they should be encouraged whenever and wherever it is feasible. As pupils develop skill in independently learning how to learn, the effectiveness of self-discovery as a method multiplies in snowball fashion. Perhaps the most effective way of achieving this goal is that of teacher-guidance of pupils' self-discovery experiences. In this role, the teacher does more leading, guiding, stimulating, and insightful questioning, and less telling, demonstrating, explaining, and illustrating.

Luchins and Luchins [37] have illustrated the process in their report of teaching sixth grade children a generalized procedure for finding the areas of various geometrical figures. First a rectangle 15 by 5 inches was drawn on the chalkboard. A pupil was asked to determine its area, using a 1-inch cardboard square with which he was supplied. "He laid off the square along the longer base 15 times, repeated this procedure to obtain a parallel row, and was about to start on a third row when he said, 'I don't have to do it again. It will always go in 15 times this way and it goes 5 times the other way, so it's 15 times 5 squares.' He computed the area as 75 square inches." [37, p. 529].

As varied applications of the idea, pupils were then supplied with scissors, rulers, yellow paper, and various-sized paper rectangles. They were directed to cut out 1-inch squares from the yellow paper and by using them, to determine the areas of rectangles. After succeeding with this, they were asked whether it was necessary to use the 1-inch square. "A number of pupils volunteered the information that it sufficed to use a rule to measure the base and the height 'to find out how many squares fit each way,' and then to multiply." Subsequently, a 10-by-4-inch parallelogram was presented. The pupils were baffled. When asked why they couldn't determine the area, they replied that the figure was "crooked," that the sides were "slanted." They were encouraged to try. "It's no good. The squares stick out on this side and they don't fill up the other side," they objected. However, after considering the scissors, ruler, yellow paper, and paper parallelogram given to her, one child "cut off the two ends to make the figure straight." Asked what she planned to do with the two ends, "she hesitated, toyed with them, put them together to form a rectangle, placed it alongside the larger rectangle, thus forming a new rectangle, and triumphantly exclaimed, 'Now nothing's wasted.'" Other pupils followed her example. Then the pupils were led by appropriate questions to discover that they could convert a parallelogram to a rectangle by cutting off one "slanted end" and using it to fill the "gap" at the other end. And eventually, by means of further guiding questions, they were led to the generalization that the area of a parallelogram can be determined by measuring its base and height (not side) and then multiplying together these two dimensions.

Thiele [54] has reported another interesting and instructive illustration of how, by appropriately arranged experiences and with guidance of their thinking by teacher questions, pupils may be led inductively to the discovery of useful generalizations. For a class of sixth grade pupils who needed to learn to multiply whole numbers by mixed numbers, the teacher planned a sequence of experiences which would lead them to discover the function of a fraction multiplier. From previous experience, these pupils had already learned that the size of a product is related to the size of the multiplier. For example, if uncertain about the product of 8×7, they would be apt to think that $4 \times 7 = 28$ and that two 28s equal 56.

To restimulate their thinking about this relationship, the teacher called the pupils' attention to list A as a multiplication exercise and asked them to give the products, which the teacher recorded as in list B [54, pp. 8–9]:

A	B
$6 \times 8 =$	$6 \times 8 = 48$
$5 \times 8 =$	$5 \times 8 = 40$
$4 \times 8 =$	$4 \times 8 = 32$
$3 \times 8 =$	$3 \times 8 = 24$
$2 \times 8 =$	$2 \times 8 = 16$
$1 \times 8 =$	$1 \times 8 = \ \ 8$

As a first step in helping the pupils to discover the meaning and function of a fraction multiplier, the pupils were asked to read and to observe carefully the multiplications of list B, from $6 \times 8 = 48$ to $1 \times 8 = 8$. They were then asked what they noted. Their responses included the following:

"8 is multiplied each time."

"As the multipliers become smaller, the products also become smaller."

"When 8 is multiplied by 1, the product is 8."

When asked to look again for significant relationships between pairs of products, they noted that:

"3 times 8 is 24. 6 times 8 is 48, which is twice as much as 24."

"The 6 is two times as much as the 3."

"2 times 8 is half as much as 4 times 8."

"4 times 8 is 4 times as much as 1 times 8."

"1 times 8 is half as much as 2 times 8."

"1 times 8 is a third of 3 times 8."

When it was apparent that the pupils understood that with a constant multiplicand, the products become proportionately smaller as the multipliers become smaller, the teacher led them to the next step. In list A, directly below "1 × 8 = 8," she wrote, "½ × 8 = ?" and asked the pupils to supply the product. Many gave it as 16. Asked again to read the column of multiplications from 6 × 8 = 48 to 1 × 8 = 8, they soon discovered, however, that 16 is the product of 2 times 8. "Individual pupils then corrected the error of thinking ½ × 8 is 16 with statements such as: 'The answer couldn't be 16 because 1 × 8 is 8. The answer has to be one half as much, or 4.'" Then "¼ × 8 = ?" and "⅛ × 8 = ?" were added to the list; and for the fraction multipliers as well as for the integer multipliers, the relation between multipliers and products was perceived. Thus by teacher-guided self-discovery experiences, "the pupils were moved on the way to a discovery of the generalization that when whole numbers are multiplied by fractions, the products are smaller than the multiplicands."

Principles of Teacher-guidance Applied

Teacher-guidance in developing in pupils effective modes of attack in learning is one of seven conditions of effective learning. In performing this important function of teaching pupils how to learn, the twelve general principles here reviewed should guide the teacher both in informal guidance of pupil learning and in the development and application of more formal methods of teaching. As examples of their applications to formal methods of teaching, plans for teaching problem solving in arithmetic and mode of attack in learning to spell are presented.

Problem Solving in Arithmetic. Within a broader range of objectives in arithmetic, skill in using computational abilities in problem solving in appropriate personal and social situations is generally recognized as of fundamental importance. For many pupils, as we earlier observed, accomplishment of this objective is often difficult. Adding, subtracting, multiplying, or dividing with integers, common fractions, or decimals, when one knows which process to use, is not especially difficult to learn. Managing the "story problems" is often, however, more baffling. Considerable effort toward devising effective arithmetic problem-solving procedures has therefore been made. Johnson, in a review of the literature [34], has noted as causes of difficulty in problem solving (1) physical and mental defects; (2) reading- and arithmetic-vocabulary disabilities; (3) lack of variety in problem-solving experience; (4) *lack of method of attacking problems;* (5) lack of skill in fundamentals; (6) poor teaching; (7) lack of knowledge of essential facts, rules, and formulas; (8) carelessness in arranging written work; and (9) lack of interest. As factors favorably affecting problem solving, even though the research is sometimes conflicting, he mentioned (1) familiarity with and an interest in the problem setting; (2) special practice prior to problem solving in computation, in selecting the correct process, and in identifying cues on how to solve different types of problems; (3) practice in estimating answers prior to solving problems; (4) practice based on weaknesses revealed through diagnostic tests; and (5) supplementary vocabulary training. Schaaf, in discussing a "realistic approach to problem-solving in arithmetic," says the approach should include (1) understanding of numbers and number relations; (2) understanding of mathematical relations as functions, including relations among time, rate, and distance, etc.; (3) ability to visualize verbal descriptions of what is known and of what is wanted, and to interpret questions; (4) agreeing with Johnson, understanding of arithmetic vocabulary; (5) understanding relevance and irrelevance of data; (6) recognizing arithmetic operations to be used; (7) analyzing two-step problems, that is, seeing that an unstated question must be answered before a second can be asked and answered; (8) estimating answer; and (9) checking answer [50].

As guides for avoiding some of the difficulties mentioned, including, of course, *lack of a method of attacking problems*, and for embodying as many favorable features as possible, several specific problem-solving patterns have been proposed and partially evaluated. Johnson [34] describes six such devices or phases of problem solving.

1. Conventional Formula Method. As a means of analyzing an otherwise more complex problem statement, the pupil is taught to ask himself the following questions: (1) What is asked for in the problem? (2) What is given in the problem? (3) How should these facts be used to secure the answer? (4) What is the answer? (These are applications of general principles 4 and 6.)

2. Graphic-dependencies Method. Supplementing the verbal analysis of the conventional method, a graphic analysis should present still more clearly the interrelationships between relevant items in the problem. As an example, the following problem is analyzed: "John had 16¢. He earned 10¢ more and then spent 15¢ for ice cream. How much money did John have left?" We ask: What is to be found? This *depends* upon what? Upon what does each other factor depend? The dependency relations are then shown graphically as follows:

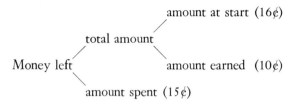

(This method is especially an application of general principle 6.)

3. Individual Method. Without direct teacher-guidance on mode of attack, pupils are simply told to solve problems by any methods which they have used before or which they may devise. (Here we have mainly applications of principles 1 and 11.) Without some teacher-help in arranging the conditions for self-discovery of effective methods, we should, according to our emphasis upon the value of teacher-guidance in directing attention to effective modes of attack, expect this method to be weak.

4. Association Method. This is a method by which concepts built up from experience in problem solving are organized for more effective application (transfer) to new problems. Similar, but not identical, problems are classified into groups, and one problem is explained, demonstrated, and copied into a notebook for reference as a model. When a child meets a new problem, he first classifies it among his "type" problems and then is guided in solving it by the model for the group it most resembles. (This method is perhaps mainly an application of principles 3 and 11.)

The two additional methods mentioned by Johnson in his review are not in themselves complete; they are only aids to using more complete problem-solving procedures.

5. Analysis Method. As practice prior to actual problem solving, pupils analyze the problem according to a modification of the conventional verbal method and then select from among multiple-choice items the procedure which they think will produce a correct solution. No computations are actually made. (This would be an application of principle 6.) This procedure lacks adequate provision for self-activity and application of perception of the effects as a condition of effective learning.

6. Vocabulary Method. Also without solving problems, pupils study arithmetic-vocabulary exercises requiring them to select from a list of terms the missing words in statements of problems. (Ensuring understanding of items is one contribution toward making the approach meaningful and is thus a partial application of principle 3.)

Although the research reported by Johnson sometimes favored one method over another (for example, the graphic-dependencies over the conventional method and the association method over both of the noncomputational methods mentioned), no one of these methods has been shown to be consistently superior to the others. Johnson cites Washburne as having found practice on many problems and individual help superior to any set, formal analysis. But such a study does not disprove the value of *some* systematic problem-solving approach. The individualized teaching, which could and perhaps should be applied with every method, may have accounted for the differences found. And the individualized help may have developed systematic, though not formal, procedures for those children who found such teaching most helpful.

Practical teaching experience has shown that children have special difficulty in problem solving in arithmetic. We have already cited experimental evidence on the general value of teacher-guidance on mode of attack in learning. Therefore, despite the inconclusive evaluation of present methods of problem solving, we shall suggest still another. It will combine some of the phases of the methods already described and will embody an application of our "essential conditions of effective learning."

7. *Derived Guide for Problem Solving in Arithmetic.* This guide involves eight steps which, with the development of skill and confidence, become telescoped into a smoother and more unified pattern of thinking.

1. Determine what is wanted—what is to be found.

2. What are the relevant facts given?

3. In a single declarative sentence, state what is wanted as a function of what is given.

4. Restate this sentence in arithmetical language (something as equal to something else), using N for unknown or to-be-found quantities.

5. This statement will be recognized as one of a few well-learned types of operations in arithmetic. The solution can then be planned. (A classified group of models such as employed in the association method would be helpful at first.)

6. Estimate an answer.

7. Make the necessary computations.

8. Check the solution: (*a*) Does the answer approximate the estimated answer? (*b*) Perform any possible arithmetical check.

As an example of the procedure, take this problem: "My mother told me to buy ¾ pound of chocolates for my party. How many 4-ounce boxes would that require?"

Items (1) and (2) in the guide are an adaptation of the conventional method. (1) To be found are the number of 4-ounce boxes required. (2) The fact given is that ¾ pound in 4-ounce packages is wanted. In stating these facts in a functional relationship (3) in a single sentence, the child should apply (transfer) (*a*) his developed knowledge of such relationships (total amount is a function of numbers and sizes of parts) and (*b*) his general knowledge from reading, from outlining, from formulating the central thought of a paragraph as a single, topical sentence, and from many other language experiences. The sentence formulated could be: "Three-fourths pound of chocolates contains how many (or N) 4-ounce boxes?" And, employing an arithmetical vocabulary (4), the sentence, translated, would be: "$\frac{3}{4}$ pound $= N$ times 4-ounce boxes"; or better, converting to like denominate numbers: "$\frac{3}{4} \times 16 = N \times 4$, which equals $12 = N \times 4$." This will be recognized (5) as a type of problem or relationship which H. Van Engen has shown occurs with great frequency. Beginning at about grade three, it continues to recur through all the grades and is included in algebraic equations in high school [58]. Its general, unifying idea is: "The product of two numbers equals a third number." If the product is unknown, as indicated by N, it is found by multiplying together the two factors. If one of the factors should be unknown, it is found by dividing the product by the known factor. In teaching this principle, the instructor would not, of course, state it simply as a verbalized rule; it should be developed and formulated inductively by the children from their experience in an appropriate variety of problems and concrete experiences.

It should be apparent from our discussion that items (3), (4), and (5) draw heavily upon the principle of transfer of training, the importance of which we can hardly overemphasize. (6) The answer is readily estimated in this very simple problem. (7) The computation, guided by the division symbol which occurs when the unifying idea above is elaborated, is also readily made mentally: $N = 12 \div 4 = 3$. And (8) as a check on the computation, we multiply the two factors together, both now being known, and are satisfied that we are correct by obtaining the originally given product: $3 \times 4 = 12$.

Mastery of this outline should give the child an efficient and systematic approach to problem solving which will have considerable transfer value not only throughout the study and use of arithmetic but in more advanced mathematics as well. As children become proficient in problem solving and use the method in solving many different kinds of problems, these steps will, of course, become considerably telescoped.

Mode of Attack in Learning to Spell. Besides mastery of the 3,000 to 5,000 words most frequently needed in the writing of both children and adults, another important objective in spelling is learning how to learn to spell words efficiently. Here research has indicated the value of a mode of attack which can be formulated fairly explicitly [29, 46]. During the primary grades, children should be taught in closely supervised spelling lessons how to apply the procedure to learning in spelling the words they need to know. As children advance through the primary grades, they can be expected to use efficient learning methods more independently. The mode of attack in learning to spell a word should involve the following phases:

1. Understanding the meaning of the word so that it can be used correctly in speaking, reading, and writing.

2. Perceiving the word correctly and efficiently—auditorily, visually, and in the motor-kinesthetic process of speaking and writing it. The child needs to hear and/or pronounce the word with accurate emphasis on the larger phonetic (syllable) elements. He should visually analyze the word into its meaningful larger phonetic elements—word roots, suffixes or prefixes, variant forms, plural endings, double letters, and the sequence of syllables and letters.

3. Generalizing from one's background of spelling experience and principles about each particular word. The child recognizes in a compound word two root words he already knows, as "rain" and "coat" in "raincoat." He sees that "jig" is spelled like the already familiar words "pig" and "big," except for the substitution of another consonant. He applies what phonetic principles he may have up to now learned inductively. He recognizes in variant forms familiar word roots. He also notes unusual spellings—beginnings, endings, and syllables. And he applies such inductively learned and self-formulated rules as the following [63]:

    a. Words ending in silent *e* (1) drop the *e* when adding a suffix beginning with a vowel ("cite, citing") and (2) keep the *e* when adding suffixes beginning with a consonant ("lame, lameness").

    b. Words ending in *y*, (1) when preceded by a consonant, change to *i* when adding any suffix ("study, studious"), except one beginning with *i* ("studying"), and (2) when preceded by a vowel, leave the base form unchanged when adding any suffix ("boy, boyish" or "coy, coyly").

    c. Monosyllables or words accented on the last syllable ending in a single consonant preceded by a single vowel, or a vowel after *qu*, double the final consonant when adding a suffix beginning with a vowel ("hit, hitting" or "quit, quitting"). If the accent is not on the last syllable, the final consonant is not usually doubled ("environ, environed").

    d. In diphthongs, *i* comes before *e*, except after *c* or when sounded as *a*, as in "neighbor" and "weigh."

4. Applying, in practicing a word, both the principles of self-recitation and of perception of the effects. After visualizing the sequence of syllables and letters in a word, the child closes his eyes and imagines the sequence, checking back to see if he has imagined correctly. Then, after getting a correct visual impression of the word, he covers the copy and writes it, checking to see if it is written correctly. If the comparison with the model reveals a misspelling, the error and how it is corrected should be examined especially closely, and item (2) should be repeated before the second trial.

5. Practicing. If the above four approaches to spelling are employed, no more than two or three correct writings are necessary in one session. But practice should be distributed and should include (1) writing the word on the initial test—and if misspelled, two or three times in the study session; (2) periodic review tests; and (3) using the word in language and other writing activities.

In summary, learning to spell a word includes knowing its meaning, perceiving it analytically, generalizing about its relation to other words and to spelling principles, practicing writing it without the model, checking it for correctness, repeating or trying again to overcome errors noted, and reviewing.

Summary

Pupil learning is a matter of goal-directed self-activity. However, this review has shown some amount and kind of teacher-guidance to be necessary in order for the learning of elementary school activities to be efficient. It can range, on a continuum of variations, from highly directive and systematic instruction to teacher-guidance of pupil self-discovery experiences in which the pupil exercises considerable initiative and resourcefulness. The extent and kind of teacher-guidance will need to be adapted to the maturity and independence of the pupil and to the nature of the particular learning activity being directed.

As guides to planning and directing learning activities by both informal and formal methods, the following principles on modes of attack should be considered: (1) Pupil learning is most efficient when there is ample provision for active self-recitation. (2) Verbal explanations, especially in supplementing demonstrations, often facilitate learning, because they make concepts and goal-directing ideas more explicit. (3) A meaningful approach to any learning undertaking is of central importance, because it takes full advantage of prior learnings and substitutes for numerous separate learnings the development and wide applications of a few unifying generalizations or principles. (4) An overview facilitates perception and insight into the interrelation of factors within a problem and is one way of making a meaningful approach to learning. (5) Proceeding from the simple to the complex, from the familiar to the new, and from the concrete to the abstract also takes advantage of prior learning and emphasizes the meaningful approach. (6) Making significant features in learning tasks identifiable by graphs, charts, outlines, etc., also facilitates insight into interrelations; and the understanding of the whole thus achieved enriches the meaning of the parts. (7) Each provisional trial in problem solving should be thorough; but flexibility and variability of approach are also necessary. (8) "Crutches" are learning devices to simplify and to aid in understanding in the initial stages. Since they are readily eliminated as the learner makes progress, they often facilitate learning without being an ultimate handicap to efficiency. (9) One approach to learning efficiency is to make a "job analysis" of alternate modes of attack to discover from the points of view of time and motion the easiest and most efficient way of accomplishing a task. (10) For some learning activities or at certain stages in learning undertakings, explicit, systematic methods of teacher-guidance are effective. Often a systematic approach promotes both efficiency and confidence. (11) Pupils can, from their own exploratory and self-discovery experiences, learn how to learn effectively. Such initiative and resourcefulness should be encouraged. (12) There are such great educational values in pupils' self-discovery approaches to learning that teacher-guidance of their self-discovery experiences should be exploited wherever and whenever feasible.

Review and Applications

1. For sharing with your classmates, observe and record behavior as a child "thinks out loud" his approach to reading a paragraph, to solving five arithmetic problems, or to spelling five words, all chosen slightly in advance of the child's present status of abilities. Classify the varied modes of attack found. Are needs for teacher-guidance indicated?

2. From observation and experiments, cite evidence on teacher-guidance as a factor affecting children's efficiency in learning.

3. Cite experimental support for and describe teaching examples of the following principles of teacher-guidance: (a) self-recitation, (b) verbal explanations, (c) meaningful approach, (d) achieving an over-all view, (e) proceeding from the simple to the complex, (f) making relevant features identifiable, (g) balancing thoroughness with variability of attack, (h) using appropriate crutches, (i) finding the most efficient approach, (j) systematic guidance, and (k) guidance of pupils' self-discovery experiences.

4. Why is learning how to learn especially important as an educational objective for every child? How can it be achieved?

5. From your reading or from observation of an example of good teaching, try to identify principles of teacher-guidance employed.

References

1. Ausubel, D. P., and H. M. Schiff: "The effect of incidental and experimentally induced experience in learning of relevant and irrelevant causal relationships by children," *J. Genet. Psychol.*, 84: 109–123, 1954.

2. Bedell, R., and E. S. Nelson: "Word attack as a factor in reading achievement in the elementary school," *Educ. Psychol. Measmt.*, 14: 168–175, 1954.

3. Bond, G. L., and L. C. Fay: "A report of the University of Minnesota Reading Clinic," *J. Educ. Res.*, 43: 385–390, 1950.

4. Brownell, W. A.: "Rate, accuracy, and process in learning," *J. Educ. Psychol.*, 35: 321–337, 1944.

5. ———: "A study of learning in one phase of arithmetic," *J. Gen. Psychol.*, 24: 457–465, 1941.

6. ———: "When is arithmetic meaningful?" *J. Educ. Res.*, 38: 481–498, 1945.

7. ———, and C. B. Chazal: "The effects of premature drill in third-grade arithmetic," *J. Educ. Res.*, 29: 17–28, 1935.

8. Cantril, H.: *The "Why" of Man's Experience*, Macmillan, New York, 1950.

9. Cole, Luella: "Instruction in penmanship for the left-handed child," *Elem. Sch. J.* 39: 436–448, Copyright, 1939, by the University of Chicago. Reprinted by permission of the University of Chicago Press.

10. Craig, R. C.: *The Transfer Value of Guided Learning*, Teachers College, Columbia University, Bureau of Publications, New York, 1953.

11. Davies, Dorothy R.: "The effect of tuition upon the process of learning a complex motor skill," *J. Educ. Psychol.*, 36: 352–365, 1945.

12. Dusenberry, Lois: "A study of the effects of training in ball throwing by children ages three to seven," *Res. Quart. Amer. Ass. Hlth. Phys. Educ. Recr.*, 23: 9–14, 1952.

13. Dynes, J. J.: "Comparison of two methods of studying history," *J. Exp. Educ.*, 1: 42–45, 1932.

14. Forlano, G.: *School Learning with Various Methods of Practice and Reward*, Contributions to Education, no. 688, Teachers College, Columbia University, Bureau of Publications, New York, 1936.

15. Gates, A. I.: *The Improvement of Reading*, Macmillan, New York, 1947.

16. ———: "Recitation as a factor in memorizing," *Arch. Psychol.*, 6, (40): 1–104, 1917.

17. Germane, C. E.: "The value of a controlled mental summary as a method of studying," *Sch. Soc.*, 12: 591–593, 1920.

18. ———: "The value of the corrected summary as compared with re-reading the same article," *Elem. Sch. J.*, 21: 461–464, 1921.

19. ———: "The value of the written paragraph summary," *J. Educ. Res.*, 3: 116–123, 1921.

20. Goodenough, Florence L., and C. R. Brian: "Certain factors underlying the acquisition of motor skill by pre-school children," *J. Exp. Psychol.*, 12: 127–155, 1929.

21. Grossnickle, F. E.: "How to find the position of the decimal point in the quotient," *Elem. Sch. J.*, 52: 452–457, Copyright, 1952, by the University of Chicago. Adapted by permission of the University of Chicago Press.

22. Hall, J. V.: "Color clarifies arithmetic processes," *Elem. Sch. J.*, 50: 96–98, 1949–1950.

23. Harlow, H. F.: "The formation of learning sets," *Psychol. Rev.*, 56: 51–65, 1949.

24. Helson, H.: *Theoretical Foundation of Psychology*, Van Nostrand, New York, 1951.

25. Hertzberg, O. E.: *A Comparative Study of Different Methods Used in Teaching Beginners to Write* (Contributions to Education, no. 214, Teachers College, Columbia University, Bureau of Publications, 1926). Cited from H. B. Reed: *Psychology of Elementary School Subjects*, p. 281, Ginn, Boston, 1938.

26. Hicks, J. A.: "The acquisition of motor skill in young children: A study of the effects of practice in throwing at a moving target," *Child Develpm.*, 1–2: 90–105, 1930–1931.

27. ———: *The Acquisition of Motor Skill in Young Children*, University of Iowa Studies in Child Welfare, ser. 4, no. 5, 1931.

28. Hildreth, Gertrude: "The difficulty reduction tendency in perception and problem solving," *J. Educ. Psychol.*, 32: 305–313, 1941.

29. ———: *Learning the Three R's*, Educational Test Bureau, Educational Publishers, Inc., Minneapolis, 1947.

30. ———: "Puzzle-solving with and without understanding," *J. Educ. Psychol.*, 33: 595–604, 1942.

31. Hurlock, Elizabeth B.: *Child Development*, 1st ed., McGraw-Hill, New York, 1950.

32. John, Lenore: "Difficulties in solving problems in arithmetic," *Elem. Sch. J.*, 31: 202–215, 1930–1931.

33. ———: "The effect of using the long-division form in teaching division by one-digit numbers," *Elem. Sch. J.*, 30: 675–692, 1930.

34. Johnson, H. C.: "Problem-solving in arithmetic: A review of the literature," *Elem. Sch. J.*, 44: 396–403 and 476–482, Copyright, 1944, by the University of Chicago. Reprinted by permission of the University of Chicago Press.

35. Kurtz, K. H., and C. I. Hovland: "The effect of verbalization during observation of stimulus objects upon accuracy of recognition and recall," *J. Exp. Psychol.*, 45: 157–164, 1953.

36. Lewin, K.: "Field theory and learning." *The Psychology of Learning*, pp. 215–242.

41st Yearbook of the Nat. Soc. Stud. Educ., Chicago, Distributed by the University of Chicago Press, 1942.

37. Luchins, A. S., and Edith H. Luchins: "A structural approach to the teaching of the concept of area in intuitive geometry," *J. Educ. Res.*, 40: 528–533, 1947.

38. Maier, N. R. F.: "An aspect of human reasoning," *Brit. J. Psychol.*, 24: 144–155, 1933.

39. Mattson, Marion L.: "The relation between the complexity of the habit to be acquired and the form of the learning curve in young children," *Genet. Psychol. Monogr.*, 13: 299–398, 1933.

40. Monroe, W. S.: *Encyclopedia of Educational Research*, Macmillan, New York, 1950.

41. Mursell, J. L.: *Successful Teaching*, 1st ed., McGraw-Hill, New York, 1946.

42. Olander, H. T., and E. P. Sharp: "Long division versus short division," *J. Educ. Res.*, 26: 6–11, 1932.

43. Priebe, R. E., and W. Y. Burton: "The slow motion picture as a coaching device," *Sch. Rev.*, 47: 192–198, 1939.

44. Pyles, M. K.: "Verbalization as a factor in learning," *Child Develpm.*, 3: 108–113, 1932.

45. Reed, H. B.: "Meaning as a factor in learning," *J. Educ. Psychol.*, 29: 419–430, 1938.

46. ———: *Psychology of Elementary School Subjects*, Ginn, Boston, 1938.

47. Riess, Anita: "Meaning of the meaningful teaching of arithmetic," *Elem. Sch. J.*, 45: 23–32, 1944.

48. Rimer, L. E., A. Wilson, and H. B. Knight: "How pupils solve problems in arithmetic," *Educ. Res. Bull.*, 3: 274–277, 1924.

49. Risden, Gladys: "What price mechanization: Some notes on arithmetic learning in the modern school," *Progr. Educ.*, 17: 86–93, 1940.

50. Schaaf, W. L.: "A realistic approach to problem-solving in arithmetic," *Elem. Sch. J.*, 46: 494–497, 1946.

51. Stevens, S. S. (ed.): *Handbook of Experimental Psychology*, Wiley, New York, 1951.

52. Swenson, Esther J.: "Arithmetic for preschool and primary grade children." *The Teaching of Arithmetic*. 50th Yearbook of the Nat. Soc. Stud. Educ., Part II, Chicago, Distributed by the University of Chicago Press, 1951.

53. Thiele, C. L.: "Arithmetic in the early grades—from the point of view of interrelations in the number system," in 16th Yearbook of the National Council of Teachers of Mathematics, Washington, 1941.

54. ———: "Fostering discovery with children," *Arith. Teacher*, 1: 6–11, 1954.

55. Thompson, G. G.: "The social and emotional development of pre-school children under two types of educational programs," *Psychol. Monogr.*, vol. 56, no. 258, 1944.

56. Thorndike, E. L.: *Human Learning*, Century, New York, 1931.

57. Tilton, J. W.: "Individualized and meaningful instruction in arithmetic," *J. Educ. Psychol.*, 38: 83–88, 1947.

58. Van Engen, H.: "An analysis of meaning in arithmetic," *Elem. Sch. J.*, 49: 321–329 and 395–400, 1949.

59. ———: "An aspect of meaning in arithmetic," *Elem. Sch. J.*, 46: 272–277, 1946.
60. Washburne, J. N.: "The use of questions in social science material," *J. Educ. Psychol.*, 20: 321–359, 1929.
61. Weaver, J. F.: "Some areas of misunderstanding about meaning in arithmetic," *Elem. Sch. J.*, 51: 35–41, 1950.
62. Wheat, H. G.: "A theory of instruction for the middle grades," in 16th Yearbook of the National Council of Teachers of Mathematics, Washington, 1941.
63. Wheat, L. B.: "Four spelling rules," *Elem. Sch. J.*, 32: 697–706, Copyright, 1932, by the University of Chicago. Reprinted by permission of the University of Chicago Press.
64. Wilburn, D. B.: "A method of self-instruction for learning the easier addition and subtraction combinations in grade I," *Elem. Sch. J.*, 42: 371–380, 1941–1942.
65. Wilson, G. M.: "For 100 per cent subtraction, what method: A new approach," *J. Educ. Res.*, 27: 503–508, 1934.
66. Winch, W. H.: "Immediate memory in school children," *Brit. J. Psychol.*, 2: 52–57, 1906–1908.
67. Woodrow, H.: "The effect of type of training upon transference," *J. Educ. Psychol.*, 18: 160–171, 1927.

Chapter 5

Practice
as a Condition
of Learning

EXPERIENCE HAS taught us well that proficiency in such skills as reading, writing, and arithmetic, or skating, drawing, and piano playing, is attained only by tremendous amounts of practice. The experimentation on learning reviewed in the previous chapters confirms the conclusion that practice is an essential condition of learning. Typical of the demonstrations of the role of practice in learning are the curves plotted for the number of trials required by the six-year-old child to find unerringly a piece of candy hidden under a certain book in a bookcase [Chapter 2, page 38] and for the improvement in speed of reading of the 12-year-old child [Chapter 4, page 103]. As an additional example of such learning curves, Figure 5-1 is presented.

This figure shows that, as practice is continued for 35 days for this child of approximately six years, there is a gradual accumulation in the number of words that he is able to recognize from their general contours as they are presented each on a separate card. In these practice periods, each word is presented many times. The word "school," for example, is not recognized with consistent certainty until after 18 exposures.

Many school concepts and skills, such as language usage, spelling, and multiplication combinations, require repetitive practice for mastery. Sometimes, however, a concept is mastered in a single attempt, as was demonstrated by the children who achieved insight into the Obstacle Peg Test

[Chapter 2, page 40]. Having on the first trial perceived how the path could be cleared from obstructions, and guided by the "cognitive map" consequently constructed, these children on a second trial slid the red peg directly along its path to the goal without error. In other instances, however, despite practice on a skill ordinarily requiring it, improvement fails to occur, even when the learner has sufficient maturity for the task.

A striking example of the failure of practice to result in improvement, which is perhaps not uncommon in elementary school practice activities, is presented in Figure 5-2.

Guided by previously established goals with respect to letter formation, alignment, and spacing, this second grade child, whose manuscript-writing

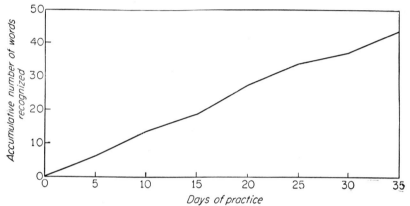

FIG. 5–1. Progress with practice in visual recognition of words by Peter (age 5–9; IQ, 101). (*Adapted from Hildreth, G.: Elem. Sch. J., 35: 606–619, Copyright 1935. Scores used by permission of the University of Chicago Press.*)

lesson is reproduced, wrote the phrase "October 1, 1949." In this instance, there is no apparent improvement from the 10 repetitions of the original writing of the phrase. Indeed, rather than improvement, careful examination reveals progressive deterioration. At the fifth trial, the day of the month is deleted; and by the tenth trial, the terminal "r" of "October" has ceased to be a part of the word and now occupies the space of the deleted date. The subject's letter formation has also lapsed slightly from her best form. Illustrations such as this make it clear that, although practice is a necessary condition of learning, it is not a sufficient condition. The other six conditions of effective learning are also essential for practice itself to be effective. Perhaps in this particular case, there was especial need for teacher-guidance in directing the child's attention to higher levels in the writing developmental sequence. She could have been encouraged to write smaller or to keep the slope more uniform; or she could have been permitted to use the skill already attained in creative writing.

Fig. 5–2. Manuscript-writing exercise shows that repetition alone fails to produce improvement; instead, it sometimes leads to deterioration.

The Role of Practice in Learning

These variations in the need for and effectiveness of practice indicate that the role of practice in learning needs further definition. In Chapter 2, practice was defined as consisting of provisional trials, or of hypothesis-guided self-activity oriented toward discovery, differentiation, and integration of more

effective patterns of behavior. But since practice has also sometimes been considered *repetitions* of specific stimulus-response patterns (such as $6 \times 7 = 42$)
for the purpose of strengthening them in the nervous system, it is pertinent to
consider here some experimentation on the role of repetition in learning.

Repetition as Practice. As a part of several such experiments, Thorndike read
and reread repeatedly to his subjects 10 sentences like the following [14,
p. 19]:

Jackson Craig and his son struggled often.
Charlotte Dean and her friend studied easily.
Mary Borah and her companion complained dully.
Norman Foster and his mother bought much.

After 10 repetitions of the selection containing these four sentences, his subjects were asked such questions as:

What word came next after "and his son struggled often"?
What word came next after "Norman Foster and his mother"?

Despite the circumstance that the facts needed for answering these two
types of question had been given the same number of repetitions, the percentages of correct answers for them were distinctly different. For the first
question, in which "struggled often" was to be followed by the beginning of
the next sentence, only 2 per cent of the answers were correct, which demonstrates practically no learning from 10 repetitions. For the second question,
calling for the predicate of the sentence beginning with "Norman Foster and
his mother," the 81 per cent accuracy of the answers shows considerable
learning. On the basis of these results and similar results from other experiments, Thorndike concludes that "Repetition of a connection in the sense of
mere sequence of the two things in time has then very, very little power,
perhaps none, as a cause of learning" [14, p. 28]. Thorndike explained the
advantage of the second question by his principle of "belonging." It is fitting to
complete "Norman Foster and his mother" with "bought much"; but as a succession to "and his son struggled often," "Charlotte Dean" does not belong.
Such a principle, however, seems unnecessary. It seems adequate to explain the
memorization of the sequence "Norman Foster and his mother" and "bought
much" mainly as a result of motive satisfaction and transfer of training in
completing a logical sequence.

In another, related experiment, Thorndike has shown how initially frequent
responses are sometimes abandoned when responses providing greater motive
satisfaction are discovered. Subject C, asked to write word completions for the

initial syllable "el-," wrote, "evate, ephant, ephant, evate, ephant, ephant, ephant, f, f, f, f, f, f, f, f." Despite the initial frequency advantage for "elephant," it was finally abandoned for "el-f." The general trend of Thorndike's subjects was to abandon longer completions for shorter ones, because they are easier [14, p. 14].

In teaching 26 concepts in fractions and denominate numbers to fifth grade children, Harap and Mapes [7] found no relation between percentage of mastery of these concepts and the frequency of their repetition in arithmetic projects. In such functional units as making candy and conducting a candy sale, the children learned and used the fraction concepts as they had need for them. For example, concept No. 2 (multiplying an integer by a common fraction) was used 51 times, while concept No. 10 (dividing a common fraction by a common fraction) was used only once. Yet the percentage of mastery for both concepts was 94 per cent. The rank-order correlation between frequency of repetition of all the concepts (ranging from 0 to 112) and percentage of mastery for corresponding concepts was found by the author to be .0. In this teaching experiment, in which understanding and meaningful use of fractions were emphasized, the relative number of repetitions proved unimportant.

Symonds [13] has also shown, in connection with mastery of correct language usage, that "pure repetition of correct forms" alone is not sufficient. No appreciable gains (only 1 per cent) in correction of usage errors were made from such practice by sixth grade pupils. Only when the teaching incorporated the learning of general principles of grammatical usage, when there was teacher-guidance in applying rules in choosing correct constructions, and when both correct and incorrect forms were presented and perceived as "right" or "wrong" did appreciable gains (from 6 to 13 per cent) occur.

Learning Requires Practice plus Other Conditions. Finding that practice, although necessary, is not alone a sufficient condition of learning should not be surprising. All three of the background theories of learning reviewed in Chapter 2 agree on the practical role of repetition in learning. Thorndike, it has been noted, who represents the trial-and-error theory, does not consider repetition a direct cause of learning. Guthrie believes that learning a stimulus-response association requires fundamentally only one trial: " . . . that conditioning is an all-or-nothing affair, like the setting of a switch rather than like the wearing of a path" [5, p. 81]. And when the preliminary conditions are developed in pupils or are arranged in situations to favor insight, the differentiation and integration of cognitive maps as guides to problem solving can often be achieved in one trial, as was illustrated in the self-discovery of how to find the area of a rectangle which was achieved by the sixth grade pupils mentioned in the preceding chapter.

It appears, therefore, that practice, not as repetitions of specific behavior patterns but as repeated attempts at discovery of more adequate solutions, is an essential condition of learning only as it provides opportunity for operation of the other essential conditions of learning. It is also apparent that the amounts of practice required for mastery of various concepts and skills will vary from only one to many trials, depending both upon the nature of those concepts and skills and upon the effectiveness of provisions for the other conditions of learning.

Learning Requiring Practice

The numerous concepts and skills in the elementary school curriculum vary in their requirements for practice. The six-year-old children mastered the Obstacle Peg Test in one trial because in one view of the entire situation they were able to perceive and to conceptualize a solution. Many single concepts in the elementary school curriculum are similarly grasped in one trial—such, for example, as understanding that "big," "dig," "fig," and "pig" are similar in

Table 5–1. Variations in the Types of Processes in Decimal Division

1 $4\overline{)8}$	16 $.2\overline{)2.4}$	31 $1.4\overline{)1.96}$	46 $7.7\overline{)399}$
2 $25\overline{)2}$	17 $.2\overline{)2.04}$	32 $1.25\overline{)1.5}$	47 $6.5\overline{)35}$
3 $44\overline{)110}$	18 $.48\overline{)7.2}$	33 $2.5\overline{)5.6}$	48 $4.5\overline{)3}$
4 $.2\overline{).4}$	19 $.48\overline{)2.4}$	34 $2.4\overline{)1.44}$	49 $30.6\overline{)2}$
5 $.04\overline{).2}$	20 $.25\overline{)2.2}$	35 $80.8\overline{)7.272}$	50 $2\overline{).6}$
6 $.02\overline{).3}$	21 $.4\overline{)1.3}$	36 $72.4\overline{)6.154}$	51 $4\overline{).24}$
7 $.04\overline{).484}$	22 $1.3\overline{).45}$	37 $2.4\overline{)1.2}$	52 $8\overline{).33}$
8 $.004\overline{).03}$	23 $3.2\overline{).096}$	38 $40.2\overline{)2.1}$	53 $12.\overline{).9}$
9 $.04\overline{).16}$	24 $1.3\overline{).487}$	39 $8.6\overline{)2.15}$	54 $4.\overline{).7}$
10 $.7\overline{).49}$	25 $1.5\overline{).3}$	40 $.4\overline{)8}$	55 $4\overline{)3.2}$
11 $.5\overline{).035}$	26 $6.4\overline{).32}$	41 $.2\overline{)1}$	56 $15\overline{)1.35}$
12 $.5\overline{).046}$	27 $2.4\overline{).36}$	42 $.4\overline{)7}$	57 $103\overline{)6.375}$
13 $.6\overline{).3}$	28 $1.2\overline{)3.6}$	43 $.4\overline{)3}$	58 $50\overline{)3.5}$
14 $.5\overline{).01}$	29 $3.06\overline{)15.3}$	44 $1.3\overline{)52}$	59 $25\overline{)4.5}$
15 $.5\overline{).06}$	30 $1.24\overline{)18.6}$	45 $2.5\overline{)5}$	60 $8\overline{)57.6}$
			61 $18\overline{)47.7}$

Source: H. W. Distad: *J. Educ. Res.*, 27: 512–518, 1933–1934.

word form and differ only in their initial consonants. One obvious reason, however, why such skills as reading, spelling, language, and arithmetic require a great many practice sessions is that they are comprised of thousands of separate, though interrelated, subconcepts and subskills. Moreover, these numerous subconcepts and subskills must be differentiated and organized for appropriate functioning in numerous different situations. For example, the major phases of computation arithmetic include adding, subtracting, multiplying, and dividing of integers, common fractions, and decimal numbers. Analyzing decimal division, Distad [3] has found 61 variations in the process of dividing with decimals. His list of types of processes is presented in Table 5–1.

Similarly in art design, the child learns to use in composition variations in line, space, shape, texture, color, and lightness-darkness; and as these concept skills are mastered, they are applied with refinements in skill to numerous art designs. Likewise in science, the truth of such a concept as the interdependence of animal life may be observed in woodpeckers eating insects, bears eating fish, owls eating rats, snakes eating frogs, etc. From such varied experiences, concepts are generalized.

An analysis of the multiple-element concepts and skills learned by children and of their numerous and varied applications reveals, as Tilton has explained [15], several types of learning tasks requiring practice:

1. Discriminations and Negative Transfer. Because such systems of learning as reading, language, spelling, and arithmetic are comprised of so many parts, it takes practice to learn the many discriminations required. A child who has just begun independent identification of words in reading may read "several" as "seven," because he relies mainly on the beginnings of words in identifying them. In language, having learned that it is correct to say, "He *did* his work well," a child may also say, "I have finally *did* my language exercises." Knowing how to spell "proceed," a child may spell the related noun "proceedure." And in learning multiplications, a fourth grade child is often confused about certain products, such as whether $7 \times 9 = 63, 72$, or possibly 54. Overcoming such negative-transfer errors and being able to make such discriminations accurately and confidently takes practice.

2. Memorizing. In memorizing a poem, the lines of a part in a play, songs, or a piano piece for one's music lesson, it takes practice to differentiate the several segments and to organize them into an integrated sequence. In such sequences, each segment is cued both to the central meaning and to the preceding part. And for the memorizing required in learning facts in such subjects as computational combinations, correct language usage, spelling, science, or social studies, the adaptive organization of these facts into various patterns for

FIG. 5–3. Well-motivated practice in singing, speaking, dramatics, art, reading, and cooperative social behavior are involved in the all-school Christmas cantata. (*Courtesy of Whittier School, Utah State Agricultural College.*)

use in many different situations requires practice in dealing with them in a variety of situations.

3. Automatization of Responses. "Automatic" responses without conscious attention to details, as in riding a bicycle, playing the piano, or rapid reading, are achieved by learning to respond to reduced cues. Reading, for example, at first requires attention both to context and to a careful visual or phonetic response to the beginnings of words, to word roots and suffixes or prefixes, or to each syllable. But through practice, the learner comes to require for comprehension fewer and fewer cues, until finally, as a mature reader, he needs to perceive only parts of some of the words in the piece being read. As another example, it may be observed that, when a child writes creative compositions smoothly and easily, without thinking specifically of sentence structure, word usage, spelling, and handwriting, he has learned through considerable practice to respond to reduced cues for these necessary subprocesses. Many skills are acquired in part from cue reductions.

4. Variations in Cues and Responses. Many responses must be cued to several different stimuli. For example, "21" is learned as a product in 3 × 7, in

FIG. 5–4. In learning such skills as dancing the minuet, observation of your more expert class-mates sometimes helps. (*Courtesy of Adams School, Logan, Utah.*)

$7 + 7 + 7$, and in checking the quotient of $21 \div 3$. Likewise, the syllable "ac" is always spelled the same whether it occurs in "accident," "account," "acquire," or in other, similar words. Children must also learn to respond differentially to the same cue, depending upon variations in its context. A child learns to interpret "line" differently in each instance when it occurs in "Write on the line," "Line up for your turn at the fountain," and "The coat is lined with satin." Learning such discriminative adaptations requires practice.

  5. *Imitating.* Teacher-guidance of learning is often accomplished through teacher- or other-pupil-demonstrations. Successful imitation of a teacher's demonstration or of the model performance of another child, as in figure skating, sewing a seam, baking muffins, or making a class report, often re-quires several trials. This is because the model, being complex, may be in-completely perceived in one trial. In each repeated demonstration, a new phase of the total performance may be grasped. Sometimes the significant cues are not readily identified, as was true of the author's attempt to imitate the figure-skating pattern before it was explicitly verbalized. In other cases it may take

FIG. 5–5. Achieving a satisfying artistic representation of one's concepts often requires provisional self-discovery trials. (*Courtesy of McGraw-Hill Text-Film Department.*)

several provisional trials, checked for correctness against the model, before the learner can reproduce it correctly, as, for example, in improving speech articulation. Teacher-guidance through demonstrations or explanations of how to do something must always be translated into pupil self-activity; and learning to perform such activities independently usually requires several trials.

6. *Problem Solving.* In such problem-solving activities as arithmetic, science, social studies, creative writing, or art, where often several alternative approaches or solutions appear plausible, correct or satisfying solutions can often be reached only by provisional self-discovery trials. Here an adequate and characteristic approach is repeated "trial and check." For example, in a science project, second grade children tried several different kinds of leaves before they discovered the kind which a milkweed caterpillar would eat. The same pattern of self-discovery trials is also applied in such subprocesses as trying out alternate visual or phonetic analyses of an unfamiliar word to find a meaning consistent with the context.

7. *Refinement of Skills.* In the developmental sequences of reading, arithmetic, language composition, and other skills, there is a period of improvement in the skill after the mastering of a fundamental process. In reading, for

example, once a child has learned to read for meaning and understands how to use, along with the context, various visual- and phonetic-analysis techniques for identifying unfamiliar words, the next developmental step is a period of rapid progress. This is accomplished by eliminating unnecessary elements, by telescoping segments, and by coordinating the parts into a smoother, better-integrated pattern. Looking at each separate word, pointing with the finger, lip reading, and extensive phonetic analysis are all eliminated. Emphasizing the meaning, the child sometimes comprehends a whole sentence from perception of the first phrase. He writes a word, after sufficient practice, as a total impulse rather than as a succession of separate letters. Again, in adding such sums as $5 + 6$, a child may at first think, "$5 + 5 + 1$"; but with more teacher-guided practice, he eliminates the unnecessary step and thinks directly, "$5 + 6 = 11$." As a result of such refinements stemming from effective practice, skills are executed more rapidly, accurately, smoothly, comfortably, and confidently.

Practice Situations in School

As is suggested in Table 5–2, observation of school learning activities reveals a wide variety of practice situations. Sometimes concepts and skills in reading, language, arithmetic, and so on are practiced as functional phases of integrated projects in social studies or science, as in the animal-diet experiment described in Chapter 1. But there are also separately scheduled periods for systematic practice in these subjects. And many concepts and skills are practiced incidentally to pupil participation in carrying on "classroom business," including accounting for milk, lunch, attendance, and some supplies; participation in making menus; making and procuring room pictures and exhibits; welcoming new students; writing letters of request and thanks; conducting pupil government; producing plays, operettas, and other school programs; participating in safety-patrol and fire drills; observing and participating in health inspection, conferences, and making records; and learning from taking tests and from excursions. In this schedule, each of the seven types of practice described in the preceding section occurs.

Memorizing, automatizing of responses, and refining skills occur both in separately scheduled systematic practice of skills and in the functional application of these skills in social studies, science, and creative writing. In the incidental practice of skills in connection with "classroom-business" activities and in other practice situations, some responses (in reading, arithmetic, language, etc.) are cued to several different stimuli, and varied responses, ac-

Table 5–2. Curriculum of a Typical Day in the Sixth Grade

Time	Activities
8:50–9:05	Informal health inspection. Business: school lunch collections and accounting, attendance records, announcements, etc.
9:05–9:20	Sharing news: child and teacher contributions.
9:20–10:40	Social studies and science: planning and organizing individual and group work, and summarizing projects, including individual reading on problems; making graphs, charts, posters, and craft constructions; observing, analyzing, discussing, and experimenting with data; individual and committee special contributions; and discussions and pupil reports.
10:40–11:00	Recess play.
11:00–11:30	On MWF, singing. On TTh, practice on arithmetic skills.
11:30–12:00	Arithmetic problem solving, both in connection with projects and from text or curriculum guides.
1:00–2:00	On MWF, language and spelling: creative writing; practice for improvement of skills, both as functionally related to projects and as preplanned systematic practice. On TTh, rhythms and dancing.
2:00–2:30	Reading, both in teacher-guided small groups and in independent library study of literature, science, health, social studies, etc.
2:30–2:50	Recess play.
2:50–3:30	Arts, crafts, and dramatics, both as separate activities and as functionally related to social studies or science projects.

Source: Whittier School, Logan, Utah.

cording to the situation, are sometimes learned to the same cue. Problem solving probably characterizes much of social studies and science learning. As children hear their classmates make reports in social studies, in science, and in "sharing" activities or achieve good results in art or craft activities, they are probably motivated to improve their own efforts by imitating some aspects of the classmate's presentation or technique. Because of the complexity of these activities and the possibilities for alternative responses in many situations, negative as well as positive transfer occurs.

As a more concrete indication of the developmental sequence in these practice situations, the record of a sixth grade child's individual reports in social studies and science over a year is presented in Table 5–3. An examination of

Table 5-3. One-year Record of Sixth Grade Child's Individual Reports
(In connection with social studies and science projects)

No.	Topic	Child's own evaluation
I	Strange Animals: (a) Platypus, (b) Koala Bear, (c) Flying Dragon, (d) Tapir, (e) Armadillo, (f) Myths of Animals	Pretty good
II	Leaves of Trees: Classification	Incomplete
III	Wild Rice: Legend of How Wild Rice Was Discovered	Pretty good
IV	Babylonia: Anciently, People and Religion	Incomplete
V	The Age of Mammals (from *Life*)	Pretty good
VI	Myths: (a) Damon and Pythias, (b) Hercules	Pretty good
VII	Greece	Excellent
VIII	Rome	Pretty good
IX	Piltdown Man	Good
X	Norse Myths	Excellent
XI	Coral Reefs	Excellent
XII	Japanese Architecture	Excellent
XIII	Denmark	Excellent (most complete)

Source: Whittier School, Logan, Utah, 1953–1954.

this sequence of reports reveals both the emergence of new concepts and techniques and the refinement of skills practiced in all of them. The child's own evaluations indicate perception of these improvements and increased satisfaction with them. The first report consisted simply of a clipped picture and a quoted description, all from the same source, of each animal. The report on Japanese architecture utilized different references, included both clipped and self-drawn illustrations, and made comparisons to other, similar architectural styles. The last report in the sequence included an organized outline; comprehensive treatment (history, geography, government, industries, education, travel interests, great people, and present status); discriminating use of several sources; clippings of magazine pictures; self-drawings of maps and architecture; careful attention to writing (paragraphing, sentence structure, spelling, and punctuation); and freer use of the child's own thinking. As each new report in the sequence was undertaken, with motivation to make a good presentation to classmates and with teacher-guidance toward new concepts, techniques, and standards, there was a gradual emergence of new features, as well as refinements in the skillful use of previously used features. For example, at first only one reference was used; then, a couple of references. Following this, as many as possible were used, but with little discrimination. Later, references were scanned for possible use, and some were rejected or used only for a particular phase of a report. Finally, references were used with careful

Fig. 5–6. The library corner in a classroom encourages varied reading interests and facilitates reading research. (*Courtesy of McGraw-Hill Text-Film Department.*)

discrimination. In treating the topic of Denmark's industries, for example, it was important, the child said, that recent references be obtained because of the economic changes which had occurred following World War II.

Using Practice Effectively

It has already been observed that practice, although necessary, is not alone a sufficient condition of learning. Moreover, practice as mere repetition of the same response pattern does not result in learning. Practice is an effective condition of learning only when all the other conditions are also provided. We have already considered in detail the need for sufficient maturity and for teacher-guidance. In later chapters, the other general conditions of effective learning will be discussed in detail. In concluding this chapter, however, we shall consider six specific conditions affecting the effectiveness of practice.

1. Effect of the Learning Environment on Practice Results. The school child's learning environment includes his classroom and school, his home, and his community. Each should make a significant and unique contribution.

The classroom, as the most specialized learning environment, needs to be

F<small>IG</small>. 5–7. Equipping the learning laboratory with appropriate tools affords practice opportunities in creative problem solving in many projects. (*Courtesy of University Elementary School, University of Minnesota.*)

more than a log with a teacher at one end and the pupil at the other. It should be equipped for a large variety of practice activities. The typical intermediate classroom, for example, needs shelves containing a variety of books in children's literature, science, social studies, and nature; reference encyclopedias; and magazines. It needs, as a minimum, shelves, desks, and tables for special activities. Plant, animal, and earth laboratories are desirable. Objects and devices for demonstrating arithmetic concepts are needed. Ample bulletin-board space and newsprint charts for pupil presentations are useful. There should be maps, globes, a variety of art materials, easels, used magazines, and equipment for mounting and filing clipped pictures. Craft tools and a work-bench serve many purposes. A pull-down screen needs to be hung and provisions made for quickly and conveniently darkening the room for projection by both pupils and teacher of clipped pictures, drawings, graphs, charts, pupils' exercises of various kinds, slides, and filmstrips. The opaque projector is an especially flexible and adaptable device for a large variety of teacher and pupil uses. And for many learning activities, a sound recorder is a useful addition to a learning laboratory. Sometimes large classrooms can be arranged for more effective use of these materials by providing a "reading nook," a plant collection, a "geology museum," an "art center," an "arithmetic laboratory," etc.

Homework should use the unique learning opportunities in the home so that it complements rather than duplicates school activities. It should extend school learning into the home and utilize home contributions in the school. Since homework is done without close teacher-guidance, it should probably emphasize independent and creative activities.

For example, in a class discussion of a suitable motif for the classroom Halloween decoration, a child felt that she had not succeeded in making clear to her classmates her idea. That evening, her self-chosen "homework" was the drawing, cutting out, and paper sculpturing of her idea of a witch, which she had failed to convey to her classmates in words alone. Next day at school, she was pleased to have her classmates accept her creative effort as a contribution to the decorating being planned.

As independent homework, Jacobs [12] suggests recreational and research reading (securing from the city library a special contribution to a social studies project); creative art experiences; craft experimentation (constructing and enjoying at home the crystal radio set studied at school); individual practice on skills (after studying, according to the systematic procedure taught by the teacher, the spelling words missed on the pretest, asking a parent to dictate them and then checking them for correctness); socially useful work (making the salad learned about at school as a part of the family dinner); exploration of the community (in relation to a science project); experimentation in relation to school science; collecting; interviewing appropriate persons (a geologist to learn about the state's oil resources); and sharing a variety of school learning experiences with the family.

Teacher-guidance of homework consists of suggesting projects suited to each child's potentialities for independent effort in the home, encouraging initiative, and seeing that homework contributions are rewarded by approval and by being incorporated into school activities.

Jacobs cites a teacher's description of how homework provided needed extended practice [12, p. 80]:

Penny, a wispy, little ten-year-old fifth grader, had done a rather ineffectual job in a group report to the class and realized it. On her own she gathered what materials she could at school, collected some at home, and got down to work. In fact, she reported her progress regularly, and when she was ready, gave a fine, well-organized report on the shoe industry, referring to maps and illustrating her talk with pictures on the opaque projector. From that day on, Penny was established, and felt herself one of the group.

FIG. 5–8. This big potato brought from home for sharing, the children learn from their references, is a product of well-nurtured soil, sunshine, water, and a cool climate. (*Courtesy of Whittier School, Utah State Agricultural College.*)

Children often need teacher-guidance in planning homework to adapt it both to parents' time, talents, and interests and to the child's talents and the demands upon his time of such other activities as music, dancing lessons, scouting, jobs, home responsibilities, hobbies, sports, church, and radio and television listening and watching.

Curricula for the attainment of several major elementary school objectives are greatly enriched by teacher-guided excursions into the community. Such excursions can motivate initiation of comprehensive projects or activities in separate subjects; they can illustrate concretely concepts related to classroom study; and they can afford opportunities for application of concepts and skills learned in the classroom. To make timely, appropriate, and effective integrations between classroom and community study, the teacher will need to inventory his community's resources for curriculum enrichment. One such intermediate grade teacher's inventory includes city health, water, fire, and police departments and facilities; a variety of specific farms, including general, dairy, poultry, vegetable, orchard, and nursery; industries, such as clothing manufacture, cheese making, canning of vegetables and fruits, candy manufacture, farm-machinery manufacture, and poultry processing; college facilities and departments, including the zoology museum, geology museum, herbarium, art exhibits, and meteorology laboratory as well as many departmental dis-

FIG. 5–9. Visiting a farm is interesting, but even better is having a part of the farm in the classroom. These children report that their hen sat 21 days and hatched seven chicks. (*Courtesy of Dilworth School, Salt Lake City.*)

plays, especially at the two-day spring college fair; animal life at the nearby national bird refuge, fish hatchery, deer-feeding station, chinchilla farm, trout farm, dog kennels, and county-fair animal exhibits, and general community exploration; plant life in a nearby mountain canyon, as well as selected gardens, a wide variety of trees, shrub, flower, and park plantings; transportation and communication, including the railroad depot, airport, telephone switchboard, telegraph station, post office, and radio station; and miscellaneous items, including different types of local architecture, new construction, different tradesmen at work, reservoirs, and other schools.

2. Systematic, Functional, and Incidental Practice. Functional practice grows out of child-interest activities and in turn results in improved effectiveness in both these and related activities. In illustrating this concept, Crosby [2] has described how child interest in studying the telegraph led to effective word study. The group were having difficulties with many unfamiliar words in their science book. These children already knew the initial consonants and consonant blends but were not sure of the vowel sounds. So to improve their independent identification of words, the teacher first helped them to learn when vowel sounds are long and when short. As practice material, words that the children could not read in the science book were written on the chalkboard. The list included "insulation," "receiving," "electromagnet," "screws," "connection," "attach," and "battery." To this list, the teacher added other words which the children already knew and which involved the same principles of pronunciation, including "into," "nation," "lady," "scrape," "black," and "bag."

Describing the method, Crosby writes [2, pp. 25–26]:

We marked all the vowels with yellow chalk.

We reviewed the long and short vowel sounds by having children give words which used both.

At this time, I did not give the children any reasons for syllabication. I simply asked them where they thought the divisions were. I divided the words correctly and told them why.

I asked them to pronounce words such as la-dy, pa-per, and to make a rule for syllables ending in a vowel. (The vowel has a long sound.)

We then pronounced words such as late, bite, and formed the rule that when syllables have two vowels, the first is long and the second silent.

We attempted to pronounce the words by using information we already knew and information we had just learned [and thus worked out "in-su-la-tion"].

The children knew "in" and "tion". They knew "sand" and "u", so they knew "su". They then pronounced "insulation".

These same principles of practice were applied to "elec-tro-mag-net" and to all the other words in their list. As a result of this functional practice, the children were able to proceed with their reading about the telegraph and related materials. And they had also learned something important about *how to learn* to read.

More comprehensive projects, such as the diet experiment already mentioned, include opportunities for considerable functional practice in reading, language, writing, spelling, arithmetic, and drawing. The special merits of such practice are that it is well motivated and meaningful and that it results in cuing responses within the skills to situations in which they are needed, thus increasing the probability of effective transfer. For developing effective functional-practice situations, Hildreth [9] lists five requirements: (1) There will be a shift from separate-subject teaching toward "life activities centering around basic experience units and activity projects" requiring improved use of the skills of reading, arithmetic, oral and written language, writing, and spelling. In the primary grades, such units as "The Post Office," "The Circus," and "Animal Pets" provide integrating opportunities. At the intermediate level, wholehearted interest and meaningful, purposeful study and applications of skills may be induced by units centering about science, social studies, or health. (2) A second requirement of functional practice is provision for learning through a variety of approaches—texts, references, personal experiences, pictures, talking about events and organized discussions, handling and working with various materials, broadening knowledge through wider community experiences, seeing and exhibiting collections, and laboratory experimenting. (3) Functional practice results from teacher-guidance of learning, so that curriculum activities emerge as children raise questions, make suggestions, and make discoveries related to their interests and needs. (4) Rather than uniform lesson assignments, participation of each child in projects should be provided according to his unique pattern of abilities, interests, and needs. (5) The interrelatedness of skills should be utilized so that they are learned in integrated patterns of activities.

When curricula are organized around child-interest-centered projects and supplemented as needed by systematic, teacher-guided practice on skills, as in the illustration above from Crosby, effective mastery of the skills is achieved, as several experiments have demonstrated. One of the most extensive of these experiments was conducted in several New York City schools by Wrightstone [16]. On comprehensive achievement tests, he compared the achievement of children who for six years had participated, in schools emphasizing projects, in interest-centered activities with the achievement of children who attended schools relatively more subject-centered. The two kinds of school, however, were not sharply differentiated in this respect; on a 5-point scale for measuring extent of "activities," the activity schools rated 3.2 and the nonactivity schools 1.6. The achievement comparisons for children in each of these two kinds of school are presented in Table 5–4.

From the data of this table, Wrightstone has concluded that "results show that the activity program was as effective as the longer established program in developing children's mastery of fundamental knowledge and skills, that it was more effective in developing children's attitudes, interests, social behavior, ability to think and ability to work on their own initiative." Comparing the mean scores for the two groups, we note that, although all the differences are small, only in the case of arithmetic is achievement in a basic skill higher for the nonactivity group. But even in arithmetic, Harap and Mapes [6, 7] have shown that an expert teacher can achieve better results from functional practice in activities than from the traditional assignment-recitation procedures.

But teacher-guided functional practice of skills in connection with interest-centered activities is not the equivalent of "incidental" or "opportunistic"

Table 5–4. Comparison of School Achievements by Pupils in Activity and Nonactivity Schools

Test	No. of classes	Mean score A	Mean score NA	Diff.	d	t ratio	%
Social performance:							
Cooperative activity..............	36	3.65	2.43	1.22	.38	3.21	1
Leadership activity..............	36	1.90	.91	.99	.28	3.54	1
Self-initiated activity............	36	4.04	2.80	1.24	.43	2.88	1
Recitational activity.............	36	4.10	5.99	−1.89	.50	3.78	1
Basic skills:							
Reading comprehension..........	36	40.85	40.55	.30	.53	.57	60
Arithmetic computation..........	36	16.84	17.76	−.92	.26	3.61	1
Spelling......................	36	54.90	53.75	.15	.67	1.73	9
Language usage................	36	28.35	27.57	.78	.37	2.09	4
Critical thinking:							
Skills in social studies...........	35	29.20	27.76	1.44	.87	1.66	10
Drawing conclusions in social studies......................	35	21.22	19.76	1.46	.68	2.15	5
Applying generalizations.........	34	14.44	13.16	1.28	.59	2.17	5
Current affairs:							
Current events.................	35	32.12	29.95	2.17	1.30	1.67	10
Attitudes and personality:							
What do you believe............	35	35.72	33.64	2.08	.87	2.39	2
Personal adaptability............	34	59.12	57.30	2.08	.84	2.17	5
Social adaptability..............	34	48.48	46.94	1.54	.83	1.86	8

Source: J. W. Wrightstone: *J. Educ. Res.*, 38: 254, 1944.

practice. In developing new word meanings in connection with reading history at the fourth grade level, Holmes [10] has shown that systematic, teacher-guided practice is superior to incidental vocabulary study. The systematic instruction consisted of preliminary study before reading of words which the teacher anticipated might give pupils difficulty. Using explanations, questions, pictures, and illustrative sentences, and calling attention to the distinctive and difficult parts, the teacher directed attention to the meaning, appearance, pronunciation, and opportunities for application in speaking and writing of each new word. This directed, systematic instruction, as compared with incidental experience in reading alone, resulted in greater vocabulary growth, more efficient reading of new material, more fluency in discussion, improved facility in writing, and better-sustained interests.

Gates and others [4] have also found systematically planned and teacher-guided learning to result in better achievement in arithmetic, spelling, and reading than that attained by a group for whom the teacher, without pre-planning, relied relatively more upon "the self-initiated urges of the pupils to read, write, spell, etc." To trust the incidental use of skills to result in their improvement would seem to place too much reliance on mere repetition as a condition of learning. And it has already been demonstrated that repetition alone is not a sufficient condition of effective learning; there must be effective provisions for the other conditions as well. Among these conditions, incidental practice perhaps lacks especially teacher-guidance toward more efficient modes of attack.

3. *Practice at the Right Time.* When practice grows out of the need for more skill in a project and is given appropriate teacher-guidance, it is usually meaningful and efficient. The ineffectiveness of meaningless practice has been demonstrated in the previous chapter. If children begin "drill" on a skill before learning efficient modes of attack, at best they will make only limited improvement in speed and accuracy because of poor procedures [1]. For example, children who practice adding 3 + 4 by counting, "3, 4, 5, 6, 7" improve only their skill in adding by counting. Their rate of progress and ultimate level of proficiency would be greater if the practice were preceded by teacher-guidance on an efficient mode of attack. Therefore, in the several situations requiring practice for development of skills, it is desirable that the practice *follow* rather than *precede* attention to meaning and to efficient modes of attack.

In addition to the quality of the learning environment, the type of organization of learning activities, and the appropriateness of the time for practice, three factors studied in experimental psychology may also affect the efficiency of practice in the elementary school. Studies have shown that the effectiveness of practice, especially in memorizing, varies with the amount of material to be learned as a unit, the distribution of practice trials and rest intervals, and the extent to which material is studied as a whole or is subdivided for practice on its separate parts. From Hovland's review [11, pp. 619–642] of these studies, the following applications to teaching elementary school children seem tenable and useful.

4. *Amount of Material.* As the amount of relatively meaningless material (nonsense syllables) is extended, the learning time required per unit is increased; but for meaningful material, the rate of increase in learning time with increased length of material is much slower. Mastery of 20 irregularly spelled words in one lesson would probably require more than twice as much time as mastery of only 10 such words. However, if all 20 words were spelled accord-

ing to the same principle or to a few principles, the longer list could probably be managed almost as easily as the shorter list. The implication is that, for systematic practice on many of the verbal and motor skills, such as spelling, handwriting, and arithmetic combinations, the assignments for each practice period should include relatively small amounts of content. But in learning meaningful concepts in science, social studies, language, or art, the units to be learned can be much larger without reducing learning efficiency. For these latter activities, provision for only a short period is quite unsatisfactory for accomplishment, as is suggested by one child's remark when asked if the picture which she had brought home had been drawn in that day's art period. "Oh, my, no," she replied, "we just get started in art, and then it is time to put the art things away."

5. *Distribution of Practice*. For learning of both verbal and motor skills, research results have favored fewer trials per practice period and relatively longer rest intervals between practice periods over massed practice. But the difference is not general; the advantages of distributed or massed practice depend upon certain conditions. Long practice periods on repetitive activities, such as handwriting, spelling, memorizing arithmetic combinations, or memorizing poetry or music are likely to lead to waning motivation, boredom, fatigue, or "retroactive inhibition" (later learning interfering with recall of earlier-learned content). For such activities, shorter practice periods with rest intervals between—an hour, or even a day—are likely to be advantageous. Intervals between practice periods are also likely to be helpful in memorizing poetry, music, or class reports, and even in swimming and skating, when the rest intervals implicitly permit opportunity for incidental, extra rehearsals or when a fresh start will free the individual from interfering mental sets in problem solving. "Massed" practice—that is, completing the assignment in one interval—is favored when a "warm-up" or "getting-set" period is required, as in creative writing, in organizing notes for a social studies report, or in art (as the example above suggested), when long rest intervals would cause too much forgetting. Longer practice periods are also better where variability of approach is needed in complex problem solving. For "activity" or project teaching in science, social studies, or creative pursuits involving correlation or integration of all or most of the school subjects, long periods are required; such endeavors are in harmony with the psychological advantages of massed practice. For the functional and systematic practice on the skills related to such projects, however, distributed practice is more effective.

6. *Whole versus Part Methods*. From several studies of the relative effectiveness of the whole and part methods of memorizing verbal material, no universal conclusions favoring either approach have emerged. A relatively short

piece with a unifying thread of meaning is usually memorized more efficiently when studied as a whole. If the content is very long, some subdivision into smaller segments is often more effective. There are advantages in both the whole and the part methods. For many individuals, and especially with children, proceeding with the learning task part by part results in better motivation. Knowledge of progress as subgoals are attained is better motivation than the long-deferred evidence of progress which often occurs when the whole method is used. But meaningfulness is also a factor affecting the efficiency of learning. And since the meaning of a piece is usually inherent in the piece as a whole, the whole method would be advantageous from this point of view. For more mature individuals, for children with higher intelligence, and for individuals who have had experience with it, the whole method seems generally superior. As Hovland writes in his summary of the literature, "the best advice seems to be to learn by using the largest units that are meaningful and within the individual's capacity" [11, p. 642].

Review and Applications

1. Explain: "Practice is a necessary, but not a sufficient, condition for mastery of skills."

2. What features of language, reading, spelling, arithmetic, and other significant parts of the elementary curriculum account for the tremendous amounts of practice required to master them?

3. From observation of some child learning activity, describe specifically the role of practice, noting the occurrence of both repetition and the discovery, differentiation, and integration of more effective behavior patterns.

4. From your observation, describe a classroom well equipped for effective practice. What features make it effective?

5. How can homework and community excursions effectively supplement practice opportunities at school?

6. In a rich project curriculum, is systematic, teacher-guided practice desirable? Why?

7. In the sequence of learning activities required to achieve understanding of concepts or mastery of skills, where is the appropriate position for practice activities?

8. How can such factors in efficient learning as amount of content in an assignment, distribution of practice, and whole versus part methods be applied to school learning?

References

1. Brownell, W. A., and C. B. Chazal: "The effects of premature drill in third grade arithmetic," *J. Educ. Res.*, 29: 17–28, 1935.

2. Crosby, Muriel: "Purposeful direction in speaking and writing," *Childh. Educ.*, 31: 22–29, 1954.
3. Distad, H. W.: "An analysis of the drill provisions in division of decimals in 10 arithmetic series," *J. Educ. Res.*, 27: 509–523, 1933–1934.
4. Gates, A. I., M. R. Batchelder, and J. A. Betsner: "A modern systematic versus an opportunistic method of teaching," *Teach. Coll. Rec.*, 27: 678–701, 1925–1926.
5. Guthrie, E. R.: *The Psychology of Learning*, rev. ed., Harper, New York, 1952.
6. Harap, H., and Charlotte E. Mapes: "The learning of decimals in an arithmetic activity program," *J. Educ. Res.*, 29: 686–693, 1936.
7. ———: "The learning of fundamentals in an arithmetic activity program," *Elem. Sch. J.*, 34: 515–525, 1934.
8. Hildreth, Gertrude H.: "An individual study in word recognition," *Elem. Sch. J.*, 35: 606–619, 1935. Adapted by permission of the University of Chicago Press.
9. ———: "Skills develop with functioning," *Educ. Outl.*, 24: 13–19, 1949.
10. Holmes, Eleanor: "Vocabulary instruction in reading," *Elem. Engl. Rev.*, 11: 103–105 and 110, 1934.
11. Hovland, C.: "Human learning and retention," in S. S. Stevens (ed.): *Handbook of Experimental Psychology*, Copyright, 1951, by Wiley, New York, and used with permission of the publisher.
12. Jacobs, L. B.: "What about homework?" *Childh. Educ.*, 31: 74–81, 1954.
13. Symonds, P. M.: "Practice vs. grammar in the learning of correct language usage," *J. Educ. Psychol.*, 22: 81–95, 1931.
14. Thorndike, E. L.: *Human Learning*, Century, New York, 1931.
15. Tilton, J. W.: *An Educational Psychology of Learning*, Macmillan, New York, 1951.
16. Wrightstone, J. W.: "Evaluation of the experiment with the activity program in the New York City Elementary Schools," *J. Educ. Res.*, 38: 252–257, 1944.

Chapter 6

Perceiving the Effects of Provisional Trials

W HAT IS the mode of approach of a child in meeting an unfamiliar problem for the first time? As has already been observed, even though his first efforts may be unsuccessful, they will be purposeful: he will try and see. Guided by hypotheses built up from his past experiences, the child will try alternative approaches and check their consequences. On the basis of his perception of the effects of these provisional trials, he will confirm or deny their validity as solutions to his problem. Such "trying and checking" is the central feature of learning. It provides the basis for revising originally vague or erroneous cognitive maps so that they become guides to improved performance. Woodworth, in answering this same question as applied to perception, has written [20, p. 124]:

When a new percept is in the making—when an obscure stimulus-complex is being deciphered, or when the meaning of a cue or sign is being discovered—an elementary two-phase process is observable. It is a trial-and-check, trial-and-check process. The trial phase is a tentative reading of the sign, a tentative decipherment of the puzzle, a tentative characterization of the object; and the check phase is an acceptance or rejection, a positive or a negative reinforcement of the tentative perception.

Perhaps in reading this paragraph the reader may experience firsthand the trial-and-check process as he draws upon his background for hypotheses to

interpret the story and checks them as he proceeds, item by item, through it
[7, p. 122]:

> Our master was a good, kind man. He gave us good food, good lodging, and kind
> words; he spoke as kindly to us as he did to his little children. We were all fond of him,
> and my mother loved him very much. When she saw him at the gate, she would neigh
> with joy and trot up to him. He would pat and stroke her and say, "Well, old pet, and
> how is your little Darkie?" I was a dull black, so he called me Darkie; and then he
> would give me a piece of bread which was very good, and sometimes he brought a car-
> rot for my mother.

In the first phase of the trial-and-check process—the trial phase of solution
learning or problem solving—the hypotheses tried out are applied because
they have proved effective in the past. The child who finds the sum for
12 + 7 to be 10 adds the digits as units because he has found this procedure
previously satisfactory in adding 1 + 2 and 3 + 7. And the child who has
finally learned, perhaps after several corrections, to spell "receive" according
to the rule "*i* before *e* except after *c*" may now misspell "ancient" with the
e before the *i*. All such hypotheses, both correct and incorrect, writes Cantril,
in fact "all ideas of what things are, where they are, and what they are good
for, and so on, are based on . . . assumptions built up from past experience
because they have proved good bets for action" [1, pp. 65–66].

Learning Involves Perceiving the Effects of Provisional Trials

It is in the second phase of this reciprocal trial-and-check process that the
reorganizations and revisions of cognitive maps dependent on perception of the
effects of each trial occur. Guthrie, in commenting on this central feature of
learning, quotes Wiener as saying, "In its simplest form, the feedback principle
means that behavior is scanned for its results, and the success or failure of this
result modifies future behavior" [5, p. 296]. In the above arithmetic-sum and
spelling examples of hypothesis-guided trials, however, the errors would probably not be immediately self-corrected. According to the pupils' standards,
they would be likely to be perceived as adequate solutions, and thus they
would be affirmed for subsequent use in similar situations. Because so many
teaching situations are like this, correcting pupil errors or providing adequate
criteria for checking the effects of goal-directed trials is an important teaching
function. Some learning situations, however, do provide opportunities for self-
correction on the basis of perception of the effects of one's efforts. For example, given three trials in copying the diamond at year 7 of the Stanford-

FIG. 6–1. How will they taste? In this instance of trial-and-check learning, "the proof is in the eating." (*Courtesy of Whittier School, Utah State Agricultural College and the U.S.A.C. Photography Department.*)

Binet intelligence scale, a six-year-old child often improves each trial on the basis of his perception of the effects of his preceding trials. His first trial, compared with the model, may be irregularly shaped and have poorly defined angles. Guided by his perception of these faults, he may on the second trial achieve well-defined angles. On a third trial he may still better define the angles and also correct the shape.

Often provision for perception of the effects will be found inherent in generally good teaching methods. This concept is implicit in Pressey and Robinson's terse explanation of learning as illustrated in explaining how three children learned to solve a jigsaw picture puzzle: "How did the girls *know* when they had found the right answer to the question of where a block belonged? The answer is obvious: the block fitted" [12, p. 395]. Similarly, when a child who reads for meaning identifies an unfamiliar word by phonetic analysis and when the word as identified fits the meaning, he knows he is right. If the word does not fit, he tries and checks again. When the computed answer to an arithmetic problem matches approximately the estimated answer, an at least tentative assumption of being correct is justified. The pitch of a note sung is recognized as right because it sounds right. And, after many attempts, the technique finally discovered for drawing a bird in flight is perceived as effective because the bird now appears to be flying. In many other learning activities, whether a solution "works" or not is a pragmatic test of its correctness.

Thus it is apparent in trial-and-error and insight learning or problem solving that perception of the effects of goal-directed trials is an essential condition of effective learning. It should also be recognized from the above examples how perception of the effects *and* motive satisfaction (or dissatisfaction) are combined as factors determining the selection of right and the elimination of wrong responses in such learning. Besides passively perceiving that the pieces of the picture puzzle "fit" when correctly assembled, the child is motivated toward correct responses by the pleasure of completing the picture and of enjoying its meaning and beauty. Similarly, the meaning achieved in reading, the problem solved, the note sung correctly, and the visual concept portrayed artistically are all both perceived as correct and are motive-satisfying. The special role of perception of the effects in learning may be demonstrated even more clearly, however, by some experimental studies of it.

Experiments on Perception of the Effects

Imagine that you were one of Davies's subjects in his archery experiment. If your first arrow had struck the target on the outermost left edge, you would very probably in the next trial, perceiving this result, have tried to correct the error by aiming more toward the right. In each successive trial, your approach would have been guided by your perception of the effects of preceding trials. But suppose you were blindfolded and given no information at all on the result of any trial. Would any improvement occur from such practice? Thorndike has tested the hypothesis that without the opportunity to perceive the effects of goal-directed trials, learning cannot occur. He instructed seven blindfolded subjects to draw lines 4 inches long, providing them with no knowledge on how correctly the lines were drawn. Except for vague kinesthetic impressions, perception of the effects of their provisional trials was absent as a condition of their learning. Their errors averaged almost an inch at the beginning of the experiment, and after 400 such trials, the errors remained practically the same at the end [18].

In another such experiment [17] subject T drew over a period of 12 days 3,000 lines intended to be 4 inches long without ever seeing any of them. The results, which are presented in Table 6–1, reveal no appreciable progress to-

Table 6–1. Subject T's Distribution of Responses in Drawing Lines to Equal 4 Inches with Eyes Closed

Response	Practice sittings											
	1	2	3	4	5	6	7	8	9	10	11	12
3.7									1			
3.8								2				
3.9												
4.0			3						3			
4.1			4	1				1	3			2
4.2		4	8			1		3	6	1	2	1
4.3		3	9	1				4	5	3		4
4.4		13	12	6			3	4	12	2	4	3
4.5	3	18	18	14	2	7	3	15	14	8	7	11
4.6		20	23	23	3	7	8	13	14	8	14	11
4.7	6	20	14	22	11	14	16	25	13	9	14	21
4.8	6	22	15	18	14	27	17	16	18	15	19	26
4.9	13	17	24	24	22	28	18	21	16	10	18	30
5.0	25	20	16	24	26	21	29	25	14	24	19	20
5.1	27	10	16	12	25	32	14	15	14	22	31	22
5.2	24	11	8	12	24	21	23	25	16	18	28	16
5.3	30	8	2	11	21	13	17	8	18	18	16	12
5.4	17	4	2	8	10	10	7	8	12	12	7	7
5.5	12	1		4	13	8	7	3	10	13	4	3
5.6	7			2	4	7	4	1	4	5	2	2
5.7	3			1	4	2	5	2	6	4	3	1
5.8				1				1		2		
5.9	1			1						1	2	
6.0												
6.1												
6.2	1						1					
Total.......	175	171	174	183	181	198	172	192	200	175	190	192
Median.....	5.23	4.83	4.77	4.93	5.15	5.07	5.07	4.96	4.79	5.13	5.09	4.96
Q.........	.16	.22	.23	.22	.19	.19	.21	.24	.33	.24	.21	.20

Source: E. L. Thorndike: *Human Learning*, Century, New York, 1931, p. 9.

ward a precise 4-inch line. The variations among the last 192 lines drawn are as great as among the first 175 lines. And the line length most frequently drawn varies from day to day. Thorndike interprets these results as demonstrating that repetition alone is not a sufficient condition for learning. Perception of the effects is also necessary, as is implied by Thorndike in his statement "Had I *opened my eyes* after each shove of the pencil during the second and later sittings, and *measured the lines* and *been desirous of accuracy* in the task, the connections leading to 3.8, 3.9, 4.0, 4.1, and 4.2 would have become more frequent until I reached my limit of skill in the task" [17, p. 13, italics supplied].

Actually, although subject T had no *visual* perception of the effects of the lines drawn, he did have a vague kinesthetic impression of them, which he could check against his own, subjective standard for a 4-inch line. Because conjectural checking was possible, some learning should have occurred. Taking the average of all lines drawn (5.01 inches) as T's subjective standard, Seashore and Bavelas [14] have shown that the deviations from the standard of the mean length of line drawn in each sitting are gradually reduced, from .22 on the first day to .05 on the twelfth day. Therefore, although improvement in drawing a *4-inch* line did not occur, some learning did take place.

In Thorndike's experiment, checking was only vague and progress thus very slight. Other experiments have shown that the more precisely the results of each trial can be perceived, the more efficient will be the learning. Trowbridge and Cason [19] directed blindfolded groups of college students to draw 100 3-inch lines under four different conditions: (1) given no information, (2) distracted by hearing E. say a meaningless nonsense syllable after each line, (3) hearing E. say "right" whenever a line came within ⅛ inch of a 3-inch line, and (4) being informed precisely (in eighths of an inch) how much each line drawn deviated, plus or minus, from a 3-inch line. Only condition (4) provided information on every trial. Under condition (3), a subject came within ⅛ inch only very rarely. The marked advantage of opportunity to perceive precisely the effects of each trial is shown in Table 6-2.

Table 6-2. Proficiency in Learning to Draw a 3-inch Line Is Related to Amount and Precision of Information Given

Condition	Lines within ⅛" of correct, av. per cent
No information given	13.6
Distracted by hearing nonsense syllable on each trial	5.1
Hearing "right" only when within ⅛ inch of correct	22.6
Precise information on extent and direction of each error	54.8

Source: M. H. Trowbridge and H. Cason: *J. Gen. Psychol.*, 7: 245–258, 1932.

Reed [13] has also demonstrated that perception of the effects is necessary and that the more precisely the learner perceives the effect of each goal-directed trial, the more effective will be his learning. He had nine college students practice drawing 4-inch lines, 2-cent-stamp-size rectangles, and penny-size circles under four conditions varying, in opportunity to perceive the effect of each trial, from being blindfolded to being permitted to measure with a rule every fifth figure drawn. For the blindfolded subjects, "change is largely an accident." With eyes open, or with the models before them (the

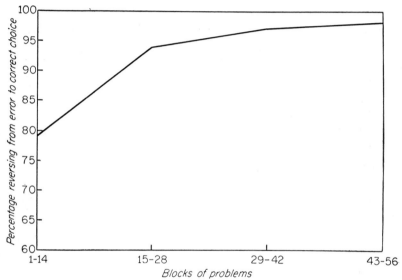

Fig. 6–2. Two- to five-year-old children learn to be guided by perception of the effects: percentages reversing on a second trial to a correct choice after an error trial. (*From Harlow, H. F., in Stolurow, L. M. (ed.): Readings in Learning. Copyright, 1953, by Prentice-Hall, Inc., Englewood Cliffs, N.J., p. 493. Reproduced by permission of the publisher.*)

second and third conditions), progress occurred. But only under condition (4) did the subjects make consistent progress throughout the training period. "This was possible because, by means of measurement, the subjects could tell at once how much error they had made and what was necessary to correct it" [13, p. 21].

Gilliland [4] has demonstrated the role of perception of the effects in learning to use a scale for judging the quality of children's handwriting. The accuracy of student teachers' appraisals improved especially after practice in grading 30 specimens of handwriting for which they checked their judgments against those made on these same specimens by an expert in the use of the scale.

In experimentation on this factor in learning, adult subjects have usually been used. Harlow [6], however, has shown that two- to five-year-old children learn from perceiving the effects of previous trials and also that they learn from their mistakes. From an error choice in a discrimination problem, they learn to infer that an alternate choice will be correct. Moreover, with increasing amounts of experience, they learn how to use this condition of learning more effectively. This latter fact is demonstrated in Figure 6–2, which shows in successive blocks of different discrimination problems gradual increases in the percentage of children reversing to a correct choice after one error choice.

Situations Requiring Special Provisions for Perception of Effects

Often one of several factors affecting or determining an event is noticed only when for some reason it is absent. When the usual provision for perception of the effects in learning is not possible, its fundamental importance is brought more strikingly to our attention. This is illustrated by the great difficulty a deaf child has in learning to articulate words correctly. Deprived of hearing—the usual cue for noting the correctness or incorrectness of our attempts at correct articulation—the deaf child must find some other way of perceiving the effects of attempts at correct articulation. Presented in Figure 6-3 is a device reported by *Life* magazine for showing a deaf child immediately and precisely how nearly his own provisional trial matches or approximates the teacher-model or oral concept he is striving to reproduce. The teacher has said "shoe" into a microphone, and the sound is represented on a grid as a certain pattern of colored lights. As the child says "shoe" into another microphone, she can tell, by observing how nearly the pattern of lights she produces matches her teacher's pattern, how near or how far away she is from the correct articulation. Thus she is guided in revising her learning efforts. With this device, the child can continue her goal-directed trials, being guided toward improvement at each subsequent trial by her perception of the effects of each previous trial.

Several years ago, Thompson [16] was remarkably successful in teaching beginning reading to deaf-mutes because, besides applying the other conditions of effective learning, she was especially ingenious in providing ways in which these handicapped children could perceive the effects of their goal-directed attempts at reading. Since they lacked both speech and hearing, she had to employ with these children various visual-action and pantomime signals. Stoelting [15] also made good use of this same principle in teaching speech and reading combined to cerebral-palsy children. It was difficult to correct the

Fig. 6–3. Illustrating how precise "perception of effects" of provisional trails facilitates attaining an otherwise vague goal, a pupil from the Tennessee School for the Deaf says "shoe" into a microphone and watches the colored lights, which tell her when she is pronouncing it correctly. (*From Life, September 22, 1952, p. 73. Courtesy, Life Magazine (c) Time, Inc.*)

speech of these children, because the teacher often could not tell from their incomprehensible articulations what they were really trying to say. Molly, for example, who had practically no understandable speech, desired to read orally. And "it was easier," writes Stoelting, "to understand her with the printed page as a check upon what she was attempting to say."

On some learning tasks, there are experimental data comparing performance without and with opportunity to perceive the effects of goal-directed trials. Merely hearing music or singing does not often improve the pitch discrimination of persons who are deficient in making such discriminations. Both McCarthy [10] and Wyatt [21] have reported that pitch discrimination is not improved as a result merely of making hundreds of such discriminations. Using the Seashore pitch-discrimination test, which requires the subject to tell whether the second of a pair of tones is higher or lower than the first for 100 pairs of tones, Wyatt had 24 adults make 500 such discriminations—100 per day for five successive days. On none of these discriminations were the subjects informed of the correctness or incorrectness of their responses. For the five successive days, their average scores were 85.71, 85.35, 87.02, 87.96, and 87.90, which show gains to be "relatively insignificant" [21, p. 9]. When, however, there were added to practice both teacher-guidance on effective modes of attack and information on the correctness of each pitch discrimination practiced, Wyatt found significant improvement in pitch discrimination for both music and nonmusic students [21, p. 51].

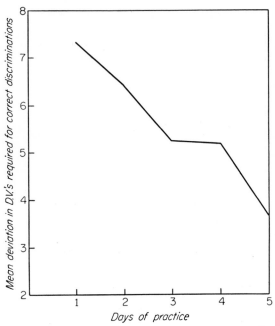

Fig. 6–4. Improvement in pitch discrimination from practice and perception of the effects of each trial. (*From Connette, E.: J. Educ. Psychol., 32: 528, 1941.*)

Connette [2] has also shown that practice in pitch discrimination with opportunity to check the correctness of each discrimination will result in improvement. Twenty-three college students were given five half-hour training sessions in discriminating pitch differences between a standard 440-double-vibration fork and forks deviating from it in either direction by 0.5, 1, 2, 5, 17, and 30 double vibrations. Immediately following each guess as to whether the second tone was higher or lower than the first member of a pair, each subject was informed as to the correctness of his judgment. From the percentage of correct judgments on each pair of tones for each day, the average amount of deviation between each pair of tones required for correct discriminations was computed. The curve of these results is presented in Figure 6–4.

As a result of providing adequately for perception of the effects in learning, Connette notes, from examination of the above curve, that the "average improvement in pitch discrimination . . . amounts to approximately fifty per cent in five days" [2, p. 531]. From the continued downward trend of the curve through the fifth day, however, it appears that even finer tone discrimination might be learned by this method.

Perception of Effects in Examinations

Adequate provision for perception of effects of goal-directed trials is desirable in many phases of teaching, but perhaps it is strategically important in connection with examinations. Examinations are useful in summarizing and evaluating a unit of learning and as a means of determining readiness for the next step in a sequence of learning activities. As such, they are highly effective teaching devices. In preparation for an examination, the learner has practiced and has organized principles and skills for application. The examination affords an opportunity for checking his understanding and mastery of them. It yields the pupil information confirming some of his provisionally tried hypotheses and indications of the need for revising others—provided, of course, that he sees and uses his corrected examination papers.

The teaching value of informing pupils on the correctness or incorrectness of their responses to examination questions has been demonstrated by Plowman and Stroud [11]. These investigators had 250 tenth and eleventh grade students, divided into two matched groups of 125 each, study textbook material on the history of bookmaking for 15 minutes. Both groups were then given a 30-item multiple-choice test on the content read, after which one group was allowed to inspect for five minutes the corrected test—a learning opportunity not permitted the other group. Then, after six days, without intervening warning, both groups took another test on the same content. The superiority on the second test of the group who had had the opportunity to

Table 6–3. Allowing Pupils to Inspect Their Corrected Test Papers
Facilitates Learning and Retention

Group	Condition	N	Means		Diff. in 2d test	S.E. of diff.	C.R.
			1st test	2d test			
1	Corrected tests inspected	125	21.5	25.2			
2	Corrected tests not inspected	125	21.5	20.0	5.2	.21	24.8

Source: Adapted from L. Plowman and J. B. Stroud: *J. Educ. Res.*, 36: 16–20, 1942.

Fig. 6–5. The teacher checks a child's beginning efforts at reading while other children work independently at prereading activities. (*Courtesy of Whittier School, Utah State Agricultural College.*)

learn from checking the correctness of their efforts on the first test (and, of course, to make self-corrections in their understanding of the content) is shown in Table 6–3. Although the groups were originally matched, a difference on the second test of 5.2 favoring the group who had inspected their test papers is noted. That this difference can be trusted not to have resulted merely from errors of sampling and measurement is indicated by the very high critical ratio of 24.8, reported as a test of the statistical significance of the obtained difference.

Implications for Teaching

This review has demonstrated that opportunity for perception of the effects of goal-directed trials is an essential condition of learning, and that the more effectively this condition is provided, the more efficient will be the learning. Though often this condition is provided as an inherent part of good teaching methods, sometimes it requires direct attention from the teacher.

Here is a report of an effort to help children gain facility in language expression [3, p. 24]:

One teacher of 11-year olds conceived the idea of using a tape recorder so that her group could hear whether or not they were saying just what they meant. [The teacher] knew that they needed to understand better the concept of change and that much discussion would be necessary in order to do this. A short simple story called *Stick-in-the-Mud* which illustrated this concept was read aloud by several children. This itself was a valuable experience, for the children learned much from learning different pronunciations, voice quality, pitch, and smooth meaningful interpretation of the material read. Discussion followed the reading, then the tape was played back. Following this was further discussion as to whether comments were relevant (and of course several were not), whether they were too long-winded or whether the thought was clearly expressed in a few words. The tape was erased; another recording was made and improvement was discussed.

In correcting children's written work in language, social studies, or arithmetic, the papers can be checked so as to give more specific guidance in correcting errors. Holland [8], in discussing several ways of overcoming difficulties in teaching long division, includes as one suggestion more informative checking of children's arithmetic papers. She suggests placing on the chalkboard a list of the most frequently made errors in long division with a symbol for it opposite each kind of error, as shown in Table 6–4. This list of errors

Table 6–4. Long-division Errors and Symbols for Marking Them

Symbol	Error	Symbol	Error
z–om	Zero omitted	s	Error in subtraction
w–q	Wrong quotient	p	Error in placement
w–c	Wrong carrying	bd	Error in number brought down
m	Error in multiplication	r	Error in remainder

Source: H. Holland: *Elem. Sch. J.*, 42: 585–596, 1941–1942. Reprinted by permission of the University of Chicago Press.

calls the pupil's attention at the outset to those which he will need to be careful to avoid. And it provides the teacher a convenient device for marking specifically and informatively his arithmetic paper. When the child sees on problem No. 2 the symbol "z-om" and on problem No. 7 the symbol "w-c," he will know he has made mistakes by omitting the zero in a quotient and in carrying. These are concepts that he will need to restudy. This device has general application in many phases of arithmetic and in language, handwriting, spelling, and possibly other subjects for which lists of commonly made errors have been inventoried [13] or can be inventoried by a teacher for a particular purpose.

There is some evidence, as in the pitch-discrimination experiments, that the time elapsing between making an error and discovering and correcting it is critical for effective learning. Keller [9] has reported improvements in Morse

FIG. 6–6. Tentative, provisional abstract concepts about fractions are checked against concrete, visual models. (*Courtesy of McGraw-Hill Text-Film Department.*)

Code training resulting from more immediate provision of knowledge of the correctness of responses to code signals. The usual practice had been for a student to respond to a set of signals (as many as 100) before checking them. Keller arranged that 100 signals be presented by the following sequential procedure: (1) presentation of the signal, (2) a pause to permit the student to write down (provisionally) the appropriate character, and (3) presentation of the correct character, by which the student could check his own response. In this way the student is given the opportunity throughout each practice exercise to perceive the effect of each goal-directed trial and to affirm or correct immediately each response.

Pupil self-checking of answers in arithmetic and social studies problem solving and in spelling is an example of immediate checking of goal-directed efforts. Perhaps the most glaring violation of this principle is the common one of frequent delay in returning to pupils their teacher-marked examinations or other written work. Immediate return (the next day) of such papers should improve their teaching value.

These are only a few examples of the trial-and-check process in teaching. The alert teacher, recognizing that provision for adequate perception of the effects of goal-directed trials is an essential condition of effective learning, will provide amply for both pupil self-checking and teacher-guidance in checking pupil learning efforts.

Summary

A central feature of learning as problem solving is the trial-and-check process. Facing a problem in learning, such as the identification of an unfamiliar word in reading, the child, on the basis of generalizations achieved in prior experiences, makes provisional trials. Perceiving the effect of a trial in relation to his goal, he either confirms it as correct and utilizes this same response more confidently the next time he meets the problem, or he perceives his provisional trial as having failed to achieve his goal and revises it in the light of his perception of its effects. Without opportunity to perceive the effects of goal-directed trials, or with only limited opportunity, learning—making improvements in response patterns—is impossible or difficult, as is illustrated by the unaided efforts of the deaf child to articulate words correctly.

Many learning activities provide their own conditions for pupil self-checking, as using the context in reading, or estimating the sensibleness of an answer in arithmetic. But many learning errors, such as the incorrect pronunciation of a word, persist because children are unaware of them. Thus teachers provide another condition of effective learning by checking and by teaching children more effective ways of checking the correctness of provisional trials in problem solving. Apparently, in such checking, explicitness and timing are important.

Review and Applications

1. Cite several examples of the "trial-and-check" phase of learning. Why is perception of the effects of goal-directed provisional trials an essential condition of learning?

2. Cite examples to show that the more precisely a learner perceives the effects of his provisional trials, the more effectively he learns.

3. What happens when learners practice without opportunity to check the results of their goal-directed trials? Cite examples.

4. In identifying an unfamiliar word in reading, in solving an arithmetic problem, or in drawing his concept of a girl swinging, how does a child often check by himself the correctness of his own provisional trials?

5. Give good examples of how teachers aid children in learning by checking or by helping children to check the correctness of their learning efforts.

References

1. Cantril, H.: *The "Why" of Man's Experience*, Macmillan, New York, 1950.
2. Connette, E.: "The effect of practice with knowledge of results," *J. Educ. Psychol.*, 32: 523–532, 1941.
3. Crosby, Muriel: "Purposeful direction in speaking and writing," *Childh. Educ.*, 31: 22–29, 1954.
4. Gilliland, A. R.: "The effect of practice with and without knowledge of results in grading handwriting," *J. Educ. Psychol.*, 16: 532–536, 1925.
5. Guthrie, E. R.: *The Psychology of Learning*, rev. ed., Harper, New York, 1952.
6. Harlow, H. F.: "The formation of learning sets" (*Psychol. Rev.*, 56: 51–65, 1949), in L. M. Stolurow (ed.): *Readings in Learning*. Copyright, 1953, by Prentice-Hall, Inc., Englewood Cliffs, N.J. Reproduced by permission of the publisher.
7. Hildreth, Gertrude: *Learning the Three R's*, Educational Test Bureau, Educational Publishers, Inc., Minneapolis, 1946.
8. Holland, Henrietta: "Difficulties in long division and some suggestions for teaching the process," *Elem. Sch. J.*, 42: 585–596, 1941–1942.
9. Keller, F. S.: "Studies in International Morse Code: A note on second-level training in code reception," *J. Appl. Psychol.*, 29: 161–163, 1945.
10. McCarthy, Dorothea: "A study of the Seashore measures of musical talent," *J. Appl. Psychol.*, 14: 437–455, 1930.
11. Plowman, Letha F., and J. B. Stroud: "Effect of informing pupils of the correctness of their objective test questions," *J. Educ. Res.*, 36: 16–20, 1942.
12. Pressey, S. L., and F. P. Robinson: *Psychology and the New Education*, Harper, New York, 1944.
13. Reed, H. B.: *Psychology of Elementary School Subjects*, Ginn, Boston, 1938.
14. Seashore, H. G., and A. Bavelas: "The functioning of knowledge of results in Thorndike's line-drawing experiment," *Psychol. Rev.*, 48: 155–164, 1941.
15. Stoelting, Frances: "A classroom teacher of a cerebral palsy group teaches speech," *Quart. J. Speech*, 35: 65–70, 1949.
16. Thompson, Helen: *An Experimental Study of the Beginning Reading of Deafmutes*, Contributions to Education, no. 254, Teachers College, Columbia University, Bureau of Publications, New York, 1927.
17. Thorndike, E. L.: *Human Learning*, Century, New York, 1931.
18. ———: "The law of effect," *Amer. J. Psychol.*, 39: 212–222, 1927.
19. Trowbridge, Margery H., and H. Cason: "An experimental study of Thorndike's theory of learning," *J. Gen. Psychol.*, 7: 245–260, 1932.
20. Woodworth, R. S.: "Re-inforcement of perception," *Amer. J. Psychol.*, 60: 119–124, 1947.
21. Wyatt, Ruth F.: "Improvability of pitch discrimination," *Psychol. Monogr.*, vol. 58, no. 2, 1945.

Chapter 7

Transfer
of Training

For children to learn to meet every specific problem as a separate task unrelated to any other would make education a highly inefficient, if not a futile, undertaking. But the learning of principles or generalizations multiplies the efficiency of each learning activity in proportion to the effectiveness of transfer procedures. We have already observed how applying the principle of transfer can improve the efficiency of primary school children in learning manuscript writing. Such applications pervade all elementary school learning. For example, as a child's reading vocabulary increases, the effectiveness of context as a clue for identifying unfamiliar words in his reading is multiplied. Again, using phonetic analysis as a mode of attack in spelling certain words achieves as a by-product the mastery of certain other words without the necessity of specific practice on them. A few art principles and techniques, once mastered, can be applied in unique creative expression whenever need for such expression occurs. And when a generally effective mode of attack in problem solving with integers and fractions as applied to certain varied types of problems is learned, a child has command of a system of understandings and skills which he will be able to apply to innumerable quantitative personal and social situations. Besides transfer of content or method or ideal within and between curriculum areas, children under effective conditions of learning achieve a more general transfer ability: they learn how to learn more effectively and confidently. But the instances mentioned here are only a few situations in which the role of transfer is especially clear.

The Role of Transfer in Learning

Since no two problems or practice sessions are ever exactly alike, and since *progress* in every area of the curriculum is always occurring for successful learners, there is some degree of transfer in every learning activity. Indeed, transfer is an essential condition of all learning; and the efficiency of learning depends significantly upon how effectively the principles of transfer are applied. In general, transfer principles improve learning efficiency by utilizing in new learning the child's background of experience as fully as possible and by reducing complex and multiple-element tasks to a few unifying generalizations. Such applications of transfer principles should occur frequently between parts of a subject (as between phonetic identification of words and independent reading, or between functional grammar and expression in language); between different subjects (as between arithmetic and social studies, or between manuscript writing and reading in the primary grades); and between school and out-of-school activities.

The history of modern education, however, reveals that trust in the efficacy of transfer principles has varied [45, pp. 522–538]. In early American education teachers trusted a few difficult subjects to discipline the mind so that people would, with improved ability to reason, manage all sorts of activities—even unrelated activities—effectively. At about the turn of the nineteenth century, a view propounded by Thorndike and Woodworth on the basis of their research [40, 41, 42] that "the mind . . . on its dynamic side is a machine for making particular reactions to particular situations" [40, p. 249] gradually came to be accepted and to discourage reliance on transfer. Numerous specific and independent facts, skills, and ideals were to be learned as specific stimulus-response connections. But further and differently planned experimentation on this important concept continued, with the result that belief in the possibilities of transfer has become established and the conditions for its favorable occurrence more clearly understood.

Orata, in reviewing 167 experiments on transfer [27], reports that in 76 per cent of these studies either "considerable" or "appreciable" positive (favorable) transfer occurred. It did not, however, always occur; sometimes there was no influence from activity A to activity B, and sometimes there was even interference. In a later, further review of research on transfer, Orata [26] listed some of the factors upon which the extent of transfer depends. Factors favoring transfer include maturity; intelligence; recency and stability of the learned pattern to be transferred; favorable attitudes toward learning and its applications; efficient methods of study emphasizing meaning, generalizing, and applying; and the organization and developmental sequences of the content learned.

At the present state of our knowledge about transfer, then, the important questions are not: "Does transfer occur?" and "Can teachers depend on this principle?" Some transfer is essential for learning, and the effectiveness of learning depends to an important extent upon how well we can provide learning conditions to promote transfer. The important question is: "How can the principles of transfer be utilized effectively in teaching?" In the main, we shall find that applying transfer principles to teaching will involve emphasizing meaning, understanding, generalizing, and the development and applications of principles. But to understand and to use transfer principles effectively in teaching, some study of the experimenting and theorizing on the concept should be helpful.

Model Transfer Experiments, Positive and Neutral

Knight's experiment [22] on the role of transfer in the addition of fractions, while not a typical model for transfer experiments, is a good illustration of the effective use of transfer principles. Two groups of children, of equal ability and both ready for the topic, were given the same amount of instruction in adding of fractions. Group A practiced on fractions which had as denominators 2, 3, 4, 5, 6, 7, 8, 9, 10, 12, 14, 15, 16, 18, 21, 24, 28, and 30. Group B practiced on fractions having as denominators only 2, 4, 6, 8, 12, and 24 and depended on transfer of this limited training for mastery of the untaught fractions. The crucial test for transfer was the T list of problems comprised of fractions with denominators of 3, 5, 7, 9, 14, 15, 18, 21, 28, and 30, which were taught to Group A but not to Group B. On this T test, Group A scored 14.50 and Group B 13.25, thus demonstrating almost complete transfer from mastery of the specifically taught fractions to mastery of the fractions not practiced specifically. Knight, in explaining the results of his experiment, wrote [22, p. 787, italics supplied]:

We get transfer in substantial amounts in relatively complex skills, such as handling fractions. *The transfer is possible, however, to the extent that the skills exist to transfer.* The groups experimented with had in their work with whole numbers very carefully constructed drills which guaranteed the mastery of the number combinations. We could not expect 2×5 in the simple skills in whole numbers to transfer to 6×7, but if 2×5 and 6×7, etc., have all been practiced in simple skills, they can be trusted to operate later in higher and more involved skills.

Transfer in such favorable amounts as these obtained by Knight is perhaps possible in other curriculum areas, but as Grossnickle's experiment demonstrates, it does not occur automatically. Grossnickle [12] attempted "to see the amount of transfer between ability to respond to multiplication facts when isolated [in multiplication] and ability to use the facts in long division." To 1,075 pupils in grades 5 to 15, he administered (1) a test of 50 multiplication facts and (2) a division test requiring these same multiplication facts. Tabulating the errors in each situation, he found that out of a total of 1,135 errors, only 371 occurred in multiplication, while 764 occurred in division; and that only 22, or 1.9 per cent, of the errors were common to both processes. The failure of transfer to occur from simple multiplication to its application in division is especially clearly indicated by the finding that over twice as many errors occurred in division as in multiplication (67.3 per cent in division, and 32.7 per cent in multiplication). In other words, a child who used correct operations in multiplication often failed to apply this knowledge when the same multiplication facts were needed in division. From these results, Grossnickle concluded that "the multiplication involved in division is a specialized ability and not a generalized reaction to multiplication facts" [12, p. 681]. He recommended that as remedial help for multiplication errors in division, pupils "should be given division examples with emphasis placed on the multiplication process." These two experiments show that, though positive transfer is possible, it does not occur automatically, even when the conditions for transfer would seem to be favorable. To understand the specific conditions upon which favorable transfer depends, we need to examine these experiments more precisely in the light of the theories of transfer. Understanding of such theories should give us better control over transfer in practical applications in teaching.

Transfer Theories

As explanations of transfer phenomena both in transfer experiments and as observed in teaching, two main theories have been proposed.

Thorndike's Theory of Identical Elements. In an explanation of how improvement in one mental function produces improvement (or interference) in another, Thorndike says [38, p. 358]:

The answer which I shall try to defend is that a change in one function alters any other only in so far as the two functions have as factors identical elements. . . . To take a concrete example, improvement in addition will alter one's ability in multiplication because addition is absolutely identical with a part of multiplication and because certain other processes, e.g., eye movements and the inhibition of all save arithmetical impulses, are in part common to the two functions.

The elements of identity between two or among more functions include content, method, and attitude. According to Thorndike again [38, p. 359]:

> Chief amongst such identical elements of practical importance in education are associations including ideas about aims and ideas of method and general principles, and associations involving elementary facts of experience such as length, color, number, which are repeated again and again in differing combinations.

Thorndike based his theory on the data obtained from some now famous experiments which he and Woodworth did in 1901 [40, 41, 42]. Six adult subjects (in some instances fewer) were tested both before and after intervening training in functions both closely similar to and somewhat different from other trained functions. In different experiments, they were trained to a "high degree of proficiency" in estimating areas of rectangles, lengths of lines, and weights and in marking words containing the letters *e* and *s* or certain parts of speech. Both before and after this training, the subjects were tested in estimating other areas ranging from similar in size and shape to differing markedly in size and shape, in estimating different weights and lengths of lines, and in marking words containing other, both similar and different, pairs of letters on both similar pages and pages of different line length, size of type, and style of matter. As examples of the data gathered, the results of two of the experiments will be cited.

Before and after training in estimating the areas of rectangles ranging in size from 20 to 90 square centimeters, the six subjects were required to estimate the areas of rectangles ranging in size from 20 to over 240 square centimeters, as well as areas of other geometrical shapes both similar and different in size to the rectangles on which they had been trained [40]. The training included looking at a rectangle to be judged, comparing it by eye with three standard rectangles with areas of 1, 25, and 100 square centimeters, respectively, estimating the size of the rectangle being judged, checking on the back of the rectangle to see what the area really was, and recording the error. In the "before" and "after" testing, only the estimates were made. As a result of the intervening training, the average error in judging the rectangles on which the subjects actually practiced was reduced to 2.43. The average error on all the test figures before training was 17.75; after training it was still 13.98, which is 78.8 per cent of the before-training error score. The improvement from the pretests to the end-tests was much less than that which occurred on the intervening practice material. It was noted, however, that "there was more improvement [from "before" to "after" tests] when test areas were similar in shape to those in the training series." The average ratio of before- to after-test error score, showing the transfer effect from training, was .56 for areas of similar shape and .90 for areas of different shape. The transfer effect from the training series proved to be greater for test areas similar in size and shape to the training series than for dissimilar test areas.

In another experiment [42], four subjects practiced marking the words in a book containing *e* and *s*, before and after which training they were tested for transfer in marking words containing *i* and *t*, *s* and *p*, *c* and *a*, and *e* and *r* on pages similar to the training pages and in marking words containing *a* and *n*, *l* and *o*, and *e* and *r* on pages different in line length, size of type, and style of matter. Again significant gains resulted from practice on the training series, and smaller gains by transfer from pretests to end-tests, as measured in terms of time, percentage of letters marked, and omissions of letters which should have been marked. And as found in judging areas, transfer gains were relatively larger for marking similar pairs of letters, especially on similar pages, than for the dissimilar material.

From such data as these, Thorndike and Woodworth concluded that: (1) Because the gains on the transfer tests were almost always less than the gains from direct training, certain quasigeneral abilities, such as "judgment," cannot account for the uneven performances found for different functions, all apparently requiring some kind of judging. They concluded that "functions of judging nearly equal magnitudes are, sometimes at least, largely separate and independent" [40, p. 261]. (2) While tending to minimize transfer effects, they did note some transfer gains. In analyzing these transfer gains, Garrett [9] observes that they range on different tests from 20 per cent to 44 per cent of the gains directly due to practice. But in attaining educational objectives, Thorndike and Woodworth, on the basis of these results, consider it better to teach for each specific objective directly rather than depend on the by-products of transfer. (3) From comparing the amounts of transfer on "before" and "after" tests differing in their degree of resemblance to the training functions, they concluded that the amount of transfer from the training to the test series decreased in proportion to the extent of difference between the training and the test series [41, p. 386]. (4) The "spread of practice occurs only where identical elements are concerned in the influencing and influenced function" [40, p. 250]. These identical elements, they believed, include, besides specific content, "ideas" of at least limited-scope applications, efficient work habits, and attitudes, such as "avoiding certain prejudices" [41, p. 395].

Both Knight, in interpreting the marked transfer in teaching of fractions, and Grossnickle, in accounting for the failure of mastery of multiplication facts to transfer to their use in division, implicitly used Thorndike's theory of identical elements. Knight [22, p. 787] explained that "transfer is possible to the extent that the skills exist to transfer." When the elements to be transferred "have all been practiced in simple skills, they can be trusted to operate later in higher and more involved skills." And Grossnickle explained that multiplication facts were not applied without error in division because "the multiplication involved in division is a specialized ability and not a generalized reaction to multiplication facts" [12, p. 681].

Judd's Theory of Transfer by Generalizing. As we have noted, Thorndike's theory focuses attention on the elements in common between learning activities in which transfer is expected to occur; transfer would occur from A_{1234} to B_{3456} because these situations have in common elements 3 and 4. According to Judd's theory, what is learned in A transfers to B because in studying A, the learner develops generalizations or principles which apply in part or completely to *both* A and B. The difference between these rival theories is perhaps only one of subtle emphasis, because, as Thorndike mentioned, among the identical elements of practical importance for education are general principles [38, p. 359]. But the principles, for Thorndike, tend to be only elements among other more specific facts, and the transfer occurs as specific applications to certain situations. For Judd, on the other hand, generalizations of broad scope, because of their potential widespread transfer value, are of paramount importance in teaching. This idea is indicated in this quotation cited from Van Engen [43]: "A central idea moves of its own accord to application, it seeks opportunity for operation in use to bring other facts into line."

Implicit in the two theories is perhaps another difference. According to the identical-elements theory, when between two learning situations identical elements exist, transfer from the first to the second should occur automatically. As the theory is developed here, however, it will be found that transfer depends upon the development of dynamic generalizations in such organizational sequences that transfer is actively promoted; that is, generalizations which transfer are achievements of learning and teaching. According to Judd [20, pp. 412–413]:

The first and most striking fact which is to be drawn from school experience is that one and the same subject-matter may be employed with one and the same teacher with wholly different effects, according to the mode of presentation. If the lesson is presented in one fashion it will produce a very large transfer; whereas if it is presented in an entirely different fashion it will be utterly barren of results for other phases of mental life. . . . Formalism and lack of transfer turn out to be not characteristics of subjects of instruction, but rather products of the mode of instruction in these subjects.

General support for this statement, incidentally, is also found in research by Thorndike, which revealed that one particular pattern of high school subjects was not appreciably more effective than another in promoting gains in general intellectual efficiency, as measured by an intelligence test [39].

The experimental basis for Judd's first formulation of this theory is historically interesting, and the presentation of this study, done in 1908, will improve our understanding of the theory. Judd writes [21, p. 37]:

In this experiment one group of boys was given a full theoretical explanation of refraction. The other group of boys was left to work out experience without theoretical training. These two groups began practice with the target under twelve inches of water. It is a very striking fact that in the first series of trials the boys who knew the theory of refraction and those who did not gave about the same results. That is, theory seemed to be of no value in the first tests. All of the boys had to learn to use the dart, and theory proved to be no substitute for practice. At this point the conditions were changed. The twelve inches of water were reduced to four. The difference between the groups of boys now came out very strikingly. The boys without theory were very much confused. The practice gained with twelve inches of water did not help them with four inches. Their errors were large and persistent. On the other hand the boys who had the theory fitted themselves to the new condition of four inches very rapidly. Their theory evidently helped them to see the reason why they must not apply the twelve-inch habit to four inches of water.

In a more recent and slightly modified experiment, in which eighth grade boys in three equated groups practiced shooting BB shots at targets first placed 6 inches and then 2 inches under water, Hendrickson and Schroeder [16] attempted to confirm Judd's results. One experimental group studied an elementary explanation of refraction. A second experimental group studied the explanation of refraction and were also explicitly warned that changing the depth of water in the second test would change the amount of refraction. Following Judd's procedure, the principle of refraction was withheld from a third, control group. In this experiment, the amounts of transfer of skill from the 6-inch depth to the 2-inch depth were 34.1 per cent for the control group, 36.5 per cent for the group given an explanation of refraction, and 40.3 per cent for the group given the explanation plus a more specific statement of how it would apply with changes in conditions. Here the principle was of only slight and uncertain advantage. But it is possible that, from a background of the science taught in modern junior high schools, these eighth grade boys in the control group discovered for themselves in the experience at the first depth the equivalent of the principle explicitly taught the experimental groups.

Judd's theory that transfer depends on applications of generalizations has been accepted and elaborated by many writers, and especially by the gestalt, or "insight," theorists. Bayles has proposed an extension of Judd's theory which we shall first illustrate by applying it as an explanation of the experiments of Knight and Grossnickle. We shall then cite further experiments in support of this concept of transfer. Bayles says that transfer depends upon (1) learning generalizations, (2) opportunity for varied applications of the generalizations, and (3) developing a mental set to be interested in and alert to further applications of the generalizations or principles [4].

According to this theory, the pupils in Group B of Knight's experiment did not learn merely how to manipulate, as denominators of fractions specifically, 2, 4, 6, 8, 12, and 24. They learned a principle of fractions: a numerator-over-denominator relationship (N/D). Regardless of the particular numbers used, the denominator indicates the size of the fractional parts and the numerator the number of them. They also learned that in adding or subtracting, the fractions must be changed to those of common denominators, and that this can be accomplished by multiplying both numerators and denominators by the same number without changing the value of the fractions. The varied applications of the N/D principle (and subprinciples), with 2, 4, 6, 8, 12, and 24 each playing the denominator role, led to this generalization. And since, as Knight pointed out, the basic skills of operations with *all* integers had already been acquired, the pupils readily inferred that, since 2, 4, 6, etc., could be denominators of fractions, any other integer (including specifically the untaught fractions) could also be a denominator (or a numerator) of a fraction, and that the same principles of operation would apply to *all* such fractions.

According to this theory of transfer, it should also have been possible with proper teaching to have obtained transfer from mastery of multiplication facts to mastery of their use in division. Multiplication in multiplication problems need not be independent from multiplication in division. According to Swenson [36, pp. 64–66]:

The most significant modern emphasis in regard to the four fundamental processes is that all four are basically processes of regrouping. This generalization, once it is understood, adds meaning to each process at the same time that it simplifies each and the interrelationships of all. . . . Addition and subtraction are opposite processes— putting together and taking apart. Multiplication and division are opposite processes— putting together and taking apart.

Addition and subtraction, continues Swenson, may be applied to unequal-sized groups, while multiplication always deals with equal-sized groups.

In learning well the facts and principles of multiplication and their inter-relationships with the other operations, the "varied applications" of multiplication for the subjects in Grossnickle's experiment should have included both multiplication and division examples. Out of such applications and with encouragement to be alert to and to seek for other possibilities of application, the set to expect to apply multiplication in all sorts of situations should have been developed. As another factor accounting for failure to secure transfer in Grossnickle's experiment, it should be noted that the multiplication facts at the time of the test for transfer had not themselves been well learned. From the point of view of either theory, as was noted in Orata's survey, transfer should be expected to be favorable only when the facts or the principles to be transferred are learned well.

Dynamic Principles of Transfer

For transfer to occur from mastery of activity A to the learning of activity B, the two activities must have some elements in common. But identity of elements, it was learned from Grossnickle's experiment, although necessary, is not a sufficient condition for transfer to occur. Judd's theory of transfer by generalizing seems both a more adequate explanation and a more effective guide to teaching. This theory, as here elaborated, assumes that transfer in learning and teaching depends upon (1) developing generalizations, (2) providing for varied applications of them, and (3) building up mental sets and alertness for continually making new applications of principles learned. Some experimental data have been accumulated supporting these assumptions.

1. Generalizing. Three experiments indicate the value of generalizing in arithmetic. Using four matched groups of 112 each of second grade children, Overman [30] compared four different methods of training them over a period of 15 days on addition of two 2-digit numbers, three 2-digit numbers, and two 2-digit and one 1-digit numbers. In method A, there was no generalizing; the teacher merely showed pupils how to write and add numbers like $45 + 23$, $52 + 32 + 13$, and $24 + 23 + 2$. In method B, requiring generalizing, the teacher showed how and helped pupils to generalize that numbers must be written so that the right-hand column is kept straight. In method C, called "rationalizing," the pupils discussed the principle that only ones can be added to ones and tens to tens, but nothing was said about keeping the right-hand column straight. In method D, employing both generalizing and rationalizing, pupils were helped to conclude that the right-hand column must be kept straight in order to add ones to ones and tens to tens. The percentage of transfer was determined by dividing the number of examples to which effects of training did spread (to untaught examples like $54 + 322 + 2$) by the number to which it might have spread had transfer been complete. The results are shown in Table 7–1.

Table 7–1. Mean Percentage of Transfer in Final Tests for Four Methods (including percentage increase of methods B, C, and D over method A)

Method		Percentage transfer	Increase over A	
			Diff.	D/σ_d
A	Teaching by showing how only...............	59.6		
B	Generalizing rule to keep right column straight	72.4	21.5	3.67
C	Rationalizing on adding ones to ones and tens to tens only.................................	62.8	5.4	.90
D	Generalizing and rationalizing...............	71.8	20.5	3.63

Source: J. R. Overman: *Elem. Sch. J.*, 31: 188, Copyright 1930–1931. Reprinted by permission of the University of Chicago Press.

As this table indicates, learning the principle of adding ones to ones and tens to tens did not produce significantly more transfer than merely "showing how." But both generalizing the rule with respect to the right-hand column and the combination of generalizing and rationalizing did produce significantly greater transfer than method A. The general implication from these results on methods of teaching is that "in addition to teaching any given type of example, we should help the pupils to use it as a basis for generalizing the process" [30, p. 190].

In teaching the 100 addition and 100 subtraction combinations to 1,300 second grade children, Olander [25] had half the classes taught all the combinations and half taught only 55 combinations from each addition and subtraction table. From his results, he concluded that "the ability gained by children on fifty-five simple number combinations in addition and on fifty-five similar combinations in subtraction transferred almost completely to the forty-five remaining simple number combinations in each of the two processes." These results suggest that, when the opportunity is provided, "a child does not learn these combinations as so many separate entities or bonds—but that he probably learns them rather as a system of interrelated experiences" [25, p. 436].

Fig. 7–1. A cooperatively created mural expressing their understanding of "Where Our Daddies Work" makes these children's study of their community more meaningful. (*Courtesy of William M. Stewart School, University of Utah.*)

Luchins has shown the value of an approach emphasizing meaning in arithmetic. Children drilled in arithmetic but lacking understanding could usually give the correct answers when tested on the material on which they had practiced. But when compared to the children taught the processes mechanically, the children who had been led to understand the processes were much superior in assimilating new content [24, cited from 15].

Archer [1], with fifth and seventh grade children, has demonstrated almost complete transfer from learning to spell certain verb forms to correct spelling, without specific study of them, of other, derived forms of these verbs. For example, the subgroup in his experiment who studied "reflect" also spelled correctly "reflects," "reflected," and "reflecting." Subgroups who learned any derived form, such as "reflecting," were found to be able to spell without additional study all the other forms. Similarly, children who at the outset misspelled both "assign" and "consigned," after learning how to spell correctly "assign," could in most instances also now spell "consigned." Sometimes, however, negative transfer occurred; for example, some children who learned to spell "create," "creates," or "created" later spelled "creating" as "createing." The explanation for this marked transfer (mainly in the positive direction) is not offered by Archer. But it is very probably the result of *generalizing*

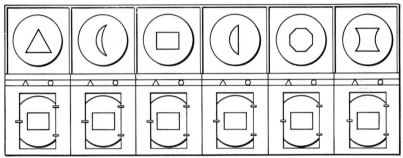

Fig. 7–2. Diagrammatic front view of six two-story boxes arranged for multiple-choice problem solving (Situation IIB, Trial 1). (*From Roberts, K. E.: Univ. Iowa Stud. Child Welf., 7, (3): 31, 1933.*)

from understanding of suffixes and prefixes which these fifth and seventh grade children had learned in previous spelling, language, and reading lessons.

2. *Varied Applications.* As an illustration of the role in determining transfer of varied applications of a principle in different but related problems, Roberts's experiment [33] is especially instructive. Using as subjects 21 preschool and 19 orphanage children ages 3 to 7 and varying in IQ from 80 to 150, she presented to them individually in succession nine different learning problems, all requiring for solution the same principle. Within each group of three problems the variations were slight, while between each two groups of three problems there was a more marked variation.

The 24-by-9-by-5-inch problem box shown in Figure 7–2, consisting of six boxes divided into upper and lower compartments, was used. Through a glass window in each upper compartment, a toy airplane or box containing toys could be seen. On each trial a concealed hook which supported a platform separating one of the upper compartments from its corresponding lower compartment was released. If the door of this particular compartment was opened, the toy above would drop down to the lower compartment, from which it might be secured by the child. The guiding principle to be discovered was that, although the correct door was changed for each trial, it always matched in some identifiable way a cue in the windows above.

The nine different situations included three major variations: I (color), II (form), and III (size). Within each of these major variations there were three minor variations: A, B, and C. In IA, the upper compartments contained six airplanes, all of the same color for any one trial; and each of the doors below was marked with a different color, only one matching the airplanes' color. In IB, there were six airplanes, each of a different color, over six doors, all of the same color, one airplane only matching the doors' color. In IC, both airplanes and doors varied through six colors, only one pair being matched for color. These three subvariations were similarly applied for the form (II) and size (III) series. Figure 7–2, of course, illustrates one trial in the IIB series, in which the six geometrical patterns on the boxes above vary and the patterns on the doors below are all the same, with only the third pair matching in this particular trial. Each successive trial required a response to a different stimulus cue, in a random order which was kept constant for each child. The nine situations were IA, IB, IC, IIA, IIB, IIC, IIIA, IIIB, and IIIC.

The directions were: "See all these airplanes" (pointing to each one), "and see all of these doors" (pointing again). "All of these doors open, but just one door will make an airplane fall so you can get it to play with. You look at all of the airplanes and all of the doors, and then you open one door and see if you can make an airplane fall." For each of the nine situations, 12 trials were given per day and continued until mastery, which was defined as four correct choices in succession.

Because the situations are of approximately equal difficulty as initial problems and because of the counterbalanced order of presentation for the three subgroups, a tendency toward a decrease in the mean number of trials required for each succeeding problem is evidence of transfer from earlier to later problems. In situations (1), (4), and (7), which are the initial problems starting each major variation, the successive means of 36.78, 9.03, and 1.23 indicate transfer through application of the principle to quite radical variations.

But perhaps the most striking indication of transfer, especially in the form of "learning how to learn," as Harlow has expressed it [14, 15], is revealed in Figure 7–3, showing the percentage of children in the two groups who demonstrated immediate mastery of the principle and therefore reached the criterion on the first trial in each of the nine situations. The curves in this figure show that within each major variation after success on an initial problem, increasing percentages of children—with minor fluctuations from situations (4) to (6) for the orphanage children—applied the principle immediately to a related problem. And the increasing percentage of children applying the principle by transfer to the initial problem in each major variation—from color to form to size (or in reversed order) in situations (1), (4), and (7)—shows marked cumulative transfer. This transfer appears to have resulted from varied applications of the principle. Only because the children had experienced application

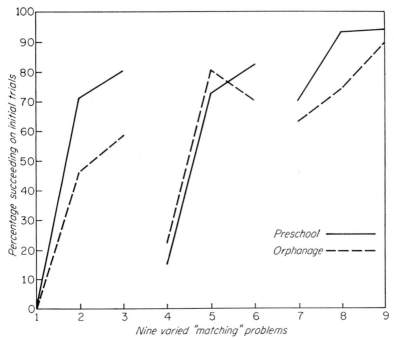

Fig. 7–3. Transfer from varied applications of a principle is indicated by percentages of children successful on first trials in each of nine different situations (for 21 preschool and 19 orphanage children). (*From Roberts, K. E.: Univ. Iowa Stud. Child Welf., 7 [3]: 50, 1933.*)

of the principle, not only to the first series—situations (1), (2), and (3)—but also to a second, quite different series—situations (4), (5), and (6)—could so many of them (about 70 per cent) apply the principle to the new conditions met in situation (7). We see, then, from this experiment that transfer is facilitated by experience with varied applications of principles learned.

Perhaps no concept in transfer is more important than that of learning how to learn. As the child meets, in every phase of his school curriculum, challenging problems with which at first he cannot cope adequately, he discovers that by learning the appropriate concepts and skills he is able to solve them. And as

FIG. 7–4. Through meeting their various needs by independent problem solving, children become resourceful problem solvers. (*Courtesy of William M. Stewart School, University of Utah.*)

he works at developing more effective modes of attack in learning, he becomes better as a learner. The child who learns how to learn effectively becomes skillful and confident in using this approach with numerous problems both in and out of school. As a specific illustration of this concept, let us consider again the 14 independent reports made by a child during her year in the sixth grade, including such topics as "Strange Animals," "Babylonia," "Norse

Myths," "Japanese Architecture," and, finally, "Denmark"— the land of her great-grandparents. By these varied applications of report writing, she learned to do each job more effectively. Each report was intrinsically self-motivated, and the child strove for improvements in each succeeding one. More and better references were sought. Organization was improved. Reports became longer and more elaborated. Artistic illustrations were included, especially in "Japanese Architecture." And increasingly more attention was given to spelling, punctuation, and sentence and paragraph structure. This child learned a generally useful way to learn about any topic which might interest her. When during the summer vacation, the family planned a trip to Canada, she immediately self-initiated a "report" on the country, independently employing the same systematic techniques she had learned to use so skillfully and confidently in school.

3. *A Mental Set for Transfer.* Out of such sequences of learning activities in which principles are applied in varied situations, there should probably emerge inductively a mental set to expect further applications of the principles, such as occurred in the case of the sixth grade child's creative reports. But teachers have also often found children failing to apply appropriate principles they have learned; and some experiments indicate a need for specific teacher-guidance in helping children become alert to opportunities for using the knowledge, skills, and ideals that they know.

It will be recalled that in Hendrickson and Schroeder's repetition of Judd's experiment, only the group who were given both the explanation of refraction and the explicit information on how it would apply to a changed depth of water profited significantly from the principle. Because of this, they wrote that "it is clearly important for a teacher to consider carefully the adaptation of any theoretical statement to the specific needs of the learner" [16, p. 110].

It was also noted that giving the second grade children in Overman's experiment the rationalization that only ones can be added to ones and tens to tens was not sufficient to increase transfer over that induced by merely showing how to add. Improved transfer occurred only when both the rationalization and the explicit principle that added numbers must be written so that the right-hand column is kept straight were given them.

Reed, using college students as subjects, found in his experiment on learning by a trial-and-error or problem-solving approach to name with nonsense syllables different groups of words classifiable by concepts, that the group of subjects who had had included in their preparation for the task a set to employ meaningful concepts learned the tasks more efficiently than the group not thus prepared [31].

Dorsey and Hopkins [7], also using college students as subjects, tested them for transfer of previously acquired pertinent knowledge of and skill in reading comprehension on a vocabulary test of Latin derivatives and on miscellaneous tests to which geometry was thought applicable. The only difference in preparation between control and experimental groups was that before each appropriate test, the experimental group was given these suggestions: (1) "Use the method of study which you have learned in studying the paragraphs," (2) "Use your knowledge of Latin in determining the meanings of words in the test," and (3) "Use your knowledge of descriptive geometry in answering the questions." The control group, although they had had the same prior training, were not thus explicitly directed to apply their knowledge to the tests. Differences on all these transfer tests favoring the group given explicit directions to apply their knowledge were significant.

Two other experiments indicate that ideals transfer only when a set for transfer is developed. Bagley [3] reports an experiment in which a teacher emphasized for third grade children neatness and accuracy in preparation of their arithmetic papers, with consequent improvement in these respects on the arithmetic papers. But measurements revealed no transfer of these ideals to their papers in spelling and language, which subjects had not been mentioned in discussing neatness and accuracy. However, in another experiment by Ruediger [34], neatness was emphasized for one class as an ideal which could be applied with advantage to *all* classes and activities, both in and out of school. With such a set for widespread application of the principle, neatness was improved not only in the class in which it had been emphasized but in other classes as well.

These experiments indicate that building mental sets for transfer—encouraging children to be alert, to expect to find occasions for using concepts, and to seek continually for applications of principles learned—should be a definite teaching objective. But from a series of such discoveries, or verified expectations, there should be developed a general habit, which has often been rewarded, of looking for further applications of principles. Then such explicitness about specific applications as was employed in some of these experiments should not be necessary. Such a habit will be developed best in an integrated curriculum arranged in such sequences that applications for both old and new principles occur continually.

Other Conditions of Transfer: Identical Elements

It has already been demonstrated that the existence of identical elements between activities A and B is not a sufficient condition for expecting transfer to occur from one to the other. But *some similarlity between them is a necessary condition for transfer.* Gates and Taylor [11] demonstrated this transfer principle in an experiment to determine the transfer effect on learning to write (copying letters) of mechanically guided tracing of letters over transparent paper. They used as subjects equated groups of kindergarten children without prior experience in writing. Fourteen children in the writing group were given 14 daily, five-minute guided practice periods in copying letters from models. For the

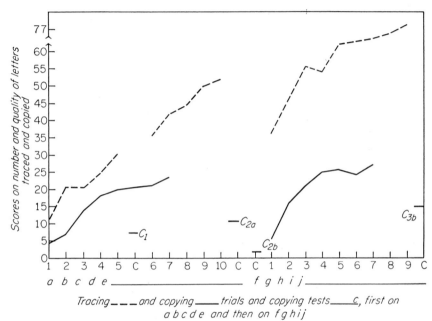

Fɪɢ. 7–5. Transfer from tracing letters to copying letters is shown to be very slight for kindergarten children. (*Adapted from Gates, A. I., and G. Taylor: Teach. Coll. Rec., 24: 459–469, 1923.*)

first seven days they practiced the letters *a, b, c, d, e,* and for the second seven days the letters *f, g, h, i, j.* Twenty-one children in the tracing group practiced for 19 days, including, in sequence, (1) five days of tracing over transparent paper the letters *a, b, c, d, e;* (2) a copying test on these letters; (3) five days more of tracing them; (4) two tests on copying—one on *a, b, c, d, e,* and one on *f, g, h, i, j;* (5) nine days' practice on tracing *f, g, h, i, j;* and (6) a final copying test on *f, g, h, i, j.*

Graphed in Figure 7–5 are the progress curves of both the copying and the tracing groups, as well as certain copying-test scores for the latter group. Scoring for both the copying and the tracing groups was based on the quantity and quality of letters written or traced.

Careful examination of Figure 7–5 yields several interesting conclusions. Progress from practice in tracing letters, which of course is a much easier skill than writing, is much more rapid than the progress made in independent writing (copying). The fourteenth score in tracing is 54, while the fourteenth score in writing is only 26. But the transfer from practice in tracing to writing is extremely meager. After five practice periods on tracing a, b, c, d, e, the copying transfer score is only 8, which score is almost achieved with only two practice periods on copying. And after five days of direct practice in copying, the score is 20. Similarly, after nine practice periods on tracing f, g, h, i, j, the copying score from transfer is only 15, which score is achieved by only two practice periods in copying these letters. Transfer from tracing a, b, c, d, e to tracing f, g, h, i, j is considerable. But this is to be expected because of the close identity between the two tasks. Mechanically guided tracing does not require conceiving the unique features of each letter, as is required in writing them. Therefore, there should be very little difference between tracing a, b, c, d, e and tracing f, g, h, i, and j; both require only following lines. The transfer from *independently* writing a, b, c, d, e to writing f, g, h, i, j, however, is less. Here the dissimilarity is greater, because the writing *does* require conceiving the unique features of five different letters. But there is some transfer from copying a, b, c, d, e to copying f, g, h, i, j: although the first day's score on f, g, h, i, j is only one point higher than the first day's score on a, b, c, d, e, after three days' practice on f, g, h, i, j, the score achieved on a, b, c, d, e only after seven days is reached.

On the whole, of course, the experiment demonstrates that practice in tracing letters is a very poor way of learning to write. Three periods in direct-copying practice results in as much improvement in writing as is achieved by 19 days of tracing. But why doesn't tracing transfer to writing? The answer seems to be simply that these processes have very little in common. Writing is largely a conceptual-perceptual process, and tracing is largely a motor process. There seem to be few if any pertinent applications to be made from tracing to writing.

Even though considerable transfer within and between learning activities is often demonstrated, whenever the teaching of skills such as writing, arithmetic, reading, or spelling is approached through an ancillary process, the transfer value of the indirect approach needs to be carefully analyzed or checked experimentally. Gates [10] has also evaluated the use of flash-card exercises as an ancillary approach to improving comprehension and speed of reading. Using equated groups of first through fourth grade children, he compared the reading progress of a group trained directly in silent reading with that of a group whose training was supplemented over a period of six weeks with daily, 10-minute flash-card exercises. Gains were greater for the group who practiced on "regular" reading material, without the flash cards. Flash-card reading (in which, among other differences, there is no reliance on context) has so little in common with meaningful reading that the identical elements necessary for transfer are lacking. Such an ancillary approach to reading and spelling as systematic training in phonetic and visual analysis of words, however, apparently does have transfer value [19, 37].

Some specific concepts or skills recur so frequently as identical elements in so many different situations that to search them out for initial and special emphasis in teaching creates an opportunity for very effective application of this transfer principle. Examples of such concepts and skills are Rinsland's basic vocabulary of elementary school children [32]; Dolch's "basic sight vocabulary," which consists of 220 words likely to occur with very high frequency in primary school children's reading [6]; Kyte and Neel's core vocabulary of the 501 words which children are most likely to need to spell [23]; and Osburn and Sheldon's inventory of syllables and root words which recur with high frequency in words children are likely to spell [29].

Kyte and Neel [23] have pointed out the high frequency of certain words that children write. For example, they note that the 500 most frequent words in Rinsland's list account for 82 per cent of the total words that elementary school children write. Using both the Rinsland list and Horn's *A Basic Writing Vocabulary* [17] (as used by adults), they have derived a core vocabulary of the 501 spelling words which children are most likely to need both as children and as adults. Teaching this list early to all children should prepare them for many of their writing needs in school. For mentally retarded children or for other children who have difficulty in learning to spell, the list is a manageable and useful list of minimum essentials. But mastery of the list, besides having transfer value in wide applications, also should result in transfer through generalizing. If spelling is taught according to transfer principles, generalizations learned in studying these 501 words should lead to ready mastery of additional words. For example, "men" and "send" are in the list; from learning these, children should by generalizing also be able to spell "mend," "lend," "tend," etc.

Osburn [28] has also adapted the Rinsland word list for effective application of the transfer principle of identical elements. In the 9,000 polysyllabic words in the list there are about 23,000 syllables. But if the 45 key syllables presented in Table 7–2 are mastered, pupils who have had guidance in recognizing these syllables as identical elements in other words will be able to learn from transfer most of the other words in the list. For example, if in learning to spell "going," "morning," "playing," and "counting," the children generalize that the final syllable (or suffix, in this instance) is always spelled "-ing," they will be able to spell this part of 877 other words in the Rinsland list which end in "-ing."

Table 7–2. A Diagnostic Test in Syllabication for Reading and Spelling
(Based on frequency of occurrence of syllables in words in Rinsland's Word List)

Initial syllable	Frequency	Medial syllable	Frequency	Final syllable	Frequency
1. re-ceived	209	1. an-i-mals	277	1. go-ing	881
2. in-to	203	2. Jan-u-a-ry	161	2. start-ed	338
3. a-round	149	3. sev-er-al	131	3. moth-er	323
4. de-cid-ed	146	4. dec-o-rat-ed	107	4. on-ly	290
5. con-tains	145	5. af-ter-noon	81	5. hous-es	212
6. ex-cept	141	6. el-e-phant	79	6. va-ca-tion	210
7. un-til	99	7. pe-ri-od	75	7. ver-y	193
8. com-mon	95	8. reg-u-lar	72	8. pret-ty	95
9. dis-cov-ered	82	9. In-di-an	56	9. re-al	84
10. en-joy	81	10. won-der-ful	44	10. ta-ble	82
11. an-oth-er	68	11. car-ni-val	40	11. af-ter	75
12. o-pen	65	12. gym-na-si-um	40	12. base-ment	73
13. e-ven	63	13. ar-ti-cle	40	13. sto-ry	69
14. pro-gram	58	14. ear-li-est	35	14. larg-est	65
15. ac-ci-dent	56	15. o-ver-alls	34	15. sev-en	48
Total	1,660	Total	1,272	Total	3,038

Source: J. W. Osburn: "Teaching spelling by teaching syllables and root words," *Elem. Sch. J.*, 55: 32–41, Copyright 1954. Reprinted by permission of the University of Chicago Press.

Other Conditions of Transfer: Practice plus Guidance

Practice alone, like the mere existence of identical elements, is not a sufficient condition for transfer. This is not surprising, of course, since it has already been demonstrated that practice without operation of the other conditions of learning produces no improvement. Three experiments together show that transfer depends *both* upon practice *and* upon either teacher-guidance or pupil self-guidance in the discovery and mastery of more effective modes of problem solving and learning.

In the interim between a variety of "before" and "after" memory tests, Sleight [35] had three subgroups of 21 sixth standard pupils each practice memorizing, with another 21 children being used as a control group. Group 1, the control group, did not practice. Group 2 listened as the experimenter read poetry and repeated it after him line by line. Group 3 listened as the experimenter read tables of number combinations and repeated them after him part by part. For Group 4, prose selections were read twice, after which the children wrote what they could remember of them. No teacher-guidance on methods of memorizing was given, and the stereotyped direction of the practice permitted little pupil initiative in discovering more effective procedures. It is not surprising, therefore, to find that on the various postpractice memory tests, gains beyond those made by the no-practice control group were neither consistent nor significant.

Woodrow [47] has also investigated the possibility of improving proficiency in memorizing. He tested and retested his subjects on memorizing poetry, prose, facts, dates, vocabulary, and digits. Using one-third of his subjects as a control group, he had a second group practice memorizing poetry and nonsense syllables without teacher-guidance. A third group was given, on the same material, practice plus teacher-guidance in effective memorizing techniques, such as learning by wholes, emphasizing meaning, employing active self-recitation, and use of rhythm and grouping. Comparing the gains from pre-tests to end-tests, Woodrow also found, as Sleight had, that those of the practice group did not exceed those of the control group. But on all six memory tests, the group given guidance in effective memorizing techniques made substantially greater gains than those made by both the practice-only and the control groups.

Winch [46], using equated groups of children, had one group memorize and reproduce in writing 100-word passages of poetry on four different days separated by three- or four-day intervals, while a control group spent the same periods in arithmetic problem solving. Comparison of the memorization scores on passages of history and geography in tests administered to both groups before and after the practice periods revealed small but significantly greater gains for the group who memorized poetry. Since practice as mere repetition does not result in either improvement in the function practiced or transfer, and since there was no teacher-guidance, how is this transfer from poetry to prose to be explained? It has already been noted that Winch's subjects in another experiment [Chapter 4, p. 122] discovered for themselves better ways of memorizing; and, compared with the stereotyped procedures imposed by Sleight, the greater freedom of approach allowed in this experiment should likewise have permitted improvement from pupil self-guided experience. Moreover, that improvement did occur from the poetry memorizing is implicit in Winch's conclusion: "Improvement, gained by practice in memorizing one subject of instruction [poetry], is transferred to memory work in other subjects [history and geography] whose nature is certainly diverse from that in which the improvement was gained" [46, p. 293]. As an explanation of the transfer found here, it seems plausible to assume that these children, on the basis of self-guided experience in memorizing poetry, discovered generally better memorizing procedures, which they applied to both the poetry and the prose.

Among the factors influencing transfer which Orata found from his review of experiments, we have thus far dealt with organization of content and methods of learning. But Orata also considered the nature of the learner an important factor; more maturity and higher intelligence being favorable to transfer.

Intelligence as a Factor Influencing Transfer

Since both an examination of intelligence-test items and a consideration of definitions of intelligence reveal an emphasis upon abstract reasoning, on generalizing, and on use of symbols to represent ideas and relationships [8], it is not surprising to discover that bright children tend to transfer their learning more effectively than do dull or even average children. The results from Carroll's experiment [5] may be considered representative of the findings on the relation of intelligence to transfer. Carroll studied "the comparative ability of bright and dull children to generalize" through a classification of the errors they made as they attempted to spell unfamiliar words. To 100 "bright" (mean IQ: 124.9) and to 100 "dull" (mean IQ: 92.0) children in three homogeneously grouped sections, each made up of fourth and fifth grade children, were dictated 318 words (50 per session) taken from spelling lists with grade placements one year in advance of the children's actual grades.

Out of a total of 62,431 words spelled, there were 32,000 spelling errors, which were classified to show the nature of spelling errors made by bright and by dull children. A careful examination of this classification shows that errors of all kinds are made by both bright and dull children. However, bright children tend to make fewer errors, and their errors are more often "reasonable" from the point of view of transfer principles. Bright children tend to make relatively more errors of doubling single letters (as "advise" spelled "addvise"), of using a single in place of a double letter (as "rabbit" spelled "rabit"), and of substituting or transposing single letters (as "fairly" spelled "fariely"). Dull children exceed the bright children in errors of adding, of omitting, of substituting groups of letters, and of substituting entire words—either synonyms or wholly irrelevant words (such as writing "boat" for "picture"). Such rare sheer guessings as writing "rszilon" for "defeated" are also produced more often by dull children.

In general, the errors of bright children relatively more often involve phonetic transfer; the dull children's errors are relatively more erratic. According to Carroll, "it appears that phonetic generalization is the dominating factor in the psychology of differences in degree in the kinds of spelling errors made by bright and dull children." The bright child, in other words, possesses in greater degree ability for translating sounds into letters [5, p. 499].

But our findings that bright children generalize more effectively than do dull children do not justify the conclusion that generalizing is for the bright child and rote memorization for the dull child. Although the dull child achieves generalizations more slowly and with greater difficulty, and although some abstract principles are beyond his comprehension, as a method of teaching for both the dull and the bright, to emphasize meanings, to lead to generalizations of principles, is the most effective approach to learning. And it should be noted from Carroll's experiment that both groups misspelled words by misapplying phonetic principles and that both groups also failed to apply them. But since the dull child generalizes less easily, he will need more and simpler, concrete inductive experiences as a basis for his generalizing. Abstract levels of reasoning will need to be approached more slowly. He will need more varied applications of principles and more explicit guidance as to when and how to adapt them for new applications.

Illustrations of Transfer in Teaching

This review of experiments and theories on transfer has yielded three dynamic and two supplementary principles, namely, that transfer depends upon (1) generalizing; (2) varied applications of these generalizations or principles; (3) building a mental set for transfer; (4) the existence of "common elements" or of the potentiality for relevant applications; and (5) teacher-guidance—either direct or by providing for pupil self-guidance—which leads to discovery of more effective work methods applicable to both the original learning and, by transfer, to other activities.

Unifying Concepts in Arithmetic. As one good application in the teaching of these principles, Van Engen's [43 and 44] illustrations of "unifying ideas" in arithmetic may be cited. As an example of a "central idea [which] moves of its own accord to application, [which] seeks opportunity for operation in use to bring other facts into line," he uses the arithmetic concept that "the product of two numbers equals a third," or, stated arithmetically, $N_1 = N_2 \times N_3$. This same concept extends as a unifying idea in problem solving from the primary grades through high school, as indicated in the following sequence:

1. Long division: $34 \times N = 563$. (N is the symbol here for the unknown number.)

2. Fractions: $\frac{2}{3}$ of what number is 15? $\frac{2}{3} \times N = 15$.

3. Area of a rectangle: $L \times W = N$ (area), $N \times W = A$, $L \times N = A$.

4. Percentage: 16 per cent of $48 =$ what? $0.16 \times 48 = N$, (or other variations).

5. Variations of principles in grades 7 and 8: $C = \pi D$, $I = PR$, $I = PRT$, $A = BH/2$, commission = rate times amount of sales, discount = rate times selling price, denominate numbers, $D = RT$.

6. Algebraic equations (grade 9).

In this sequence of arithmetic problems, children would discover (under teacher-guidance) that a very great variety of problems, when stated arithmetically according to the suggestions on problem solving given in Chapter 4, all reduce to the familiar pattern: "$N_1 = N_2 \times N_3$." And if either N_2 or N_3 should be the unknown, it can be found by dividing N_1 (the product) by N_2 or N_3 (the known factor).

Among many other applications in the elementary school curriculum, the principles of phonetics, as applied to both reading and spelling, illustrate well the economy of emphasizing transfer in teaching.

Phonetics in Spelling. Hanna and Moore [13] have explained how, in both the organization of words within the spelling curriculum and the method of teaching spelling, the principle of transfer contributes to an important extent to learning efficiency. "If the child is taught, beginning with the simplest sound-symbol patterns, to relate sound and written symbol, he will soon be able to arrive inductively (to generalize) at the spelling of most of the words that he can pronounce. This ability to transfer from one word to another the knowledge of phonetic patterns which are similar is what we call 'spelling power' " [13, p. 337].

Children need to learn to spell the words of highest frequency in the writing *and* speaking vocabularies of adults and children; and if these words can emerge (in part) from lessons in social studies, literature, and science, spelling will be better motivated and applied. But from the point of view of transfer principles, such words need to be graded and organized so that "principles rather than individual words" will be emphasized [13, p. 334]:

Materials properly graded would present, in the early years of instruction, primarily those words in which the phonemes [phonetic units, such as "p," "i," and "n" in "pin"] have a high degree of spelling consistency, in order to develop accurate responses to those speech sounds which are of relatively high spelling reliability. This grading of instructional materials would further present, in later periods of instruction, irregular spellings of words in groups according to their deviation from the [phonetic] principles of the English language.

This is possible because, as Hanna and Moore report that their study reveals, many spelling principles, despite many phonetic imperfections [18], have a high degree of consistency [13, pp. 333–334]:

> Approximately four-fifths of the phonemes contained in words comprising the spelling vocabulary of the elementary school child are represented by regular spelling. Nearly three-fourths of the vowel phonemes are spelled by their regular letter representations from about 57 per cent to about 99 per cent of the times they occur. . . . The single consonant phonemes . . . are represented by their regular spellings about nine tenths of the times they occur. The phonemes b, d, g (hard), h, i, m, n, p, r, t are either spelled only by the single letter representing the sound or by the doubled letter representing the sound [the latter occurring with a frequency of less than 1 per cent].

As for method, assuming that the words to be taught are in the child's oral or reading vocabularies and are also words that he will be likely to need in written expression, Hanna and Moore have four suggestions: (1) The child must hear and pronounce the word correctly. (2) "By selecting from the child's spoken vocabulary [groups of] simple words that begin or end with the same sound, and by helping him note that we use the same symbol to write this sound, we aid the child to arrive inductively at a generalization about translating the sound into a symbol" [13, p. 336]. Such generalizations are expected to transfer to other words, making it possible for a child to spell, on occasions when they are needed, words he may not have been taught specifically. (3) "Care must be taken to avoid giving the child the impression that the 'right' or only way to spell speech sounds is the regular spelling. Our efforts throughout must be to give him a sense of word patterns—a feeling for both the consistencies and the inconsistencies in the phonetic structure of our language" [13, p. 336]. (4) The relatively few inconsistently spelled words which the child needs must be individually memorized.

To illustrate more specifically the transfer application of phonetic principles, consider how children may learn to combine the consistently spelled consonant phonemes with groups of words ending in the same sound and in the process deduce generalizations which lead to "spelling power." After children have learned from reading and spelling experiences to translate the regular consonants *b, d, g, h, l, m, n, p, r,* and *t* into their sounds as a means of identifying and reading words in their oral vocabulary, and to translate these sounds into their symbols in writing, they are ready to learn to spell such a group of words as "bate," "hate," "mate," and "late." In studying these words, they are led to note that the ending, "-ate", is the same for all these words. By combining the proper symbols for the initial sounds of these different words with "-ate," they spell them correctly. From this generalization and from the above four varied applications of the principle, the children should then be able to transfer the principle to the spelling of "date," "gate," etc. As another variation of the principle at the same level, the spelling of "able," "cable," "table," and "fable" might be undertaken. From these experiences, along with more marked variations of the general principle (as in different groups including "sat," "pad," "met," "riddle," "time," "tune," "jump," etc.), a broader generalization about spelling words or parts of words with different endings should emerge.

Besides learning to spell by transfer additional words within a group, because of the cumulative effects of transfer, the children are also learning *how to learn* to spell efficiently. Later it may be noted that even the exceptions have some consistency. For example, *c* (hard) may be represented by *c* (as in "cat" and "cattle") or by *k* (as in "kit," "kitten," and "kettle"). And the *n* sound is sometimes preceded by *k* (as in "knit," "knife," and "knot"), or even by *p* (as in "pneumonia" and "pneumatic"). But such variations are not frequent in the elementary school child's vocabulary. When they do occur, they should be taught according to suggestions (3) or (4) above from Hanna and Moore.

Transfer Principles in Reading. Artley [2], with greater emphasis on broader and more variable generalizations, explains how transfer may be applied to teaching modes of attack in identifying unfamiliar words in reading. He applies the concept that general principles transfer more effectively than identical piecemeal elements to the evaluation of methods for developing competence in word perception in reading. As techniques for perceiving or identifying unfamiliar words, excessive single-letter phonics (as sounding "dance" as "du-a-n-ts-e"), rote emphasis upon word families, and the practice of looking "mechanically" for "little words in big words" (as finding in "washer" "was-her" or "w-as-her") are all found inefficient because they tend toward a piecemeal approach, resulting in numerous exceptions where these methods ought to but do not apply. Instead of too much piecemeal analysis into constant word elements, Artley thinks transfer will be greater by applying phonetic and visual analysis of unfamiliar words to larger, more meaningful units. Always the meaning context is to be relied upon, both for perceiving unfamiliar words and for checking (through perception of effects) the validity of word-analysis techniques. Moreover, initially the child's attention should be "on the word whole rather than on some phonetic unit." Recognizing that phonetic or visual word elements may have various sounds and meanings in different words, a child checks a provisional word interpretation against the context to see if it makes sense; if it does not, he will try another sound or meaning. Applying these principles of context and of variability of sounds and meanings for the same word elements, the child who analyzes "washer" as "was-her" in the sentence: "Mother put the dirty clothes in the washer" will try again, eventually arriving at "wash-er."

As a part of this generalizing approach, such word-analysis techniques as "the consonant substitution procedure" (suggested above for spelling), "looking for meaning units and/or syllables in words," certain "vowel principles," and mastery of initial consonant sounds are found helpful. Using the substitution procedure, "making mental substitutions of elements makes possible the working-out of a whole group of words from one known word." For example, if a child recognizes "make" but not "take" and observes that they are similar in form, "by a process of mentally substituting the sound of *t* for the sound of *m*, he identifies the unfamiliar word as *take*." In analyzing words into meaning units and/or syllables, the child "is learning to search for elements which not only will help him to understand the meaning of a word but will also furnish a key to unlocking its pronunciation." Seeing the root "wash" and the suffix "er" in "washer" illustrates this technique. Other examples are finding "butter" and "fly" in the compound word "butterfly," "boy" in the plural "boys," and the familiar root "jump" in the variants "jumps," "jumping," and "jumped." Recognizing a prefix, suffix, or ending, such as "-s," "-er," "-ing," and "-ed," the child learns (generalizes) to look for familiar roots as a key to identifying the word. As an example of a vowel principle which would make possible "unlocking of words like *take*, *time*, and *refuse*," Artley mentions that "if a word or syllable ends in an *e* preceded by another vowel, the first vowel is usually long and the final *e* is silent." Such rules would, of course, be developed gradually and inductively, as generalizations by the children under teacher-guidance.

Conclusions on How to Teach for Transfer

As has been demonstrated by experiments and illustrated by several teaching examples, transfer of training is a powerful teaching concept. By application of transfer principles, the learner profits in two important ways. He applies in each new problem or learning undertaking as many as are pertinent of his already acquired generalizations. And very often he can simplify otherwise complex and multiple-element tasks by reducing them to the repeated application of a few unifying principles. In general, this review has shown that transfer depends upon the nature of the content to be learned, on the methods of teaching, and on the nature of the learner. From the experiments and theories on transfer the following practical teaching principles are derived:

1. In one important sense, transfer depends upon there being "identical elements" between the transfer content and the areas of applications. Tracing letters does not transfer to learning to write because these functions have so little in common. Visual and phonetic analysis of words, however, *are* applicable to both spelling and reading. As Thorndike himself mentioned, the most significant common elements for education are principles. As one way of promoting transfer, the organization and sequential arrangement of the curriculum should be such that principles learned will have continual and increasingly wider application.

2. Even though relationships for potential transfer exist, it will not occur automatically; the method of teaching must be directed toward securing transfer. Practice alone is not sufficient; teacher-guidance toward efficient work methods is also necessary.

3. Transfer depends upon the mastery of general principles. Such principles will be developed by emphasizing meaning, by studying and organizing experiences inductively for the purpose of arriving at generalizations, and by looking for the interrelationships among ideas and techniques.

4. If the general principles learned are to transfer to new situations in which they are appropriate, practice should be on varied applications of the principles in the initial mastery of them. Only by applying a principle to different kinds of situations will the nature of a principle be understood, namely, that it is an idea which is not limited to a specific situation. And from a sufficient number of varied applications of a principle there should often emerge the set to expect even further applications.

5. But the experiments have indicated that the emergence of this set to be alert to new applications of principles cannot be left to chance. By suitable sequential arrangements of content and by methods of teaching which encourage initiative and reward efforts at applying previously learned principles in meeting new problems, children should be made alert to and develop the habit of seeking for new applications and extensions or adaptations of previously learned principles.

6. As with other phases of learning, attention to individual differences in maturity, intelligence, and pattern of abilities will be necessary for effective

learning. But this does not mean that only bright children should be encouraged to generalize. On the contrary, emphasis on transfer through generalizing is equally important for the dull child. He will need in his generalizing, however, more and simpler kinds of concrete inductive experiences. And it should be recognized that some generalizations may be beyond some children.

7. Transfer of training as a condition of learning will be effective only when provision is also made for effective application of the other six essential conditions of learning.

Review and Applications

1. What two general features of transfer of training explain the way it facilitates learning efficiency?

2. Compare the "identical-elements" and the "generalization" theories of transfer.

3. Cite some of the evidence or examples to show that transfer in learning depends upon (1) generalizing, (2) experiencing varied applications of the generalizations, (3) an expectation to make transfer applications, (4) the potentiality for relevant applications, and (5) teacher- or self-guidance in more effective methods.

4. Why is "learning how to learn" one of the most important applications of transfer principles?

5. Why, despite the fact that bright children achieve generalizations more effectively than do dull children, should transfer principles be emphasized in teaching both dull and bright children?

6. From reading about or observing an example of effective teaching, point out the application of as many transfer principles as you can find.

References

1. Archer, C. P.: *Transfer of Training in Spelling*, University of Iowa Studies in Education, 5(5): 1–62, 1930.

2. Artley, A. S.: "Pattern versus principle in developing competence in word perception," *Elem. Sch. J.*, 51: 147–151, Copyright, 1951, by the University of Chicago. Reprinted by permission of the University of Chicago Press.

3. Bagley, W. C.: *Educational Values*, Macmillan, New York, 1911.

4. Bayles, E. E.: "An unemphasized factor in current theories regarding the transfer of training," *J. Educ. Psychol.*, 27: 425–430, 1936.

5. Carroll, H. A.: "Generalization of bright and dull children: A comparative study with special reference to spelling," *J. Educ. Psychol.*, 21: 489–499, 1930.

6. Dolch, E. W.: "A basic sight vocabulary," *Elem. Sch. J.*, 36: 456–460, 1936.

7. Dorsey, Mattie F., and L. T. Hopkins: "The influence of attitudes upon transfer," *J. Educ. Psychol.*, 21: 410–417, 1930.

8. Garrett, H. E.: "A developmental theory of intelligence," *Amer. Psychologist*, 1: 372–378, 1946.

9. ———: "Transfer of training," in *Great Experiments in Psychology*, Appleton-Century-Crofts, New York, 1941.

10. Gates, A. I.: "Functions of flash-card exercises in reading: An experimental study," *Teach. Coll. Rec.* 27: 311–321, 1925.

11. ———, and G. Taylor: "Acquisition of motor control in writing by pre-school children," *Teach. Coll. Rec.*, 24: 459–469, 1923.

12. Grossnickle, F. E.: "Transfer of knowledge of multiplication facts to their use in long division," *J. Educ. Res.*, 29: 677–685, 1936.

13. Hanna, P. R., and J. T. Moore: "Spelling—from spoken word to written symbol," *Elem. Sch. J.*, 53: 329–337, Copyright, 1953, by the University of Chicago. Reprinted by permission of the University of Chicago Press.

14. Harlow, H. F.: "The formation of learning sets," *Psychol. Rev.*, 56: 51–65, 1949.

15. ———: "Thinking," in H. Helson (ed.) : *Theoretical Foundations of Psychology*, Van Nostrand, New York, 1951.

16. Hendrickson, G., and W. W. Schroeder: "Transfer of training in learning to hit a submerged target," *J. Educ. Psychol.*, 32: 205–213, 1941.

17. Horn, E.: *A Basic Writing Vocabulary*, University of Iowa Monographs in Education, ser. 1, no. 4, 1926.

18. ———: "A source of confusion in spelling," *J. Educ. Res.*, 19: 47–55, 1929.

19. Hudson, J. S., and Lola Toler: "Instruction in auditory and visual discrimination as a means of improving spelling," *Elem. Sch. J.*, 49: 466–469, 1949.

20. Judd, C. H.: *Psychology of High-school Subjects*, Ginn, Boston, 1915.

21. ———: "The relations of special training to general intelligence," *Educ. Rev.*, 36: 28–42, 1908.

22. Knight, F. B.: "Transfer within a narrow mental function," *Elem. Sch. J.*, 24: 780–788, Copyright, 1924, by the University of Chicago. Reprinted by permission of the University of Chicago Press.

23. Kyte, G. C., and V. M. Neel: "A core vocabulary of spelling words," *Elem. Sch. J.*, 54: 29–34, 1953.

24. Luchins, A. S.: "Mechanization in problem-solving: The effect of Einstellung," *Psychol. Monogr.*, vol. 54, no. 248, 1942.

25. Olander, H. T.: "Transfer of learning in simple addition and subtraction," *Elem. Sch. J.*, 31: 358–369 and 427–437, Copyright, 1931, by the University of Chicago. Reprinted by permission of the University of Chicago Press.

26. Orata, P. T.: "Recent research studies on transfer of training with implications for the curriculum, guidance, and personnel work," *J. Educ. Res.*, 35: 81–101, 1941.

27. ———: "The transfer of training and educational pseudoscience," *Math. Teacher*, 28: 265–289, 1935.

28. Osburn, W. J.: "Teaching spelling by teaching syllables and root words," *Elem. Sch. J.*, 55: 32–41, Copyright, 1954, by the University of Chicago. Reprinted by permission of the University of Chicago Press.

29. ———, and C. J. Sheldon: *A Syllabic Inventory*, University of Washington Book-store, Seattle, 1954.

30. Overman, J. R.: "An experimental study of the effect of the method of instruction on transfer of training in arithmetic," *Elem. Sch. J.*, 31: 183–190, Copyright, 1930–1931, by the University of Chicago. Reprinted by permission of the University of Chicago Press.

31. Reed, H. B.: "Factors influencing the learning and retention of concepts, I.: The influence of set," *J. Exp. Psychol.*, 36: 71–87, 1946.

32. Rinsland, H. D.: *A Basic Vocabulary of Elementary School Children*, Macmillan, New York, 1945.

33. Roberts, Katherine E.: *Learning in Preschool and Orphanage Children; An Experimental Study of Ability to Solve Different Situations According to the Same Plan*, University of Iowa Studies in Child Welfare, 7(3): 1–94, 1933.

34. Ruediger, W. C.: "Indirect improvement of mental functions through ideals," *Educ. Rev.*, 36(4): 364–371, 1908.

35. Sleight, W.: "Memory and formal training," *Brit. J. Psychol.*, 4: 386–457, 1911.

36. Swenson, Esther J.: "Arithmetic for preschool and primary-grade children." *The Teaching of Arithmetic*. 50th Yearbook of the Nat. Soc. Stud. Educ., Part II. Chicago, Distributed by the University of Chicago Press, 1951.

37. Templin, Mildred C.: "Phonic knowledge and its relation to spelling and reading achievement of fourth grade pupils," *J. Educ. Res.*, 47: 441–454, 1947.

38. Thorndike, E. L.: *Educational Psychology*, vol. II, *The Psychology of Learning*, Teachers College, Columbia University, New York, 1914.

39. ———: "Mental discipline in high school studies," *J. Educ. Psychol.*, 15: 1–22 and 83–98, 1924.

40. ———, and R. S. Woodworth: "The influence of improvement in one mental function upon the efficiency of other functions, I." *Psychol. Rev.*, 8: 247–261, 1901.

41. ———: "The influence of improvement in one mental function upon the efficiency of other functions, II." *Psychol. Rev.*, 8: 384–395, 1901.

42. ———: "The influence of improvement in one mental function upon the efficiency of other functions, III." *Psychol. Rev.*, 8: 553–564, 1901.

43. Van Engen, H.: "An aspect of meaning in arithmetic," *Elem. Sch. J.*, 46: 272–277, 1946.

44. ———: "Unifying ideas in arithmetic instruction," *Elem. Sch. J.*, 42: 291–296, 1941.

45. Webb, L. W.: "Transfer of learning," in C. E. Skinner (ed.): *Educational Psychology*, Prentice-Hall, Englewood Cliffs, N.J., 1951.

46. Winch, W. H.: "The transfer of improvement in memory in school children," *Brit. J. Psychol.*, 2: 284–293, 1906–1908.

47. Woodrow, H.: "The effect of type of training upon transference," *J. Educ. Psychol.*, 18: 160–171, 1927.

Chapter 8

Motivation and Learning

L ISTEN," SAID seven-year-old Gerald; and as his classmates became quiet, the "chr-r-r, chr-r-r" sound came again. Their curiosity was aroused by the strange sound. Guided both by their previously learned ideas of searching and by the almost constant sound, the children undertook "a short and extremely quiet search which led to the discovery of a big black cricket" [18]. "He makes a lot of noise," observed Gerald. "I wonder how he does it?" questioned Gary. Alert to the interest the cricket aroused in these second grade children, their teacher channeled it toward further problem-solving experiences by her direction, "Let's find out." This science interest, as it was encouraged and expanded, sustained and directed the learning efforts of these children for a "couple of months of insect study." From observing the cricket in a glass jar, Gerald was led to conclude, "When he moves his wings he makes his noise." The children's well-motivated study included experimenting, field trips, collecting a variety of insects, some dissecting, and the use of books as references. The answer to Sue's question: "Can a cricket hear?" for example, was found in a book, which informed the children "that a cricket's ears are on his knees." Because of the satisfying consequences to which they led, such problem-solving methods would be further reinforced for these children as procedures for satisfying their curiosity and interests.

Motives Defined

This example illustrates how motives, as internal conditions, arouse, sustain, direct, and determine the intensity of learning efforts, and also define the satisfying or unsatisfying consequences of goal-directed trials. Motives, however, are themselves modified by learning, as is suggested in the example. In the beginning they lack direction and specific associations with environmental objects. James was probably right in describing the newborn's perspective of his world of stimuli as a big, blooming, buzzing confusion. At first, motives merely arouse the infant to activity; but upon his experiencing (and learning) the consequences of motivated activity, the behavior becomes goal-directed. The hungry infant soon learns to direct his behavior toward the breast or bottle which he has discovered satisfies his need. On the basis of such experiences, motives acquire direction and attachments to goals. They become motive-incentive conditions. "Incentives" are the goal conditions or situations which the child has learned will satisfy his internal motivating conditions. Teachers usually provide incentives which appeal to children's motives and which may be attained as a result of learning effort. Both teaching experiences and experiments have shown that passive, perfunctory participation in an activity, or mere repetition of it, does not result in improvement; efficient learning requires high and sustained effort. It should be recognized therefore that attention to motive-incentive conditions is an important teaching function.

Classroom Illustrations of "Good" Motivation

Teachers consider appeals to curiosity, novelty, and interests effective motives. Interests of children are aroused, they report, in a lush environment, such as is found in nature trips; visits to a store, farm, factory, park, garden, or museum; care of pets; experimentation; dramatizations; and such projects as the earlier-mentioned diet experiment. Television and radio programs may arouse interest in topics and projects to be pursued further in school. Seasonal activities provide interest themes. The Thanksgiving holiday, for example, may motivate civic appreciation and the study of history integrated with language, drama, art, and music.

One teacher found an approach combining novelty with an already developed interest in a community activity especially effective. She motivated the reading activities of second grade children by suggesting that they build a setting for a motion-picture show. The children drew pictures and, with the teacher's help, wrote scripts for each one. Pasted together on a long roll, the pictures and

FIG. 8–1. Interest in creative activities has sustained these children through identifying, splatter-painting, labeling, and now using as classroom decoration leaves collected on an excursion to a park. (*Courtesy of Adams School, Logan, Utah.*)

scripts were arranged to tell a story. "The children were fascinated with this device and loved nothing better than to give a show, taking delight over the privilege of turning the crank that unfolded the roll and being especially pleased at each scene that they themselves had helped to create."

Interests may be especially impelling when they are related to significant community goals, as for example, a concrete study of possibilities for community beautification or for improved employment opportunities in the children's own community.

Teachers also report that creating situations for significant uses of what is being studied constitutes effective motivation. According to one teacher, "One of the best ways to motivate handwriting practice is to give the children a real job that needs to be done, such as writing letters, being the teacher's secretary, or writing notices for the school's bulletin board." Another teacher changed a boy-scout troop's indifference to their activities to enthusiasm for them by appealing to interest and usefulness as a combination of motives. Capitalizing on the already developed interests of these boys in overnight camping, the teacher motivated them to learn how to identify plants; to identify and to understand the habits and habitats of birds and other animals in the area; and to learn how to take care of their food and safety needs while camping—all in anticipation of using these concepts and skills on a camping trip they had planned at the outset. Besides the motive satisfactions in anticipation, enjoyment of the adventure itself, which was enhanced by their new knowledge and skills, reinforced this approach to learning.

Another motivation concept mentioned by some teachers is that of relating the specific behavior of children to their self-concepts or to self-identifications in which they can experience enhanced values. The experience of "enhanced value" is apparent in Judy's development of a new self-concept. Success in reading and arithmetic had not been among her accomplishments. "Suddenly, on her own, she struggled with the compact style of arithmetic problems, and her exultant feeling" of enhanced self-evaluation from her success is apparent in her comment: "Look at these problems. I think I know how to read each one and can work them. I did two. Are they right?" [13].

Another teacher, recalling her own experience as a child, thinks that the first basis for achieving real self-confidence came from attaining her desire to play in the school orchestra. In her experience there are indications of both identification with loved persons and enhanced self-evaluation as motives. As she progressed, she writes, "Gradually I came to feel, because of the approval of the teacher and my parents, that I was able to accomplish something satisfactorily, and I was stimulated beyond words to want to live up to the expectations of my family and teacher, who seemed to have so much confidence in me. And after I was made to feel that I was progressing successfully on my horn, not only did my classroom work improve, but I began to feel that maybe goals that had seemed utterly beyond my reach might be attainable after all."

From such identifications with more mature roles, whether actual, as in this instance, or dramatized, children experience motive satisfaction from enhanced values—from being "better" in ways defined by their culture.

Teachers also say that, when a child recognizes progress toward his goals, he is stimulated to even greater effort. One points out, "If a child slow at learning to read is given an opportunity to hear himself on a tape recorder as he read a month ago, he realizes that his recent learning efforts have been fruitful, and he becomes more receptive to further instruction."

Finally, and with no attempt to be comprehensive, among these suggestions for "good motivation" made by students in the author's course is the recommendation to show pupils approval and appreciation for their contributions and efforts.

In further exploration of classrooms for examples of good motivation, two

FIG. 8–2. Children enjoy identifying with self-ideal roles in dramatizing stories and social studies events. (*Courtesy of Whittier School, Utah State Agricultural College.*)

observations from the point of view of the pupils are pertinent. Gorman reports [14] being surprised one day when he substituted for an ill teacher to find that such a large proportion of the pupils in this high school class (27 out of 29) had fully prepared the assigned citizenship lesson. The pupils, upon being asked what had motivated them to prepare this lesson, gave the following reasons: (1) "The assignment is something we can do. It is within our ability, both as to difficulty and amount." Because of this, these students could feel a sense of achievement or mastery. (2) "There is always something different. It isn't the same kind of work all the time." Apparently appeals to curiosity and novelty are effective. (3) "We like the up-to-dateness of the subject. Much of it deals with the here and now." Perhaps the motives appealed to here are "prestige" and use. (4) "Much of the subject is close to us. It is near to our lives. It deals with problems that are real to us." Activities related to significant personal and community goals invite identification and sincere effort. (5) "The teacher always allows part of the class period for study." Starting the study in the classroom probably develops a desirable set and sufficient confidence for completing it as homework. (6) "We know what we're supposed to do." With definite, attainable goals, progress is probably easily recognized. (7) "The teacher is always sure to check on us and to find out whether or not we did the work." Approval is anticipated. (8) "The teacher is fair." Perhaps an implication here is that pupils work well when they feel secure and have respect for their teacher.

In another evaluation of motive-incentive conditions from the point of view of pupil opinion, 284 pupils in grades 4 to 6 answered a questionnaire, expressing their preferences between pairs of incentives [25]. As incentives for "studying harder," the majority favored "useful and interesting knowledge" (74 per cent) over "short and easy lessons" (26 per cent); having a personal responsibility (74 per cent) over a class-membership responsibility (26 per cent); "working because I like the teacher" (75 per cent) over working "for fear of being punished (25 per cent); "striving for a high mark on a test" (82 per cent) over competing in a contest (18 per cent); and studying for "being checked on by an examination" (85 per cent) over for "praise from my teacher" (15 per cent).

Both teachers and pupils apparently think that certain motive-incentive conditions, including interest, use, knowledge of progress, identifications with more mature roles, mastery, significance, approval, and security, are effective in motivating learning effort. As a next step in this analysis of motives, some experimental and theoretical appraisals of the general role of motives in learning are considered.

Experimental Demonstrations of the Role of Motivation

Relatively early in the scientific study of education, Chapman and Feder demonstrated the favorable influence on learning of special motivation [7]. Using as learning tasks over a period of 10 days' practice (1) 10 minutes on addition, (2) five minutes on substitution, and (3) one minute on cancellation, they compared the progress of two equated groups of 16 each of fifth grade children. Group B was motivated only by "novelty," "interest," and "conditions of serious school work." Group A was motivated by these appeals plus (1) publishing the previous day's results for each individual, (2) graphing the class results, and (3) awarding stars to both those who on the previous day had scored in the upper 50 per cent and those who in "gross improvement" were in the upper 50 per cent.

The effects of this extra motivation are presented in Table 8–1. This table shows that Groups A and B were approximately equal on all three tasks on trial 1; but the extra motivation given Group A resulted in superior performance in succeeding trials, especially on the two longer tasks. On the one-minute cancellation task, however, there was no significant advantage.

Table 8-1. Motivation Makes a Difference in Learning
(Average scores of Group A, given extra motivation, and Group B, given usual
motivation, on learning three routine speed tasks)

Trial	Addition		Substitution		Cancellation	
	A	B	A	B	A	B
1	14.7	14.0	81	79	32.0	34.0
2	18.6	11.7	155	131	46.8	47.9
3	20.2	11.9	215	181	55.2	51.2

Source: Adapted from J. C. Chapman and R. B. Feder: *J. Educ. Psychol.*, 8: 469–474, 1917.

In a different approach to evaluating the role in learning of motivation, Turney [41] with high school students and Frandsen and Darke [12] with college students found significant correlations between teacher ratings on intensity of motivation and on school achievement. In the latter study, the correlation between high school teachers' ratings of their students on "industriousness" and marks earned by these students as college freshmen was found to be .47, thus showing a relationship between motivation and school achievement approximating that usually found between intelligence and achievement.

Chapman and Feder's experiment illustrates only one kind of motivating procedure. In developing practical guides for providing motivation as a condition for effective learning, it will probably be useful to list more comprehensively and to evaluate the motives and incentives commonly appealed to in teaching.

School Motives and Incentives

School motives and incentives develop out of four basic kinds of human motive: (1) innate physiological drives, including hunger, appetite, thirst, alternating needs for activity and rest or sleep, elimination, sex, release from anxiety and other disturbing emotional states, escape from pain, and equilibrium for various other homeostatic needs; (2) general positive, striving activity drives—impulses to use energies and emerging capacities in motor, intellectual, and perceptual activities in ways, defined by the child's culture, which result in "self-actualization"; (3) learned social motives universal to the individual's culture, including need for attention and the presence of other people, love and affection, approval and blame avoidance, security, mastery, progresssive achievements, ascendancy in competition, etc.; and (4) learned individual interests, ideals, and identifications.

The physiological drives depend upon specific inherited body structures and conditions, which develop as the body matures and are modified in their functioning by learning. The general activity drives and the striving toward self-actualization, although developed through learning, are also assumed to be based on innate human characteristics, as yet undefined. Both the universal social motives and the individually acquired interests are learned by conditioning, wherein personal satisfactions are derived from an extending range of stimuli. For example, the infant at first experiences pleasure only from satisfaction of physiological drives, such as from being fed. But as a part of the combination of stimuli connected with his satisfaction from eating, the mother or another person is nearly always present. Thus, according to the formula for conditioning, the general satisfaction experienced in the eating situation is extended to the presence of another person. In the same general way individual interests are acquired. For a person interested in art, for example, art media have become conditioned stimuli for pleasure. If art media are associated with smooth-going activity, mastery, and approval (stimuli already adequate for evoking pleasure), the art media in themselves come to elicit interest or an anticipation or set for pleasure.

Out of such motivation-learning experiences, numerous school motives and/or incentives develop. The following list is identifiable in discussions of elementary school teaching methods:

1. Satisfaction of *interests* by acquisition of knowledge, understanding, and skill—as in reading, in group study of a social studies project, or in creative expression with art media.

2. *Using* what is learned in achieving one's interests and purposes—as using one's skill in spelling and writing to write a letter or to write about one's research on cheese making.

3. *Mastery* of challenging undertakings—as reading with understanding at a new level, solving an arithmetic problem, or completing an experiment in nature study. To be relatively sure that the child *does* experience mastery and thus is motivated to further efforts, the teacher is careful to adjust the learning undertaking to each child's level of maturity and pattern of abilities.

4. *Knowledge that one is progressing* in mastery of some skill—as may be revealed in a progress-curve graph of quality or speed in handwriting, reading comprehension and speed, words spelled correctly on the "Friday tests," etc.

5. Feeling that one is *enhancing one's potentialities* or *talents* for self-expression and useful social contributions. This kind of motivation is related to "knowl-

edge of progress" in specific activities, but it is broader and emphasizes the enhanced valuation of the self as the child identifies with more mature roles.

6. *Curiosity* and *desire to understand one's world and oneself*—through science, social studies, literature, and various experiences.

7. *Love* and *affection* of the teacher, *identification* with loved and admired persons, and a *sense of belonging*—such as being accepted by one's classmates, by a committee, or by other peer groups.

8. *Praise* or *approval* by teacher, classmates, or parents for meritorious learning effort or achievement.

9. *Blame* and *criticism*, as a corrective for mistakes, lack of effort, and undesirable behavior, and to promote in the future blame-avoidance behavior.

10. *Rivalry for ascendancy* in individual and group competition—as in spelling matches and various other school contests wherein the reward is some distinction or prize—as a star by one's name.

11. *Cooperation* in achieving group goals—such as working out a project in social studies or decorating the classroom for Halloween—wherein each child contributes according to his interests and talents.

12. Opportunity to win *special privileges*—as going to the library for "free reading," being excused from spelling, taking charge of distribution of art paper, etc.

13. *Sympathy* for one's limitations and shortcomings from teacher and classmates.

14. Feelings of *security* about one's status with respect to achievement, school promotion, and social and affectional relationships.

15. Threat of *insecurity*—as in possibility of failing a test unless one studies with effort and succeeds, of not being promoted, or of being disliked and rejected by teacher or classmates for not meeting their standards.

16. *Punishment*, including corporal punishment, isolation from the classroom, expulsion, scolding, sarcastic comments, and personal criticism.

Evaluation of Motive-incentive Conditions

The student may well ask which one motive-incentive condition or combination of conditions out of this rather long list would most effectively motivate school learning and behavior, from the points of view of both learning efficiency and accomplishment of the general aims of education. Teacher experience, which has already been partially cited, and experiments in educational psychology provide at present only piecemeal but nevertheless helpful answers to this question.

Security versus Threat of Failure. Early in the history of education [5, 21], scolding, ridiculing, threats, and other punishments were used to motivate children to learning effort and conformity to rather rigid standards of conduct. But with developing emphasis on democratic citizenship, on happy and effective interpersonal relationships among children and adults, and on emotional health as aims of education, and with better understanding of the conditions for effective learning, appeals to such motives have been abandoned. In 1927 Briggs [3] asked high school principals and teachers whether, as children, various incentives had "made them work better, the same, or worse" and reported that these teachers considered "that commendation, praise and encouragement are superior to censure, ridicule, threats and punishment." Similarly Elsbree, in discussing "school practices that help and hurt personality" [9], observed that every child desires success, recognition, sympathy and affection, and adventure-exploration of the new, and that practices that thwart these needs, such as retention or demotion, competition for marks, and disciplinary treatment (punishments) of symptoms of maladjustment hurt personality.

One experiment has compared threat of failure and security with respect to promotion as motivating conditions of school achievement. For equated groups of both second and fifth grade children, Otto [32] compared the gains made on the Stanford Achievement Test of a group periodically threatened with the possibility of nonpromotion if achievement were not satisfactory and of a group reassured at the same times that they needed to feel no concern about being promoted. In both grades, the nonthreatened group's achievement gains exceeded slightly those of the threatened group. The differences were actually not statistically significant; but the important fact to note is that the threat of nonpromotion is unnecessary to motivate learning effort. And from other points of view, such as discussed above by Elsbree, it is undesirable.

Competition. A step in advance from negative, coercive methods of motivation was the appeal to rivalry and various competitive situations. As an example of this kind of motivation, a suggestion offered by Monroe and Streitz [31, p. 169] for motivating effort to improve reading speed and comprehension is quoted:

The teacher tells the children that they may race to see who can read the most in a given time, say three minutes. At a signal the children turn to a designated page in their books and read silently until the teacher says "Time!" The pupils then place a dot after the last word read and count the total number of words read during the three minutes. The pupil who read the most words stands at the front of the room and is questioned by members of the class on the content of his reading. If he fails to answer a question, the one who read the next highest number of words is questioned, and so on. The one who read the farthest and can correctly answer all questions asked of him is declared the winner of the contest.

Such appeals to competition have been found experimentally to intensify learning effort.

Chapman and Feder's experiment has already been mentioned. Hurlock [20] divided 155 fourth and sixth grade pupils into matched rivalry and control groups and compared their progress in learning addition. The rivalry group was subdivided into two competing groups. For five days the names of the members of the winning group were read at the beginning of the next practice period, and their average score was posted on the blackboard. The gains and the average scores of the rivalry group each day exceeded those made by the control group, for whom no "special" motivation was instituted.

Maller [28], also using additions as the learning tasks, compared as motivating conditions for 814 pupils in grades 5 to 8 (1) control or no special motivation, (2) individual competition for a personal prize, and (3) group competition (and cooperation) for a class prize. Both individual and group competition resulted in better performance than did no special motivation. Average scores for sums completed were as follows: for no special motivation, 41.4; for group competition, 43.9; and for individual competition, 46.6 Moreover, both in terms of number of examples completed in 13 one-minute tests and in terms of number of times working for an individual prize was preferred over working for a group prize, individual competition was favored. Preference for individual versus group competition depends, however, upon the nature of the group. When given opportunities for working in groups as teams, partnerships, teacher-divided groups, or the class as a whole, the children chose most frequently to work for themselves. The only exception where children chose more often to work for the group than each for himself was when boys were pitted against girls.

Vaughn and Diserens remark that "in one way or another competition has been used as a motivating influence during the entire history of pedagogy" [42, p. 81]. From their review of many learning experiments from both educational and general psychology, they conclude that "competitive conditions of one sort or another generally increase efficiency of work and facilitate learning" [42, p. 92]. In some cases, however, they note when "the competitive spirit" is aroused in situations where failure is anticipated, it may "disrupt the individual or result in a change in the direction of competitive effort" [42, p. 92]. This is more likely in complex mental processes than in simpler motor and mental processes. Besides the disadvantage that competition may not be helpful in complex learning activities and may even impair efficiency in some learning situations, there are other possible adverse effects. Elsbree, as cited above, has remarked on its possible harm to the emotional health of some children. If winning becomes highly important but difficult or impossible for these children, they may resort to cheating [17]—although dishonesty is not always an outcome of competition [16]. Another limitation of competition as a school incentive is that it may interfere with the attainment of an important social objective: "that of getting along well in work and play."

Stendler, Damrin, and Haines [38] have compared seven-year-old children's social behavior when in painting a classroom mural they (1) worked with the possibility of winning an individual prize, or (2) worked cooperatively to create a mural which, if it should be considered worthy of hanging on the wall, would result in a prize for every child. During cooperative activity, there were relatively more friendly conversation, sharing of material, and mutual help. During individually competitive work, there were relatively more unfriendly conversation, self-appropriation of material, and obstruction or domination of the work of another child. Competition, therefore, besides often evoking intensified effort, may produce several undesirable by-products. But because it does facilitate learning effort in some situations, there are probably occasions where competition as a motivating condition can be wisely employed. The situation cited from Monroe and Streitz is probably relatively free of disadvantages in that cheating is not possible and that participation is fairly widespread.

Praise. Teachers' opinions that praise and encouragement are more effective as motives than censure and ridicule are well supported by an experimental study by Hurlock [19]. Using as subjects 106 fourth and fifth grade children, she had them practice for 15 minutes on each of five days on a series of addition tests of equal difficulty. On the basis of the first exercise, the children were divided into four equated groups: (1) a control group, who were in a separate room and were given no special motivation; (2) a praised group, who on each succeeding day were praised for the excellence of their work on the preceding day; (3) a reproved group, who regardless of their performance, were scolded for their poor work, careless mistakes, and failure to improve; and (4) an ignored group, who heard each day a third of their classmates praised and a third of them reproved but were not mentioned themselves.

The results from these four different motivating conditions are shown in Figure 8-3. As is indicated, both reproof and praise motivated children on the first day to greater effort, with resultant improvement in test scores on the second day. On succeeding days the praised group continued to improve; they did not even after three successive days of praise begin to rest on already attained laurels. But the reproved group, after a spurt of effort on the second day which was only followed next day by another reproof, declined in effort and achievement on succeeding days. There are individual differences in reactions, of course, to both praise and blame [10]; but in general it seems that praise motivates effort toward achievement more effectively and also probably promotes more healthy social and emotional adjustment.

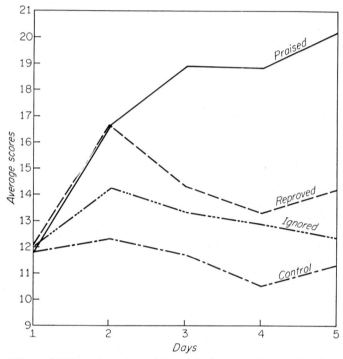

FIG. 8–3. Effects of different incentives—being praised, reproved, ignored, and control—on average scores made on arithmetic tests for four groups on five successive days. (*Adapted from Hurlock, E. B.: J. Educ. Psychol., 16: 149, 1925.*)

Guided by the results of this experiment, teachers should find some reason for approving *every* child, so that this kind of motivation may be fairly evenly distributed. To this purpose, de Groat and Thompson [15] offer some suggestions, such as praising for neat work, for some feature of a paper handed in, for good recitations, for good manners, and for other desirable behavior. They also suggest various ways of indicating approval. Besides verbal comment, approval may be indicated by choosing a monitor, by calling on a pupil to answer questions when a visitor is present, by giving parts in plays and assemblies, by putting work on the bulletin board, by selection for errands, and by arranging many self-rewarding activities.

As a general motivating procedure, praise is probably always better than reproof; but in situations where motivation is already good, as indicated by progress in learning, praise may not always increase the learning efficiency of school children [2]. And like competition, unless applied sincerely and with discrimination, praise may sometimes produce undesirable results. Taft [40] has suggested that praise may set perfectionistic standards which are maintained only at a cost of constant anxiety. It may divert the child from activities otherwise pursued for intrinsic interest. It may make the child feel uncomfortable about experimenting—trying himself out in new activities even though he may fail in some of them. And it may make a child defensive about his realistic limitations. "There is, however [according to Taft], a respectful, sincere appreciation based on objective understanding of what the other has tried to do, or a spontaneous joy in a given result, a sharing in the happiness of the creator, which is educationally sound and the truest encouragement which can be offered" [40, p. 50].

Success. Related to teacher praise and blame, but probably better as motives because they are intrinsic consequents of pupil activity, are actual success and failure. This kind of motivation has also been evaluated experimentally. Lantz [27], as a means of measuring the influence of success and failure experiences on the efficiency of immediately following intellectual performances, used alternately with 212 nine-year-old boys equivalent parts of the "L" and "M" forms of the Stanford-Binet intelligence scale as pretests and end-tests. Between the pretests and end-tests, half of the boys experienced success in problem solving and won a prize; the other half (equal in ability) experienced failure (because of the manipulations of the experimenter) in this same problem-solving effort and failed to win a prize offered for success. As a result of comparing the pretest and end-test scores for the success and failure groups, Lantz concluded: (1) A successful experience raises the average scores on an immediately following mental test (although for this comparison the difference was not statistically significant when the usual practice gain was taken into account). (2) Failure serves as a depressant on such performance (and here the differences were so large as to be clearly statistically significant). (3) Examiner ratings on such test behavior as willingness, self-confidence, social confidence, and attention are raised after success experience and lowered after failure experience.

Another kind of motivation experiment has shown how success and failure experiences affect a child's level of aspiration. In a succession of tasks clearly scorable and of equal difficulty, but where learning or increased effort may result in improvement, an individual may be asked to estimate on the basis of a previous performance his score on the next exercise. He may predict that he will do better, resulting in a positive discrepancy between his level of aspiration and his past performance, or he may set his goal lower, resulting in a negative-discrepancy score. Sears [36], working with fourth, fifth, and sixth grade school children and using as learning tasks reading and arithmetic, found that children who in the past have consistently experienced success, both subjectively in their actual school work and in school marks, continue to set aspiration levels just beyond their past achievements. Because such aspiration levels are realistic and continue to be reached, the sequence, writes Sears, is "gratifying and becomes self-perpetuating." However, when children have been continually frustrated in their day-to-day learning efforts and have consistently received low marks, their "aspiration levels are set much less realistically"—either too high or too low. Such a child, while he has actually little or no expectation of reaching his goal, may set it high and experience temporary, imagined social approval for his good intentions and recognition of the progress which he has learned is expected of every child. Or, "he may set his goal low, in overt denial of the social norm, and derive satisfaction from over-reaching it" [36, p. 530].

The "moral" to draw from the studies on success and failure is, of course, that *every* child needs, from the points of view of both efficient learning and healthy development of personality, *a curriculum in which he can succeed*. This is not to say that problem-solving tasks should not be challenging. In this connection Keister [24] has shown how children can be helped to meet more effectively what appear to be impossible tasks, but which with persistence and an effective problem-solving approach can be mastered. On the basis of their usual approaches to a difficult problem, she chose for special training out of a group of 81 preschool children the 12 who were most immature in their attack—those who gave up quickly, were excessive in their requests for help, were destructive, rationalized, whined, sulked, cried, or yelled in anger. The training, over a six-weeks' period, consisted in working through a series of problems (picture-puzzle, assembly, and block-building) graduated in difficulty. But as verbal motivation, rather than calling attention only to successful or failing outcomes, the teacher commented approvingly on the child's mode of attack: "That was fine! You are learning to try hard and not have anyone help you"; or, "Good for you! You kept right on trying until you found the way to do it, didn't you?" Sometimes she suggested such approaches as: "Try that piece some more different ways." Or she reminded, "Remember how you did the puzzles in the story about the horse? You kept right on trying until you got it right." Before- and after-training tests showed that this group of most ineffective problem solvers increased in interest and in their attempts to solve problems independently and asked another to solve or help solve the problems less often. Rationalizing decreased, and destructive behavior and such emotional expressions as sulking, crying, whining, and yelling were eliminated.

Knowledge of Progress. In a learning undertaking, progress is expected by the pupil and by his teacher, and experiments have shown that, if the learner has clear knowledge of his progress, he is motivated to even greater learning effort. As an illustration of this kind of motivation, the graph of progress of the child in remedial reading might be reexamined [Chapter 4, p. 103]. Keeping this chart of her own progress very likely was one factor in this child's rapid improvement. Such graphs may be prepared for or by children in several school skills, including reading, spelling, arithmetic, writing, various motor skills, etc. Brown [4], using as learning material a review drill on fundamental operations in grade 5A and fractions and decimals in grade 7A, divided 138 children into equated groups and had them practice 10 minutes per day for 20 days. The teacher each day scored the papers for both groups; but only for the experimental group did he each day give each child his score for him to graph and return to him. Thus the graph revealed to each child in the experimental group his progress for each day. Brown noted that the experimental group (with knowledge of progress) "made more continuous gains than control sections." And when the groups were alternated with respect to having knowledge of progress, "each section when knowing its results made higher scores and a more consistent gain than when ignorant of results" [4, p. 551]. Panlasigui and Knight also found, for fourth grade pupils who practiced mixed fundamentals over a period of 20 weeks, a "clear advantage from the use of individual and class progress charts" [33, p. 619]. Equated groups, beginning the experiment with equal mean scores, differed at the conclusion of the experiment by 11.34 points in favor of the group given knowledge of results.

Interests. The development of child-interest-centered curricula ("activity curricula," "projects," or "unified curricula"), besides having other values, is generally presumed to be an effective way of motivating pupil learning. According to Stroud, "the stimulus to group activity is a motivational factor of great worth. Children like to communicate with each other and interchange ideas and observations. They like to make things and to do things individually and in groups. These normal interests of children can be turned into educational capital of great value" [39, p. 638].

Besides this general child interest in purposeful, social activities, it is possi-

FIG. 8–4. Capitalizing on children's interest in animals effectively motivates reading for beginners and creative writing for older children. (*Courtesy of William M. Stewart School, University of Utah.*)

ble to develop in children differentiated special interests, as in art, music, dancing, art crafts, literature, science, etc.; and these special interests may become abiding motives which serve to integrate into effective patterns of knowledge learning experiences in areas of expanding scope over relatively long periods of time. Such interests are probably developed by associating, as conditioned stimuli, the activities in which the teacher hopes to interest the pupil with responses which are reinforced by satisfying activity, mastery, intrinsic use, and approval. The cultivation of such interests, besides motivating learning, are in themselves important educational objectives.

The development of such an interest in a child who early in the primary grades achieved some success in drawing is cited as an example. Because her art products were intrinsically satisfying to herself and encouraged by her parents, teachers, and classmates, who showed spontaneous and sincere appreciation for a veritable stream of creative effort, she has developed now, at 12 years of age, an abiding interest in drawing. Each day, motivated only by her interest, this child finds some occasion for practicing, experimenting, or creative expression in art. Sometimes the art is an independent activity; often it is used to illustrate concepts in social studies, science, health, or literature.

Thus, highly motivated, given some teacher-guidance and with much self-guidance, and supplied amply with art media, this child has achieved a deep and satisfying interest, considerable skill, and confidence in art as a mode of self-expression. Some indication of her development is suggested in Figure 8–5, in which are reproduced a drawing made at age 7 and another made at age 12.

Despite its importance, little well-conducted experimental evaluation of interests as motives seems to have been accomplished with children as subjects. Dean [8] has found among high achievers in reading, arithmetic, spelling, and language in the fifth grade greater percentages of children expressing preferences for these particular subjects than among low achievers. Sheldon and Cutts [37] have found being a good reader to be related to interests in social studies, science, music, and reading as an out-of-school hobby. At the college level, Frandsen [11] found between interest in science, as measured by the Kuder Preference Record, and long-range achievement in natural science the significant correlation of .50. Teacher experiences already cited, educational theory, and some experimentation all indicate that interest-motivated school learning is both effective and highly desirable from the point of view of educational objectives generally.

Self-enhancement. Because children are continuously growing and learning, they experience year by year and week by week the emergence of new abilities and improvement in skills for accomplishing goals which their culture has defined as worthwhile. At first, a child reads only with teacher-help; then he masters some techniques for identifying some words independently; and finally he feels confident that he can read anything. In swimming, the "beginner" is confined to the wading-depth part of the pool. As an "intermediate swimmer," he tries himself out in a less restricted range. And finally, he has the thrill of being classified as a "swimmer" and swims with confidence anywhere in the pool. Judy is having difficulty with arithmetic; then, as a result of her renewed efforts, she experiences an important success, and her striving continues with greater confidence. The child who cannot play a musical instrument but who desires, though without much hope, to play in the school orchestra, first sees the goal as realistic when she begins to master the horn. Eventually, she enjoys the profound pleasure of playing in the orchestra for a school assembly. These developmental patterns of emerging capacities for ever greater accomplishment provide the basis both for man's characteristic striving and for his highest motivational satisfaction.

Striving is continually being rewarded in emotionally healthy children, and thus it becomes a well-motivated general pattern of behavior. Even before

Fig. 8–5. Development in art is a product of sustained interest and talent. J. drew the robin at age 7 and the wolf-duck design at age 12.

FIG. 8–6. Children experience the highest of motive satisfactions in creative and socially constructive uses of their talents. (*Courtesy of Whittier School, Utah State Agricultural College and the USAC Department of Photography.*)

important goals are attained, well-justified *anticipations* of attaining them make the striving approach itself intrinsically satisfying.

According to May, "to the extent that we do fulfill our potentialities as persons, we experience the profound joy to which the human is heir" [30]. And Cantril [6], who has developed this concept most systematically, thinks that man's highest and most effective motivation to constructive and creative effort is the feeling that one is enhancing one's potentialities or talents for self-expression and useful social contributions. Defining the concept further, Cantril says that "the richness of the quality of our experience will depend on the opportunity we have to share experiences with others [and] on the extent to which we can create some order, some meaning, and some direction in life situations through our participation in them" [6, p. 27]. Applying this concept to the elementary school curriculum, it is not surprising to find that children find especial satisfaction in constructive and creative participation, each according to his talents, in purposeful, social, useful, unified curriculum projects.

In accounting for a child's or an adult's striving for enhanced constructive and creative achievement, Cantril explains how each growing person develops a hierarchical system of values by which each new experience is evaluated: A value attribute pervades every experience. And as a result of each person's accumulated experiences—studying, working, creating, playing, eating, sleeping, and all his other individual and social experiences—he builds a standard scale or pattern of values. Against this standard derived from past experiences, the individual evaluates each new experience as "worthwhile," "satisfying," "pleasant," "unpleasant," or "disappointing." Such comparative evaluations are possible because out of a variety of value experiences, one's developing value patterns become organized into a hierarchy—a scale from lower to higher values. But the hierarchical organization of values is never static; it is always tentative and in process of reconstruction. Because children are continuously growing and learning, they become justified in the constant expectation of enhanced values, especially from creative and constructive efforts. "What is experienced as an increment of value today becomes part of the [accumulated] value standard tomorrow" [6, p. 30]. And as compared to the new "standard," still higher values are sought. Thus "the ultimate," the most generalized goal of man is what can be called the *enhancement of the value attributes of experience*. . . . It is the capacity man has to *sense added value* in his experience that accounts for his ceaseless striving, his search for a direction to his activities, for his characteristic unwillingness to have things remain as they are" [6, p. 28, italics supplied].

Such motivation explains the thrill in creative effort. It accounts for children's eagerness for increased responsibilities and for opportunities for making greater contributions to their social groups. Such motivation is also effective in long-range undertakings and projects; it sustains the pupil over periods of difficulty and frustration. Since "we fit our specific actions into larger patterns of purpose," we can tolerate temporary frustrations because we anticipate eventually enhanced value in the long-range experience and take satisfaction even immediately in the anticipation. Children also experience enhanced values in identifying with the more mature roles they see exemplified by loved and admired parents, teachers, peers, and other real and fictional ideal characters.

Summary on Evaluation of School Motives. As was anticipated, this evaluation of school motives and incentives is piecemeal; we have achieved no complete, over-all evaluation of the motive-incentive conditions listed on pages 219 to 220. Both teacher experience and experimental results agree, however, in finding that the quality of motivation makes a difference in learning. Indeed, motivation is an essential condition of learning; and the more appropriate the motivation, the more efficient the learning will be. They also agree that attempts to motivate pupil learning by scolding and ridicule, threats of failure, and other punishments of various kinds are both ineffective and harmful to the attainment of such important educational objectives as healthy emotional and social adjustments. Children need to feel secure, accepted, successful, and approved. Arrangements of individually competitive conditions, while they usually result in intensified effort, often produce as by-products undesirable social behavior and personality disturbances. It is found that sincere appreciation for constructive effort and achievement is effective and healthy; but even praise, though much better than reproof in the long run, needs to be used carefully and with awareness of some hazards.

Perhaps the most generally effective motivating procedure discovered in this review is that of providing children with opportunities for constructive and creative participation, each according to his talents, in purposeful, social, useful, child-interest-centered, unified projects. In such projects and in the systematic practice of skills related to them, children will experience and strive continually for "enhanced values." Such motivation will also involve appeals to interest, use, and knowledge of progress, which both teacher experience and experimental results have found to be effective and in harmony with general educational objectives. As a concept which will make the teacher's handling of motivation as a condition of learning more systematic and confident, an attempt should perhaps be made to formulate an over-all theory of motivation which will integrate the findings of this review.

A Theory of Motivation

A theory of motivation which recognizes all the data just reviewed needs to take into account man's positive, creative striving. Moreover, several observers of human behavior have been impressed by man's characteristic striving, which, unless distorted by unhealthy life circumstances, is readily channeled by the dominant culture into constructive and socialized effort [1, 6, 23, 26, 29, 30, 34]. May has mentioned the "profound joy" in fulfilling our potentialities as persons [30]. Jersild is impressed by the child's "activity drives"—his impulses to put his energies and emerging capacities to use [23, p. 301]. Kluckhohn, Murray, and Schneider assume that creative intellectual activity is intrinsically gratifying [26, pp. 15–16]. And although it seems justifiable to assume an innate basis for activity drives, Cantril [6] has explained how characteristic human striving may be learned: as the child grows and learns, he is continually rewarded by experiencing "enhanced values."

Allport recognizes the "tension-reduction" demands of such physiological drives as hunger, thirst, elimination, and anxiety; but it is only the emotionally maladjusted, he says, who are preoccupied with seeking relief from such tensions. "Normal people, by contrast, are dominated by their 'preferred patterns' of self-actualization. Their psychogenic interests are modes of sustaining and directing tension rather than escaping it" [1, p. 117]. They seek opportunities for constructive and creative expression of their talents in their fields of interest.

"As a deep conviction growing out of many years of experience" in therapy, Rogers concludes that man's nature and motivation are positive and constructive [34]. He views man as "an organism able to achieve, through the remarkable integrative capacity of its central nervous system, a balanced, realistic, self-enhancing, other enhancing behavior." Freed from defensive self-distortions, man's behavior becomes "constructive" and "socialized" because man learns in his society that he achieves his potentialities most completely by constructive, socialized behavior. Among the adherents of this theory, perhaps Maslow's statement [29] is the most systematically developed explanation of man's creative striving.

According to Maslow, all an individual's capacities and energy are always mobilized in the interest of any strong motivational need. And although behavior is usually determined by multiple needs, only in its absence does a motivational need become an important determinant of behavior. Food, for example, would be a poor school-work incentive, because most children's hunger needs are taken care of by an almost automatic schedule of eating. Teacher approval, say, is better, because the need for this boost to one's self-esteem is more constantly active. Further, according to Maslow, motives are hierarchically arranged; and only as more basic motives are satisfied (at least to some extent) do motives higher in the hierarchy become potent behavior determinants. But when motives lower in the hierarchy *are* satisfied, then automatically, because of the inherent nature of man, motives higher in the hierarchy motivate activity and effort. Because of the nature of the motives in Maslow's hierarchical list, it is apparent that man will never be satisfied, except when rest is needed, to be completely inactive. His motivational needs higher in the hierarchy will keep him continuously striving as lower needs are satisfied. Maslow's list, in its hierarchical order from lowest to highest needs follows:

1. Physiological needs, such as hunger, thirst, activity, rest, etc.

2. Safety needs, security, and release from anxiety aroused by threats of various kinds.

3. Love needs, including love, affection, acceptance, and feeling of belonging in one's relationships with parents, teachers, friends, and other social groups.

4. Esteem needs, including both self-esteem from mastery and confidence in one's worth, adequacy, and capacities, and esteem from social approval.

5. Need for self-actualization through creative self-expression in personal and social achievements; need to feel free to act (within the limits of general social needs), to satisfy one's curiosity, and to understand one's world.

The first four needs in Maslow's list are to a certain extent self-centered, narcissistic needs; "a healthy man," however, "is primarily motivated by his needs to develop and actualize his fullest potentialities and capacities." The highest motivational satisfaction would come from expressing one's interests and talents constructively and creatively in useful activity. The emergence of this fifth level of motivation, however, depends upon the prior satisfaction of the lower-order needs. A child who is hungry, insecure, or unloved, whose confidence has been undermined by failures, or who feels disapproved would not be expected to reach this fifth level; consequently he would not be expected to devote his efforts constructively and creatively to his school tasks and projects. All his energies would be mobilized in his efforts to allay hunger, or to relieve anxiety, or to win love (or in a counter-aggressive attack against those who he feels reject him), or to win esteem (but not necessarily by constructive effort). But when all a child's lower-level needs *are* satisfied, he would not need to be pressed into constructive and creative study and work. In such activity for such a child, the opportunity for self-actualization in expression of talents and interests offers its own intrinsic, high reward. According to this theory, a teacher does not drive or press a pupil to constructive effort; she *releases* his energies for such effort from lower-order needs and she does this by helping the child in every way possible to satisfy amply the lower-level needs. An example from a series of case studies in *These Are Your Children* [22] will illustrate the theory as applied in the teaching and guidance of children.

Illustrating Maslow's Motivation Theory. Before a psychological examination revealed Robert[1] to be "superior" in intelligence, "Miss M. became almost certain that she had a mentally retarded child in her group" of first grade children. Besides his poor school progress, it was also apparent that Robert had emotional problems. He "cried frequently and whined even more often. He chewed his nails incessantly. He was destructive. He shuffled when he walked,

---

[1] From *These Are Your Children*, expanded ed., by Jenkins, Shacter, and Bauer. Copyright 1953, by Scott, Foresman and Company, and used with their permission.

and his speech was confined to monosyllables. His whole demeanor suggested reluctance to meet the unfamiliar and a fearfulness in social situations. He did not join the playground games. He seemed unable to follow the procedures in the classroom."

Investigation of Robert's home relationships indicated that he might very justifiably have felt rejected by his parents, and by generalizing (as he probably did), by people in general. His mother "declared petulantly that she did not see why she deserved such a burden. The boy's father said bluntly that Robert was the most exasperating kid he had ever known and that no matter what they did, they seemed unable to make him change." They had tried "bribing" him (with a bicycle he was afraid to ride), punishment (when his obedience was not prompt), and threats "of being deprived of the nice new possessions if Robert did not mend his ways." Robert's anxiety showed that he felt insecure. He could not have felt loved nor had much self-esteem. All his energies were mobilized in the interests of these needs—mainly in trying to feel safe and in some counter-aggression to his frustrating situation. There was no energy left for constructive and creative efforts in school; so, despite his superior intelligence, he was not succeeding.

Pressure toward constructive effort was not the remedy, according to Maslow's theory. Rather, it was to provide, through changes in his home, his school, and his relations with his playmates, for satisfaction of Robert's lower-order needs for security, love, and esteem. Parent-teacher conferences were arranged. "Fortunately, Robert's parents were eager for help. Their distress about the boy was genuine, and although their methods thus far had been poorly conceived, they had not thought that their ways were the only ways of treating a child. They agreed that spankings had not helped; they would stop them. They granted that they had thoughtlessly set their standards too high. They could see that their love for the boy had not been proved to him. And they could appreciate that the new baby had been so appealing that the older child had often been ignored or given little consideration and had inevitably felt rejected, unloved, and uncertain of his place in the family group. They were most receptive to Miss M.'s explanations and suggestions, and chagrined at their part in Robert's difficulties. And they were relieved that the boy was definitely not dull" [22, p. 130]. Miss M. also "planned first of all to show Robert that she was his friend. She made it a point to help Robert go over again the beginnings of the reading approach, so that his lack of accomplishment during the early part of the school year did not penalize his progress for the remainder of the year." And she facilitated a better adjustment to his classmates. "She selected one of the children in the class who was an easy-going, protective sort of boy, and saw to it that Robert was seated near him and was his partner in some of the group games."

The result was that "when his emotional problems were eased"—that is, when all his energies were no longer mobilized in the interests of safety and love—and "he could use the good ability which was his, he made progress with his school work. . . . *He learned to plan and to carry through an activity and he had pleasure in doing so*" [italics supplied]. According to Maslow's conception of motivation, Robert had emerged to the level of motivation where constructive use of talents and expression of interests provide their own rewards.

Summary Evaluation of Maslow's Theory. Besides finding that Maslow's theory of motivation is in harmony with good modern educational practice, we should note that it is further supported by at least some of the experimentation and theory discussed earlier in this section. Cantril's view [6] that "enhancing one's potentialities or talents for self-expression and useful social contributions" is the "ultimate, the most generalized goal of man" is entirely consistent with Maslow's placement of the need for self-actualization at the top of his hierarchy of motives. Also in support of the theory is Otto's experimental finding [32] that "threat of failure" did not motivate second and fifth grade children to achievement superior to that of those not confronted with this threat. In fact, freed from this threat to their safety, the secure group seemed to be influenced toward even greater achievement by motives higher in Maslow's hierarchy. The experimental findings demonstrating the effectiveness as motives of appeals to *interests*, of providing for constructive *use* of concepts and skills learned, of *success* as compared with failure experiences, and of the value of providing *knowledge of progress* are also all in harmony with this theory.

The theory is perhaps even more specifically supported by such findings (more of which will be given in the next chapter) as those of Schoeppe, Haggard, and Havinghurst [35]. They found that progress in social maturing, as indicated by the accomplishments of "adolescent developmental tasks," is related to satisfaction of the basic motives in Maslow's hierarchy. Adolescents who feel safe and loved and possess self-esteem approach their developmental tasks constructively and attain high levels of socialization. But when deprived of these basic motive satisfactions, other adolescents are retarded in their social maturing. As examples, Martha and Ned, who are starved for affection, "exert all their energies toward seeking the love of which they have been deprived, but they do so in different ways." Martha, by passive submission, strives compulsively to avoid condemnation. Ned, who is openly rejected and also stronger, expends his energies in compulsive hostility. Both are self-

defeating in their efforts to win the friendship they crave. More fortunate
are Herbert and Ann, who grew up in homes where they were secure, accepted,
loved, and "made to feel that they counted as individuals" and where they had
"harmonious interaction" with members of their families. They learned both
the need for and enjoyment in working, and they enjoyed identifications with
their parents' social roles. "On this foundation the youngsters began school,
and because they were well-socialized, the school eagerly accepted them and
they worked to further their socialization. Each new successful accomplishment made the next one easier for Ann and Herb."

Review and Applications

1. Explain the roles of motivation in learning.
2. Describe an example of especially effective motivation of school children. What
motives were appealed to?
3. Summarize the experimental evaluations of school motive-incentive conditions.
4. What motives are appealed to when children are provided opportunities for constructive and creative participation, each according to his talents, in purposeful, useful,
child-interest-centered, unified projects?
5. Cite observations and/or experimental data in support of Maslow's theory of
motivation.
6. Apply Maslow's theory of motivation in explaining an example of well-motivated
school learning.

References

1. Allport, G. W.: "The trend in motivational theory," *Amer. J. Orthopsychiat.*, 23:
   107–119, 1953.
2. Auble, D., and E. V. Mech: "Partial verbal reinforcement related to distributed
   practice in a classroom situation," *J. Psychol.*, 36: 165–186, 1953.
3. Briggs, T. H.: "Praise and censure as incentives," *Sch. Soc.*, 26: 596–598, 1927.
4. Brown, F. J.: "Knowledge of results as an incentive in school room practice,"
   J. Educ. Psychol., 23: 532–552, 1932.
5. Brubacher, John S.: *A History of the Problems of Education*, McGraw-Hill, New
   York, 1947.
6. Cantril, H.: *The "Why" of Man's Experience*, Macmillan, New York, 1950.
7. Chapman, J. C., and R. B. Feder: "The effect of external incentives on improvement," *J. Educ. Psychol.*, 8: 469–474, 1917.
8. Dean, S. E.: "Relation of children's subject preferences to their achievement,"
   Elem. Sch. J., 51: 89–92, 1950.

9. Elsbree, W. S.: "School practices that help and hurt personality," *Teach. Coll. Rec.*, 43: 24–34, 1941.

10. Forlano, G., and H. C. Axelrod: "The effects of repeated praise or blame on the performance of introverts and extroverts," *J. Educ. Psychol.*, 28: 92–100, 1937.

11. Frandsen, A.: "Interests and general educational development," *J. Appl. Psychol.*, 31: 57–66, 1947.

12. ———, and R. Darke: "An evaluation of personality ratings and intelligence in predicting scholarship," *Utah Educ. Rev.*, 29: 127–130, 1935.

13. Gans, Roma: "Reading and personal satisfactions," *Childh. Educ.*, 29: 132–133, 1952.

14. Gorman, B. W.: "How to get pupils to prepare assignments," *Sch. Rev.*, 53: 237–239, Copyright, 1945, by the University of Chicago. Reprinted by permission of the University of Chicago Press.

15. deGroat, A. F., and G. G. Thompson: "A study of the distribution of teacher approval and disapproval among sixth-grade pupils," *J. Exp. Educ.*, 18: 57–75, 1949.

16. Gross, Sister Mary Mynette: "The effects of certain types of motivation on the honesty of children," *J. Educ. Res.*, 40: 133–140, 1946.

17. Hartshorne, H., and M. A. May: *Studies in the Nature of Character*, vol. I, *Studies in Deceit*, Macmillan, New York, 1928.

18. Hill, Rocelia: "Science experiences afford opportunities for common interests of all ages," *Childh. Educ.*, 29: 84, 1952.

19. Hurlock, Elizabeth B.: "An evaluation of certain incentives used in school work," *J. Educ. Psychol.*, 16: 145–159, 1925.

20. ———: "The use of rivalry as an incentive," *J. Abnorm. Soc. Psychol.*, 22: 278–290, 1927.

21. James, H. W.: "Punishments recommended for school offenses," *Elem. Sch. J.*, 29: 129–131, 1928–1929.

22. Jenkins, Gladys G., Helen Shacter, and W. W. Bauer: *These Are Your Children*, expanded ed. Copyright, 1953, by Scott, Foresman and Company, Chicago, and used with their permission.

23. Jersild, A. T.: *Child Psychology*, 4th ed., Prentice-Hall, Englewood Cliffs, N.J., 1954.

24. Keister, Mary E.: "The behavior of young children in failure," in R. G. Barker, J. S. Kounin, and H. F. Wright (eds.): *Child Behavior and Development*, McGraw-Hill, New York, 1943.

25. Kirkendall, L. A.: "The influence of certain incentives in motivation of children," *Elem. Sch. J.*, 38: 417–424, 1938.

26. Kluckhohn, C., H. A. Murray, and D. M. Schneider: *Personality: In Nature, Society, and Culture*, Knopf, New York, 1953.

27. Lantz, Beatrice: "Some dynamic aspects of success and failure," *Psychol. Mongr.*, 59(1): 1–40, 1945.

28. Maller, J. B.: "Cooperation and competition, an experimental study of motivation,"

in L. W. Crafts et al.: *Recent Experiments in Psychology*, McGraw-Hill, New York, 1938.

29. Maslow, A. H.: "A theory of human motivation," *Psychol. Rev.*, 50: 370–396, 1943.
30. May, R.: *Man's Search for Himself*, Norton, New York, 1953.
31. Monroe, W. S., and Ruth Streitz: *Directing Learning in the Elementary School*, Doubleday, New York, 1932.
32. Otto, H. J.: "An attempt to evaluate the threat of failure as a factor in achievement," *Elem. Sch. J.*, 35: 588–596, 1935.
33. Panlasigui, I., and F. B. Knight, "The effect of awareness of success or failure," *Research in Arithmetic*, pp. 611–619. *29th Yearbook*, Nat. Soc. Stud. Educ., Part II. Chicago, Distributed by Univ. Chicago Press, 1930.
34. Rogers, C. R.: "Some directions and end points in therapy," in O. H. Mowrer (ed.): *Psychotherapy: Theory and Research*, New York, The Ronald Press Co., 1953.
35. Schoeppe, Aileen, E. A. Haggard, and R. J. Havighurst: "Some factors affecting sixteen-year-old success in five developmental tasks," *J. Abnorm. Soc. Psychol.*, 48: 42–52, 1953.
36. Sears, Pauline S.: "Levels of aspiration in academically successful and unsuccessful children," *J. Abnorm. Soc. Psychol.*, 35: 498–536, 1940.
37. Sheldon, W. D., and W. C. Cutts: "Relation of parents, home, and certain developmental characteristics to children's reading ability," *Elem. Sch. J.*, 53: 517–521, 1953.
38. Stendler, Celia B., Dora Damrin, and Aleyene C. Haines: "Studies in cooperation and competition, I.: The effects of working for group and individual rewards on the social climate of children's groups," *J. Genet. Psychol.*, 79: 173–197, 1951.
39. Stroud, J. B.: *Psychology in Education*, Longmans, New York, 1946.
40. Taft, Jessie: "The catch in praise," *Child Stud.* 7: 133–135, 1930.
41. Turney, A. H.: "Intelligence, motivation, and achievement," *J. Educ. Psychol.*, 22: 426–434, 1931.
42. Vaughn, J., and C. M. Diserens: "The experimental psychology of competition," *J. Exp. Educ.*, 7: 76–97, 1938.

Chapter 9

Mental Health
and Learning

MARY IS a "bright-normal" ten-year-old who, although she is in the fourth grade, in which considerable independent study is expected, still does not read. At best, she reads only the relatively few words she remembers as "sight words." Lacking both the confidence to try and any skills in the independent identification of unfamiliar words, she can only wait dependently for either her mother or her teacher to "tell her" when she comes to a word she does not know. She feels anxious, inferior, and guilty. Her mother feels frustrated and alternates between exasperation—because she sometimes feels that Mary could learn if she would only try harder—and discouragement about the futility of her efforts to help her. Practice sessions in the evenings—with Mary misreading words and needing to be told repeatedly the same words—have been tense experiences for both of them. There was always the hazard for Mary that she would "guess" a word wrongly and would immediately either hear her mother's reproof or sense disapproval in her mother's facial expression. Finally, Mary has become fearful of risking a trial even at a word which she should easily infer from the context. Why Mary did not succeed in her initial attempts at learning to read is not known. But now her general lack of self-confidence, her dependency, and her fear of making a mistake impair seriously her learning efficiency. Such emotional disturbances of learning develop from frustration and conflict experienced in the school, from unhealthy parent-child relationships, or from other unfortunate personal or social experiences.

241

Emotional Health and Effective Learning

According to the general two-factor theory of learning, while a child by a trial-and-error or problem-solving approach is acquiring such skills as identification of words, understanding of social studies concepts, or understanding and skill in arithmetic, he is also by conditioning developing important attitudes toward himself and his environment. If all six of the already discussed conditions for effective learning are effectively operating, and provided also that he is otherwise free from anxiety and distorting emotional attitudes, the learner will in the main experience success in his learning undertakings and will perceive and feel himself making progress. As a consequence, he will develop self-confidence, eagerness and interest in acquiring knowledge and skills, and improved efficiency and confidence in learning as an approach to all sorts of problems. But if, because his curriculum is unsuited to his maturity or pattern of abilities or because of inadequate teacher-guidance or inadequate provision for any of the essential conditions of learning, he fails in his learning undertakings, he will gradually be conditioned to respond to subsequent learning activities with negative rather than positive attitudes. He will come to feel in learning situations insecure, confused and frustrated, inadequate, and even unworthy and guilty because he has failed to reach his own and his parents' and teachers' standards for him. As defenses against the anxiety thus aroused, he may rebel against school learning, become overdependent, withdraw in various ways, or develop other compensatory modes of adjustment which interfere with his efficiency in learning.

Often a child's learning difficulties result from poor parent-child relationships or from other social conflicts. Sibling jealousy, parental overprotection, parental rejection, social-class differences, general home insecurity, personal handicaps, and other conditions producing feelings of anxiety, aggression, inferiority, and guilt have all been associated with learning difficulties [69]. Unfortunately, emotionally disturbed children are far from rare. In one recent elementary school survey [13], teachers reported 11 per cent of the children as emotionally disturbed. Another survey of elementary school children has classified 12 per cent as "seriously maladjusted" and another 30 per cent as "poorly adjusted" [28]. When the criteria of child maladjustment are broader in scope (including unmet needs for belonging, love and affection, achievement, economic security, freedom from fear and guilt, sharing, and understanding), the percentage of "poorly adjusted" children has been reported as high as 55 per cent [10]. Emotional disturbances do not, however, always disturb a child's school adjustment. But the cultivation of emotional health itself is an important school objective and one toward which good teachers contribute very significantly. Therefore, whether or not emotional disturbances interfere with school adjustment and regardless of whether the major causes are in the school or in the home, the teacher is concerned with, and effective in, their prevention or correction.

Examples of Emotional Disturbances Impairing Learning Efficiency. The cases of Mary, just mentioned, and of Robert, mentioned in the previous chapter, illustrate how children of above-average or even superior intelligence may, because of emotional disturbances, fail to make satisfactory school progress. Mary lacked confidence and resourcefulness. Robert, feeling rejected, unloved, and harshly treated by his parents, had developed a generalized attitude of fearfulness, resistance, and counter-aggression to all relations and directed activities with adults [7].

Teachers can often cite instances of aggressive resistance toward school learning. Homer, who is in the seventh grade, is described by his teacher as ranking in achievement at the fourth grade level and as being especially poor in reading. "He could do better," she says, "but he spends his time being a 'smart aleck' and is always doing silly things to make other children laugh. And he answers questions by silly remarks not related to the subject." The "children who hate" studied by Redl and Wineman, having from infancy experienced severe parental rejection and harsh treatment, have as preadolescents developed paranoid attitudes and counter-aggressive modes of attack toward adults in general. They have lost the ability for effective participation in constructive, socializing activities under adult guidance, and they use their intelligence only for promoting and defending the "delinquent" roles with which they have identified. As for profiting from school experiences, Redl and Wineman write: "Good education is not enough for the cure of children who hate. Rather the reverse comes closer to the truth; in order for good educational diet to take hold of these children at all, their basic ego disturbances must be repaired first" [50, p. 247].

A child need not react to his anxiety with aggression to have his learning efficiency impaired; he can also be as "good as gold" and yet fail in school, as another case from *These Are Your Children* illustrates [27, pp. 143–146]. Johnny, age 7, who until recently had been successful in school, began to fall behind. He tried in every way possible to please his teacher and parents. However, in order to please his dominating mother, he felt that he must do everything perfectly. But because of starting projects carefully and slowly, rechecking, erasing, and doing things over, he could rarely complete tasks. He would have preferred being more like his easygoing and somewhat careless father, but his anxiety compelled him to follow as a model his perfectionistic mother. His anxiety resulted in part from his conflict concerning which parent to identify with and in part from fear of his own irrepressible impulses of resentment toward his mother for her strict discipline and for imposing on him so many irksome home chores. Fearful of the consequences should these impulses be expressed, Johnny overcompensated by being "as good as gold"; and as is usual in anxiety-motivated behavior, he overdid his perfectionism to the extent of being self-defeating.

An example of still another reaction to anxiety illustrates how the efficiency of a child, already poor because of low ability, may be further impaired by anxiety and distorting self-attitudes. Tom came to the clinic with his third grade teacher and his mother for help about his reading. Although beginning his third year in school, he still did not read at all. His mother described how for the latter half of the first year at school and all during the second year, she had supplemented his teachers' persistent efforts with almost nightly sessions at helping him with his reading—all without success. They all were baffled and worried. That is, they were all baffled except Tom; and he was also less worried, since he had discovered the "cause" for his inability to learn to read. When he was given a book to demonstrate his attempts at reading, the book jiggled in his hands. He explained, "That's why I can't read, books always jiggle." But nothing else jiggled for him—only books.

An intelligence test at his current age of nine years revealed an IQ of 80 and a mental age of 7-3. According to the minimum mental age of about $6\frac{1}{2}$ years found necessary by Morphett and Washburne [45] for success in first grade reading, Tom should, during the last year, have been able to make some progress in beginning reading. But consider the probable level of his mental maturity when he was first attempting reading in the first grade at just six years of age. At that time his mental age was probably about 4-10 (MA = IQ × CA), at which mental age Morphett and Washburne's investigation showed no child succeeding with reading.

So even though Tom began his attempts in learning to read with confidence and wholehearted effort, he was almost certain to experience failure, frustration, confusion, and, with the pressure from teacher and parents, tension. In this state, Tom observed that the book jiggled, and his frustrating situation was no longer so baffling. It was also more comfortable to think of reading as being impossible for him because books jiggled than because *he* was unable to learn, as he had begun to think. After this discovery he could justifiably cease to try to read. Consequently his practice sessions would be at best perfunctory, consisting of just holding the book while it jiggled. Even when, at about eight years of age, he had developed sufficient mental maturity for the expectation of success in beginning reading, the distorting attitude acquired when he was too immature to succeed now interfered with the effort and the confidence which success in learning to read requires.

Edelston [14] has reported on a group of 18 emotionally maladjusted children ranging in intelligence from "average" to "very superior" who, except for one case, were failing to make satisfactory progress in school because emotional disturbances were impairing their learning efficiency.

Emotional Disturbances Appearing in Problem Solving. Efficient problem solving requires an integrated, systematic attack upon problems. It involves anticipation, planning ahead, thorough persistence balanced with variability of approach, the application of a functionally organized background of experience, and a set to learn—to be guided by experience in the problem situation. These features of efficient problem solving require self-confidence, self-reliance in the face of difficulties, and a willingness to try promising leads even while experiencing some frustration. Emotionally healthy children often demonstrate this pattern of problem solving as teachers observe them individually in school learning activities; and it is also apparent to the psychologist as he observes a child at work in the individual psychological-testing situation.

But the psychologist, like the teacher, also often observes in emotionally maladjusted children impaired efficiency in problem solving. Rather than a directed, persistent problem-solving approach, he may observe such emotional responses to temporary difficulties as negativism, sulking, resistance and aggression or refusals to try, withdrawing, overdependence, insecurity and anxiety, and excitement panic. He sometimes sees the child reacting to anticipated failure in problem solving with various defense mechanisms: rationalization; overcompensation in the form of overpretentious and false intellectualizing; substitute activities (as turning attention away from directions to something else, talking about rather than trying to solve the problem, etc.); regression to less mature levels of response; repression; sympatheticism; phantasy; and various combinations of these and other adjustment mechanisms. And with children who have become conditioned to anticipate failure, he may observe such defensive "dodges" from a direct problem-solving approach as perseveration and failure to shift mode of attack, free-associative responses, egocentric confabulations, random guessing rather than saying "I don't know," or reasoning, saying, "I can't" too readily, an uncritical attitude, and special disabilities in abstracting, analyzing, and synthesizing.

Below are cited several examples of such emotionally impaired efficiency. The children included are a miscellaneous group referred to a clinic for a variety of achievement and personality problems. Common to them all, however, are varying degrees of insecurity and anxiety.[1]

R.S. is a bright child age 5 with an IQ of 121. His insecurity and self-distrust were indicated by the very tiny circles, squares, and diamonds he drew when requested to copy models of these figures and by his self-depreciatory comments. About paper folding, for example, he remarked, "Mine isn't as good as yours." About copying the examiner's model of a bead chain, he said, "Maybe I'll forget to make mine like yours." Although he succeeded in these items, in the block-counting test his insecurity and self-distrust led to error. When asked for three blocks, he first correctly placed three blocks on the paper before the examiner; then, prompted by his anxiety, he added two more, remarking, "That's not enough, is it?" When asked for seven blocks, he placed the correct number on the paper; then, again distrusting himself, he removed some, commenting, "No, that's too many."

H.Y., age 10 to 11 and with an IQ of 90, is unable to use his "average-range" intelligence effectively because of distracting anxiety, personal apprehensions, and defensive overintellectualizing. Although his mental age of 9-10 is about equal to the average of fourth grade children, his reading is at the second grade level. His sight vocabulary is limited, and he lacks both skill and confidence in identifying unfamiliar words. But needing to appear to read well, he rapidly read "cat" as "car," "same" as "summer," and "long" as "lost." His personal apprehension is suggested by his answers to questions about similarities. "Snake," "cow," and "sparrow" are alike, he said, in that "they all could kill." And "knife blade," "penny," and "piece of wire" are "all dangerous, they are sharp." Sometimes he compensates for his uncertainty by overelaborate responses, as in his explanation of how an ocean and a river are alike and how they are different: "An ocean is a lot bigger than a river, and a river is like an ocean, but it is not as big. Ocean has fish in it and so has a river. An ocean doesn't have a fence or weeds around it like a river, and it doesn't have a bridge going over it." Then, needing to boast a little, he added, "I'm smart enough to know that." Even when he didn't know something, however, he tried to appear informed. "Peculiarity" was defined as: "Means makes you want to find out what it is and you get peculiar about it and sneak around and find what it is and it usually brings you into trouble." H.Y.'s boasting and overelaborate explanations sometimes annoyed his classmates, which only increased his ineffective striving for status.

---

[1] It should be clearly understood that these test responses are not the sole basis for diagnosing these children as insecure and anxious. They illustrate *how* such emotional disturbances (diagnosed from more comprehensive data) may impair learning and problem solving.

G., age 8 and with an IQ of 92, feeling insecure, and lacking in acceptance and status was reported as "uncooperative and resistant to participation in school activities." In the tasks he attempted, he was overcautious, arranging overprecisely the blocks which he was merely asked to count out and erasing and reerasing the diamond to be copied. But when a task appeared too challenging, he rationalized an escape: Asked, "What is foolish about that picture (a scene of a man and woman sitting outside in front of their house while it is raining)?" he said, "I can't tell a story about that picture because it's too dim." (The picture is actually clearly drawn, but the crosshatched lines drawn over it to indicate rain gave him his excuse.) That he felt guilty about his resistance is suggested by his egocentric distortion in answering the question: "What's the thing for you to do when you have broken something which belongs to someone else?" He answered, "Should get a spanking from Mother and Daddy if they find out."

B., age 18, IQ 124, did very well when solutions were a product of immediate insight, but she could not stand the mild frustration of the time required for problem solving; instead she abandoned problem solving for impulsive guessing. For the problem: "If a man buys 8 cents' worth of stamps and gives the clerk 25 cents, how much change should he get back?" she distracted herself after three seconds with such self-aggressions as: "Might as well forget it, I'm no good at that," and "Eight?—Oh, how dumb can you get, that's wrong, it's 13."

Sometimes aggressive impulses arouse anxiety, and as a defense children may distort their perception of aggressive situations. R.H., age 11 and with an IQ of 88, was shown a picture (of a pioneer, about to be attacked by two very nearby Indians with tomahawks while he is short-sightedly shooting at a much more remote third Indian) and was asked, "What's foolish about that picture?" Being diverted from the point by his fear of aggression, he replied, "They should be friends instead of fighting each other." G., age 11 and of "average" ability, who is having difficulty in his play relationships and feels that he is loved less than an older brother, explained about the same picture, "If he shoots one of the warriors, that makes them mad at him."

And R.J., age 8 and with an IQ of 133, who is a new boy in his neighborhood and is overconcerned about pleasing people and being a "good boy," explained what was foolish about: "I read in the paper that the police fired two shots at a man. The first shot killed him, but the second did not hurt him much," by saying, "Shouldn't kill a man, should just arrest him and ask him what he was doing or something." Similar conflicts and worries can distort thinking. Asked to recall who had given the Shetland pony to Dick and Betty, L., whose mother is separated from his alcoholic father, said, "Their grandfather" rather than "Their father," which was correct for the story. And for T.H., age 12 and with an IQ of 89, the fears with which he was preoccupied intruded. "Constant" was defined as: "Something gets on your mind all of the time." And in completing the paragraph ending with: " . . . saying [to the nearest policeman] that he had just seen hanging from the limb of a tree a _____. A what?" T.H. said, "Ghost" rather than "man," which would have been more plausible.

.   For H., age 11 and with an IQ of 90, anxiety is so disorganizing and distracting that, although he reads almost perfectly the paragraph for year 10 of the Stanford-Binet, he cannot recall any of the 22 ideas, except the date— "September 5th."

Sometimes mentally retarded children, already handicapped by developmental immaturity, have their limited intellectual efficiency further impaired by emotional disturbances which divert them from problem solving. D., age 11 and with an IQ of 65, who said, "I do ugly work. Everything I do is not right," often substituted perseverative and associative responses for directed problem solving. He failed to count nine blocks because he persisted in his original pattern of counting by pairs; thus he could not shift to one block in proceeding from 8 to 9. Instead he placed 10 blocks and counted them as "nine." "Mars" he defined as: "Somebody gives you more of something." 'Skill is somebody kills you or something." And for: "What is a juggler?" he asked uncertainly, "Couldn't be a jug, could it?" In giving a similarity between "wood" and "coal," he free-associated from "coal," "They're black." He also perseverated with free associations for the two following pairs of similarities. For: "In what way are an apple and a peach alike?" he said, "White." And for "a ship and an automobile," he said, "Blue."

T., age 9, IQ 72, and lacking confidence, responded unnecessarily often with: "I can't get that." When asked to draw a man, rather than risk failure by an attempt at actually drawing it, he preferred to show by gestures only *how* he would go about drawing it. And for a series of cards, each showing five objects (four alike and one different), when asked to point to the one which was not the same as the others, he stereotyped his behavior by always pointing to the object on the extreme left, regardless of its character.

These examples both from the school and from the psychological-testing situation have illustrated a variety of specific ways in which emotional disturbances may impair learning and problem solving. For a more systematic understanding of the factors involved and of the dynamics of the process, it will be helpful to study the experiments and theories on emotional disturbances of learning.

Frustration and Behavior Related to Learning

Although the above examples include a wide variety of ineffective problem-solving and learning techniques, it may be noted that in nearly every instance these *insecure* children abandoned systematic problem-solving effort when they began to experience the frustration of anticipated failure—an anticipation, to be sure, which the situations did not always really justify. Several experiments have revealed a variety of patterns of reaction to frustration. Aggression toward the frustrating agent may be evoked. Or the aggression aroused may be displaced toward other people or situations, or even turned inwardly upon the frustrated child himself. Frustration may elicit in different children aggression, dependency, withdrawal, phantasied or rationalized solutions, anxiety-produced distracting impulses, or intensified and more effective problem-solving effort, depending upon each child's general background of experience and specific training and probably to some extent upon his innately determined temperament [18, p. 197].

Maier and Ellen, in generalizing on the effects of frustration, say that, according to frustration theory [39, p. 436]:

When an individual is placed in a problem situation, he first shows problem-solving behavior which is characterized by variability and goal seeking. When, however, the problem is insoluble, when escape is prevented and when pressures force the individual into the problem, he will become frustrated at one stage or another . . . Problem-solving behavior [learning] is now replaced by aggression, regression, and fixation [learning ceases], and these may appear separately or in various combinations. None of these behaviors is oriented toward the initial goal; in fact, they most frequently separate the individual farther from the initial goal.

Lazarus, Deese, and Osler, in reviewing experiments on the effects of psychological stress upon performance, conclude that stress, induced by failure (or threat of failure) or by task pressure (difficulty, excessive demands, or distractions) may impair performance. Results may include stereotyping, distraction of attention, disorganization of activity, increased overt activity, autonomic disturbance, and ego-defensively motivated behavior, such as ceasing effort and maintenance of self-esteem by unadjustive behavior (including irrational, altered modes of attack) [34].

Sears [54], it will be recalled from the preceding chapter, found disturbances in the aspiration levels of some children frustrated by continued school failure. Their aspirations were distorted either in being unrealistically high, as in the case of H.Y., or in being unrealistically low as in the case of D. And Lantz [33], also mentioned previously, found a failure experience to impair for some children both intelligence-test performance and attitude toward taking tests.

In an interesting experiment using 30 bright children (mean IQ: 122) with a mean age of approximately four years, Barker, Dembo, and Lewin [4] have indicated that a frustrating experience can for many children reduce the constructiveness level of their free play and can change negatively their emotional expressions, moods, and actions. Observations of emotional behavior and ratings on play constructiveness were made both before frustration and during frustration for each child individually as he played in a standardized playroom equipped with doll and housekeeping toys, truck and trailer, boats and water toys, and crayons and paper arranged on three squares. In the prefrustration period each child played in a part of the room where only the toys mentioned were visible. Frustration was introduced during a second play period by first removing the partition which had divided the room and exposing to the child, in addition to the familiar toys, a larger assortment, including much more interesting and attractive toys. After the child had become interested in the more attractive toys, the experimenter gathered up the first set of toys and returned them to their original places in the part of the room played in first. The child was also led to the "old" part of the room and directed, "Now let's play at the other end." A wire screen was then drawn across the room, preventing the child further access to the more attractive toys but leaving them visible to him.

The negative emotional changes noted were a decrease in freedom of expression and in happiness of mood. Increased were unhappy expressions and "motor restlessness and hypertension as revealed by loud singing and talking, restless actions, stuttering, and thumb sucking." There was also an increased aggressiveness—hitting, kicking, breaking, and destroying.

The measure of play constructiveness was a 7-point scale ranging from "rather primitive, simple, little-structured activities to elaborate, imaginative, highly developed play." As an example of its application, the observation record: "Sits on floor and takes truck and trailer in hand," (10 seconds) was rated 2. The following observation record was rated 7: " 'Here's a car truck, and it's going out fishing, so we have to take the trailer off. First, we have to go to the gas station. Toot! Toot! Now, he's going to the gas station. Ding, ding, ding.' Gets gas. Now back for trailer and the fish pole; child has truck and takes the motor boat; attaches it to truck and trailer. 'Hmmmm! Here he goes.' Behind Square 2 to Square 1. 'Quack! Quack! Mr. Ducky come.' Places on truck and trailer. Goes to Square 3. 'Here's the sailboat' " (225 seconds)·

In the prefrustration, free-play situation, the mean constructiveness rating was 4.99; after frustration, the rating was reduced to 3.94. That this regression of 1.05 points on the scale is significant statistically is indicated by a $D/\sigma d$ of 4.39. Since ratings on play constructiveness and mental age were found to correlate .73, it is possible to estimate the regression in play constructiveness in terms of mental age. The decrement thus estimated was found to be equivalent to 17.3 months of mental age. In other words, after frustration, the play of these children on the average corresponded to that of children about 17 months less mature than their "normal," or before-frustration, standard.

The most marked reaction of these four-year-old children to frustration of their play was a decrease in constructiveness. But reactions varied, including for different children attack and destructive aggression, restless activity, loud singing and talking, unhappy expressions, thumb sucking, and (for five children) improved constructiveness of play. As an explanation for the loss by several children in play constructiveness, Waterhouse and Child have proposed the hypothesis that "frustration will produce a decrease in the quality of on-going performance to the extent that the frustration evokes other responses which interfere with that on-going performance" [66, p. 298].

In an effort to determine some of the causes of children's different reactions to frustration, Davitz [13a], using as subjects 40 seven-to-nine-year-old children, extended the design of Barker, Dembo, and Lewin's experiment to include appraisal of the influence of specific training. His experimental design included, in sequence, (1) ratings on aggressiveness and constructiveness during free play with toys permitting either aggressive or constructive activities; (2) training of 20 children in one group in aggression and of an equated group of 20 in constructive behavior; (3) frustration of both groups; and (4) reratings of both groups for aggressiveness and constructiveness. The aggressive training consisted of seven 30-minute sessions of aggressive play, such as competing in tearing the "scalp" (a piece of cloth attached to each child's arm) off other children while protecting one's own and breaking other children's ping-pong balls while protecting one's own. The constructive training consisted of rewarding subjects for constructive work in making murals and jigsaw puzzles, for an equal number of sessions. The frustrating experience for both groups consisted of being deprived of candy and of having films they were seeing abruptly interrupted.

As a result of the training, the majority of the children in each group changed in the directions expected; but the changes were not universal. As reactions to frustration after training, 14 out of the 20 given aggressive training and 6 out of the 20 given constructive training became more aggressive. Of the children who improved in constructive reactions to frustration, 12 were from the 20 trained in constructive behavior, and 4 were from the 20 trained in aggressive behavior. Apparently children's reactions to frustration can be modified by training; but regardless of this particular training, some children persist in being aggressive, and other children continue in their tendencies toward constructive reactions to frustration. Davitz concludes that "the total past history of the individual must be considered in predicting and understanding his behavior after frustration" [13a, p. 315].

Maladjusted Children Lack Frustration Tolerance. It should be recalled in this connection that the children described earlier as demonstrating intellectual impairment in problem solving on what were for them frustrating intelligence-test items were in varying degrees emotionally maladjusted children. This would suggest that *emotionally maladjusted children* tend to make negative rather than constructive reactions to frustration. Emotionally healthy children may demonstrate more frustration tolerance [3]. Such a hypothesis is also supported by several experimental investigations.

Sherman [56, 57] has observed that, when frustrated in a learning situation, neurotic (emotionally maladjusted) children are more emotionally disturbed, as revealed both by physiological measures and by observed disintegration of their behavior, than are well-adjusted children. "Not only did the neurotic children react [emotionally] more quickly to frustration, but they also returned more slowly to the normal level" [56, p. 98].

Hutt [26] has found "poorly adjusted children" less able than "well-adjusted children" to tolerate the frustration inherent in taking the Stanford-Binet intelligence scale according to the standard directions. These directions involve proceeding in order from a level where all six tests for the given age group are passed to a level where all six of the tests are failed. Toward the end of the test, according to these directions, a larger number of the tests will be failed than passed; and in concluding the test, a child will have failed to pass in succession six to eleven items. It is possible, however, to adapt the directions by proceeding from the outset with alternately easy and more difficult items, thus minimizing failure frustration. When 33 pairs of well-adjusted children, matched for age, grade, and vocabulary, and 24 similarly matched pairs of poorly adjusted children were tested, one member of each pair in both groups being given the Stanford-Binet according to standard directions and the other according to adaptive directions, it was found that the mean IQs obtained for the well-adjusted groups did not differ significantly, being 109.6 and 110.4, respectively. But the poorly adjusted children were found to be more sensitive to the frustration imposed by following standard directions. The group of poorly adjusted children tested according to standard directions scored 11 IQ points lower than the matched group of poorly adjusted children for whom frustration was lessened by adaptive directions, the means being 91.7 and 102.7, respectively.

Anderson [1], in reporting a study of 3,200 children nine to eighteen years of age, has demonstrated a relationship at all age levels between affective attitudes of such children and their classification on adjustment inventories

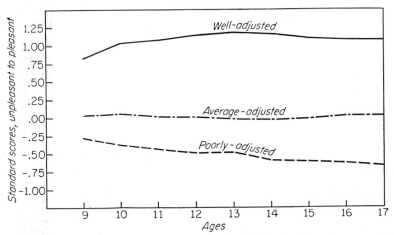

FIG. 9–1. Affective index (pleasant-to-unpleasant attitudes) is related to adjustment. (*From Anderson, J. E.: Education, 73: 212, 1952–1953.*)

and teacher's ratings as (1) well adjusted, (2) fairly well adjusted, and (3) poorly adjusted. The affective attitudes (pleasant, neutral, or unpleasant) were appraised by classifying the children's responses to a 30-item sentence-completion test, including such items as: "When I go home from school, I _____." The child who filled in the blank with: "I have a good time," would be credited with a pleasant attitude on this item. "I go by the store" would be classified as neutral. And "The boys tease me" would be rated unpleasant. Mean ratios of number of pleasant responses to number of unpleasant responses, converted to standard scores, for the three adjustment groups at each age level are graphed in Figure 9–1.

As an explanation of this relationship between maladjustment and "unpleasant" attitudes, it seems plausible to assume that the maladjusted child, because of frustration at school, unhappy parent-child relationships at home, and

Fɪɢ. 9–2. Learning to enjoy people, activities, and places is essential to mental health. (*Courtesy of Whittier School, Utah State Agricultural College.*)

frequent ineffective and unrewarding behavior in many situations, becomes conditioned to anticipate life generally as unpleasant. And apparently because of frequent reinforcement of this attitude, it tends to become more intense and generalized with age, as is suggested by the gradual separation of the curves.

In addition to these formal experiments on the relation of frustration tolerance to maladjustment, the observations of Redl and Wineman on the children who hate are pertinent. They found these seriously disturbed delinquent children extremely susceptible to frustration. "Even in the midst of a happily enjoyed game the slightest additional hurdle to be met or mild frustration to be added would throw the whole group into wild outbursts of unstructured bickering, fighting, disorganization, and griping" [50, p. 77].

Emotionality and Repression as Related to Learning

Sometimes as a result of associating words, ideas, or actions with anxiety and guilt-producing experiences, the words, ideas, or actions become, through conditioning, effective conditioned stimuli in eliciting anxiety. As a defense against such anxiety, however, the individual also unconsciously learns (by problem solving, according to the two-factor theory) to react to the incipient anxiety with repression or avoidance of giving attention to the anxiety-producing words or ideas. This concept is illustrated by Peter, who at five years nine months learned from repeated presentations of them to recognize 43 sight words. Peter was fascinated by the street which he watched from behind a fence; but because he was strongly impressed with the command that he "must never cross or go near the street," he was also conditioned to react to it with anxiety. Among the words presented to him were "school" and "street." He learned "school" after 18 exposures; but "street," which symbolized the anxiety-arousing street, was after 98 exposures still not consistently recognized. "Instead of looking at the word fixedly as was his custom with other words, he turned away from it" [25].

Several experiments also suggest the validity of this hypothesis. McGinnies [41], for example, found the perceptual exposure time required for recognition of emotionally toned or anxiety-arousing words to be greater than for neutral words. He presented to 16 adult subjects in a succession of brief exposures (from 0.01 second upward) 11 emotionally neutral words (as "apple," "dance," and "child") and seven emotionally toned words (as "raped," "whore," and "bitch"). He measured the exposure time required for recognition of the words; and by the galvanic skin response, he also measured during the prerecognition period the physiological emotional reactions elicited by these words. Even before they could be correctly recognized, the emotionally toned words produced in the subjects significantly greater ($t = 5.10$) emotional reactions, and the exposure times required for correct perception of them was reliably longer ($t = 3.96$), than for the neutral words. "The findings are interpreted as representing conditioned avoidance of verbal symbols having unpleasant meanings to the observer" [41, p. 251]. The resistance to recognizing the emotionally toned words is a perceptual defense "designed to delay the greater anxiety that accompanies actual recognition of the stimulus" [41, p. 250].

In a similar experiment, there were presented under seven different degrees of illumination (from below the threshold of visibility to adequate illumination) to adult subjects sentences representing both sexual and aggressive content and neutral content. The sentences embodying the anxiety-arousing content required greater illumination for perception and were sometimes distorted by the subjects to make them less disturbing [52].

In another experiment, Williams [68] has demonstrated how avoidance or repression of ideas associated with aggressive impulses threatening to the ego may interfere with learning. In studying learning by paired associates (after memorizing, presentation of one member of a pair being expected to elicit the other), he found college students retarded in their rate of learning hostile items (as "dark–blow" and "square–harm") as compared with both neutral ("cold–bird") and food ("dark–food") items.

In the above-mentioned experiments on the role of repression as a defensive device for avoiding in perception and learning anxiety-arousing stimuli, presumably well-adjusted subjects were used. Since maladjusted subjects apparently have much less tolerance for anxiety and are therefore more prone to be defensive, repression and distortion of perception and recall should be more marked in such subjects.

Sperry, Staver, and Mann have contributed additional and more concrete data on 30 emotionally disturbed children which are indicative of the ways in which repression may impair learning [60]. They hypothesize that injury or illness to a child or to a member of his family may emphasize or confirm the child's phantasies about destroying or being destroyed. As a defense against anxiety, guilt, and threat, the child may repress perception of certain content or distort verbal or motor expression in certain situations which have become symbolically related to the anxiety experiences, with consequent impairment of learning efficiency. The case of Janet, an eleven-year-old child with an IQ of 81 who was retarded in the third grade because of her inability to read, illustrates their concept.

For Janet, "looking" had become equivalent to "destroying by cutting." And as a defense from anxiety aroused by her own aggressive and sexual impulses, she inhibited her perception—seeing only a conglomeration of details, or only the middle parts of words. Words had become conditioned stimuli for anxiety in Janet, because they symbolized her younger brother Donald's scarred head and her mother's abdomen. These objects aroused her anxiety because of the guilt she experienced from the unconscious aggression, jealousy, and sexual rivalry she felt toward Donald. Consciously, she denied even looking at Donald's scar, for which, because of her aggressive impulses toward him, she felt vaguely responsible. Guilty about sex knowledge, she also denied knowing what distinguishes boys from girls and recognizing signs of pregnancy in women. Donald, she said, was brought in a moving truck (the ambulance), the letters on which she could not read; but reading letters had become associated with looking at her mother's abdomen with the baby inside before Donald was born. Such confusion and conflict could arise in Janet because of her parents' severe restraint, their inability to discuss disturbing situations, their failure to give Janet sex information, and their manifestations of negative attitudes toward her aggressions and the sexual connotations of her doll play.

Liss thinks that such learning disturbances are not especially rare. "For some students the implication that the contents of the learning process are sexual suffuses that activity with such taboo implications that the acquisition of facts is endowed with inordinate guilt and ultimately accentuated anxiety" [37, p. 520]. Sex guilt, however, is not always repressed by avoiding knowledge. A compulsive quest for knowledge and excessive intellectualizing may also screen otherwise disturbing sexual fantasies [38].

Summary: Effect of Emotional Disturbances on Learning

Our review of observations in school situations, of behavior observed in the psychological-testing situation, and of some related experiments indicates that for insecure and maladjusted or neurotic children, anxiety and distorted attitudes may impair learning efficiency in several ways. Faced with challenging or only mildly frustrating learning or problem-solving tasks, *attention* may be *distracted* by a variety of fear and escape impulses. Acute anxiety may result in almost complete *disorganization* of *behavior*. Confident, integrated, and systematic *problem-solving effort* is *abandoned* for *impulsive guessing, perseveration, free-associative responses, egocentric confabulations*, or *"giving up."* The learner often becomes *rigid* and *stereotyped* in his approach to problems so that varied provisional trials are no longer possible. He may *counter-aggressively resist teacher-guidance, attack himself*, or *overdependently* wait without initiative for too much teacher-guidance. In defense against anxiety, he may be partially "blinded" by *repression* or *distortion* of *perception* and *memory* of *facts* and *ideas* pertinent to his activities. And often, feeling inadequate, unworthy, and guilty, he will react to anticipated failure or other personality threats by a variety of other *ego-defensive* modes of adjustment, including withdrawal, phantasy, rationalizing, compulsive perfectionism, regression, assumption of unrealistic aspirations, and development of hysteric symptoms which justify his assumption that success in learning is impossible. Such emotional disturbances of thinking and learning are especially likely to impair efficiency in situations calling for initiative, resourcefulness, improvising, and organizing in problem solving and for creative productivity [20, 22, 44, 63].

A Dynamic Theory: Emotional Maladjustment and Learning Efficiency

A healthy personality, including efficiency in learning and problem solving, is a developmental achievement. The infant is born relatively helpless; but if, as he matures through childhood, he manages his developmental tasks successfully, he will develop a concept of himself as adequate, worthy, confident, and secure in dealing with tasks and in interpersonal relations. From the point of view of Maslow's hierarchy of motives, when a child is free from anxiety, excessive amounts of his energy will not be mobilized in seeking satisfaction of physiological needs, safety, love, and esteem. Such a child will be free for constructive and creative expression of his talents in various fields of interest.

The child's self-concept or self-image is a product of his socializing experiences. Modeling his behavior in a variety of situations largely after individuals whom he has come to love, he tries out various modes of attack: persistent effort at acquiring skills, playing fair, sharing, showing respect for his teachers, succeeding in school tasks, and other effective problem-solving techniques. And according to the conditions of learning, including perception of the effects and motive satisfaction, he incorporates into his personality and self-concept those patterns of behavior and ideals which significant adults in his environment have rewarded. Bennett has pointed out that, for full acceptance and approval in the culture of Western civilization, the individual, as he matures, must attain the ideal of "status—through success—through personal competence" [5]. Thus in the typical ideal self-image, attitudes of self-adequacy, self-capability, and self-sufficiency, because they are so universally rewarded in our culture, are emphasized.

General Conditions for Developing Mental Health. In presenting a concise but comprehensive view of the general requirements for developing a comfortable self-image and a healthy personality, Heffernan [24] has adapted Erikson's concept of the "eight stages of man" [19]. For development of a healthy personality, the individual needs to achieve, as he develops, (1) a *sense of trust* —from the care and love of adults, during his first year of relatively greatest dependency; (2) a *sense of autonomy*—from being permitted choices, independent action, and individuality in a safe environment, during the second and third years when he is making such strides in basic motor abilities, in language, and in exploration of himself and his environment; (3) a *sense of initiative* or *confidence*—from trying himself out in a variety of constructive and tentative role-playing experiences, during the fourth and fifth years when he is growing so rapidly in knowledge and skills, in independence, in effective social participation, and in ability to do many things for himself; (4) a *sense of worthwhile accomplishment*—from successful achievement in school, at home, and in play, during the period from six to twelve; (5) a *sense of identity*— from discovering, clarifying, accepting, and becoming effective in his major life role as he works successfully through the special "developmental tasks of adolescence"; (6) a *sense of intimacy* in the relations of love, friendship, and inspiration—as he accomplishes the social adjustments of courtship and marriage; (7) a *parental sense*—from productivity and creativity in family and responsible-adult roles, during the "working," productive, family-rearing years of life; and (8) a *sense of integrity*—from satisfaction and self-respect with one's roles in life.

These eight major attainments of healthy personality are not, of course, confined to the age periods mentioned in connection with each. Once achieved, each attainment continues to operate and to develop throughout the person's life. But cumulatively, accomplishment of preceding attainments constitutes preparation for the next developmental stage, and they all culminate in the "sense of integrity" mentioned last.

General Conditions Leading to Maladjustment. When a child's life at home, in school, and with his playmates fails to provide opportunities for developing a sense of trust, of autonomy, of confidence, of accomplishment, of comfortable identity with worthy life roles and when fulfillment of his ideal self-image of self-adequacy and personal competency are threatened, he will be vulnerable to development of maladjustive modes of behavior. Threatened with loss of esteem, love, and safety, all or most of his energy will be mobilized in excessive effort to secure only these basic needs. There will be little energy available for objective and constructive learning and for efficient problem solving. Having often experienced in the past rejection, disapproval, and harsh treatment for his "mistakes" at home, having frequently experienced failure at school, or, because of his own inadequacies and lack of interpersonal skills, having had many unhappy play experiences with his peers, he will have become conditioned to respond to a great many school and play tasks and interpersonal relations with feelings of inadequacy, inferiority, and guilt.

How Maladjusted-behavior Patterns are Learned. As protection from the anxiety thus aroused and in defense of his ideal self-image, each individual will by trial-and-error behavior learn the particular pattern of adjustive mechanisms which seems to satisfy his basic needs. But because of the ways in which reactions to anxiety can impair learning, he will often learn maladjustive modes of behavior. In striving compulsively to protect, at least partially, his self-image ideal, he will lose capacity for objective and constructive learning and creative productivity in general. And once maladjustive patterns are learned, even though in the long run they are self-defeating, they are clung to tenaciously. This occurs because through them a measure of anxiety reduction is achieved and because in defense of his ideal self-image of adequacy and self-competence, the individual, by repression, rigidity, and other defense mechanisms, selects and distorts his perception and recall of himself and of his life situations [5].

This concept of how maladjustive behavior is learned is illustrated by many of the children in the cases already cited. Janet allayed her anxiety over her aggressive and sexual impulses by not looking closely at things, especially words; but this defense for anxiety impaired her reading. Mary, fearful of the anxiety which might result from a mistake in reading, avoided an increase of anxiety by not risking a provisional guess; but this restriction of her trial-and-check learning efforts prevented further progress in reading. Both Johnny and H.Y. prevented intolerable anxiety by their compulsive perfectionism. Both children felt unloved or in danger of losing love. If Johnny should express the resentment he felt toward his mother for her impositions, he might lose her love. But doing things over and over to get them perfect allayed his anxiety (and prevented him from getting his school work done). And H.Y. could not risk doing a thing simply, such as defining a word unpretentiously. In these instances and in the others cited, anxiety-motivated behavior, although in the long run it proved self-defeating, was persisted in tenaciously because it provided immediate relief and because the consequences of these behavior patterns were not perceived.

In his more systematic explanation of how maladjustive behavior patterns are learned, Shoben [58, 59] assumes that they begin in faulty early socializing experiences. Because of these damaging socialization experiences, emotionally disturbed individuals do not learn to live comfortably and "to relate themselves to others in ways that are mutually evaluated as fulfilling" [59, p. 132]. As observed in the cases previously cited, pervading or easily aroused anxiety is common to all emotional maladjustment. The anxiety is acquired as a conditioned response to punishments—including the threat of loss of love. It is anticipatory and is attached primarily to those of the individual's own impulses which have been punished and forbidden—including sexual impulses, unjustified aggression, overdependency, seeking achievement and status in ways not culturally approved, and expressing affection in certain culturally forbidden relationships. By generalizing, *all* such impulses become conditioned cues for anxiety which "may be conceived as fear of one's self" [59, p. 132].

To the anxiety thus often aroused, the individual reacts by attempts at problem solving; but in this process, his efficiency is impaired by the blinding effect mainly of repression, which is a prepotent response because of its immediate, even though temporary and only partial, effectiveness in reducing anxiety. But as Shoben points out, the diminution of anxiety is purchased at a high price. Because repression excludes from verbalization and perception the impulses which elicit anxiety, the individual is left unable to interpret his own experience. (H.Y. did not know why he had to define a word either in flowery terms or not at all, nor that he could obtain the affection and respect which he wanted so much of his classmates more effectively by doing things casually and simply rather than with his habitual pretentiousness.) This leads to "neurotic stupidity" and to other expressions of the incompletely repressed impulses, including dreams, incipient motor responses, vague but troublesome symbolic meanings attached to objects and events, and feelings of dread and apprehension without recognition of any specific persons, objects, or events to justify the vague fears.

The maladjusted individual, "driven by anxiety and unable to symbolize the sources of the stress in his repressed impulses, desperately pursues first one set of goals and then another, giving up each as his strivings fail to bring him satisfaction. Forever dissatisfied, he develops an image of himself contrary to his self-ideal." Instead of feeling successful and competent, he perceives himself as inadequate—as unable to cope with demands of his own existence. "And these self-concepts lead to even more intolerable anxiety, under motivation of which he develops various strategies ['being perfect,' 'not looking at forbidden things,' 'being dependent,' etc.] for rationalizing or denying his experience to himself and to others." But these adjustments, although they partially allay anxiety, lead to failure in important life activities and therefore to social disapproval and self-blame—"thus producing an ever-increasing spiral of neurotic involvement" [59].

"Without realizing how it happened," these maladjusted individuals are forced, because of their ineffective efforts and consequent self-recrimination and social disapproval, "to the painful realization that they have fallen short" —that they are failures. And since feeling inadequate, inferior, and guilty is incompatible with their incorporated cultural ideals, there is a powerful tendency to deny this embarrassing self-image, to attribute it to others, to seek protection, to rebel, to be counter-aggressive, to be compulsively perfectionistic, or to demonstrate in some way the untruth of the strongly felt inadequacy. But this aggression and failure to assume self-responsibility and these false pretensions lead to further disapproval and guilt. The whole trend becomes a vicious circle: sexual, aggressive, and other culturally disapproved impulses → punishment → anxiety and general fear of self → repression → "neurotic stupidity" → social disapproval and self-disapproval → to further anxiety and guilt → to more perceptual distortion and neurotic stupidity—in a self-sustained cycle.

This theory on how emotional maladjustment may impair learning efficiency may be summarized in the light of the two-factor theory of learning. As a result of an unfortunate psychological history, the individual has become conditioned to respond with anxiety to a wide variety of tasks and interpersonal situations. As defenses against anxiety, he learns by trial-and-error problem solving a variety of techniques and self-attitudes, which, except for partially and temporarily reducing anxiety, are ineffective and self-defeating. But despite their ineffectiveness, they are maintained and applied generally —in school, in psychological testing (as has been noted above), at home, and in other social and personal situations—because these defensive techniques and attitudes are not perceived by the child as contributing to his maladjustment.

Theory of Treatment for Maladjusted Children. Their treatment, it would seem, will require first, counter-conditioning (as was done for Peter) to help them learn security, comfort, and confidence as responses to the cues and impulses which heretofore have led to anxiety; and second, when they are free from anxiety and distorting self-attitudes, helping them learn by problem solving more effective patterns of adjustment.

Counter-conditioning to feel comfortable and trustful of people again rather than anxious, suspicious, or hostile occurs in the child because his teacher and counselor are nonthreatening. They are interested, sympathetic, loving, accepting despite his maladjustive behavior, encouraging, and confident in him. In this situation, as he begins to behave more freely and less defensively, they help him to perceive more clearly the consequences, both good and bad, of his behavior. As he tries out in self-perspectives, verbal expressions, and actions new and sometimes more constructive behavior, he is rewarded both by their approval and by the intrinsic satisfaction of adopting more resourceful and effective modes of adjustment. And as he practices in his relations with his teacher and counselor these new modes of adjustment, they are generalized and gradually (by transfer) applied generally in and out of school. Thus, according to the conditions of effective learning, not only is subject matter learned, but emotional health is restored. Whether children learn, as they are maturing, healthy or unhealthy patterns of adjustment depends upon the quality of their care, interpersonal relationships, and guidance in both their homes and schools.

Role of the Home in Emotional Control in Learning

The basis for a healthy, confident, efficient approach to school learning is largely a product of good child-parent relationships before the age for entering school. According to Heffernan, as already mentioned, from such child-parent experiences the emotionally healthy child has developed by six years of age a sense of trust, a sense of autonomy, and a sense of self-confidence and initiative.

And according to Maslow's hierarchical concept of motives, if he is accustomed to adequate provision for his physiological needs and feels safe, loved, and esteemed, the child will be free for constructive and creative use of his talents. Adapting from both Nimkoff [46] and Katz and Lehner [29], the child-parent relationships desirable for the child's development of healthy emotional control may be summarized as follows: Every child needs two emotionally healthy parents

1. Who have themselves developed a sense of integrity in their life roles and who love each other.

2. Who love him and demonstrate amply their love of him, thus helping him to achieve feelings of trust, security, and confidence.

3. Who achieve some understanding, as he matures, of his talents, interests, and aspirations.

4. Who further his development by providing opportunities, guidance, encouragement, and democratic discipline.

5. Who provide, as he matures, appropriate amounts of help and guidance, opportunities for independence, respect and pleasure in his developmental achievements, and freedom for development—at his own rate, following his own interests, and finding his own talents.

6. Who accept him as he is and are permissive with respect to emotional expression, even of fears, angers, and jealousies.

7. Who provide within the family a sense of belonging, opportunities for democratic planning and social action, and opportunities for consideration and help with both individual and family problems.

How a child about to enter the first grade of school who has experienced most of these beneficial child-parent relationships behaves in the psychological-testing situation is indicated from an excerpt from the psychologist's report on Marilyn:

Besides meeting the minimum mental age requirements for success in a first grade curriculum (M's MA was 6-11 and her IQ was 118), she demonstrated several other traits which may be equally important as factors favoring a good adjustment in the first grade. In vocabulary, she is at the eight year level of development, and she expresses herself freely, accurately, and concisely ("An envelope is something you put a letter in."). Also at the eight year level, she was successful in comprehending the story read to her and concentrated well enough to recall all six items asked about the story. On relatively difficult items, permitting three successive trials (drawing a diamond and recalling digits), she persisted in problem-solving, and in improving on the successive trials, showed her capacity for learning from experience. In her relations with the strange examiner, she showed unusual poise and spontaneity in initiating and in participating in conversation ("Sometimes I help Mama bathe my baby brother."). Despite her spontaneity in expressing herself, she maintained a high degree of attention (no direction had to be repeated) and complied willingly and promptly with all directions. And she took pleasure in her problem-solving efforts and achievements. In general, she should be a very teachable and creative child.

Too often, however, homes fail to provide these child-parent relationships considered necessary for healthy emotional development and control. When in place of these conditions, the child experiences rejection, inadequate guidance, and harsh treatment, he will be vulnerable to emotional maladjustment and sometimes to resulting impairment of learning and problem-solving efficiency.

McCarthy proposes the "hypothesis that emotional insecurity, usually stemming from unwholesome parental attitudes of rejection and over-protection, is the basic cause of most educational disabilities and learning failures which are not due to mental defect." This "emotional insecurity," she writes, "is the cause of the entire syndrome of behavior maladjustment and the poor learning in whatever area it manifests itself" [40, p. 95]. In support of this hypothesis, she states that "three-fourths of all our nonreaders [in her clinic] show clear evidences of parental rejection, or over-protection, or both." In reaction to the frustration of parental rejection or overprotection, these nonreaders developed one or the other of two different patterns of behavior. An aggressive group, exemplified by Ted, who scribbled on his teacher's board and blotter, were characterized by quarrelsomeness, defiance, jealousy of siblings, bad temper, stubborn and demanding attitude, fears, lack of friends, and lack of motor skills, normal interests, and ability in athletics. The submissive group, more similar to "good-as-gold" Johnny, also exhibited jealousy of siblings and lack of skill in sports, but were quiet, docile, immature and helpless, and fearful and anxious, and did not dare show antisocial behavior.

As a concrete example both of how such emotional attitudes may interfere with effective learning and of the treatment of such emotional disturbances, we may cite a case from Axline's study of nondirective therapy for emotionally disturbed nonreaders [2, pp. 64–65]:

Dick was a thin, hollow-eyed boy, almost nine and still in the second grade. He stayed on the outer edge of the group. He watched the others, said very little to anyone, and drifted around the room leaving behind him a trail of unfinished work. When, for a moment on rare occasions, he joined in the activities of the group there was soon a flare-up of trouble because Dick had moments of displaying a violent temper. He bit other children, hit them, kicked them, shoved them. He was bigger than they. And just as quickly as it flared up, it died down, and he cried out his remorse, "I'm sorry!

I'm sorry! I didn't mean to do it." Dick played truant quite often. When he did his truancy was followed by reports from other children on the way to and from school, from the neighbors, store-keepers, and the police. Dick stole, set fires, and committed acts of vandalism. Dick was not at all interested in reading, or in any other school work.

One day, during the children's "work period," Dick decided to paint. The teacher sat down beside him, smiled at him. Dick looked at her with a sad expression in his eyes. He was slopping black paint over his paper. Then suddenly he said to her, "Know what? I'm a bastard—just a dirty bastard and I ain't got no father and I never did have. My stepfather told me he wished I'd never been born. You know what a bastard is, don't you?"

"Yes," said the teacher, "I know. And it makes you unhappy when you think about it—and when your step-father talks to you like that."

"I've got a sister," said Dick, and there was a note of pride in his voice. "She's pretty, like a doll. She's three. She's taking dancing lessons." He smiled briefly, then suddenly glowered. "I hate her," he said, "I hate her. She gets everything. They love her."

"She's a pretty little sister—and kind of nice, but sometimes you hate her because she gets things and you don't—and you think they love her better than they do you."

"Yeah!" Dick said. He smeared the paper vigorously. He stabbed it with his brush. Then he looked at the teacher again with a brief smile. "She's got yellow curls all over her head," he said, "bright as the sun." He paused momentarily. "She's so sweet," he said. His smile changed again to a glower. "Someday, I'll get the scissors and cut them off," he said. "I'll take the scissors and cut her throat. Then they'll feel bad."

"You think she's a sweet little girl—and pretty—but sometimes you feel like hurting her to get back at your mother and stepfather because of the way they treat you, hm?"

"Yeah," Dick answered soberly. "I wouldn't hurt her, I'd kill her and get rid of her so they wouldn't have her."

"Oh," said the teacher, "You mean you would kill her just to take her away from your parents."

"Yeah," Dick answered, glumly. He placed his other hand down on the wet black paint and smeared it around. "I wouldn't though," he said quietly. "I wouldn't hurt her. Not really. She's the only one at home who likes me. She runs out to meet me. I take good care of her. If anybody ever hurts her, why, I fight them until they bleed."

"Then you really think a lot of your little sister and she thinks a lot of you—and you wouldn't hurt her or let anyone else hurt her."

"I'll say I wouldn't. It's my stepfather I really hate."

There the teacher had a brief glimpse into Dick's inner thoughts. And there were many other times when the teacher sat down beside Dick, who had a very real problem and was not interested in reading, writing, or anything else. First of all he must find some release from these tensions and feelings of conflict. First of all he must feel accepted.

Before Dick could learn efficiently, he must first be given freedom from anxiety and distorting emotional attitudes. Axline's report shows that, when these children were given the kind of therapy which we have shown was given to Dick, in 19 out of 37 children, during the $3\frac{1}{2}$ months between pretests and end-tests, the gains on the Gates Primary Reading Tests exceeded $3\frac{1}{2}$ months of growth in reading age.

There are other writers who also see in unfortunate parent-child relations the origin of emotional disturbances which impair efficiency of learning in school. Missildine [43] reports on 30 children ages 7 to 13 and with IQs of 91 to 140, all with reading disabilities, whose case histories, selected from the files of the children's psychiatric service of the Harriet Lane Home for Children, were examined for information on parent-child relations. Of these 30 children, who were all functioning inefficiently in school, the mothers of 10 were characterized as "critical, hostile, and rejecting." Ten other mothers were described as "tense, coercive, perfectionistic," and as demanding strict obedience. And the fathers of these 20 children also were in various ways lacking in support, guidance, or love. Among the remaining 10 children, four of them had problems of sibling rivalry over a new baby; two were indulged until they entered school and then were neglected; two were considered "over-protected"; and one child was disturbed over adjusting to a new school in a new city to which he had been moved: "All of these children," writes Missildine, "with at most one or two exceptions, had this in common: They harbored a serious affect disturbance in connection with some member or members of their family. Some assumed a restless, indifferent, happy-go-lucky pose in reacting to this disturbance. Others felt crushed, unhappy, inadequate. With one exception, all were acutely ill emotionally" [43, p. 271].

Blanchard has shown that children who, because of unfortunate relations with their parents, develop emotional conflicts toward them, often involving anxiety over repressed hostility, are handicapped both in establishing healthy relations with other people and in their learning efforts. Children like to please and to imitate loved and admired parents. When they come to feel rejected or cheated by their parents, they may become counter-aggressive and unconsciously resist their guidance. These positive or negative attitudes may be transferred by children to their teachers, with consequent enhancement or impairment of their learning to read or to achieve effectively in other curriculum areas [7, pp. 411–412]. Overdependence as well as resistance, however, may be transferred from child-parent relations to child-teacher relations [61].

In a study by Hattwick and Stowell [23] relating ratings on parent-child relations to ratings on adjustment in school, it was found that in both effectiveness of work habits and in quality of social adjustment, children rated as either "pushed by parents" or "babied by parents" were inferior to children who enjoyed "well-adjusted" relations with their parents.

Finally, we may cite the conclusion of Jenkins, Shacter, and Bauer, who write that "those who work with problems of adjustment place a major emphasis upon the influence of early emotional experiences in the home in determining how a child feels toward other people, and his capacity for weathering the strains and frustrations which everyone will have from time to time." In support of this view, they cite the experience of Dr. Lauretta Bender of Bellevue Hospital, New York, who, as a result of studying "more than six thousand maladjusted youngsters, feels that almost all of these children have suffered from lack of adequate parent-child relationships in infancy and early childhood" [27, p. 222].

Role of the School in Emotional Control of Learning

For children who bring to the school a "sense of trust," a "sense of autonomy," and a "sense of confidence and initiative," the school experiences over the years between approximately six and twelve can provide opportunity for another important phase in the development of mental health—that of developing a "sense of accomplishment." And for children who feel safe, loved, and esteemed, it can provide opportunities for a high level of motive satisfaction in constructive and creative expression of their talents. These opportunities would further enhance the confidence, efficiency, and interest of children in learning and problem-solving activities.

But unfortunately, the school, like the home, also sometimes provides conditions for acquiring the reverses of these attitudes and modes of adjustment. Some children develop a sense of inferiority rather than a sense of accomplishment; and rather than feeling safe, loved, and esteemed, some children come to feel threatened, unlovable, and guilty. There are desirable procedures in at least five areas of school experience which can help to implement a child's development of healthy emotional control and efficient learning: a suitable curriculum, effective and otherwise appropriate teacher-guidance and methods of teaching, supervision and guidance of the child's in-school social experiences, help in dealing with his personal problems, and indirect aid through helping his parents to better understanding of his needs.

1. Suitable Curriculum. A curriculum of learning activities for each child suited to his maturity, interests, needs, and pattern of abilities should lead in the main to success experiences and thus result for the child in a sense of accomplishment. Being able to do something well contributes to a child's healthy acceptance of himself, his feeling of worth, and his self-confidence. And because children are typically characterized by wide intraindividual trait variations—varied motor abilities, art abilities, music abilities, craft skills, social abilities, and intellectual abilities—a child is most likely to find something he can do well if his school provides great diversity of curricular opportunities and guidance in finding his talents in them. Making progress in such a curriculum should result in feelings of enhanced value and worth as a person. From success in varied learning and problem-solving experiences, the child will learn how to learn more effectively and will develop increasing confidence in learning and problem solving as general modes of adjustment. Because of his increasing skill and confidence as a learner and problem solver, he will make better adjustments in his life in general—with his playmates, with his siblings and parents, and in other interpersonal relations.

To provide the same standard curriculum for every child in a classroom, however, ignores the fact of marked individual differences and for many children results in frustration, confusion, and failure. From such experiences in school, children are likely to develop self-attitudes of inferiority, guilt, or counter-aggressive rebelliousness. Rather than developing confidence and skill in learning and problem solving, the child who has found his learning efforts frustrated will turn away from learning and problem solving as modes of adjustment and thus will be handicapped for dealing with tensions arising in many of his life situations. Such children who have experienced too much failure can sometimes be helped to return to more effective learning and problem-solving procedures by specially contrived success experiences [30, 31, 42] and by remedial teaching.

The statement of aims given in Chapter 1, which includes both child development and subject-matter objectives, is a good guide in providing a suitable curriculum. It is apparently easier, however, for teachers to accept such principles on a verbal level than to translate them into actual curricula and teaching practices. Oliver, in working with 119 elementary teachers, found that they believed it desirable to provide for individual differences, to relate learning to maturity levels, to provide "experience units," and to relate learning to child interests and previous experiences. But he also found a correlation of only .31 between their belief scores and the scores on an evaluation of their *teaching practices* in these areas [47]. Because a curriculum suited to each child's maturity and pattern of abilities is crucially related to most of the conditions for effective learning and because it is so difficult to create, providing it will require of teachers very serious and persistent effort and study.

A curriculum rich in opportunities for resourcefulness and creative expression, besides correcting the shyness and overdependency of some children, should contribute to the emotional health and motivational satisfaction of all children. During the course of the elementary school years, children should be exposed to many creative media and should be encouraged to try their hand at using them. As children begin to explore their world through excursions, in unified curriculum projects, and in science, social studies, reading, health, and other subject activities, they begin to use the objects and materials around them to express their thoughts and feelings. To encourage free and resourceful creative expression, their home and school environment should provide abundantly a variety of simple media and needed guidance in exploring their uses. Art activities, crafts, puppets, dramatic play, rhythms and dancing, music, creative writing, construction, and science and social studies projects are all rich in opportunities for creative expression. As children are thus encouraged to experiment freely with various arts and crafts media, they may find the need for certain techniques and skills. At these points, appropriate teacher-guidance will lead to improved competence and confidence in creative expression.

2. *Teaching Procedures.* Sometimes faulty teaching methods, especially inadequate guidance in modes of attack in reading, spelling, arithmetic, and other subjects, can result in pupil frustration, confusion, and failure [8]. As a consequence of such experiences, the pupil may develop attitudes of inferiority or rebellion which will impair subsequent learning efforts. To motivate learning by threats, by competition with one's peers, or by excessive concern for success and avoidance of failure may impair learning efficiency in some instances. Teachers who reward pupils with approval for learning efforts, for persistence in problem solving, and for using good modes of attack, rather than confine their approval and disapproval to successful and failing *outcomes*, will find that they can distribute their approval of learning efforts more widely. Keister has shown that such motivation can help children with emotional disturbances connected with learning and immature modes of attack to become more effective as learners [30, 31]. But besides employing efficient modes of attack in teaching and appealing to motives (which show a concern for both personality and subject-matter goals), the teacher can through appropriate teacher-guidance indicate to a child her concern and interest in and her affection for him, thus promoting feelings of trust and self-worth. This is illustrated interestingly in an example from Redl and Wattenburg [51, p. 191]:

Ned was having trouble with decimal points in a multiplication problem. From her desk, Miss Jenks noticed the frown on his face. She walked to his seat and asked him

FIG. 9–3. Encouragement and teacher-guidance on a problem at the right time are likely to result in its satisfying completion and in self-confidence rather than failure and guilt. (*Courtesy of Whittier School, Utah State Agricultural College.*)

what was wrong. He said that he couldn't do the problem. With patient questions she helped him figure out the answer and, in doing so, to understand the rule and reason for it. Then she gave him another problem. Later, when he had solved it, he brought the paper to her desk. All she said was, "That's right."

Such incidents have an emotional as well as intellectual meaning. To Ned, Miss Jenks's first approach meant that when he was making mistakes an adult did not punish him or reject him but stood by him. The trouble she took told him that he was pretty important as a person; at least, he was worth bothering about. The fact that he was led to find the answer for himself was a way of declaring that Miss Jenks had confidence in him, and he was justified in respecting his own ability.

Another aspect of teaching in which the possibility of arousing undue anxiety needs to be considered is that of necessary criticism. Perception of the effects is an essential condition of effective learning; children must recognize, correct, and avoid their mistakes. But with due concern for the possibility of arousing anxiety or resistance to learning, the teacher will try to give criticism in proper amounts, at the right times, and in the right way. If a third grade child has pointed out to him *all* the errors in his composition at the same time, he may be overwhelmed by his limitations or by the task's complexity. He can make improvements more confidently and effectively if he attacks one or two kinds of errors at a time. In undertaking a new project, initial success, indicating that he will be able to manage it, may be more helpful to a child than being confronted immediately with all his errors. Or when general confidence depends upon being right, as was true of the child who thought she knew how to write her name correctly on the first day of school, correction of errors should be deferred. Later, when confidence in one's capacity to master the task has been developed and when he feels more secure in general, the child will welcome criticism as a means to self-improvement.

Heed for the right way to give criticism is illustrated in a specific example from Stoelting, who, as the classroom teacher of a group of cerebral-palsy children, was especially concerned with the teaching of speech. When Willie heard his speech on the recorder (used as an aid in perceiving the effects of his speech trials), he seemed quite shocked; he had thought that he spoke much better. He argued that everyone had been well recorded except himself. When the children told him that it did sound just like him, "he was finally convinced it was a true record, and he was horrified. His teacher said: 'Willie, don't start hating yourself because you didn't like your speech. We hear you all the time but we like you. You have to like yourself too. We can work with the recorder and try to improve your speech'" [62].

Attention to *methods of attack*, rather than to outcomes only, and to the correctness of only some aspects of a child's learning efforts can lessen the hazard that teacher-corrections may make a child fearful of making mistakes and thus restrict desirable variability in his problem solving. For example, when a retarded reader reads "seventeen" as "silver" in the phrase "seventeen families lost their homes," the teacher need not say, "Oh, my, no, not 'silver'; the word is 'seventeen'!" Instead, he can say something like: "That was a good trial on 'seventeen'! you used your knowledge of both the 's' and 'v' sounds. It didn't come out completely correct because we have found that we need to learn more about the other parts of words like 'seventeen.'" Then, using material containing fewer words unfamiliar to the child so that he can also use the context more effectively, the teacher will give guidance in combining consonants with vowels in their long, short, silent, and "r" forms and in analyzing words into syllables and meaning units.

Overaggression, excessive timidity, tense speech, uncompleted tasks, and such behavior as thumb-sucking are indications of need for more security, for less frustrating conditions in home or school, and for understanding, support, and guidance. Guided by sensitivity and alertness to such unhealthy developmental trends and to symptoms of pupils' emotional disturbance, appropriate teaching at the right time can serve a therapeutic role.

The teacher can lessen frustrations for the overaggressive child by providing a curriculum in which he can succeed, by giving guidance in effective methods of learning, and by being accepting, permissive, encouraging, and democratic in her guidance of him. For children whose aggression arises from the frustration of autocratic and harsh home control, the teacher can provide especially opportunities for self-planning and choice of activities. Sometimes opportunities for legitimate expression of aggression need to be provided, as in physical play, art, dancing, crafts, and "talking it out." For the young child, Read suggests acceptance, permissiveness of expression, explanation, and guided diversions (such as: "You feel just like hitting someone, I know. Let's run as hard as we can over to that corner. That may make you feel better" [49, p. 142], or: "I know you feel like hitting him because he has the tricycle you want. When you feel like that, you can hit our punching bag or do some pounding at the table" [49, p. 164]). By her example and explanations, a teacher of older children helped George's classmates to understand and to deal with his impulsive hostilities—reactions to abandonment by his parents and punishments from the aunt with whom he lived. When his classmates complained about his unprovoked, bullying attacks upon them, the teacher would say, "When you see George in one of his mean streaks, stay away from him and tell me. I'll try to help him. When he's having a good day, be friendly. He has a hard life" [67, p. 134]. Teacher-explanation leading to both understanding and tolerance of other children's aggression is illustrated in Read's example: "Never mind. He's calling you names only because he is mad. It's your turn on the swing and he wants it to be his. It makes him feel better to call you 'Dope.' You don't need to let it bother you" [49, p. 167].

For shy, overdependent, and helpless children, both general training and specific guidance at the appropriate time will help them to become more resourceful. Jacks [42] has found that training in skills needed for effective social participation helps shy children to develop more confidence and initiative. As another means of developing initiative, resourcefulness, and a problem-solving approach to frustrations and problems, teacher-guided self-construction of needed material is suggested. "Because there was only one easel and so many of us to use it, we had to take turns, the rest of us painting at our desks or on the floor" [53, p. 233]. Finding this very unsatisfactory and having no funds for the purchase of extra easels, the class, in a cooperative, problem-solving approach, constructed them. Experiencing satisfaction in such resourcefulness, "the boys and girls in our class are learning slowly that we, ourselves,

FIG. 9–4. From "self-help" in meeting some of their needs, children develop resourcefulness and problem-solving attitudes. (*Courtesy of McKinley School, Tremonton, Utah.*)

can do something about our lack of things. If we really need it, we can make it" [53, p. 233].

As an example of meeting the child's need at the appropriate time, Wattenburg's illustration is pertinent [67]. Jack, who often left work unfinished for fear of failure and criticism (his parents often criticized him for failing to meet their too-high standards for him), merely stared at his just-begun arithmetic problem. His alert teacher, sensitive to Jack's need at such occasions, relieved his fear by her manifestation of interest and encouragement: "It's right as far as you've gone." This help at the right time was enough to encourage Jack to go on to satisfying completion of the lesson and to take a step toward greater self-confidence.

Such teaching recognizes that, as children are learning reading, arithmetic, or science by teacher-guided problem solving, they are also by conditioning acquiring either emotional health or illness. By understanding children, by being alert and sensitive to the meaning of their behavior, and by appropriate action at the right time as opportunities occur in daily teaching situations, teachers can help children to build emotional strength—security and confidence. Understanding involves recognition that behavior always has a purpose. Both "good" behavior and socially unacceptable behavior are attempts at meeting needs "to be loved, to belong to a group, to have a feeling of self-respect, to conquer fears of inadequacy, to earn approval of one's fellow-humans, or to satisfy curiosity" [67, p. 135]. Such understanding—seeing the child and his situation from his point of view—should guide the teacher in taking at the right time appropriate action for each child's emotional health.

3. *Supervision of Social Relations.* Each child needs to feel accepted, loved, and esteemed by his classmates. If he feels rejected and disapproved by them, he may withdraw, he may react counter-aggressively with general displaced aggression, as did Dick, or he may, in excessive and compulsive efforts to win their approval, set such unrealistic and pretentious standards for himself that other children come to regard him as a show-off, as was true for H.Y. In any case, the child's anxiety-motivated behavior will probably prove ineffective in winning friends, and he will not be left free for constructive and creative effort in school activities.

Teachers can help such children by friendly, professional, intelligent supervision of children's social activities in the classroom, in the lunchroom, at school parties and special events, and on the playground at "recess" periods. Such supervision should be guided by democratic principles [35]. It will require knowledge and skill in suggesting, guiding, and providing a sufficient variety of interesting and otherwise appropriate social activities. By providing for each child opportunities for expressing his talents, self-confidence rather than overconformity or overdependency will be cultivated. For children who have special difficulties in establishing friendly relations with other children, the teacher can provide opportunities to come into contact with potential friends —through arrangement of seating, appointments to working groups, committees, etc. [16]. For children whose social skills and standards are unacceptable to their group, special coaching on their specific needs will often help. By using opportunities to select pupils for helping with school routines (distributing the materials for art, watering the plants, arranging materials on the bulletin board, etc.), children who need confidence-building experiences and more social contacts can be given such experiences.

Through parent-teacher conferences, teachers can help parents to arrange for more out-of-school social experiences with classmates for children who, because of the remoteness of their homes or for other reasons, rarely meet their classmates, except in school. And for children whose personality problems make their own efforts at winning friends self-defeating, arrangements for counseling and specially planned experiences will be needed.

Sometimes a teacher can enlist the help of an unhappy child's classmates in efforts to improve his social relations. Elaine is a colored child who had been highly aggressive toward her classmates because she felt rejected by them

Fig. 9–5. Coaching in sports and social skills can sometimes give a child the skill, confidence, and peer status he needs for achieving better social relationships. (*Courtesy of Standard Oil Company of New Jersey.*)

("They're mean to me"). The teacher, in Elaine's absence, asked her classmates, "Are there any ways in which we can make Elaine feel happier?" After the discussion, the children tried to put their suggestions into practice, as is indicated by such later comments as: "Elaine can jump pepper," proudly announced by one of her classmates after a recess period, and by Elaine's comment that she was going to walk home from school with Jane, who had suggested that they walk home together.

Apparently academic achievement and good social adjustment are to some extent reciprocally related, each affecting favorably the other and both being conditions of emotional health [11].

4. Teacher-help with Personality Problems. There are three ways in which teachers can help to alleviate personality problems which hinder efficient learning: They can be alert to symptoms of maladjustment; they can treat some problems of maladjustment and can cooperate in the treatment of all school children; and they can refer seriously emotionally disturbed children to the school psychologist or counselor or to other appropriate professional help.

Emotional maladjustment is evidenced when a child achieves less than he is capable of achieving; is easily provoked to anger and hostility toward other children, teacher, and other older people; is destructive and steals; is excessively timid and worried; is depressed; is oversensitive to slights or imagined slights; is overanxious to achieve perfection; violates school regulations often; shows little or no affection; hesitates to begin tasks; withdraws and prefers "just sitting"; often appears confused; is perpetually fatigued [64, 65]. These and other, similar symptoms are indicative of emotional maladjustment and indicate a need for teacher-investigation of possible causes. The child's school day, his play activities, and (through the parent-teacher conference) his home activities and child-family relations should be examined for possible frustrations of his needs for security, love, esteem, and achievement opportunities. Every possible adjustment to eliminate such frustrations should be made. As was done for Dick, the teacher, during supervision of informal class activities (as during art periods) and in afterschool child-helping periods should provide opportunities for permissive expression of feeling. If the problem appears to be one which friendly acceptance, affection, and teacher-guidance can help, such guidance should be given. Otherwise the child should be referred for more professional mental-hygiene service.

A further example from Redl and Wattenburg illustrates effective teacher-help for an emotionally disturbed child [51, p. 199]. Ira was so fearful of making mistakes that, to play safe and to remain less insecure, he did little or nothing.

At first teachers thought that he might have some illness that had sapped his energy. He had a peculiar inability to complete any task. However, only a passing glance at the playground showed that there he was a little powerhouse. The contrast was so great that they decided he was willfully lazy. They sent for his mother. She was no help. Her story was that he was the same way at home. There, he never seemed to get anything right. She claimed that she and his father did all they could to give the boy high standards. The wording of her summary was revealing: "His father is at him all the time, and I'm even worse." In as much as nagging and punishment had not worked at home, obviously the school should try another attack. A clue was supplied when a student teacher was asked to watch him closely. She reported that he started tasks but either destroyed his work or left it undone. Following this lead, his teacher waited until he was halfway through a lesson, then walked over and looked at the paper. He glanced up with the look of a dog expecting to be beaten. She said, "You have the idea," smiled, and went to another pupil. With variations, she repeated the same performance. Ira improved a little. He began to finish some tasks and take them to the teacher for approval. It was plain to see, though, that he was still very unsure of himself. His teacher was afraid to be critical when his work was faulty lest he be frightened back into his old defense. That was not a healthy situation, but a start had been made toward correcting Ira's trouble.

Sometimes a teacher can aid an emotionally disturbed child by inviting him to share with her some special afterschool activity, such as getting the art materials ready for the next day's project. Jersild has pointed out the therapeutic possibilities in such a relationship [28, pp. 282–283]:

The common task makes it possible for the child to be silent when he chooses, yet his nearness to the adult makes it possible for him to talk about the work or about himself if he so desires. The work makes it possible for him to make mistakes and to observe that he will not be condemned, to proceed slowly and observe that this adult is not going to hurry him, to venture a little criticism while observing that it brings no retaliation, to express self-reproach about his own lack of skills while observing that he is not therefore abandoned as a failure, and so on. . . . The child, without having to ask for help, or seem like a weakling or a beggar, can explore this relationship, exploit it, and venture into an expression of his feelings and grow in his understanding of what might be expected of others, as well as in an awareness of his own wishes and his own rights.

5. *The Parent-teacher Conference*. Because, as we have already learned, a child's maladjustment is often largely a result of unfortunate child-parent relationships, he can be helped indirectly by working with his parents. A technique teachers are learning that makes for better child-parent and -teacher relations is the parent-teacher conference. It was mentioned in the case of Robert, in the previous chapter, and in the case of overperfectionistic Johnny, in this chapter. The teacher will approach the parent or parents at school or at their home with a friendly, noncritical attitude, stating that she thinks that by learning something of the child's behavior at home and by working cooperatively with his parents, she will be able to help him more effectively at school. By listening with interest and by being accepting and noncritical of the parents, a friendly teacher can help allay some of their probable anxiety, guilt, and defensiveness with respect to the child's maladjustment as they talk with her. If a calm, objective, and interested attitude toward the child's problem can be achieved, teacher and parent can proceed in problem-solving fashion to consider ways of helping the child toward more healthy development. If the parents remain anxious and defensive, more expert professional help will be needed.

Fig. 9–6. The common task shared with his permissive and interested teacher provides the child with an opportunity both to express and to clarify, if he chooses, disturbing and perplexing feelings, and to experience an intimate, friendly relationship. (*Courtesy of Adams School, Logan, Utah.*)

Sometimes the teacher is aided by the school psychologist or counselor in detecting emotional disturbances in children, and very often such professionally trained persons are able to assist the teacher in making a diagnosis and plans for remedial treatment. In general, the diagnosis begins with a consideration of the behavior symptoms, followed by a search for causes in the child's school activities, family relationships, and play relationships and in a personality study of the child. On the basis of a better understanding of the child and of the factors affecting his behavior, plans are made for giving him the experiences he needs for satisfying his basic motives of security, love, mastery, approval, and expression of talents and interests, and for developing healthier, more effective modes of adjustment.

The methods of treatment include consulting with other teachers on provision for successful regular classroom activities in an atmosphere of acceptance and friendly, warm approval; diagnostic and remedial instruction; counseling and/or play therapy, such as was used with Dick [3]; changes in parent-child relationships through parent-psychologist conferences; help for the teacher in supervision and guidance of the child's play and of other relationships with his classmates; and other environmental manipulations.

Summary

Even though all the other conditions of effective learning are provided, problem-solving learning will be efficient only if the learner, through appropriate home and school experiences, has become conditioned to approach learning activities with feelings of security, eagerness, and confidence. If such experiences have conditioned him to feelings of insecurity, inferiority, and guilt to the extent that he becomes emotionally maladjusted, he will defensively attempt to protect his self-image ideal and to allay his anxiety by adjustment mechanisms which often impair his efficiency in problem-solving learning. How the home and the school can help to free the child from anxiety and emotionally distorting percepts and attitudes has been considered. As a concluding summary to this chapter, some general principles for promoting emotional health and for preventing or correcting maladjustment are here listed:

1. For development of emotional health, children need from their parents and teachers care, security, love, understanding, opportunities, and guidance, regardless of their abilities, achievements, and behavior.

2. For constant experience in zestful, constructive, and creative accomplishment and to avoid too much frustration, each child needs a curriculum suited to his maturity, pattern of abilities, needs, and interests.

3. Skillful and friendly teaching—including adequate teacher-guidance, ample individualized teaching, and remedial procedures as needed—contributes to emotional health.

4. Emotional health is favored by motivating learning effort through appeals to the child's "natural" creative and constructive impulses, through approval, and through love, rather than through negative criticism and pressure.

5. Parents and teachers who are warm, friendly, tolerant, and accepting make it possible for children to express disturbing emotions and thus to gain an advantage in learning to deal more effectively with them.

6. The child's own self-confidence reflects to some extent the confidence that others have in him. Without pressuring them, parents and teachers need always to show confidence in children's abilities and potentialities for constructive and useful accomplishment.

7. Acquiring useful skills and a problem-solving approach to difficulties and pursuing tasks to satisfying completions lead to confidence and to satisfaction in constructive effort.

8. As children grow and progress in their accomplishments, parents and teachers need to accept and to provide for their needs for both independence and dependence.

9. Guiding children by helping them to have fun and to look for and expect to find pleasant and satisfying elements in most school experiences should aid in cultivating healthy attitudes.

10. Both by arranging situations for them and by improving children's social skills and social attractiveness, children may be helped to acquire satisfying friendships with other children.

11. In promoting emotional health and in correcting emotional disturbances, healthy group interaction is necessary. Healthy group activities are promoted by (a) pupil-teacher planning in which pupils' goals and interests become dominating motives, (b) cooperative participation in creative projects, (c) subgrouping in terms of pupils' talents and social needs, (d) training in the skills needed for communication and for effective cooperative work, and (e) skillfully and often gradually inducting isolates into confident and accepted group participation.

12. Being sensitive to the special needs of the aggressive, shy, or overdependent child and being ready to give appropriate guidance and support at the right time serves both a teaching and a therapeutic purpose.

As general corrections of emotional maladjustments and as steps toward positive emotional health, Shaw [55] proposes three principles for focusing the child's attention on his potentialities for productive and creative accomplishment:

13. For "resourcefulness anxiety," which "can be thought of as the sense of helplessness that arises from inability or felt inability to meet demands, responsibilities, or challenges presented by one's environment," he proposes "fostering experimentation with new forms of behavior"—fostering a "try-and-see" approach without a need for assured perfection.

14. For "repression anxiety," which serves the individual by covering intolerable ways of perceiving himself, Shaw proposes that he seek new, different self-perspectives. "Many potentially bright people," he notes, "are not as bright as they might be simply because they have never thought of themselves as people capable of having ideas." In implementing this principle, the teacher will constantly seek opportunities for discovering and revealing pupils' talents.

15. And for "inhibitory deficit," definable as inability to restrain oneself from self-defeating behavior, he proposes helping the individual to see "that it is his own behavior which gets him into trouble," as in the example of the child who strove intensely to win his classmates' approval by being "very expert" in pointing out all their mistakes.

Review and Applications

1. Cite examples of how emotional disturbances may impair learning and problem-solving efficiency.

2. What are some of the factors which determine how children react to frustrations?

3. What are the components of the ideal self-image of children growing up in our society? Why are these particular components idealized?

4. Explain how some children may come to feel inadequate, inferior, and guilty and how, in defense of their self-image ideal, they may develop and cling tenaciously to maladjustive patterns of behavior.

5. Explain according to the integrated theory of learning developed in Chapter 2, how emotionally disturbed children learn more healthy patterns of adjustment.

6. How can parent-child relations either help or hinder a child in development of mental health and effectiveness in learning and problem solving?

7. Cite examples of how the school, by providing a suitable curriculum, through appropriate teacher-guidance and teacher-child relationships, through constructive supervision of social relations in the school, by help with personality problems, and through parent-teacher conferences, can correct emotional disturbances and promote the mental health of children.

References

1. Anderson, J. E.: "The relation of attitude to adjustment," *Education*, 73: 210–218, 1952–1953.
2. Axline, Virginia M.: "Nondirective therapy for poor readers," *J. Consult. Psychol.*, 11: 61–69, 1947.
3. ———: "Play therapy: A way of understanding and helping reading problems," *Childh. Educ.*, 26: 156–161, 1949.
4. Barker, R. G., Tamara Dembo, and K. Lewin: "Frustration and regression," in R. G. Barker, J. S. Kounin, and H. F. Wright (eds.): *Child Behavior and Development*, McGraw-Hill, New York, 1943.
5. Bennett, E. M.: "A socio-cultural interpretation of maladjustive behavior," *J. Soc. Psychol.*, 37: 19–26, 1953.
6. Bettelheim, B.: *Love Is Not Enough*, Free Press, Glencoe, Ill., 1950.
7. Blanchard, Phyllis: "Reading disabilities in relation to difficulties of personality and emotional development," *Ment. Hyg.*, 20: 384–413, 1936.
8. Bond, G. L., and L. C. Fay: "A report of the University of Minnesota Reading Clinic," *J. Educ. Res.*, 43: 385–390, 1950.
9. Bower, E. M.: "The need for punishment," *Calif. J. Elem. Educ.*, 21: 41–48, 1953.
10. Bullock, Burleen J., and W. H. Brown: "Screening a fourth grade class for emotional needs," *Understand. Child*, 22: 116–120, 1953.
11. Buswell, Margaret M.: "The relationship between the social structure of the classroom and academic success of the pupils," *J. Exp. Educ.*, 22: 37–52, 1953.
12. Cederquist, Helen T.: "The 'good mother' and her children," *Smith Coll. Stud. Soc. Wk.*, 19(1): 1–26, 1948.
13. Clancy, Nora, and Faith Smitter: "A study of emotionally disturbed children in Santa Barbara County schools," *Calif. J. Educ. Res.*, 4: 209–218 and 222, 1953.
13a. Davitz, J. R.: "The effects of previous training on postfrustration behavior," *J. Abnorm. Soc. Psychol.*, 47: 309–315, 1952.
14. Edelston, H.: "Educational failure with high intelligence quotient: A clinical study," *J. Genet. Psychol.*, 77: 85–116, 1950.
15. Elkins, Deborah: "How the classroom teacher can help the emotionally disturbed child," *Understand. Child*, 20: 66–73 and 79, 1951.
16. Elliot, M. H.: "Patterns of friendship in the classroom," *Progr. Educ.*, 18: 383–390, 1941.
17. Elsbree, W. S.: "School practices that help and hurt personality," *Teach. Coll. Rec.*, 43: 24–34, 1941.
18. English, H. B.: *Child Psychology*, Holt, New York, 1951.
19. Erickson, E.: *Childhood and Society*, Norton, New York, 1950.
20. Farber, I. E., and K. W. Spence: "Complex learning and conditioning as a function of anxiety," *J. Exp. Psychol.*, 45: 120–125, 1953.

21. Forel, O. L.: "Resentment: An obstacle to re-education," *Ment. Hyg.*, 33: 177–199, 1949.
22. Gaier, E. L.: "Selected personality variables and the learning process," *Psychol. Monogr.*, vol. 66, no. 17, 1952.
23. Hattwick, LaBerta W., and Margaret Stowell: "Relation of parental over-attentiveness to children's work habits and social adjustments in kindergarten and the first six grades of school," *J. Educ. Res.*, 30: 169–176, 1936.
24. Heffernan, Helen: "The organization of the elementary school and the development of a healthy personality," *Calif. J. Elem. Educ.*, 20: 129–153, 1952.
25. Hildreth, Gertrude: "An individual study in word recognition," *Elem. Sch. J.* 35: 606–619, Copyright, 1935, by the University of Chicago. Reprinted by permission of the University of Chicago Press.
26. Hutt, M. L.: "A clinical study of 'consecutive' and 'adaptative' testing with the Revised Stanford-Binet," *J. Consult. Psychol.*, 11: 93–103, 1947.
27. Jenkins, Gladys D., Helen Shacter, and W. W. Bauer: *These Are Your Children*, expanded ed. Copyright, 1953, by Scott, Foresman and Company, Chicago, and used with their permission.
28. Jersild, A. J.: *Child Psychology*, 4th ed., Copyright, 1954, by Prentice-Hall, Englewood Cliffs, N.J., and reproduced by permission of the publisher.
29. Katz, B., and G. F. J. Lehner: *Mental Hygiene in Modern Living*, Ronald, New York, 1953.
30. Keister, Mary E.: "The behavior of young children in failure," in R. G. Barker, J. S. Kounin, and H. F. Wright (eds.): *Child Behavior and Development*, McGraw-Hill, New York, 1943.
31. ———, and Ruth Updegraff: "A study of children's reactions to failure and an experimental attempt to modify them," *Child Develpm.*, 8: 241–248, 1937.
32. Keliher, Alice V.: "When will we do as well as we know?" *Childh. Educ.*, 26: 148–151, 1949.
33. Lantz, Beatrice: "Some dynamic aspects of success and failure," *Psychol. Monogr.*, 59(1): 1–40, 1945.
34. Lazarus, R. S., J. Deese, and S. F. Osler: "The effects of psychological stress upon performance," *Psychol. Bull.*, 49: 293–317, 1952.
35. Lippitt, R., and R. K. White: "The social climate of children's groups," in R. G. Barker, J. S. Kounin, and H. F. Wright (eds.): *Child Development and Behavior*, McGraw-Hill, New York, 1943.
36. Liss, E.: "The failing student," *Amer. J. Orthopsychiat.*, 11: 712–717, 1941.
37. ———: "Learning difficulties: Unresolved anxiety and resultant learning patterns," *Amer. J. Orthopsychiat.*, 11: 520–523, 1941.
38. ———: "Learning: Its sadistic and masochistic manifestations," *Amer. J. Orthopsychiat.*, 10: 123–128, 1940.
39. Maier, N. R. F., and P. Ellen: "Can the anxiety-reduction theory explain abnormal fixations?" *Psychol. Rev.*, 58: 435–445, 1951.

40. McCarthy, Dorothea A.: *Personality and Learning*, American Council on Education Studies, 13: ser. 1, no. 35, Washington, 1948, pp. 93–96.

41. McGinnies, E.: "Emotionality and perceptual defense," *Psychol. Rev.*, 56: 244–251, 1949.

42. Meek, Lois H. (reporting findings of Lois M. Jacks): "A child's relation to the group," *Progr. Educ.*, 18: 212, 1941.

43. Missildine, W. H.: "The emotional background of thirty children with reading disabilities with emphasis on its coercive elements," *Nerv. Child*, 5: 263–272, 1946.

44. Montague, E. K.: "The role of anxiety in serial rote learning," *J. Exp. Psychol.*, 45: 91–96, 1953.

45. Morphett, Mabel V., and C. Washburne: "When should children begin to read?" *Elem. Sch. J.*, 31: 496–503, 1931.

46. Nimkoff, M. F.: *The Child*, Lippincott, Philadelphia, 1934.

47. Oliver, W. A.: "Teachers' education beliefs versus their classroom practice," *J. Educ. Res.*, 47: 47–55, 1953.

48. Otis, Nancy B., and B. R. McCandless: "Responses to repeated frustration of young children differentiated according to need area," *J. Abnorm. Soc. Psychol.*, 50: 349–353, 1955.

49. Read, Katherine H.: *The Nursery School: A Human Relations Laboratory*, Saunders, Philadelphia, 1950.

50. Redl, F., and D. Wineman: *Children Who Hate*, Free Press, Glencoe, Ill., 1951.

51. ———, and W. W. Wattenburg: *Mental Hygiene in Teaching*, Harcourt, Brace, New York, 1951.

52. Rosenstock, I. M.: "Perceptual aspects of repression," *J. Abnorm. Soc. Psychol.*, 46: 304–315, 1951.

53. Rudolph, Adele: "When we need it we make it," *Childh. Educ.*, 30: 233–236, 1954.

54. Sears, Pauline S.: "Levels of aspiration in academically successful and unsuccessful children," *J. Abnorm. Soc. Psychol.*, 35: 498–536, 1940.

55. Shaw, F. J.: "Counseling from the standpoint of an interactive conceptualist," *J. Couns. Psychol.*, 1: 36–42, 1954.

56. Sherman, M.: *Basic Problems of Behavior*, Longmans, New York, 1941.

57. ———: "The secret that will win you success," *Magazine Digest*, May, 1946, pp. 1–5.

58. Shoben, E. J.: "Counseling and the learning of integrative behavior," *J. Couns. Psychol.*, 1: 42–48, 1954.

59. ———: "A theoretical approach to psychotherapy as personality modification," *Harv. Educ. Rev.*, 23: 128–142, 1953.

60. Sperry, Bessie M., Nancy Staver, and H. E. Mann: "Destructive fantasies in certain learning difficulties," *Amer. J. Orthopsychiat.*, 22: 356–365, 1952.

61. Staver, Nancy: "The child's learning difficulty as related to the emotional problem of the mother," *Amer. J. Orthopsychiat.*, 23: 131–141, 1953.

62. Stoelting, Frances: "A classroom teacher of a cerebral palsy group teaches speech," *Quart. J. Speech*, 35: 67–70, 1949.

63. Taylor, Janet A., and K. W. Spence: "The relationship of anxiety level to perform-ance in serial learning," *J. Exp. Psychol.*, 44: 61–64, 1952.

64. Topp, R. F.: "Behavior difficulties in childhood as portents of future emotional dis-orders," *Elem. Sch. J.*, 51: 196–200, 1950.

65. ———: "Preadolescent behavior patterns suggestive of emotional malfunctioning," *Elem. Sch. J.*, 52: 340–343, Copyright, 1952, by the University of Chicago. Re-printed by permission of the University of Chicago Press.

66. Waterhouse, I. K., and I. L. Child: "Frustration and the quality of performance, III.: An experimental study," *J. Pers.* 21: 298–311, 1953.

67. Wattenburg, W. W.: "Teachers can build emotional strength," *Education*, 74: 133–137, 1953.

68. Williams, M.: "Rate of learning as a function of ego-alien material," *J. Pers.* 19: 324–331, 1951.

69. Young, N., and E. L. Gaier: "Implications in emotionally caused reading retarda-tion," *Elem. Engl.*, 28: 271–275, 1951.

Chapter 10

Learning Theory and Teaching

IN THE preceding seven chapters, applications to teaching of *each* of the essential conditions of learning have been pointed out. However, as was illustrated in connection with the teaching of manuscript writing in the "overview" chapter on learning theories, effective learning *always* requires the simultaneous application of *all* seven conditions. Therefore, in a concluding chapter on learning theory, let us consider some additional examples of all these conditions in action at the same time. The examples chosen are from reading, arithmetic, art, science, and social development. Before proceeding with these analyses of teaching, the outline of learning theory is here resummarized.

Conditions of Effective Learning

Learning results from reacting purposefully to problem situations and involves a change in or a reorganization of an individual's perceptual, cognitive, and motivational-emotional structure which may be utilized as a guide to more adequate adjustments both to the original and to related situations. According to Mowrer's two-factor theory, such learning involves both problem solving and conditioning.

Descriptively, problem-solving learning involves the following phases: (1) a motivated person, who, upon meeting (2) a situation to which he cannot adjust adequately on the basis of either innate behavior patterns or prior learning, (3) makes multiple, goal-directed, provisional tries. (4) Experiencing the effects of these trials, both perceptually and as motive satisfaction or dissatisfaction, he (5) selects ("differentiates" or "integrates"), often from several trials, a pattern of behavior which promises to meet more adequately the motivating conditions. (6) When the same or a similar situation arises again, the more adequate pattern will recur more directly and with less attention and effort.

As the individual is learning, by problem solving, concepts, verbalizations, and motor skills, he is also acquiring, by conditioning, interest and confidence in or distaste for and anxiety about the activities, depending upon the favorable or unfavorable conditioning aspects of the situation. When such a motivational-emotional response has been elicited by a combination of stimuli frequently enough to make the conditioned stimulus a significant part of the combination of both already adequate and to-be-conditioned stimuli, the conditioned stimulus alone becomes effective in eliciting the response. Thus a reading situation, originally neutral as an emotional stimulus, may become a conditioned stimulus for either confidence or anxiety in a child, depending upon whether his reading efforts are successful or result in failure and humiliation.

Both from this definition of learning and from the background of theories which led to the definition, the following conditions are derived. In previous chapters they have been experimentally supported as essential for effective learning.

1. Maturity and an Appropriate Pattern of Abilities. Initial success and satisfactory progress in learning depend upon the child's having sufficient mental maturity and an appropriate pattern of abilities. Signs of a child's readiness for learning are chronological and mental age norms, status in developmental sequences, performance on tests of readiness, and manifestations of interest.

2. Teacher-guidance. The child profits from teacher-guidance in directing his attention to goal-directing hypotheses, to efficient modes of attack, and to new stages or standards in learning sequences. Such teacher-guidance on *how* to approach a problem is accomplished by explaining, demonstrating, correcting the pupil's provisional trials, and promoting pupil self-discovery experiences by teacher arrangement of learning sequences and by leading questions.

3. Practice. Although practice alone is not a sufficient condition for learning and although its effectiveness depends upon the other conditions, it is necessary. Effective practice, however, does not consist merely in repetitions of responses; it consists of active provisional trials or of hypothesis-guided self-activity oriented towards discovery, differentiation, and integration of more effective patterns of behavior.

4. Perception of Effects. Since problem-solving learning is a "trial-and-check" process in which improvement depends upon discovery of better response patterns, perception of the effects of each trial is essential for effective learning. Such perception of the effects of provisional trials makes possible checking their correctness and adequacy, confirming correct responses, and making revisions as needed in subsequent learning efforts.

5. Transfer. Effective learning for a child depends upon his full utilization in new problems of previously mastered generalizations and skills and upon his finding the unifying principles in otherwise complex and multiple-element tasks. This requires the application in teaching of such transfer principles as teaching to recognize "identical elements" in learning sequences, giving guidance in learning how to learn efficiently, emphasizing mastery of general principles, providing for varied applications of these principles, and developing sensitivities for and habits of seeking new applications and extensions of them.

6. Motivation. Motivation is a necessary condition of learning because motivational processes arouse, sustain, direct, determine the intensity of learning effort and, in cooperation with perception of the effects, define and evaluate the consequences of provisional trials. There are many ways to motivate pupil learning; but perhaps the best way is to provide for the child's natural desire for "activity satisfaction" in the constructive and creative use of his talents and to help him find opportunities in learning for constructive self-expression in social situations. Related to reliance on such "self-actualization" motivation are appealing to interests, providing for constructive use of concepts and skills learned, arranging opportunities for mastery of worthwhile learning tasks, and providing knowledge of progress.

7. Freedom from Emotional Disturbances in Learning. As a final essential condition for effective learning, the child needs to feel secure; trustful of his parents, teacher, and classmates; accepted, loved, and esteemed by them; and comfortable and confident in his self-concept and role. Otherwise, defenses motivated by anxiety and feelings of inadequacy, inferiority, and guilt may impair or prevent effective learning.

The following examples[1] of good teaching are analyzed as applications of this outline of the conditions for effective learning.

Teaching Reading Comprehension

In his recent book, *Teaching Elementary Reading* [8], Tinker's aim "is to present a clear, simple, and straightforward exposition of the principles and practices underlying sound reading instruction." If he has succeeded, and

---

[1] For their generous courtesy in permitting extensive quotations from the following five examples of teaching, the writer is very grateful to both authors and publishers.

provided also that our analysis of the conditions of effective learning is valid, they should be found illustrated in his book. The scope of activities in learning reading includes "(1) word identification and recognition, (2) vocabulary meanings and concepts, (3) comprehension, (4) rate of reading, (5) study skills, (6) specialized reading skills, (7) oral reading, (8) attitudes, and (9) interests and tastes" [8, p. 286]. In order to limit the space requirements for this analysis, however, attention will be focused only upon comprehension and upon the related concepts and skills upon which it is closely dependent. Since reading is considered a process of understanding, reasoning, and creative thinking, comprehension is of central importance.

1. Maturity and an Appropriate Pattern of Abilities. Learning to read is regarded by Tinker as a developmental process, and in adapting instruction to the child's maturity, most of the signs of readiness are employed.

Developmental norms are applied. "Provided there are no special handicaps," writes Tinker, "the child may begin to read when he reaches a mental age of about six years" [8, p. 38]. In addition to attaining this mental age norm, the child's pattern of abilities for beginning reading should include satisfactory language skills, abilities for visual and auditory perceptual discriminations, social maturity, and emotional health.

Tinker observes that the process of learning to read follows a developmental sequence, to which each child's progress is related. "In the beginning, learning to read is learning that symbols (queer, senseless-looking marks to the child) stand for speech. He learns to say the word that stands for a particular printed or written mark. . . . During this first stage in reading, skill in word recognition has a continuous development, and as time goes on, occurs at a faster pace. The child's list of sight words grows. Soon familiar phrases are recognized as meaningful units. In addition to the accumulation of sight words, the child gradually learns to work out words by their sounds so that he less frequently has to be told what a new word says. And gradually there is less and less need for speaking the words aloud. As the reading becomes inaudible, lip and tongue movements tend to cease. . . . With progress in reading beyond the beginning stage, skill in recognition, if properly mastered, becomes largely automatic so that the reader's attention may be largely devoted to understanding, reflection, and evaluation" [8, pp. 11–12].

In adjusting instruction to each child's general maturity and particular pattern of abilities, continuous testing and evaluation are necessary. For example, readiness for learning phonetics is apparently reached when the child has acquired visual and auditory discriminations adequate for differentiating between letter forms and between letter sounds, when he has acquired a considerable stock of sight words, when he has attained a mental age of approximately seven years, and when he is making some progress in formal reading situations. Such diagnostic evaluations of pupil abilities, status, and development are followed by teaching adapted to individual differences. For example, "where inefficient vision cannot be remedied, the teaching should be adapted to the child, as by emphasizing auditory rather than visual methods of instruction" [8, p. 30]. Intraclass grouping "based upon pupils' abilities, experiences, and needs is employed to facilitate instruction." And individualized instruction characterizes the day-to-day program, in which "it is desirable to diagnose difficulties promptly and then carry out the indicated remedial measures."

2. *Teacher-guidance.* Teacher-guidance in helping children learn to read is of the "utmost importance" at every stage. At the prereading stage, for example, children are taught to discriminate similarities and differences by such exercises as: "Mark another word in the list which is the same as the first: apple— pail, shovel, cat, mouse, monkey, apple" [8, p. 61]. In teaching an initial sight-word vocabulary, the teacher *explains* how different objects in the classroom have been labeled, and she may *demonstrate* reading the labels. She may also write on the chalkboard a story composed by the children from their experience. Then, pointing to the succession of words, she may read their story to them. "At first, the child is repeatedly told the name of the word," until he learns it as a sight word. When the child has begun to read by means of sight words, he "needs techniques for independently identifying the sound or pronunciation that belongs to a new word form so that the sound may be associated with the printed word form to facilitate recognition when the word is met again" [8, p. 91]. A variety of techniques for independently identifying and recognizing words is taught.

Picture Clues. Before a child reads a story, he may be directed to scan the pictures which illustrate it, both to aid in comprehending the story as a whole and to aid in recognizing some specific words. Teacher-guidance in this reading activity "draws attention to numerous details and relationships that otherwise might have been missed. Thus attention may be directed to the details of clothing worn by a postman and how they differ from those of other men, or to the relative sizes of dolls and children" [8, p. 133].

Verbal Context Clues. The context of an unfamiliar word in an otherwise familiar and meaningful sentence provides the clues for recognizing it. With the emphasis upon reading by reasoning and for meaning, such verbal context clues are of central and pervading importance. Tinker observes, however, that "few children will make maximum use of these clues without training" [8, p. 137]. Examples of the needed teacher-guidance suggested are (1) the teacher's

It is Lee Anns Birthday
Happy Birthday! Lee Ann

Fig. 10-1. Especially in the earliest stages of learning, familiar contexts and picture clues are helpful in identifying and recognizing words. (*Courtesy of McKinley School, Tremonton, Utah.*)

pausing at appropriate places in her reading for children to give the next word; (2) encouraging a child to "read all the sentence and then return to the unknown word and try to supply a word which will fit into the context" [8, p. 137]; and (3) teacher questions and suggestions which help children make use of such clues.

Word-form Clues. "No child," Tinker says, "can become a proficient and rapid reader unless he learns to employ word-form clues." Word recognition depends upon noticing the visual characteristics of words. "The main problem is to develop sensitivity to the total configuration with some analysis of the factors which produce characteristic word forms, such as the contributions of word length, patterns composed of the alternation of short letters (a, n, c, and so on) and long letters (l, t, p, and so on). This may come from class discussion and from teacher explanation" [8, p. 139].

Phonetic Analysis. By sounding out unfamiliar printed letters and letter combinations, the child identifies and recognizes words already in his oral vocabulary. Phonetic analysis should be taught *in the reading situation* as a supplement to context clues in identifying unfamiliar words. Teacher-guidance in learning initial-consonant sounds may begin "soon after beginning formal reading."

Frequently the initial consonant plus context clues are sufficient for identifying one unfamiliar word in a sentence. Thus in the sentence: "Jane put on her hat and coat," "the clue from the sound of c plus the context may immediately lead to identification of *coat*." Other words will require more complete phonetic analysis. "Emphasis should be placed upon employing only the degree of analysis necessary as a supplement to other clues [8, p. 143]. After mastery of initial consonants, guidance in phonetic analysis should be continued to include syllabification and recognition of phonetic "families" occurring at the beginnings or ends of familiar words (such as in "bed" and "beg," or in "car" and "far").

Structural Analysis. "Structural analysis consists of identification of those parts of a word which form meaning units or pronunciation units" [8, p. 145]. These meaning or pronunciation units include parts of compound words (such as "schoolhouse"); base words (such as "fall" in "falling"); suffixes (such as "-ing" in "falling"); prefixes (such as "re-" in "return"); and various inflected forms of nouns, adjectives, and verbs, formed by adding "-s," "-ing," "-er," and "-ed" (such as "dolls," "eating," "colder," and "looked"). When the root words in such words are already known, the child identifies the whole word from recognition of the prefixes or suffixes and their meanings.

Combination of Clues. For effective independent identification of words, the child will need to acquire skill in using these techniques with versatility in combinations and in hierarchical orders. Except for the context clues provided by emphasizing reading for understanding, no single clue should be used exclusively or predominantly. How verbal context clues, word-form clues, and phonetic analysis may in combination contribute to identification of a word is illustrated by a child's identification of "tame" in the sentence: "When the children came home, Jack saw a tame rabbit." In word form, "tame" is like the familiar word "came," except that it begins with a *t* instead of a *c*. "Context clues plus a knowledge of the initial sound t can lead to identification of the word 'tame.'" In efficient reading, context is the predominant clue. It is supplemented to the extent needed by word-form clues and, but only as a last resort, by phonetic analysis.

Reading comprehension requires the aforementioned skills in independent identification and recognition of words; but it is a more comprehensive process. Word meanings, sentences, paragraphs, and longer units must all be understood in organized interrelations for reading with comprehension. In order to understand sentences, children need teacher-guidance in "phrasing, proper use of punctuation, understanding of figures of speech, use of context, and identification of the ideas involved." In comprehending paragraphs, they "need

Fig. 10–2. Teacher-guidance in reading meets each child's needs more effectively in small groups. (*Courtesy of McKinley School, Tremonton, Utah.*)

guidance in identifying the topical sentence containing the key idea and in interpreting its relation to the explanatory or amplifying sentences. In a similar manner, some attention should be devoted to the relation between paragraphs in longer selections." They also need guidance in learning skills appropriate to different purposes, such as skimming, following and predicting the sequence of events in a narrative, apprehension of details, following directions, generalizing, and critical evaluation of concepts. Moreover, children need guidance in adjusting their speed of reading to their rate of comprehension.

3. *Practice.* In Tinker's treatment of the teaching of elementary reading, practice is regarded as a necessary although not a sufficient condition for effective learning and progress. In prescribing practice, care is taken in introducing the proper amounts, in distribution, in arranging concepts and skills in their proper order according to difficulty, and in providing for transfer advantages and for retention through properly spaced reviews. Several examples illustrate these principles of effective practice. In developing a sight vocabulary, there must be "continual repetition of the old words in meaningful situations all the while new ones are gradually added" [8, p. 86]. To secure sufficient practice on the words most needed, Dolch's sight vocabulary of 220 words should be

taught early [8, pp, 88–89]. The introduction "of new words should be so spaced that most of the words in a given selection are familiar, that is, about 95 per cent should be familiar" [8, p. 167]. And "following initial presentation, provision should be made . . . for systematic reviewing of the word" in varied contexts, so that meanings are clarified and broadened. But although repetition is essential, "it is not sufficient to provide time and assume that the child is reading comprehendingly. He may be sitting idly and thereby acquiring harmful habits" [8, p. 123]. Practice will be effective only as the other essential conditions of learning are also provided.

4. *Perception of the Effects of Goal-directed Trials.* Teacher-guided or self-initiated practice results in the discovery of improved patterns of response only when provisional trials are checked for correctness. Often interrelated features within a learning activity provide the checks for confirming or denying the correctness of a response, and thus the learner is self-guided to improvement. At other times the teacher must help the pupil to evaluate the correctness of his goal-directed efforts. Both of these ways of providing for perception of the effects of goal-directed responses are implicit in *Teaching Elementary Reading.*

The use of several word-recognition clues in combination illustrates the former procedure. When the child identified "t-ame" on the basis of the initial consonant and the word form as "tame," the context clue permitted him also to perceive it as correct—it fitted. Tinker's emphasis upon reading for meaning provides for the continual operation of this principle of self-checking. "Only when the sound and meaning are familiar [in using phonetics] can the reader check his analysis in terms of meaning context derived from the sentence" [8, p. 142]. And in employing syllabification, "the final check on the derived pronunciation is whether it sounds like a known word and whether this fits the meaning context of the sentence" [8, p. 143].

There are also many instances in which the teacher helps the child to check the correctness or incorrectness of his efforts. In beginning reading, for example, oral reading is helpful because it permits the teacher "to check the accuracy of matching sight and sound" [8, p. 100].

In exercises for improving apprehension of details, "questions should be phrased to call for details related to the main idea. Furthermore, the work should be so arranged and supervised that through checking and discussion the errors are readily seen and improvement appreciated" [8, p. 188]. Again, in teaching reading to follow directions, the teacher "should be sure that the pupils clearly understand each step, and that the steps are kept in proper sequence. Checking the end product, as in a construction or sewing job, ordinarily will reveal to both pupil and teacher whether the directions were properly read and followed" [8, p. 189]. In learning to generalize from reading problem-solving material, "in many instances the discussion of a conclusion may reveal the need for further reading to gain sufficient information to justify the tentatively formed conclusion" [8, p. 190]. In teaching word recognition, "observation of a child's responses from day to day may indicate to the teacher that the child is not making desirable progress in learning to use a clue or technique that is being taught. Some individual checking with the child will more clearly identify the source of the trouble and determine the seriousness of the difficulty" [8, p. 213]. And more generally, "the teacher takes down a complete record of errors as the child reads. As the child finishes reading each paragraph, the teacher takes notes on the characteristics of the reading performance, noting such items as too slow or too fast reading, word-by-word reading without phrasing, failure to correct errors by use of meaning context, distinctness of enunciation, unwillingness to try or inability to carry out adequately phonetic analysis, indications of nervousness, and any other behavior which may seem of importance" [8, pp. 213–214]. Often the corrective measures, consisting of more efficient modes of attack, are indicated by such analyses. "At times, some additional individual diagnosis is necessary for a clearer definition of the deficiency. This is followed by the corrective instruction indicated by the diagnosis" [8, p. 219].

5. Provision for Transfer of Training. By effective application of the principles of transfer, the value of each learning effort is multiplied severalfold; and without some transfer, improvement from trial to trial could not occur. Transfer in learning is facilitated by emphasis upon proper sequence and organization among learning activities, by emphasizing meanings, and by mastering principles of wide-scope application. All these ways of promoting transfer are implicit in Tinker's discussion of the teaching of elementary reading.

The developmental approach pervades the entire book. It is expressed explicitly in such statements as this: "Progress in reading is developmental and continuous. Each stage prepares for what is coming next. The teaching of the new follows naturally what has been learned before" [8, p. 13]. Tinker gives several specific examples of transfer principles. Probably influenced by the "identical-elements" interpretation of transfer, he advises that in developing visual discrimination during the prereading stage, "it is doubtful that training to discriminate geometric forms will have any important effect on ability to discriminate words" [8, p. 60]. The training should be on words themselves, and preferably on words which the child will later learn to read. According to the same principle, Dolch's list of basic words is recommended for teaching children a sight vocabulary because these words have been found to occur most frequently in the books which children will later learn to read. Teaching both oral and silent reading in beginning reading takes advantage of the transfer from oral language to oral reading to silent reading. In Tinker's words "In beginning reading, word meanings aroused by printed symbols are derived from one's background of oral word meanings accumulated in prior language development. Oral reading, therefore, can become the basis for learning to think meanings into content reading. Complete non-oral reading instruction eliminates this meaningful [transfer] link and thus represents a narrow approach" [8, p. 103].

As mentioned previously, use of the principles of transfer multiplies learning effort. By emphasizing the verbal context clues in identifying and recognizing words, Tinker recognizes this advantage: "Verbal context clues become increasingly useful as reading proficiency grows through the grades and on into adult life. At all grade levels, the clearer the meanings derived from verbal context, the more useful verbal context clues can become in aiding word identification and recognition" [8, p. 135]. Recognizing that structural analysis must be deferred until certain prerequisite skills and understandings have been acquired is a specific acknowledgment of the transfer principle as applied to sequence in learning activities. For the beginner, initial-consonant substitution is a very general principle in learning to identify new words. Knowing all the initial consonants as well as such word forms as "-ake," children are able, after learning to recognize a word like "make," to identify independently such similar words as "bake," "take," and "cake." As an advantage in this technique, Tinker notes that "it is easier for the child to learn consonant substitution in word analysis than to learn long lists of phonograms. Furthermore, attention is directed to complete pronounceable units instead of to [meaningless] vowel-consonant combinations." And "mastery of the substitution technique will facilitate the identification of many new words . . . throughout the elementary grades" [8, p. 150].

6. *Motivation.* The importance of motivation as a condition of effective learning is explicit in Tinker's statement that "motivation is perhaps the most potent factor determining success in learning and is intimately related to the operation of all other basic principles involved in learning" [8, p. 97]. As motives for learning to read, appeals are made to interests, using the skills in achieving purposeful personal and social adjustments, mastering skills and problems, experiencing growth in reading abilities and in enhanced values from

reading, satisfying curiosity and achieving understanding, and experiencing vicarious pleasures from reading.

According to Tinker, "many needs of the child can be met through reading activities. . . . The emphasis now placed upon reading to learn, rather than upon learning to read, is merely another way of saying that one reads to satisfy needs" [8, p. 6]. "Interest which provides motivation is derived from at least two sources: the individual interests which the child brings to the reading situation, and the interests developed by the teacher in her guidance of the pupil in directed reading activities" [8, p. 97]. On mastery as a motive, Tinker writes: "Success in these first experiences in reading practically assures pleasing emotional reactions and fosters the desire for more reading. . . . And as the child progresses through the year, it is desirable that the pace, content and methods of instruction insure continued success by each child in reading" [8, p. 98]. On purpose, "From the beginning, all reading should be *purposeful to the child*" [8, p. 98]. Again, on interests and success: "Motivation is maintained by guiding the child to material which is interesting to him and which is pitched at just the proper level of difficulty so that the context will yield a maximum amount of intelligible clues to the meaning of the new word. . . . Correct guidance in wide reading leads to exploration of many areas of experience, promotes extension of interests, and brings contact with many new words" [8, pp. 161–162].

7. Freedom from Anxiety and Distorting Emotional Attitudes. If the above-mentioned motives are satisfied so that the child experiences success and pleasure as he learns to read, he will acquire as conditioned responses to reading situations attitudes of self-confidence and interests in reading materials. And if he experiences enhanced pleasure from reading better literature, he will become conditioned to respond with "taste" to it. Therefore, by problem-solving effort, he will learn varied ways of satisfying his interests and tastes. On the other hand, if in reading situations most of these motives are frustrated, he will become conditioned to respond to reading situations with attitudes of inferiority or with rebellion and dislike for reading activities. Because of the anxiety and other emotional disturbances which reading situations may elicit in some children, they will, by problem-solving effort, learn to avoid reading and to resist reading instruction. It should also be remembered, however, that such attitudes are developed not only in the school; they may be aspects of general feelings of security and confidence or of rejection and inferiority which have arisen out of fortunate or unfortunate home relationships and conditions.

Tinker refers in several instances to the need for maintaining favorable attitudes and for avoiding or correcting unfavorable attitudes. The "exposure to the teaching of reading prior to adequate mental development may have unfortunate results." The child "has tasted failure, which may be a bitter experience and leave him with a feeling of frustration and a distaste, if not for reading in general, at least for the reading situation in school" [8, p. 27]. On the need for security and confidence, Tinker writes: "Other things being equal, the happy, well-adjusted child who feels secure in the school situation will make the better progress in learning to read. In addition to general social orientation, the readiness program should furnish experiences which foster more adequate personal and social adjustment. Such experiences should be so arranged that they encourage active interests and self-expression. Frequently special guidance is needed to develop confidence and self-reliance in a child. Participation and success in both classroom and play activities are important for developing a feeling of security in the timid, shut-in child. It is equally important to help the child who is compensating for a feeling of inferiority by resorting to aggressive and bullying behavior. He needs sympathetic understanding as well as success in participation to gain self-confidence and to bring about his cooperation in the school activities. Sometimes it is necessary to consult with and get the cooperation of the parents in order to achieve development of better personal and social adjustment of the child" [8, p. 58]. Finally, we may mention Tinker's opinion on how such emotional attitudes may be dealt with in a specific situation: "To require a child of poor reading ability or one ill prepared to read orally before a group is likely to produce unfortunate emotional reactions. The consequent humiliation and frustration produce feelings of insecurity and thus adversely affect personal adjustment. On the other hand, well prepared, skillful reading aloud to groups promotes self-confidence and poise in social situations involving oral communication" [8, p. 238].

Since we find amply illustrated in *Teaching Elementary Reading* the seven conditions of effective learning, perhaps the teacher who is guided by this book in his teaching of reading is justified in assuming that he is providing good conditions for children to learn to read with understanding, skill, interest, and confidence. Other examples of good teaching illustrate these same principles of learning.

Teaching Division in Arithmetic

Purdy and Kinney [6] have reported an illustration of what they regard as especially effective guidance in learning division. If their appraisal is correct, their example also should illustrate the seven conditions of effective learning.

Since the report is brief, the teaching process will first be described completely and then analyzed.

"The process of problem-solving, until it has been perfected, must be guided at each level. . . . The skilled teacher has techniques suitable for guiding and perfecting each step. Teaching becomes the external counterpart of the active process of learning." And the ultimate test of effective teaching becomes, "Have they learned to learn?" This concept is illustrated in Ruth Feiring's teaching of division with a remainder to fourth grade children:

Step I. Background skills and concepts requisite to dividing with remainders were insured by testing and checking, "and, when need was shown, remedial experiences were provided."

Step II. Varied situations in the classroom calling for use of a process of dividing with remainders were called to pupils' attention. "For example, members of the class were to walk to the library with partners. Questions were raised such as, 'Will everyone in each section have a partner?' 'How many pairs will there be?'. . . . The children improvised solutions, some pairing plastic disks, while others counted by two's." Another such question was, "How many groups of 3 each can view the turtle, and how many will be in the last group?" And so forth.

Step III. Inductive discovery and development of efficient generalized procedure: The teacher led pupils to discovery of the common elements in these problems and their improvised solutions. "In each situation the questions had arisen as to how many two's or three's were contained in some other number, each leaving a remainder. Thus, pupils and teacher agreed, study of the new situations where remainders occur seemed desirable.

"Each pupil was given twenty strips of colored paper, and the class experimented with arranging strips in groups of two to illustrate odd and even numbers and remainders. Likewise, other concrete objects, such as books, pupils, chairs, were grouped for this purpose.

"Next, pupils drew pictures to illustrate division of chairs and other objects into groups of two, the division of nine chairs into two's being depicted as hh hh hh hh h. The word remainder was introduced for 'the one left over.'

"The pupils were led to the generalization that the quotient for each odd dividend is the same as that for the even dividend just below it (that is, in the example, $2\overline{/13}$, one can think: '2 × ? gives a number one less than 13?').

"At this stage the pupils made charts showing the quotients and remainders upon division by two.

"2 divided by 2 gives 1 with remainder 0
"3 divided by 2 gives 1 with remainder 1
"4 divided by 2 gives 2 with remainder 0

"As they saw the nature and need for the new process, the pupils were introduced to important details:

"1. The pattern for carrying out the process. They were shown why we use the form:

$$
\begin{array}{r}
3 \\
2\overline{/7} \\
6 \\
\hline
r = 1
\end{array}
$$

"2. The procedure of checking the work. Here the relation between subtracting 6 (as three 2's) and subtracting 2 three times (in the form $7 - 2 = 5$, $5 - 2 = 3$, $3 - 2 = 1$) was discovered. The new aspect here was the remainder to the product of the quotient and the divisor.

"3. Keeping up with the specialized arithmetic vocabulary. The new and old vocabulary—odd, even, uneven, remainder, compare, and quotient—were used continually as the class worked.

"The pupils' familiarity with all these details was carefully checked to make certain their understanding was adequate."

Step IV. Practice. "The pupils practiced use of the process, by means of seat work, including vocabulary exercises. The first practice was in order, as $2/1$, $2/2$, $2/3$, and so on. Later practice was on random recall. As individuals or small groups encountered difficulties, Miss Feiring had them return to manipulation of objects, paralleling the work using the algorism."

Step V. Varied applications. "When pupils demonstrated that they could perform the operation, they returned to the type of problems that were solved in Step I (for which improvised solutions had been developed) using the new approach. At this stage, each pupil made up several problems that could be solved using division by two (both from the textbook and from class activities).

"As situations were found that required division, they were listed on the board. All the pupils in the class were alerted to search their daily environment for ways in which to apply this new skill."

Analysis of this example of teaching reveals that provision for sufficient *maturity* and an appropriate *pattern of abilities* is made in the first step, where "testing and checking" to ensure requisite background skills and concepts are mentioned. In teaching these children how to divide with remainders, *teacher-guidance* is recognized as needed, in such statements as: "The skilled teacher has techniques suitable for guiding and perfecting each step." Sometimes the teacher explained and demonstrated: "They were shown why we use the form:

$$
\begin{array}{r}
3 \\
2\overline{/7} \\
6 \\
\hline
r = 1
\end{array}
$$

But mainly the teacher relied upon leading children by questions and arranged sequences of observations and actions to self-discoveries of principles and methods. For example, the "teacher led pupils to discovery of the common elements in these problems and their improvised solutions." Their progress was carefully guided: "As they saw the nature and need for the new process, the pupils were introduced to important details." They were led gradually from concretely experienced division through pictorial representations to abstract, symbolic formulations of the process. The division process was *practiced* in a variety of situations: the children formed pairs to walk; they counted groups of three to view a turtle; they grouped strips of colored paper, books, chairs, and pupils into various combinations; they practiced on a variety of numerical examples; and then they returned to the original practical problems. At each step their provisional solutions were *checked:* "The pupils' familiarity with all these details was carefully checked to make certain their understanding was adequate." *Transfer* principles were emphasized throughout the teaching and learning processes. Pupils drew upon their backgrounds of experiences. The principles were met and demonstrated in varied situations. The children were led to discovery of the common elements in these problems and their improvised solutions. The charts aided in making common elements more readily identifiable. And "the pupils were led to the generalization that the quotient for each odd dividend is the same as that for the even dividend just below it." The relation to subtraction was discovered; thus division was perceived as an extension of an already familiar process. And they were sensitized and alerted to possible new applications of the principle and skill they had just mastered: "At this stage, each pupil made up several problems that could be solved using division by two" and: "As situations were found that required division, they were listed on the board. All the pupils in the class were alerted to search their daily environment for ways in which to apply this new skill."

As *motivation* for this learning, the teacher appealed to the children's interest in their own activities, to satisfaction in extending their skills, to successful mastery, and to useful applications of the skill learned. *Security* and *confidence* were maintained by skillful teaching, by gradual progress from the familiar to the new, and by making sure that understanding was adequate for each new step. Anxiety was avoided by returning individual children or small groups of them to a more familiar and concrete level when they encountered difficulties with the abstract algorism.

It should not be surprising to find *all* the conditions of effective learning applied in this teaching example, because "mastery and retention tests showed a high level of skill that endured."

F_{IG}. 10–3. Second only to words is drawing as the child's medium of conceiving and expressing his ideas and feelings. (*Courtesy of Whittier School, Utah State Agricultural College.*)

Teaching Art

A visit to almost any elementary school classroom confronts one dramatically with the importance of art in the elementary curriculum. The development of understanding and skillful expression in art seems intrinsically worthy of the child's efforts. But art is also integrated into almost every other aspect of the curriculum. In a variety of media, both individually and in groups, children apply their developing art skills in more effective expression in literature, science, social studies, and many integrated curriculum projects [5, p. 113].

Art for the maturing child is a delightful and effective system of symbols, comparable in importance to gestures and words, by which he grasps the meaning of his expanding world of things and relationships and expresses his differentiating feelings and ideas. Using lines, shapes, values, textures, and hues in an infinite variety of patterns, sizes, and intensities, the child defines and expresses his growing conceptions and feelings about his world and himself.

In Figure 10–4, six-year-old J. has portrayed her concept and joy in imagining two children playing ball. Her visual concept of her dog and the fun she has in playing with him are expressed in Figure 10–5, drawn at age 7. Expression of a new and exciting idea is often shared in the school, as in Figure 10–6, in which a group of fourth grade children have conceived the pre-Columbus concept of a flat world and Columbus's mission of discovery. With art media, children often symbolize self-identifications with animals, as in Figure 10–7, in which an artistically talented eleven-year-old has expressed her comfortable and affectionate feelings for the "human-animal" characters which delight her both as she finds them in such books as Grahame's *The Wind in the*

It would ~~like~~ be fun to play a game of catch.

Like This

FIG. 10–4. Expressing her understanding of and pleasure in playing catch, J. at six years of age applies Schaefer-Simmern's first four art principles.

Willows and in firsthand experiences. This same child at ages 11 and 12 projects more personal self-identifications into drawings, such as Figure 10–8, in which emerging, tentative romantic interests are suggested. With these same art symbols, an unhappy child may express deep gloom or intense aggression, as is revealed in Figure 10–9, which was drawn by a nine-year-old boy who said he hated everybody except his teacher, in whom he was beginning to confide his painful and disturbing feelings. Drawing as a medium of conceiving and expressing may, of course, symbolize both concrete percepts and feelings, as in Figures 10–4 to 10–9, and more abstract conceptions, moods, or even sheer aesthetic line and color delights, as in Figure 10–10. Typically, however, children's drawings contain, in varying degrees, both representative and abstract features.

How to develop in children both free, creative interests and proficiency in art expression has been a perplexing problem for teachers. Does creative ex-

Fig. 10–5. J.'s growth from age six to seven in visual conception and in art skills includes use of the first seven of Schaefer-Simmern's principles.

Fig. 10–6. As for so many new and interesting concepts, these fourth grade children, using art media, have dramatically expressed the pre-Columbus concept of a flat world. (*Courtesy of Adams School, Logan, Utah.*)

FIG. 10–7. J. at age 11, delighted with her new skills in portraying depth and distances, does her best with a loved animal figure for Father's birthday present.

Fig. 10–8. At age 12, in expressing emerging, tentative romantic interests, J. also demonstrates her command of a variety of techniques for portraying depth, tridimensionality, and relative distance.

FIG. 10–9. Needing emotional expression, an unhappy nine-year-old finds symbolic expression safer and healthier than acting out his hostility.

Fig. 10–10. Children use art mainly for conceiving and portraying concrete ideas and feelings; but they also enjoy sheer abstract combinations of lines, shapes, and colors, as this design by a twelve-year-old illustrates.

pression develop spontaneously from maturation alone, or does it require teacher-guidance? Fearful of smothering creative interests and expression with imposed techniques, many teachers have accepted as their teaching philosophy for art the "doctrine of self-expression" [7, p. 5]. But without guidance, Professor Schaefer-Simmern believes, "the growth of a child's artistic abilities" is retarded [7, p. 5]. He resolves the dilemma of either teaching too much or too little by adapting the teaching of art to what he regards as a "natural unfolding and development of artistic abilities" [7, p. 8]. As in speaking and writing, the child's developing proficiency in art expression depends upon maturing, upon his spontaneous uses and self-guided problem-solving efforts, and upon effective teacher-guidance. Indeed, as our analysis of Schaefer-Simmern's *The Unfolding of Artistic Activity* [7] and Napper's "A guide for teachers directing creative art experiences in elementary schools" [5] show, all seven of the conditions of effective learning are as applicable to teaching art as they are to teaching any other school subject or activity.

1. Sufficient Maturity. The child's development in artistic expression parallels his growing understanding of his world and his mastery of art principles and techniques. The child needs to understand his world, and he satisfies this need, Schaefer-Simmern believes, "preponderantly by means of perceptual experience" [7, p. 29]. By organizing and differentiating his perceptions of the world of objects, he achieves visual conceptions characterized by meaning and "unity of form." His art is the pictorial realization of these "visual configurations" or concepts [7, p. 26]. As he grows and learns, his capacity for more differentiated and better organized visual conceptions develops; and as a consequence, his artistic creations gradually become more complexly organized. This growth in complexity of expression is based on his mastery, in approximate sequence, of an accumulating system of art principles, explained and illustrated in Schaefer-Simmern's book [7]:

1. The first principle is the simple, intentionally outlined figure on a background, emphasizing figure-ground contrast relations—such as the circle drawn on the background of a plain sheet to portray the sun in the sky.

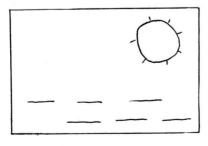

2. A second principle is the simple figure extended or elaborated vertically, horizontally, or in both directions—illustrated in the figure of a man.

3. A third principle is the simple line amplified by the greatest contrast of directions—that is, in both the vertical and horizontal. This is also illustrated in the figure of a man, with vertical body and legs and horizontal arms, or by a simple tree.

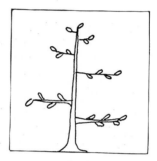

4. Variability of directions of lines develops as a modification of the simple vertical-horizontal contrast, and now movement is conceived and portrayed. This is illustrated in the oblique lines for both the branches of the second tree and the legs of the cow.

The second grade children's drawings in Figure 10-3 and the six-year-old child's drawing in Figure 10-4 illustrate all of these first four principles.

5. Extended and differentiated application of the principle of variability of direction gradually occurs. The principle is applied to both the primary and

secondary parts of figures: limbs of a tree have smaller branches, arms are differentiated at joints, and hands have fingers—as in the fifth illustration and in Figure 10–5.

6. These principles—figure-ground, vertical-horizontal direction, variability of direction, and differentiations of them—may be combined in more integrated representations or creations—as in Figure 10–6.

7. Coherence of direction is also achieved with maturity. Young children sometimes draw people, animals, and plants at right angles to their bases, regardless of the position of the bases. With more maturity, the child achieves total coherence of direction, and now all figures stand or "grow upward in one direction from the earth" [7, p. 18].

8. With the still greater maturity usually reached at ages 9 to 12, children come to perceive objects as having depth, or tridimensionality, and as being differentiated in their distances from the observer. There are five techniques for achieving such differentiated perceptions: (a) by arranging figures one above the other, as in Figure 10–3; (b) by gradual diminution in size of figures toward the top, as in Figure 10–8; (c) by the principle of geometrical variability of direction of lines, as in the building in Figure 10–8; (d) by shading parts with either figural or ground meaning, as in Figure 10–7 especially and also in Figures 10–8 and 10–10; and (e), for the effect of spatial depth, by gradually changing nuances of color tones—only suggested in the black-and-white reproductions of Figures 10–7, 10–8, and 10–10.

To chronicle the signs of artistic maturing, Schaefer-Simmern follows the individual through this developmental sequence. Napper, on the basis of much experience with children throughout the elementary grades, suggests also some grade norms. First grade children, employing the principle of the "intentionally outlined figure on a background," he says, draw "clumsy" circles for heads, "draw simple, one-sided, proportionless houses, omitting many details," and often limit themselves to one color [5, p. 50]. During the second and third grades, they use more colors and "a greater variety of lines, sizes, and shapes" and differentiate more detail in their drawing. "The simple one-sided house in the first grade becomes, in the sixth, a house with tile or shingled roof, with brick, cinder block, stucco, slab, or log walls, with any one of several architectural styles, and perhaps with complicated color schemes" [5, p. 51]. Understanding of art principles also depends not only upon learning but upon maturing as well. "A fourth grade child can understand the meaning and use of such terms as variety of lines, shapes, sizes, colors, values, and textures. In the fifth grade the average child can use these elements with force and imagination, and many of the principles [of function, harmony, unity, proportions, balance, rhythm and movement, emphasis, variation, dominance, subordination, and simplicity] as well. The majority of the sixth grade children can be expected to use most of these elements and principles effectively and be able to understand the meaning of all of them" [5, p. 57].

2. *Teacher-guidance.* The pattern of artistic development just reviewed does not develop spontaneously without guidance, as an observation of Margaret Mead's strikingly demonstrates. "Very intelligent . . . keen, alert" Manus children of New Guinea, who are left to themselves all day long, "unhampered by supervision or suggestions from the adult world" were for the first time supplied with art media, but with no teacher-guidance. They immediately began drawing avidly, happy to relieve their "endless boredom." "Through five months their interest did not flag." But "they produced nothing which remotely resembled art" [4, p. 110]. For artistic development in children, what kinds of guidance are needed?

Napper says that "the creative spirit should permeate all art activities" [5, p. 53] and that "all art experiences should start with the interest of the pupil" [5, p. 59]. Out of rich curriculum experiences, the child finds an abundance of ideas and feelings which he feels impelled to conceive or express in art media. And because of his increasingly more differentiated perceptions and his continual need for enhanced satisfaction in self-expression, he is always meeting problems of *how* to achieve more satisfying expression of his concepts and feelings. A seven-year-old, delighted in seeing from the window in front of her breakfast table a robin pulling a worm from the lawn, tried repeatedly to draw it "so it really looked like it was pulling up the worm." By means of such varied problem-solving efforts, the child may sometimes discover by himself the principle or technique which fills his needs [7, p. 40]. In meeting such problems, however, the child often needs teacher-guidance—an explanation, a demonstration, a suggestion, or a hint toward a self-discovery experience which will lead to the appropriate art principle. In this instance, her teacher's suggestion to change the direction of the robin's legs helped the child to achieve the satisfying result shown in Figure 8–5, page 230.

Without needed guidance, the child's frustration may lead to discouragement and resistance to creative effort. On a rainy day the oldest of three children ages 10, 7, and 6 suggested that they amuse themselves by drawing. On being provided with crayons and paper, two of them began their drawing immediately; but the seven-year-old boy just sat. Asked if he didn't want to draw, he said, "Yes, I'd like to draw a boy riding a horse; but I don't know how." Upon being shown how he could represent an animal's body, neck, head, and legs by varied-sized ovals (a variation of the principle of the intentionally outlined figure), he immediately adapted the principle to his needs and happily executed his conception of a boy riding a horse.

When Miss E. found her cows "too flat," she was guided through a self-discovery experience to the principle of shading for portraying depth and roundness. Professor Schaefer-Simmern "suggested that she make a relief of her cow by cutting it out of a plate of plaster of paris" [7, p. 142]. From studying her modeled cow, "she received so definite an idea of this new stage of visual conceiving that she was able to realize it on canvas" [7, p. 144].

Sometimes encouraging, constructive, but critical evaluation of a child's efforts directs his attention to the area where improvement is needed. As an example, Napper suggests: "I like Jack's trees. They have interesting shapes. His sky is nice too. But it looks as if he has the same trouble as I have with the dark and light colors" [5, p. 58].

Such nondirective teacher-guidance should not stifle creative interests or impose rigid patterns on the child's modes of expression; rather it should, in freeing the child from frustrations, enhance his creative interests, and develop his proficiency in artistic expression.

3. *Practice.* The seven-year-old girl's *repeated efforts* at achieving a result which "really looked like a robin pulling up a worm" are typical of children's learning efforts in artistic expression. The "woodchuck" [Figure 10–7], presented as a father's birthday present, is the culmination of several trials. Portraying a man of satisfying proportions necessitated measuring an actual person's head, torso, legs, and arms; making a trial sketch; checking; and trying again—over and over. The pictorial realizations of a child's visual conceptions are not often achieved in one trial, unless all the art principles have been thoroughly mastered in previous trials. Schaefer-Simmern's pupils clearly reveal in their self-observations the role of practice in learning artistic ex-

pression: "I knew exactly how to draw the wagon of hay, as I made *several* sketches . . . " [7, p. 146, italics supplied]; "I tried over and over again, attempting to differentiate the trees, branches, and leaves by different colors and different shaped leaves . . . " [7, p. 154]; and "Finally, after long and sustained effort to achieve clarity, it occurred to me to enclose the branches and leaves of the tree into an outlined treetop form" [7, p. 154].

Such examples as these demonstrate that in acquiring art skills, just as for other complex skills, practice *is* an essential condition. It is also apparent, especially from these pupil self-observations, that practice is not merely repetitions of responses; it rather consists of repeated attempts at discovering more adequate behavior patterns, guided by provisional, goal-directing ideas and improved in the light of perception of the effects of each goal-directed trial.

4. Perception of the Effects. As the child's percepts and visual conceptions become more differentiated and realistic, he looks at his pictorial representations of them more sharply. As he achieves understanding of more art principles, he also asks, with a more critical concern, "Is my picture unified?" "Are the proportions right?" "Have I achieved interesting variations of line, size, shape, color, and texture?" and so on, guided by other art principles. Thus continually seeking enhanced satisfactions in artistic expression, he confirms or makes corrections in his learning efforts in the light of his perception of the effects of each trial.

Often the pupil checks and corrects his own efforts. J., in observing her drawing of a man, commented, "His arms are too short; *your* hands extend below your hips." "Miss E. observed her drawings for about 10 minutes, and then, with the remark, 'I think I've got a better idea,' went on with another drawing" [7, p. 133]. In another instance, she observed, "The high moments in working always come when I *stand back to see how* the new painted object takes its place in the whole picture. If it harmonizes well with other objects and its effect brings further life to the picture, then I can go to bed happy. If, however, it does not harmonize with other objects, then I can at least wipe it out before the paint dries and save the painting from ruin" [7, p. 160, italics supplied]. Sometimes, however, the child needs guidance in evaluating his tentative product. As an example appropriate for a primary grade child, Napper suggests such constructive encouragement as: "Isn't this an interesting elephant? How different! He has such a long trunk. Can you see some way to make it even better? I wonder if the ground could be darkened so the elephant could be seen more easily. Would you also like to color the sky?" [5, p. 56]. For the older child, he suggests helping him to check his drawing according to the art principles he has mastered and to search for applications of the principles which might lead to improvement [5, p. 55].

5. Provision for Transfer. Beginning with our discussion of maturity as a condition of learning, in connection with Schaefer-Simmern's eight developmental principles, and in discussing the other conditions of learning, we have referred repeatedly to *principles* of artistic expression. It is mainly upon mastery of art principles (not necessarily verbalized) that growth in artistic expression depends. Specific art problems grow out of the child's needs for and interests in creative expression. His teacher should guide him in mastering the art principles which help solve for him these specific problems. As the child applies these same principles in new and varied art activities, he discovers their generality. He also becomes more competent, confident, and creative in applying them in expressing his unique ideas and feelings. J., for example, after learning in separate problems the principles of spatial depth and distance, applied them all in Figure 10–8 and in varied subsequent drawings. Miss E., writes Schaefer-Simmern, found that by drawing a dark line under her cows and grass, she made them appear to be standing on the ground rather than left floating. Subsequently she anchored shocks of grain, trees, shrubs, and people by varied applications of the same principle [7, pp. 147–149]. Because of their importance in developing freedom and proficiency in creative expression, Napper believes that a major teaching responsibility is to "provide opportunity for children to obtain a working knowledge of the art principles and elements, and to develop sensitivity or taste in the application of them" [5, p. 3].

6. Motivation. Creative, artistic activity is well motivated. It is intrinsically motivated both by the need to conceive the world of objects meaningfully and by the inherent satisfaction in creative self-expression. Both of these needs motivate continual effort toward improvement. With maturing, the development of greater differentiation and complexity in visual conceiving demands corresponding differentiation and complexity of pictorial representation. Of Miss E., Schaefer-Simmern writes: "Her spontaneous step forward in reaching a more differentiated stage was based upon an inner compulsion which became the underlying drive for development" [7, p. 144]. The child's creative products often afford him aesthetic pleasure. And like other learning activities, effort toward progress in artistic activity is also motivated by mastery, knowledge of progress, warm approval, self-esteem, and the satisfaction of experiencing enhanced self-value and growing confidence. According to Napper, "creativity flourishes when nourished by the foods of satisfaction, recognition, approval, security, and confidence" [5, p. 59]. These are provided in a successful achievement shared with one's classmates, by teacher and parent approval of one's efforts, and by seeing one's product contribute to the interest and beauty of a classroom wall or hall.

7. *Freedom from Anxiety.* If they feel secure and confident, children (and adults) often find their greatest pleasures in creative expression. Following some very successful progress, Miss E. remarked, "I look forward to an undisturbed evening of painting with a joy that actually fills my whole being and is even reflected in my daily activities" [7, p. 148]. Napper also remarks that "creative activity develops spontaneously once the child has experienced the joy and adventure in the delightful discovery of new things to do" [5, p. 53]. Too much anxiety may produce opposite effects.

Frustration for lack of guidance in achieving pictorial representation of visual conceptions, overrigid teacher imposition of goal-directing ideas, unrealistic standards for an individual's maturity or stage of progress, or overcritical evaluation of products can stifle creative interests, result in stereotyped performances, or provoke attitudes of resistance and distaste for art activities. From his experience, Napper concludes that, just as creative interest in the child thrives on the assurance that his efforts and products will be appreciated, "insincerity or ridicule will destroy all desire and courage for originality" [5, p. 57]. A father's thoughtless remark about his sixth grade child's first attempt at abstract design ("What kind of crazy stuff is that?") ended the child's interest in abstract art [5, p. 57]. Often in his initial trials in a new activity, when his own uncertainty makes him insecure, the child is especially vulnerable to frustration or criticism.

Schaefer-Simmern reports that Selma, a mentally immature pupil, showed her first drawing "fearfully." "Anxiety" again appeared when she was requested to show the second. An "inner compulsion" for security kept her drawings rigidly repetitive for a long time. When asked if she "could draw these parts better," she expressed signs of anxiety and said, "No." But with lack of pressure, with freedom to set her own standards and pace, with warm encouragement, and with success, gradually emerging improvements, and attendant satisfactions, her initial anxiety was replaced by more "spontaneous activity" and a developing "passionate enjoyment in her work" [7, pp. 36–49].

Teaching Science

Although they are not obvious, it is also possible to find implicit applications of the seven conditions for effective learning in Miss Hopkinson's informal report [3] of her "continuing" lessons in science for second grade children. Her report:[1]

"What is it? Where did it come from?"

"I think it's a worm."

"No, it's a caterpillar."

"It looks like the picture of a caterpillar in this book," declared Mary, as she went to get *Johnny and the Monarch* by Margaret Friskey.

These were the excited comments made by second-grade children as they observed a milkweed caterpillar which I had brought to class early in September.

We compared our caterpillar with the picture in the book and agreed that they were alike. After reading the story of the caterpillar's metamorphosis, the children asked, "Will that happen to our caterpillar?"

"Let's watch and see," I suggested.

Our caterpillar would not eat leaves we put into its new milk-bottle home. "Why?" the children wondered.

"Maybe it just likes milkweed leaves. I know where we can find some," volunteered Ronald.

A trip to a nearby field proved that the "milkweed" was really ragweed. The caterpillar didn't like it.

Next morning, however, we had an ample supply of milkweed leaves. The parents had helped in the search after school.

For a few days the caterpillar just ate and ate. Then it fastened itself upside down on a twig in the bottle. The children described it as "wiggling and resting" as it changed into a beautiful green chrysalis with gold dots and "a gold zipper."

Within two weeks, the chrysalis turned a blue-black color. Each morning the children anxiously watched to see whether this was the day that the butterfly would emerge.

One morning when we came to school, we saw a beautiful monarch butterfly clinging to the split chrysalis. Reactions varied from bewilderment to extreme delight. The wings, still damp, were folded close.

Then ever so carefully we picked up a drop of sugar and water on a pinpoint and offered it eagerly to the butterfly. Quickly its tongue uncurled and claimed the droplet.

After an amazingly short time, the butterfly was able to fly around the room. At that point the children agreed they should open the window and let their butterfly go free.

"Where will the butterfly go?" plaintively asked little Susie. To answer her question, the class did a little "research." As one result, a picture of a bush covered with cutout butterflies was made by the class to show how monarch butterflies winter in the South.

---

[1] This illustration was suggested by Mrs. Sherman Eyre, as a student in educational psychology.

HOW CHILDREN LEARN

Others turned from *art* to *verbal expression*. For example:

"See the chrysalis
 Pretty and green.
 Inside is a butterfly
 That can't be seen."

"Out in the field
 On a milkweed tall
 Caterpillars crawl
 Eating leaves till fall."

While we were waiting for the butterfly to emerge, Barbara Sue brought a shoe box to school that contained five of the fattest and ugliest tomato caterpillars I ever saw. But they kept crawling out of the shoebox. So Albert made a wooden box for them, which we partially filled with soil.

Next we wondered what to feed them. That was easy! We canvassed the neighborhood for tomato plants and then, with a magnifying glass, we watched the caterpillars eat.

One by one the caterpillars disappeared.

"Let's see if they have made a chrysalis."

"Let's dig in the soil and see."

Jimmie dug and the tension and expectation were as great as if he were on the verge of discovering gold. Great was the delight when Jimmie found a brown chrysalis.

After much discussion the children decided to cover the box with a screen and wait to see what would happen in the spring.

No need to moralize on this little "continuing" story. But I do believe that these children, with freedom to wonder and explore and work together, are learning many things besides scientific facts about the world they live in.

The children's sustained curiosity and interest in the creatures of their environment and their thrilling creative discoveries *motivated* these lessons. But their interest required arousing and directing. The teacher brought a milkweed caterpillar to school, about which the children asked questions, made guesses, and sought answers—"It looks like the one in this book!" Hearing the teacher read the story of the caterpillar's metamorphosis raised further questions: "Will it happen to ours?" "Will it be a butterfly?" "Where will it go?"

The *teacher guided* them in effective, scientific problem solving. Reading *Johnny and the Monarch* to them had suggested hypotheses. Now, her answer to their questions: "Let's watch and see," led to systematic observations and self-discoveries.

FIG. 10–11. Guided by their teacher, children's interests in their natural environment lead to scientific observing, recording, and thinking; to reading; and to creative expression in writing and art. (*Courtesy of McKinley School, Tremonton, Utah.*)

Practice for these children consisted of field observations, experimenting with different foods, searching books for answers, and expressing their discoveries in language and in art.

They *checked* their hypotheses against the book, they noted the caterpillar's reactions to different foods, they compared by observations the development of the milkweed caterpillar and the tomato caterpillars, and their verbal and art expression was elicited to match their observations. In these lessons, the concepts learned were checked scientifically. Some hypotheses were confirmed, but others had to be rejected: the caterpillar *was* a milkweed caterpillar, but what was thought to be milkweed proved to be ragweed.

There are many examples of *transfer* in these lessons. The children learned how to learn by observing and experimenting. They utilized prior experiences. They generalized: since a milkweed caterpillar makes a chrysalis, perhaps a tomato caterpillar does also. They checked this hypothesis by the same kind of observation that they had applied to the first caterpillar. Similarly, after the trial-and-error discovery that milkweed caterpillars eat milkweed, they generalized that tomato caterpillars probably also eat the plants on which they are found. Mainly, they learned how to use in problem solving all the concepts and skills at their command.

These children at the second grade level were mature enough to wonder about other life in their environment, to reason, to maintain sustained interest, and to use some skills in reading, language, and art; so the project proved suited to their *level of maturity*.

The teacher contributed to the *security, confidence, and interest* in learning of these children in several ways. There was, for example, her friendly interest in them and in their interests. By leading them, through their own self-discovery experiences, to make satisfying interpretations of their world and by guiding them in learning how to learn, she helped them to become more secure and confident.

A Lesson in Courtesy

Our final illustration of the conditions of effective learning as applied in teaching is a student teacher's report and analysis of her observation of an incident in social learning achieved by sixth grade pupils:[1]

I had never realized before that teaching children to be respectful and courteous to other people requires the same conditions for effective learning as learning to read or to write. My observations of an effective lesson in courtesy, however, have taught me that these conditions of learning are general.

All over the nation, people were observing United Nations Week. The sixth grade I visited was planning and preparing a play about the U. N. for presentation to the children of the entire school. While their regular teacher, Miss M, was rehearsing a few members of the class in the auditorium, the remainder of the pupils in the classroom were taught by Miss H, a practice teacher.

As soon as Miss M had left the room, the children began to see just how far they could go with Miss H. There was much whispering and giggling and throwing of paper. Miss H, being unprepared for such behavior, became nervous and upset. Fortunately, it was soon time for the recess period and the children went out to play.

When the children returned to their classroom, they found Miss M again in charge of the class. And having had a report about their behavior while Miss H had been in charge, she was displeased.

Miss M explained to the class that she was not angry, but was very disappointed to learn that her class would act so disrespectfully to anyone. Then she asked if anyone could explain the meaning of respect. Several children volunteered definitions. She then asked if they were reminded of any recent discussions of respect. Several immediately recalled discussion of respect in connection with their study of the United Nations.

[1] Contributed by Miss Annette Hansen.

They had learned that one of the purposes of that organization was to create respect for all people.

The children were then asked if anyone would like to express his feelings about his recent behavior in the classroom. No one was forced to say anything. No one was called upon. But several children said that they had participated in the mischief making, and they were now sorry and ashamed of their actions. Miss M then asked the children for suggestions about better behavior in such situations. One boy suggested that he should apologize to Miss H for his disturbing conduct in the class. Several believed that they had behaved much too childishly for sixth graders. The class also concluded that if they could make the practice teacher feel more comfortable with them, she would probably be a better teacher, which would result in a happier and more interesting class for all.

The student goes on to report that

. . . the children soon had an occasion to put into practice their new plans for being respectful to their practice teacher, and they experienced the improvement they had predicted.

Moreover, the student also learned

. . . that the children became increasingly respectful to other people, not only to other practice teachers and to classroom visitors, but also to each other. They didn't abandon all mischief. That couldn't be expected of active eleven- and twelve-year-olds, but the social relations in their classroom became much more courteous.

In her analysis of this learning episode, the student points out applications of the seven conditions of learning:

1. The children showed their readiness and maturity for this lesson by their immediate recognition that their conduct had been inappropriate and disrespectful and by their suggestions for improving their classroom behavior.

2. By her leading, thought-provoking questions, the teacher guided their thinking toward the self-discovery of more appropriate social behavior and attitudes.

3. The initial class discussion, the opportunity for trying out their new plans for more respectful behavior with the practice teacher, and subsequent opportunities with other practice teachers and visitors provided practice in self-discipline in the classroom.

4. Because pupils perceived that the improved and happier classroom situation resulted from their more respectful behavior and because they experienced greater satisfaction in it, the new patterns of behavior were reinforced.

5. Understanding of respectful behavior was generalized from the United Nations discussions to their own social behavior. Transfer was also illustrated in the spread of courteous behavior to everyone in their classroom and possibly elsewhere.

6. Probably the main motive for their changed attitude and behavior was the "enhanced value" these children experienced in their more mature self-concepts. They

enjoyed identifying with the "respectful" leaders of the United Nations. Acting like "second graders" was perceived to be inconsistent with this self-concept; and they experienced greater satisfaction in playing more mature sixth grade roles.

7. The teacher by "criticizing" the mischief of these children without anger or threat, provoked no fear or anxiety. They did not need to become defensive about their behavior. And she gave them an opportunity to solve the social problem themselves; thus they felt more mature and confident.

Summary

Analyses of several examples of effective teaching—from reading, arithmetic, art, science, and social development—reveal in all of them applications of the seven conditions of effective learning. The *scientific* validity of these principles of learning has been established in previous chapters in which the pertinent experimental literature was cited. These applications to teaching demonstrate their *practical* value as guides to effective teaching. The set of principles should therefore be useful to the teacher in evaluating or in creating new methods. They can serve as general criteria for directing children's day-by-day learning activities. And they can be used as a frame of reference for analyzing pupils' learning difficulties. If any condition should not be applied effectively in some child's learning activity, he might be expected to make no or little progress. His learning ability could probably be improved by providing more effectively for the misapplied conditions. As an exercise to improve the student's awareness of the application of these conditions of effective learning, it is suggested that he use them as criteria for evaluating other examples of effective teaching [1, 2].

Review and Applications

1. Why are the seven conditions listed and defined at the beginning of this chapter considered *essential* for effective learning?

2. From the point of view of the conditions of effective learning, why does it seem desirable to teach children versatility in using a combination of word-identification techniques in which verbal context clues predominate?

3. In the illustration of teaching division with a remainder, which condition of learning seems most effectively applied?

4. In the discussion of teaching art, point out several instances of pupil initiative and self-teaching—of learning from self-discovery experiences. Why should such learning be encouraged?

5. What conditions of effective learning are applied especially well in the science lesson?

6. Suggest desirable ways of achieving good classroom discipline. Do your suggestions embody applications of the seven conditions of effective learning?

7. Find, from observation or reading, an especially interesting illustration of teaching, and analyze it for applications of the seven conditions of effective learning.

References

1. Artley, A. S.: *Your Child Learns to Read.* Copyright, 1953, by Scott, Foresman and Company, Chicago.
2. Fitzgerald, J. A.: "The teaching of spelling," *Elem. Engl.* 30: 79–85, 1953.
3. Hopkinson, Margaret: "Their own special butterfly," *Nat. Educ. Ass. J.,* 42: 567, 1953.
4. Mead, Margaret: "The meaning of freedom in education," *Progr. Educ.,* 8: 108–111, 1931.
5. Napper, D. G.: "A guide for teachers directing creative art experiences in elementary schools," unpublished master's thesis, Utah State Agricultural College Library, Logan, 1951.
6. Purdy, C. R., and L. B. Kinney: "Directing learning in arithmetic," *Elem. Sch. J.,* 54: 285–290, Copyright, 1954, by the University of Chicago. Reprinted by permission of the University of Chicago Press.
7. Schaefer-Simmern, H.: *The Unfolding of Artistic Activity,* University of California Press, Berkeley, 1950.
8. Tinker, M. A.: *Teaching Elementary Reading,* Appleton-Century-Crofts, New York, 1952.

Chapter 11

Remembering
and Forgetting

EARNING, REMEMBERING, transfer, and forgetting are
interrelated processes which occur simultaneously
as children progress through school and life. The beginner in reading, for example, can recognize only a few words. But as is illustrated in Figure 11–1, as he
progresses through school, he learns to recognize an increasing accumulation of
words [19]. Such an accumulating reading vocabulary can be mastered
gradually only by remembering words learned earlier. Transfer also facilitates
mastery of such an accumulating list. Having learned the concept of compound
words, for example, a child who has learned to recognize "base" and "ball"
may apply his retention of these words to recognition of "baseball" without
specific learning. But while these "positive" processes are going on, forgetting
is also taking place. It is as though a child takes three steps forward and one
step backward. As an illustration, in reading Gray's Oral Reading Paragraphs,
a child whose reading level was grade 1.4 and who had recognized these words
correctly in some contexts now read "then" as "there," "boy" as "dog," and
"pig" as "big." Since he had not mastered any of them well, it is easy to
understand how he could confuse these similar words. As a preliminary to the
presentation of a more systematic theory of remembering and forgetting, it will
be instructive to explore further some informal illustrations.

Examples of Remembering and Forgetting

A bright child, who had at 10 years of age barely learned to associate the
names of the capitals with their states, was asked two years later to recite
them. She now recalled correctly only Salt Lake City (in her home state),

Indianapolis (in the other state in which she had lived), Sacramento, Boise, Cheyenne, Phoenix, Santa Fe, Oklahoma City, and Austin. Since in her own state and in the state in which she had lived temporarily, the capitals are the largest cities, it probably seemed logical to "reconstruct" in her recall the capital of Nevada as Reno and of New York as New York City. Butte,

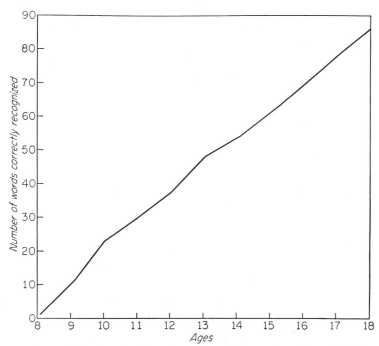

FIG. 11–1. Accumulative learning depends on remembering and transfer, as is indicated by these vocabulary scores on the Gates Reading Survey Test. (*Teachers College, Columbia University, Bureau of Publications, New York, 1942.*)

Kansas City, and Miami intruded as capitals possibly because they are frequently associated with their respective states. Mobile, Alabama, was perhaps recalled for a similar reason. For the remaining 32 states, she couldn't make even a plausible guess. Apparently, for unmeaningful associations, initially only poorly learned and rarely reviewed, retention is very limited and inaccurate.

The same child was asked both "specific-memory" and "understanding" questions from her paper on Denmark, written the previous year. Asked to name in order the kings of Denmark, she named, "Gorm, Bluebeard [for Bluetooth], Sweyn . . . then I can't remember until Christian I," followed by "Valdemar I, Christian II, Valdemar II, Christian III, Valdemar III, Christian

IV, Valdemar IV," and so on to "Christian IX, who is the present king. And the next king will be named Valdemar IX," she said, "because they alternate between Christian and Valdemar." In recalling the kings, she recalled the first three and then the general alternating pattern, from which she filled in the specific names. But again her recall was erroneously "reconstructed." The more familiar "Bluebeard" replaces "Bluetooth," and after Valdemar IV, according to her paper, the succession proceeded with the alternating names of Frederick and Christian, instead of Valdemar and Christian. The "understanding" questions were: "What is the latitude of Denmark?" "How cold is it?" and "Why?" Her answers were, respectively: "As far north as northern Canada and Alaska." "It is not as cold as northern Canada and Alaska; it is more like Seattle, Washington," and "It is warmed by the Gulf Stream and the protecting warmed sea which surrounds it." She explained that she had determined the location by thinking that "Sweden is just north of Denmark, Greenland is just west of Sweden, northern Canada and Alaska are west of Greenland, and both are just south of Greenland, so Denmark is as far north as Alaska and northern Canada." She knew it would not be especially cold in Denmark "because the Gulf Stream warms every place it touches."

In these illustrations, meaningful concepts are apparently remembered better than detached details. The beginning and the end of a sequence are remembered better than the middle part. And in both instances, general patterns and principles are recalled first, from which the details are reconstructed at the time of recall.

The same principles seem to operate in instances of more remote recall. The same child at age 12 was asked to recall a nursery rhyme which she had first learned at age 3 and which, because of the pleasure it gave her parents, she had been asked to recite several times up to about age 6.

The original:

> One misty, moisty morning,
>   When cloudy was the weather,
> I chanced to meet an old man
>   Clothed all in leather;
> He began to compliment,
>   And I began to grin——
> "How do you do," and "How do you do,"
>   And "How do you do" again!

Her recall:

> Twas a misty, moisty morning,
>   When cloudy was the weather . . .

(something about an old man in an overcoat or raincoat.)

> He began to compliment,
> And I began to ———— . . . ?
> "How do you do," and "How do you do."
> And "How do you do" again!

There is a second verse, but I can't remember it.

For this well-learned rhyme, reviewed several times with rewarding approval, retention over approximately a six-year interval is almost complete. The general structure of the rhyme, including the weather, the old man, his complimenting, and the pleasant alliterative features, are all retained almost unchanged from the original. But recall as construction is also apparent. The old man's being "in an overcoat or raincoat" is constructed to fit the logic of the moisty situation. Her own role is forgotten, as is indicated by her failure to recall "I chanced to meet" and "grin." Perhaps "to grin" was not recalled because grinning in such a situation is inconsistent with her present self-concept. And the need for a second verse intruded to suit her present idea of the length of such a rhyme.

A final example, besides illustrating again the reconstruction process in recall, also reveals both the role of interference from other learning and the saving from retention achieved in relearning. J., who has studied piano for about four years, was asked to play from memory some pieces she had memorized for recitals two or three years earlier but had not played since. "Rustic Chapel," a difficult and therefore not a well-learned piece, could not be recalled. She thought at first that she could not recall "Soldiers' Chorus"; then the general nature of the melody came to her, and in a few trial-and-error attempts she reconstructed it. She recalled "Playful Rondo" as "a gay piece which I liked"; but she could recall bits of the melody only. As she worked at its reconstruction, she observed, "I don't know whether all these parts are from "Playful Rondo" or from "The Doll's Dream." Actually, when the music was checked, she found that she had been confusing bits from the "Playful Rondo" and from "The Music Box" rather than "The Doll's Dream," both of which have "gay things in them." Now she remembered that after she showed delight in "The Music Box," her teacher had assigned her "Playful Rondo." Because these two pieces are alike in mood and in pattern and had been learned in close succession, bits from "The Music Box" intruded to interfere with accurate recall of "Playful Rondo."

But more was retained than seemed apparent from the recall efforts alone. Originally it had required approximately 50 trials to memorize "Playful

Rondo" and almost as many trials to memorize the slightly easier "The Music Box." J. now practiced to relearn "Playful Rondo." It required only 11 trials, which is 39 fewer than were originally needed. Because of the original learning three years earlier, she was saved 78 per cent of the trials which would have been otherwise required. This may be an overestimate, however, of the amount of her retention. Since the original learning she probably has learned something about how to learn music, which she transferred in relearning "Playful Rondo." Such a transfer effect was clearly demonstrated in the relearning of "The Music Box," which she undertook immediately after relearning "Playful Rondo." Relearning of this piece, similar in mood and pattern and in the same key, now required only six trials.

These informal observations have illustrated the interrelation among learning, remembering, transfer, and forgetting and have suggested some of the factors affecting these processes. In the remainder of this chapter, the experimentation and theorizing on remembering and forgetting are presented more systematically.[1]

General Patterns of Retention

Studies of retention after initial learning have shown that what has been learned may be forgotten rapidly and almost completely, may be retained without appreciable loss, or may be recalled even more efficiently after an interval of time than it was originally.

In his historically important study of retention of nonsense syllables, Ebbinghaus found that forgetting was extensive and rapid, especially immediately after learning. The record of his results is shown in the lower curve of Figure 11–2. The upper curve shows only slight early loss from forgetting and then relatively stable retention over a 30-day interval for answers to questions on the content of "interesting pictures" which had been observed. In the same article [20], Gilliland reports 81 to 98 per cent retention on the contents of two films (one an action film and one on Kellogg's *Ape and the Child*) which had been seen a week earlier. And Jones [25] has reported stable retention of a conditioned emotional reaction in infants over a 31-day interval.

Ballard [3] has discovered that under certain conditions, recall may be more efficient after two or three days than it is immediately after learning. He had 5,192 school children learn long selections of poetry under time limits insuffi-

---

[1] Because the experimentation with children on this topic has been insufficient to establish general principles, relatively more frequent references to the literature on adults will be cited in the next three parts of this chapter.

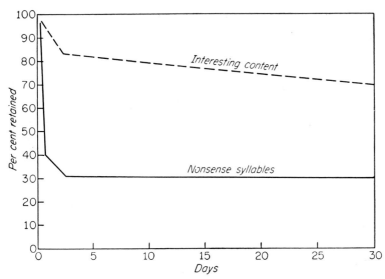

FIG. 11–2. Retention of answers to questions on observation of interesting pictures compared to Ebbinghaus's retention of nonsense syllables. (*From Gilliland, A. R.: J. Educ. Psychol., 39: 23, 1948.*)

cient for mastery, using different subjects for each condition. Recall tests were given immediately and, without advance notice, one, two, three, four, five, six, or seven days later.

The delayed recall, expressed as percentages of the immediate recall, is presented in Figure 11–3. Incomplete recall of "The Ancient Mariner" is shown to be 6 to 9 per cent better after two or three days than it was immediately after learning. Several hypotheses have been proposed to explain this phenomenon, which has been named "reminiscence" [23]. Practice from the initial test is not the full explanation, because, as in Ballard's experiment, there was no immediate test for the groups tested a day or more after learning. It has been found to occur in situations where there have been attempts to prevent "rehearsal" during the intervening time. It has been suggested that rapid forgetting of irrelevant responses which interfere with effective immediate recall may permit better recall later. Between immediate and later recall there may be a change of attitude toward the task. For example, attention may be focused immediately upon *all* the details of a poem—an attitude in which the "trees obscure the forest." Later, when the child's attention is returned to the recall task, he may consider the poem as a whole. And having recalled the structure as a whole, he may, in the reconstruction process already

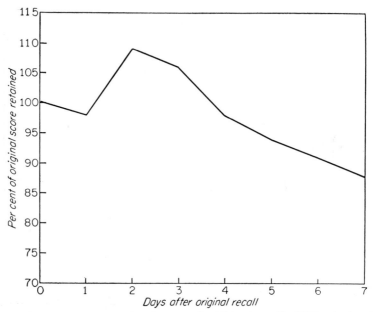

Fig. 11–3. Reminiscence curve of twelve-year-old children's recall of "The Ancient Mariner," tested immediately and after varying delay intervals. (*From Ballard, P. B.: Brit. J. Psychol. Monogr. Suppl., 1–4 (2): 5, 1911.*)

referred to, fit in the details even more efficiently than could have been done originally.

A General Theory of Remembering

Man is motivated and, possessing a nervous system, is equipped to achieve an economical, adaptive relationship to his environment. As a result of accumulating learning experiences, he develops systems of hypotheses or assumptions and relatively stable "cognitive maps" as guides to satisfying behavior. On the basis of past experiences, he remembers how to meet recurring situations, because the systems of hypotheses and the cognitive maps are registered in his nervous system as "memory traces." One can only speculate that these hypothetical traces may be electrochemical organizations in the nervous system which correspond to the psychological organizations observable in behavior. The "traces" themselves have not been observed.

In the interest of economy of behavior, the individual classifies and organizes his cognitive guides to action into integrated systems of responses. He also tends to respond to the "class," or abstract features, of objects rather than to the specific features of each. For example, oranges varying somewhat in shape, size, color, and taste are all responded to as spherical, as approximately the size of a baseball, as orange in color, and as good to eat. Repeated perception of the effects of and motive satisfaction from actions guided by these hypotheses have established them as valid assumptions, and they have been registered as relatively stable in the individual's organization of traces. Similarly, the child's assumptions about capitals being large cities, the Gulf Stream's warming influence, an old man's need for a raincoat in moisty weather, and bits of "The Music Box" being parts of "Playful Rondo" were firmly established. When, however, in learning experiences, one's perception of the effects of acting on these assumptions proves them wrong, a change in the individual's cognitive structure occurs. As a residual of such learning experience, the "trace system" is altered. Because of these changes in the trace system, subsequent responses to these situations are modified. The corresponding changes in behavior constitute learning or forgetting (which, of course, are similar processes differing only in direction).

These general concepts are now related to a more specific theory of remembering. It has already been suggested in the interpretations of the earlier cited examples of remembering that remembering is at least in part a process of reconstruction. When the child recalled "Misty, Moisty Morning," the influence of the specific original trace was apparent in her recall of the general form, the atmosphere, and some striking details of the poem. But the influence of the subsequently developed, integrated organization of traces was also apparent. This total organization of traces influenced her to construct a completed poem which met her present demands of logic: If it was moisty, the old man was probably wearing a raincoat. Bartlett [4], who originally developed this theory, writes that "remembering obviously involves determination by the past." From past experience the individual develops an active organization of traces, which Bartlett calls "schemata." In remembering, however, Bartlett thinks that the individual in part *infers* the past from his present hypotheses, assumptions, interests, and attitudes. It is as though the individual said, "This and this and this must have occurred in order that my present state should be what it is." Remembering, therefore, "appears to be far more decisively an affair of construction than of mere reproduction. . . . When a subject is asked to remember, often the first thing that emerges . . . is an attitude. The recall is . . . a construction" which justifies the attitude. (When J. tried to recall "Playful Rondo," she recalled gay, well-liked bits of melody from *both* "The Music Box" and "Playful Rondo.") The original trace probably determines the attitude and the general form, and from these the individual "constructs the probable detail." In this construction process, "condensation, elaboration, and invention are common features." Bartlett summarizes: "Remembering is an imaginative reconstruction, or construction, built out of the relation of our attitude towards a whole active mass of organized past reactions [traces], and to a little outstanding detail which commonly appears in image or in language form" [4, p. 213].

This theory of remembering also takes into account the role of motivation in behavior. The trace effects of intervening learning sometimes prevent accurate reproduction. But at the need for recall, imaginative reconstructions which agree with the individual's attitudes, interests, and logic are often more motive-satisfying than reproductions.

Bartlett's evidence for his theory consists of the changes he finds for several subjects in their repeated recalls of verbal and pictorial materials. Our example of the child's recall of "Misty, Moisty Morning" illustrates well his data

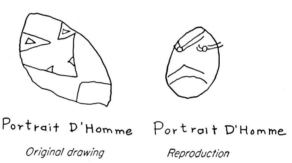

Portrait D'Homme   Portrait D'Homme

Original drawing   *Reproduction*

FIG. 11–4. The original is transformed in memory reproduction to resemble more nearly the cultural concept. (*From Bartlett, F. C.: Remembering, Cambridge, New York, 1932, p. 178.*)

on verbal recall. The similar transformations in recall of his pictorial material are illustrated in Figure 11–4. The individual first observed the original drawing, named "Portrait of a Man." Then from memory, which was influenced both by the specific trace left by the observation and by the general trace representing his cultural concept of man, he reproduced *and* reconstructed the compromise shown in the second drawing. The result is apparently a product of a specific trace interacting with earlier developed trace systems or schemata.

Several studies have contributed data in support of Bartlett's theory. Northway [34] found that, as different children ages 10 to 15 reproduced in succession a story, only its general outline or a significant detail was retained. By changes, additions, deletions, and substitutions, the original story was molded into a form more in harmony with the concepts of the group. Carter and Schooler [11] have demonstrated the role of motivation as a determinant in memory. Asked to match with circles of light the sizes of coins recalled rather than observed, poor children remembered them as larger than they really were, while rich children made reasonably accurate estimates of their sizes. The magnified value of the coins for the poor children distorted their judgments of sizes in recall. When they were matched from observation, however, both groups judged the coins fairly accurately. Carmichael, Hogan, and Walter [10] have shown that the trace from hearing a neutral form (such as two small circles joined by a straight line) named affects some memory reproductions in the direction of conformity to the named object. Hearing the neutral form called "glasses" resulted in some reproductions resembling lenses in a nosepiece. Hearing the form called "dumbbell" resulted in some dumbbell-shaped reproductions. Allport [1] found that children ages 10 to 13 in reproducing immediately, two weeks later, and four months later the S-B designs (a Greek key and a truncated pyramid) which had been exposed for 10 seconds, tended to construct smaller, simpler, and more symmetrical designs. This tendency is

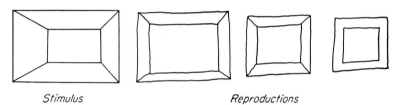

Stimulus   *Reproductions*

Fig. 11–5. In reproducing designs from memory, children tend to make them smaller, simpler, and more symmetrical. (*From Allport, G. W.: Brit. J. Psychol., 21: 138, 1930.*)

illustrated in the one immediate and the two delayed reproductions of the truncated pyramid shown in Figure 11–5.

Tiernan [44] had children ages 7 to 14 study sets of 12 incompleted figures, such as hearts, circles, or diamonds, with a small omitted segment of each and then reproduce them from memory at intervals of 11, 46, and 130 days. A tendency to reproduce these familiar figures as closed—that is, to reproduce them to conform to their concepts of them—was found. The tendency was more marked for the younger children. Williams and Knox [46], in summarizing these dynamic factors affecting memory, note that (1) reproductions are affected by naming objects; (2) they tend toward symmetry, simplicity, and completeness; and (3) their traces are affected by organizational processes, by interaction with other traces, and by attitudes.

General Factors Affecting Forgetting

It has already been implied in noting that learning and forgetting are basically alike that forgetting is not merely the fading away in time of traces in the nervous system. As the individual remembers and learns, there is continuous interaction between memory traces and new learning; and this "interaction works both ways, modifying both" the organization of the traces and the new learning [47].

That forgetting is an active process in which new experiences interact with the trace systems from prior learning to interfere with recall of them is indicated by the fact that forgetting is more rapid during the activities of

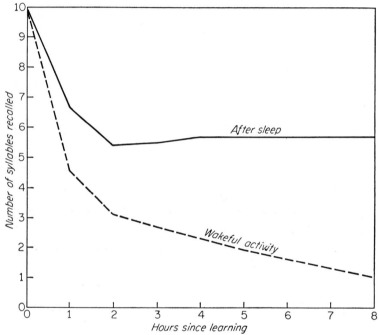

FIG. 11–6. Retention of nonsense material after sleeping compared with retention after equal periods of wakeful activity. (*From Jenkins, J. G., and K. M. Dallenbach: Amer. J. Psychol., 35: 610, 1924.*)

wakefulness than it is during the relative inactivity of sleep. As is indicated in Figure 11–6, forgetting of nonsense syllables occurred much more rapidly for Jenkins and Dallenbach's subjects while they were awake than while they were asleep [24]. What, then, are the activities which cause forgetting? In answering this question, Deese [15] mentions six causes.

1. Retroactive and Proactive Inhibition. When two similar patterns of behavior are learned in succession, at recall of either, there is likely to be competition between them. At recall of the first, intrusions from the second may interfere ("retroactive inhibition"). And at recall of the second, intrusions from the first may interfere ("proactive inhibition"). In trying to recall "Playful Rondo," the child was confused by the interfering recall of bits of similar melody from "The Music Box" (proactive inhibition). Had her intent been to recall the first-learned piece, "The Music Box," undoubtedly bits of melody from "Playful Rondo" would have interfered (retroactive inhibition). Similarly, there was interference from retroactive inhibition of the child's reading. After the beginner had learned to recognize "then," "boy," and "pig," he also learned to recognize "there," "dog," and "big." Since his mastery of these words and his general proficiency in reading were far from thorough, the latter learning interfered with recall of the former. He read "then" as "there," "boy" as "dog," and "pig" as "big." This is probably the most important single factor in forgetting. One forgets a learned response to a situation because in the meantime he has learned another response to the same or to a similar situation.

2. *Changes in Attitudes, Interests, and Cognitive Structure.* In one of the original stories which Bartlett read his subjects, there were references to a young man joining some ghosts in a war party. The structure of the story as a whole was not very logical and coherent. In succeeding recalls of this story, in order to make it conform to their naturalistic beliefs and logic, his subjects often deleted the ghosts and constructed the story more logically. Similarly, to the child who recalled "Misty, Moisty Morning," it seemed logical because of the weather to provide the old man a raincoat. And in trying to recall "Playful Rondo," "The Music Box" intruded because they are both gay in mood and provoked a similar attitude: she liked them both. If between original learning and recall, children learn new attitudes, beliefs, or logical systems, the traces from these new learnings may be expected to modify their recall of the original learning.

3. *Mental Set for a Given Activity.* Suddenly confronted with a request to play some recital pieces she had not played for two or three years, the child was at first baffled. She could not recall "The Old Mill Wheel" at all. At first she could not remember "Soldiers' Chorus" either; but as she tried, an idea of the melody occurred. Then, in a trial-and-error process, she reconstructed it —first the melody and then even the accompaniment. As she "warmed up" to the task, achieving a set to recall these pieces, recall of them became easier. When the mental set changes in the time between original learning and the time for recall, recall is more difficult.

4. *Changes in the Recall Situation.* The child who sometimes confused "then" and "there," "boy" and "dog," and "pig" and "big" did not always do so. In the original piece in which he had learned to recognize "then," "boy," and

"pig," he could still do so. Only in new situations, in which some of the original cues for recall were absent and in which new, distracting cues were present, was he inaccurate. The student may have experienced this phenomenon in trying to recall the name of a person whom he has met but who is not at the time present. Though he is unsuccessful, when he again comes into the presence of the person, the name is promptly recalled. The role of a changed situation in interfering with recall was also illustrated when Grossnickle found pupils unable to use in division multiplication facts which they had practiced only in the multiplication situation [21].

5. Repression. As a protective device for avoiding anxiety, the individual may fail to recall certain emotionally disturbing ideas. It will be remembered that a five-year-old child learned to recognize "school" after 18 exposures; but "street," which was connected with his anxiety about the street in front of his yard, could not be recognized correctly even after 98 exposures. Likewise, perhaps the child failed to recall her grinning in the presence of the complimentary old man because such a self-concept would be embarrassing. Levine and Murphy [31] found students forgetting more rapidly propaganda content contrary to their own biases than content favorable to them.

6. Disuse and Metabolic Changes in the Nervous System. This factor was at one time considered to be the primary cause of forgetting; but with the accumulation of evidence for the active interferences with retention, it has come to be considered less and less important. Since the first five psychological factors appear not to account completely for the observed decrements in retention, however, the physiological factor is also assumed to be a possibility, although the evidence for it is not specific. Woodworth and Schlossberg [47], although they consider retroactive factors primarily responsible for forgetting, think that "there is evidence that metabolic activities play some part" in erasing memory traces from the nervous system.

General Factors Affecting Retention

Retention is related to the nature of the material learned, to the methods of learning, to the degree of learning, and to the characteristics of the learner.

1. Meaningfulness of Material. Compared with nonsense syllables or detached details, meaningful concepts and content organized around principles are much better retained. This difference was illustrated by the child's poor retention of the detached capital-state associations and by her excellent retention of an understanding of Denmark's climate. The composite of findings collected by Davis and Moore [13] from several studies which have compared the retention of meaningful versus meaningless material is presented in Figure 11-7 [12, p. 211]. In their review of these studies, Davis and Moore point out that the retention curves for both kinds of material are similar in form—showing rapid loss early and then leveling off; but as the curves show, the retention of meaningful prose and poetry is maintained at a much higher level than the retention of nonsense syllables.

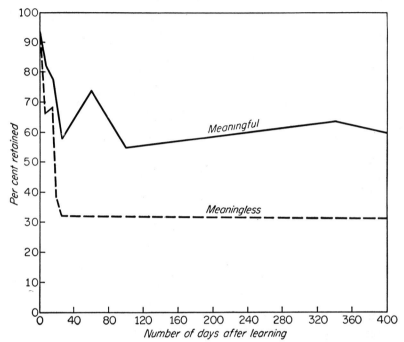

FIG. 11-7. Composite retention curves for 18 studies of meaningless material and 24 studies of meaningful material. (*From Davis, R. A.: Psychology of Learning, McGraw-Hill, New York, 1935, p. 211.*)

In a recent study, Hall [22] has shown meaningful, well-organized verbal content to be quite resistant to retroactive inhibition. Forty-five college students, subdivided into three groups, all studied for three minutes a day a story about the customs and characteristics of a hypothetical primitive tribe. The story consisted of an introductory statement and 30 sentences such as: "Women perform most of the *domestic* tasks." Immediately following the study, all three groups were tested for memory of the content just read by a 30-item completion test in which one key word was deleted from each—for example, "domestic" in the above sentence. Then, before a delayed retention test 45 minutes later, a different kind of activity was interpolated for each of the three groups. The control group took mechanical aptitude tests whose content had no relation to the original content but prevented them from rehearsing the story. Experimental Group I studied a second, but different, 30-sentence story about another hypothetical tribe. As an example of the variations between the two stories for Experimental Group I, the sentence: "The tribe is located in *northern* Africa," in the original was changed to: "The tribe is organized into *numerous* divisions," in the interpolated story. Experimental Group II studied a second story more similar to the original story. Twenty of their interpolated items were the same as for Experimental Group I; but 10 of the 30 items were identical with those in the original story except for a single changed word. For example, "The tribe is located in *northern* Africa," from the original story, was changed to: "The tribe is located in *southern* Africa," in the interpolated story.

Forty-five minutes after study of the original story and the immediate test on it, the original 30-item completion test on this story was repeated. It was repeated again 21 days later.

It was anticipated, of course, that in the process of trying to recall the originally learned items, items from the interpolated sentences might intrude, especially from the similar sentences. Instead of recalling the tribe as located in "northern Africa," for example, it was considered likely that the subjects would recall the location as "southern Africa." Despite the possibility, however, of retroactive-inhibition effects, by which items from the interpolated stories for the experimental groups might interfere with accurate recall of items from the original story, retention was very high after 45 minutes; and it continued to be good after 21 days. After 45 minutes, the percentages of items recalled by all three groups ranged from 91 to 101 per cent; and after 21 days, these percentages ranged from 81 to 83. Since the scores of both experimental groups equaled the retention scores of the control group, there were no retroactive effects demonstrated either from similar or from dissimilar interpolated activities. These unusual results, however, seem well explained by Bartlett's theory of remembering.

These short, fairly well learned, coherent paragraphs probably left as a trace a unitary impression from which the details could be logically reconstructed. Set to recall customs about a primitive tribe, one might very well infer the missing word in such a sentence as: "Women perform most of the _____ tasks." For women to perform "domestic" tasks is in harmony with well-learned cultural concepts.

Several studies of school learning also show that meaningful, organized content is better remembered than isolated details. Pressey and Robinson [37] have summarized studies indicating that two-thirds of students' original knowledge of detailed facts from high school and college courses is forgotten after two years. But Frutchey [18], with high school students, and Tyler [45], with college students, while confirming the findings on rapid and extensive forgetting of isolated details, have shown that generalizations and general, meaningful principles are retained very well for long intervals. Schrepel and Laslett [38] have reported that, while junior high school pupils lose some computational skill over the summer vacation, their ability to apply general principles of arithmetic is retained. And Steele [40] found, with equated groups of fifth and sixth grade pupils, that the group taught fractions with emphasis upon understanding and inductive discovery of principles did better both on end-of-course tests and retention tests seven months later than the group taught without such emphasis.

2. *Organization of Principles and Spheres of Knowledge.* A conception of the globe map as a whole helped the child to locate the latitude of Denmark. It was almost possible to remember the names of the later Danish kings because they alternate between Christian and Frederick. Even the accompaniments of some piano pieces could be recalled after two or three years because the child by age 12 had achieved some sense of the rules of harmony; she had a sense of what was fitting. A child who otherwise might not recall the product of 7×9 may arrive at it by mentally locating it in the multiplication table. Postman [36] has demonstrated experimentally that "learned rules of organization can systematically influence both the amount and quality of retention." For his subjects, explicit, verbal formulations of principles governing the content to be remembered improved their retention. The more explicit and differentiated the principles, the less susceptible is memory to retroactive inhibition. In time, "as the detailed features of the original stimuli are forgotten, the subject makes increasing use of these rules in reconstructing what he has learned." Therefore, especially over long intervals of retention, organizational categories for classifying or interpreting details determine the number and quality of ideas retained. Irrelevant items are forgotten, or if retained, are modified in the direction of conformity to principles.

3. *Methods of Learning.* Efficient methods of learning also result in good retention. Provision in learning for self-recitation, distributed practice, verbalization of principles, a meaningful approach, an over-all view, making relevant features identifiable, and such transfer principles as generalizing, making varied applications, and developing a set for continued application all contribute both to efficient learning and to sustained retention [23 and 47].

4. *Thorough Mastery.* Retroactive inhibition caused the immature reader to read "then" as "there" and "boy" as "dog" mainly because recognition

FIG. 11–8. Organizing their findings from well-motivated research on the uses of trees should aid these children in remembering and understanding. (*Courtesy of Dilworth School, Salt Lake City.*)

of these words had not been thoroughly mastered. Eventually, with continued practice, the child will cease to confuse such words. Content that is learned so that it can just barely be recalled once is likely to be soon forgotten. "Rustic Chapel," for example, which was too difficult for thorough mastery and which had been learned just sufficiently to be played at the recital, could not be recalled two years later. "Material that one wishes to retain for a long period needs to be studied and re-studied" [47, p. 730].

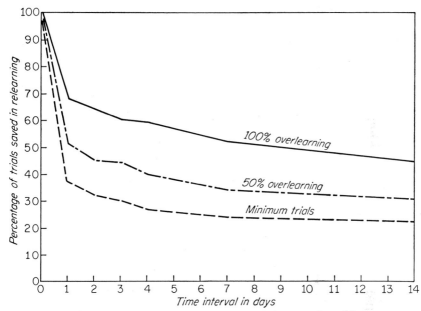

FIG. 11–9. Overlearning sustains retention: curves comparing retention of finger-maze performance for groups given (*a*) minimum trials for mastery, (*b*) 50 per cent added trials, and (*c*) 100 per cent added trials. (*Adapted from Krueger, W. C. F.: J. Exp. Psychol., 13: 155, 1930.*)

Using a finger maze as his learning material, Krueger [30] has demonstrated the advantage for sustained retention of such overlearning. After three groups of subjects had had the minimum number of trials needed to be able to trace the maze correctly, he gave one group 50 per cent and a second group 100 per cent more practice. The trials added for overlearning were not perfunctory repetitions but consisted of active efforts to improve proficiency and confidence on the maze. Krueger's results are presented in Figure 11–9. The curves show that for this relatively meaningless material, considerable forgetting occurs, especially for the group who practiced just to the point of mastery. But the more thoroughly the material is mastered, the better it is retained.

5. *Review.* The gradual progress which children make in school achievement from year to year (illustrated for reading in Figure 11–1) occurs because in the sequences of their learning activities, while new components are always being added, the accumulations of prior learnings are also being repeatedly reviewed. It will be recalled that Tinker suggested that only about 5 per cent of the words for practice in reading comprehension should be unfamiliar. Similarly, as children make progress in arithmetic, the earlier-learned computational skills in adding, subtracting, multiplying, and dividing with integers are continually reviewed throughout the grades as they are used with fractions, decimals, and denominate numbers and in a wide variety of problem-solving applications. Two experimental studies are cited to show the effect of reviewing upon retention.

Stroud and Johnson [42] had about 600 pupils in grades 7 to 9 read a 1,750-word article on the making of paper. They were then subdivided into three pairs of comparable groups for a 40-item multiple-choice retention test taken, by different groups, 1 day, 15 days, and 29 days later. For one group of each pair, a 12-minute rereading review of the material was permitted before the retention test; the other group in each pair was denied this opportunity for review. The results are presented in Table 11–1. As is indicated in the table, without review more of the content of the article is forgotten as the retention interval is increased. But a short review prior to the retention test restores retention, even up to 29 days, to the level of performance attained after only one day after the original study. The need for the review increases, of course, as the retention interval is increased. After only one day, review produces an advantage of 14.7 per cent; after 29 days, the advantage is 59.7 per cent.

Word and Davis [48] have also demonstrated experimentally the role of review in reporting the retention by seventh grade pupils of factual information

Table 11–1. Effectiveness of Rereading Review before a Retention Test
(Spaced at 1, 15, and 29 days after original learning, for seventh, eighth, and
ninth grade pupils)

Condition	Time, days	Mean	Diff.	t	Increase in effect., %
Retention without review	1	21.7			
Review and retention	1	24.9	3.2	4.2	14.7
Retention without review	15	19.4			
Review and retention	15	24.2	4.8	6.7	24.7
Retention without review	29	15.4			
Review and retention	29	24.6	9.2	15.6	59.7

Source: J. B. Stroud and E. Johnson: *J. Educ. Res.*, 35: 618–622, 1941–1942.

in general science. Their review devices included repeated testing, providing continued use for previously learned facts, and attempts to interrelate and to integrate the accumulating information with principles. At the conclusion of each two-week assignment, the pupils were tested both on the newly acquired content and on retention of content from the preceding two-week assignment. Their accumulated scores on both kinds of tests, recorded biweekly over a period of 18 weeks, are presented in Figure 11–10. This sequential development of concepts plus the biweekly tests comprised of both new content and

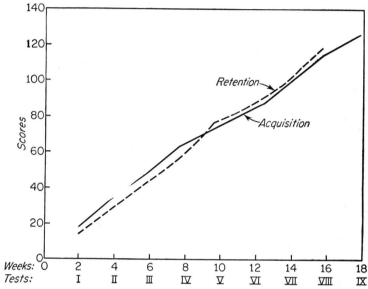

Fig. 11–10. Reviewing sustains retention and facilitates new learning, as is shown by acquisition and retention scores plotted cumulatively. (*From Word, A. H., and R. A. Davis: J. Educ. Psychol., 30: 121, 1939.*)

reviews of earlier-learned concepts not only kept the facts alive but probably also promoted transfer gains in that facts took on enriched meanings through the broader organizing concepts that were developed.

In order to prevent effectively the losses which would otherwise occur from forgetting, the reviews need to be spaced taking into account the findings from curves of forgetting. To prevent the typical rapid forgetting following shortly after initial learning, a thorough review should be given early. Then, still comprehensive but with smaller samplings, reviews can be spaced at longer and longer intervals. For example, in spelling, the words for the week should be reviewed on Friday. Words missed should be included in the next week's lesson. Other comprehensive reviews might be spaced at the end of a month,

FIG. 11–11. Understandings related to abiding interests are enhanced rather than forgotten over the summer vacation. (*Photographed by Prof. H. R. Reynolds.*)

at the end of each term, and at the beginning of the following school year. For some school content, such systematic scheduling of reviews is needed. But probably the best review procedure is to provide for periodic and continual use of accumulating knowledge and skills in interesting and worthwhile projects.

6. Interests. Capitalizing on children's interests or developing their interests in curriculum activities not only motivates original learning effectively but results in sustained retention. If children enjoy a learning activity, they exercise initiative in seeking more of it. For example, the children who enjoyed studying the rats in the diet experiment were happy to find and to study the report of another and more thorough experiment which later appeared in the local newspaper. Thus, their originally learned concepts were revived and extended.

7. Set to Recall. Often before earlier-learned concepts or skills can be recalled, a child must "warm up" to the specific task. As J. practiced recalling her earlier-learned piano-recital pieces, she was able to recall pieces which at first seemed completely forgotten. As the warm-up proceeded, traces from general musical concepts and related clue traces were revived to assist recall, and attention was diverted from distracting traces and cues. Perhaps as a device in learning how to learn, this factor affecting retention can be used to good advantage. It often seems futile to attempt some tasks because they seem too difficult; and they *are* difficult until one gets into them. Children need, however, to learn to make trial efforts. Cultivating resourcefulness generally may aid children in getting through the warm-up period. As an example of such a use of set, it will be recalled that in learning to spell an unfamiliar word, the children are encouraged to draw upon any and all generalizations available from their prior spelling experience. The transfer principles of cultivating sets to remember and of applying what one learns should also aid in retention.

Principles Applied to Retention of School Content

In the foregoing discussion of principles, forgetting has been conceived mainly as an active process. It is caused by retroactive and proactive inhibition; by changes in attitudes, interests, concepts, and beliefs; by changes in mental set; by changes in the recall situation; by repression; and (to a limited extent) by metabolic changes in the nervous system. Recall is a complex process involving both the influence of memory traces and creative reconstruction. Retention is influenced by meaningfulness of material, organizing principles and functional classifications of knowledge, methods of learning, thoroughness of mastery, reviews, interests, and appropriate mental sets. These principles are now applied here in interpreting several studies in retention of school content, involving mainly retention over the summer vacation.

1. Differential Effects of Summer Vacation on Retention. Several investigations indicate that the effects on retention of interrupted instruction over the summer vacation vary with the subject and with the grade level of the pupils [9, 17, 26, 29, 35, and 41]. In these studies, scores on retention tests given early in the fall are compared with initial-achievement-test scores earned the previous spring— often on different forms of the same tests. At the intermediate grade levels, where the majority of pupils have developed considerable mastery and interest in reading, average gains over the summer are quite uniformly reported [9, 17, 29, 41]. Not all pupils at these levels gain, however. Elder [17] found 27 per cent of pupils in grades 3 through 6 sustaining losses from spring to fall and 15 per cent remaining unchanged. For primary grade pupils, whose skill in reading is less mature, slight losses often occur over the summer [41]. Largest losses are usually reported in arithmetic—varying, however, from inappreciable [35] to considerable [9, 26]; and they are sometimes larger for computation

Fɪɢ. 11–12. Used skills are improved rather than forgotten over the summer vacation. (*Courtesy of D. Allred, Logan, Utah.*)

than for problem solving [9]. Some losses are also usually found in spelling, especially for the primary grades [41]. Data on retention of language skills are varied, some investigators reporting gains [26] and others losses [9]. Retention of information in science and social studies also varies with unreported conditions. Bruene [9] reports small gains in science and small losses in history for grades 5 and 6. On the other hand, Keys and Lawson [26] report a gain in history and a loss in science for grades 4 to 8.

Not all the factors determining the differences in retention for these subjects and pupils are clearly indicated in these experiments of oversimplified design. The role of thoroughness of mastery, however, is suggested in the poorer retention in reading and spelling of primary as compared with intermediate level pupils. And perhaps the gains in reading and sometimes in science and history are due to the reviewing which occurs in the summer activities of some pupils at the intermediate level. Many of these children have learned how to identify words independently—they have learned how to learn. So, by further practice in reading, they increase their reading vocabularies, with consequent improved skill in using the context to identify new words. Having learned how to teach themselves, they are able to make rapid progress for awhile without close teacher-guidance.

2. Recovery and Prevention of Losses from Forgetting. Because of reviews, the development of organizing principles, and the reestablishment of appropriate mental sets, relearning in the fall soon results in recovery of the losses which are sustained in some subjects over the summer. Keys and Lawson report that by October the "typical pupil . . . had recovered an average educational status approximating that of the previous May." [26].

Morgan [32] has shown that by bringing recent achievement in the spring to a higher level of mastery, the usual summer forgetting can be prevented and test performance the following September even be made to exceed that of the previous May. Using equated experimental and control groups of sixth grade children, he gave them tests in reading and in arithmetic computation and reasoning on May 11, May 25, and September 4. For the experimental group, between the May 11 and May 25 tests he provided two weeks of intensive diagnostic and remedial teaching based on the individual needs discovered in the May 11 tests. For this group, the special teaching resulted in gains in all three subjects from May 11 to May 25; and these gains were maintained without loss over the summer vacation. For the control group, from whom the special spring teaching was withheld, there were no mean gains from May 11 to May 25; and in September, the mean computation score was lower than the May 11 score. For reading and arithmetic reasoning, the control group's scores did not change appreciably in either direction.

3. Mastery and Retention. Level of maturity and degree of mastery have already been suggested as affecting retention in reading and spelling. Several other investigations support and extend the application of this hypothesis. Ashbaugh [2] found net losses in spelling over the summer vacation for third grade children. But in the fifth and seventh grades, by which levels children had accumulated a greater background of spelling generalizations and skill in learning how to spell, gains exceeded losses. Kolberg [28] found losses in American history only for his duller seventh grade pupils; those pupils less able to master concepts initially also retained them less well. And throughout the range of intelligence, Kolberg found retention better for familiar, well-learned information items than for new, less well-learned facts. Brueckner [7] found no forgetting over the summer of the relatively well-learned additions (sums under 10) and subtractions (minuends under 10) for either grade 2A or grade 2B pupils. The 2A pupils also studied the 100 addition facts and retained them without appreciable loss. But in the less well-learned 100 subtraction facts, these 2A pupils sustained some loss over the summer vacation. Similarly, Kirby [27] found greater loss over a summer in division skills than in the probably better-learned addition and subtraction facts. Brueckner and Distad

[8] compared the summer-retention losses of first grade children who had had 12, 24, and 36 weeks of reading instruction. That the extra amounts of instruction increased the level of mastery in reading is shown by the scores in the June tests of 9.7 for 12 weeks and 15.1 for 24 weeks on the easy test, and of 7.6 for 24 weeks and 17.4 for 36 weeks on the more advanced test. For children given 24 or 36 weeks of instruction in reading, there were no appreciable losses. But for the children given only 12 weeks of teaching, a significant loss occurred over the summer in their poorly developed skills. Level of initial mastery is closely related to retention of history content, as is revealed in a study by Brooks and Bassett [6], who found a correlation of .81 between initial-test scores and retention scores for 64 seventh grade pupils after 16 months.

4. *Retention as Related to Nature of Practice, Use, and Need.* Practice alone, unguided and without goal-directed effort, does not result in either sustained retention or improvement. Under such conditions, Beales [5] reports deterioration in pupils' handwriting. And Nelson [33] has shown that, when "no special drill was given" and when "teachers were not aware that the successive tests were to be given," it took six weeks or more in the fall to recover the status of the previous spring on tests in arithmetic and spelling. When, however, "much time is spent . . . in drilling on similar material," the spring status in arithmetic was reached by the end of the second week.

But perhaps the best way to retain and to improve earlier-learned skills is to provide for continuing need and use for them. Davis and Rood [14] demonstrated the validity of this hypothesis by testing every four to seven months during the seventh and eighth grades for retention of computation and problem-solving skills learned in the elementary grades. In the intervals between the tests, continued instruction in arithmetic required the use of previously learned concepts and skills. During the first semester of the seventh grade, there were reviews of the four fundamental processes as applied to integers, decimals, and fractions. In the eighth grade, percentage was reviewed and applied to interest, insurance, and other problems. Throughout the two years, pupils also reviewed by taking periodic short tests from their text on addition, subtraction, multiplication, and division. In this succession of tests, each child was motivated to try to better his previous record. The results on five retention tests given at intervals of from four to seven months over the two-year period are graphed in Figure 11–13. These data appear to justify Davis and Rood's conclusion that "continued study in a field of subject matter will cause learning to be retained to the extent that it draws upon important facts and principles and presents new topics and problems in an orderly arrangement with reference to recurring concepts."

5. *Review Testing and Retention.* Besides showing the effectiveness in sustaining retention of providing for continuous use of earlier-learned concepts, Davis and Rood's data also yield evidence on the specific value of testing [14]. Of problems performed correctly on the first test but, because of forgetting, incorrectly on the second test, there was considerable recovery on

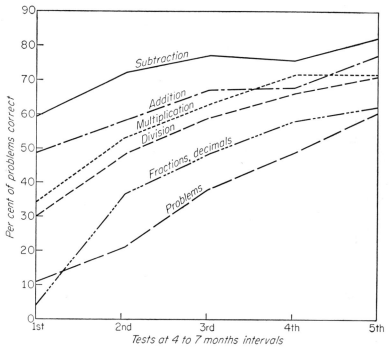

FIG. 11–13. Retention and improvement of concepts and skills occur when review, need, and use of them are provided. (*Adapted from Davis, R. A., and E. J. Rood: J. Educ. Psychol., 38: 216–222, 1947.*)

subsequent tests—especially on the very next test. For example, of the addition problems missed on the second test after being solved on the first test, 82.5 per cent were corrected on the third test, 8.8 per cent more were corrected on the fourth test, and an additional 2.9 per cent were finally corrected on the fifth test. The successive testing resulted in an eventual total recovery of 94.2 per cent of concepts initially forgotten. Repeated testing, with intervening opportunities for self-corrections, is apparently a good device both for remedial teaching and for sustaining retention.

Periodic review tests, with opportunities for children to confirm or to revise concepts on the basis of studying their corrected test papers, not only sustain retention but also produce the improvements noted in Figures 11–10 and 11–13. To test children and not take advantage of the learning opportunities in their perceiving the effects of their provisional trials limits unnecessarily the effectiveness of testing; nevertheless, some studies [6, 16, 39, 43] show that merely taking review tests without checking the corrected papers apparently aids somewhat in retention.

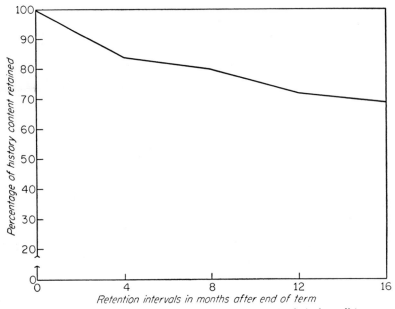

FIG. 11–14. Retention of facts in American history is sustained relatively well by repeated testing. (*From Brooks, F. D., and S. J. Bassett: J. Educ. Res, 18: 201, 1928.*)

De Weerdt [16], by a series of 11 consecutive daily tests, motivated 49 fifth grade pupils to make considerable improvement in adding, multiplying, and speed of reading. After four months, two review tests restored multiplication ability to end-of-training status, approximated this status for adding ability, and restored reading speed to 67 per cent of the end-of-training speed.

Brooks and Bassett [6] repeated at four-month intervals for 64 seventh grade pupils a factual objective test in American history, which resulted in the moderately declining retention curve shown in Figure 11–14. After 16 months, the mean retention score is still 69 per cent of the average close-of-term score.

Studies by Tiedeman [43] with fifth grade and by Spitzer [39] with sixth grade pupils are similar in content, design, and results. In both experiments,

the pupils read articles on geography content and were tested both for immediate recall and for deferred retention (up to 63 days for some groups) by
multiple-choice items such as: "To which family of plants do bamboos belong?
( ) trees, ( ) ferns, ( ) grasses, ( ) mosses, ( ) fungi." The article
included the sentence: "These plants are members of the grass family" [39].
Deferred recalls, from 7 to 63 days after reading the articles and without intervening tests, were compared with deferred recalls on the same days for groups

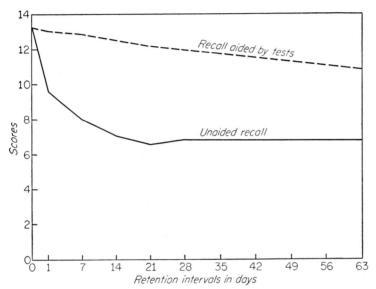

Fig. 11–15. Retention curves on geography facts for subjects aided by prior recall tests and
for subjects unaided by recall. (*From Spitzer, H. F.: J. Educ. Psychol., 30: 647, 1939.*)

who had been given the same test twice before, at different times for different groups, during the intervening interval. Spitzer's results, which are typical
of both studies, are graphed in Figure 11–15.

Both Tiedeman and Spitzer conclude that review tests given immediately
after learning and spaced appropriately over the retention interval aid in sustaining retention. It has already been noted that effectiveness in promoting
both learning and retention could be increased, of course, if each review test
were followed by study of the corrected test.

Summary

Learning results from reacting purposefully to environmental situations and
produces a change in the individual's cognitive structure which serves as a

guide to more effective behavior in the future. Each learning experience leaves a residual "trace" in the nervous system, which interacts with the organization of trace systems previously established from one's entire background of prior experiences; thus new experiences are constantly changing the organization of trace systems. It is more correct, therefore, to think of learning as a *reorganization* of the individual's cognitive structure. The accumulated learnings characteristic of children's progress through school are the products of the interrelated processes of learning, remembering, and forgetting. When a learned behavior pattern is recalled, the reproduction is affected by the residual trace from the original learning experience. But it is also affected by the individual's total organization of trace systems, with which the original trace and the traces from all intervening experiences have interacted. Recall is, therefore, both a reproduction and a reconstruction. The specific trace produced by the behavior pattern to be recalled probably determines its general form and some distinctive details. But the general system of traces developed up to the moment of recall results in condensations, elaborations, substitutions, and inventions to suit the individual's *present* attitudes, interests, and logic. This theory of remembering is in harmony with the varied experimental data from deferred retention tests, which sometimes show rapid and extensive forgetting, in other instances reveal long-sustained retention, and in still other situations, because of the operation of transfer principles, demonstrate better performance in the deferred retention tests than immediately after learning.

According to this theory, forgetting is conceived as mainly an active process in which intervening learnings intrude to interfere with accurate recall of earlier-learned specific behavior patterns. Specifically, forgetting is caused by interactive inhibitions; by more recently acquired attitudes, concepts, and beliefs; by differences between the learning and recall situations; perhaps by repression in some cases; and probably, to a limited extent, by intervening metabolic changes in the nervous system. But some of the processes of forgetting can be counteracted. And by the arrangement of learning experiences and the application of transfer principles, through which the components of original learning may take on an expanded meaning, retention performance may even be made to exceed performance at immediate recall.

Sustained retention of worthwhile understandings, skills, and attitudes can be achieved by making the child's curriculum meaningful; by teaching him organizing principles and establishing functional classifications of his knowledge; by teaching him how to learn efficiently (that is, by effective methods); by leading him to thorough mastery of useful concepts and skills; by reviewing (which can be accomplished best by arranging a continuous, developmental sequence of opportunities for applying his accumulating concepts and skills in unified curriculum projects); by relating the curriculum to his interests, so that he takes some initiative in using and in extending his knowledge; and by developing mental sets appropriate to generalizing, to applying principles wherever possible, and to becoming resourceful in using understandings and skills in an increasing variety of problem-solving situations.

Review and Applications

1. Test a child's recall of an earlier-learned poem, piece of music, or set of social studies facts. Try to explain your results.

2. Explain under what conditions retention tests of children's learning may reveal (a) rapid forgetting, (b) no appreciable loss, and (c) better recall later than immediately after learning.

3. Explain how remembering is a process of reproduction and reconstruction, in which both past experiences and present hypotheses, assumptions, interests, and attitudes determine what is remembered.

4. Cite examples to show that remembering is an active and complex process affected by (a) interfering learnings, (b) changes in cognitive structure and attitudes, (c) mental set, (d) changes in the recall situation, (e) repression, and (f) metabolic changes in the nervous system.

5. Cite examples demonstrating effective retention from (a) a meaningful approach to learning, (b) functionally organizing concepts, (c) efficient methods of learning, (d) thorough mastery, (e) reviewing, (f) following interests, and (g) developing a set to apply learned concepts and skills at every opportunity.

References

1. Allport, G. W.: "Change and decay in visual memory image," *Brit. J. Psychol.*, 21: 133–148, 1930.

2. Ashbaugh, E. J.: "Variability of children in spelling," *Sch. Soc.*, 9: 93–98, 1919.

3. Ballard, P. B.: "Obliviscence and reminiscence," *Brit. J. Psychol. Monogr. Suppl.*, 1–4(2), 1911.

4. Bartlett, F. C.: *Remembering*, Cambridge, New York, 1932.

5. Beales, Beulah P.: "Trends in handwriting," *Balt. Bull. Educ.*, 20: 29–32, 1944.

6. Brooks, F. D., and S. J. Bassett: "The retention of American history in the junior high school," *J. Educ. Res.*, 18: 195–202, 1928.

7. Brueckner, L. J.: "Certain arithmetic abilities of second grade pupils," *Elem. Sch. J.*, 27: 433–444, 1927.

8. ———, and H. W. Distad: "The effect of summer vacation on the reading ability of first-grade children," *Elem. Sch. J.*, 24: 698–707, 1924.

9. Bruene, E.: "Effect of summer vacation on the achievement of pupils in the fourth, fifth, and sixth grades," *J. Educ. Res.*, 18: 309–314, 1928.

10. Carmichael, L., H. P. Hogan, and A. A. Walter: "An experimental study of the effect of language on visually perceived form," *J. Exp. Psychol.*, 15: 73–86, 1932.

11. Carter, L. F., and K. Schooler: "Value, need, and other factors in perception," *Psychol. Rev.*, 56: 200–207, 1949.

12. Davis, R. A.: *Psychology of Learning*, McGraw-Hill, New York, 1935.

13. ———, and C. C. Moore: "Methods of measuring retention," *J. Gen. Psychol.*, 12: 144–155, 1935.

14. ———, and E. J. Rood: "Remembering and forgetting arithmetic abilities," *J. Educ. Psychol.*, 38: 216–222, 1947.

15. Deese, J.: *The Psychology of Learning*, McGraw-Hill, New York, 1952.

16. De Weerdt, E. H.: "The permanence of improvement of fifth grade school children in certain mental functions," *J. Educ. Res.*, 16: 127–131, 1927.

17. Elder, H. E.: "The effect of summer vacation on silent reading ability in the intermediate grades," *Elem. Sch. J.*, 27: 541–546, 1927.

18. Frutchey, F. P.: "Retention in high school chemistry," *J. High. Educ.*, 8: 217–218, 1937.

19. Gates, A. I.: *Manual of Directions for Gates Reading Survey Test: For Grade 3 (Second Half) to Grade 10*, Teachers College, Columbia University, Bureau of Publications, New York, 1942.

20. Gilliland, A. R.: "The rate of forgetting," *J. Educ. Psychol.*, 39: 19–26, 1948.

21. Grossnickle, F. E.: "Transfer of knowledge of multiplication facts to their use in long division," *J. Educ. Res.*, 29: 677–685, 1936.

22. Hall, J. F.: "Retroactive inhibition of meaningful material," *J. Educ. Psychol.*, 46: 47–52, 1955.

23. Hovland, C. I.: "Human learning and retention," in S. S. Stevens (ed.): *Handbook of Experimental Psychology*, Wiley, New York, 1951.

24. Jenkins, J. G., and K. M. Dallenbach: "Obliviscence during sleep and waking," *Amer. J. Psychol.*, 35: 605–612, 1924.

25. Jones, H. E.: "The retention of conditioned emotional reactions in infancy," *J. Genet. Psychol.*, 37: 485–498, 1930.

26. Keys, N., and J. V. Lawson: "Summer vs winter gains in school achievement," *Sch. Soc.* 46: 541–544, 1937.

27. Kirby, T. J.: *Practice in the Case of School Children*, Contributions to Education, no. 58, Teachers College, Columbia University, Bureau of Publications, 1913.

28. Kolberg, O. W.: "A study of summer-time forgetting," *Elem. Sch. J.*, 35: 281–287, 1934. Reprinted by permission of the University of Chicago Press.

29. Kramer, Grace A.: "Do children forget during vacation?" *Balt. Bull. Educ.*, 56–60, 1927.

30. Krueger, W. C. F.: "Further studies in overlearning," *J. Exp. Psychol.*, 13: 152–163, 1930.

31. Levine, J. M., and G. Murphy: "The learning and forgetting of controversial material," *J. Abnorm. Soc. Psychol.*, 38: 507–517, 1943.

32. Morgan, L. D.: "How effective is specific training in preventing loss due to summer vacation?" *J. Educ. Psychol.*, 20: 466–471, 1929.

33. Nelson, M. J.: "How much time is required in the fall for pupils in the elementary school to reach again the spring level of achievement?" *J. Educ. Res.*, 18: 305–308, 1928.

34. Northway, M. L.: "The influence of age and social groups on children's remembering," *Brit. J. Psychol.*, 27: 11–29, 1936.

35. Patterson, M. V. W.: "The effect of summer vacation on children's mental ability and on their retention of arithmetic and reading," *Education*, 46: 222–228, 1925–1926.

36. Postman, L.: "Learned principles of organization in memory," *Psychol. Monogr.*, 68(3): 1–24, 1954.

37. Pressey, S. L., and F. P. Robinson: *Psychology and the New Education*, Harper, New York, 1944.

38. Schrepel, Marie, and H. R. Laslett: "On the loss of knowledge by junior high school pupils over the summer vacation," *J. Educ. Psychol.*, 27: 299–303, 1936.

39. Spitzer, H. F.: "Studies in retention," *J. Educ. Psychol.*, 30: 641–656, 1939.

40. Steele, D. C.: "Teaching and testing the understanding of common fractions," *Univ. Pitts. Bull.* 37(3): 317–328, 1941.

41. Stroud, J. B.: "Experiments on learning in school situations," *Psychol. Bull.*, 37: 777–807, 1940.

42. ———, and Ethel Johnson: "The temporal position of review," *J. Educ. Res.*, 35: 618–622, 1941–1942.

43. Tiedeman, H. R.: "A study of retention of classroom learning," *J. Educ. Res.*, 41: 516–531, 1947–1948.

44. Tiernan, J. J.: "The principle of closure in terms of recall and recognition," *Amer. J. Psychol.*, 51: 97–108, 1938.

45. Tyler, R. W.: "Permanence of learning," *J. High. Educ.*, 4: 203–204, 1933.

46. Williams, R. D., and G. W. Knox: "A survey of dynamic principles governing memory," *J. Gen. Psychol.*, 30: 167–179, 1944.

47. Woodworth, R. S., and H. Schlossberg: *Experimental Psychology*, Holt, New York, 1954.

48. Word, A. H., and R. A. Davis: "Acquisition and retention of factual information in seventh-grade general science, during a semester of eighteen weeks," *J. Educ. Psychol.*, 30: 116–125, 1939.

Chapter 12

Appraising
Individual Differences
in Abilities

O NE OF the most firmly established facts in scientific
education is that individuals differ. No two chil-
dren are exactly alike. Because of the wide extent of individual differences
among children in intelligence and in every other important dimension of personality, every phase of their teaching and guidance requires recognition and
appraisal of individual differences. A striking illustration of the extent of
differences in capacity for school achievement is the fact that some nine-year-
old children (with IQs of 140 or higher), who would normally be completing
the third grade of school, could already have succeeded in mastering the elementary school curriculum at the sixth grade level if they were given the
opportunity to do so [23]. And, at the other end of the distribution continuum
of intelligence, other nine-year-old children (with IQs as low as 70) would
only by then have reached sufficient mental maturity for expectation of success with first grade level reading and other such verbal-abstract activities
[39].

Complicating further the problem of individual differences, it must be
recognized that children cannot be classified satisfactorily according to a single
dimension of ability. Besides abstract-verbal intelligence, a child's mental
abilities include such traits as number facility, word fluency, memory, perceptual speed, inductive and deductive abstract reasoning, visualizing of space
abilities, and other primary mental abilities [52, 55]. For any given child,

these different mental abilities are typically unevenly developed [53]. To appraise them requires a profile of scores rather than a single score. So, besides a wide range of interindividual differences, teachers need to consider also the pattern of each child's intraindividual differences.

Moreover, in addition to both interindividual and intraindividual differences in abilities, children also differ in interests, personality traits, prior learning experiences, and home environmental experiences, which affect their behavior and development. At every level of abilities, some children will have particular interests in art, music, science, social studies, or arithmetic. And for some children it will require special alertness to discover or to develop *any* interests related to school activities. At each level of ability, some children will be confident, socially secure, and competent in using their abilities. Others will be anxious, shy, or rebellious and will be unable to use their abilities efficiently. With respect to parent-child relationships, some children will feel accepted, secure, loved, and esteemed, and because of these satisfactions will be able to use their abilities freely in constructive and creative efforts. Other children will lack adequate satisfaction of these needs, and some will feel outright parental rejection. There will be a wide range among their homes of economic, social, and educational determinants related to child development and school progress. All these factors affect significantly children's school progress and patterns of achievement. In this chapter, however, we shall be concerned only with the nature and appraisal of children's mental abilities.

General Intelligence

One important personality trait significantly affecting a child's academic progress, and many of his out-of-school adjustments as well, is his general mental ability. The significance of this trait is implied in a broad and practical definition of intelligence as "the general *capacity* to learn and to solve problems."

Children demonstrate a wide range of differences in general learning and problem-solving capacities by variations in their performance on intelligence tests, in school activities, in self-initiated creative projects, and in many other personal and social activities. The more intelligent child solves intellectual problems more accurately and rapidly. He understands more quickly and grasps more complex concepts. He perceives finer differentiations in situations and concepts. He poses problems and asks questions more readily and answers them more effectively. Both his school and his other activities are characterized by independence, originality, and inventiveness. He uses language and other symbols more appropriately, precisely, and effectively. Since he learns more rapidly and can apprehend more complex concepts, he knows more. Moreover, his knowledge is functionally organized for more effective application and approaches to new problems. And his problem-solving approach is more integrated, unified, flexible, adaptive, and efficient. Stoddard, in summarizing the ways in which intelligence is manifest, has written that "intelligence is the ability to undertake activities that are characterized by (1) difficulty, (2) complexity, (3) abstractness, (4) economy, (5) adaptiveness to a goal, (6) social value, and (7) the emergence of originals" [48, p. 255].

In analyzing through intelligence-test performance and other intellectual activities the central abilities underlying an individual's capacity to learn and to solve problems, Garrett has arrived at a more restricted and precise definition of intelligence. He writes that "intelligence includes abilities demanded in solution of problems which require comprehension and use of symbols," especially words, numbers, diagrams, equations, and formulas which represent ideas and relationships [15, p. 372]. Applying Garrett's concept, teachers will recognize that abilities to comprehend and to use such symbols effectively in reading, language, science, social studies, arithmetic, and other abstract school activities are necessary for progress in them. Therefore, since intelligence tests sample these same abstract abilities for dealing effectively with symbols, it is not surprising to find that variations in the intelligence-test scores of children are significantly related to variations in their school achievements, and especially to achievement in abstract, or academic, subjects. Intellectual efficiency, however, as revealed both in school achievement and in intelligence-test performance, needs to be differentiated from basic capacity for dealing with abstract symbols.

As has already been indicated in several preceding chapters, a child's intellectual efficiency, besides being dependent upon his *capacity* for using symbols in learning and problem solving, is also affected by other conditions. A child's intellectual efficiency depends upon his basic capacities, prior opportunities for learning, the quality of his work methods or how effectively he has learned how to learn and to solve problems, his degree of motivation and concentration, and his degree of freedom from anxiety and other emotional disturbances. The intelligence test is an attempt to measure potential capacity while differences due to these other factors affecting intellectual efficiency are at least partially controlled. Psychologists attempt to control variations in prior learning opportunities by using as intelligence-test items either novel problems unrelated to prior experience (especially to school content) or measures of knowledge for which opportunities for acquisition have been ample, unrestricted as to level capable of being reached (except by capacity), and approximately equal.[1]

On the basis of the relative amount of a child's accumulated knowledge meeting these criteria, an inference is made about his capacity for learning. A bright child's range of information and understanding of test concepts is greater than the average child's not because he has had better opportunities for learning such items but because, it is assumed, he has more capacity for learning. Variations in work methods are partially controlled by the directions for the test, to which the trained examiner adheres very carefully. Motivation is controlled by keeping it high, both by the intrinsic challenge and interest appeal of the test items and by the rewarding approval of the examiner. Emotional disturbances are reduced to a minimum by building confidence in the child by giving him items at the beginning of the test on which he can surely succeed and by warm, friendly approval of his efforts throughout the examination. And for emotionally maladjusted children whose intellectual efficiency is sometimes impaired by uncontrollable emotional disturbances, the skilled examiner can make allowances for this factor in estimating basic capacity. Most of these factors affecting a child's demonstration of his capacity are controlled more effectively in tests given individually than in group tests administered to many children at one time.

These general concepts of intelligence testing, as well as some additional concepts to be developed, are illustrated here more specifically by reference to typical individual and group intelligence tests.

Stanford-Binet Intelligence Scale

A pioneer, and still the test most generally used [32] with children, is the individual Stanford-Binet intelligence scale, abbreviated "S-B." Defining intelligence as "the general ability to do abstract or conceptual thinking," Terman, basing his work on Binet's pioneer efforts, has constructed a developmental mental age scale. The 1937 revision of this scale by Terman and Merrill [50] includes 129 items of great variety in each of two equivalent forms ("L" and "M"). All these items were selected according to four criteria. They sample conceptual thinking. Between each successive age level, from 2 years to mental maturity (which is at 16 years for this test), there are significant increments in the percentages of children passing the items. In order

---

[1] In present tests these goals are only partially achieved. Probably few, if any, tests are entirely free of socioeconomic or geographic biases.

to measure *general* intelligence, only items which showed a significant correlation with the scale as a whole are included. And finally, the items are meant to be equally fair to all the native white population of the United States, for whom the test is intended.

These 129 items in each scale are organized on the basis of standardization data on about 3,000 representative individuals from 2 to 18 years of age into a hierarchy of 20 mental age levels, with six items at each level, from a 2-year level to superior-adult levels, I, II, and III. At each level, the percentages of individuals passing the six items are only approximately equal, varying from about 40 per cent to over 70 per cent for most of the items in the middle range of the scale. At the lower levels, the percentages passing items are relatively higher; and as maturity is approached, the percentages passing items is relatively lower. After age 16, where average percentage increments passing items cease on this scale, items passed by fewer than 50 per cent were selected for the above-average-adult levels. At superior-adult level III, the percentages passing the six items range from only 8 per cent to 30 per cent, in Form L. Thus, a mental developmental scale was created, ranging in level from age 2 to superior-adult ability, against which any individual tested can be matched or placed.

The technique of testing, which requires considerable psychological training, involves first some exploratory testing at levels below that at which an individual might be expected to succeed, to find the level at which all six tests can be passed. From here the examiner proceeds up the scale to the level at which all six tests are failed. By adding to the basal age, at which all tests are passed, the appropriate months of mental age for the tests passed beyond this level, the child's placement on the scale, or his mental age, is determined. And by dividing the child's obtained mental age (MA) by his chronological age (CA), his intelligence quotient (IQ) is computed.

How the S-B samples a child's abilities for learning and problem solving and how from his test performance inferences are made about his general capacity for accomplishment in school and in some other activities can be suggested concretely by examining some of the test items. A 45-word vocabulary test illustrates how mental capacity is inferred from measuring previously acquired knowledge. In the standardization of this S-B subtest, it was found that at each succeeding age, the average number of words defined correctly increases. Average six-year-old children know six of these words; seven-year-olds know seven; eight-year-olds know eight; nine-year-olds know nine; ten-year-olds know eleven; eleven-year-olds know thirteen; and twelve-year-olds know fifteen words [9]. Since it is assumed that the opportunities for learning these words have been ample, unrestricted, and approximately equal for the children for whom the scale is suitable, from the number of these words which a given child defines, his capacity for such learning is inferred. If a ten-year-old child should define 15 of the words, it would be assumed that he has superior capacity for such learning, since this is the average score found in the norm group for representative twelve-year-olds. Here are some examples of the more novel problem-solving items in the S-B: at year 6, reproducing from memory a bead chain demonstrated by the examiner; at year 7, generalizing the similarity between two things like "iron" and "silver"; at year 8, being able to recall several events from a story just read by the examiner; at year 9, determining how much change one should get back if he were to purchase 4 cents' worth of candy and should give the storekeeper 25 cents; at year 10, detecting the absurdity in a picture; at year 11, repeating after one auditory presentation a 15-word sentence; and at year 12, analyzing and reporting completely three significant events to be observed in a single action picture.

Despite the great variety of items in the S-B scale—including manipulating objects, copying patterns from memory, observing and identifying objects, perceiving similarities and differences, making practical judgments, interpreting situations, memorizing, and reasoning, and using in all of these processes verbal, numerical, and pictorial and spatial symbols—the scale as a whole is mainly a measure of verbal learning and reasoning. This is indicated especially by the fact that the correlations between the vocabulary subtest and the scale as a whole are so high (correlation coefficients being .71, .83, and .86 for ages 8, 11, and 14, respectively) [2, p. 186].

The standardization population of approximately 3,000 American-born whites living in 17 different communities from 11 geographically representative states included 200 children at each age from 6 to 14 and 100 at each age below and above this range from 2 to 18. Since from these standardization data the tests were scaled into a hierarchy of age levels, the average level attained by each age group is interpreted as an equivalent mental age. Thus, according to this scale, if a ten-year-old, mentally maturing rapidly, attains the level on the scale of representative twelve-year-old children, he is assigned a mental age of 12. Another child of 10 who reaches only the level attained on the scale by the representative eight-year-olds would be assigned a mental age of 8. By converting scores to mental ages, children's intelligence-test scores are thereby interpreted against a scale of mental maturation age levels. According to this scale, the ten-year-old who earns a mental age of 12 is accelerated two years in mental growth, and the ten-year-old whose mental age is only 8 is retarded two years in mental growth.

Another way of expressing a child's rate of mental growth or his relative brightness is to divide his mental age on a test by his chronological age, thus determining his intelligence quotient, or IQ. In the hypothetical examples just cited, the bright child has an IQ of 1.20 (IQ = MA/CA = $12\!/\!10$), and the dull child has an IQ of .80 (IQ = MA/CA = $8\!/\!10$). It is conventional, however, to eliminate the decimal points in IQs by multiplying them by 100; so these IQs would be written as 120 and 80, respectively. It should be observed that as indices of intelligence, mental age indicates a child's *level* of mental

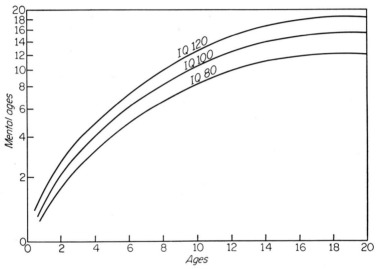

Fig. 12–1. Theoretical mental growth curves, illustrating differential rates of growth for children with IQs of 80, 100, and 120.

maturity and IQ his *rate* of mental growth and relative brightness. The IQ, as will be demonstrated later, remains relatively constant as a child matures, while the mental age increases continuously from birth to mental maturity— for each child at a rate determined by his IQ.

These concepts are represented graphically in Figure 12–1. On the assumption that a given child's rate of mental growth remains relatively constant, this figure portrays theoretical patterns of mental development for three children whose rates of growth are different—one slow, one average, and one fast. For the average child, each year of chronological age from birth up to maturity is paralleled by an increment of one year of mental age; and the IQ, as an index of this average growth rate, remains constantly at 100. For the child whose IQ is only 80, at each age his mental age is only 80 per cent of his chronological age. Since he develops constantly at a slower rate, his mental age retardation gradually becomes greater. At 6 years, he is mentally retarded about one year; at 10 years, his mental age is only 8; and at maturity (which is 16 years on the S-B scale), his mental age is only 12, which is three years below the average "adult" mental age of 15[1] on this scale. For the superior child whose IQ is 120, the advantage of his faster rate of mental growth produces a deviation from the average mental age which gradually becomes greater. At 5 years, this child has a mental age of 6 (6 = 1.2 × 5). At 10 years, his mental age is 12. And at maturity, he has gained a mental age advantage of three years, having an S-B mental age of 18, as compared to 15 for the average sixteen-year-old.

Besides the concepts of mental age and IQ, two other ideas are implicit in this figure. At maturity, which is 16 years for the S-B, mental age levels off and ceases to increase with chronological age. Among the representative standardization subjects, the seventeen- and eighteen-year-olds did not exceed the average score of the sixteen-year-olds. By portraying mental age increments with wide spaces for young ages and by gradually making them narrower (logarithmically) for older ages, an observed fact about mental growth is made apparent. Differences in levels of mental development characteristic of different age levels are much more marked at younger than at older ages. Differences in mental ability between typical two- and four-year-old children are readily apparent; between ages 10 and 12, differences are much less easily discerned.

Two other commonly used indexes of intelligence which are applicable to the S-B should be mentioned here, although they will be illustrated in greater detail later. These are standard-deviation scores and percentiles. The "standard deviation" is a measure of variability or divergence from the mean of a distribution of test scores. The distance along the base line of a distribution of scores covered by the 34 per cent of individuals falling just above or below the mean is 1 standard deviation. On the S-B scale, this distance of 1 standard deviation is approximately 16 IQ points at most ages. At ages at which the standard deviation is appreciably greater or smaller than 16, IQs can be corrected to make them comparable for an assumed standard deviation of 16 at each level [36]. Thus a S-B IQ of 116 is 1 standard deviation above the mean IQ of 100. An IQ of 132 is, of course, 2 standard deviations above the mean.

"Percentiles" are scores converted to ranks of from 0 to 100, the highest rank being 100, the median rank 50, and the lowest rank 0. Any percentile score indicates the percentage of scores below it in a distribution. A percentile score of 84, for example, means that such a score exceeds 84 per cent of the

[1] A technicality in the construction of the scale requires the assignment of 15 rather than 16 as the average mental age of "adults" at age 16.

ranked scores in the distribution. Since 84 per cent of a distribution of scores, counted from the lower end, includes the 50 per cent below the mean and 34 per cent immediately above the mean, the 84th percentile corresponds to a standard deviation of 1. Throughout their ranges, IQs, standard-deviation scores, and percentiles can be made equivalent. Thus an IQ of 116 is equivalent to 1 standard deviation above the mean and to the 84th percentile. Each of these indexes for interpreting test scores has certain merits, as will be perceived as the discussion proceeds.

Wechsler Intelligence Scale for Children

The Weshcler Intelligence Scale for Children [56], abbreviated "WISC," is an individual, diagnostic intelligence scale for children ranging in age from 5 to 15. The test is subdivided into verbal and performance scales, so that it yields comparable verbal-scale, performance-scale, and full-scale IQs. These are deviation IQs, indicating for every four-month interval from ages 5 to 15 a child's degree and direction of deviation from his own age group. The scores of the norm group, including 100 representative boys and 100 representative girls at each age level, were statistically treated to produce at each age a distribution of IQs having a mean of 100 and a standard deviation of 15. Provided that the standardization groups are equal in ability, this should make WISC IQs roughly comparable to S-B IQs, for which the means and standard deviations at each age are approximately 100 and 16, respectively. Several investigations, however, show that S-B IQs tend to be slightly higher than WISC IQs. One fourth grade group of children of about average ability earned a mean IQ on the S-B 3.5 points higher than on the WISC [13].

The verbal and performance scales of the WISC are each comprised of five (plus an alternate) subtests. The verbal subtests measure range of information (example: "Who discovered America?"); verbal comprehension (example: "Why are criminals locked up?"); arithmetic problem solving (example: "If 3 pencils cost 5¢, what will be the cost of 24 pencils?"); ability to generalize verbal similarities (example: "In what way are a piano and a violin alike?"); and vocabulary—plus an alternate test requiring both forward and backward recall of digits. The performance subtests measure ability to detect missing parts in pictures (such as the missing shaft in a pair of scissors); to arrange series of pictures so as to tell sensible stories (such as rearranging into a sensible sequence separate pictures of shucking corn, hauling corn, growing corn, and planting corn); to analyze designs and to reproduce the patterns with identical blocks colored differently on their six faces; to assemble jigsaw-like picture puzzles; and to learn and to code a series of number symbols (such as "÷" stands for 1, ")" for 2, etc.).

Like the S-B, this test includes both prior-learning items (such as range of information and vocabulary), from which capacity for learning is inferred, and novel problem-solving items. Because the subtests are diverse and yet interrelated, it would seem that they may be assumed to measure both *general* capacity for learning and reasoning with verbal, numerical, and spatial symbols and some *specific* abilities tapped by each subtest. At the 10-year level, for example, the median intercorrelation among the verbal subtests is .61. Among the performance subtests the interorganization is less close, the median r (correlation coefficient) being .37. Between pairs of verbal and performance subtests the median r is .38 [56]. Some independence between the traits measured by verbal-scale and those measured by the performance-scale tests is indicated by the moderate correlation of .52 found between them for 54 fourth grade children [13]. That the scale as a whole measures much the same kind of intelligence as is measured by the S-B is indicated by a correlation of .80 found between them at the fourth grade level [13]. The verbal scale, however, is more closely related to the S-B ($r = .71$) than is the performance scale ($r = .63$). Since the 11 subtests are only moderately intercorrelated and since they are standardized to yield comparable scores (means of 10 and standard deviations of 3 at each age), they permit some extra diagnostic possibilities just as the verbal-versus-performance-scale comparisons do.

Group Tests of Intelligence

As one helpful guide to teachers in adjusting each child's curriculum to his level of maturity, a group intelligence test is both economical and, for most children, valid. A group intelligence test can usually be administered to an entire class within an hour, and in another three or four hours all the tests can be scored. There are several such tests available at the elementary school level. Citing here examples of five of them will illustrate their general nature, their uses in sampling pupil learning and problem-solving abilities, and some of their specific and unique characteristics.

1. The Davis-Eells Test. This test [10], items from which are illustrated in Figures 12–2 to 12–5, was designed specifically to yield an index of problem-solving ability, which, when desirable, may be considered as an IQ. The test, prepared for three levels (grade 1, 30 items; grade 2, 47 items; and grades 3 to 6, 62 items) is "composed of mental problems of a kind found in most of the basic areas of children's lives: school, home, play, stories, work." It is a *problem-solving* test in which interference from variations in children's prior-learning experiences is reduced to a minimum. Since all the items are pictorially represented, no reading is required. Special care was taken to exclude problems for which specific training at home, at school, or in play relationships would be likely to contribute solutions. Moreover, the situations and pictures "are about equally familiar to all American urban cultural groups."

Fɪɢ. 12–2. Demonstration item from Davis-Eells Test of General Intelligence; a "probability" item ("What happened?"). (*World, Yonkers, N.Y., 1953.*)

For solving the problems of this test, the authors of it say that such mental processes as making associations, logical classifications, discriminations, seeing analogies, drawing conclusions, organizing elements into meaningful patterns, and gaining insight and foresight are required. Despite the use of pictorial content, however, because of the verbal directions and the verbal symbols probably used in reasoning through the problems, "the test is highly verbal."

To illustrate more specifically how this test measures problem-solving abilities, demonstration items from the four kinds of problems found in the

Elementary Form for grades 3 to 6 are presented. For 20 items like Figure 12–2, the child marks the correct one among three statements such as:

1. The man fell down and hit his head.
2. A ball came through the window and hit his head.
3. The picture does not show how the man got the bump on his head.

The next eight items in this form of the test are "money" items, for which a demonstration item is shown in Figure 12–3. The child is told that on each

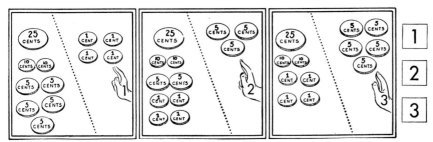

FIG. 12–3. "Money-problems" item for Davis-Eells Test of General Intelligence ("Which is the best way to put down on the right side of the diagonal line 40 cents?"). (*World, Yonkers, N.Y., 1953.*)

FIG. 12–4. "Best-ways-problems" demonstration item from Davis-Eells Test of General Intelligence ("Which boy is starting the best way to get over the gate?"). (*World, Yonkers, N.Y., 1953.*)

table pictured, "the hand has to use all the money that is on its side of the table [right of the dotted oblique line], and that every hand can use all the money it needs from the other side of its table. Which hand is starting the best way to put down 40 cents on its side of the table?

Items (29) through (46) are illustrated by Figure 12–4, in which the problem is: "Which boy is starting the best way to get over the gate?"

The test is concluded with 15 analogy problems, illustrated by the demonstration item in Figure 12–5, for which the direction is: "The foot helps the boy walk. This animal foot does the same thing for what?"

To develop norms for this test, it was given to 19,000 pupils in grades 1 to 6 in 16 cities and two counties in 15 states of the East, Middle West, and South of the United States. For the Elementary Form, median scores at each three-month age level were computed. For example, the "adjusted" median at

FIG. 12–5. "Analogies-problems" item from Davis-Eells Test of General Intelligence ("The foot helps the boy walk. The animal's foot does the same for what?"). (*World, Yonkers, N.Y., 1953*).

age 8-0 to 8-2 is 32.4; at 9-0 to 9-2, 37.8; at 10-0 to 10-2, 41.2; at 11-0 to 11-2, 46.1; and at 12-0 to 12-2, 49.2 [10, p. 63]. Using the mean scores and the standard deviations of the distributions at each six-month age level, scores are converted into either IQs or equivalent IPSAs ("indexes of problem-solving ability"), for which the mean is 100 and the standard deviation 16. For example, if a child at age 10-2 earned a score of 41, his IQ or IPSA would be approximately 100. If his score were 1 standard deviation above the mean of his age group, his IQ or IPSA would be 116.

Data on the reliability and validity of this test will be presented when these factors are considered for all the intelligence tests to be discussed here. One critical comment is pertinent, however, at this point. Generally intelligence tests for children are considered to be indexes of mental development or maturation. As such, they should discriminate significantly between successive age levels. In this test, however, the median scores for ages 8 to 12 (above) show very small increments of gain from year to year. This characteristic may limit the validity of the test in predicting school progress and achievement. To determine the significance of this principle as a factor affecting the validity of intelligence tests in predicting elementary school achievement, Grimes [17] compared the Davis-Eells test, which doesn't discriminate well between age levels, and the Kuhlmann-Finch tests, which emphasize age-level discrimination, in predicting achievement at the fifth grade level as measured by the Iowa Every-pupil Achievement Tests. The validity coefficients are .61 for the test with good discrimination between age levels and only .44 for the test which does not effectively apply this principle.

2. The Kuhlmann-Finch Tests. The Kuhlmann-Finch tests [28] include five kinds of item which appear to require reasoning and mental manipulations of verbal, pictorial-diagrammatic, and numerical symbols. Separate test booklets for each grade from 1 through 6 and for junior and senior high school levels provide a maximum number of items of appropriate difficulty at each level. An example of each type of item at the grade 4 level will illustrate the kinds of mental processes tested.

There are 24 verbal analogies, such as: "Eye is to see as ear is to (1) sound, (2) hear, (3) noise, (4) music, (5) head."

A second type, including 20 items, requires children to analyze a figure and to match it with one among four other, similar figures from which it must be discriminated. For example: "Find the picture with arms held like the beginning picture."

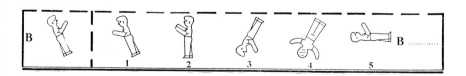

The third type, including 20 items, requires a generalization and an application to numerical symbols of the rule derived. For example: "Find out how the first five numbers go together, and then tell what number comes next: 88664 ____ (a) 5, (b) 6, (c) 16, (d) 8, (e) 4."

Another 20 items require a similar generalization and application of a derived rule to spatial symbols. For example: "See how the first three pictures go together with one other picture, and then find the missing picture."

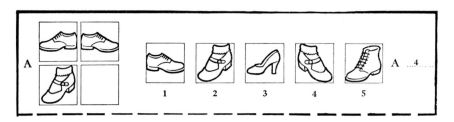

And a final set of 24 items, again using verbal symbols, also require a generalization and a discriminating application of it. For example: Which one of these five words "does not belong with the other four: (1) spoon, (2) cup, (3) door, (4) fork, (5) dish?"

Kuhlmann and Finch consider an intelligence test a measure of general mental development. Therefore, the most fundamental principle governing the selection of test items is to discover experimentally those tasks in which children "become more proficient each year, as they progress toward mental maturity." To discover such tasks, over 1,600 items were tried out on children over a wide age range; and from the percentages at each age found to pass an item, graphs such as that shown in Figure 12–6 were plotted for the item.

In addition to discriminating significantly among age levels, three other criteria for selecting test items were used: variety (five different kinds of item with a median correlation among them of .45); freedom from effects of specific training (vocabulary kept simple and school content excluded); and avoidance of cultural bias (relationships among familiar symbols expressed only in terms of the universal concepts of form, position, size, number, and familiar vocabulary).

In order to avoid the undue influence of any single high or low subtest score, the general score is taken as the median of the five subtests. The norms are based on the scores of about 1,000 pupils at each age level from "carefully selected schools in widely scattered geographic areas" to represent "the average ability level." Using a convenient scale based on these normative data, the median scores are converted to "standard IQs," for which the mean is 100 and the standard deviation 16 at each month age level. When mental ages are desired, they are determined by the formula: MA = IQ × CA.

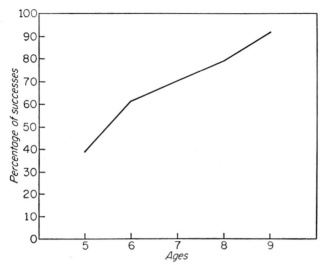

FIG. 12–6. Item A, showing satisfactory discrimination between children at succeeding ages (*N* = 81 to 110 in each group), was selected for Test II, grade 2. (*From Kuhlmann, F., and F. H. Finch: Tests for Elementary and High School Levels: Kuhlmann-Finch Manual, Educational Test Bureau, Minneapolis, 1952, p. 17.*)

3. *The Otis Quick-scoring Mental Ability Tests.* For the elementary school there are two forms: "Alpha," for grades 1 to 4, and "Beta," for grades 4 to 9. The new edition [42] of the "Alpha" test consists of 45 sets of four pictures or diagrams each, such as:

The child goes through all 45 items twice: first, to permit an appraisal of his "nonverbal"intelligence, and second, for a measure his "verbal" intelligence. The nonverbal test directions require the child to mark with a horizontal line the one picture or diagram in each set of four which is different from the others. This would seem to require for each different item formulation of a classifying generalization and a discriminative deduction (which, despite the "nonverbal" designation of the test, pupils will probably often formulate in verbal symbols). For the verbal part of the test, the pupil must comprehend and execute a specific, orally presented direction for each item. For the above item, for example, the direction is: "Mark the lines that appear to run most nearly in the direction of telegraph wires."

The manual includes a table giving the median score for each age from 5-0 to 12-11. As is illustrated below, significant increments in the median score occur during each full-year interval:

Ages:	5-0	6-0	7-0	8-0	9-0	10-0	11-0	12-0
Medians:	22	33	44	55	63	71	78	83

A child's mental age may be found by locating his score in a table (from which the above is an excerpt) and then reading off the corresponding mental age. For example, if a child at 6-0 should earn a score of 44, his mental age on this test would be 7-0. By dividing his mental age by his chronological age, an IQ could be computed. In this instance, the IQ would be $\frac{7}{6} \times 100$, or 117.

The "Beta" form of the Otis Quick-scoring Mental Ability Test, intended for grades 4 to 9, utilizes a variety of items to yield a single total score, from which a mental age and an IQ are derived. This form includes vocabulary and arithmetic items, which are justified because "in a given community in which all children have approximately the same educational opportunities," it is reasonable to assume "that differences in school progress are indicative of differences in learning ability." Some of the variety among the 80 items of the test is suggested in the following:

1. The opposite of weak is (1) poor, (2) sick, (3) tall, (4) strong, (5) young.

2. Three of the four designs at the right are alike in some way. Which one is not like the other three?

3. Fur is to rabbit as feathers are to (1) a pillow, (2) a bird, (3) a hair, (4) an animal, (5) a nest.

4. If grapefruit are 4 for a quarter, how much will two dozen cost? (1) 23¢, (2) 60¢, (3) 96¢, (4) $1.50, (5) $1.00.

From an age-norm table for Beta scores (from which the following is an excerpt), mental ages may be derived for ages 7-1 to 19-2. However, above age 13, the MAs are extrapolated rather than based on actual mean scores at these ages.

Age or MA:	7-1	8-0	9-0	10-0	11-0	12-0	13-0	14-0	15-0	16-0
Scores:	1	7	14	21	28	35	41	48	54	61

Beta IQs are still another variation of IQ. They are deviations from a mean set equal to 100 and are computed from the formula: IQ = 100 ± the deviation of the score from the age norm. For example, if a ten-year-old earned a score of 28, his IQ would be 100 + (28 − 21), or 107.

4. The California Test of Mental Maturity. Except for 3 of the 13 subtests which depend upon previously acquired vocabulary and arithmetic knowledge, the California Test of Mental Maturity [49] appears to be a test of problem-solving or reasoning ability, involving verbal, numerical, pictorial, and spatial symbols. The Elementary Series includes forms for kindergarten to grade 1, grades 1 to 3, and grades 4 to 8. The test yields mental ages, IQs, and per-centile scores on the total test, on a language part, and on a nonlanguage part. It is further subdivided to yield profiles of separate mental ages and percentile scores on five "factors," including memory, spatial relationships, logical reasoning, numerical reasoning, and verbal concepts.

As measured in the Elementary Series for grades 4 to 8, the memory factor includes both immediate recall (paired associates) and delayed recall (recalling items from a story after 30 minutes). The spatial factor includes tests of imaginal manipulation for left-right orientation and for diagrammed patterns,

such as identifying this pattern: among these:

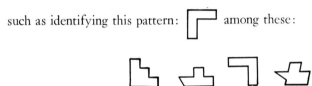

The logical-reasoning factor includes three pictorial tests and one verbal test (a syllogism test) involving generalizing and deductive reasoning. For example, looking at pictures of seven objects, the child must generalize that the first three (a suit coat, a dress, and a pair of pants) are all articles of clothing and then choose, or deduce, which one among the next four objects (a clock, a sweater, a teacup, and a bird) is like the first three. The numerical-reasoning factor includes items on deducing the principle governing the organization of a number series (for example: "18, 15, 13, 12, 9, 6, 3: Which number is wrong?"); items on making change; and arithmetic reasoning problems, such as : "Richard saw a bicycle advertised for $21 at one-third off for cash. How much money will he need to buy it?" Finally, the verbal-concepts factor is covered by a 50-word vocabulary test.

Intercorrelations (based on 1,048 pupils in grades 4 to 6) among the major parts and subfactors show that they are only partially independent of one another [49]. Between the language and nonlanguage parts, r equals .75. This fairly high correlation indicates that 56 per cent ($r^2 = .56$) of what these two major parts of the total test measure they have in common. They probably both measure, largely, reasoning, but with different symbols —one verbal, and the other pictorial and spatial. Intercorrelations among the five less reliably measured subfactors range from .25 to .60. Between logical reasoning and numerical reasoning, r is .50. Memory correlates with vocabulary .60. The spatial-relations factor is most independent of other factors, r's being from .25 to .32. That the whole test, however, is heavily weighted with verbal-reasoning factors is indicated by the fact that the single factor correlating highest with the total test is the vocabulary subtest ($r = .86$).

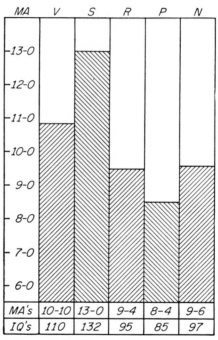

Fig. 12–7. Profile of primary mental abilities for child age 9-10. (*From SRA Primary Mental Abilities: Examiner's Manual for ages 7 to 11, Science Research, Chicago, 1954, p. 13.*)

The authors report that the test was standardized on a "controlled (stratified) sample of over 125,000 cases which constituted a normal distribution of mental ability." The means and standard deviations of these scores at each age are converted to IQ distributions with means of 100 and standard deviations of 16.

5. *The SRA Primary Mental Abilities.* Like the California Test of Mental Maturity, the SRA Primary Mental Abilities tests [54], besides yielding a measure of "general level of learning ability," provide a five-factor profile of a child's primary mental abilities, such as is illustrated in Figure 12–7. Except for one test dependent on vocabulary and another on addition skill,

all the tests for measuring these five factors are novel problem-solving tasks requiring mental manipulations of pictorial, diagrammatic, and verbal symbols.

V, the *verbal-meaning* factor, is "the ability to understand ideas expressed in words" and is considered to be the most important "index of a child's potential for handling school work." It is measured by two tests: (1) 36 vocabulary items, such as: "Mark the word with the same meaning as the first word in the line: big———— (*a*) fair, (*b*) wind, (*c*) soft, (*d*) large," and (2) a vocabulary test in picture form.

S, the *space* factor, is "the ability to visualize and think about objects in two or three dimensions" and is thought to be especially important in art and craft activities. This test includes 30 items such as: "Mark the drawing that will make the first figure a complete square:

R, the *reasoning* factor, which is "important in all school subjects," is measured by two "word-grouping" and "figure-grouping" exercises which require the child to generalize and to discriminate exceptions. Examples are: Find the word (or object) that does not belong with the group: "(*a*) red, (*b*) blue, (*c*), heavy, (*d*) green" and:

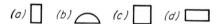

P, the *perceptual-speed* factor, is "the ability to recognize likenesses and differences between objects or symbols, quickly and accurately." It may be important in attaining advanced skill in rapid and precise reading. This factor is measured by tests requiring perceptual analysis and discrimination to determine the identical pairs among groups of four pictures or forms, such as:

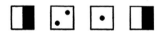

N, the *number-ability* factor, is a measure of a child's speed and accuracy in computational arithmetic. This ability is sampled by 45 simple addition problems, ranging from examples like $\begin{matrix} 6 \\ +7 \end{matrix}$ to others like $\begin{matrix} 72 \\ 49 \\ +87 \end{matrix}$.

Except for the perceptual-speed and number-ability tests, which are speed tests, ample time allowances eliminate speed as an important determinant of proficiency in these tests. A table of equivalent mental ages for each factor, corresponding to the mean scores for each age as determined from the norm data, is provided. IQs, according to the formula (IQ = MA/CA), may also be read from this table.

In addition to IQs, or "Quotient Scores," on the five factors, a total IQ is computed by weighting appropriately and summing the scores on the five tests. In this procedure the word-meaning test is weighted most heavily. The separate test scores may also be recombined to provide separate estimates of a nonreading IQ (based on verbal-pictures, figure-grouping, and perceptual-speed tests), a reading-aptitude score (based only on the word-meaning test), and an arithmetic-aptitude score (based on the verbal-meaning, reasoning, and number-ability factors).

This test was developed especially to reveal the *pattern* of a child's abilities —his special abilities and disabilities. The child age 9-10 whose profile of primary mental abilities is presented in Figure 12–7 is about average in the *reasoning* and *number-ability* factors. He is above average in *verbal meaning* and especially high in *visualizing space*. In *perceptual speed* he is relatively low. Anastasi [2], however, has pointed out that the reliabilities of the factor tests are too low (probably below .80) and the intercorrelations among the factors too high (as high as .41 to .70) to justify sharp discriminations in such analyses of a child's pattern of abilities. Because of these limitations, unless the profile shows very marked differences between factors, differences may be due to chance errors of measurement rather than representing real differences in pattern of abilities. In the above profile, therefore, analysis should probably be limited to noting that this child is especially high in visualizing space and is relatively low in perceptual speed.

Reliabilities of Intelligence Tests

A useful and trustworthy measure of intelligence should be reliable; that is, it should be accurate and self-consistent in repeated applications, unless of course in the meantime the abilities being measured have changed. When a second grade child who, despite persistent efforts to teach him, seemed unable to learn to read earned an S-B IQ of 110, his teacher doubted the accuracy of the result. However, when he earned an IQ of 109 on a second, similar test, she concluded that the child's intelligence had been reliably measured. Usually the reliability of a test is determined by testing and retesting a large, representative group of children, most desirably at single age levels, and then computing the correlation between the two sets of scores. If it is available, an alternate form of the test is often used for the retest. In determining the reliability of the S-B, for example, both the "L" and "M" forms were used. If there is only one form, however, the same test may be repeated after a time interval, or it may be subdivided for scoring into two parts of odd and even items, respectively. In this latter case, it is assumed that, if both parts are measuring reliably the same trait, the scores should be the same on each half, except for relatively small errors of measurement. Correlations between tests and retests taken at the same time (as on odd and even parts) or with only a short interval between them are indications of test-retest equivalence. When the interval between initial test and retest is longer, the correlation coefficient indicates the stability over a period of time of the scores. Both of these concepts of reliability are useful in appraising intelligence tests.

As an indication of the reliabilities of the typical intelligence tests discussed in this chapter, certain odd-even and test-retest correlations, computed from their use with various populations, are assembled in Table 12–1. As a more meaningful measure of test reliability, the standard errors of measurement, computed from the reliability correlations and the standard deviations, are also included for most of these tests.

As determined from single age groups, the reliability coefficients for these group and individual tests of intelligence range, in the main, from about .85 to .95. The reliabilities for both individual intelligence tests, except for the preschool-age groups, are .90 or higher. The Davis-Eells test has the lowest reliabilities among these tests, ranging from .68 to .84, except for the one test-retest reliability coefficient of .91 obtained at the fourth grade level. The split-half or odd-even reliabilities reported for the California Mental Maturity Scale of .92 to .95 tend to be spuriously high, since they are based on a grade *range* of from 4 to 6 rather than on single age groups.

Perhaps the most meaningful indication of a test's reliability is an interpretation of the test's standard error of measurement ("$\sigma_{meas.}$."). This is computed, from the reliability coefficient and the standard deviation of the distribution of test scores, by the formula: $\sigma_{meas.} = \sigma_{dist.} \sqrt{1 - r}$, where r stands for reliability. According to this formula, the median standard error of measurement for S-B IQs is 5.3, or $16 \sqrt{1 - .91}$. This means that out of 100 S-B retests, for example, 68 of them may be expected to vary from the initially obtained IQs by $\pm$ 5.3 IQ points. Or, more specifically, about two-thirds of the retests for a child whose IQ was initially found to be, say, 105 could be expected to range from 100 to 110—that is, 105 $\pm$ 5. For the remaining 32 retested children in our hypothetical example, retest IQ's could be expected to vary by a larger amount. But only about 5 per cent of retests on the S-B should vary by more than 2 standard errors of measurement, or by more than 10.6 IQ points. For each test reported in Table 12–1, the standard

Table 12–1. Reliability Data on Typical Intelligence Tests

Test	N	Age	Grade	Correlations		σ IQ	σ measurement	
				Split-half	Test-retest		Score	IQ
Davis-Eells problem-solving-ability	163		1	.68		16	2.5	8.0
	165		2	.82	.71	16	2.8	
	165		3	.84		16	3.4	5.3
	165		4	.83		16	3.4	
	165		5	.82	.91	16	3.5	
	165		6	.81		16	2.5	
Kuhlmann-Finch	370	8		.95		16		3.5
		9		.95		16		3.5
Otis:								
Alpha			3	.87	.73	16		3.5
Beta			4	.89	.98	16		3.9
			5	.84	.83	16		4.5
			6					
California mental-maturity (grades 4–8):								
Total	725		4–6	.95		16		3.5
Language factors	725		4–6	.94		16		3.9
Nonlanguage factors	725		4–6	.92	.85–.95	16		4.5
Stanford-Binet	About 200 at each age	Separate ages 2 to 6 each age Above 6 each age			.91 (med.) .88 (med.) .93 (med.)	16.4		6.2–3.5 5.6 4.2
For IQs:								
130 and over					.90			5.24
110–129					.91			4.87
90–109					.92			4.51
70–89					.94			3.85
Below 70					.98			2.21
Wechsler's children's intelligence:								
Full scale	100 each age	7, 10, 13		.92, .95, .94		15		3.7
Verbal scale		7, 10, 13		.88, .96, .96		15		3.0
Performance scale		7, 10, 13		.86, .89, .90		15		4.7

error of measurement shows the expected extent of IQ variation. Two-thirds of the retests will probably vary as much or less than 1 standard error of measurement, and one-third will vary in either direction by a greater amount.

Extent of Differences in Intelligence

In any typical classroom, children are found to differ both in level of mental maturity (MA) and in rate of mental growth, or relative brightness (IQ). Perhaps the most representative sample of the complete range of IQs which may be expected in a school population is the distribution of IQs reported by Merrill [37] for the S-B standardization sample of 2,904 children ranging in age from 2 to 18. This distribution, together with a set of classification terms indicative of broad subdivisions of degrees of intelligence, are presented in Table 12–2 as a frequency distribution and in Figure 12–8 as a frequency curve.

Table 12–2. IQ Distribution and Classification of 2,904 Representative Children, Ages 2 to 18

IQ	N	Percentage	Classification
160–169	1	0.03	Very superior; at 9 years may equal academic achieve-
150–159	6	0.2	ment of average 12-year-old
140–149	32	1.1	
130–139	89	3.1	Superior; needs enriched curriculum
120–129	239	8.2	
110–119	524	18.1	Bright; should succeed well in average curriculum
100–109	685	23.5	Average
90–99	667	23.0	
80–89	422	14.5	Below average; needs adjusted curriculum
70–79	164	5.6	Slow learner; may achieve 5th or 6th grade level by age 16
60–69	57	2.0	Mentally retarded; needs special class
50–59	12	0.4	
40–49	6	0.2	Mentally retarded, usually unable to learn to read
30–39	1	0.03	

Source: Adapted from M. A. Merrill: *J. Educ. Psychol.*, 29: 650, 1938.

Both the frequency distribution of IQs and the corresponding frequency curve show that IQs of representative, unselected children tend to be distributed normally—according to a bell-shaped curve. They range from a very few extremely low IQs through the majority at the average range of intelligence to a very few extraordinarily high IQs. Using this distribution as representative, the expected range of IQs in a typical class may be predicted. In a group of 35 to 40 pupils, there would be, possibly, one mentally retarded child; three slow-learning children; five below average in capacity for learning and problem solving, who could be expected to experience considerable frustration unless the regular curriculum were adapted to their limited mental maturity and patterns of abilities; 16 in the middle range of intelligence; six or

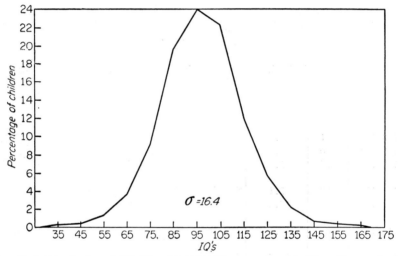

Fig. 12–8. Distribution of S-B IQs of 2,904 children ages 2 to 18. (*From Terman, L. M., and M. A. Merrill: Measuring Intelligence, Houghton Mifflin, Boston, 1937, p. 37.*)

seven who would be bright; about four superior children, who would need an enriched curriculum; and possibly one very superior child, who would need a greatly enriched or accelerated curriculum for his achievement to match his distinctively high capacities.

As an index of capacity for achievement at various levels, the mental age is more meaningful than the IQ. For example, a child whose mental age is about 6-6 is ready for academic learning at the first grade level. A child at mental age 8-6 is usually ready for third grade level reading and other such activities. And a child whose mental age is 12-0 should be making average progress at the sixth grade level. Just as for IQs, at any age or grade level, there is considerable variation among pupils' mental ages.

A typical distribution of mental ages for a school population is presented in Table 12–3. This table shows that the average mental age of these eleven- to thirteen-year-old sixth grade children is 12.4. But at this single grade level there is a range of nine years in mental maturity—from MA 7 to MA 15. The sixth

Table 12–3. Distribution of CMM Mental Ages of Sixth Grade Children, Logan, Utah

Mental age	Frequency
15-0 to 15-11	12
14-0 to 14-11	21
13-0 to 13-11	36
12-0 to 12-11	43
11-0 to 11-11	38
10-0 to 10-11	30
9-0 to 9-11	4
8-0 to 8-11	6
7-0 to 7-11	1
Mean = 12.4	N = 191

grade child whose mental age is 7 has only the average mental maturity of second grade children, while the 12 top sixth grade children with mental ages of from 15-0 to 15-11 equal in mental maturity the average of tenth grade students.

Pupil Variation in School Achievement

The individual differences among pupils are fully as large in school achievement as they are in intelligence. Cornell [7], in administering the Stanford Achievement Tests to the children of an entire New York community, found the range of achievement of 585 ten-year-old pupils to spread from second grade to ninth grade performance, the middle 80 per cent spreading over four grades—3A to 6A. "To provide instruction for the middle 80 per cent of ten-year-olds, therefore, we need work which we have traditionally regarded as appropriate for 3A, 4B, 4A, 5B, 5A, 6B, and 6A, a range of seven half-years, while for the entire range of ten-year-olds, we need work representing the entire elementary and junior high school levels" [7, p. 8].

The range of variations in over-all school achievement for each age from 7 to 12 and the overlapping in achievement among these ages are graphically shown in Figure 12–9. For this figure, scores on the total Stanford Achievement Test have been converted to grade equivalents. This is accomplished in the standardization of the test by setting the mean score earned at each grade equal to the corresponding grade level. A grade equivalent of 6.5, for example, would be assigned to every pupil whose score equaled the average score of pupils from the standardization population in the fifth month of the sixth grade. Thus interpreted, the figure shows that eight-year-olds range in performance from below the average of second grade pupils to the average of sixth grade pupils. Similarly wide ranges of achievement are found for all ages represented. Another generally observed phenomenon found in this figure is that with advancing ages, the range of differences appears to increase. It is also

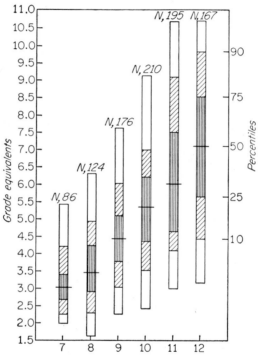

Fig. 12–9. Stanford Achievement GEs for children ages 7 to 12 (from fourteen New York rural districts combined). (*From Cornell, E. L.: Educational Research Studies, State University of New York Bulletin 1, 1937, p. 26.*)

apparent that the overlapping among age levels is so great that some pupils at seven years of age equal the achievement of some pupils 12 years of age.

A similar range of achievement in the separate subjects of the Iowa Every-pupil Tests of Basic Skills in sixth grade classes of a school system is revealed in Table 12–4. In this table, it may be observed that sixth grade children range in reading skills from five pupils who equal the average performance of representative children just beginning the third grade to four pupils who match in reading skills the average of tenth grade pupils. For the other subjects repre-

Table 12–4. Iowa Every-pupil Tests of Basic Skills, Combined Totals for 5 Sixth Grade Classes, Logan Utah, 1951

Grade equivalent	Reading	Work-study skills	Language skills	Arithmetic
11.0–11.4	...	1		
10.5–10.9	4	4		
10.0–10.4	4	1	1	1
9.5– 9.9	8	5	1	2
9.0– 9.4	7	7	3	3
8.5– 8.9	10	5	8	3
8.0– 8.4	8	10	6	10
7.5– 7.9	16	16	11	8
7.0– 7.4	21	23	13	20
6.5– 6.9	15	19	17	35
6.0– 6.4	21	21	13	31
5.5– 5.9	15	19	31	25
5.0– 5.4	19	25	33	31
4.5– 4.9	21	21	21	16
4.0– 4.4	10	12	20	7
3.5– 3.9	9	4	5	3
3.0– 3.4	5	1	2	
2.5– 2.9	...	...	3	
2.0– 2.4	...	...	2	
1.5– 1.9	...	...	2	
1.0– 1.4	...	...	2	
Number........	193	194	194	195
Median........	6.36	6.36	5.61	6.25

sented, variations in achievement are similar, being especially marked in language skills.

These data on pupil variations in intelligence and in school achievement show that for both these traits children in typical classes of unselected groups are characterized by marked individual differences. Since intelligence has been defined as the general capacity for learning and problem solving, it would seem logical to expect that pupil variations in intelligence are related to their variations in achievement. Moreover, the comprehension and use of symbols seem to be important both for effective performance on typical intelligence tests and for success in academic school subjects. But in terms of precise measures of correlation, how close is this assumed relationship? Or, how valid are intelligence tests for predicting school achievement?

Validity of Intelligence Tests in Predicting School Achievement

Data from a study by Frandsen and Higginson [13] show a typical relationship between intelligence and school achievement at the elementary school level. A scatter diagram showing the relationship for 50 fourth grade children between the Stanford-Binet IQs and the total grade-equivalent scores on the Stanford Achievement Test (which measures achievement in reading, language, arithmetic, literature, social studies, science, and spelling) is presented in Table 12–5. This diagram, in which are plotted the IQ and grade-equivalent

Table 12–5. Correlation between S-B IQs and School Achievement
for 50 Fourth Grade Children

Stanford achievement grade equivalents

IQ's	3.0	3.3	3.6	3.9	4.2	4.5	4.8	5.1	5.4	5.7	6.0	f
135								I				1
130										I	I	2
125						I						1
120			I b				I	II	I	I		6
115						I	II	I	I			5
110		I			II	I	I	II				7
105						I		I	I			3
100					IIII	I					I a	6
95		I	I	II	I		I					6
90	I	II		I			II					6
85			I		III							4
80	I		I	I								3
f	2	4	4	4	10	5	7	7	3	2	2	50

Source: Adams School, Logan, Utah.

score for each child, shows a definite tendency for higher achievement to correspond to higher IQs and for pupils of relatively lower IQs to score lower on the achievement test. The coefficient of correlation for this table is .63, which, using the coefficient of determination to interpret it (r^2), indicates that 40 per cent of the variation in achievement of these pupils can be accounted for by variations in their intelligence. The other 60 per cent of the variation in achievement is probably related to differences among the pupils in motivation, efficiency of work methods, nature of previous school experiences, emotional control, pattern of aptitudes other than general intelligence, and errors of measurement and sampling. Examining the scatter diagram more closely, we may surmise that for pupil A, whose IQ is only average (100 to 104) and whose grade equivalent is between 6.0 and 6.2, these other factors have been especially favorable. For a pupil such as B, whose IQ is between 120 and 124 and whose grade-equivalent score in achievement is only 3.6 to 3.8, these other factors have been presumably unfavorable and, of course, need correcting. These two children, however, are exceptions to a tendency for close correspondence between IQs and achievement scores.

The validities of the other intelligence tests discussed in this chapter, as expressed by their correlations with both total achievement and achievement in separate subjects, are indicated in the data assembled in Table 12–6. The validity coefficients in this table are not all comparable, since they are not all based on the same population. But as a whole they indicate that intelligence, as measured by any of these tests, is in some degree related to school achievement. Since these correlations, while significant, tend not to be high, they also indicate that intelligence is only one significant factor among others determining variations in achievement. In predicting total achievement, the median correlation is .60, and the range is from .44 to .76. Correlations between intelligence and the separate subjects vary from .24 to .83, and the median r is .55.

As was illustrated for the correlation between S-B IQs and grade equivalents on the Stanford Achievement Test at the fourth grade level, one meaningful way of interpreting a validity correlation is to convert it to a coefficient of determination by squaring the r. When the correlation between intelligence and achievement is as high as .60 (the median r with total achievement in this table), variations in intelligence account for 36 per cent ($.60^2 = .36$) of the variations in achievement. When the correlation is only .44 (the lower range of r with total achievement in this table), only 19 per cent of the variations in achievement are accounted for by the variations in intelligence ($.44^2 = .19$). In this instance, 81 per cent of the variations in achievement are accounted for by factors other than intelligence, plus errors of measurement. And when the validity coefficient is as high as .76 (the upper range of r with total achievement in this table), 58 per cent of the variations in achievement are related to variations in intelligence. In this instance, all the other factors affecting achievement, plus errors of measurement, account for only 42 per cent of the variations in achievement.

Often predictions of children's school achievement are sharpened by the teacher's knowledge of these other factors affecting achievement. For example, if it is known that a child, in addition to having an IQ of 125, is well motivated, is emotionally healthy, is given expert teacher-guidance, and has ample opportunity for efficient practice, a reliable prediction of very high academic achievement may be made. On the other hand, if all or some of these

Table 12–6. Correlations (Validity Coefficients) between Intelligence and School Achievement

Test	Grade	Study skills	Word mean.	Read. comp.	Lang.	Arith.	Soc. stud.	Sci.	Spell.	Total ach.
S-B [13]	4	...	...	.67	.64	.48	.61	.46	.45	.63
WISC [13]	4	...	...	.68	.55	.64	.71	.45	.55	.76
WISC [F*]	5	.39	...	.48	.47	.59	...	...	...	.58
Davis-Eells [10]	4	...	...	.43	.40	.41	...	...	...	...
Davis-Eells [F*]	4	.43	...	.35	.31	.43	...	...	.24	.46, .53
Kuhlmann-Finch [F*]	4	.59	...	.48	.54	.51	...	...	...	.44
Otis, Alpha [42]	1	...	.31	.32	...	.51	...	...	...	.61
	2	...	.51	.56	...	.60	...	...	.43	
	3	...	.55	.56	.48	.52	...	...	.50	
	4	...	.60	.62	.55	.63	...	...	.34	
Otis, Beta [42]	5	...	.83	.77	.70	.67	...	...	.44	
California mental-maturity [F*, 4]	6	.74	...	.77	.70	.67	.78	.76	.75	.66
SRA Primary mental abilities [2]	2	...	...	.72	.77	.68	...	...	...	.50–.70

* Personal data.

other significant factors affecting achievement are unfavorable for him, despite superior intelligence his school achievement is likely to fall short of matching it.

In using a pupil's IQ or another index of his relative intelligence as one factor in predicting his subsequent school achievement, especially in the long run, it is assumed that his degree of brightness or rate of mental growth will remain relatively constant. In explaining the IQ as a measure of rate of mental growth, IQ constancy was assumed in the graphic illustration of the concept (Figure 12–1, page 362). Some of the supporting data for this assumption are now here examined.

Constancy of the IQ

Our previous examination of the errors of measurement for typical intelligence tests, based on test-retest reliability studies, show that over relatively short intervals of time, retest IQs fluctuate from initial IQs up to about 5 points in either direction for about two-thirds of the retests and somewhat more than this for another third. There have also been several studies on the stability of IQs over longer intervals.

In one investigation of 58 children ages 2 to 5, in which retests were given six months after the initial tests, 59 per cent of the IQs changed only from 0 to 5 points; 24 per cent changed from 6 to 10 points; and 17 per cent changed from 11 to 15 points—both positively and negatively in all groups [12]. In another study of 252 children ranging in age from 2 to 18 years over the age period from 6 to 18, almost 60 per cent of the group changed by 15 or more IQ points [24]. Bradway [5] has reported IQ changes in children who had been initially tested 10 years earlier, some at ages 2 and 3 and some at ages 4 and 5. Of the children tested initially at ages 4 and 5, one-third changed less than 5 points, three-fifths changed less than 10 points, and three-fourths changed less than 15 points. The correlation between IQs at ages 4 and 5 and retest IQs earned 10 years later is .67. Jones [26] points out that the correlations between initial and retest IQs increase as the age of initial testing is increased and as the interval between the initial tests and retests is shortened. Between initial tests at age 2 and retests at age 5, r equals .32; between ages 3 and 6, $r = .57$; between ages 4 and 7, $r = .59$; between ages 5 and 8, $r = .70$; between ages 7 and 10, $r = .78$, and between ages 9 and 12, $r = .85$ [26, p. 637].

As concrete examples of such test-retest variations in IQ, Woodworth [60] cites the IQs of specific children retested several times. The IQ of child A at age 6-8 is 83; at 7-1, 75; at 8-2, 84; at 8-7, 81; and at 12-10, 77. Child B earned an IQ of 105 at age 6-6; at 7-2, 95; at 8-3, 107; at 9-6, 101; and at 12-8, 103. A gifted child, tested first at age 5-3, earned an IQ of 176; at age 6-2, 153; and at age 11-5, 143—still in the highest 1 per cent of Terman's standardization group, but lower by 33 points than the initial IQ. Such drops, however, are not characteristic of gifted children; testing initially high, they tend to maintain their high rates of mental growth [20, 29, and 51]. The sustained high rate of mental growth of gifted children is clearly indicated in Figure 12–10, which presents graphically the S-B IQs obtained from repeated testing over a six-year period of three gifted children and one child of average ability [21].

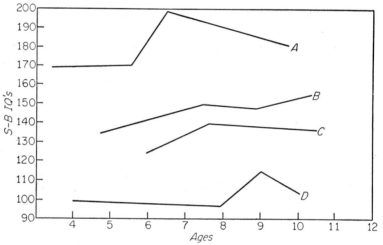

Fig. 12–10. S-B IQs from repeated tests for three gifted children (A, B, C) and one child of average ability (D). (*From Hildreth, G.: J. Genet. Psychol., 85: 243, 1954.*)

Even during relatively long intervals of time, then, IQs tend to remain fairly stable. For the three-year interval from 9 to 12 years of age, for example, the test-retest correlation of .85 would yield for the S-B a long-range standard error of measurement of 6.2. This means that the middle two-thirds of the re-tests at year 12 varied from the tests at year 9 by about ± 6 IQ points. On the whole, however, the long-range test-retest correlations are less than .85. Therefore, since the reliability of predictions is proportionate to the length of the interval between tests, when crucial guidance plans are being made for a child, a fairly recent appraisal of intelligence should be used.

Related to the question of the constancy of the IQ, or the stability of the rate of mental growth, is the important and practical question of whether the rate of mental growth can be accelerated, which would be indicated by a significant rise in IQ.

Improvement of Intelligence

Intelligence tests yielding IQs are standardized to produce constancy of IQs in representative populations, that is, to produce mean IQs of 100 and, usually, similar variability of scores throughout the age range for which the test is appropriate. Thus in retesting of representative children in successive years in "normal" school situations, the mean IQs remain constant. But the significant question here is: What happens to the rate of mental growth when children are subjected to unusual environmental stimulation? Only a few of the numerous experimental investigations [47] of this problem are cited.

In contrast to the traditional elementary school curriculum in which IQs remain constant, Lamson [30] has tested experimentally the hypothesis that an individualized, vital, activity, interest-centered curriculum which emphasizes the physical, social, emotional, and intellectual development of each child may accelerate the rate of mental growth. For 141 children who had enjoyed these special experiences in a teacher's college activity school for two, three, or four years, she determined possible S-B IQ gains from the time of entrance to the completion of the fourth grade. Her results are presented in Table 12–7.

Table 12–7. IQ Gains in an Activity School
(From grade 1, 2, or 3 to completion of grade 4)

Period of attend., yrs	N	Grades	Mean initial IQ	Mean final IQ	Diff.	P.E. of diff.	D/P.E.d
4	51	1–4	112.95	111.42	−1.53	1.36	1.12
3	74	2–4	108.31	109.79	1.48	1.18	1.25
2	89	3–4	110.39	110.45	.06	1.07	.05

Source: E. E. Lamson: *J. Educ. Psychol.*, 29: 69, 1938.

The absence of IQ gains revealed in this table justifies the conclusion that "participation in a rich and vital school curriculum," while it has many educational advantages for children, apparently does not accelerate the rate of mental growth as measured by the S-B. As in traditional schools, the IQs of children as they progress through the grades of an activity school remain relatively constant.

Of the 58 preschool children already mentioned who were tested with the S-B and retested six months later, 30 of them experienced the enriched social, emotional, and intellectual guidance provided by a college nursery school. The other 28 otherwise equated children did not have this opportunity. The nursery school group gained, on the average, 3.34 IQ points, as compared with a mean gain of 0.53 point for the control group [12]. Although larger gains from nursery school attendance have been reported [57], this relatively small advantage of 2.81 points of IQ gain from nursery school attendance has been confirmed by several investigations [47]. And similar or slightly larger gains associated with kindergarten attendance have been explained as resulting from improved test behavior acquired from making the initial adjustment to a school situation "rather than [from] actual growth in intelligence" [35, p. 32].

In this somewhat controversial field of investigation, one investigator [45] has reported phenomenal increases in IQ when mentally retarded children are transferred from regular school classes, where they are often unable to profit from the instruction provided, to "special classes," where curricula and methods of teaching are adapted to each child's mental maturity and pattern of abilities. The methods and conclusions of this particular investigator's study, however, have been severely criticized [27]. And Hill, from the results of another very carefully planned and conducted study of the influence of special-class education for mentally retarded children, concludes that "there seems to be no reason to believe that a well-planned special education program will result in upward IQ variations" [22, p. 224]. Testing 107 mentally retarded children at the time they were placed in special classes especially suited to their needs and retesting after a mean interval of three years and nine months, he found a mean difference of $-.33$ IQ point. Test-retest fluctuations ranged from $+22$ to -22 points; but about three-fourths of the variations over this interval of almost four years were from 0 to 7 points.

Two studies [8 and 38] indicate that, when borderline feeble-minded children are placed in institutions for the feeble-minded, they tend to decline slightly in IQ as they mature. Apparently such institutions, which rightly emphasize practical, nonverbal training, limit children slightly in learning how to manage the somewhat verbal items in intelligence tests intended for children in a more normal environment. When children at this deficient level of ability are placed in an orphans' home instead of in an institution for the feeble-minded, no decline in IQ seems to occur [8]. And one investigator has suggested that children in the 50- or 60-to-70-IQ range are more likely to make good occupational and social adjustments when they are provided opportunities for adjusting to normal society than when they are given institutional care [40].

As was suggested in the chapter on emotional disturbances of learning, poor parent-child relations may produce emotional disturbances which actually impair intellectual efficiency. Expert individual diagnostic intelligence testing attempts to control this factor in estimating basic capacity for learning and problem solving; but in the usual intelligence test, an emotionally disturbed child may not demonstrate his potential capacity. According to this hypothesis, when children who have lived in homes where child care and parent-child relations are very inadequate are transferred to good foster homes, their improved opportunities for healthy emotional adjustment should also result in raised IQs which reflect more nearly their potential capacities. Several studies confirm this hypothesis. In one study, a moderate mean-IQ gain of 4 points occurred in a retest given at a median interval of 13 months after foster-home placement of the children [46]. Among these studies, the investigator reporting the largest IQ gain from foster-home placement found an estimated gain, during the four years since placement at the age of eight years, of 5 points for children placed in homes of average quality and of 10 points for children placed in better foster homes [14].

It has already been pointed out that in making inferences about children's mental capacities from their present knowledge and problem-solving abilities, it is assumed that they have had ample, unrestricted, and approximately equal opportunities for learning the content on which the tests are based. It is not especially surprising, therefore, to find that children living in an isolated settlement cut off from all contact with the outside world (absence of telephones, lights, newspapers, automobiles, radio, movies, etc.) earn relatively low IQs on tests intended for children living in a more normal culture [33]. And it is also reasonable to expect that, when the economic, cultural, and educational opportunities of a handicapped region are improved, the IQs of children living in such a region may rise. This hypothesis is supported in the higher IQs reported by Wheeler [58] for children ages 6 to 16 tested in 1940 than for children from the same families tested at the same ages in 1930. During this period, this region experienced considerable improvement in transportation, economic, educational, and cultural conditions.

Finally in this review of some of the factors affecting IQ constancy, let us consider indirect and direct medical efforts to accelerate children's rates of mental growth. As an example of the indirect approach, Rogers's study [44] of the effect on general intelligence of removal of diseased tonsils may be cited. Testing 28 boys before tonsillectomies and retesting six months later, he found a mean gain of 2.25 IQ points. For a control group of children, not operated upon, with tonsils in similar condition to those of the first group, he found a gain of 3.28 IQ points. Between these small gains, the difference is not statistically significant, and both gains probably reflect only the practice effect from taking the test a second time.

As an example of the direct approach, two well-designed studies on the effect of feeding glutamic acid to feeble-minded children are cited. In these studies, the S-B IQs of both experimental and control subjects remained practically constant. The prefeeding mean IQ of McCullock's [34] subjects was 44.4; after six months of feeding, it was 43.4. For the control group, the corresponding mean IQs were 39.1 and 41.1. For Quinn and Durling's [43] subjects, the initial mean S-B IQ of the experimental group was 53.2. After six months of standard glutamic acid feedings, the final mean IQ was 55.3. For the control group, treated in the same way except for absence of glutamic acid feedings, the initial and final mean IQs were 49.4 and 51.3, respectively. These authors conclude that "the present experiment does not furnish much support for the proposition that the administration of glutamic acid to mentally deficient subjects results in improved test ratings" [43, p. 229].

This review of attempts to improve the rates of mental growth or to raise the IQs of children does not offer promise of much success, except for some children who have been subjected to impoverished environmental influences. When teachers have justification for assuming that an appraisal of a child's intelligence represents his potential capacity, rather than attempting to change his capacity for learning and problem solving, they provide a curriculum suited to his mental maturity and pattern of abilities. For all children, but especially for children of limited general intelligence, it is highly important that the exploration of their possible special talents be extensive and that adequate provision be made for worthwhile use and training of these special talents. Furthermore, to assume that it is usually not possible to raise children's IQs does not mean that teachers are not concerned about improving their pupils' intellectual efficiency. This is an important teaching aim. It is accomplished by providing suitable curricula for each child's pattern of abilities, by giving guidance in efficient work methods, and by promoting in every way possible his emotional health.

In this chapter, intelligence has been defined broadly as the general *capacity* for learning and problem solving. More specifically described, intelligence includes the abilities for comprehension and use of symbols. Several tests for appraising these abilities have illustrated the important concepts of intelligence testing. Evaluation of these tests has found them reliable, valid as one factor in predicting school achievement, and descriptive of a fairly stable characteristic in which individual children differ significantly. Although intelligence is only one of several factors affecting a child's progress in school, teachers need to appraise this factor for understanding and effective guidance of children. As a conclusion to this chapter, four methods of doing this are considered.

Procedures for Appraising Intelligence

As procedures for appraising intelligence, teachers have available (1) reports from a school psychologist of individual intelligence-test results and (2) group tests of intelligence yielding either a single total score or a profile of primary mental abilities. They also often estimate a child's intelligence from (3) their observations of his performance and behavior in school activities and (4) from his performance on school achievement tests. What are the merits and limitations of each of these procedures?

1. Individual Intelligence Tests. The most important limitation of the individual intelligence test is the expense. Only one child can be examined in an hour, and another half hour is usually required for writing a report. Moreover, only a psychologically trained person, such as a school psychologist, school counselor, or psychologically trained teacher, is competent to administer and to interpret such a test. Its advantages, which fully justify the added expense, are that it is more reliable for unusual cases and that it yields, besides a mental age and IQ, other data very useful in the clinical study of children. The unusual cases include children whose scores on a group test are low, children who are retarded in school achievement, and children who appear to be emotionally disturbed. The additional useful data are the by-products of an intimate "clinical interview" with a trained examiner, which constitutes the child-examiner relationship in individual diagnostic testing. The clinical interview affords an opportunity to observe a child's learning and problem-solving methods, indicating whether the child learns from problem-solving experience and whether his problem solving is unified and integrated or piecemeal, sporadic, and easily abandoned for guessing, for pretentiousness, or simply by "giving up." Degree of emotional control and personal and social attitudes are often manifest. And because the tests sample a variety of mental processes, special abilities and deficiencies suggested can be related to the specific problem for which the child is being examined, such as reading retardation or readiness for the first grade. These concepts have already been illustrated in the S-B reports cited in the chapters on maturation, teacher-guidance, and emotional disturbances. As another illustration, the test details on the child retested because his teacher doubted the reliability of the first test are instructive.

Because Allen, age 7-7, seemed unable to learn to read and appeared immature generally, his second grade teacher asked the school psychologist to give him an individual intelligence test as an aid in understanding both his retardation and her frustration in trying to teach him. An S-B IQ of 110, however, classified him as "bright"—at the 73d percentile, according to Terman and Merrill's norms. His mental age of 8-4 indicated that in mental maturity he equaled average third grade children. Since this brightness and level of mental maturity were inconsistent with his inferior school progress and unresponsiveness to teaching efforts, the retest was requested. A month later, however, on Wechsler's Intelligence Scale for Children, Allen earned a full-scale IQ of 109, a verbal IQ of 104, and a performance IQ of 114. Allowing for the usual three- or four-point mean difference between the S-B and WISC, favoring the S-B, the WISC full-scale IQ of 109 is slightly better than the previously obtained S-B IQ of 110. The WISC subtest pattern of his performance is shown below.

	Standard Score		*Standard Score*
Information	13	Picture Completion	14
Comprehension	13	Picture Arrangement	9
Arithmetic	8	Block Designs	13
Similarities	13	Object Assembly	12
Vocabulary	10	Coding	12
Digit span	7		

The differential scores and the "clinical data" brought out in these individual tests help to explain the discrepancy between Allen's underachievement and his above-average capacity and also indicate his potential teachability.

The relatively low standard scores in the digit-span subtest (7) and in arithmetic (8) suggest that Allen's abilities for attention and concentration are being disturbed, possibly by anxiety. His need for persistent encouragement to continue with the tests to their completion also suggests lack of confidence and giving up easily as reactions to challenges. His feelings of anxiety are even more specifically indicated in his attempted definition of "nitroglycerine" as: "When you can't go to sleep at night and your're afraid there is a bear and you talk in your sleep."

A 52-word reading paragraph, a subtest in the S-B, also provided an opportunity to observe Allen's reading performance. He did not even attempt to comprehend the paragraph, and he recognized as sight words only "the," "fire," and "houses." Habitually, he waited dependently for the examiner (as with his teacher or mother) to tell him each word as he progressed through the paragraph. Asked to try to identify independently the word "girl," he guessed blindly without reference to the context, asking, "Is it 'lion'?" Since his articulation was also found to be immature ("The wabbit is wunning this way," he said in the S-B), it is not surprising that his teacher had assumed that Allen was probably immature generally.

Allen's potential capacity for progress at his own grade level is indicated, however, both by his general test-score classification as "bright" and by the quality of many of his responses. His verbal formulations were meaningful, precise, and complete. Defining "roar," for example, he said, "When a lion roars, he makes a loud sound." Explaining why oil floats on water, he said, "'Cause it is lighter than water." And in problem solving, although he showed that he lacked arithmetic information, he could even be inventive. Asked how much change he should get back if he bought 4 cents' worth of candy and gave the storekeeper 10 cents, he held out his 10 fingers, turned down four fingers, and counted off the remaining six fingers. Then he announced his solution as 6 cents. Moreover, his problem-solving ability, when applied to abstract, spatial, and pictorial symbols, as shown by his WISC performance IQ of 114, indicates that in basic problem-solving ability he exceeds about 80 per cent of children of his age.

The individual diagnostic testing of Allen indicates that he has capacity for good-to-superior school achievement and that he needs remedial reading instruction and therapy for his emotional disturbance. With the increased confidence that will come from beginning to make progress in reading and from being freed emotionally for constructive and creative use of his talents, his school achievement should eventually match his capacities for learning and problem solving. In such cases as this, however, should the child's intelligence be appraised by a group test requiring any appreciable amount of reading or even unencouraged persistence, the teacher's suspicion of both achievement *and* mental retardation might be falsely confirmed.

2. Group Tests. Compared to the individual intelligence tests, group tests are, of course, economical of time. An entire class can be tested within an hour or less, and the scoring can be done within five minutes or less per pupil. For the normal child, some group intelligence tests are probably as reliable and valid in predicting school achievement as are individual tests. They do not, however, provide opportunities for the clinical interview, which is a valuable part of the individual test. When group tests are used, retesting with an individual test would be highly desirable for children retarded in school achievement, for those who score low in the group test, and for emotionally maladjusted children.

As an approach to understanding children's capacities for learning and problem solving in various areas of the curriculum, the concept of pattern or profile of primary mental abilities is both psychologically sound [18] and educationally useful. The profile of abilities presented in Figure 12–7 (page 374) is typical of the variation in abilities which children exhibit. Such patterns are reflected both in tests of "factors," such as measured by the California Test of Mental Maturity and the SRA tests of primary mental abilities, and in profiles of achievement in different subject areas [3, pp. 459–464]. For example, 25 pupils, all near 11 years of age and all having IQs of 106, were

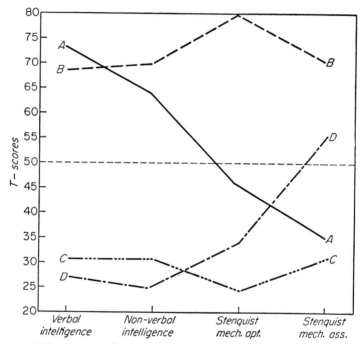

Fig. 12–11. Ability patterns for four thirteen-year-old boys given Haggerty Intelligence Test, Pintner Non-language Mental Test, and Stenquist's Mechanical Aptitude and Mechanical Assembly Tests. (*From Brown, A. W.: Contributions to Education, no. 220, Teachers College, Columbia University, Bureau of Publications, New York, 1926, p. 108.*)

found to vary markedly on the five factors of the California Test of Mental Maturity. On the memory factor, they varied from 120 months to 180 months; on the spatial factor, from 101 to 180 months; on the reasoning factor, from 130 to 154 months; and on the verbal factor, from 98 to 156 months. Such patterns are also demonstrated when several separate tests of different aptitudes are given to the same person.

Figure 12–11 shows the variations in ability patterns of four thirteen-year-old boys, as reflected by different tests of intelligence and of specific aptitudes. In this figure, boys A and B are of superior intelligence, as indicated by both the verbal and nonverbal intelligence tests. One of these boys is also superior in mechanical aptitudes. The other intellectually superior boy is considerably below average in mechanical aptitudes. Of the two boys C and D, who score very low on both intelligence tests, one is equally low in mechanical aptitudes. But the other boy is relatively higher in mechanical aptitudes, being above average in the nonverbal mechanical-assembly test.

In another study [59] of variations in pupils' abilities, eleven-year-old pupils, all of whom had S-B IQs of 140 or higher, were administered seven special-aptitude tests. In general, these very superior children also demonstrated superior abilities in art judgment, music, memory, science, and mechanical abilities. But there were also marked variabilities in the profiles of their scores. In art judgment, their scores ranged from 59 to 107; in musical ability, from 1 to 221; in general science, from 12 to 37; and in mechanical aptitude, from 15 to 60. Such differentiated patterns of aptitudes may be a product of development.

Garrett [15] has proposed a developmental theory of intelligence which assumes that "abstract or symbol intelligence changes in its organization as age increases from a fairly unified and general ability to a loosely organized group of abilities or factors." More research is needed for verification of this theory and to determine, if the theory is confirmed, at what age levels the emergence of more differentiated abilities occurs. In the meantime, however, using the present, imperfect tests of primary mental abilities, tests of achievement, and observation for manifestation of special abilities, teachers can guide children more effectively by being alert to the emergence of the particular pattern of talents in each child. Discovery of pupil talents and provision for constructive development and use of them should result both in especially efficient learning in differentiated activities and in development of healthy, satisfying self-concepts. At later ages, such preliminary exploration for individual talents should become the basis for guidance into differentiated areas of study and work.

3. *Teacher Estimates of Intelligence.* If teachers were to estimate the intelligence of their pupils from their appearance—of face, eyes, forehead, or mouth—their judgments would be worthless. Correlations between such estimates and tested intelligence are .0 [19]. But teachers have better bases than appearance for estimating intelligence. They have many opportunities for comparing and evaluating pupils' learning and problem-solving performances in reading, language, arithmetic, science, social studies, and other activities involving comprehension and use of symbols. On the basis of performance in these activities, one child may be judged by his teacher as "very superior,"

another as "bright," and still another as "seriously retarded." Often such judgments are confirmed by succeeding teachers as children progress through the grades of a school. How do these estimates agree with tested intelligence?

In one attempt to answer this question, Alexander [1] asked 35 teachers of grades 2 to 8 with a median of 12 years of teaching experience to list in order their five most and five least intelligent pupils after six months' experience with them. Of 199 pupils classified among the five highest in intelligence, 57.3 per cent were also so classified by the intelligence tests. Of 185 pupils classified by their teachers among the lowest five, 57.8 per cent were similarly classified by the tests. In a similar study, Lewis [31] also found that elementary school children rated by their teachers as "extremely mentally retarded" and as "geniuses" tended to score low and high, respectively, on intelligence tests. But the full range of IQs (from below 70 to over 120) was represented both in the group estimated as "mentally retarded" and in the group estimated as "geniuses."

In some situations, however, teachers have apparently learned to estimate intelligence more precisely. Olander [41], for example, found between the average of four teachers' estimates of children's IQs and the children's IQs on a group test of intelligence a correlation of .74. Despite the tendency for some agreement between teacher estimates and tested intelligence, however, many discrepancies occur. Gibbons [16] has noted a constant error in such teacher judgments of intelligence: superior pupils, while often rated above average, tend to be underrated; and dull pupils, while often rated below average, tend to be overrated. Apparently when teachers judge intelligence without the use of intelligence tests, they fail to recognize the very great extent of individual differences. But perhaps teacher estimates of pupils' intelligence can be improved. Being aware of the concepts of intelligence in this chapter should help. And with both improved understanding of the manifestations of intelligence and experience in judging pupils under circumstances in which estimates can be checked against reliable and valid test results, teachers' judgments of intelligence should become more reliable and valid. One recent study [25] indicates that teachers actually have learned to estimate intelligence more accurately. In this study of four schools, the median correlation between tested and estimated IQs was found to be .72, which is compared with a median correlation of .57 obtained in five earlier investigations (1922–1924).

4. *Inferring Intelligence from Achievement Tests.* Finally, as a device for judging their pupils' intelligence, teachers often have available achievement-test results. The median correlation between intelligence-test scores and achievement in the elementary school is probably about .60. But just as intelli-

gence scores can be used to predict achievement, so achievement scores can be used to infer intelligence. Or, still more useful, since from variations in achievement-test scores one can infer differences in capacity for learning, early achievement-test results can be used to predict subsequent achievement. This will be true, of course, only when the achievement tests meet the same criteria as intelligence tests with respect to ample, unrestricted, and approximately equal opportunities for learning their content. Especially in "core" subjects, such as reading, language, and arithmetic, in which pupils have ample and common experiences, variations in achievement at early grades (reflecting variations in capacity for learning) are related to variations in achievement in later grades.

In one school, achievement-test results obtained at the beginning of the fourth grade (using the Iowa Every-pupil achievement test) predict very well variations in achievement at the conclusion of the sixth grade. The correlations between early and later achievement were for reading, .78; for social studies skills, .71; for language skills, .57; and for arithmetic, .66.[1] These correlations indicate that variations in later achievement can be predicted just as well from prior-achievement tests as from intelligence tests. In fact, these earlier-to-later-achievement correlations tend to be slightly higher than the intelligence-achievement correlations, the median r's being .68 for the former and .60 for the latter. By converting the median r of .68 to a coefficient of determination, it may be noted that 46 per cent of the variation in achievement at the beginning of the fourth grade is directly related to the variations in achievement at the end of the sixth grade.

But in using achievement-test scores to estimate capacity for learning and problem solving, there is even greater need than when group intelligence tests are used for rechecking with individual tests children who score low in the achievement tests or who are emotionally maladjusted. For such children, present achievement tests are not always reliable in reflecting their potential capacities.

Review and Applications

1. Define intelligence and indicate the ways in which children manifest different degrees of intelligence.

2. What are the meanings of (*a*) mental age, (*b*) intelligence quotients, and (*c*) percentile scores?

---

[1] The author is grateful to Dr. Parry Wilson, director of guidance services in the Logan, Utah, schools, for the achievement data on 172 pupils on which these correlations are based.

3. Describe the specific features of and mental processes measured by a few different intelligence tests. In what ways are they similar? How are they different?

4. What are the potential merits of tests which yield a profile of mental abilities?

5. What are the expected ranges of (*a*) intelligence and (*b*) achievement of children in a typical classroom?

6. To what extent are variations among children in intelligence related to their differences in achievement in reading, arithmetic, and other academic activities? Why is this relationship not higher?

7. To what extent and under what conditions do IQs of school children tend to remain constant?

8. Under what circumstances are retests of children's intelligence likely to show significant gains?

9. Evaluate as procedures for appraising the intelligence of school children (*a*) individual testing, (*b*) group testing, (*c*) observation of behavior and performance, and (*d*) use of achievement-test results.

References

1. Alexander, Audrey M.: "Teacher judgment of pupil intelligence and achievement," *Elem. Sch. J.*, 53: 396–401, 1952–1953.
2. Anastasi, Anne: *Psychological Testing*, Macmillan, New York, 1954.
3. ———, and J. P. Foley, Jr.: *Differential Psychology*, Macmillan, New York, 1949.
4. Bailey, Helen K.: "A study of the correlations between group mental tests, Stanford-Binet, and Progressive Achievement Test used in the Colorado Springs elementary schools," *J. Educ. Res.*, 43: 93–100, 1949–1950.
5. Bradway, Katherine P.: "IQ constancy on the revised Stanford-Binet from preschool to the junior high school level," *J. Genet. Psychol.*, 65: 197–217, 1944.
6. Brown, A. W.: *Unevenness of Abilities of Dull and Bright Children*, Contributions to Education, no. 220, Teachers College, Columbia University, Bureau of Publications, New York, 1926.
7. Cornell, Ethel L.: "The variability of children of different ages and its relation to school classification and grouping," *Educational Research Studies*, State University of New York Bulletin 1, 1937.
8. Crissey, O. L.: "The mental development of children of the same IQ in differing institutional environments," *Child Develpm.*, 8: 217–220, 1937.
9. Cureton, E. E.: "Mental age equivalents for the revised Stanford-Binet vocabulary test," *J. Consult. Psychol.*, 18: 381–383, 1954.
10. Davis, A., and K. Eells: *Davis-Eells Test of General Intelligence or Problem-solving: Manual*, World, Yonkers, N.Y., 1953.
11. Frandsen, A. N.: "Mechanical ability of morons," *J. Appl. Psychol.*, 19: 371–378, 1935.
12. ———, and Frances Barlow: "Influence of the nursery school on mental growth." *Intelligence: Its Nature and Nurture*, pp. 143–148. 39th Yearbook of the Nat. Soc.

Stud. Educ., Part II. Chicago, Distributed by the University of Chicago Press, 1940.

13. ———, and J. B. Higginson: "The Stanford-Binet and the Wechsler Intelligence Scale for Children," *J. Consult. Psychol.*, 15: 236–238, 1951.

14. Freeman, F. N., et al.: "The influence of environment on the intelligence, school achievement, and conduct of foster children." *Nature and Nurture: Their Influence upon Intelligence*, pp. 103–217. 27th Yearbook of the Nat. Soc. Stud. Educ., Part I. Chicago, Distributed by the University of Chicago Press, 1928.

15. Garrett, H. E.: "A developmental theory of intelligence," *Amer. Psychologist*, 1: 372–378, 1946.

16. Gibbons, C. C.: "A comparison of Kuhlmann-Anderson test scores and teachers' estimates," *Sch. Soc.*, 47: 710–712, 1938.

17. Grimes, J.: "Age level discrimination and the validity of intelligence tests for elementary school children," unpublished master's thesis, Utah State Agricultural College Library, Logan, 1955.

18. Guilford, J. P.: "Human abilities," *Psychol. Rev.*, 47: 367–394, 1940.

19. Gurnee, H.: "An analysis of the perception of intelligence in the face," *J. Soc. Psychol.*, 5: 82–99, 1934.

20. Hildreth, Gertrude: "Stanford-Binet retests of gifted children," *J. Educ. Res.*, 37: 297–302, 1943.

21. ———: "Three gifted children: A developmental study," *J. Genet. Psychol.*, 85: 239–262, 1954.

22. Hill, A. S.: "Does special education result in improved intelligence for the slow learner?" *J. Except. Child.* 14: 207–213, 224, 1948.

23. Hollingworth, Leta S.: "An enrichment curriculum for rapid learners (130–200 IQ) at public school 500: Speyer School," *Teach. Coll. Rec.*, 39: 296–306, 1938.

24. Honzik, M. P., J. W. Macfarlane, and L. Allen: "The stability of mental test performance between two and eighteen years," *J. Exp. Educ.*, 17: 309–324, 1948.

25. Hubbard, R. E., and W. R. Flesher: "Intelligent teachers and intelligence tests— do they agree?" *Educ. Res. Bull.*, 32: 113–122, 139–140, 1953.

26. Jones, H. E.: "The environment and mental development," in L. Carmichael (ed.): *Manual of Child Psychology*, 2d ed., Wiley, New York, 1954.

27. Kirk, S. A.: "An evaluation of the study by Bernardine G. Schmidt entitled: Changes in personal, social, and intellectual behavior of children originally classified as feebleminded," *Psychol. Bull.*, 45: 321–333, 1948.

28. Kuhlmann, F., and F. H. Finch: *Kuhlmann-Finch Tests for Elementary and High School Levels: Manual*, Educational Test Bureau, Minneapolis, 1952.

29. Lamson, Edna E.: "High school achievement of fifty-six gifted children," *Pedag. Semin. J. Genet. Psychol.*, 47: 233–238, 1935.

30. ———: "To what extent are intelligence quotients increased by children who participate in a rich, vital school curriculum?" *J. Educ. Psychol.*, 29: 67–70, 1938.

31. Lewis, W. D.: "Some characteristics of children designated as mentally retarded, as problems, and as geniuses by teachers," *J. Genet. Psychol.*, 70: 29–51, 1947.

32. Louttit, C. M., and C. G. Broune: "The use of psychometric instruments in psychological clinics," *J. Consult. Psychol.*, 11: 49–54, 1947.
33. Ludeman, W. W., and J. R. McAnelly: "Intelligence of colony people," *J. Educ. Psychol.*, 21: 612–615, 1930.
34. McCullock, T. L.: "The effect of glutamic acid feeding on the cognitive abilities of institutionalized mental defectives," *Amer. J. Ment. Def.*, 55: 117–122, 1950–1951.
35. McHugh, Gelolo: "Changes in IQ at the public school, kindergarten level," *Psychol. Monogr.*, vol. 55, no. 2, 1943.
36. McNemar, Q.: *The Revision of the Stanford-Binet Scale: An Analysis of the Standardization Data*, Houghton Mifflin, Boston, 1942.
37. Merrill, Maud A.: "The significance of IQ's on the revised Stanford-Binet scale," *J. Educ. Psychol.*, 29: 641–651, 1938.
38. Minogue, B. M.: "The constancy of the IQ of mental defectives," *Ment. Hyg.*, 10: 751–758, 1926.
39. Morphett, Mabel V., and C. Washburne: "When should children begin to read?" *Elem. Sch. J.*, 31: 496–503, 1931.
40. Muench, G. A.: "A follow-up of mental defectives after 18 years," *J. Abnorm. Soc. Psychol.*, 39: 407–418, 1944.
41. Olander, H. T.: "Can teachers estimate IQ?" *Sch. Soc.*, 44: 744–746, 1936.
42. Otis, A. S.: *Otis Quick-scoring Mental Ability Tests*, rev. ed., and manuals for Alpha A-s, grades 1–4, and Beta EM and FM, World, Yonkers, N.Y., 1954.
43. Quinn, K. V., and Dorothy Durling: "I. New experiment in glutamic acid therapy: 24 cases classified as mental deficiency, undifferentiated, treated with glutamic acid for six months," *Amer. J. Ment. Def.*, 55: 227–234, 1950–1951.
44. Rogers, M. C.: *Adenoids and Diseased Tonsils: Their Effect on General Intelligence*, Archives of Psychology, no. 50, Columbia University Press, New York, 1922, pp. 1–70.
45. Schmidt, Bernardine G.: "The rehabilitation of feeble-minded adolescents," *Sch. Soc.*, 62: 409–412, 1945.
46. Schott, E.: "IQ changes in foster home children," *J. Appl. Psychol.*, 21: 107–112, 1937.
47. Stoddard, G. D. (Chairman): *Intelligence: Its Nature and Nurture*, 39th Yearbook of the Nat. Soc. Stud. Educ., Chicago, Distributed by the University of Chicago Press, 1940.
48. ———: "On the meaning of intelligence," *Psychol. Rev.*, 48: 250–260, 1941.
49. Sullivan, E. T., W. W. Clark, and E. W. Tiegs: *California Test of Mental Maturity—Elementary Series (Grades 4–8)* and manual, California Test Bureau, Los Angeles, 1951.
50. Terman, L. M., and Maud A. Merrill: *Measuring Intelligence*, Houghton Mifflin, Boston, 1937.
51. ———, and Melita H. Oden: *Genetic Studies of Genius*, vol. IV, *The Gifted Child Grows Up*, Stanford University Press, Stanford, Calif., 1947.

52. Thurstone, L. L.: "A new conception of intelligence," *Educ. Rec.* 17: 441–450, 1936.

53. ———: "Testing intelligence and aptitudes," *Hygeia*, 23: 32–36, 52–54, 1945.

54. ———, and Thelma G. Thurstone: *SRA Primary Mental Abilities: Examiner's Manual for Ages 7 to 11*, Science Research, Chicago, 1954.

55. Thurstone, Thelma G.: "Primary mental abilities of children," *Educ. Psychol. Measmt.*, 1: 105–116, 1941.

56. Wechsler, D.: *Wechsler Intelligence Scale for Children*, Psychological Corporation, New York, 1949.

57. Wellman, Beth L.: "Mental growth from pre-school to college," *J. Exp. Educ.*, 6: 127–139, 1937.

58. Wheeler, L. R.: "A comparative study of the intelligence of east Tennessee mountain children," *J. Educ. Psychol.*, 33: 321–334, 1942.

59. Wilson, F. T.: "Some special ability test scores of gifted children," *Pedag. Semin. J. Genet. Psychol.*, 82: 59–68, 1953.

60. Woodworth, R. S.: *Psychology*, 3d ed., Holt, New York, 1934.

Chapter 13

Providing for Differences in Abilities

THE CHILDREN in a typical elementary school class-room are alike only in being approximately at the same age. Otherwise, as the preceding chapter has revealed, they are very heterogeneously grouped. They differ in mental maturity, in patterns of abilities, in level and patterns of school achievement, in interests, in social and emotional adjustment, and in needs for guidance and instruction [38, 83]. The children entering a typical fourth grade will vary in mental age at least from 7 through 12; and in standardized tests in reading, language, social studies, or arithmetic, there will be similar ranges in achievement of from grade equivalents 1 or 2 to 6. According to Cook, "when a random group of six-year-olds enters the first grade, two per cent of them will be below average four-year-olds in general mental development and two per cent will be above average eight-year-olds. Disregarding the extreme two per cent at either end, there will be a four-year range in general intelligence" [15, p. 141]. And since individual differences increase with age, "in any grade above the primary level will be found the complete range of elementary school ability" [15, p. 141]. Further, "when the educational achievement of a typical sixth grade class is measured, we find a range of approximately eight years in reading comprehension, vocabulary, arithmetic reasoning, arithmetic computation, the mechanics of English composition and other forms of achievement" [15, p. 141]. Moreover, for any single child, there will often be marked variations within his

404

pattern of abilities and achievements. A nine-year-old may have a mental age of 9, a reading age of 7, a social studies age of 8, and an arithmetic age of 10. Furthermore, the "causes" of each child's achievement status are often different.

Nine-year-old Harold is unable to keep up with his fourth grade classmates because he is unable to read. He recognizes only the few sight words he remembers and lacks completely skill and confidence in independent identification of the many unfamiliar words he meets. But Harold has an S-B IQ of 110 and a mental age almost equal to the average of fifth grade pupils. He needs remedial teaching for his ineffective work methods and therapy to overcome emotional handicaps which interfere with effective use of his good ability.

Walter is another frustrated nine-year-old fourth grade child. Like Harold, he reads at the first grade level. His S-B IQ is only 70, however, and his mental age, which is only slightly over 6, is just at the minimum for expectation of success at the first grade level. He needs patience from his teacher and parents, a curriculum radically adjusted to his very slow rate of mental maturing and to his possible special talents, and beginning, systematic instruction in reading at the first grade level.

Irene is still another nine-year-old fourth grade child. Her achievement is apparently quite satisfactory. Her grade-equivalent score in reading is at the fifth grade level, and, except for arithmetic, which is just at her grade level, her other achievement scores are also slightly above average. But her S-B IQ is 140, and her mental age of 13-2 is equal to the average of representative seventh grade children. It is quite probable that Irene is not using efficiently her distinctively high capacities for abstract learning and problem solving, with a resultant loss both to herself and to her society. Hollingworth has remarked that children with IQs above 140 "earn high marks without effort and waste one-half or more of their time during the school day either in idleness or in performance of routine tasks" [13].

How can teachers meet the needs of such heterogeneous groups of pupils? Obviously such a provision as a uniform "fourth grade" curriculum through which all nine-year-old children can be encouraged or prodded is an impossible solution [83]. Each child needs during each year of school—in fact, during each day—a worthwhile curriculum in which he can experience success, see himself making progress, and find opportunities for constructive and creative expression of his talents. His curriculum experiences and his relations with his teacher and classmates should provide each child a feeling of being adequate, accepted, recognized and loved for himself, and esteemed for his contributions [38]. Uniform curricula and standards would frustrate these needs for all but

Fɪɢ. 13–1. The "free period" recognizes and cultivates independence, and encourages creative effort in each child's field of interest. (*Courtesy of Dilworth School, Salt Lake City.*)

a few pupils in a classroom. Better provisions for individual differences among school children have, however, been suggested [66].

General Suggestions on Providing for Individual Differences

Cook [15] has proposed that the teaching and guidance of elementary school children should include (1) provision for understanding *each* pupil's pattern of abilities, interests, background, and needs, and (2) provision of curricula and instruction adapted to the individual characteristics thus discovered in each child. Such curricula and teaching methods, he thinks, should (1) be varied with respect to goals requiring differences in ability; (2) free the teacher for attention to individual development of pupils; (3) be broad enough for a wide range and varied combinations of interests and aptitudes; (4) be organized around large units or projects in social studies and natural science; (5) appeal to varied interests; (6) utilize reading material varied in difficulty and content; (7) utilize varied media—literature, moving pictures, radio, newspapers and magazines, museums, and field trips; and (8) involve a wide range of pupil activities—reading, research, reports, interviewing, planning, organizing, generalizing, dramatizing, craft construction, literature, music, art, arithmetic, graphs, maps, diagrams, taking responsibility, cooperating, etc. In such a curriculum, there would be both teacher-guided and independent pupil activities, individually and in groups. The well-equipped, workshop-type classroom described in the chapter on practice would be desirable. There would be flexible daily schedules. "Free periods" for work in the library, in the workshop, in the art center, or in committees would be needed [86].

Washburne [83] has suggested for meeting the problem of individual differences a combination of (1) highly individualized instruction and (2) socialized, cooperative work on projects. For mastering the skills of reading, spelling, language, and arithmetic, he proposes a self-instruction program in which each child begins when he is ready and progresses at his own rate in each different subject. Teacher-guidance is highly individualized. Using individual, workbook-type materials and diagnostic testing, the teacher gives each child instruction as he needs it. Balancing the individual work, the socialized projects in social studies, science, and arts involve group planning and discussing, excursions, committee activities, "research," listening to the teacher's talks and demonstrations, group singing and dramatics, and creative work in crafts, art, music, and writing. In these projects, each child participates and contributes according to his interests, talents, and needs.

Procedures for Adapting to Individual Differences

Suggestions for providing for individual differences in abilities have included (1) adjusting each child's rate of progress through the grades to his rate of mental maturing, (2) homogeneous or ability grouping, (3) intraclass grouping, (4) a variety of individualized-instruction procedures, (5) diagnostic and remedial teaching, and (6) special provisions for slow learners and for gifted children. There are probably some merits and perhaps some limitations in each of these procedures. Probably no one method is best for every pupil in every situation. We need to determine under what conditions and for which pupils each provision or combination of provisions would be best. It is from this general point of view that these specific devices, together with the principles just discussed, will be evaluated.

1. Adjusting Pupil Progress to Rate of Mental Maturation. Traditionally, and especially according to present practice, elementary school children usually spend one year in each grade, being "promoted" to the next grade at the end of each school year. Most of the above suggestions, such as adapting projects and other varied curriculum activities to individual differences, assume that class grouping according to age is good practice and provide for individualized teaching within this plan. According to Washburne [83, p. 147]:

At the end of the year children have all progressed, in varying degrees, to mastery of appropriate parts of the common skills. All have had a rich year of experience in many fields. If the children have got along fairly well together and can work and play as a team, the teacher has no hesitancy about letting them continue their group experiences together [in the next grade] next year, knowing that her successor will carry each child on from where he left off in that fraction of the curriculum where common mastery is necessary.

Exceptions to such regular yearly promotions, however, are sometimes considered. Slow-learning children are sometimes expected to repeat a grade;

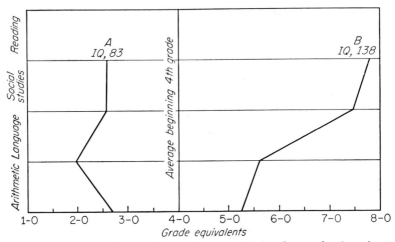

FIG. 13–2. Iowa Every-pupil Basic Skills Achievement Profiles for two fourth grade pupils, one with CMM IQ 83 and one with CMM IQ 138.

superior children may skip a grade, or part of it; and in some schools, flexible rates of progress are being tried. For example, let us consider the two children about to begin the fourth grade whose achievement profiles are portrayed in Figure 13–2. Some teachers might think it desirable to retain pupil A in the third grade for another year, since he is now about a grade and a half below the fourth grade average in reading, social studies, language, and arithmetic. And they might consider accelerating pupil B's rate of progress. Since at the beginning of the fourth grade, his achievement grade equivalents range from 5-3 in arithmetic to 7-8 in reading, it is apparent that he has already mastered the usual fourth grade curriculum content. Perhaps he should be advanced immediately to the fifth grade or during the year complete both grades 4 and 5.

Actually, these two children continued at the usual one-grade-per-year rate of progress. At the end of the sixth grade, after three years of further growth and learning, pupil A's grade-equivalent scores are in reading, 3-4; in social studies, 4-3; in language, 2-6; and in arithmetic, 4-7. He has made only very limited progress during these three years. Pupil B, already advanced at the beginning of the fourth grade, has continued during the next three years his rapid rate of maturation and learning. At the end of the sixth grade, his grade-equivalent scores are in reading, 11-0; in social studies, 10-3; in language, 10-4; and in arithmetic 9-5.

RETARDATION. If mentally immature children enter the first grade at mental ages of 4 or 5 (as some of them do), because of their slow rates of mental maturing, it will require one, two, or even three years of growth before they have sufficient mental maturity for success with reading and other such academic activities. A child whose IQ is 80, for example, will not attain a mental age of $6\frac{1}{2}$ until he is eight years of age. If his IQ were only 70, he would be nine years old before his mental age was $6\frac{1}{2}$ (CA = MA/IQ). While such children are advancing at a rate of one grade per year through grades 1, 2, or 3, they will need a prereading curriculum of worthwhile activities in which they can succeed. And in the third or fourth grade, when many of their classmates are reading skillfully and rapidly, they will only then be ready for the gradual and systematic introduction to reading which first grade teachers often consider their major job. Teachers of third or fourth grade children, occupied as they are with many other activities, sometimes think they lack time and competency for teaching such children beginning reading [55]. One solution proposed is to retard the grade progress of such children. The entrance of a child with an IQ of 80 into kindergarten might be delayed until he is six years of age. He might then remain in either the kindergarten or first grade for two years, so that during the year he becomes eight and attains a mental age of $6\frac{1}{2}$ he will participate with a first grade group in learning to read. If such a child happens to be physically small and socially immature, he might also adjust well socially to younger classmates.

The chief argument against retardation, however, is that many retarded children become emotionally and socially maladjusted. Several studies tend to support this contention. Sandin [72], using a variety of observation, interview, teacher-rating, and sociometric techniques, found 139 pupils who had failed at least once to be promoted in grades 1 to 8 to choose more often companions above their grade levels, to be regarded less favorably as companions or seatmates, to be rated less favorably on personality traits, to wish more often to quit school, and to feel discouraged or unfairly treated more often than their regularly promoted classmates.

Bedoian [6] discovered that overage sixth grade pupils are chosen less often in sociometric tests as "a team captain," as "president of the class," or as "someone to help with school work" than either at-age or underage pupils. And in these sociometric tests, the overage pupils earned from their classmates "significantly higher rejection scores." Both Anfinson [3] and Turner and Eyre [81] report less favorable self-ratings for repeaters than for nonrepeaters on a personality inventory. And in a study by McElwee [64], fewer retarded children were rated favorably by their teachers and more unfavorably than were either normal-progress or accelerated pupils. However, in none of these studies did retardation result universally in unfavorable effects. In McElwee's study, 61 per cent of the retarded pupils were rated "gets along well with others"; 52 per cent "interested in school work"; and 40 per cent "making a good effort in school." Only 15 per cent were rated "quarrels with others" and only 32 per cent "indifferent toward school." The differences between the retarded pupils and the nonrepeaters are *average* differences. On favorable traits normal and accelerated pupils are checked only *relatively* more frequently and on unfavorable traits *relatively* less frequently than are retarded children.

Retardation of slow learners is proposed, of course, as a device for facilitating learning. On this criterion, Cook [15] and Washburne [83] agree with Goodlad that "studies into the achievement of repeaters indicate that these children do no better than children of like ability who are promoted" [30, p. 150].

In evaluating grade retardation as a device for adjusting the curriculum of slow-learning children to their retarded rate of mental maturing, it cannot be considered universally satisfactory. Experimental investigations, while in need of better design and control, find, on the average, learning efficiency not improved and a tendency for greater frequency among retarded children of social and emotional maladjustment. In individual instances, however, especially at entrance into school, there may be some children who could learn more effectively if their entrance or promotion were delayed and who would adjust happily to an age group younger by a year or two.

ACCELERATION. Intellectually gifted children, both with and without actual grade acceleration, often advance rapidly in their mastery of the elementary school curriculum [41, 60, 80]. For example, when he began the fourth grade, the median grade-equivalent score on the Iowa Every-pupil achievement test of pupil B in Figure 13–2 (page 408) was already 6-5; and as he completed the sixth grade, the median of his achievement profile was grade 10-4. Such rapid progress in learning, Hollingworth has shown [41], is typical for intellectually superior children. She found that a group of 50 children whose S-B IQs were 140 or higher had reached at the conclusion of the third grade seventh grade status on the Stanford Achievement Tests. And Terman and Oden have observed that "it is a conservative estimate that more than half of the children with IQs of 135 or above have already mastered the school curriculum to a point two full grades beyond the one in which they are enrolled, and some of them as much as three or four grades beyond" [79, p. 28]. It is obvious that such children need either an accelerated rate of grade progress or a greatly enriched curriculum.

Accelerated school progress, besides providing a more challenging curriculum to these children intellectually maturing at a rapid rate, would also make possible in adulthood earlier completion of the long period of professional training which many of these gifted individuals need. Because of this saving in time for training, these individuals would enjoy and their society would profit from an earlier and longer period of their highly productive and creative services.

Despite these advantages, however, intellectually superior children are rarely accelerated in grade progress. Terman and Oden note that, while tests showed their school achievement to be 44 per cent in advance of average children of their age, their gifted children were advanced only 14 per cent in grade progress [80]. School administrators and teachers are reluctant to accelerate children because of the difficulties that they fear younger children will have in adjusting socially to children one, two, or three years older than themselves, especially in preadolescence. Several studies, however, indicate that accelerated superior children adjust very well both academically and socially.

In contrast to both normal-progress and retarded pupils, McElwee [64] found accelerated children more frequently checked by their teachers on such favorable traits as "gets along well with others" and "interested in school work." And she found them checked much less frequently on such undesirable traits as "quarrels with others" and "restless," "stubborn," or "listless." When judged by their classmates on sociometric devices, underage sixth grade pupils were found by Bedoian [6] to receive significantly higher social-acceptance scores than either at-age or overage pupils.

When the effects of elementary school acceleration on high school achievement and social adjustment are appraised, the results also are favorable to acceleration [1, 48, 53, 84, 85]. Johnson [48] reports that, when elementary school children are selected for acceleration on the basis of advanced S-B MA, relatively high achievement-test scores, size not under the norm for a year below their new associates, and social age equal to that of their new associates, their high school achievement is equal to and their social adjustment better than those of nonaccelerated children. He recommends gradual acceleration: one-half year in grades 1 to 4 and another one-half year in grades 5 to 8. Adams and Ross [1], however, find that "under reasonably favorable conditions skipping is a satisfactory method of accelerating pupils of superior ability." Keys [53] discovered that 113 boys and girls who graduated from high school at ages from one to three years younger than normal were superior to an equated group of nonaccelerated children in scholarship, study habits, and personal and social adjustment. Wilkins found students graduating from high school at ages 15-5 to 16-11 because of acceleration in elementary school "superior" in achievement [84] and socially well adjusted [85]. The majority of these accelerated pupils expressed in high school a preference for academic subjects (mathematics, science, English, foreign languages) and for playmates their age or (slightly more often) older. According to Wilkins, the "typical accelerated pupil," besides enjoying such intellectual activities as reading, is also highly social. He likes strenuous play, parties and dances, and the company of friends [85, p. 451].

Pressey has evaluated the acceleration of superior students through elementary and secondary schools in terms of its effects on their achievement and behavior in college. "Practically all research findings," he writes, "are in support of early entrance," which acceleration makes possible. "Younger students make better grades in college than students entering at average or older ages. They less often present disciplinary problems. . . . And they are *not* especially subject to social maladjustment; in fact, some investigators have found them more often and more prominent in extra curricular activities than students of average age" [68, p. 36].

Because of these almost universally favorable findings, Keys [52] recommends acceleration of one, two, or even three grades as one means of adjusting the curriculum of the superior child (IQ of 120 to 140 or over) to his intellectual maturity. For children for whom acceleration seems appropriate according to all criteria, perhaps one year should be accomplished by rapid progress in the kindergarten and primary years; and if a second year seems desirable for a particular child, it could be achieved in either the primary or the intermediate years. In any event, if acceleration is to be used as one device for adjusting the curriculum to the mental maturity of the intellectually superior child, some of the acceleration should probably occur early in the child's education program.

FLEXIBLE RATES OF PROGRESS IN WIDER AGE-RANGE GROUPING. Another way of adjusting children's progress through a sequence of curriculum activities to their different rates of mental maturation is to apply modifications of the principles of acceleration and retardation to grade groups of wider age range. DeLong [20] has suggested combining grades 1 and 2 into one primary unit in which a sequence of six reading levels are differentiated—from prereading to fairly rapid and skillful independent reading at beginning third grade level. Within this sequence of reading levels, there is no "promotion" until a child completes the sixth level and is ready for promotion to the third grade. Each child progresses through the sequence at his own rate, which may require from as little as a year to more than three years. Readiness to advance from prereading to the first reading level is determined by readiness tests; and advancement to succeeding levels depends upon mastery of the preceding level. Several books on each level of difficulty are provided, so that a child can practice as little or as much as he needs for mastery without repetition of the same content.

Recently an adaptation of this plan extended over all the elementary grades has been tried and informally evaluated by elementary schools in several states [8]. Typically, these schools group together, with one teacher for every two years, children covering a span of three years in age. In Group I, there are children from the usual grades 1 and 2; Group II includes children from grades 2 and 3; Group III draws children from grades 3 and 4; Group IV takes children from grades 4 and 5; and in Group V, children from grades 5 and 6 are combined. Each child's placement in an appropriate group is decided in conference with the teachers concerned, the principal, and the parents. Their criteria for placement are the child's size, interests, and mental, social, and emotional maturity. To illustrate how the criterion of mental maturity is applied, a mentally immature eight-year-old might be placed in Group I with children whose ages range from 6 to 8. A bright seven-year-old might be placed in Group II, among the seven-to-nine-year-olds. An intellectually superior seven-year-old might even be placed in Group III, which is comprised mainly of eight- and nine-year olds but may include an unusual child of seven or ten years of age.

Rate of progress through the groups is flexible. If it is determined that a given child, after spending three years in groups including grade levels 1, 2, and 3, has not completed all the curriculum experiences available to him and has not progressed as much as he might with more time in the group, he may be retained for another year, provided that it appears that he will remain well adjusted mentally, emotionally, and socially. Similarly, a bright child may reach the fourth grade level in fewer than the usual three years. In at least one of the schools trying this plan, predictions of rate of progress are made early on the basis of careful observations of each child's learning and social progress. These predictions are then used in planning with the parents the entire elementary school sequences for each child.

Without citing objective data, the several authors [8] reporting on this plan for flexible progress in wider age-range groups say that it is one effective way of meeting the problem of individual differences. They say that children make "satisfactory" progress, are interested, achieve good emotional and social adjustment, and learn to recognize and to accept individual differences among themselves. They say also that teachers become better acquainted with the children and come to understand their individual and group needs better. Because of the modified application of the principles of acceleration and retardation, teachers find fewer different reading groups required. Thus the plan facilitates use of intraclass grouping.

On the question of the possible effect on achievement of wider age-range grouping, there has been at least one objective study. Adams [2], in comparing gains in achievement on the Progressive Achievement Test of fifth grade pupils grouped separately and fifth grade pupils grouped together with fourth grade pupils, discovered no significant differences.

2. Homogeneous Grouping. A plan for adjusting to the individual differences in mental ability of pupils of the same age, applicable in large schools, is to classify children in each grade into sections according to IQs. If the school population is large enough, three sections of equal size can be arranged in each grade by classifying in the highest section pupils whose IQs are 108 and higher, in the middle section children with IQs from 93 through 107, and in the lowest section children whose IQs are 60 through 92. For these three sections of each grade, now more homogeneous with respect to IQ, there should be three differentiated curricula. The middle group should progress through school with the usual curriculum. For the highest group, the curriculum should be enriched. And for the lowest group, the curriculum should consist of minimum essentials and should aim at more limited academic goals. There should also presumably be some differentiation in methods of teaching, perhaps involving more concrete experience and greater amounts of varied practice on the lowest level and proceeding more directly to abstract generalizing on the highest level.

Homogeneous grouping was invented and became popular early in the history of intelligence testing in schools. Uniform assignments, general recitations, and other activities conducted with the class as a whole are considered easier to manage when pupils are grouped homogeneously. In general, the research on ability grouping has revealed "slightly superior achievement and better personal adjustment" for homogeneous than for heterogeneous groups [77]. Barthelmess and Boyer [5] found for equated groups of fourth grade pupils an achievement gain of 12.8 months for homogeneous classes during a school year, while heterogeneous classes gained 10.4 months. Sorenson, however, considers the evaluative evidence on ability grouping "far from adequate" [77, p. 237]. And in at least one comparative study [23], the gain in reading achievement for fifth and sixth grade pupils was slightly greater for the group of wider IQ range than for the narrower-range group. Of groups of equal mean IQ (104.7 and 104.4), the group with the wider IQ range (41 points) gained 8.54 months of reading age, while the group with a narrower IQ range (29 points) gained 8.02 months. Such diversity of experimental results suggests that achievement depends more upon other factors, such as the quality of teaching and how well it is adapted to the nature of the group, than it does upon the degree of homogeneity of the group.

In evaluating homogeneous grouping arranged on the basis of IQs, it should also be remembered that the correlation between intelligence and achievement is far from perfect. In the previous chapter, for the limited data there considered, the median r between intelligence and achievement in separate subjects was found to be .55. Since the coefficient of determination for a correlation of .55 is only .30, this means that 70 per cent of the variation in achievement is unrelated to variations in intelligence. Therefore, even though pupils are classified homogeneously with respect to IQs, they are still left relatively heterogeneously grouped for achievement in different subjects.

This fact is illustrated in Table 13–1, where the grade-equivalent scores in achievement of selected fourth grade pupils from three different narrow-range levels of intelligence are presented. The three intellectually superior fourth grade pupils exhibit three levels of achievement: R.K., below average for fourth grade; S.C., average; and L.G., distinctly superior. One of the pupils in the average category for IQ (B.N.) exceeds the achievement of one (R.K.) of the intellectually superior pupils and equals the achievement of another (S.C.). Similarly, the pupil whose IQ is only 79 (C.J.) exceeds in achievement the pupil whose IQ is 101 (C.B.). Moreover, there is a variation in the pattern of achievement for each pupil. For example, the pupil at the low level of ability whose achievements in reading, social studies, and language are all at the level of grade 1 (P.H.) approaches the average of his grade in arithmetic. And further, despite the fact of significant correlations between early and later

Table 13–1. Variations in Achievement of Children with Similar IQs
Beginning Grade 4 at Three Different Levels

Level	Child	IQ	Grade equivalents			
			Reading	Soc. studies	Language	Arithmetic
High..........	L.G.	138	7–8	7–5	5–6	5–3
	S.C.	134	5–4	4–3	3–9	4–4
	R.K.	152	4–8 (11–2)	3–1 (10–5)	2–5 (7–8)	3–8 (7–6)
Average........	B.N.	107	5–0	4–1	3–8	4–8
	D.B.	108	4–1	3–7	3–8	3–8
	C.B.	101	2–0	1–5	2–1	3–2
Low..........	C.J.	79	3–0	3–4	2–1	3–0
	S.H.	82	2–6	2–6	2–0	2–7
	P.H.	83	1–8	1–2	1–0	3–2

achievement, the relative achievement statuses of many pupils change. An especially marked change occurs for R.K. At the beginning of the fourth grade, his achievement, when compared to his very superior intelligence, is very low. By the end of the sixth grade, however, his achievement matches his superior capacity, his grade equivalents being for reading, 11-2; for social studies, 10-5; for language, 7-8; and for arithmetic, 7-6. Such observations as these suggest that grouping should be flexible and should be arranged separately for each subject or activity.

An example of such modification of the concept of homogeneous grouping is Floyd's report [26] on reclassifying for reading the fourth, fifth, and sixth grade pupils in a school. On the Iowa every-pupil basic-skills test in reading, the pupils in these grades ranged from grade equivalents 1.1 to 9.2. And although the mean scores for grades 4, 5, and 6 increase progressively (being 4.25, 5.3, and 6.3, respectively), almost the complete range of scores is represented in each grade. In order to provide a narrow range of reading ability for each teacher—one in which the teacher-guidance and materials would be suitable for most of the group—all the pupils were reclassified into five groups on the basis of their scores on the reading test. Group I included pupils with grade-equivalent scores of from 1.1 to 2.9; Group II, 3.0 to 4.3; Group III, 4.4 to 5.5; Group IV, 5.6 to 6.9; and Group V, 7.10 to 9.2. Each group included pupils from all three grades. During daily 45-minute reading periods the pupils were regrouped according to their specific needs for instruction in reading, as determined by the reading test. After this reading period, the pupils returned to their regular classes, which provided 25 minutes more of reading with materials suited to each child's reading level. Another form of the Iowa reading test was used as a retest after four months of such homogeneous instruction. The reading gains, in months, were for fourth grade pupils, 6.5; for fifth grade, 8.7; and for sixth grade, 13.5. It is also reported that both pupils and their parents expressed satisfaction with the new reading program.

3. Intraclass Grouping. A more popular modification of homogeneous grouping involves subgrouping and regrouping for a variety of different activities within a single class which, as a whole, is heterogeneous with respect to IQ. Several writers[39, 66, 83] think that acceleration, retardation, and homogeneous grouping into class sections on the basis of IQ are unsatisfactory solutions to the problem of individual differences. They believe that children of widely different patterns of ability can all advance together, at the rate of one grade per year, efficiently and happily. In a school environment which is rich and varied in curricular opportunities and materials, individual differences are best provided for, they say, by combinations of intraclass grouping and individualized instruction. According to this plan, standards, curricula, and methods are flexible. Each pupil is assigned to a subgroup within the class (which changes for different activities) suited to his mental maturity and unique pattern of abilities, which meets at the time his particular needs for teacher-guidance. A child's entrance into a particular subgroup will also depend upon the social role in which he needs experience, upon his need and most likely possibility for cultivating desirable friendships, and upon his own preference [16, 29, 39]. A fourth grade child may join a particular subgroup because the project on which the group is working needs his talent in art and because he needs the confidence-building experience of recognized and appreciated leadership. This same fourth grade child may, because he greatly needs to improve his reading, join a group to which the teacher is giving guidance in beginning independent identification of words. Other children from his art group may at this time join a group doing advanced, independent research reading in such mature library references as *The National Geographic Magazine*.

In a room equipped for varied activities, the teacher is occupied mainly in going from subgroup to subgroup, giving guidance as needed and always cultivating in children efficient, independent work methods. For example, before she leaves the retarded-reading group, she may instruct the temporary group leader that, when a child taking his turn at reading comes to an unfamiliar word, the leader may help him more by reminding him *how* to identify the word than by "telling" it to him. Or the group may be left alone for independent silent reading, each child being helped to choose a book in which he is especially interested and which is at a vocabulary level not beyond his reading maturity [76]. Only on such appropriate occasions as planning a

Fig. 13–3. When independence is cultivated, small groups work effectively by themselves, permitting the teacher to concentrate on each in turn. (*Courtesy of Lincoln School, Brigham City, Utah.*)

project or hearing children's contributions to it, guiding the summarization of a problem-solving activity, or teaching or leading a song will the teacher direct the class as a whole.

Elise Martens [63] has reported an intimate view of such intraclass grouping, with the teacher taking advantage of the arrangement especially to develop each child's special abilities and interests. As is suggested in Figure 13–4, in such a classroom individual children or small groups of them are busily and often independently engaged in a variety of practice and creative activities in work centers set up in various parts of the room—for science, reading, art, arithmetic, construction, or special projects. The teacher is found moving from group to group, pausing to give individual or group guidance as needed.

From her observations of several such classrooms, Williams presents a striking composite view of the varied possibilities of providing effectively for individual differences by using intraclass grouping for developing efficient and creative uses of independent work periods [86, pp. 188–189]:

Near well-stocked library shelves children had gathered to read books of their own choosing. In another part of the room a small group was sitting together to share books

FIG. 13–4. Busy, independent activities and close teacher-guidance are possible through well-planned intraclass grouping. (*Courtesy of Whittier School, Utah State Agricultural College.*)

they had enjoyed—"friendship reading" they called it. At a round table near the back of the room, another small group was using a flannel board and cutouts to work number combinations from a stack of flash cards. Many devices for helping children to understand number relationships through use of concrete objects were at hand.

At easels about the room, smocked children expressed their ideas and emotions with long-handled brushes dipped in cans of bright poster paint. Material for finger painting was found at the work table and children applied paste, sprinkled dry color from salt shakers and worked out amazingly intricate and beautiful designs. A group of boys was seen working zealously at building high towers, ramps, garages, bridges, and airports with blocks or tinker toys using toy trucks, planes, boats, and people. They dramatized with keen imagination the work life of the world about them.

On a side wall where a long strip of wide paper covered the pinning board, a group of children was at work on a mural depicting the hibernation of animals. Squirrels with their winter hoard were shown in trunks of trees, birds were winging their way to the Southland. Underground, the rodent burrows were plainly shown; and under the water of a pond and in the mud of its banks, fish, toads, and turtles were shown asleep for the winter.

By themselves or with a friend or two, children were putting puzzles together, modeling with clay, writing stories for the class book, making entries in the science log,

Fig. 13–5. Experimenting with seeds and soil gives these children opportunities for initiative, scientific problem solving, and thrilling self-discoveries. (*Courtesy of Whittier School, Utah State Agricultural College.*)

writing stories for their own book, making birthday and greeting cards, and writing letters to absent schoolmates.

One small bright-eyed boy who had not yet learned to read searched diligently through science books and pamphlets for pictures and words for the teacher to read which would tell more about the wriggling garter snake which reposed in a fruit jar near by. His grandmother had helped him to catch it.

Other interesting and purposeful activities may be found in classrooms where teachers and children plan together the work time of the day.

While their teacher is working directly with a single small group, as in Figures 13–3 and 13–4, other children are not merely kept "busy" and "quiet." They are directed toward achieving important educational goals; they are learning "by exploring, experimenting, investigating, and discovering—in situations which are meaningful to them." As is suggested in Figure 13–5, while they are learning to work independently, they are developing initiative and learning to make intelligent choices, to work effectively together, and to use freedom with responsibility. To make possible the achievement of these goals, Miss Williams points out, requires careful preplanning, provision, and arrangement of materials. The children need teacher-guidance in developing "standards of neatness, order, fair play, and cooperation which are right for the maturity level of the children and which are acceptable to them." They need to be shown how to make correct use of tools, paints, brushes, scissors, clay, and other materials. If children are to learn to act decisively, they need to share in planning and to be permitted to make choices. But the teacher needs to help a child, especially at first, to make choices of activities which he can manage by himself. Choices and execution are improved, however, by taking time for evaluation of independent work activities.

To ensure systematic practice of skills at appropriate maturity levels, intra-class grouping is sometimes accomplished by testing and by arranging systematic teaching schedules. For example, Johnson [45] reports grouping sixth grade pupils according to their arithmetic ages on a test: the low group (A) includes arithmetic ages from 8-3 to 10-9; the middle group (B), from 10-5 to 12-10; and the high group (C), from 12-5 to 14-2. A 45-minute daily period for arithmetic is scheduled thus:

Time	Group A	Group B	Group C
9:00 to 9:15	Teacher-guidance	Study	Study
9:15 to 9:30	Study	Teacher-guidance	Study
9:30 to 9:45	Study	Study	Teacher-guidance

Uniform standards for all having been abandoned, each child is helped to make his own maximum potential growth in each subject. The range of the present achievement of these sixth grade children in arithmetic is from the beginning of grade level 3 to grade level 8.

Examples of such differential rates of progress for "fast" and "slow" sub-groups of second grade children in reading, as measured by nine successive monthly administrations of the Detroit Word Recognition Test [59], are shown graphically in Figure 13–6. Apparently by intraclass grouping, provision can be made for subgroups which progress at markedly different rates. In this second grade group, by the third month the fast group had made greater progress than the slow group made in nine months. It also seems to be an effective arrangement for providing for each child both appropriate social experience and the development of his special talents and interests. The plan thus permits considerable individualized instruction [38].

4. Individualized Instruction. Both in heterogeneous groups and in groups classified more homogeneously according either to IQ or to more specific criteria, some individualized instruction is desirable. From a background of accumulating understanding of each pupil's pattern of abilities, interests, and achievements, the effective teacher organizes her teaching activities so as to give to *each* pupil specific individual instruction at the times he needs it. Such individualized guidance and instruction is applied both in the socialized projects of social studies, science, and arts and in the systematic practice of skills.

In a comprehensive and unified project, teacher and pupils together plan, study, discuss, engage in constructive and creative activities, share, and evaluate. But each pupil participates and contributes according to his particular

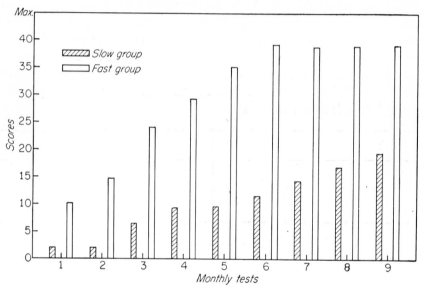

Fig. 13–6. Illustrating different rates of progress in reading of "slow" and "fast" groups, a second grade class is subdivided into three groups for reading. (*Adapted from Lampman, P.: Elem. Sch. J., 44; 358–360, 1944. Reprinted by permission of the University of Chicago Press.*)

talents, interests, and needs for academic or social experience. As Smith [75] points out, children of widely different reading abilities can all participate and contribute in study and discussion within a common interest unit and yet read different materials suited to their various reading levels. For example, in studying how children and their families live in different lands, one fifth grade child may read Louise Ranklin's *Daughter of the Mountains;* another may read something as simple as *Pepper Moon* or *Kintu, the Congo Boy;* and an intellectually superior child may read *Heidi* or *The Good Master.*

Several experiments have yielded results favorable to individualized teaching, especially as applied to reading [50, 56, 90]. Guiding principles for such teaching are that each pupil should find material suited to his level of maturity,

Fig. 13–7. Children learn to carry on independently a variety of efficient study procedures. (*Courtesy of Lincoln School, Brigham City, Utah.*)

pattern of abilities, and interests; that teacher guidance should meet his particular needs; and that his initiative, independence, and resourcefulness should be cultivated. Individualized-teaching activities include independent silent reading for information or enjoyment, teacher-guided word-study sessions for small groups with similar learning needs, independent pupil efforts at improvement in skills needed, group discussion and sharing of different contributions, and teacher-pupil conferences on book selection, for checking of vocabulary and comprehension, and for planning how to practice needed skills independently. Typical of the advantage in gains reported for a year of such individualized instruction as compared with uniform group instruction are the approximately 2½-month greater gain in reading, arithmetic, and spelling age found by Jones [50] and the 0.4-grade greater gain in reading found by Kottmeyer [56].

In order to save his time for individualized guidance of pupils in the practice of skills, the teacher will need to initiate a variety of worthwhile, interesting, and efficient study procedures which children can carry on independently. Many occasions for effective independent practice should grow out of needs for specific skills discovered in carrying on interest-centered curriculum

Fig. 13–8. Johnny shares with interested classmates his creative reaction to reading *The Three Bears*. (*Courtesy of Dilworth School, Salt Lake City.*)

projects. There are also a variety of workbooks for independent study (which, however, need to be selected carefully according to all three of the above criteria—as being worthwhile, interesting, and efficient). A number of exercises such as the following may be devised by teacher and pupils [14].

Following a period of silent reading for enjoyment of stories, third to sixth grade children may be encouraged to draw pictures to illustrate them. Then in a group period, they may share with their classmates their reactions to a story by putting, each in turn, his pictures on the flannelboard. If several children have read the same story, their different interpretations may be enjoyed.

As an aid both in exploring for interests and in independent selection of books, the teacher may encourage children to classify books they read into patterns, such as books about animals, foreign countries, myths, or the sea. If it should be brought out in a pupil-teacher conference that a child likes especially sea stories, for example, he might be guided in finding other titles to add to his list of such stories.

For children who need further practice in blending different consonants with phonograms as a means of independent identification of words in reading, the disk device pictured in Figure 13–9 may be interesting, worthwhile, and effective. When the outer disk is rotated around the inner one, each consonant in turn is matched with all the phonograms to make as many meaningful words as children can recognize or identify. Thus, *b* is combined with "ack," "ake," "ad," etc., to make "back," "bake," "bad," etc. It should be noted that from the phonograms presently on the disk, the principles for determining the long and short sounds of the vowels may be derived. After some teacher-guidance

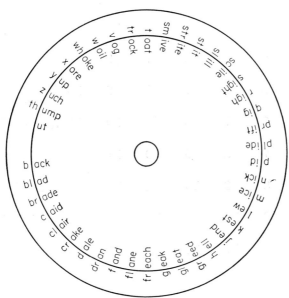

Fig. 13–9. Double cardboard disks fastened together with a wing staple so that the inner disk can be turned on the outer disk to match different consonants with different phonograms; for example, b-ack, b-ad, or b-ake.

of a group in using the device, pupils may be left to compile lists of words independently. As the blending with consonants of one group of phonograms is mastered, a new inner disk with additional phonograms may be substituted. Pupils may pair with classmates for checking their lists and may be checked also occasionally by the teacher.

As a reading-vocabulary-building exercise, pupils may be directed to write (in manuscript style) on small, separate cards all the words they encounter in reading which they cannot identify. Then on scheduled occasions, each pupil brings his cards for presentation, one at a time, to a small group of three or four other teacher-selected children for help in learning them. After hearing his classmates read them and explain *how* they identified them, each pupil studies his own list, placing in one stack the words he recognizes and in another those he still cannot identify. Then, in his turn, he re-presents those he has not yet learned to his small group; and so on. The list of words mastered grows in each practice session; and as each child continues his reading, new words are added to the list of words which each needs to learn to identify. As the teacher supervises individually such groups, she can be especially helpful in teaching children to explain *how* they identify words, so that children learn to become more independent in this skill.

	1	2	3	4	5	6	7	8	9	10
2	3	4	5	6	7	8	9	10	11	12
3	4	5	6	7	8	9	10	11	12	13
4	5	6	7	8	9	10	11	12	13	14
5	6	7	8	9	10	11	12	13	14	15
6	7	8	9	10	11	12	13	14	15	16
7	8	9	10	11	12	13	14	15	16	17
8	9	10	11	12	13	14	15	16	17	18
9	10	11	12	13	14	15	16	17	18	19

Fig. 13–10. Key for checking addition combinations for pairs of digits 1 to 9. (Similar keys can be prepared for differences and products.)

For independent practice in computational skills, a deck of playing cards from which the face cards have been removed may be enjoyed by a pair of children. For example, child A shuffles the cards and deals them in successive pairs to child B, who is expected to add the pair (or, depending upon the skill being practiced, to subtract or multiply them). A keeps a record of B's successes (or errors). B then reshuffles and deals the pack in pairs to A, who also reports the sum, etc., for each combination. Whichever child's score of successes is higher deals again, until his score is equaled or exceeded by that of the other child, who then takes the role of dealer. Thus the practice continues for the period or until the combinations are mastered. As a check on the accuracy of his partner, the dealer can refer to a key, such as is shown in Figure 13–10 for addition.

For individualized instruction in handwriting, a recent sample of each child's handwriting may be analyzed for illegibilities, letter formation, slant, alignment, evenness of lines, spacing, and size. Each child's errors should be encircled. Then, through group instruction for errors common to most of the children and through individualized instruction for particular errors, each child should be shown how to correct his own errors. This instruction should be followed by independent and individually supervised practice and self-checking for correctness. In checking his practice writing, the child should compare it both with the sample containing his encircled errors and with a model of correct writing.

Finally, let us note a suggestion for this type of individualized practice for improvement of skills as applied to spelling. For a week or for a longer period of time, each child's spelling lessons should include the words he has missed in a dictation test of words he will need to know, plus words he has misspelled in his writing. After children have been taught the efficient procedure outlined in Chapter 4, each child, guided by this procedure, studies independently a few words (at each period) from the list of words *he* has misspelled. When he thinks he has learned them, he joins a partner; each then dictates to the other the other's list. Each child then checks his spelling against a correctly spelled list. In this way children, by studying independently and testing themselves in pairs, complete their study of words for the week. When three or four children's own records indicate that they have mastered their complete lists, they may take them to the teacher for a dictation test and checking. The teacher will be able to test three or four children at a time by dictating successively from their separate lists; that is, while the first child is writing his first word, the teacher is dictating the second child's first word; and so on.

The teacher interested in individualized-practice activities will invent many such exercises. Cole, who suggests most of the above devices, has included many more like them in her book [14].

5. Diagnostic and Remedial Teaching. Diagnostic and remedial teaching, as the phrase implies, is individualized teaching based on a diagnosis of a child's strengths and weaknesses as related to his educational objectives. Diagnostic procedures used for this purpose include observation of pupils' classroom performance—reading, oral contributions to class discussions, and behavior in a variety of problem-solving activities; examination of their products—themes and papers in arithmetic, spelling, social studies, etc.; interviewing, in which a child describes his study procedures or "thinks out loud" as he solves arithmetic problems or identifies unfamiliar words in reading; and diagnostic tests of intelligence, of detailed patterns of achievement, and of interests and adjustment. Diagnostic tests, inventories, and rating scales for this and other purposes will be described in Chapter 14.

As a first step in diagnostic testing, a profile of test scores such as is shown in Figure 13–11 may be obtained. The figure reveals that this child of nearly eleven years is only at the 6-to-7-year levels in spelling and reading. But that this marked retardation is not the result of general mental retardation is indicated by the fact that both his mental age and his arithmetic age are equal to his chronological age. Some specific factors have interfered with normal development in spelling and reading. What these specific factors are should be

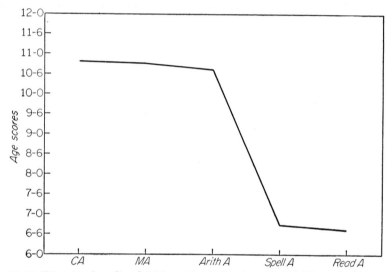

Fɪɢ. 13–11. Educational profile of child age 10-8 in fourth grade (S-B IQ: 100). (*From Kirk, S. A., and G. O. Johnson: Educating the Retarded Child, Houghton Mifflin, Boston, 1951, p. 61.*)

determined by more specific diagnostic achievement testing in reading and spelling, by observation of the child's performance, and by interviewing. Often diagnostic study of such children has revealed faulty methods of approach, with the need for more effective teacher-guidance being indicated.

But a diagnostic study of different children may reveal ineffective application of any one or combination of the seven conditions of effective learning. A child's curriculum may be unsuited to his mental maturity or to his particular pattern of abilities. A phonetic approach in reading, for example, may be unsuited to a child with hearing deficiencies. Practice may be inefficient. A child may continue to make errors because he has not learned how to self-check his problem-solving efforts. He may be poorly motivated. Or, despite otherwise effective and appropriate teaching, emotional disturbances may handicap a child in using his intellectual capacities efficiently.

PRINCIPLES OF REMEDIAL TEACHING. The seven conditions for effective learning, besides being a guide for diagnosis, can also serve as an outline for formulating some general principles of remedial teaching. Every child in serious need of remedial teaching has experienced the frustration of failure. The fourth grade child whose achievement profile is presented in Figure 13–11 has experienced five years of failure in his attempts at learning to read. He may feel inferior and guilty or rebellious. It may be difficult to motivate him to wholehearted effort in reading again. He is likely to be confused about modes of attack. His practice is perhaps perfunctory. And the reading materials provided him at the fourth grade level are very probably beyond his present level of maturity in reading. Remedial instruction for him will consist of a more effective application than previously of all the conditions of effective learning [21, 28].

Sufficient maturity and appropriate pattern of abilities. A child's fear of failure will be confirmed at the outset of remedial reading unless he finds a measure of success in the first lesson. Success will require material at the child's current level of development. The sixth grade child mentioned in Chapter 4 as in need of remedial reading began with third grade material because that was found to be her level. The fourth grade child cited in Figure 13–11 would need material at the first grade level. But because the content for remedial reading needs to be both interesting and also at a relatively low level of difficulty, the use of primary readers written for younger children is unsatisfactory. Reading material about his own interesting experiences, sometimes dictated by him, may be written for a child. Fortunately, however, many books have been written specifically for remedial-reading purposes. Smith [76] has prepared a bibliography of books and pamphlets covering a variety of interests and maturity levels but with vocabulary levels one to five years below the age levels of interest.

Teacher-guidance. Effective remedial teacher-guidance is based on a thorough understanding of the processes of learning reading, arithmetic, spelling, speech, or whatever the subject in which a child needs remedial instruction. It is also based upon a careful analysis of the child's current modes of approach, as determined by hearing him read or by listening as he "thinks out loud" his mode of attack in solving problems. In helping a child substitute effective, systematic procedures in which he can feel confident for confused and ineffective work methods, the teacher applies the general principles of teacher-guidance explained in Chapter 4.

Practice. The time allowance for practice in remedial reading needs to be generous. But it should not be an "extra" activity which deprives the child of recess play or requires him to remain in school after other children have left. Remedial instruction should be arranged as an important part of the school program. It should involve both individual and group activities, including projects, library visits, independent study, teacher-guided study, and check-up activities. Exercises should be repeated for new purposes—to discover new concepts or to improve skills—and reviews should be varied. It is especially important in remedial teaching to distribute practice to avoid fatigue and anxiety. Several short periods in which specific goals are accomplished are better than long periods. The remedial instruction should be continued long enough to habituate the pupil to the improved techniques.

Perception of effects of trials. As in other instruction, a child's progress in remedial instruction will depend upon detecting and correcting his errors. For this purpose, both teacher-checking and pupil self-checking exercises are helpful.

Transfer. Reteaching to correct errors should always emphasize general principles, so that the teaching will correct not merely a specific error but all such errors. For example, if a child makes a mistake in multiplication, such as $90 \times 32 = 272$, he is taught the place value of units, tens, and hundreds and the meaning of zero in a way which proceeds from the concrete to the abstract. To illustrate: The teacher writes $24 \times 10 = $ on the board. He asks 10 children to stand in a row to demonstrate the problem. Then he asks how many sticks each of the 10 children should hold. The answer is two packs of ten sticks and four single sticks. The product is checked by having the children put all their sticks together for counting. How many sticks in all? Forty sticks are found. How many tens can be made from 40 ones? Four tens. Then all the tens are counted. Twenty-four tens in all are found. How many hundreds in 24 tens? Two hundreds and four tens are found. These are placed in the pockets of the number chart showing units, tens, hundreds, etc. Then the example is done abstractly. The concept of zero may also be demonstrated by giving a child no sticks four times and then asking him how many he has. This is then compared with giving him one stick four times [37].

$$
\begin{array}{r}
24 \\
\times 10 \\
\hline
40 \\
200 \\
\hline
240
\end{array}
\quad
\begin{array}{l}
\text{(10 times 4 ones)} \\
\text{(10 times 2 tens)}
\end{array}
$$

Motivation. Harris thinks that successful remedial reading is fundamentally a problem of arousing and sustaining motivation [36]. Since children needing remedial instruction have become accustomed to expect failure, success at the outset must be assured. And as the child continues, his progress should be made clearly apparent to him. The instructional materials should be highly interesting. The skills mastered should be put to worthwhile use in activities important to the child. The child should feel that his teacher thoroughly accepts him, is interested in him, enjoys with him his successes, and is tolerant of his difficulties. Moreover, the remedial-teaching activities should be pleasant and enjoyable.

Freedom from emotional disturbance. The previous failures of children who need remedial instruction have often led to anxiety, feelings of inferiority, and guilt [18]. These unhealthy feelings and self-concepts must be replaced by feelings of security, self-respect, and confidence. Dolch [21, 22] suggests that this is accomplished by cultivating a friendly, happy pupil-teacher relationship; by substituting systematic for confused modes of approach; by finding an area for beginning in which, because of his ability or already acquired skill, the child can feel confident; and by utilizing in each new step previously established areas of confidence. Most of the principles of treatment of emotional problems discussed in Chapter 9 are applicable to remedial teaching.

EXPERIMENTAL EVALUATIONS OF DIAGNOSTIC AND REMEDIAL TEACHING. Several experimental evaluations of teaching based on diagnoses of pupils' specific learning needs have shown it to be effective. Bond and Fay [9], after a thorough diagnosis of each of 23 children's reading difficulties, taught each child to substitute systematic and efficient word-identification techniques for his uncertain and faulty procedures, adjusted the reading materials to his level of maturity, improved his motivation, and corrected his negative attitudes toward school and reading. Over a five-week period of remedial teaching, this group made an average gain of five months. The gain expected on the basis of their past experience was only one month. Fogler [27] reports the experience of two regular teachers with special training in remedial reading who were assigned for one or two hours per day for six months to diagnostic and remedial teaching of 17 children who were retarded two or more years in reading and whose average IQ was 81. Eleven of the 17 pupils made significant gains in reading. Johnston, Coleman, and Guiler [49] gave fifth grade pupils 18 weeks of remedial instruction individually or in small groups to correct difficulties the pupils experienced as they worked through some systematic, self-administering and self-testing reading-comprehension exercises. While a control group who "pursued their regular work in reading" gained 0.7 school grade on the Iowa Silent Reading Tests, the remedial-reading group gained 1.1 grades.

As examples of the effectiveness of remedial instruction in arithmetic, three studies are cited. Sister Mary Jacqueline reports gains in computation and problem solving for 11 children who, outside of regular class periods, were given remedial instruction based on test results [43]. Using equated groups of children, Guiler and Edwards [34] gave the experimental group two periods (out of each of several five-period weeks) of individualized, remedial instruction in arithmetic, based upon specific difficulties discovered in pretests. Over a 23-week term, the experimental group gained 27.3 per cent, while the control group who pursued the course without diagnostic testing gained 19.3 per cent. And by testing and reteaching to correct errors discovered, Harvey reports [37] a reduction of about 72 per cent in multiplication errors by sixth grade pupils from six months' instruction. As was illustrated in the above discussion of transfer in remedial teaching, in correcting an error, the *general principle* basic to a correct mode of attack was always emphasized.

Davis [19] reports that the pupils in a school who were having most difficulty with spelling were helped by three weeks of individualized, remedial instruction consisting of teaching more efficient modes of attack in learning to spell words and by attempts to improve confidence and attitudes. Weekly pretests and end-tests were given; and during study periods, each child was helped to overcome his particular difficulties.

Grant and Marble [31] discovered from a survey test in handwriting that 54 per cent of 3,500 sixth grade pupils wrote with sufficient skill so as to require no further instruction, except that needed to maintain their proficiencies. They concluded that half of the pupils still in need of further instruction in writing could be helped best by diagnostic and remedial teaching to overcome their particular defects in letter formation, size, spacing, slant, and in other features necessary for legible and efficient writing. The other half would need to have systematic and intensive instruction in the essentials of writing continued beyond the sixth grade.

Teaching based on testing is apparently generally economical. It ensures that pupils are not merely repeating what they already know but are striving to master what they need to learn. Moreover, the principle may be applied to every phase of the curriculum—not just to reading, arithmetic, spelling, and writing. Wolner and Pyle [89] have even improved the pitch discrimination and singing skill of pitch-deficient children by diagnostic and remedial teaching. And Unzicker and Flemming report, from their experience in applying remedial teaching to the improvement of general study habits of children ranging in IQ from 95 to 144, that "an analysis of work during the past three years shows in every instance a gain definitely beyond the progress normally to be expected from regular class instruction" [82, p. 413].

These evaluations of five general procedures—adjusting rate of school progress to rate of mental maturing, homogeneous grouping, intraclass grouping, individualized instruction, and diagnostic and remedial teaching—for meeting the teaching problem of individual differences show that all of them have merit. By using these procedures effectively and appropriately, the teacher will be able to adjust the curriculum and methods of teaching to the individual characteristics and needs of most school children. At the extremes of the intelligence distribution, however, special provisions may be needed for both mentally retarded and intellectually gifted children.

6. *Mentally Retarded Children.* Among the feeble-minded, those below IQ 50 are rarely able to profit from school experience. They require permanent family or institutional care. The approximately 2 per cent of school children at the lower end of the intelligence distribution whose IQs range from 50 to 75 are educable in reading, writing, arithmetic, and unskilled and semiskilled occupations. But they are so limited in self-direction, learn so slowly and with such difficulty, and have such inferior generalizing and problem-solving abilities, that they require special curricula and educational guidance if they are to achieve even up to their limited potentialities. At six years of age, a child whose IQ is 50 has a mental age of only 3-0. He will not be ready to begin first grade reading until he is about 12 years of age, at which time his mental age will be about 6-0. If he enters school at the usual age, he will need to spend the first six years in a prolonged preacademic curriculum [67]. Even if a child's IQ is as high as 75, at six years of age his mental age is only 4-6. Not until he is about eight years old will his mental age be 6, at which level some success with beginning reading should be possible. But even when mentally retarded children reach sufficient mental maturity for learning reading and other academic activities, they often fail.

Kirk and Johnson [55] believe that teachers of regular classes often lack understanding of these mentally retarded children and of their special curricular needs. Moreover, in large classes teachers have insufficient time to give the individualized instruction such children require. Therefore, frustrated in their first attempts to master the usual curriculum for their grade placement, mentally retarded children often come to feel confused, inferior, anxious, and rejected by their teachers, parents, and classmates [46]. One such child, now in the fifth grade and mentally mature enough for reading, can only pretend that she does. Because of her anxiety, she strives excessively to be friendly. Another is often fighting with other children. Still another wanders about her classroom and the school halls, not participating in any activities with her fourth grade classmates; at recess periods she plays with younger children.

One sixth grade boy was found seated in a corner of his classroom where he could not disturb other children; and when the school psychologist asked his teacher for the boy's birth date, she turned to the class and asked, "Class, when is John's birthday?" John was not supposed to know anything.

Studying heterogeneous groups of children in grades 1 through 5 of a school which included one or more mentally handicapped children in each grade, Johnson [46] found the handicapped children often isolated or rejected, and considered by their normal peers as prone to bullying or fighting. Innately handicapped in possibilities for school achievement at the outset, the mentally retarded face the hazard that they will develop defensive reactions to the early frustrations they meet which will interfere with efficient use of the limited

CA	IQ	MA	Grade	Reading	Arith.	Spelling	Writing	Geog.	Language
13			VIII						
12			VII						
11	80		VI						
10			V						
9		9-1	IV						
8			III						
7			II						
6			I						
5			Kgn						

Fig. 13-12. Profile of mental age and achievement grade equivalents for a retarded boy age 11-4. (*From Benda, C. E., in Carmichael, L. (ed.): Manual of Child Psychology, 2d ed., Wiley, New York, 1954, p. 1123.*)

abilities which they do have. As they mature sufficiently for some school learning, emotional disturbances impair their effectiveness.

A case described by Benda [7] illustrates this hazard. According to his mental age of 9-1, this eleven-year-old sixth grade boy's school achievement should be at the third to fourth grade level. Actually, as is shown in Figure 13–12, his achievements in reading, arithmetic, spelling, writing, geography, and language are only at the first and second grade levels.

Because mentally retarded children often fail to achieve even up to their limited capacities and also frequently become socially maladjusted in regular classes, experts [42, 55] believe that their educational needs can be met more adequately by specially trained teachers in "special classrooms," which should, however, be located in schools attended also by normal children.

THE SPECIAL CLASS. An ungraded special class for educable mentally retarded children (with IQs ranging from 50 to 75) usually includes from 10 to 15 children ranging in age from 6 to 13 or 14. Most of the children entering at age 6 would need to continue in a preacademic program until ages 8 to 12, at which time they would be mentally mature enough for the academic program. Beginning the academic curriculum at ages 8 to 12, by ages 13 or 14 they should be able to attain second to fourth grade levels of achievement [55].

A typical group of mentally retarded children at the intermediate or "academic" level of a special class is illustrated in Table 13–2. In chronological age, these special class children have a median age of 11-5, which approximates the age of average children about to begin the sixth grade. Their median mental age of 7-7, however, is nearer the average of unselected children beginning the second grade. When their actual achievements in reading and arithmetic, as indicated by their grade-equivalent scores, are compared with their capacities for learning, as indicated by their mental ages, it appears that these special-class children are achieving in these subjects up to their capacities. And their relative social maturity, as appraised by the Vineland Social Maturity Scale, is slightly higher than their intelligence quotients, which means that their social maturing is slightly in advance of their mental maturing. What should be the educational goals for such children?

Table 13–2. A Typical Intermediate Class for Mentally Retarded Children

Child	CA	S-B MA	S-B IQ	Reading grade	Arithmetic grade	Soc. Mat. G.
1	9-4	6-9	72	2.0	1.9	80
2	9-8	7-2	74	1.5	2.1	68
3	10-1	6-5	64	1.8	1.5	75
4	10-3	7-7	74	2.2	2.5	85
5	10-6	6-4	60	1.6	1.5	71
6	10-9	6-2	57	1.0	1.4	67
7	11-3	7-11	70	1.5	1.8	69
8	11-7	8-11	77	2.9	3.0	87
9	11-9	7-6	64	1.4	2.5	73
10	11-10	8-4	76	3.3	3.7	84
11	12-2	6-10	56	1.0	1.4	74
12	12-8	7-10	62	2.7	3.1	84
13	12-10	8-5	66	1.5	2.1	71
14	13-6	7-10	59	2.5	2.8	68

Source: S. A. Kirk and G. O. Johnson: *Educating the Retarded Child*, Houghton Mifflin, Boston, 1951, p. 181.

EDUCATIONAL GOALS. With suitable training and with some continued casual supervision from social-welfare agencies, these children can be freed from dependence upon institutional care and prepared to make satisfactory economic and social adjustments in their communities [4]. Their education should be focused on helping them to meet independently the specific personal and social needs in their various daily-life activities [25, 42, 55]. (1) Development and maintenance of physical and emotional health, including specific health habits, emotional security, independence, and confidence, should be emphasized. (2) By a program reduced to the minimum essentials in reading [54], spelling [57], manuscript writing [61], arithmetic [70], and taught from the viewpoint of practical solutions to various life-activity needs, these children should attain eventually second to fifth grade levels. (3) Adequate, comfortable, and happy participation in community and family life should be stressed. (4) Wholesome leisure and recreational habits, attitudes, and skills should be developed. (5) The education of these children, especially as it is continued beyond the elementary level from ages of about 14 to 16, should prepare them for unskilled and semiskilled occupations, differentiated in so far as possible according to each child's special talents. As preparation for their working lives, they need to develop pride and satisfaction in efficient work methods, in being dependable, and in getting along happily with fellow workers in whatever job they have. Their occupational preparation should include understanding various workers' roles in society, information about suitable jobs, how to find jobs, preemployment experience, placement, and follow-up guidance to aid them in learning on the job how to improve both their efficiency at work and their social adjustments.

CURRICULUM AND METHODS. As for normal and gifted children, the curriculum for mentally retarded children should include provision both for scheduled, systematic practice of skills and for community-interest-centered projects. The latter should dominate their activities, so that what they learn may be meaningful and so that they may have ample occasions for concrete applications of concepts and skills to situations in their school-created, miniature society. The projects should develop out of real-life experiences—home activities, explorations of the community, a visit to the food market, selecting and preparing foods, caring for children, decorating a room, making a garden, nature explorations, jobs different workmen do, and other interesting and practical activities. They should provide for participation in groups, each child according to his interests, abilities, and needs. A given child may contribute to a group project ideas learned from his simplified reader. Another may express himself in art media. Another child may employ his craft skill in supplying a needed construction. And still another child may report what he has learned from an individual community exploration. All of them will need warm approval and encouragement for their efforts and contributions.

Even though mentally retarded children be homogeneously grouped with respect to IQ (50 to 75), each child is still an individual problem. Diagnostic testing will be helpful in understanding their characteristics and needs. Flexible intraclass grouping and individualized instruction will also be desirable. Because many of these children have experienced serious frustration, attempts to make them feel comfortable, wanted, secure, approved, and successful are highly important. Because, in general, they are most limited in abstract, verbal abilities, a great amount of interesting picture-book material and reading material of simplified vocabulary will be needed. Learning to read a word, for example, may take 10 to 20 times as many repetitions in varied contexts as for the child of average verbal ability. In teaching family, community, health, and work concepts, reading should be supplemented and often replaced by pictorial and auditory presentations and by firsthand experiences. In social studies, for example, projects should lead to interpretations of the child's environment through pictures, films, exhibits, excursions, and dramatized role-playing. Again, in arithmetic, only the most simple and practical concepts should be taught, and in concrete, meaningful situations. Many varied applications of each concept are required for mastery. And applications should be made to the specific situations in which the concepts are likely to be needed by the children. In every field, concepts should be simplified, amount of concrete experiences increased, more detailed explanations given, more varied repetitions provided, and more guidance in generalizing and applying given [24].

In providing suitable curricular experiences for the age range from 6 to about 14, both a preacademic and an academic program are needed, preferably in two separate groups. Kirk and Johnson [55, pp. 175–176] have suggested for the primary, or preacademic, level (ages 6 to 9 or 10) the following aims:

(1) To establish, or re-establish, the confidence of the child in his own abilities by giving particular attention to mental and emotional factors in development.

(2) To develop habits of physical health and safety according to the needs of such children.

(3) To provide parent education so that parents will accept the child for his abilities and his worthwhileness.

(4) To emphasize the importance of social adjustment and social participation, and to achieve the goal of social competency.

(5) To develop language abilities in these children since this is one of their major deficiencies.

(6) To develop quantitative concepts at the pre-arithmetic level.

(7) To develop better thinking ability through special guidance.

(8) To develop visual perception abilities as a preparation for reading activities.

(9) To develop auditory abilities as preparation for reading activities.

(10) To facilitate the use of their muscles for better coordination.

(11) To develop more adequate speech.

(12) To develop, in general, habits and attitudes of work which will permit them to obtain maximum benefits from group participation in the classroom.

For the intermediate, or academic, level (ages 10 to 13 or 14), Kirk and Johnson propose two major areas of study: (1) the skill subjects, up to second to fourth grade levels by age 13 or 14, and (2) experience units in daily-life activities. The experience units should aid the child in (1) adjusting to his physical environment—home, school, police department, fire department, businesses, industries, farms, neighborhood, community, transportation, etc.; (2) adjusting to his social environment—working with others and being tolerant, honest, friendly, and constructive in various areas of activity; and (3) healthy personal adjustments—personal habits, cleanliness, posture, healthful dress, care of body, exercise, preparation of healthful foods, safety, etc.

RESULTS OF SPECIAL-CLASS EDUCATION. Several investigators have indicated that the limited and specific goals set for mentally retarded children are attainable in special education programs. Featherstone [25] has reported that "project teaching," supplemented by individualized teaching of reading, arithmetic, spelling, and writing, results in satisfactory progress in these subjects and also produces desirable personality changes. She observed changes in children from "insecurity, fear, futility, pre-delinquency, truancy, inferiority" to "security, self-assurance, cooperativeness, dependability, optimism." Janes [44] has reported on the progress in reading of children with IQs of from 50 to 80 who were transferred from regular to special classes. Five teaching principles guided their teachers: (1) new words presented should be paced more slowly; (2) reading time should be increased; (3) motivation should be enhanced by providing a greater variety of reading materials at suitable levels of difficulty; (4) assignments should be shortened to avoid waning motivation and fatigue; and (5) the material selected should be about actions and incidents familiar to the child through experience and pictures. The *rate* of progress of these mentally retarded children (averaging during one year from 8 to 10 months of gain in reading age) was beyond that expected for their maturity level. This progress, however, was a matter of making up relatively rapidly retardation in reading previously accumulated. "No child exceeded the grade level expected for his mental age but all made progress within the range of the child's known ability" [44, p. 53].

Despite these reports of better educational results from special-class instruction of the mentally retarded, some writers believe that, where the classes are not too large, teachers of regular classes have available effective resources for educating them. Stevens and Stevens [78] believe that rural schools with small enrollments can, by intraclass grouping and individualized instruction and by effective use of their school and community environmental resources, achieve the previously mentioned educational goals for mentally retarded children.

7. *Gifted Children*. According to the criterion of *general* capacity for learning and problem solving, gifted children include the highest 1 or 2 per cent of the intelligence distribution. In IQ, they equal or exceed 130 or 140, depending upon the specific standard applied in a given selection of gifted children [40, 41, and 80]. Often, however, the criteria for selection of "gifted" children are broadened to include those exhibiting special talents in specific areas, such as arts, music, crafts, mechanics, science, social relations, leadership, and organizing abilities [87].

CHARACTERISTICS. Carroll has observed that gifted children are distinguished by their intellectual power, alertness, keenness in observing, curiosity, and insight into complex relationships [13]. Besides being extremely superior throughout their lives [13, 79] in abstract intellectual activities, these children have been characterized by Terman and Oden [80] as (1) slightly above average physically; (2) having relatively advanced play interests, according to developmental norms; (3) equaling the norm in physical-activity interests and being superior in social and intellectual interests; (4) participating normally in such social organizations as scouting, Sunday school, and group athletics and enjoying both indoor and outdoor recreation; and (5) superior in both healthy-personality and ethical-character traits. On school-achievement tests, such children exceed their age norms by 44 per cent, being especially superior in reading, language, arithmetical reasoning, science, literature, and arts [60 and 80]. Typically, they have high educational and professional aspirations [10]. Because success in school comes so easily, however, they may not always learn to work efficiently.

These potentialities of intellectually gifted children are manifest early in their lives. In administering the S-B intelligence scale to gifted children (IQs of 130 to 168) ages 3 to 9, Hildreth reports that favorable notations of intellectual, personality, and character traits were made five times as frequently as they were for children whose IQs averaged 115. The notes indicate that "the gifted group were superior to the control group in energy, physique, language, information, judgment, reasoning, sense of humor, and willingness to face difficulties. They fatigued less quickly than the control, had more experiences to relate, showed more skill and proficiency in the arts, were more active and vivacious, more independent and self-assured" [40, p. 309].

NEEDS FOR DEVELOPING POTENTIALITIES. In every field of useful work—agriculture, industry, the sciences, literature, music, arts, education, medicine, social relations, government—society needs the creative services of its most gifted leaders. Intellectually gifted children in whom there are also developed the drive to achieve, healthy personalities, and attitudes of social interest and responsibility are society's greatest potential leaders. Therefore, as Lorge says, "society should make good use of the developed abilities of its most superior members" [62]. But it is also important from the point of view of the gifted children themselves that they develop their talents to the fullest extent, as it is for children of every other level of ability. For as May has said, a person's most profound joy comes from fulfilling as completely as possible his potentialities.

IDENTIFICATION. For full development of the potentialities of gifted children, it is necessary that they be given, from kindergarten through college, the guidance, education, and other environmental opportunities suited to the development of their talents. It has been found that gifted children develop more frequently into successful adults if they are recognized and encouraged early in childhood by appreciative parents or teachers [79, 87]. It is, therefore, important to identify the potentially gifted as early in their lives as possible. Perhaps the best single device for identifying the intellectually gifted is the individual intelligence test. But group tests of general intelligence and of primary mental abilities are also useful. For identifying children's special talents in art, music, crafts, mechanics, etc., specific aptitude tests are helpful; but at present they are limited in scope and in practical value.

Teachers can supplement psychological testing by being alert to indications of superior general ability and of special talents in profiles of achievement tests and as manifest in pupils' demonstration of initiative, interest, creative contributions, and leadership in various school activities. In this connection, Lally and La Brant [58] have suggested that talents in such areas as art are best indicated by sustained interest, perseverance of effort, exorbitant expenditure of energy on a creative project, sensitivity to artistic situations, ability to combine many elements in creative productions, and tendency to collect and remember more effectively perceptual experiences. Finally as an aid in identifying potentially gifted children, parents' reports are also worth heeding. Reports of a child's quick understanding, insatiable curiosity, extensive information, retentive memory, large vocabulary, unusual and wide interests, and early development of reading and other skills are indicative of superior ability [87].

GOALS. As for every child, the educational goal for the gifted child is the fullest possible development of his talents—for his own happiness and for society's welfare. But especially for the gifted child, capacities for initiative, independence, originality, and creative self-expression need to be cultivated.

FIG. 13–13. Gifted children's abilities and interests in experimenting especially need to be nurtured. (*Courtesy of Whittier School, Utah State Agricultural College.*)

His abilities "to plan, to discover, and to invent" [33] need to be nurtured and related to a simultaneously developed interest in his society and its advancement. He needs to learn to think, to discuss, and to work in leadership and cooperative roles with associates of varied levels and patterns of abilities. Because of his ability to learn at least twice as fast as children of average intelligence, he needs to learn more—to develop diversified, many-sided, and well-rounded interests. But he also needs to go deeply into ideas and projects. He needs to learn efficient habits of study and work and to take pride in superior workmanship, in constructive achievement, and in creative contributions. And besides these intellectual and social traits, if he is to realize his capacities, he also needs to develop a drive to achieve and a healthy personality.

CURRICULUM. Even though some acceleration of school progress for gifted children would partially challenge their extraordinary learning and problem-solving capacities, it would not provide for achieving the uniquely valuable goals of which they are capable. These special goals can be achieved only by a greatly enriched curriculum [10, 12, 13, 33, 41, 51, 62, 69, 80, 88]. Allowing half the school day for gifted children to master the fundamental skills, the

Fig. 13–14. Planning and working together on such projects as a class play provide both for creative expression of varied talents and interests and for satisfying social contributions. (*Courtesy of McGraw-Hill Text-Film Department.*)

other half is available for added experiences. What experiences would be most valuable for these gifted children and for their society? Hollingworth, as the pioneer thinker on the nature of an enriched curriculum for gifted children [41], proposed that it should utilize their superior creative abilities and orient them to thinking about society's need for creative services and contributions. As meeting these criteria, she suggested study of (1) the evolution of common things—food, shelter, clothing, transportation, sanitation and health, trade, timekeeping, illumination, tools and implements, communication, law, government, education, warfare, punishment, labor, recreation; (2) biographies of creative persons; (3) foreign languages; (4) science of nutrition; (5) general science; (6) music and art; (7) crafts; and (8) games of intellectual skill. Several writers have accepted Hollingworth's general proposals and have suggested the following further enrichments for attaining the educational goals for gifted children:

1. Scientific and thorough explorations of the environment, including trees, animals, flowers, zoological and botanical gardens, industrial processes, museums, legislatures, and places of historical interest [10, 13, 51, 80].

FIG. 13–15. Children's special talents and interests are enhanced in learning to understand and operate the school's varied equipment. (*Courtesy of Dilworth School, Salt Lake City.*)

2. Experimenting and exploring in science, constructing models to illustrate the evolution of common things, organizing material and contributing to projects, and writing comprehensive research reports [10, 13, 33].

3. Taking differentiated assignments in class projects suited to special talents and interests, including reading extensive collateral sources for greater understanding and deeper penetration, using mature references, making special reports, and preparing special scientific demonstrations [10, 12, 33].

4. Encouraging intensive creative work in fields of special interest and talent—writing, crafts, art, music, social leadership, science, etc. [74].

5. Encouraging and guiding extensive and varied independent reading, each child according to his interests, from library books, magazines, and newspapers [33, 80].

6. Developing skills in rendering helpful school services, including handling of teaching equipment (projectors, recorder, mimeograph, etc.); creating and maintaining a nature center; preparing illustrations; assisting the principal with school reports; assisting the school nurse with health examinations; etc. [10, 51].

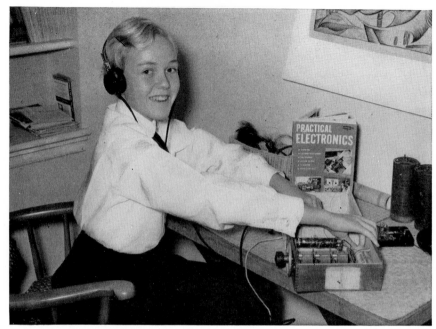

FIG. 13–16. Hobbies foster initiative in creative expression of special talents and interests. (*Courtesy of Herald Journal, Logan, Utah.*)

7. Carrying on hobbies and participation in clubs, including science experiments; construction—a pinhole camera, telegraph set, crystal radio, etc.; photography—taking, developing, printing, and enlarging pictures; collecting —butterflies, minerals, stamps, etc.; studying animals (mammals, reptiles, birds, insects, etc.)—their habits, size, shelter, color, food, number of young, methods of protection, length of life, strength, etc.; plants; gardening; music; art; crafts; dramatics; creative writing; cooking; serving; dancing; athletics; etc. [35, 80].

METHODS. Teaching methods are intimately related to goals and to curriculum. By striving to understand each child both as an individual and as a participant in projects carried on with his group, the teacher helps him in an enriched curriculum to develop as fully as possible efficient, constructive, and creative use of his high intellectual ability and unique talents. The teacher adapts the general methods of teacher-guidance discussed in Chapter 4 to the characteristics and special goals of gifted children. By emphasis on their capacities for initiative and creative achievements, gifted children should be helped to become their own best teachers. As such, they should learn how to learn efficiently. Their learning and problem-solving methods should be characterized by self-recitation, by emphasis upon meanings, by achieving comprehensive views of problems, by carrying concepts to complex and abstract levels, by learning short cuts and the most efficient approaches, and especially by ability to learn from their own self-discovery experiences. They should be encouraged to penetrate more deeply into concepts, to discover interrelations between ideas, and to generalize more broadly. Although gifted children will need their share of teacher-guidance, a part of this guidance should be directed toward helping them become effective in independent use of the rich learning environment described in Chapter 5. In this enriched environment, including both the classroom and the community, they should be encouraged to follow their interests in explorations to find answers to their numerous questions.

There needs to be a shift in emphasis in teaching gifted children from routine practice to consideration of their unique needs. Because of their superior abilities, they will often need fewer practices or varied trials to master skills or to generalize concepts. Rather than being held to every practice exercise in their texts, such as solving every computational example and problem in the arithmetic book, they should be freed for and encouraged to carry their already mastered principles into new and creative applications. They need guidance in learning scientific methods of problem solving and in research-report writing, such as the child's extensive report on Denmark which was described in Chapter 5. It is also especially important that gifted children become proficient in leadership techniques. As an example, Ryan [71] has described a pattern for effective participation in group discussion, including (1) appreciation of the need for a clearly stated goal to guide participants; (2) taking initiative in making and evaluating problem-solving suggestions; (3) listening to others' suggestions, being sensitive to them, and integrating them into one's own thinking; and (4) building on what others have said so that group problem solving is carried forward rather than going off on a tangent, or rather than making only destructive criticisms. (As an example of effective group discussion, see Chapter 14, page 501.)

ORGANIZATION. Each of several administrative provisions for gifted children has its advocates. While recognizing that intellectually superior children learn more rapidly, grasp more complex concepts, exercise more independence and originality, and achieve deeper insights, Seegers [73] believes that they can still participate effectively and profitably in discussions and creative projects suited to a wide range of mental abilities. He believes, therefore, that differentiated participation in projects and individualized teaching in heterogeneous classes is the best provision for gifted children. Johnson [47] also believes that "individual treatment which keeps each child engaged in work suitable to his capacity and related to his interests" can be managed in a regular classroom. Cutts and Moseley [17] have suggested a number of procedures by which teachers of heterogeneous groups can enrich the regular curriculum for gifted children, including choosing them for suitable leadership; encouraging them in independent research work; inviting them to make class reports requiring initiative and creative scholarship; directing them in broader and more mature library reading; encouraging creative effort in writing, art, and science; permitting them to carry on individually or as group leaders projects involving reference reading, interviewing people, experimenting, and constructing; arranging for each child to progress at his own rate in reading, arithmetic, language skills, and writing; encouraging participation in athletics, on the school paper, on the student council, etc.; providing educative tasks aiding the teacher, such as tutoring, mimeographing, etc.; and individualized teacher-guidance.

Terman [80] and other writers already mentioned believe that intellectually gifted children should be accelerated to the extent that they enter college at age 16 or 17. And several writers believe that a special class for gifted children is the best provision for them [13, 41, 62]. Experimental evaluations by Gray and Hollingworth [32] and by Nelson and Carlson [65] of special-class education for gifted children have failed to reveal advantages in tested achievement; but these writers believe that it furnishes a richer background and greater intellectual stimulation. Studying with their intellectual peers, these investigators say, taught these gifted children to "probe more deeply into subject-matter, and to use a many-faceted approach." They acquired research techniques and developed vast intellectual enthusiasm. Witty says that most authorities recommend some acceleration, plus enrichment of the curriculum [87]. But he sees merit, as provisions for gifted children, in (1) acceleration in elementary school up to two full grades; (2) special classes; (3) enrichment and differentiated participation in regular classes; (4) enrichment by extension of experiences in workshops, clubs, and library reading; and (5) individualized guidance [88].

Regardless of the organization for gifted children, enrichment seems very desirable. Among letters collected by Ryan, Strong, and Witty on children's reactions to stimulating teaching in enriched programs, one from a seven-year-old girl suggests the possibilities of developing both enthusiasm for learning and creative expression: "I loved the first grade. We learned so much. We learned to read and to write and do interesting things. Like caring for fish and watching turtles. Planting seeds and watching them grow. We took walks and watched the seasons change. We listened to the sound of the wind and smelled the flowers and leaves. It was a happy year. It was really not like school. It was like living in a make-believe land" [71, p. 110].

Summary

Children can achieve full development and expression of their talents only in a school situation which provides for a wide range and for varied patterns of individual differences. To meet the challenges of providing effectively for individual differences requires of the teacher understanding of individual children and a high level of professional teaching skill. Available to him as procedures and devices are (1) adjusting a child's school progress to his rate of mental maturing, (2) homogeneous grouping, (3) intraclass grouping, (4) individualized instruction, (5) diagnostic and remedial teaching, (6) special curricula and adapted teaching for mentally retarded children, and (7) enriched curricula and stimulating teaching for gifted children. On the basis of a careful appraisal of the physical, social, mental, and achievement characteristics of each child, an appropriate application of one or a combination of these procedures should result in curricular and teaching adjustments suited to each child's needs.

Review and Applications

1. What are the consequences of uniform curricula and methods of teaching for *all* children of the same age? How can *every* child, as he progresses through school, develop his potential talents and achieve a sense of accomplishment, of personal worth, and of confidence?

2. Describe and evaluate as ways of providing for individual differences (*a*) adjusting each child's rate of progress through the grades to his rate of mental maturing, (*b*) ability grouping, (*c*) intraclass grouping, (*d*) individualized teaching, (*e*) diagnostic and remedial teaching, and (*f*) special provisions for slow learners and for gifted children.

3. Outline suitable goals, curricula, teaching procedures, and guidance for (*a*) Harold, (*b*) Irene, and (*c*) Walter. (See page 405.)

4. Teachers believe that making suitable provisions for individual differences among school children is highly important; yet observations in their classrooms often reveal inadequate provisions for such differences. What seem to be the obstacles to achieving this teaching function?

5. Describe, from your observation or reading, examples of excellent provisions for individual differences among school children.

References

1. Adams, J. E., and C. O. Ross: "Is skipping grades a satisfactory method of acceleration?" *Amer. Sch. Bd. J.*, 85: 24–25, 1932.
2. Adams, J. J.: "Achievement and social adjustment of pupils in combination classes enrolling pupils of more than one grade level," *J. Educ. Res.*, 47: 151–155, 1953.
3. Anfinson, R. D.: "School progress and pupil adjustment," *Elem. Sch. J.*, 41: 507–514, 1941.
4. Baller, W. R.: "A study of the present social status of a group of adults who, when they were in elementary schools, were classified as mentally deficient," *Genet. Psychol. Monogr.*, 18(3): 165–244, 1936.
5. Barthelmess, Harriet M., and P. A. Boyer: "An evaluation of ability grouping," *J. Educ. Res.*, 26: 284–294, 1932.
6. Bedoian, V. H.: "Social acceptability and social rejection of underage, at age, and over-age pupils in the sixth grade," *J. Educ. Res.*, 47: 513–520, 1954.
7. Benda, C. E.: "Psychopathology of childhood," in L. Carmichael (ed.): *Manual of Child Psychology*, 2d ed., Copyright, 1954, by Wiley, New York, and used with publisher's permission.
8. Bennett, Erma, Norma Rowan, Florence Kelly, Ruby Schuyler, and W. B. Segar: "Schools can change grouping practices," *Childh. Educ.*, 30: 64–67, 1953.
9. Bond, G. L., and L. C. Fay: "A report of the University of Minnesota reading clinic," *J. Educ. Res.*, 43: 385–390, 1950.
10. Brown, M. V.: "Teaching an intellectually gifted group," *Elem. Sch. J.*, 49: 380–388, 1949.
11. Brueckner, L. J.: "Diagnosis in arithmetic." *Educational Diagnosis*. 34th Yearbook of the Nat. Soc. Stud. Educ., Chicago, Distributed by the University of Chicago Press, 1935.
12. Brumbaugh, Florence: "A school for gifted children," *Childh. Educ.*, 20: 325–327, 1944.
13. Carroll, H. A.: "Intellectually gifted children: Their characteristics and problems," *Teach. Coll. Rec.* 42: 212–227, 1940.
14. Cole, Luella: *The Elementary School Subjects*, Rinehart, New York, 1946.
15. Cook, W. W.: "Individual differences and curriculum practice," *J. Educ. Psychol.*, 39: 141–148, 1948.
16. Cornelius, Ruth: "Reading with six-year-olds," *Childh. Educ.*, 26: 162–163, 1949.
17. Cutts, Norma E., and N. Moseley: "Providing for the bright child in a heterogeneous group," *Educ. Admin. Supervis.*, 39: 225–230, 1953.
18. Dahlberg, C. C., F. Rosewell, and J. Chall: "Psychotherapeutic principles applied to remedial reading," *Elem. Sch. J.*, 53: 211–217, 1952.
19. Davis, G.: "Remedial work in spelling," *Elem. Sch. J.*, 27: 615–626, 1927.
20. DeLong, V. R.: "Primary promotion by reading levels," *Elem. Sch. J.*, 38: 663–671, 1938.

21. Dolch, E. W.: "A remedial-reading specialist in every school," *Elem. Sch. J.*, 41: 206–209, 1940–1941.

22. ———: "Success in remedial reading," *Elem. Engl.*, 30: 133–137, 1953.

23. Edmiston, R. W., and J. G. Benefer: "The relationship between group achievement and range of abilities within the groups," *J. Educ. Res.*, 42: 547–548, 1948–1949.

24. Engel, Anna M.: "The challenge of the slow learning child," *Educ. Lead.*, 11: 151–155, 1953.

25. Featherstone, W. B.: "An experience curriculum for slow learners at public school 500: Speyer School," *Teach. Coll. Rec.* 39: 287–295, 1937–1938.

26. Floyd, C.: "Meeting children's reading needs in the middle grades: A preliminary report," *Elem. Sch. J.*, 55: 99–103, 1954.

27. Fogler, S.: "Remedial reading for selected retarded children," *Elem. Sch. J.*, 51: 22–30, 1950.

28. Gates, A. I.: *Improvement of Reading*, Macmillan, New York, 1947.

29. Glad, D. D.: "Grouping for development," *Childh. Educ.*, 25: 354–356, 1949.

30. Goodlad, J. I.: "Research and theory regarding promotion and nonpromotion," *Elem. Sch. J.*, 53: 150–155, Copyright, 1952, by the University of Chicago. Reprinted by permission of the University of Chicago Press.

31. Grant, A., and M. M. Marble: "Results of Cincinnati handwriting survey," *Sch. Rev.*, 48: 693–696, 1940.

32. Gray, H. A., and Leta S. Hollingworth: "The achievement of gifted children enrolled and not enrolled in special opportunity classes," *J. Educ. Res.*, 24: 255–261, 1931.

33. Gray, W. S.: "Education of the gifted child: With special reference to reading," *Elem. Sch. J.*, 42: 736–744, 1942.

34. Guiler, W. S., and V. Edwards: "An experimental study of instruction in computational arithmetic," *Elem. Sch. J.*, 43: 353–360, 1942–1943.

35. Hahn, Julia L.: "Hobby clubs for children with special gifts," *Educ. Meth.*, 18: 21–26, 1938.

36. Harris, A. J.: "Motivating the poor reader," *Education*, 73: 566–574, 1953.

37. Harvey, Lois F.: "Improving arithmetic skills by testing and reteaching," *Elem. Sch. J.*, 53: 402–409, 1953.

38. Heffernan, Helen: "Each child is a custom job," *Childh. Educ.*, 30: 109–112, 1953.

39. ———: "Grouping pupils for well-rounded growth and development," *Calif. J. Elem. Educ.*, 21: 42–50, 1952.

40. Hildreth, Gertrude H.: "Characteristics of young gifted children," *Pedag. Semin. J. Genet. Psychol.*, 53: 287–311, 1938.

41. Hollingworth, Leta S.: "An enrichment curriculum for rapid learners (130–200 IQ) at public school 500: Speyer School," *Teach. Coll. Rec.* 39: 296–306, 1938.

42. Ingram, Christine P.: *Education of the Slow-learning Child*, Ronald, New York, 1953.

43. Jacqueline, Sister Mary: "An experiment in remedial teaching in arithmetic," *Elem. Sch. J.*, 41: 748–755, 1940–1941.

44. Janes, H. P.: "Is remedial reading effective with slow learners?" *Train. Sch. Bull.*, 50: 51–53, 1953.

45. Johnson, C. E.: "Grouping children for arithmetic instruction," *Arith. Teacher*, 1: 16–20, 1954.

46. Johnson, G. O.: "A study of the social position of mentally handicapped children in the regular grades," *Amer. J. Ment. Def.*, 55: 60–89, 1950.

47. Johnson, G. R.: "Educating bright children," *J. Except. Child.*, 10: 41–44, 1943.

48. Johnson, W. H.: "Program for conserving our superior elementary school students," *Educ. Admin. Supervis.*, 29: 77–86, 1943.

49. Johnston, J. W., J. G. Coleman, and W. S. Guiler: "Improving the reading ability of elementary school pupils," *Elem. Sch. J.*, 42: 105–115, 1941–1942.

50. Jones, Daisy M.: "An experiment in adaptation to individual differences," *J. Educ. Psychol.*, 39: 257–272, 1948.

51. Kellogg, Roberta M.: "Skills instruction for the gifted child in the regular classroom," *Nat. Elem. Principal*, 29: 37–40, 1949.

52. Keys, N.: "Should we accelerate the bright?" *J. Except. Child.*, 8: 248–254, 269, 1942.

53. ———: *The Underage Student in High School and College: Educational and Social Adjustments*, University of California Press, Berkeley, Calif., 1938.

54. Kirk, S. A.: *Teaching Reading to Slow-learning Children*, Houghton Mifflin, Boston, 1940.

55. ———, and G. O. Johnson: *Educating the Retarded Child*, Houghton Mifflin, Boston, 1951.

56. Kottmeyer, W.: "Improving reading instruction in the St. Louis schools," *Elem. Sch. J.*, 45: 33–38, 1944.

57. Kyte, G. C., and V. M. Neel: "A core vocabulary of spelling words," *Elem. Sch. J.*, 54: 29–34, 1953.

58. Lally, Ann, and Lou LaBrant: "Experiences with children talented in the arts," in P. Witty (ed.): *The Gifted Child*, Heath, Boston, 1951.

59. Lampman, Permilla: "Finding the correct reading group for each child in grade II," *Elem. Sch. J.*, 44: 358–360, Copyright, 1944, by University of Chicago. Reprinted by permission of the University of Chicago Press.

60. Lamson, Edna E.: "High school achievement of 56 gifted children," *J. Genet. Psychol.*, 47: 233–238, 1935.

61. Lewry, Marion E.: "Improving manuscript writing in primary grades," *Elem. Sch. J.*, 47: 508–515, 1947.

62. Lorge, I.: "Superior intellectual ability: Its selection, education, and implications," *J. Hered.*, 32: 205–208, 1941.

63. Martens, Elise H.: *Curriculum Adjustments for Gifted Children*, U.S. Office of Education Bulletin 1, 1946.

64. McElwee, Edna W.: "A comparison of the personality traits of 300 accelerated, normal, and retarded children," *J. Educ. Res.*, 26: 31–34, 1932.

65. Nelson, E. A., and E. F. Carlson: "Special education for gifted children, III: Evaluation at the end of three years," *J. Except. Child.*, 12: 6–13, 24, 1945.

66. Parker, J. C., and D. H. Russell: "Ways of providing for individual differences," *Educ. Lead.*, 11: 168–174, 1953.

67. Patterson, Ruth M.: "The curriculum of a prolonged preacademic program," *Amer. J. Ment. Def.*, 51: 666–673, 1947.

68. Pressey, S. L.: "Acceleration and the college student," *Ann. Amer. Acad. Pol. Soc. Sci.*, 231–232: 34–41, 1944.

69. Pritchard, Miriam C.: "The contributions of Leta S. Hollingworth to the study of gifted children," in P. Witty (ed.): *The Gifted Child*, Heath, Boston, 1951.

70. Reed, H. B.: *Psychology of Elementary School Subjects*, Ginn, Boston, 1938.

71. Ryan, W. C., Ruth Strang, and P. Witty: "The teacher of gifted children," in P. Witty (ed.): *The Gifted Child*, Heath, Boston, 1951.

72. Sandin, A. A.: *Social and Emotional Adjustments of Regularly Promoted and Non-promoted Pupils*, Child Development Monographs, no. 32, Teachers College, Columbia University, Bureau of Publications, New York, 1944, pp. ix, 142.

73. Seegers, J. C.: "Teaching bright children," *Elem. Sch. J.*, 49: 511–515, 1949.

74. Sexson, J. A.: "Teaching the gifted child," *Amer. Childh.*, 16: 3–6, 1930.

75. Smith, Dora V.: "Caring for individual differences in the literature class," *Education*, 74: 294–299, 1954.

76. Smith, Nila B.: "Helpful books to use with retarded readers," *Elem. Sch. J.*, 53: 390–397, 1952.

77. Sorenson, H.: *Psychology in Education*, 2d ed., McGraw-Hill, New York, 1948.

78. Stevens, G. D., and H. A. Stevens: "Providing for the education of the mentally handicapped child in the rural school," *Elem. Sch. J.*, 48: 442–446, 1948

79. Terman, L. M., and Melita H. Oden: *Genetic Studies of Genius*, vol. IV, *The Gifted Child Grows Up*, Stanford University Press, Stanford, Calif., Copyright, 1947, by the Board of Trustees of Leland Stanford University, and reprinted with the permission of the author and the publisher.

80. ———: "The Stanford studies of the gifted children," in P. Witty (ed.): *The Gifted Child*, Heath, Boston, 1951.

81. Turner, E., and M. B. Eyre: "A study of the emotional stability in elementary school students in grades four to eight," *Psychol. Bull.*, 37: 595, 1940.

82. Unzicker, Cecilia E., and C. W. Flemming: "Remedial instruction an aid to effective study," *Teach. Coll. Rec.*, 34: 398–413, 1933.

83. Washburne, C. W.: "Adjusting the program to the child," *Educ. Lead.*, 11: 138–147, 1953.

84. Wilkins, W. L.: "High school achievement of accelerated pupils," *Sch. Rev.*, 44: 268–273, 1936.

85. ———: "The social adjustment of accelerated pupils," *Sch. Rev.*, 44: 445–455, 1936.

86. Williams, Margaret: "What are children learning through independent work periods?" *Childh. Educ.*, 31: 183–190, 1954.

87. Witty, P. (ed.): *The Gifted Child*, Heath, Boston, 1951.

88. ———: "What is special about special education? The gifted child," *J. Except. Child.*, 19: 255–259, 1953.

89. Wolner, M., and W. H. Pyle: "An experiment in individual training of pitch-deficient children," *J. Educ. Psychol.*, 24: 602–608, 1933.

90. Worlton, J. T.: "Individualized instruction in reading," *Elem. Sch. J.*, 36: 735–747, 1936.

Chapter 14

Appraising
School Achievement

As was observed in the preface, the important functions of teaching include (1) formulating objec-
tives, (2) choosing appropriate curriculum experiences, (3) giving children
guidance and creating other conditions for effective learning, (4) recognizing
and providing for individual differences, and (5) appraising the outcomes from
learning experiences. Evaluation and measurement of achievement status and
progress in learning are directly or indirectly related to all the other functions.
But the major purpose of evaluation and measurement in each teaching function
is to facilitate learning [6].

The comprehensive outline of elementary school objectives sampled in
Chapter 1 and presented completely in Kearney's report [26] is especially
significant for appraisal[1] of achievement because, besides being *desirable* from
the point of view of philosophical analysis, these objectives are considered to
be *attainable*. Guided by the results of numerous prior evaluation and measurement studies of children, the elementary education and child development
specialists selected these objectives tentatively as appropriate to the primary
and intermediate levels of the elementary school. However, because they are

---

[1] As used in this chapter, "measurement," "evaluation," and "appraisal" all refer to the
appraising of attainment or achievement of both subject-matter and child development objectives, but with some differences in connotations. "Measurement" implies relatively precise
appraisal according to some quantitative dimension or scale. "Evaluation" implies less precise appraisal, and is applied to noting merely the presence or absence of a trait or behavior
pattern, or in noting its presence in only loosely defined degrees. "Evaluation" is applicable
to a wider scope of objectives than is "measurement," and includes appraisal of some of the
so-called "intangible" objectives. "Appraisal" is used as a more general term to include both
"measurement" and "evaluation."

453

described in terms of overt and observable behavior, so that they are susceptible to measurement and evaluation, their appropriateness can be more
precisely established by further appraisal studies. Moreover, in specific learning situations, measurement and evaluation serve to define objectives more
clearly. As Cook observes, children attain most effectively objectives on which
they are tested [6, p. 6]. But appraising achievement facilitates learning also
because of its relation to the other teaching functions.

The scientific selection, organization, and sequential arrangement of suitable
curriculum experiences depend largely upon appraisal of outcomes from experimental trials of different curricula. For example, appraisals of progress in
handwriting have revealed manuscript to be more suitable than cursive writing
for primary level children. A curriculum organized around centers of child
interest has been shown, by measurement of outcomes in mastery of skills,
to be as effective as the traditional subject-matter organization. And measurement has been employed in many studies to determine readiness for learning
different aspects of reading, arithmetic, language, and some other subjects.

As learning is a process of repeated "trial and check," so effective teaching is
a process of testing, teaching, retesting, and reteaching—of constant progress
toward new goals. Evaluation of achievement at each stage of learning reveals
what a child has already learned and what he needs to learn. It permits a continuous adjustment of instruction to the changing achievement status of the
child. Testing motivates learning by providing knowledge of progress. Examinations themselves are effective learning experiences. Properly made tests
require recall, organization of knowledge learned into functional concepts, and
the making of provisional applications of principles. In correcting or in seeing
his corrected test, the child checks his provisional trials, affirms or revises
concepts, and as a consequence, he becomes more effective and confident in
further applications of the concepts or skills he learns.

Measurement also functions in adjusting the curriculum to individual differences in abilities, achievement status, and needs. Flexible rates of grade
progress, intraclass grouping, individualized instruction, and especially diagnostic and remedial teaching all require appraisals of pupil status and progress.

Finally, in this analysis of the purposes of evaluation and measurement, it
should be noted that devices for appraising achievement reveal to teachers, to
school administrators, to parents, and to pupils themselves the extent to which
the educational goals which they have set are being accomplished.

Achieving these purposes of evaluation, however, is not a simple task. In
the first place, appraisal is concerned with the attainment of *significant* objec-

tives which are not always easily tested. Their scope is broad, and mastery of immediate curriculum content is not always equivalent to attainment of significant, ultimate objectives.

Measurement and Evaluation in Relation to Scope of Objectives

It will be recalled from Chapter 1 that elementary school objectives include knowledge and understandings, skills and competencies, attitudes and interests, and action patterns in nine curriculum areas: (1) physical development and health, (2) individual social and emotional development, (3) ethical behavior and values, (4) social relations, (5) the social world, (6) the natural environment, (7) aesthetic development, (8) communication, and (9) quantitative relationships [26]. As was illustrated by the fifth grade diet experiment, any curriculum project is likely to contribute toward attainment of a variety of these objectives. In appraising the extent of their achievement, several different evaluation and measurement procedures are likely to be required.

Referring again to the diet project, *knowledge* and *understanding*, such as "food combinations required for a wholesome meal,"[1] can be measured by the familiar information tests, either teacher-made or commercially prepared. Such tests might include such items as: "On one day a child has eaten bread and butter, meat, orange juice, potatoes, spinach, and applesauce. In order to balance his diet by including some food from each of the 'seven basic food groups,' he should also eat _____." Attainment of such an objective as strengthened "*habits* of eating wholesome food" [italics supplied], however, might be better evaluated by observing a child's behavior in the school cafeteria or by asking his parents about his eating habits in a parent-teacher conference. "Interest and pride in his physical growth and development, health and strength" might be evaluated by parent-teacher conferences, by teacher-pupil interviews, by an accumulation of behavior anecdotes, or by a self-inventory. "Social and emotional development" objectives, such as "volunteering to assume responsibilities and to carry them out," could be evaluated by pupil sociograms, by observation and anecdotal records, or by a rating scale. These same devices would be appropriate for evaluating such ethical-behavior objectives as "ethical values strengthened through satisfying acts of cooperating, sharing, taking responsibility, and subordinating self-interest in working with

---

[1] The objectives quoted in this chapter are from N. C. Kearney: *Elementary School Objectives*, Russell Sage, New York, 1953.

others." Such social-skills objectives as "leadership of a group or being a co-operative member of peer groups" and such characteristics as "being a courteous speaker or listener" could be evaluated by observation, by sociograms, or by a participation chart. Such science skills as "observing accurately and describing carefully the results of individual investigations" could be appraised by examining as "child products" children's notes and papers reporting their experiments. Such quantitative skills as "measuring, weighing, constructing and reading graphs" could be measured by tests of actual performance. The appropriate appraisal of several other objectives attained in the diet project could be suggested. But from this partial analysis of the problem, it is probably apparent that the appraisal of *all* the objectives will require a variety of evaluation and measurement devices. Because appraisal of objectives affects so markedly the learning effort directed toward their attainment, it is highly desirable that the degree of attainment of *all* types of significant objectives be evaluated. If attainment of only *certain* objectives is appraised, learning effort may be diverted from other, even more worthwhile objectives.

As a means of estimating, among the practical and available devices, those which might be useful in appraising *all* the elementary school objectives, the author has matched a list of appraisal devices against Kearney's list of objectives [26]. As the author studied each objective in the list, he considered which appraisal device or devices would be suitable for evaluating or measuring its attainment. The results of this subjective analysis are presented in Table 14–1. As is indicated in this table, each of the 15 different appraisal devices is considered appropriate for evaluating some objectives. Teacher observation is useful in appraising attainment of knowledge, skills, attitudes and interests, and action patterns in every curriculum area. Survey, separate-subject, diagnostic, and teacher-made tests are mainly considered appropriate for measuring knowledge and understandings. Attitudes and interests and some action patterns may often be appraised by inventories and rating scales. Social-behavior objectives can often be appraised by these same devices plus the sociogram. The parent-teacher conference appears useful especially for appraising action patterns.

Thus it appears that some devices are applicable over a wide scope of objectives, while others are especially useful for appraising certain outcomes. For effective appraisal of all the elementary school objectives, teachers need to learn the uses, merits, and limitations of all these devices. In the next section the general characteristics of good evaluation procedures will be discussed, and in the following sections each device will be described and evaluated separately.

Table 14–1. Procedures for Appraising Attainment of Elementary
School Objectives

Area and objective	Survey tests (1)	Subject tests (2)	Diagnostic tests (3)	Teacher-made tests (4)	Observation (5)	Child products (6)	Teacher-pupil interviews (7)	Anecdotal records (8)	Rating scales, check lists (9)	Sociograms (10)	Participation charts (11)	Self-inventories (12)	Performance tests (13)	Parent-teacher conferences (14)	Cumulative records (15)
1. Health															
(a) Knowledge	x	x		x	x										
(b) Skills									x				x	x	
(c) Att.'s & interests					x		x				x	x			
(d) Actions					x				x					x	X
2. Social & emotional															
(a) Knowledge	x				x							x		x	
(b) Skills					x		x							x	
(c) Att.'s & interests					x		x		x	x		x		x	x
(d) Actions					x		x	x	x	x				x	x
3. Ethical															
(a) Knowledge	x			x	x							x			
(b) Skills					x		x		x		x			x	
(c) Att.'s & interests					x		x		x					x	
(d) Actions					x			x	x		x				
4. Social relations															
(a) Knowledge	x			x	x							x		x	
(b) Skills					x				x	x	x	x	x		
(c) Att.'s & interests					x				x		x			x	
(d) Actions					x				x	x	x	x	x	x	x
5. Social world															
(a) Knowledge	x	x	x	x	x										
(b) Skills	x	x	x	x	x				x		x		x		

Table 14–1. Procedures for Appraising Attainment of Elementary
School Objectives (*Continued*)

Area and objective	Survey tests (1)	Subject tests (2)	Diagnostic tests (3)	Teacher-made tests (4)	Observation (5)	Child products (6)	Teacher-pupil interviews (7)	Anecdotal records (8)	Rating scales, check lists (9)	Sociograms (10)	Participation charts (11)	Self-inventories (12)	Performance tests (13)	Parent-teacher conferences (14)	Cumulative records (15)
(c) Att.'s & interests	x				x			x	x	x		x			
(d) Actions					x				x	x		x	x	x	x
6. Natural environment															
(a) Knowledge	x	x	x	x	x	x			x				x		
(b) Skills	x	x	x	x	x	x							x	x	
(c) Att.'s & interests					x	x		x	x			x			x
(d) Actions					x	x		x	x			x	x	x	x
7. Asthetic															
(a) Knowledge	x				x	x							x		
(b) Skills	x				x	x		x	x				x		
(c) Att.'s & interests					x			x	x			x			
(d) Actions						x			x			x		x	
8. Communication															
(a) Knowledge	x	x	x	x	x										
(b) Skills	x	x	x	x	x	x	x	x					x		
(c) Att.'s & interests					x				x			x			
(d) Actions					x	x			x		x				
9. Quantitative															
(a) Knowledge	x	x	x	x	x		x								
(b) Skills	x	x	x	x	x		x								
(c) Att.'s & interests												x			
(d) Actions					x							x			

General Characteristics of Good Measuring and Evaluating Devices

Good devices for evaluating and measuring school achievement should be valid, reliable, useful in facilitating learning, and efficient.

1. Validity. Tests are said to be valid to the extent that they measure what they are intended to measure. Procedures for evaluating and measuring school achievement should, therefore, appraise attainment of significant educational objectives. They are valid to the extent that they accomplish this purpose. The desirable educational objectives for elementary school children have been very carefully selected and formulated [26] as the knowledge and understandings, skills, attitudes and interests, and action patterns which they will need for personally satisfying and socially valuable participation in their society. Valid tests for elementary school children should measure attainment of these particular and significant objectives. They sometimes fail to do so, however.

Consider, for example, for the "health" part of an elementary survey test, such an item as: "Carbohydrate is a (1) food nutrient, (2) drug, (3) body fluid, (4) waste product." Would this item contribute validity to a test intended to measure *useful* understandings and knowledge of personal health? As a health objective, children need at the elementary level knowledge of the "food combinations for a wholesome meal" [26], and pertinent knowledge about carbohydrates would probably contribute toward fulfilling such an aim. But the facts tested in this item are too remote from this objective. Facts selected for testing should be relevant to important and useful general concepts or principles which can be applied as guides to effective action, to the solution of important personal and social problems, or in facilitating further learning [29]. To return to the illustration, children *can* use in selecting food for a wholesome meal knowledge of the role of carbohydrates in body nutrition. Such a test item as: "The most important food nutrient for quick body energy is (1) protein, (2) carbohydrates, (3) fats, (4) vitamins," would measure such knowledge. And to test children's understandings of *how* to select carbohydrates for their diets, the following item would be appropriate: "An example of a food rich in carbohydrates is (1) meat, (2) cheese, (3) bread, (4) butter." The item first proposed for the health section of the survey test, however, does not appear to be so specifically valid. It is difficult to conceive how a child might make significant use of his knowledge that carbohydrate is not a drug, a body fluid, or a waste product. And merely knowing that it is a food is too indefinite to be helpful.

There are two practical approaches to selecting or preparing valid tests of achievement. Guided by a statement of the significant objectives in the course or unit for which achievement is to be appraised, the teacher may select or construct a test whose items match an adequate and comprehensive sample of these objectives. A test which fails to cover several objectives in the unit or course which *should* be appraised or which measures many objectives which are irrelevant to the course or unit is not likely to be valid. A second approach to determining test validity requires that the teacher already have one valid measure of the area of achievement to be appraised. If a newly purchased or constructed test correlates fairly high with this valid measure of achievement in the area, the new test may then also be assumed to be a valid measure of the same pupil accomplishment.

2. *Reliability.* Reliability as a feature of a good test refers to the test's self-consistency—to the degree to which the test agrees with itself. A reliable test is comprised of an adequate sample of clear, unambiguous items for which both child performance and scoring are free from irrelevant factors. Such a test should accurately represent a child's ability in the function measured. Scores on retests of the same trait should not fluctuate outside the limits of a reasonable error of measurement, except to indicate real changes which may have occurred between testings in the trait being reappraised. Correlations between test and retest scores for a single age or grade group in reliable tests of knowledge and skills in elementary school subjects should range from .85 to .95 [35], just as they do for reliable intelligence tests. The reliability of achievement tests may be determined by test-retest correlations, by correlating odd against even items of the test, or by determining the correlation between two forms of the test.

If a test samples only a very limited section of the area it is intended to measure, scores on it are likely to be unreliable. For example, if a child who knows only how to add fractions when they have common denominators is given two 10-item fraction tests, one containing only three and the other six items with common denominators, his scores on the two tests are likely to be inconsistent. Reliable tests sample adequately *all* the objectives in the area covered by the test. An example of a test meeting this criterion well is Harap and Mapes's test for understanding fractions at the fifth grade level [22]. An analysis of the concepts of fractions to be taught in their activity curriculum revealed 14 different concepts, from "finding a fractional part of an integer, using unit fractions only" (such as $\frac{1}{4}$ of 12) up to "dividing a mixed number by a mixed number," (such as $30\frac{5}{6} \div 3\frac{1}{2}$). Their test covered all 14 concepts. Reliability was further assured by formulating three problems for each concept, thus avoiding an undue influence on the scores of computational errors. Success on two of the three problems was considered indicative of mastery of the concept.

The attention to the possible influence of computational errors on a test to measure understanding of fraction concepts also illustrates the attempt to improve reliability by control of irrelevant factors which might influence performance. Some problem-solving tests in arithmetic eliminate the influence of computational skill by not requiring computations; instead, they merely ask the children to indicate the *processes* for solving a set of problems. Essay tests are often unreliable because of the effect both on the performance and on the scoring of the function being measured of irrelevant variations in legibility and speed of handwriting or in effectiveness of expression [34, p. 57]. Objective tests constitute an attempt to eliminate this source of unreliability. Essay questions are also often faulty in being ambiguous—in failing to indicate clearly what is wanted. According to this criterion, the item: "Discuss food combinations for wholesome meals," is probably less reliable than: "Using the chart of 'seven basic foods,' plan a well-balanced diet for the three meals of a day." The second item is clearer, of course, because it explicitly states the point of view and the background of information from which it is expected that the question will be answered. But reliable objective-test items also require very great care in their formulation. Otherwise an unintended interpretation of a question, rather than lack of knowledge, may elicit "wrong" answers from some children on some occasions.

3. *Utility in Facilitating Learning.* As has already been suggested, tests facilitate pupil learning primarily when they direct attention to significant objectives. But there are also other test features which facilitate learning. Harap and Mapes's test of fractions, because it indicated for each pupil his *extent of mastery* of computations with fractions, was an effective guide to economical pupil learning effort. If a child's score at the end of the term indicated that 12 of the 14 concepts were now mastered, whereas on the pretest his score had been only 4, he knew he had made progress. He also found that he had two more concepts to master. And he knew from the test results which particular concepts he needed to study in order to complete his mastery of the topic.

Extent of progress made over a term or a year may be even more meaningfully indicated by converting pretest and end-test scores into age or grade equivalents. It was by such a device that the relatively rapid rate of progress of gifted children was indicated. Tests which yield profiles of scores (such as is illustrated in Figure 14–1, page 463) are especially useful in pupil guidance. Tests are also more useful if the items are classified to indicate specific strengths and weaknesses, as a guide to what children need to learn next, and for use in diagnostic and remedial teaching. Such tests are, of course, most useful in guiding learning when pupils have an opportunity to see their corrected tests relatively soon after taking them.

4. Efficiency. The three features of good tests just discussed contribute to their efficiency in facilitating learning. In addition, such features as ease of administration, economy of time in scoring, and meaningful presentation of derived scores all contribute to their efficiency.

In summary, good achievement tests should appraise attainment of significant objectives, measure them consistently, yield results which contribute to effective and worthwhile learning, and be economical of the time and effort of pupils and teachers. These concepts will be further illustrated as they are applied in describing and analyzing the 15 different types of appraisal device required in measuring and evaluating the attainment of elementary school objectives.

Survey Tests of School Achievement

For measuring attainment of general knowledge and understandings, skills and competencies, and (to a limited extent) attitudes in several curriculum areas of the elementary school, there are available several standardized survey tests [20, pp. 564–581]. These tests usually include, in one battery, subtests of language, reading, spelling, arithmetic, social studies, natural science, health, and some study skills, such as map and chart reading and use of dictionaries and references. Such tests yield scores which permit a teacher to determine the status of her particular class in comparison with representative national, state, or school-district norms. By using two or more forms of such tests for testing and retesting, pupil growth in achievement over a term, a year, or a longer period can be appraised. In experimental situations, the relative effects on achievement of variations in curricula or methods of teaching can be evaluated by such tests. Or, a given pupil's achievement status or progress may be evaluated with reference to class or national norms or by comparison with his own previous rate of progress. Perhaps the most distinctive advantage of a survey battery, however, is that, because the several tests have been standardized to yield comparable scores, a profile of the pupil's scores can be plotted to show his relative achievements in different curriculum areas.

In brief examinations of four such tests, general concepts of testing will be further illustrated. These examinations should help the student to become familiar with the specific features of some currently used tests, and he should learn some principles and techniques which he can apply to self-construction of tests as a teacher.

The Stanford Achievement Test. Covering the elementary school, the Stanford Achievement Test is comprised of three batteries: Primary, for grades 1.9 to 3.5; Elementary, for grades 3.0 to 4.9; and Intermediate, for grades 5 and 6 [27]. The five different forms of this test provide unusually well the repeated testing required for studies of growth in achievement. The content areas of the intermediate-level battery are shown in Figure 14–1, which also illustrates the profile interpretation of the several comparable scores of the test.

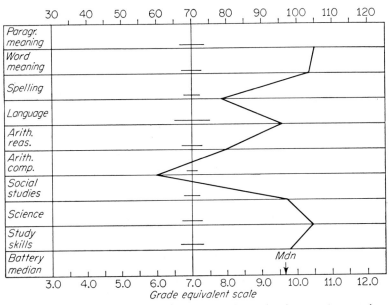

Fig. 14–1. Stanford Achievement Test profile for child age 11-8 about to enter seventh grade.

In their attempt to construct valid tests, the authors of the Stanford Achievement Tests state they have based their items on an examination of current goals, texts, and courses of study and the professional literature on such tests. They further claim to have "recognized the trend toward teaching of meanings or understandings, rather than mere factual knowledge." By allowing pupils ample time for completing them, the tests emphasize power rather than speed. Items were chosen that would measure the achievement of important objectives. But it was sought to have the tests measure *growth* in achievement as well. Items were therefore selected which had been shown by a preliminary tryout to have been passed by significantly increasing percentages of children at successive grade levels. We cite a few typical items from the Elementary

Battery, although they can only suggest how well the tests measure significant objectives.

1. *Reading comprehension* is measured by 50 items on paragraph meaning, such as:

There are three kinds of bees in a hive—the queen bee, the worker bees, and the drones. The queen bee is the mother who lays the eggs. The busy workers gather honey. The _____ do not do any work at all. (Choose the correct word from item 29 to fill the blank.)

29. bees, queens, females, drones

and by 38 items on word meaning, such as:

A customer is one who _____ (plants, works, buys, learns).

2. *Spelling* is measured by a dictation test for which validity is achieved by selecting "words frequent in children's reading and writing." Of the 30 words in the primary test, 26 come from the first 500 words, representative of second and third grade usage, from the Rinsland list.

3. *Language* measurement covers usage, capitalization and punctuation, and sentence structure, using at each level content "suitable to the appropriate grade level." Typical of the alternate-choice items are:

$$\text{Will you} \begin{array}{c} 3 \text{ teach} \\ \\ 4 \text{ learn} \end{array} \text{me to jump rope?}$$

$$\text{Can you come to my} \begin{array}{c} 3 \text{ birthday} \\ \\ 4 \text{ Birthday} \end{array} \text{party on} \begin{array}{c} 5 \text{ saturday} \\ \\ 6 \text{ Saturday} \end{array} \text{at about half past} \begin{array}{c} 1 \text{ twelve} \\ \\ 2 \text{ Twelve} \end{array} ?$$

4. *Arithmetic-reasoning* items include solving verbal problems, understanding concepts, and arithmetical judgments, with hypothetical situations within the experience of pupils and with computational and vocabulary demands kept simple. An example of the 45 items in the elementary test is:

Bob's mother had 7 quarts of ice cream. The boys ate a gallon. How many quarts were left? _____.

5. *Computation* at the elementary level is measured by such problems as these:

$$\begin{array}{cccccc} 60 & 69 & 63 & & \frac{2}{3} & \$ \\ +29 & -67 & \times 14 & 3\overline{)156} & +\frac{1}{3} & 5\overline{)\$4.29} \end{array}$$

6. *Social studies* are measured by informational items considered "crucial" to other desirable outcomes. The authors have tried to achieve a balance between facts of history and geography and facts of community life and civics. Examples of intermediate-level items from each area are:

The "forty-niners" were seeking chiefly (5) free land, (6) gold, (7) adventure, (8) furs.

Midwestern farmers work in the fields least in the (5) spring, (6) summer, (7) fall, (8) winter.

The highest officer of a city is usually the (1) alderman, (2) mayor, (3) chief of police, (4) councilman.

7. *Science* measurement samples life science, earth, conservation, health and safety, and elementary physics and chemistry. Items included test knowledge of facts, discernment of cause-effect relations, ability to draw inferences, and information on conservation and health. An example at the intermediate level is:

For his bones to harden well, a child needs plenty of (5) sugar, (6) starch, (7) fat, (8) calcium.

8. *Study-skills* measurement covers pupils' skills in interpreting charts, tables, and maps; skills in using the dictionary and other references; and ability to draw inferences and to think in quantitative language. The following is an example at the intermediate level:

6. How many papers did Joe sell on Wednesday? (e) 25, (f) 30, (g) 35, (h) 40.

7. How many papers did Joe sell on Tuesday and Wednesday together? (a) 60, (b) 70, (c) 80, (d) 90.

8. On which day did Joe sell 10 more papers than on the day before? (e) Tuesday, (f) Wednesday, (g) Friday, (h) Saturday.

9. On which day did Joe sell 45 papers? (a) Monday, (b) Tuesday, (c) Thursday, (d) Friday.

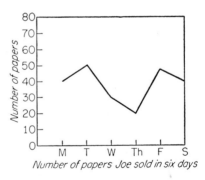

Number of papers Joe sold in six days

As is appropriate, the primary tests are restricted to parts 1, 2, and 4, and they cover only reading, spelling, and arithmetic. The elementary-level battery adds to these three parts the test of language. At the intermediate level, all seven parts are included.

Adequate reliabilities of the separate Stanford Achievement Test subtests are indicated by the correlations between odd and even items presented in Table 14–2, which are based on single grades with populations of from 235 to 298.

Table 14–2. Odd-Even Reliabilities of Stanford Achievement Subtests

Level	Read. paragr. mean.	Word mean.	Spell-ing	Lan-guage	Arith. reas.	Arith. comput.	Social studies	Sci-ence	Study skills
Primary.........	.91	.83	.94	...	.73	.91			
Elementary......	.91	.92	.95	.87	.92	.90			
Intermediate.....	.90	.92	.93	.81	.89	.87	.92	.91	.88

Source: T. L. Kelley et al.: *Stanford Achievement Test, Forms J. K, L, M, N* and Manual, World, Yonkers, N.Y., 1953.

The standard errors of measurement based on these reliabilities and the corresponding standard deviations, at the intermediate level, are shown in the short horizontal lines of the profile in Figure 14–1 (page 463). The lengths of these lines indicate the extent of chance or error variation from test to retest (when there is no appreciable time interval between them) which may be expected in about two-thirds of children's retest grade-equivalent scores. For example, two-thirds of the immediate retests in reading can be expected to vary from the initial test by from 0 up to 0.5 grade.

Perhaps the uses in teaching and guidance of this survey test can be appreciated best by referring again to Figure 14–1. The mid-line above grade equivalent 7.0 indicates that this child is about to begin the seventh grade. These grade equivalents, into which raw scores have been converted, are based on mean scores of 345,736 pupils distributed throughout the grades indicated from 363 representative school systems in 38 states. Compared with these national grade norms, this child's general achievement is very superior. In reading and science she reaches tenth grade norms. In language, social studies, and study skills, she has attained ninth grade levels. And in spelling and arithmetical reasoning, she approximates the eighth grade level. Only in arithmetic computation is her performance below her grade level, being 6.0 rather than 7.0. A diagnostic examination of the arithmetic-computation items indicates that this relatively low score resulted from proceeding too slowly. All items attempted are correct. She needs, therefore, to cultivate greater speed and confidence in this area. But the profile indicates that this child's greatest need is for a challenging and enriched curriculum in varied reading, science, social studies, and language projects. Had another form of this test been used as a pretest, a comparison between beginning- and end-of-year profiles could have shown the growth[1] achieved during the year. And similar profiles of class

[1] A more accurate measurement of growth achieved could be shown by converting the scores to K scales that are approximately equal throughout the entire range. A unit in the K scales is equal to one-seventh of the standard deviation for fifth grade scores [27, p. 14].

mean scores could reveal the relative status and progress of the class as a whole in these curriculum areas.

Concerning the efficiency of this test, it may be observed that directions are clear. Scoring is simplified so that the entire battery may be scored in 7 to 10 minutes per pupil. And scores are readily converted to grade equivalents from a table which appears at the end of each subtest.

In order to illustrate as many test concepts as possible, this test has been reviewed in some detail. For the remainder of our sample of achievement tests, they will be described more briefly.

The Iowa Every-pupil Tests of Basic Skills. In making up a test "designed to measure and evaluate the pupil's functional mastery of a wide variety of critical skills involved in reading, work-study, language, and arithmetic," the authors of the Iowa tests, Bryan thinks, have succeeded very well in sampling "those that are crucial to total educational growth" [4]. Four comparable forms permit measurement of growth over a range of eight years. An examination of the Elementary Battery [37] for grades 3, 4, and 5 will indicate the general nature of this test.

1. The tests on *silent-reading comprehension*, including 59 paragraph-comprehension items and 40 vocabulary items, measure the skills needed for locating and understanding significant details, for organizing ideas, and for appreciating the total meanings of selections read. Following is an example of a paragraph-comprehension item:

When a cowboy died, his horse with its empty saddle was usually led to the grave-yard on the day that the man's body was buried. This custom of the cowboys has led to the building of a strange monument near Dalhart, Texas. On the main road just north of town stands a large stone base with a flat top. On this flat top is a pile of rocks over which rests an empty saddle. Beside the saddle is the head of a cow. On the side are written the letters XIT. This monument was raised in honor of the cowboys now dead who once worked on the famous XIT ranch near Dalhart.

Two of five questions on the paragraph are:

20. What is a good title for this article? (1) Texas Cowboys, (2) The XIT Ranch, (3) An Unusual Monument, (4) Dalhart, Texas.

22. If you went from the monument to Dalhart, in what direction would you go? (1) South, (2) East, (3) West, (4) North, (5) The paragraph does not tell.

Here is an example of a vocabulary item:

Cease playing [means] stop, being, tire of, like.

2. The *work-study-skills* tests include actual work samples of map reading, use of indexes and the dictionary, and alphabetizing and information about use of references.

3. *Basic-language-skills* tests include actual work samples of punctuation and

□ is

capitalization; true-false items on usage ("The marbles □ are large.") and on

R W

sentence sense ("□ □ The big dog."); and a multiple-choice spelling test.

4. *Basic-arithmetic-skills* tests include items on vocabulary and fundamental knowledge ("For what does oz. stand? (1) gallon, (2) foot, (3) point, (4) ounce," or: "In which of these numbers does the 4 stand for four hundred? 849, 2471, 604, 4026."); skills in adding, subtracting, multiplying, and dividing with integers, money, and fractions; and problem solving as applied to a variety of practical situations (for example, given a picture of a fruit stand displaying

nine different fruits with prices marked, | Peaches / 4 for 5¢ | , a typical problem is: "What would 20 peaches cost?").

Intended especially to facilitate learning, the diagnostic possibilities of the test are emphasized, as is indicated in the profile presented in Figure 14–2. Compared with the grade-equivalent norms for this test based on mean scores of 196,851 pupils from the various grades of 350 different school systems, the midyear-test profile for this fifth grade pupil reveals about "average" over-all achievement. He is superior (reaching sixth grade levels) in language and in some related study skills. His weakest skills are in arithmetic—especially in "fundamental knowledge." Compared with the profile for the previous year, except for language—in which he has made a full year or more of growth—his growth has been very limited (in arithmetic and in work-study skills) to moderate (in reading).

Besides the profile for providing diagnostic leads, a further item analysis of each subdivision to determine more specific errors and strengths is suggested. For example, the punctuation subdivision includes use of period, question mark, comma, apostrophe, double quotation marks, and colon. A table in the test manual classifies items into each of these punctuation categories; thus whether a pupil is having difficulties with the period, the question mark, or the comma can be specifically determined. Even the specific nature of comma or period errors are indicated. From such analyses, data in the test booklet for each pupil can lead directly to some remedial instruction.

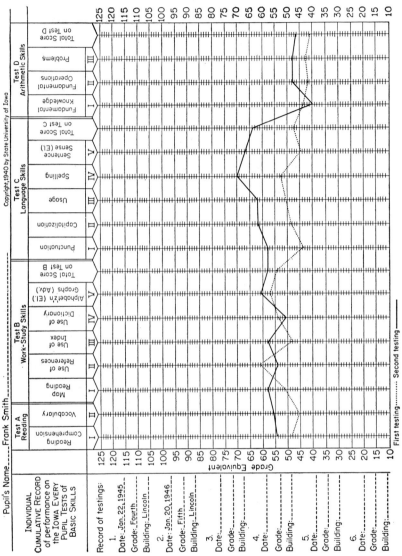

Fig. 14–2. Profile of achievement on the Iowa Every-pupil Test of Basic Skills, showing status, indicating growth, and suggesting diagnostic leads. (From Spitzer, H. F., et al.: Iowa Every-pupil Tests of Basic Skills Manual, Houghton Mifflin, Boston, 1945, p. 12.)

The California Achievement Tests. This series of tests provides continuous measures of growth from grades 1 through 12. Except for the reading part, however, the Primary Battery, for grades 1, 2, and 3, is considered because of its difficulty to be too frustrating for satisfactory use with young children [10]. The Elementary Battery, for grades 4, 5, and 6, will be described here

Tests	Score	G.P.	Grade placement 3.0 4.0 5.0 6.0 7.0 8.0 9.0
Reading vocabulary	79	6.5	
A. Word form	22	4.2	
B. Word recognition	20	7.0	
C. Meaning of opposites	19	7.3	
D. Meaning of similarities	18	7.3	
Reading comprehension	14	4.1	
E. Following directions	5	4.2	
F. Reference skills	2	3.5	
G. Interpretations	7	4.3	
Arithmetic reasoning	24	5.0	
A. Number concepts	5	4.2	
B. Signs and symbols	13	7.0	
C. Problems	6	5.1	
Arithmetic fundamentals	36	5.8	
D. Addition	10	5.3	
E. Subtraction	13	6.3	
F. Multiplication	6	5.5	
G. Division	7	6.0	
English and grammar	27	5.3	
A. Capitalization	9	5.3	
B. Punctuation	3	5.0	
C. Words and sentences	15	5.4	
Spelling	9	4.5	
Total language	36	4.9	
Total test	189	5.4	

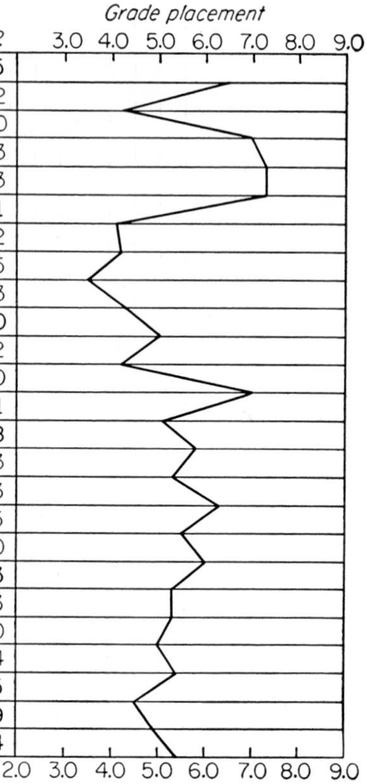

2.0 3.0 4.0 5.0 6.0 7.0 8.0 9.0

Fig. 14–3. California Achievement Tests profile for fifth grade pupil age 10-4; MA: 11-0), (*From Tiegs, E. W., and W. W. Clark Manual, California Achievement Tests, Elementary Battery, California Test Bureau, Los Angeles, 1951, p. 6.*)

[42]. By allowing sufficient time for 90 per cent of the children to finish, "power" rather than "speed" is emphasized. As the profile in Figure 14–3 shows, this test covers reading vocabulary and comprehension, arithmetic reasoning and computations, language, and spelling.

Like those of the Iowa Every-pupil Tests of Basic Skills, the authors have tried to provide diagnostic guidance for facilitating learning by subdividing the major categories of the profile into a total of 18 subcategories. This diagnostic advantage, however, may have been purchased at the cost of unreliable measurement of some significant objectives. For example, while the six basic areas have satisfactory reliabilities, ranging for the fifth grade from .88 to .93, "Interpretations," which is one of three components under "Reading Comprehension," is sampled by only three short paragraphs. In measuring such an important reading objective at the intermediate level, more representative sampling of the child's performance seems desirable. It could have been achieved without lengthening the total test by omitting less important items (such as those on word form) at this level. If this limitation is recognized, however, the test should be useful in facilitating learning, because the range of objectives covered is broad and because often the items test significant understandings in functional form [10]. Scoring of this test is especially economical.

The Coordinated Scales of Attainment. These batteries, including a separate one for each of the grades from 1 to 8, cover spelling, language, reading, social studies, science, literature, arithmetic computation, and arithmetic-problem reasoning [11]. The authors emphasize especially their measurement of the content specifically being taught at each grade level and their conversion of raw scores into equal, scaled units of measurement "along the whole distribution of raw scores." These features are intended to make the tests good measures both of objectives and of growth, over a limited grade range. Test items, the authors say, were chosen from the "areas of agreement" in 30 state courses of study in 15 city curricula and were constructed by subject specialists. On the basis of preliminary "tryouts," items were also selected so as to be of medium difficulty for the middle 50 per cent of pupils at each grade level and to show significantly higher proportions of correct answers in the grades for which they are intended than in the grades immediately below. In appraising these tests, Schindler [36] says that for a curriculum stressing information and skills, they are "a good choice." Illustrations of their content are only suggested here.

1. *Spelling* is measured by a 45-word dictation test of words occurring commonly in children's writing and in spelling books. The child first writes the word and then matches his spelling with four common variant spellings or with "D" (to indicate that his spelling differs from any given). For example, "anyone" is dictated, and the child matches his spelling with (1) "enyone," (2) "ennyone," (3) "annyone," (4) "anyone," or (5) "D."

2. *Language* is measured by true-false items on punctuation, capitalization, and usage. Examples of items for each of these areas are, respectively:

(R or W) "Where is my cap?" asked Willard.
(R or W) There are nine great dams in the *Tennessee Valley*.
(R or W) The folks *set* down to dinner early that night.

3. *Reading* comprehension and context vocabulary are measured by 13 complete narratives on interesting life situations intended to require the reader to grasp the central thought, to note details, to interpret content, to integrate dispersed ideas, to draw inferences, and to identify certain words from their context. Here is an example:

The flock that was corralled each night on Merino Ranch was tended by Moss, a tall mountaineer who had strayed to the Texas plains from North Carolina. In the lonely cabin lived Moss and a cowboy from Montana who cooked the meals and fed the sheep mornings and evenings. A stove occupied one end of the cabin and a fireplace the other. The men slept on blankets on the floor. Ben, the shepherd dog, slept in front of the fire. He was broad of chest, with curly black hair and brown eyes like Moss, strong in limbs and great in height, weight, speed and courage, with a jaw that promised ill for an enemy. Often he dreamed and told of his dreams in low, snuffling barks or moans that meant he was having a hard time somewhere. Moss would wake him with a caress.

46. The cowboy who lived with Moss came from (1) North Carolina, (2) Montana, (3) Texas, (4) South Carolina, (5) Oregon.

47. When Ben barked or moaned in his dreams, Moss woke him up with a (1) yell, (2) slap, (3) gentle stroke, (4) pull on his hair, (5) kick.

48. Moss (1) cared nothing for Ben, (2) cared nothing for the cowboy, (3) hated Ben, (4) loved Ben, (5) loved the cowboy.

49. Ben slept (1) in front of the fireplace, (2) in a blanket, (3) in front of the fireplace [*sic*], (4) in front of the stove, (5) in back of the stove.

50. The meaning of "occupied" in the sentence, "a stove occupied one end of the cabin and a fireplace the other" is (1) burned in, (2) adorned, (3) heated, (4) decorated, (5) took up.

4. *Social studies* measurement, including separate history and geography subtests, is comprised of a preponderance of informational items but includes 13 items on maps and graph interpretations. Here are three examples:

For writing, the Babylonians used (1) pencil, (2) pen, (3) stylus, (4) quill, (5) needle.

One would expect flat roofs on houses (1) in wet places, (2) in dry places, (3) in cold places, (4) in mountains, (5) on islands.

From reading a map on the test paper on which a strait is marked "2," the child is expected to answer such multiple-choice items as:

Number "2" on map E shows the location of a (1) river, (2) canal, (3) bay, (4) strait, (5) estuary.

5. *Science* understanding is measured by items on animals, plants, agriculture, the earth, weather, physics, astronomy, chemistry, health, and hygiene. Following is an example:

A bird that builds a hanging nest is the (1) robin, (2) sparrow, (3) bluebird, (4) oriole.

6. *Literature* items, including mythology, folk stories, classics, poetry, and miscellaneous stories, are intended to appraise the "scope of pupils' experience in good reading, rather than his memory of details." Here is an example:

What character belongs in Robin Hood? (1) Br'er Fox, (2) Gluck, (3) Prince Dolor, (4) Leif the Lucky, (5) Will Scarlet.

7. *Arithmetic-computation* items "sample broadly among the arithmetic fundamental operations taught at each particular grade level." At the fourth grade level for example, they include adding, subtracting, multiplying, and dividing, mainly with integers but also with decimal money and with such fractions as $\frac{1}{2}$, $\frac{1}{3}$, $\frac{1}{4}$, and $\frac{1}{8}$.

8. *Problem-reasoning* items, without computations, require the pupil to indicate which of four methods will produce the correct solutions to a variety of arithmetic-social problems, for example:

Isabel paid 48 cents for 4 loaves of bread. How much did a loaf cost? (1) Multiply 48 by 4. (2) Subtract 4 from 48. (3) Divide 48 by 4. (4) Add 48 and 4.

That the computation and problem-reasoning tests measure different functions is indicated by the correlation of .46 between them, which shows that only 21 per cent (r^2) of the variation in problem-reasoning scores is related to variations in computation.

Since these tests are not timed, their reliabilities are fairly accurately determined by odd-even-item correlations. These are, at the fifth grade level: spelling, .96; language, .76; reading, .92; history, .87; geography, .89; science, .87; literature, .74; arithmetic computation, .93; and problem reasoning, .91.

Raw scores for the separate tests in the battery are converted to comparable scaled units, and from these derived scores to grade equivalents, to age equivalents, or to percentile scores. Any one of these derived scores may be profiled to show the comparative status of a pupil on the 10 tests. The norms for the derived scores are based on "carefully selected sampling of pupil attainment in all sections of the country," using populations at each grade of from 1,122 to 9,887 and totaling 50,039 for the eight grades.

Separate-subject Tests

The distinctive feature of survey batteries of achievement tests is the profiles which they yield of comparable scores in several subjects. In each of the elementary school subjects, however, separate tests are available [20]. Often by selecting separately tests for different parts of the curriculum, teachers can achieve more adequate measurement of the objectives being emphasized in their particular school. This is especially true of such subjects as social studies, science, and health, where adaptations are often made in the curriculum to take advantage of local environmental opportunities and to meet local needs. Some teachers may agree with Findley [10], who would use only a reading test for instructional purposes in the primary grades. He thinks that survey batteries are undesirable for use in the primary grades because they may impose undue stress and may divert teaching emphasis from more important child development objectives. Of the numerous separate-subject tests, only Gates's reading tests are selected for illustration here. Four tests cover the elementary school grades.

1. The Gates Primary Reading Tests. These tests for grades 1 and 2 measure level and range of abilities for three aspects of beginning reading: (1) recognition of representative primary level *words*; (2) ability to read and understand representative *sentences* composed of words commonly found in primary reading materials; and (3) ability to read thought units with understanding of *paragraphs* as a whole. "In general, the tests measure all-round reading competence, with more emphasis on accuracy, range, and level of comprehension than upon sheer rate" [14, p. 7]. How these reading objectives are measured is suggested by an example of each kind.

Word-recognition measurement is comprised of 48 items such as:

Draw a ring around the one word that tells about the picture.

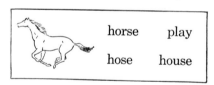

Sentence-reading measurement includes 45 items such as:

Draw one (/), two (//), or three (///) lines on a picture that tells about each sentence.

The goat is eating grass. I

Here are a hammer and nails. II

Father is milking the cow. III

Paragraph-reading ability is sampled by 26 items such as:

Read the story, then take your pencil and do *exactly* what the story tells you to do.

15. Draw a line from the robin to its nest. You will find the nest in the tree on the left side of the picture.

Raw scores on each part are converted, on the basis of extensive norm data, into either grade equivalents or age equivalents. The manual suggests some diagnostic "leads" in the patterns of the three comparable scores. For example, at the end of grade 1, pupil B's grade-equivalent scores are 2.2, 2.0, and 1.4, respectively, in the three types of reading. The first two scores indicate good progress in recognition vocabulary and in ability to comprehend single sentences. But the relatively low score in paragraph reading indicates a deficiency in ability to get the central idea in bigger and more complex thought units. This child needs teacher-guidance and motivated practice in acquiring "the subtle skills essential to reading and understanding more exactly and fully reading units of greater size and complexity." Reading interesting material for challenging, specific problem-solving purposes should help. Specific exercises might include reading "to get the main idea," "to tell what comes next," "to find the best reason," "to get ideas for illustrating," etc.

2. The Gates Advanced Primary Reading Tests: For Grade 2 (Second Half) and Grade 3. These tests are like the primary reading tests, except that they contain only word recognition and paragraph reading and that they reach higher levels of difficulty so as to challenge the ablest pupils of grades 2 and 3 [13].

3. The Gates Reading Survey Test: For Grade 3 (Second Half) to Grade 10. This test measures (1) reading vocabulary, (2) level of reading comprehension, (3) speed, and (4) accuracy of reading [17].

Range of representative reading vocabulary is measured using words from the Thorndike word list, ranging from easy words found in the first 1,000 to difficult words in the twentieth 1,000. Meanings are tested by 85 multiple-choice items such as:

Underline the word which means the same or nearly the same as the first word. *bashful*, shy, short, bold, brave, cheap

Level of reading comprehension is measured by multiple-choice questions on a graduated series of 35 paragraphs ranging in level of complexity from third grade to college, for example:

19. There are no ears on a frog's head that we can see. This does not mean, however, that he cannot hear. A short distance behind each eye are two holes, inside of which is an inner ear. Beyond this is the middle ear. In this ear   A   is carried by a special   B   to the brain where the   C   is actually done.

A	sight	sound	light	smells	feeling
B	trunk	messenger	police	blood	nerve
C	coughing	smelling	seeing	hearing	touching

Speed of reading is measured by one simple multiple-choice question on each of 64 brief paragraphs, all easily comprehended, such as:

24. At night huge electric signs make Broadway a fairyland of light and color. This is one of the most famous streets in the world. How does it look?

    dull   noisy   bright   dark

Accuracy of reading is appraised by determining the percentage correctly answered of the speed-test paragraphs.

A table of norms, from which Table 14–3 is excerpted, makes possible conversion of raw scores into grade equivalents.

Table 14–3. Grade Equivalents for Scores on Gates Reading Survey Test, Form II

Skill	Grade equivalents										
	2.6	3.5	4.4	5.2	6.2	7.2	8.4	9.3	11.3	11.4	12.4
Vocabulary................	1	11	23	29	37	47	53	61	69	78	85
Level of comprehension.....	1	18	36	47	55	62	69	75	79	82	83
Speed....................	8	14	19	24	28	33	38	42	44	48	56

Source: Teachers College, Columbia University, Bureau of Publications, New York, 1942, p. 3.

By sampling very extensively each phase of reading measured, Gates has produced relatively high reliabilities. Correlating Form 1 against Form 2 for a total of 3 fourth grade classes, the correlations obtained are: for vocabulary, .91; for comprehension, .87; for speed, .88; and for accuracy, .82 (17, p. 13).

That these four parts of the reading survey test actually measure different reading functions is indicated by the relatively low intercorrelations among them, presented in Table 14–4.

Table 14–4. Intercorrelations among Three Phases of the Gates Reading Survey Tests, Grade 4

	Comprehension	Speed	Accuracy
Vocabulary...............	.53	.33	.34
Comprehension............	...	.50	.38
Speed....................	...	...	.20

Source: A. I. Gates: *Manual of Directions for Gates Reading Survey Test: For Grade 3 (Second Half) to Grade 10*, Teachers College, Columbia University, Bureau of Publications, New York, 1942, p. 14.

4. The Gates Basic Reading Test: For Grade 3 (Second Half) through Grade 8. Supplementing the survey test, this team of four tests [16] measures "a pupil's speed and accuracy in reading relatively and uniformly easy material" for four different reading purposes.

Type A, reading to appreciate general significance, measures skill in getting an accurate general impression from casual reading of a passage, as in newspaper or fiction reading. It includes 24 items such as:

Read each paragraph, and underline the word that tells best how the person felt. . . .

13. Betty had gone shopping with mother for a whole morning. She had looked and looked at all the pretty things until her eyes ached. Then her feet began to drag behind her. She found that she could hardly lift them from the floor. She saw a nice soft chair over in one corner. Stumbling over to it, she sank down with a deep sigh.

Draw a line under the word that best tells how Betty felt.

    afraid   joyful   weary   naughty   playful

Type B, reading to predict the outcome of given events, requires grasping the general significance of a passage plus reasoning to implications and predictions of likely outcomes and subsequent events. It includes 24 items such as:

Read each paragraph, and underline the sentence that best tells what is coming next. . . .

13. An American boy was in Mexico with his father. He saw Mexican men playing games with large seeds that moved. His father told him they were "jumping beans" that grew on bushes. The boy wanted some. One day he saw many little things moving about under a bush. They were jumping beans. Dozens of them rolled about at his feet.

He thought how good ice cream would taste
He filled his pockets with the beans
He told stories to the Mexican children
He bought one of the large Mexican hats

Type C, reading to understand precise directions, measures rigid, careful, exact reading for selecting, organizing, and retaining relevant details as a guide to action. It includes 24 items such as:

Read and do exactly what each paragraph tells you to do. . . .

13. Walter had these three pieces of money. He wanted to buy a valentine for the school valentine box. He found valentines for fifty cents, ten cents, and twenty-five cents, but no one was to pay more than ten cents. Draw a line under what Walter paid for the valentine.

Type D, reading to note details, measures ability to comprehend several points in a paragraph without the organization demanded in Type C. It includes 24 items such as:

Read each paragraph, and underline one word as the best answer to each question about it. . . .

15. There are many ways one can make a fire. Man found out these ways long before matches were made. One way is to rub two pieces of dry wood together until they become very warm. This will make enough heat to set fire to dry grass. Another way is to hit two pieces of rock together until sparks fly off and set the dry grass on fire. What did man rub together to get enough heat to set grass afire?

        clay   coal   grass   wood

What did he hit together to make sparks?

        rock   wire   matches   grass

What kind of grass was used to start the fire?

        moist   green   dry   fresh

Each test yields a score on (1) items attempted, (2) number correct, and (3) percentage of accuracy (which is the number correct divided by the number attempted). The scores are converted either to grade equivalents or to age equivalents. These different scores on each of the four types of reading lead to a variety of diagnostic- and remedial-teaching suggestions [15].

Like the other tests in this Gates series, adequate sampling of the functions measured has resulted in satisfactory reliabilities. For 136 fourth grade pupils, the reliability correlations are: for Type A, .90; for Type B, .89; for Type C, .85; and for Type D, .94—all on number of items correct [16, p. 18].

Unlike the different aspects of reading measured by the survey test, however, the different functions measured by the four types of the basic reading test are rather closely related, as is indicated by the correlations for 136 fourth grade pupils presented in Table 14–5. For example, the correlation of .85

Table 14–5. Intercorrelations among Items Correct on Measures of Reading [For general significance (A), to predict outcomes (B), to follow directions (C), and to note details (D)]

	B, outcomes	C, directions	D, details
A, significance.............	.85	.72	.78
B, outcomes...............	...	.66	.80
C, directions..............	...	...	.76

Source: A. I. Gates: *Manual of Directions for Gates Reading Survey Test: For Grade 3 (Second Half) through Grade 8*, Teachers College, Columbia University, Bureau of Publications, 1942, p. 18.

between reading to appreciate general significance (A) and reading to predict outcomes (B) indicates that 72 per cent (r^2) of the variations in Type A of these 136 pupils' scores are related to their variations in Type B scores.

Diagnostic Testing of Achievement

Because diagnostic testing is so important in facilitating effective learning, the diagnostic possibilities, as we have noted above, have been fully exploited in both the survey batteries and the separate-subject tests. This has been accomplished mainly by a comprehensive coverage of objectives and by organizing items for scoring into meaningful diagnostic categories. Some tests, in their efforts to explore for *causes* of learning difficulties, have still further emphasized this phase of achievement testing. As illustrations of diagnostic tests, the Gates Reading Diagnostic Tests and the Freeman Handwriting Scale are cited.

1. The Gates Reading Diagnostic Tests. For the school psychologist and for teachers who achieve the expert's understanding of how children learn to read, the Gates Reading Diagnostic Tests [15, pp. 577–652] supplement the diagnostic clues obtainable from the previously described tests. These tests are given individually and include (1) analysis of the child's oral reading, from which the examiner appraises expression, word-identification techniques, maturity and correctness of articulation, nature of errors, confidence or emotionally disturbing attitudes toward reading, and ability to learn from experience; (2) oral vocabulary; (3) tests for tendency to reverse words (such as reading "on" as "no"); (4) ability to perceive phrases such as "the big ship" in flash (one-half-second) exposures; (5) perception of single words both in flash exposures and with ample time and encouragement to try to identify them by phonetic- and visual-analysis techniques; (6) tests of spelling, for analysis of the child's mode of attack in learning to spell; (7) specific testing of visual-perception techniques, such as combining syllables into words, recognition of syllables and phonograms, blending letter sounds (such as "f-o" into "fo"), and giving the sounds of letters; and (8) testing of auditory perception and techniques, such as giving letters for sounds, supplying other words that begin with the same initial sound, and giving words than end in the same sound.

These several specific tests provide a comprehensive analysis of the component abilities and skills required for an effective mode of approach in reading. Guided by the results of preliminary testing and by hearing the child read, the examiner employs whichever of these tests he thinks may aid in revealing the child's specific difficulties and his strengths and weaknesses. Remedial instruction is then adapted to the child's needs and to the pattern of reading abilities revealed.

2. The Freeman Handwriting Scale. This scale [12] is comprised of 15 standard samples of cursive handwriting, varying from lowest to highest quality of five features of handwriting: (1) uniformity of slant, (2) uniformity of alignment, (3) quality of line, (4) letter formation, and (5) spacing. To diagnose a child's handwriting, a sample of his copying of the Gettysburg Address is obtained. This sample is then matched with the standard scale samples for each feature and is rated from 1 to 5, depending upon which standard it most nearly matches. To aid in matching for uniformity of slant, vertical lines drawn through several letters on the child's sample may be compared with those drawn on the standard samples. Similarly, in matching carefully for uniformity of alignment, horizontal lines may be drawn at the tops and bottoms of the child's one-space letters. Quality of line is judged for smoothness, firmness, and evenness. In evaluating letter formation, a number of common illegibilities are especially noted: (1) open or closed loops in a, d, f, g, s, and v; (2) high or low stroke in such letters as b, f, k, and l; (3) slurring over letters so that the characteristic form is lost; (4) substitution of angles for curves, and vice versa, in such letters as m, n, and w; (5) substitution of loops for return strokes along the same line, or the reverse, in c, d, e, f, i, t, etc.; (6) substitution of a return stroke for an open curve or of an open curve for a return stroke in such letters as r, and y; (7) faulty direction or placement of a stroke in t, u, x, etc.; and (8) confusion of small letters or capitals because of their sizes, such as a, c, g, m, n, etc. No letter should be sufficiently varied to be confused with another, and consistency should be maintained. Spacing is judged for appropriate distances between letters and between words. Common faults in this respect are either crowding letters or spreading them too far apart, and crowding of words.

Ratings of "1" or "2", depending upon the general maturity level of the child, suggest needs for improvement. As suggestions of causes of different difficulties (and, by implication, of leads to improvement), Freeman has constructed the analysis chart presented in Table 14–6.

Table 14–6. Analysis of Writing Defects and their Causes
(According to Freeman's Handwriting Scale)

Defect	Cause
Too much slant	1. Writing arm too near body 2. Thumb too stiff 3. Point of nib too far from figure 4. Paper in wrong position 5. Stroke in wrong direction
Writing too straight	1. Arm too far from body 2. Fingers too near nib 3. Index finger alone guiding pen 4. Incorrect position of paper
Writing too heavy	1. Index finger pressing too heavily 2. Use of wrong pen 3. Penholder of too small diameter
Writing too light	1. Pen held too obliquely or too straight 2. Eyelet of pen turned to side 3. Penholder of too large diameter
Writing too angular	1. Thumb too stiff 2. Penholder too lightly held 3. Movement too slow
Writing too irregular	1. Lack of freedom of movement 2. Movement of hand too slow 3. Pen gripping 4. Incorrect or uncomfortable position
Spacing too wide	1. Pen movement too fast to right 2. Too much lateral movement

Source: F. N. Freeman: *Teaching of Handwriting*, Riverside Educational Monographs Houghton Mifflin, Boston, 1914, p. 74.

Teacher-made Achievement Tests

An important outcome of study of the foregoing commercially prepared tests is the discovery of principles and techniques which can be applied to the construction of good teacher-made tests. Like so-called "standardized" tests, the teacher's self-constructed tests should be valid, reliable, useful in facilitating learning, and efficient. The same principles and techniques by which "experts" achieve these purposes are applicable in the construction of tests which teachers make for various teaching purposes. Without "lifting" actual items from the commercially prepared tests (which would, of course, be unethical and illegal), sometimes quite direct adaptation of principles can be made.

Woltring [45], for example, has suggested an adaptation of the Freeman Handwriting Scale for effective teacher and pupil use. At any grade level—say, from 3 to 6—a teacher might select from samples of pupils' handwriting[1] typical examples of "poor," "average," and "good" quality of each of Freeman's five features. These, arranged on a classroom wall chart with the names of pupils omitted, can become a scale by which pupils can be taught to analyze and to find guidance in correcting their own handwriting. The idea can be adapted to either manuscript or cursive writing.

Another such adaptation of a commercial test can be made from Buckingham's Extension of the Ayres Spelling Scale [5]. A source of teacher-made spelling tests, this list of 1,505 words includes 1,000 words selected by Ayres according to their "frequency in written discourse" plus 505 words added by Buckingham as being common to several spelling books. The words are presented in 32 columns; in each column all the words are of approximately equal difficulty. At the head of each column are the percentages of words which pupils from the several grades of representative schools have been found able to spell correctly.

By similar procedures, a school system might prepare a master source of spelling tests comprised of words especially appropriate according to more recent or local criteria. In making such a test, the teacher selects from a column of appropriate difficulty for the grade about 20 words (50 for a more reliable sampling). For example, at the fourth grade level, if the words are drawn from column O, children should spell correctly about 70 to 76 per cent of them. If a fourth grade list is taken from column R, the percentage of correct spellings should be from 46 to 54. As examples of the very great variety of tests which can be derived from the list, two 20-word lists from columns O and R are presented in Table 14–7.

Another place for adapted tests is in individualized teaching. The effectiveness of individualized instruction, as was pointed out in the previous chapter,

[1] If it should seem likely that a pupil might recognize and be embarrassed about the display of his handwriting, the samples could be selected from a different class.

Table 14–7. Examples of Spelling Lists
(Derived from Ayres's Lists O and R)

O		R		Grade	Median percentage expected O	R
1. eight	11. refuse	1. forenoon	11. publication	2	27	12
2. afraid	12. district	2. lose	12. machine	3	50	27
3. uncle	13. restrain	3. combination	13. toward	4	73	50
4. rather	14. royal	4. avenue	14. success	5	84	66
5. comfort	15. objection	5. neighbor	15. drown	6	92	79
6. elect	16. pleasure	6. weight	16. adopt	7	96	88
7. aboard	17. fourth	7. wear	17. secure	8	99	94
8. jail	18. population	8. entertain	18. honor	9	100	98
9. shed	19. proper	9. salary	19. promise			
10. retire	20. Navy	10. visitor	20. wreck			

depends in part upon the provision for worthwhile and efficient independent pupil learning activities. Teacher-made tests can effectively facilitate such independent learning [44]. In silent-reading periods, for example, individual children should select books from the classroom library suited to their particular reading maturity levels and interests. To determine whether the level of a book is suitable for the child, to check and to correct his comprehension, to aid in organizing his thinking about what he has read, and to motivate his continued effort toward self-improvement, a quickly administered and scored test, taken by the child after reading the book, should be very helpful. And such silent reading and self-checking by pupils through tests would free the teacher for other teaching functions. In preparing a file of brief tests on reading comprehension for a variety of frequently chosen books, the teacher might use as models Gates's basic reading tests. All four types—reading for general significance, to predict outcomes, to understand directions, and to note details—would probably find appropriate applications in such a file of mimeographed tests. The type of items used should, of course, be appropriate to each of the varied kinds of reading tested. Such a file of tests should be developed and continually revised over some period of time.

But perhaps the most general application of the test experts' principles and techniques to teacher-made tests is in the writing of valid, reliable, and useful items for measuring knowledge and understandings for the day-by-day tests needed for guiding learning in the various curriculum areas. It is for this purpose that so many items have been quoted as examples. Validity of items can be achieved by relating them both to the curriculum content which pupils have been studying and (especially) to significant educational objectives, such as those outlined in Chapter 1. Reliability can be attained by an adequate sampling of all significant objectives through unequivocal items. As a guide to the formulation of clear items, Ebel [8] has suggested that the test writer use words of precise meaning, qualify statements as necessary, and avoid non-functional words, nonessential specificity, irrelevant inaccuracies, and irrelevant cues.

As the test items quoted have shown, several forms are available to the test-item writer. Multiple-choice items seem to be favored; but in measuring each objective, the form should be chosen as appropriate to the particular content for which the item is being written. As a summary of these forms, a few test items for appraising objectives in the fifth grade unit on diet will be constructed, according to Ebel's suggestions [8], in examples which also illustrate validity and teaching utility.

1. Short-answer and Completion Items. These should be employed only for questions which can be answered by a unique word, phrase, or number. In the completion form, after a clear and complete statement of what is wanted in the answer, only one or two blanks calling for a significant idea or ideas should occur; and they should be toward the end of the statement. Examples:

What nutritional element supplies quick body energy? _____.
An essential nutritional element for body growth and repair is _____.

2. True-false Statements. These are suitable only for ideas which are true or false without qualifications and without regard to a particular context. They should be related to significant choices or actions. Example:

( ) Eating a wide variety rather than restricted choices of foods is more likely to supply the essential nutritional elements.

3. Multiple-choice Items. These are adaptable to a wide variety of concepts requiring reasoning, discriminating, and evaluating between right and wrong alternatives or among problem solutions of variable quality. They are thought to be especially appropriate for testing understanding of definitions, purposes of things or skills, cause-and-effect relations, association or connections between concepts, evaluations of actions or processes, recognition and applications of principles, and recognition of errors [35]. The stem should be clear and either an incomplete statement or a direct question. All the alternatives should be appropriate to the stem and should have some plausible relation to it, but only one should be clearly correct or be a best solution—unless, of course, the subject is directed to choose more than one alternative. In the interest of conciseness, the stem should include parts of the alternatives which would be otherwise repeated. Examples:

( ) The best source of protein among the following is (1) beefsteak, (2) orange juice, (3) grain cereal, (4) string beans.

( ) A child has already eaten bread, butter, milk, orange juice, potatoes, spinach, and applesauce. In order to balance his diet for the day, what else should he eat from the "seven basic food groups?" (1) cheese, (2) meat, (3) grapefruit, (4) cereal

4. Matching. This form is suitable for measuring ability to differentiate or make discriminating applications of different aspects of some complex concepts. Matching items are especially suitable for testing understanding of associations between paired "systems" of things, such as events and dates, events and persons, events and places, terms and definitions, principles and specific applications, tools and their uses, causes and effects, and conditions and results [35]. Like the alternatives of a multiple-choice question, the parts of a matching question should all be interrelated and plausible. The primary statements should be brief and not too numerous, so that they can be easily remembered or scanned as each response is matched with one of them. There may be unmatched responses, or a response may match more than one premise. A clear introductory statement should explain the relation of the responses to the primary statement. Example:

Match the following nutritional elements with a good source of each:
( ) carbohydrates   1. salmon
( ) fats   2. butter
( ) proteins   3. oranges
( ) minerals
( ) vitamin C

5. Interpretation Exercises. These are work-sample items in which interpretations may be asked about a selection, table, chart, map, or diagram. As an example, the growth curve (Chapter 1, page 27) showing Reddie's and Blue Boy's weight gains might be reproduced, and such questions asked as:

( ) What was the first day on which Reddie's weight exceeded Blue Boy's by 2 grams? (1) sixth, (2) seventh, (3) eighth, (4) ninth

6. Essay Questions. These are intended to measure novel problem-solving understandings and skills, where the child can use facts and concepts to relate, compare, contrast, discriminate, draw inferences, detect relationships, select pertinent information, state conclusions, or make interpretations. For several reasons essay tests are likely to be unreliable. Since so few questions can be answered within a reasonable time, the test is not likely to cover an adequate and representative sample of objectives. As often constructed, they are subject to ambiguous interpretations. And their scoring is subject to the influence of irrelevant factors, such as writing facility. Such an item as the following, however, avoids some of these limitations:

> Compare the effects of adequate and "snack" diets on the growth, health, and "personalities" of Reddie and Blue Boy and, by inference, on children.

This item is related to several of the significant objectives of the unit. It states explicitly the source of facts needed, the three aspects to which they are to be applied, and the inference to be made. It could be scored fairly objectively by allowing 1 or 2 points each for stating the effects of the two diets on "growth," "health," and "personalities," plus an additional 1 to 3 points for drawing justifiable inferences.

Thus far, the validity, reliability, and uses in facilitating pupil learning of teacher-made tests have been considered. Suggestions on constructing and using them *efficiently* may also be appropriate. Efficient writing of teacher-constructed test items should be a long-range, evolving process rather than a specific job to be done each time a test is needed. Whenever a good item occurs to a teacher—in studying objectives, in reading pupil texts and references, in conducting learning activities, when a particular concept or skill is discovered to be especially needed, when an error is found that needs correcting, and so on—the item should be written, or a plan should be determined for writing it. Each item should be written on a 3- by 5-inch card, so that it can be filed conveniently in a box divided by labeled guide cards. Guide cards should indicate both the general curriculum areas and subtopics within them. Intermediate level science, for example, might be subdivided into (1) life processes, (2) animals, (3) plants, (4) earth, (5) conservation, (6) health, (7) safety, (8) physics, and (9) chemistry. And in some instances, these subcategories might be further subdivided. In such a file, our examples of diet items would, of course, be filed in the subdivision of health. As items are collected, the file grows.

Whenever a test is needed, appropriate items are drawn from the file for mimeographing or dittoing. As items are used and critically evaluated and as better ideas for items occur, some items are discarded or revised. Thus as a teacher grows in experience and in professional competency, his file of test items for a variety of areas and purposes grows in both size and quality—that is, in validity, in reliability, and in teaching utility. The teacher can use his file of tests efficiently by being alert to *all* the appropriate times and places for testing—not merely for "final" appraisal of pupil achievement, but at every step where they might facilitate learning. In addition to other ways, already mentioned, for using tests to facilitate learning, teachers should show pupils their corrected tests very soon after they take them if the tests are to serve effectively for confirming or revising concepts.

Several of the following appraisal devices, like teacher-made tests of knowledge and understanding, are dependent on teacher initiative.

Observation in Evaluating Attainment of Objectives

As was noted in Table 14–1, no other appraisal device has such general utility as teacher observation of pupils' behavior. As the teacher observes her pupils in both individual and group activities in the classroom, auditorium, library, lunchroom, and playground, she has numerous occasions for noting attainment of each type of objective in every area of the curriculum. In oral reading, for example, she observes understandings, skills, attitudes, and action patterns. Attainment of some objectives can be evaluated well only by teacher observation. Under the category of physical development, health, and body care, attainment of skills and competencies in such activities as games and social groups, beginning skill in social dancing, personal grooming, and use of craft tools are evaluated mainly by observation. Such attitudes as eagerness and confidence in learning and trying out new games and such action patterns as covering the nose and mouth with a handkerchief when sneezing or coughing are evaluated only by observation. In the area of individual social and emotional development, observation will reveal the attainment of such objectives as skill in making oral announcements, facing difficulties frankly and honestly, and of such action patterns as volunteering to assume responsibilities and carrying them out. Similar analysis of the remaining seven categories reveals objectives which depend upon observation for their evaluation. As will be indicated in subsequent sections of this discussion, however, observation of attainment of such objectives can be effectively supplemented by anecdotal records, by rating scales and check lists, and by cumulative records.

Examination of Child Products

Teacher examination of children's completed assignments and especially of their creative productions in writing, language, art, crafts, arithmetic, science, social studies projects, and so on will reveal the attainment of many significant objectives. Examples of the attainment of objectives from Kearney's list which

Fig. 14–4. Teacher examination of child products, such as these creative essays in arithmetic, is a good way to appraise attainment of many objectives. (*Courtesy of McGraw-Hill Text-Film Department.*)

may be evaluated by examining child products are "using quantitative terms to summarize data"; "making science collections"; "interest in drawing pictures of plants and animals"; "skill in constructive science hobbies"; "skill in using art work in connection with study themes—pottery, pictorial maps, murals, decorative fabrics, and illustrating"; "voluntarily writes stories and poems and independently proofreads and corrects his own productions"; and so on.

Interviewing to Evaluate Achievement

The individual teacher-pupil interview has already been mentioned in a previous chapter as an effective device for appraising work methods and as a basis for guiding children toward more effective modes of attack in learning and problem solving. It will be remembered that the interview revealed *how* a child obtained the erroneous sum indicated in "12 + 7 = 10." Since he added digits as units regardless of their place values, his need for instruction on the place value of numbers was indicated. Having children "think out loud" as they solve problems or explain *how* they learn to spell a word, identify an unfamiliar word in reading, or organize notes for a science report will reveal the effectiveness of their modes of attack. Such evaluating has great teaching utility in helping children to learn how to learn efficiently. Attainment of such objectives from Kearney's list as the following are appraised especially appropriately by teacher-pupil interviews: "insights about himself in relation to others," skill in "confiding his uncertainties and worries," "can relieve personal tension through constructive activities and from adult assistance in meeting his emotional problems," and "attitudes of becoming critical of his own work and makes greater effort to improve."

Such evaluative interviews need to be conducted in a warm, friendly, non-critical atmosphere. The interview can be guided by the teacher toward its evaluative purposes by questions and suggestions or directions; but at the same time, the teacher can make the child feel free to express himself without fear of criticism, in his own way, and in the order in which his thoughts come to him. As the interview proceeds, the child's efforts at self-revelation and self-understanding can be reinforced by teacher approval and support.

Sometimes the evaluative interview is combined with other appraisal devices. For example, as an important aid in diagnosing reading skills, the Gray Standardized Oral Reading Paragraphs [19] may be used as an interview test.

Table 14–8. The Easiest and the Most Difficult of Gray's Standardized
Oral Reading Paragraphs

---

1. A boy had a dog.
   The dog ran into the woods.
   The boy ran after the dog.
   He wanted the dog to go home.
   But the dog would not go home.
   The little boy said,
   "I cannot go home without my dog."
   Then the boy began to cry.

12. The hypotheses concerning physical phenomena
    formulated by the early philosophers proved
    to be inconsistent and in general not universally
    applicable. Before relatively accurate principles
    could be established, physicists, mathematicians,
    and statisticians had to combine forces and work
    arduously.

Source: W. S. Gray: *Standardized Oral Reading Paragraphs*, Public School, Bloomington, Ill., 1915.

Fig. 14–5. Observation and diagnostic analysis of a child's mode of attack in reading is helpful in guiding him to improvement. (*Courtesy of Whittier School, Utah State Agricultural College.*)

Handing the child, in the interview situation, a copy of 12 paragraphs graduated in difficulty (see Table 14–8), the teacher directs him to read them in succession (until he makes seven or more errors in each of two paragraphs) as well as he can without help. The examiner on another copy of the paragraphs records (1) the time for each paragraph and (2) the nature of each error, according to a suggested key. Words wholly or partially mispronounced are wholly or partially underlined. Or, the "substitutions" may be written in over the mispronounced words, (as "house" for "home") as a means of indicating more precisely the extent of the child's phonetic-analysis techniques. Omitted words are encircled. Insertions of extraneous words may be written in without underlining. Repetitions are designated "P," and reversals are indicated by "R." Lines skipped may be indicated by "skl."

Following the child's reading, the examiner may also rate or otherwise appraise more specifically (1) quality of expression; (2) effectiveness of word-recognition techniques used; (3) articulation—noting specific misarticulations; (4) appropriateness of speed; (5) attitudes; and (6) responsiveness to "teaching" (when help is given on a paragraph).

Besides the remedial-teaching suggestions provided by the above diagnostic clues, the interview test also yields a grade-equivalent score which indicates the level of difficulty at which the child is able to read.

Such combined interview-test evaluations of achievement can be applied in a great variety of teacher-made tests. Ramharter and Johnson [33], following testing with interviewing, found sixth grade pupils employing both good and poor modes of attack as they solved different types of problems in subtraction of fractions. And Brownell and Watson [3], as they listened while children solved out loud the problems in Table 14–9, found that some fifth grade children needed greater understanding of processes.

Table 14–9. Fifth Grade Diagnostic Test in Addition of Fractions

(1)	$\frac{1}{5}$ $+\frac{2}{5}$	(2)	$\frac{1}{8}$ $+\frac{5}{8}$	(3)	$\frac{2}{7}$ $+\frac{5}{7}$	(4)	$\frac{4}{5}$ $+\frac{2}{5}$	(5)	$\frac{4}{6}$ $+\frac{4}{6}$	Common denominators occur in both fractions.
(6)	$\frac{1}{2}$ $+\frac{1}{4}$	(7)	$\frac{1}{2}$ $+\frac{2}{8}$	(8)	$\frac{2}{3}$ $+\frac{3}{6}$	(9)	$\frac{4}{8}$ $+\frac{3}{4}$	(10)	$\frac{3}{8}$ $+\frac{1}{12}$	Common denominators occur in only one of the fractions.
(11)	$\frac{1}{5}$ $+\frac{2}{4}$	(12)	$\frac{2}{4}$ $+\frac{7}{11}$	(13)	$\frac{3}{7}$ $+\frac{3}{4}$	(14)	$\frac{3}{6}$ $+\frac{4}{5}$	(15)	$\frac{7}{9}$ $+\frac{5}{6}$	Common denominators must be found.

Source: W. A. Brownell and B. Watson: *J. Educ. Res.*, 29: 666, 1936.

As an example of the data yielded by the personal interviews associated with this test, a child's comment on his solution to item (4) is cited. The child said, "When you add fractions, you change the numbers around, so you write $\frac{5}{6}$ instead of $\frac{6}{5}$ for the answer." The child has revealed, of course, his dependency on a "mechanical" manipulation of numbers and his need for understanding the meaning of the numerator and denominator terms of fractions.

$$\frac{4}{5}$$
$$+\frac{2}{5}$$
$$\frac{5}{6}$$

When teachers are interested in diagnosing children's learning and problem-solving procedures, supplementing testing with interviewing is both more reliable and more valid than testing alone [3].

Anecdotal Records

Anecdotal records, as a supplement to observation, are valuable in appraising development toward many objectives but they are especially useful in appraising development of certain action patterns in nearly every curriculum area. When a child's *behavior* seems to illustrate the attainment of (or the failure to attain) some significant objective, the teacher should record in her file of anecdotal records a specific and accurate description of what the child did and said in the situation. From her background of understanding of the child's behavior and development (as indicated in earlier records), she may also formulate interpretive hypotheses. These hypotheses should be checked and affirmed, elaborated, or modified on the basis of further recorded observations. In order to realize the value of anecdotal records in facilitating teaching, confirmed hypotheses should, of course, become bases for planning desirable and needed educational experiences.

As examples of anecdotal records meeting these criteria, two anecdotes from a long sequence on "Pressley" are quoted [23, pp. 118–119].

November 18. Pressley came to school early. Said his foot hurt him a lot after he had fallen down. Got up from rest before he was asked to, but went back willingly when reminded. While reading the "Run-away Engine," Pressley often interrupted to say that just the same thing that happened to the engine had happened to his grandfather when he drives his engine. Even when the runaway engine jumped the drawbridge, and the coal car fell onto a barge below, that happened to his grandfather too.

Later in the afternoon, when some mules passed the window as the children were cleaning up the room,

Pressley said his grandfather has two mules, one is white and one is red. [He] pulled up one trouser leg before scrubbing tables—said that helped him work— . . . . I saw him from a little distance going home, his trouser leg still up and his arm tucked into his shirt with the sleeve hanging empty as though he was playing "broken arm."

Are Pressley's excessive phantasy and imaginary role-playing his responses to insecurity and lack of satisfaction and confidence in his own real life role and self-concept? Let us consider the second anecdote:

November 25. Pressley came very dirty and thinly dressed, though it was a cold day. He painted two pictures in a desultory way, then wanted to play on train. When taking care of self during reading time, Pressley changed from one thing to another quickly. But in reading, he stuck to the job well. Was interested. Volunteered often. Interrupted story often. In a familiar story, he anticipated what was coming and gave it before time came. In the playtime, wandered over to big boy's bike again. But joined game and seemed to have a good time. When a child was telling about how a cow chased him, Pressley said, "Maybe that was our cow that ran away." One of the children said, "Oh, no, it wasn't. You ain't got no cow." Pressley was silent.

Pressley likes to conform to teacher suggestions and group requirements. But some insecurity or anxiety probably distracts him from sustained interest and keeps him restless. It seems that his good verbal ability is used both in constructive imagination (interpreting reading) and in excessive phantasying of a more satisfying role than he feels he has.

In order to confirm her hypotheses, it seemed desirable to this teacher to visit Pressley's parents. From her interpretation of the parent-teacher interview, she writes [23, p. 125]:

It is apparent that his family are unaware of Pressley's needs as a person. This is indicated under (1) the ways in which the family neglect him, and also under (2) where it was pointed out that Pressley's little sister is the family pet. The family does not see his great need for love as expressed in physical affection, in an underlying tone of relationship with him, and in being sensitive to his needs and fundamental desires. . . . His fantasies as seen in the anecdotal records are all an inflation of himself or something connected with himself and when seen in the light of knowledge about his home life and of his daily behavior are an expression of his insecurity.

This interpretation would lead the teacher to strive to arrange for Pressley, directly at school and indirectly in his home, more security and confidence-building experiences. He needs to feel comfortable, lovable, approved, accepted, and self-esteemed in his own roles.

Among the "action patterns" from Kearney's list of objectives, development of such behavior patterns as the following, from each of the nine areas, could be appraised especially well by anecdotal records: "taking responsibility for health and safety of self and others at play and at work"; "is able to channel anger into some constructive activity rather than hurt persons, destroy property or bottle up his emotions"; "shows increased sympathy and understanding of why others behave as they do"; "reads newspapers and current events magazines occasionally and is beginning to relate items of local history to state and national history"; "brings science material to school to share with others"; "initiates and carries art and craft projects to completion"; "reads in order to be able to contribute to his group or to verify and fortify his opinions and arguments"; and "shows a growing tendency to deal with quantity, as he encounters it, in precise and definite terms."

It is recognized that the anecdotal record is expensive of time. But significant behavior related to the above objectives is not always producible at convenient testing periods. Therefore when such behavior does occur in special incidents, it would seem to be efficient evaluation procedure to make anecdotal records of them.

Rating Scales and Check Lists

Rating scales and check lists are devices for summarizing, organizing, and quantifying an accumulation of prior observations of children's behavior. They are applicable, therefore, to appraisal of the same kinds of objectives as have been cited as appropriate for evaluation by observation and by anecdotal records. Using the standard procedures for constructing rating scales [21, 30, 32], the teacher might make up scales for appraising any one of the above-listed objectives. For example, in summarizing and quantifying a teacher's observations on how well a child "is able to channel anger into some constructive activity rather than hurt persons, destroy property or bottle up his emotions," an item from the Haggerty-Olson-Wickman Behavior Rating Schedules [21] might be used. The item reads: "How does he react to frustrations or to unpleasant situations?" It is answered by checking the appropriate position to describe his *typical* behavior on the graphic scale, on which the numbers indicate behavior from favorable (1) to unfavorable (5).

Very submissive, long-suffering	Tolerant, rarely blows up	Generally self-con-trolled	Impatient	Easily irritated, hot-head, explosive
(3)	(2)	(1)	(4)	(5)

In constructing a rating scale, the teacher selects an interrelated but not overlapping set of objectives which are subject to appraisal by ratings. The traits should be manifest in observable behavior. Next, each trait is clearly defined, as in the above instance, by a question. Then degrees of possession of the trait are described in terms of specific behavior manifestations which can be identified in the child. These varied descriptions of manifestations of the trait are then arranged in a hierarchy which can be scored numerically, from 1 through 3, from 1 through 5, or even from 1 through 7.

As an example of such a scale, see the sample of a school-adjustment rating scale in Table 14–10. For this scale, a total score and a score for each of the six traits may be obtained. If these scores are recorded opposite the names of the children in a class and under a row of the six trait labels, an over-all appraisal of the class can be made which is suggestive to a teacher of needs for promoting better adjustment of his pupils [2].

The check list is also a device which can be used for summarizing and organizing teacher observation on the attainment of objectives. Topp, for example, has collected a list of 40 behavior manifestations of emotional maladjustment in preadolescents, which can be used as a check list [43]. As an illustration, the first 10 of these "behavior patterns" are presented in Table 14–11. Only when several of the 40 items are checked as characteristics of a child is maladjustment indicated.

Table 14–10. Suggested Items for a School Adjustment Rating Scale*

For each of the traits listed below, recall typical instances of children's behavior indicative of the trait, and then make your rating of the child by comparing his behavior with that typical of his classmates. Indicate your rating by putting a check (√) in the one appropriate parenthesis for each trait.

I. WORK HABITS

( ) 1. *Very Effective*—Pupil works carefully, thoughtfully, and independently. He uses his initiative and is very resourceful. His work habits are of the very best.

( ) 2. *Adequate*—Work habits enable him to achieve all that would usually be expected of one of his ability.

( ) 3. *Promising*—The pupil does only what is required of him. Uses little initiative. Habits developed are not adequate, but show some improvement and promise of becoming so.

( ) 4. *Inadequate*—Has work habits that are adequate only for simple situations. Limited by lack of development of some elements that make for efficiency in attacking problems.

( ) 5. *Ineffective*—The pupil is careless and negligent. Has not developed such work habits that will enable him to do what he is capable of doing.

II. SELF-DIRECTION

( ) 1. *Responsible and Resourceful*—Not only carries through whatever is undertaken, but also shows versatility and initiative in enlarging upon undertakings.

( ) 2. *Conscientious*—Completes without external compulsion whatever is assigned, but unlikely to enlarge on assignments.

( ) 3. *Generally Dependable*—Usually carries through undertakings, self-assumed or assigned by others, requiring only occasional reminder or compulsion.

( ) 4. *Unreliable*—Can be relied upon to complete undertakings only when they are of moderate difficulty, and then only with much prodding and supervision.

( ) 5. *Irresponsible*—Cannot be relied upon to complete any undertaking, even when constantly prodded and guided.

III. SOCIAL ADJUSTMENT

( ) 1. Works well with others. Goes out of the way to assist others. A "born leader."

( ) 2. Can work with others, and sometimes affects the opinions, ideals, and activities of associates.

( ) 3. Cooperates moderately. Inconsistent in ability to adjust intelligently to group.

( ) 4. Cannot work with others. Has no definite influence on others.

( ) 5. Obstructive to others in group. Unwilling to sacrifice own interests for good of the group.

( ) 6. A timid nonparticipant. Withdraws and remains quietly alone.

IV. EMOTIONAL CONTROL

( ) 1. Has unusual balance of responsiveness and control.

( ) 2. Well balanced. Shows self-control. In touch with realities.

( ) 3. Tends to be overemotional. Introspective; dreamy; feels inferior.

( ) 4. Emotional reactions get in his way. Moody; changeable.

( ) 5. Easily upset emotionally. Tantrums; outbursts of tears or anger.

Table 14–10. Suggested Items for a School Adjustment Rating Scale* (*Continued*)

V. CONFIDENCE AND PERSISTENCE

( ) 1. Does not give up; if one approach is unsuccessful, confidently tries alternate modes of attack.
( ) 2. Gives everything a fair trial.
( ) 3. Persists until convinced of inability to continue independently.
( ) 4. Gives up before adequate trial.
( ) 5. Melts before slight obstacles or criticisms.

VI. EAGERNESS TO LEARN

( ) 1. Enthusiastic and wholehearted interest in participating and/or leading in all learning activities.
( ) 2. Complies readily with all teacher directions and participates as a matter of course in every learning activity.
( ) 3. Readily participates and responds willingly to teacher-direction in most learning activities, but resists a few.
( ) 4. Resists many learning activities, or requires constant prodding to keep him working at most learning activities.
( ) 5. Strong, outright resistance to participation in learning activities and to teacher attempts to motivate learning effort.

  * Items (1) to (4) from McCormick [30], other items suggested by the Haggerty-Olson-Wickman Behavior Rating Schedules [21].

Table 14–11. Check List of Behavior Patterns Indicative of Emotional Maladjustment
(First 10 items from a list of 40)

( ) 1. Flies into fits of anger on slight provocation.
( ) 2. Shows signs of excessive "worriedness" and anxiety on such occasions as a school fire drill or rehearsal for a play.
( ) 3. Frequently depressed in appearance; almost never smiling or joking with fellow students.
( ) 4. Repeatedly steals small articles from fellow students despite severe punishments.
( ) 5. Frequently appears to be lost in his daydreams.
( ) 6. Exhibits habitual facial grimaces or tics, particularly when under slight emotional stress.
( ) 7. Although of adequate intellectual ability, cannot apply his ability to his work and, as a result, does an inferior job, despite the fact that he seems to be conscientiously trying.
( ) 8. Very sensitive over real or imagined slights; feelings easily hurt.
( ) 9. Physically energetic and active to such a degree as to lack control over actions; restless and practically unable to remain quiet even for short periods of time.
( ) 10. Shows evidence of being excessively cruel to younger or smaller children or animals; enjoys seeing other creatures suffer.

  Source: R. F. Topp: *Elem. Sch. J.*, 52: 340–343, 1952. Reprinted by permission of the University of Chicago Press.

As an example of how the teacher might prepare a check list for appraising attainment of significant educational objectives, the "health and body care" objectives at the primary level from Kearney's list are arranged as a check list

Table 14–12. Check List of Action Patterns Concerning Physical
Development, Health, and Body Care at Primary Level

( )   1. Habitually washes hands before eating and after toilet.
( )   2. Gives attention regularly to personal cleanliness.
( )   3. Covers nose and mouth with handkerchief when coughing or sneezing.
( )   4. Keeps hands and objects out of mouth.
( )   5. Eats wholesome variety of food.
( )   6. Uses only own personal articles, such as towels and toothbrush.
( )   7. Rests when tired.
( )   8. Engages in quiet activities after eating.
( )   9. Avoids contact with people who have communicable diseases.
( ) 10. Shows concern for proper room temperature and light.
( ) 11. Practices safety in playing and working and with vehicles.
( ) 12. Shows no fear of the doctor, dentist, or nurse.

Source: N. C. Kearney: *Elementary School Objectives*, Russell Sage, New York, 1953.

in Table 14–12. The extent to which a child has attained the objectives in this category is indicated by the proportion of items checked for him from the list. Unchecked items, of course, indicate specific desirable health habits he needs to learn.

Sociometrics

In evaluating a child's attainment of some objectives, especially in the area of social relations, the teacher's observations are often effectively supplemented by the observations and opinions of the child's classmates. A few among many other objectives in Kearney's list by which pupils can help in appraising one another are "has several friends"; "follows pupil leadership"; "assumes group leadership on occasion"; "abides by the group's rules"; "shares toys, tools, and materials with others"; and "behaves appropriately when differences of opinion occur." Sociometry is a procedure for summarizing, organizing, and, to a limited extent, quantifying children's opinions on the social acceptability of and relationships with their peers. The usual technique for evaluating these factors involves four steps. First, the objectives on which pupils are to be appraised are expressed as "directions" or questions, for example: "List on the small piece of paper your very best friends," or: "Who in the class are always willing to share toys, tools, and materials with others?" Second, sincere answers to such questions are obtained from all the members of the class. Third, these answers are charted in a form like Table

14–13—which shows, for example, that child A checked child B and child D as his "very best friends." Finally, the "choices" shown in the chart are plotted on a sociogram, such as Figure 14–6.

Table 14–13. Chart of Pupil Responses When Requested to List Very Best Friends

	A	B	C	D	E	F	G	H	I	J	K	L	M
A		x		x									
B				x		x							
C		x					x		x				
D		x				x					x		
E				x			x		x				
F		x		x								x	
G				x					x				
H						x							
I		x											
J					x				x				
K				x									
L				x									x
M												x	
Total....	0	5	0	6	1	4	1	2	2	1	1	1	1

Each child in the classroom is represented by a circle. Lines with arrows indicate the direction of choice of friendship relationships. Children D, B, and F are most popular and are reciprocal friends, as indicated by arrows pointing both to and from each of them. Six arrows pointing to D indicate that six children aspire to friendship relationships with her. Both A and C aspire to friendship relationships with other children; but their aspirations are not reciprocated, and no other children choose them as "best friends." With respect to friendship relationships, these two children are "isolates."

The study of such apparent patterns of friendship relationships can be supplemented by teacher observation, anecdotal records, interviewing, and other procedures. If such further study should confirm the sociogram in indicating that pupils A and C have no friends among their classmates, the teacher is alerted to try to provide for them the kinds of experiences which will make them acceptable and give them opportunities for establishing friendships. The sociogram, supplemented by other devices, is thus a guide to remedial social guidance.

Olson [31] has found that a child's friendship status (isolate to popular) on the sociogram is related to (1) distance of his home from the school, (2) extent

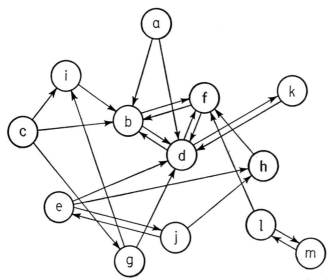

Fig. 14–6. Sociogram shows relative acceptability as a "very best friend" of each child in a classroom.

of home relationships with his classmates, (3) socioeconomic status and education of his parents, (4) carrying of lunch to school or not, (5) selection by the teacher for classroom responsibilities, (6) general maturity of development, and (7) ratings for emotional-social-problem tendencies. For the isolate child, these factors can be investigated and in some instances favorably changed when necessary. As procedures for improving friendship relationships in the classroom, Elliot [9] has suggested (1) providing opportunities for developing friendly relations, (2) enhancing children's social attractiveness by improving their skills and social-adjustment standards, and (3) building appropriate attitudes and confidence in friendship roles. Following teacher-guidance in improving friendship relationships (or other social development), the sociometric study can be repeated to measure possible changes.

Participation Charts

Participation charts, like sociograms, give organization and some quantification to observations of social behavior in certain situations. Attainment of such objectives as "participates effectively with others in group meetings," "reacts thoughtfully to discussion," and "does not monopolize a conversation or discussion, but feels free to contribute timely comments when it seems advisable" can be appraised by participation charts. Class recitations, panel discussions, committee work, and other group activities provide opportunities for guidance, for practice, and for trial and improvement of the skills and attitudes appropriate in such activities. Evaluation of the behavior patterns employed should facilitate improving them. As a standard for evaluating social behavior,

Evaluation of contributions	Participants					
	Chuck	Lyle	Doris	Gerry	Margaret	Kent
Major	|''''|'	///'	///||	|		
Minor	'/'|' |/	'/	|||'	///		
Passive or doubtful	|	////''		|	'|	'|
Distracting	~	///	'			

Fig. 14–7. Discussion-participation chart. Number and lengths of tallies indicate frequency and lengths of each type of oral contribution. (*From Thomas, R. M.: Judging Student Progress, Longmans, New York, 1954, p. 232.*)

Thomas [39] has defined effective group participation as including willing acceptance by a child of his share, contributing to discussion, keeping on the topic or problem, abiding by majority decisions, and permitting others to express their views. By observation of the discussions of such groups, a teacher can make general appraisals of the effectiveness and development of the participants. By systematic charting of their participation, the accuracy and meaning of the observations can be sharpened.

Figure 14–7 shows a teacher's charted observation and evaluation of six children's participation in a committee appointed to plan a phase of a social studies project. By drawing a line of appropriate length and in the appropriate cell as each child contributed to the discussion, the teacher produced a graphic record of the frequency, length, and value of the child's contributions. The discussion for which the chart was recorded follows [39, pp. 230–232]:

[By voting on slips of paper, the group had chosen Chuck as chairman just before the following dialogue began.]

CHUCK: Well, now here's what we're supposed to be doing. . . . Make a plan for showing how our town depends a lot on modern transportation for the way we live.

LYLE: Let's get this straight. Is our committee supposed to do all the work on showing this modern transportation? And how long do we have to do it?

DORIS: The way I understand it, we're supposed to do it all. Just like in that last unit on the town government, every committee has one job.

CHUCK: That's right. And Mr. Corning says this unit's to last about three weeks. Okay?.

LYLE: Yeah. But I'm kind of confused about what we're supposed to do.

CHUCK: Well, let's get some different ideas first. Then maybe it'll be clearer what we should do. What do you think would be a good way to show how our town depends on modern transportation?

LYLE: You mean some way to show the rest of the class? A report or something?

DORIS: Of course, that's why we're doing it.

CHUCK: Kent, you have any ideas?

KENT: No.

CHUCK: Gerry, any ideas about this?

GERALDINE: Well, some way we ought to show all the different kinds of modern transportation . . . like trains and the airfield and cars and trucks.

LYLE: Oh, sure, and bikes and scooters and kiddy-cars. Ha!

CHUCK: Well, Gerry's idea is a start. Margaret, any other ideas.

MARGARET: Gerry's suggestion is all right. The different kinds of modern transportation. But then that really doesn't show how important transportation is.

DORIS: That's right. Just think what it'd be like if all the cars and trains and trucks and airplanes stopped. What would it be like then?

LYLE: Maybe there's an idea. Maybe we could figure out what would happen if all kinds of transportation stopped. Like she says.

CHUCK: Then put on some kind of thing so the class would understand it?

LYLE: Sure.

GERRY: Thing? You mean a program, like a talk or a committee report?

CHUCK: Well, something like that.

DORIS: Oh, let's not have another report. I get bored by them all the time.

LYLE: Well, we have to do it some way . . . a report or something. We always have to report to the class.

DORIS: Well, I about fall asleep every time some committee gets up there and just talks.

LYLE: Yeah, remember when Harry read that big long thing and we snored in the back of the room?

DORIS: And Corning jumped on you for making so much noise?

LYLE: (loud whisper) Shh. He's right behind you.

(Several in the group giggle)

CHUCK: Look. We have to give a report, but we don't want it dull. So why don't we make it like a radio program. You know, like trucks and trains all stopped and this is a news broadcast?

LYLE: You mean, a war or death rays stop everything. And then we see what our town would be like?

GERRY: That might be all right.

DORIS: Say, I know. You know that microphone and that . . . that big thing they use for the square dances in the gym.

CHUCK: You mean the loudspeaker?

LYLE: That's a public-address system. P-A systems, they call them.

DORIS: Well, maybe we could get that and put it in the other room.

GERRY: What in the other room?

DORIS: The microphone . . . and we'd get in there and broadcast. Then the class wouldn't see us, and they'd hear it just like on the radio here in class.

GERRY: How would they hear us if we're in the other room?

DORIS: You just put the microphone in the other room and then run the cord out and put the loudspeaker in this room.

LYLE: Yeah, those P-A systems have a long cord. That'd work.

CHUCK: That sounds good, Doris. Does everybody agree we should do it like that?

LYLE: Okay by me.

GERRY: Me too.

MARGARET: Yes.

CHUCK: How about you, Kent?

KENT: Sure.

CHUCK: All right, now let's see what we've decided so far. We'll have a radio program and broadcast like news flashes. Have maybe some kind of rays shot down from Mars that stop all transportation. And the news broadcast will tell what it would be like if all modern transportation stopped. Agreed? (All nod and say yes.)

The chart indicates that Chuck and Doris participated frequently and most constructively. Lyle participated as frequently as they did, but his contributions were as often passive or doubtful and distracting as they were constructive. Gerry's participation was moderate but tended to be constructive. Margaret and Kent participated only rarely, and then only passively.

When such charts are examined and discussed freely by the participants, they become useful in facilitating social learning. During the group discussion, the participants are often distracted from self-observation of their own roles. The chart permits them to perceive clearly the extent and nature of their participation. It thus becomes a basis for confirming as satisfactory or for correcting their social efforts. And subsequently made charts of other group discussions may reveal progress and thus motivate further effort.

Self-inventories

Among the objectives from Kearney's list about which the child's feelings or attitudes and interests may be appraised are "desires to be clean and attractive"; "feeling a sense of adequacy, personal worth, and esteem"; "interest in stories about other children, their adventures and pets"; "development of tolerance and taste for wide variety in music"; "enjoys various types of literary material—poems, drama, science stories, biographies"; and many others in every curriculum area. Such attitudes and interests are often indirectly appraised by making inferences from observation of children's behavior. If a child often chooses to read science stories, for example, it is assumed that he is interested in them. And if he smiles, talks cheerfully, and works constructively at school tasks, it is inferred that he feels adequate and worthy and esteems himself. But since attitudes and interests reflect the child's own personal and subjective feelings, it has appeared appropriate to some people to ask the child himself to appraise directly his attitudes and interests.

In both the indirect and direct approaches, certain difficulties are incurred in achieving valid and reliable evaluations [7]. Children do not always reveal their true feelings in outwardly manifested behavior. The child may read science to please his parents or because knowing science alleviates his anxiety. Similarly, his self-appraisals of interests and attitudes may reflect his need to please the questioner, rather than constituting an honest and accurate self-appraisal. Even when children are not defensive about revealing their true feelings, they often have difficulty in self-appraisals, because both self-understanding and the skill required for translating feelings into words are achievements dependent upon some maturity. But despite their limitations, the self-inventories, as supplements to other procedures, are useful to the teacher in appraising interests in curriculum areas and in evaluating social and emotional adjustment. Perhaps their chief value, however, is in suggesting *how* more specific objectives in these areas may be inventoried. Three such devices will illustrate the general features of self-inventories.

The Specific Interest Inventory [38] is a list of 100 specific activities classified subjectively into 20 interest areas. Children are instructed to rate these activities from "dislike" to "like" on a 5-point scale. The areas include art, commercial activities, creative imagination, emotional expression, aesthetics, experimenting, social leadership, literary activities, manual activities, arithmetic, mechanical work, music, scientific observing, making orderly arrangements, outdoor activities, physical activities, science, social activities, studying, and vocal expression. The five items sampling art interests illustrate the nature of items in all these areas:

How do you like _____	Dislike		Neutral		Like
1. To sketch picture outlines of trees, people, houses, etc.?	1	2	3	4	5
2. To draw maps or charts?	1	2	3	4	5
3. To copy cartoons or draw original pictures?	1	2	3	4	5
4. To make sketches of dresses, hats, furniture?	1	2	3	4	5
5. To model or carve figures or vases from clay?	1	2	3	4	5

A very recently published similar inventory of children's interests [40] classifies 294 items into eight categories and yields a profile of standardized percentile scores indicative of interests in (1) art, (2) music, (3) social studies, (4) quiet play activities, (5) active play activities, (6) craft constructions, (7) helping with things around the house, and (8) science. The following items, one from each of the above categories, suggest the specific interests appraised by this "what-I-like-to-do" inventory:

Would you like to:

	No	?	Yes
1. Make pictures with crayons?	☐	☐	☐
2. Play in an orchestra?	☐	☐	☐
3. Hear about life in the jungles of Africa and South America?	☐	☐	☐
4. Play baseball?	☐	☐	☐
5. Listen to stories on the radio—or watch stories on TV?	☐	☐	☐
6. Make model airplanes or model boats?	☐	☐	☐
7. Wash or iron clothes?	☐	☐	☐
8. Find out why salt is so necessary for good health?	☐	☐	☐

A valid appraisal of such a pattern of interests would be very useful in the teaching and guidance of children. But using the "what-I-like-to-do" inventory and checking it against other procedures reveals some limitations. For example, the profile for a twelve-year-old child for whom close observation and evaluation of her art products have revealed sustained and intense interest in creative art shows her at only the 20th percentile in art interest. On the art section quoted above from the Stewart-Brainard Specific Interest Inventory, however, this child achieves the relatively high score of 21, earning 5 points each on items (1), (3), and (5). She earns only 2 points on item (4) because, as she said, "I don't particularly like to draw sketches of dresses, hats, and furniture; I like to draw pictures of people and animals." The inconsistency between these two inventories of art interests and the failure of one of them to reflect her true interests suggest two limitations of some such inventories. They are subject to error from "response sets" [7, pp. 50–55]; and the items are not always validly representative of the category title.

The error resulting from the particular response set taken by this child on the "what-I-like-to-do" inventory is indicated by her comment: "I marked 'yes' for 'make pictures with crayons,' 'carve things out of wood,' and 'draw unusual designs' because I like *very much* to do *them*. I also like to 'look at famous paintings'; but I don't enjoy that quite so much as the first three, so I marked the '?' for it." Only the "yes" answers, however, are counted in scoring. Another child with only a mild interest in art but with less concern for discriminative self-evaluations might have said "yes" to all four items. Thus it appears that a child with only mild art interests might actually score higher in art on this inventory than a child with intense art interests. If the child intensely interested in art had been permitted to indicate her intensity of interest, as is possible on the Stewart-Brainard Specific Interest Inventory, she would have rated the first three items 5, ("like very much") and the item on looking at famous paintings 4 ("like it somewhat"). This would have resulted in greater consistency between the two inventories of art interests. The error from inclusion of heterogeneous and unequally representative items in an interest category is indicated in the child's explanation of why she wrote "No" for the item: "Would you like to trace stencils to make pictures?" She said, "I don't like to *trace* pictures; I like to draw them myself." According to this child, *"tracing* pictures" does not belong in a list of items considered to be indicative of interest in art.

Despite the limitations of particular inventories, as a technique the self-inventory is useful and readily adaptable in appraising attainment of many interests set up as educational objectives in Kearney's list. In constructing such inventories, teachers are alerted to try to avoid by careful directions ambiguous response sets and the inclusion in a single category of heterogeneous items.

As an example of the use of the self-inventory in appraising such attitudes from Kearney's list as "feeling a sense of adequacy, personal worth, and esteem," the Elementary Series of the California Test of Personality [41] is here described briefly. Depending upon how the child answers 12 questions in each of the 12 subcategories of the inventory, the quality of the child's self-adjustment and social adjustment are measured. In order to suggest more explicitly the meaning of the traits measured in the California Test of Personality, a sample question and its favorable answer from each subdivision are quoted:

Self-reliance: "Do you usually keep at your work until it is done?" (Yes)
Sense of Personal Worth: "Can you do most of the things you try?" (Yes)
Sense of Personal Freedom: "Are you allowed enough time for play?" (Yes)
Feeling of Belonging: "Do you think that nobody likes you?" (No)
Freedom from Withdrawing Tendencies: "Are people often mean or unfair to you?" (No)
Freedom from Nervous Symptoms: "Do you bite your fingernails often?" (No)
Social Standards: "Is it necessary to thank those who have helped you?" (Yes)
Social Skills: "Do you help new pupils talk to other children?" (Yes)
Freedom from Antisocial Tendencies: "Do you often have to make a 'fuss' or 'act up' to get your rights?" (No)
Family Relations: "Do your folks seem to think that you are just as good as they are?" (Yes)
School Relations: "Does it seem to you that some teachers have it in for pupils?" (No)
Community Relations: "Do you sometimes help other people?" (Yes)

Sums of favorable answers, ranging from 0 to 12 in each subdivision, are converted into percentile scores. The higher the percentile, the better the adjustment is presumed to be.

A profile of the adjustment traits measured is shown in Figure 14–8. It reveals this fourth grade girl as feeling generally well adjusted, both personally and socially. Only one score—that indicating some restriction in her "sense of personal freedom"—appears significantly low. Here the 25th-percentile score resulted from only three unfavorable answers: she answered "No" to the items: "May you usually choose your own friends?" "Are you allowed to do most of the things you want to?" and "Are you given some spending money?" There is little justification for assuming that a child's unfavorable answers to three such questions are valid and reliable indications of his *general* lack of a "sense of personal freedom." The meaning of these answers, however, should be explored further in interviews with both the child and her parent. The child might very well be asked to tell about the specific experiences that led to her answers and to elaborate further on her feelings about them. She may actually feel comfortable about relations with her parents despite these three answers—which is suggested by her favorable answers to nine such questions as: "May you usually bring your friends home when you want to?" The parent-teacher conference might also yield further understanding of the parent-child relationship—whether it is democratic, flexible, and warm, or autocratic, rigid, and coercive for the child. This example, therefore, should suggest that such inventories are not to be trusted alone for valid and

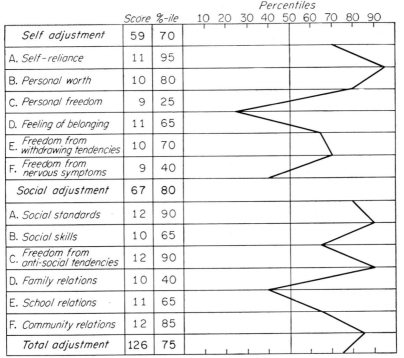

	Score	%-ile	Percentiles
Self adjustment	59	70	
A. Self-reliance	11	95	
B. Personal worth	10	80	
C. Personal freedom	9	25	
D. Feeling of belonging	11	65	
E. Freedom from withdrawing tendencies	10	70	
F. Freedom from nervous symptoms	9	40	
Social adjustment	67	80	
A. Social standards	12	90	
B. Social skills	10	65	
C. Freedom from anti-social tendencies	12	90	
D. Family relations	10	40	
E. School relations	11	65	
F. Community relations	12	85	
Total adjustment	126	75	

FIG. 14–8. California Test of Personality profile is indicative of personal and social adjustment of a fourth grade girl age 9-9. (*Chart, not the scores, adapted from California Test of Personality—Elementary, Form A: A Profile of Personal and Social Adjustment, California Test Bureau, Los Angeles, 1951.*)

reliable appraisals of the attitudes which they are intended to measure. But as supplements to other procedures, they are useful.

Performance Tests

Performance tests sample skills and proficiencies directly in typical every-day-life situations. Instead of asking the subject to express his knowledge and understanding indirectly through "pencil-and-paper" tests, firsthand work samples of proficiency are often obtained by requiring him to manipulate objects, tools, or machines or to demonstrate in "real-life" performances. Performance tests, either standardized or teacher-made, are well suited to measuring attainment of such objectives as skills in "folk dancing with figures and sets and a variety of rhythmic steps"; "increasing motor coordination and dexterity, for girls, in sewing and handling cooking utensils and, for boys, in using hammer, saw, screw driver, plane, square, chisel, brace and bit";

"operating household appliances and making some of the minor repairs and adjustments about the home"; "blending his voice in part or unison singing or playing some simple musical instrument"; and "can write legibly 40 letters a minute or 60 letters a minute if the material is repetitive with a quality of 50 on the Ayres scale."

The essential steps in developing performance tests for appraising such objectives as these are (1) selection of appropriate and representative performances for sampling, (2) collecting the necessary test materials, (3) writing clear directions for eliciting efficient performances, (4) establishing performance norms on the basis of representative school children, (5) checking the reliability of the tests, and (6) revising them when desirable. The use of norms for interpreting behavior on performance tests is illustrated here for motor skills and for handwriting.

Table 14–14 from Jenkins's study [25] of primary children's skills in a variety of common motor-play activities shows the average performances of children at ages 5, 6, and 7. The table indicates that during these years children

Table 14–14. Mean Scores in Various Motor Performances.

Motor test	Ages					
	5 years		6 years		7 years	
	Boys	Girls	Boys	Girls	Boys	Girls
35-yd dash, sec.........................	9.3	9.7	8.5	8.8	7.9	8.0
50-ft hop, sec............................	10.8	10.3	9.2	8.9	8.8	7.6
Baseball throw, ft.......................	23.6	14.5	32.8	17.8	41.4	24.4
Soccer-ball kick, ft......................	11.5	8.0	18.4	10.1	25.4	15.0
Beanbag toss at 20 ft, in. from target.......	23.7	39.3	15.7	29.5	15.6	23.3
Standing broad jump, in..................	33.7	31.6	39.3	38.0	42.2	41.0
Running broad jump, in..................	34.4	28.6	45.2	40.0	58.8	50.8
Jump and reach, in......................	2.5	2.2	4.0	3.5	5.0	4.3

Source: Lulu M. Jenkins: *A Comparative Study of Motor Achievements of Children Five, Six, and Seven Years of Age*, Contributions to Education, no. 414, Teachers College, Columbia University, Bureau of Publications, New York, 1930, pp. 22–43.

are making rapid gains in these skills. For example, at five years, the *average* distance which a boy can throw a baseball is 24 feet; at six years, it is 33 feet; and at seven years, it is 41 feet. Wide ranges of individual deviations, of course, are expected about these averages.

The Ayres scale for measuring handwriting [1] consists of eight samples of handwriting varying in legibility and in general quality from a low value of 20, through an average value at the sixth grade level of 50 to 60, to a very high level of 90. Three levels of this scale are reproduced in Figure 14–9. In apply-

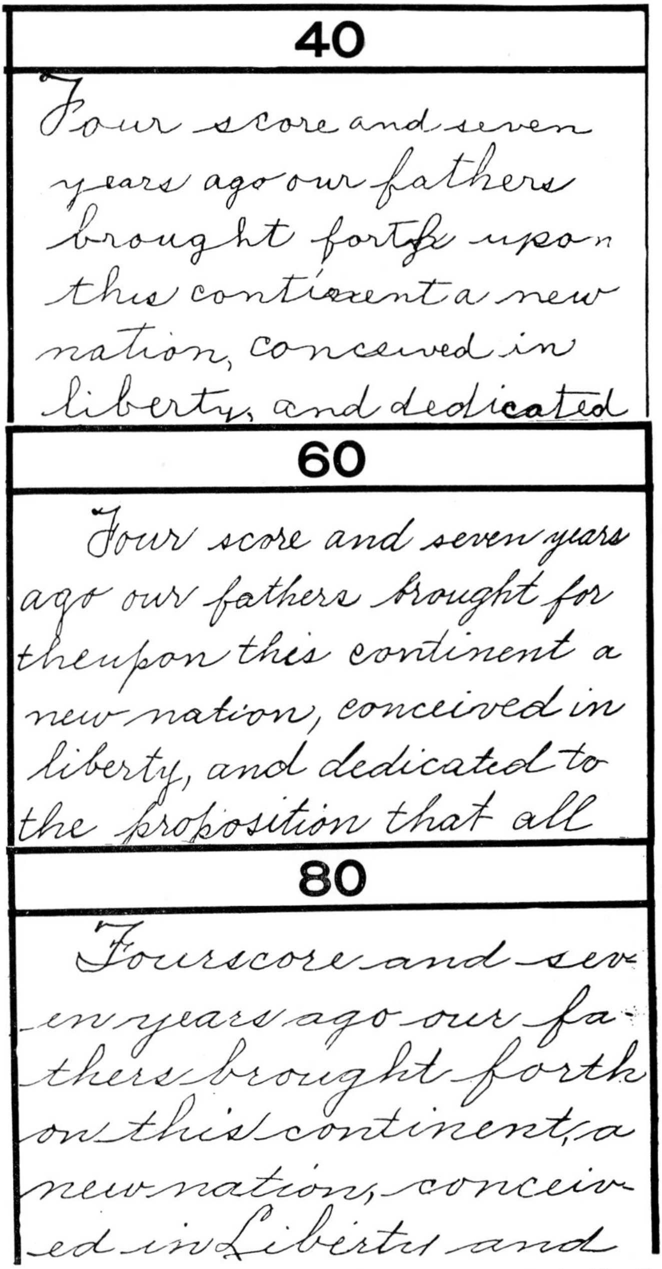

Fig. 14–9. Samples of quality 40, 60, and 80 from the Ayres Handwriting Scale, which measures quality from levels 20 through 90. (*From Ayres, L. P.: A Scale for Measuring the Quality of Handwriting of School Children, Department of Education Bulletin 113, Russell Sage, New York, 1912.*)

ing the scale, a work sample of a child's handwriting performance is rated by determining the standardized scale sample it most nearly matches. The speed of writing, in number of letters written per minute, is determined by counting the letters written in one minute of the Gettysburg Address.

Performance norms on this test, for both quality and speed, are indicated in Figure 14–10. According to the norm data supplied by Ayres [1], an average sixth grade child writes with a quality between 50 and 60 and at a speed of

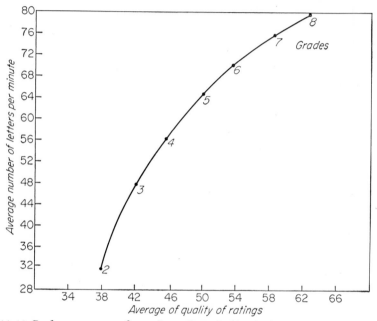

Fig. 14–10. Performance norms for quality and speed of handwriting. (*From Ayres, L. P.: A Scale for Measuring the Quality of Handwriting of School Children, Department of Education Bulletin 113, Russell Sage, New York, 1912.*)

about 70 letters per minute. The same norm data, however, reveal that the *range* in legibility of sixth grade pupils' writing is from quality levels 20 to 90.

Parent-teacher Conferences in Evaluating School Achievement

In playing their complementary roles in educating children, parents and teachers achieve several purposes by regular conferences. One of these important purposes is evaluation of child achievement and progress; and because it is a purpose in which both are interested, it affords a good basis for establishing cooperative attitudes and mutual educational efforts. The teacher has the major responsibility for evaluating a child's achievements; and in the parent-teacher conference, she often interprets her appraisals to the parents. Parents, however, have better opportunities than teachers to observe the attainment of such objectives from Kearney's list as "habitual washing of hands before eating and after going to the toilet," "can spend up to an hour an evening on constructive projects without parental supervision," "performs his proper duties and chores and shares responsibilities of the family," and many other, similar objectives. In the parent-teacher conferences, parents can contribute to evaluation of such objectives by reporting on their home observations of their children. Thus in sharing the responsibility of appraising pupil achievement and progress, parents and teachers each make unique contributions. In these joint efforts, the teacher will probably contribute statements of significant objectives to be evaluated and also supply such techniques as the check list described on page 497. She will also keep records of the evaluations.

Cumulative Records

Appraisal of pupils' achievement is worthwhile only when it facilitates their learning and development. This important function of evaluation is accomplished most effectively when the appraisal records are studied and interpreted both in their interrelations and developmentally. Comprehensive and cumulative records make this goal of evaluation attainable. For example, in Table 13–1 (page 416) it appears that at the beginning of the third grade R.K.'s achievement is only slightly below the average for that of his classmates. In reading, his grade equivalent of 4-8 is above average; in arithmetic, his grade equivalent of 3-8 is about average; and in social studies (3-1) and language (2-5) he is below average. Comparing these ratings with his distinctively high capacity for achievement and learning (IQ. 152), however, he is very retarded in all phases of achievement. With a mental age of about 13½, he should have probably attained grade-equivalent scores nearer to 8. Perhaps some understanding of his failure to achieve up to his potential capacity and guidance in correcting it could have been attained by more comprehensive evaluative and diagnostic study. Unfortunately the records of such study are not available. But his mother reports from her recollection of parent-teacher conferences that his fourth grade teacher, alerted by the test results, began to recognize R.K.'s high intellectual abilities, to take a friendly interest in him, to give appropriate guidance and encouragement to his learning efforts, and to enrich his curriculum. Over the next three years, R.K. made remarkable progress, attaining at the end of grade 6 in reading, social studies, language, and arithmetic grade equivalents of 11-2, 10-5, 7-8, and 7-6, respectively.

This unusual progress is not surprising, however, when it is interpreted in *relation* to the record of his superior intellectual capacities.

Understanding and effective guidance of child development and accomplishments require comprehensive evaluation of pupil characteristics and achievements in *all* the curriculum-objective areas. There should be provision in the records for reporting physical characteristics, intelligence and special abilities, interests, personality, nature of parent-child relationships, and for recording regular appraisals of understandings, skills, interests, and attitudes in the areas of (1) physical development, health, and body care; (2) social and emotional development; (3) ethical behavior; (4) social relations; (5) the social world; (6) the natural environment; (7) aesthetic development; (8) communication; and (9) quantitative relations [26]. Moreover, the comprehensive records need to be accumulated as the child progresses through school, so that whenever they are studied for child guidance purposes, they can be interpreted developmentally.

As another example of this need, it is noted that Harold (Chapter 13, p. 405), at the mid-term of his fourth grade year, earns a grade-equivalent score of 2-9 on Gray's Standardized Oral Reading Paragraphs. Since the record shows that Harold has an IQ of 110, from the cross-section point of view this grade-equivalent score of only 2-9 looks bad. But considered from the developmental point of view, it is really just cause for the elation that both Harold and his teacher feel. At the *beginning* of the year, the record indicates that he "recognizes only the few 'sight words' he remembers and lacks completely skill and confidence in independent identification of the many unfamiliar words he meets." Now, in the mid-term follow-up diagnostic report, it is noted that "Harold is acquiring skills in using the context and in applying phonetic and visual analysis of words as independent word-identification techniques." Moreover, "even though he still has obvious difficulties in reading, his approach is systematic and confident and he is pleased with himself." Apparently, Harold is responding nicely to the remedial instruction and treatment for emotional handicaps which diagnostic study at the beginning of the year indicated were needed. And this indication of his *progress* is more significant than his present status.

The record form for cumulative evaluation needs to be carefully considered. If a 9- by 11½-inch manila folder is used, provision might be made on the front, inside pages, and back for recording test scores periodically. Such a folder can also be used for filing inside anecdotal records, parent-teacher-conference notes, check lists, etc. However, in order to keep the file from becoming too bulky and to make it easier to interpret, such records should be summarized at the end of each year and only the summaries left in the folder. Each teacher needs a file for safekeeping of the cumulative records. At the beginning of each year they are, of course, transmitted to the child's new teacher for her guidance and contributions.

Summary

Evaluation and measurement of pupil achievement is integrally related to every important teaching function. Because appraisal of objectives often facilitates learning, as is illustrated especially in diagnostic and remedial teaching, it is important that extent of attainment of *all* significant objectives be evaluated. Using Kearney's statement [26] as a comprehensive list of worthwhile objectives for elementary school children, it is observed that a wide variety of appraisal procedures are needed to evaluate or measure attainment of understanding, skills, interests, and attitudes in the several curriculum-objective areas. Fourteen different evaluation and measurement devices have been described and partially evaluated for their validity, reliability, teaching utility, and efficiency in appraising the objectives for which each device is appropriate. Continual and effective use of these and possibly other procedures may be expected to facilitate learning [24 and 28]. Finally, in order to interpret pupil-achievement status and progress from the points of view both of inter-relationships and of development, comprehensive and cumulative records are needed.

Review and Applications

1. How can measurement and evaluation facilitate pupil learning and attainment of desirable objectives?

2. Why is it important to appraise attainment of representative samples of *all* the elementary school objectives? How can this teaching function be accomplished?

3. What are the general characteristics of good testing devices? Describe a specific device which you think satisfactorily meets these criteria.

4. For some limited elementary school learning activity of your choice—reading comprehension at a particular level, understanding a social studies unit, understanding of a phase of fractions, etc.—construct tests for appraising attainment of the important objectives. Ask your classmates to evaluate your tests in the light of the criteria in this chapter.

5. Which of the fifteen appraisal devices could you use for appraising attainment of objectives (*a*) in the nutrition unit described in Chapter 1, (*b*) in a teaching project you have observed, (*c*) in a teaching project you have planned?

References

1. Ayres, L. P.: *A Scale for Measuring the Quality of Handwriting of School Children*, Department of Education Bulletin 113, Russell Sage, New York, 1912.

2. Blackham, G. J.: "The diagnosis and treatment of children's personality and behavior disorders," unpublished master's thesis, Utah State Agricultural College Library, Logan, 1952.

3. Brownell, W. A., and B. Watson: "The comparative worth of two diagnostic techniques in arithmetic," *J. Educ. Res.*, 29: 664–676, 1936.

4. Bryan, M. M.: "Iowa Every-pupil Tests of Basic Skills," in O. K. Buros (ed.): *The Fourth Mental Measurements Yearbook*, Gryphon, Highland Park, N.J., 1953.

5. Buckingham, R. B.: *Buckingham's Extension of the Ayres Spelling Scale*, Public School, Bloomington, Ill. 1918.

6. Cook, W. C.: "The functions of measurements in the facilitation of learning," in Lindquist, E. F. (ed.): *Educational Measurement*, American Council on Education, Washington, 1951.

7. Cronbach, L. J.: *Essentials of Psychological Testing*, Harper, New York, 1949.

8. Ebel, R. L.: "Writing the test item," in Lindquist, E. F., (ed.): *Educational Measurement*, American Council on Education, Washington, 1951.

9. Elliot, M. H.: "Patterns of friendship in the classroom," *Progr. Educ.*, 18: 383–390, 1941.

10. Findley, W. G.: "California Achievement Tests," in O. K. Buros (ed.): *The Fourth Mental Measurements Yearbook*, Gryphon, Highland Park, N.J., 1953.

11. Fitzgerald, J. A., et al.: *Coordinated Scales of Attainment: Master Manual*, Batteries 4–8, Educational Test Bureau, Minneapolis, 1949.

12. Freeman, F. N.: *Teaching of Handwriting*, Riverside Educational Monographs, Houghton Mifflin, Boston, 1914.

13. Gates, A. I.: *Gates Advanced Primary Reading Tests: For Grade 2 (Second Half) and Grade 3*, rev. ed., Teachers College, Columbia University, Bureau of Publications, New York, 1942.

14. ———: *Gates Primary Reading Tests* and manual, rev. ed., Teachers College, Columbia University, Bureau of Publications, New York, 1942.

15. ———: *The Improvement of Reading*, Macmillan, New York, 1947.

16. ———: *Manual of Directions for Gates Basic Reading Test: For Grade 3 (Second Half) through Grade 8*, Teachers College, Columbia University, Bureau of Publications, New York, 1942.

17. ———: *Manual of Directions for Gates Reading Survey Test: For Grade 3 (Second Half) to Grade 10*, Teachers College, Columbia University, Bureau of Publications, New York, 1942.

18. Gray, H., D. R. Votaw, and J. L. Rogers: *The Gray-Votaw-Rogers General Achievement Tests*, Steck Co., Austin, Tex., 1948.

19. Gray, W. S.: *Standardized Oral Reading Paragraphs*, Public School, Bloomington, Ill., 1915.

20. Greene, H. A., A. N. Jorgenson, and J. R. Gerberich: *Measurement and Evaluation in the Elementary School*, Longmans, New York, 1953.

21. Haggerty, M. E., W. C. Olson, and E. K. Wickman: *Haggerty-Olson-Wickman Behavior Rating Schedules*, World, Yonkers, N.Y., 1930.

22. Harap, H., and Charlotte E. Mapes: "The learning of fundamentals in an arithmetic activity program," *Elem. Sch. J.*, 34: 515–525, 1934.

23. *Helping Teachers Understand Children*. American Council on Education, Commission on Teacher Education, Washington, 1945.

24. Henmon, V. A. C.: "Improvement in school subjects throughout the school year," *J. Educ. Res.*, 1: 81–95, 1920.

25. Jenkins, Lulu M.: *A Comparative Study of Motor Achievements of Children at Five, Six, and Seven Years of Age*, Contributions to Education, no. 414, Teachers College, Columbia University, Bureau of Publications, New York, 1930.

26. Kearney, N. C.: *Elementary School Objectives*, Russell Sage, New York, Copyright, 1953, by the Russell Sage Foundation.

27. Kelley, T. L., et al.: *Stanford Achievement Test, Forms J, K, L, M, N* and manual, World, Yonkers, N.Y., 1953.

28. Keys, N.: "The influence on learning and retention of weekly as opposed to monthly tests," *J. Educ. Psychol.*, 25: 427–436, 1934.

29. Lindquist, E. T. (ed.): *Educational Measurement*, American Council on Education, Washington, 1951.

30. McCormick, C. F.: "The anecdotal record in appraisal of personality," *Sch. Soc.*, 53: 126–127, 1941.

31. Olson, W. C.: "The improvement of human relations in the classroom," *Child Educ.*, 22: 317–326, 1946.

32. *Personality Report*, Revision B, American Council on Education, Washington, 1929.

33. Ramharter, Hazel K., and H. C. Johnson: "Methods of attack used by 'good' and 'poor' achievers in attempting to correct errors in six types of subtraction involving fractions," *J. Educ. Res.*, 42: 586–597, 1949.

34. Remmers, H. H., and N. L. Gage: *Educational Measurement and Evaluation*, Harper, New York, 1955.

35. Ross, C. C., and J. C. Stanley: *Measurement in Today's Schools*, Prentice-Hall, Englewood Cliffs, N.J., 1954.

36. Schindler, A. W.: "Coordinated Scales of Attainment," in O. K. Buros (ed.): *The Fourth Mental Measurements Yearbook*, Gryphon, Highland Park, N.J., 1953.

37. Spitzer, H. F., et al.: *Iowa Every-pupil Tests of Basic Skills: Elementary Battery*, Houghton Mifflin, Boston, 1945.

38. Stewart, F. J., and P. P. Brainard: *Specific Interest Inventory*, Forms B and G, Psychological Corporation, New York, 1932.

39. Thomas, R. M.: *Judging Student Progress*, Longmans, New York, 1954.

40. Thorpe, L. P., C. E. Meyers, and M. R. Sea: *What I Like to Do: An Inventory of Children's Interests* and examiner's manual, Science Research, Chicago, 1954.

41. ———, E. W. Tiegs, and W. W. Clark: *California Test of Personality—Elementary, Form A: A Profile of Personal and Social Adjustment* and manual, California Test Bureau, Los Angeles, 1942.

42. Tiegs, E. W., and W. W. Clark: *California Achievement Tests—Complete Battery* and manual, California Test Bureau, Los Angeles, 1951.

43. Topp, R. F.: "Preadolescent behavior patterns suggestive of emotional malfunctioning," *Elem. Sch. J.*, 52: 340–343, Copyright, 1952, by the University of Chicago. Reprinted by permission of the University of Chicago Press.

44. Wilson, L. A.: "Techniques for the integrated procedures within the classroom," *Educ. Admin. Supervis.*, 40: 395–404, 1954.

45. Woltring, Clara: "Analyzing the form of handwriting in the second grade," *Elem. Sch. J.*, 29: 358–365, 1928–1929.

Glossary

This glossary is a convenient supplement to an unabridged dictionary. It includes definitions of all the technical terms and of many common words as they are used in this text.

ABSTRACT — Symbolic of the general, common features of a class of things or events, rather than of a particular thing or event.

ABSTRACTING — Responding to the common features of a variety of things or events to achieve a general concept; generalizing.

ACCELERATION — Advance more rapid than the average. As applied to rate of grade progress in school, it refers to skipping grades or to completing more than one grade in a year.

ACQUISITION — Act of gaining or acquiring something; act of learning a concept or skill.

ACTIVITY CURRICULUM — A unified curriculum organized around children's interests both in their own activities and in society's major functions.

ACTIVITY DRIVES — Inherent impulses to activity and motive satisfaction in activities, including all the motor, perceptual, and intellectual activities of which the individual is capable.

ADAPTIVE — Capable of adjusting behavior through problem solving so as to meet varied situations effectively.

ADJUSTMENT — The quality of an individual's efficiency and happiness in his relationship to his environment, especially in his interpersonal relations.

ADJUSTMENT INVENTORY — A classified list of questions which an individual answers about himself, intended to appraise the quality of his self- and social adjustment

ADOLESCENCE — The period of life from the onset of puberty (sexual maturity) to adulthood, roughly from age 13 to 20.

ADVENTITIOUS — Extrinsic; accidental; not essentially related to other events.

AFFECTIVE — Pertaining to the pleasant or unpleasant qualities of emotional experience.

ALLITERATIVE — Repeating the same letter or sound at the beginning of two or more words in sequence.

ANALOGY — A relationship, similarity, or congruence between things or events.

ANALYTICAL — Resolving into elements or constituent parts.

ANCILLARY. Subservient; auxiliary; of preliminary help to another process.

517

ANECDOTAL RECORDS — Recorded observations of significant (child) behavior episodes.

ANXIETY — A persisting fear of threat to oneself, arising from severe insecurity or from the expression of dangerous impulses and involving feelings of apprehension, dread, and uneasiness.

APPRAISE — To estimate, judge, or evaluate the quality or excellence of performance or results.

APTITUDE — Potential capacity for learning and becoming proficient in some particular area, such as music, art, or mathematics.

ASPIRATION, LEVEL OF — The level of performance in a succession of learning tasks with established possibilities for improvement which an individual sets for himself and aspires toward in a later trial.

ASSIGNMENT-RECITATION PROCEDURE — A traditional method of teaching whereby the teacher assigns a lesson which the pupils study and then recite in some question-answer fashion to the teacher.

AUTOMATIZATION OF RESPONSES — Reduction to internal-response-produced stimuli of the cues needed for guiding behavior.

AUTONOMIC — Referring to processes not consciously controlled but involuntarily regulated by the autonomic nervous system.

AUTONOMY — Independence; self-control; self-management.

BEHAVIOR PATTERN — An organization or configuration of specific responses, adapted to some purpose.

BELONGINGNESS (Thorndike) — The logical appropriateness or fittingness of learned stimulus-response connections.

CAPACITY — The innate basis of potential abilities.

CHECK LIST — As an appraisal device, a list of traits or behavior patterns which a rater checks to indicate which items are characteristic of an individual.

CLINICAL INTERVIEW — A diagnostic interview in which the school counselor or psychologist appraises from samples of behavior an individual's strengths and weaknesses—in language, methods of work or problem solving, attitudes, defenses of self-ideal, and emotional control.

COEFFICIENT OF DETERMINATION — The square of the coefficient of correlation (r^2), which indicates the proportion of variation in one trait related to the variation in the trait with which it is correlated.

COGNITIVE — Pertaining to the mental or intellectual processes of perceiving and conceiving, or of knowing or comprehending.

COGNITIVE MAP — Figuratively, a mental map by which behavior is guided; presumably a brain process, subject to organization and reorganization by learning activity, which controls conscious behavior.

COMPENSATORY — Referring to defensive overemphasis of some pattern of behavior because of frustrated motives and threatened loss of self-esteem in another area.

COMPONENTS — The elements, constituents, or parts of a whole.

COMPULSIVE — Referring to stereotyped, irrational, anxiety-motivated patterns of behavior.

CONCEPT — An idea or generalization which represents a class of things or events, such as carbohydrates as a class of foods.

CONCEPTUALIZE — To interpret, understand, or conceive things or events in terms of concepts or generalizations.

CONCRETE — Pertaining to direct experience with real, actual, specific things.

CONDITIONED RESPONSE — An acquired response which an individual has learned to make to stimuli which originally did not elicit it.

CONFABULATION—Fabrication to compensate for lack of ability or knowledge in meeting a problem. For example, a child is employing confabulation when, unable to read, he "makes up" what he naïvely hopes will be an acceptable story.

CONFIGURATION — The pattern or arrangement of parts constituting a whole.

CONNECTION (Thorndike) — The association of a specific response to a specific stimulus.

CONNECTIONIST (Thorndike) — One who accepts the general theory that learning consists of establishing specific stimulus-response connections and that complex behavior can be analyzed into such stimulus-response components.

CONNOTATIONS — Implied or suggested meanings.

CONTEXT CUES — Clues for recognizing or identifying a word from the meaning suggested by the sentence as a whole.

CONTIGUITY — Position or occurrence of things or events close together in place or time.

CONTROL GROUP — A group of subjects used for comparison with an experimental group on whom the effect of some special treatment is being tested. Both groups are pretested, end-tested, and otherwise treated in the same way, except for the absence in the control group of the special experimental treatment which is being studied.

CORRELATION — A numerical index of the degree of relationship between two variables or measures on the same population, such as intelligence and reading achievement for a group of school children. Coefficients of correlation range from $+1.00$ (perfect relationship) through .00 (no relationship) to -1.00 (perfect inverse relationship).

COUNTER-AGGRESSION — Reciprocated hostility; counter-attack.

COUNTERBALANCED ORDER — An order of presentation of learning tasks or tests being compared in an experiment to prevent unequal practice effects from one activity to another. For example, in comparing mastery of learning tasks A and B, half the subjects (randomly chosen) would learn A first and B second, while the other half would learn B first and A second.

CREATIVE PRODUCTIVITY — Extent to which one's talents and resources are fully used for personal and social ends; degree of realizing one's potentialities.

CRITERION — The level of learning achievement or test performance considered indicative of mastery or adequate for the purpose of the experiment.

CRITICAL RATIO — The ratio of an experimentally obtained difference on some measure to the size of the differences which could be expected to occur from chance errors of sampling and measurement. For relatively large samples, ratios of 2.58 and 1.96 indicate that such obtained differences could have occurred by chance less than 1 or 5 times in 100, respectively. Such differences are considered to be "very significant" or "significant."

CRUTCH — An auxiliary device sometimes helpful in the initial stages in learning a process, usually abandoned for a more efficient mode of attack as the learner becomes more proficient and confident.

CUING — Guiding behavior by discriminated stimuli or cues.

CULTURAL BIAS — A tendency of some tests intended for general use to give an experience advantage to particular groups or segments of a culture, such as the tendency for children from urban as contrasted with rural cultures to have an advantage on certain intelligence tests.

CULTURAL HERITAGE — The organized sum of knowledge accumulated by previous generations of society and available for transmission to each new generation.

CUMULATIVE RECORDS — Continuous records on significant aspects of a child's progress throughout his school years, including data on physical growth and health, abilities, interests, emotional and social adjustment, and achievement.

CURRICULUM — The sum of all the learning experiences from which educational objectives are to be attained.

CURSIVE WRITING — (See MANUSCRIPT WRITING.)

DEDUCE — To derive logically; to draw a conclusion.

DEDUCTIVE REASONING — Application of a generalization to a particular instance; inferring a specific outcome from a general principle.

DEFENSE MECHANISMS — Adjustments to frustration and threats to loss of self-esteem by avoiding, not recognizing, or covering up personal traits which would otherwise provoke anxiety and guilt. Withdrawal, repression, overcompensation, and projection are examples.

DETERMINANT — A cause of an event or action.

DEVELOPMENTAL — Referring to the gradual emergence of children's traits and behavior patterns.

DEVELOPMENTAL SEQUENCE — An orderly succession of "stages" which children go through as a result of both maturing personally and learning in the areas of reading, arithmetic, art, and social development.

DEVELOPMENTAL TASKS — The common major personal accomplishments required of children as they mature. Some common developmental tasks of adolescents, for example, are becoming more independent, achieving appropriate and comfortable heterosexual relationships, identifying with a vocational role, and achieving a satisfying participant role in the community.

DEVIATION IQS — A device for quantitative interpretation of certain intelligence test scores, in which deviations above or below a mean IQ of 100 are computed in terms of the standard deviation in the distribution of scores, often arbitrarily equated to 15 IQ points.

DIAGNOSTIC (DIAGNOSTIC TEST) — A test, usually an achievement test, for which items are constructed and arranged to yield scores indicative of an individual's specific strengths and weaknesses.

DIAGNOSTIC AND REMEDIAL TEACHING — A sequence of testing and teaching activities in which teaching is guided by knowledge of children's specific learning difficulties and of their resources for overcoming them.

DIFFERENTIATION — Change from a general, homogeneous pattern or function to a more discriminate and categorized pattern or to more specific functions.

DIMINUTION — Act of making smaller; reduction in size.

DISCIPLINE — (*a*) To train for general intellectual effectiveness. (*b*) To establish personal or social control appropriate to the social activity of one's group.

DISCRIMINATION — Perception of a difference between two or more stimulus objects or events.

DISPLACED AGGRESSION — Misdirected aggression; attacks on innocent persons and objects rather than on the true cause of the frustration.

DISTRIBUTED PRACTICE — Division of the total time required for mastering a learning task into several short periods with rest intervals between them.

DRILL — Repetitive practice intended to improve proficiency of skills.

DYNAMIC — Active; energizing; effective as a determiner of action.

ECLECTIC — Choosing and combining ideas from various sources and systems of ideas.

EGO — The individual's conception of himself; the perceived and controlling self.

EGOCENTRIC — Self-oriented, rather than being responsive to tasks or to other people.

ELICIT — To draw out, to bring forth, or to stimulate a response.

EMERGENCE OF ABILITIES — The appearance as a child matures of new fundamental abilities, such as walking, talking, drawing a square, or riding a bicycle, rather than mere refinements in the skillful performance of these activities.

EMOTIONAL HEALTH — Self-integration and emotional control suited to the individual's maturity, so that anxiety, guilt, excessive aggression, or other disturbing emotions do not impair the individual's personal efficiency and happiness.

ENRICHED CURRICULUM — A school curriculum providing for superior or gifted children greater depth of study, more scope and variety of activities, and more creative learning in fields suited to each child's special talents.

EQUATED GROUPS — Groups made equal; experimental and control groups selected so as to be equal with respect to sex, age, and intelligence.

ERRORS OF SAMPLING AND MEASUREMENT — The variations in mean test scores of successive samplings of a population which occur because of the inadequacy of each sample as representative of the population and because of the unreliability of the test applied.

EVALUATE — To judge, estimate, or appraise carefully the amount, quality, or value of performance or results.

EXPERIENTIAL BACKGROUND — A resultant of accumulated experience; a product of having lived through events or activities.

EXPLICIT — Openly, directly, and unambiguously expressed; not merely implied.

EXTRACURRICULAR ACTIVITIES — Activities carried on beyond and usually more independently than the "academic" activities of the school, including participation in clubs, athletics, etc.

EXTRAPOLATE — To extend the range of norms or expected scores on a standardized test by predicting the extrapolated (extended) scores from the trend of known scores.

FACILITATE — To aid or assist; to make easier.

FACTORS — The elements or constituent parts of a whole, such as the relatively independent primary abilities comprising intelligence.

FEEDBACK — The perceptual reactions of a person to his own responses; a process by which goal-directed responses are checked and corrected.

FIGURE-GROUND — Differentiation in perception such that distinctive, differentiated objects or events appear as figures on a homogeneous, less differentiated background.

FIXATION — Act of becoming fixed, stable, or firmly stereotyped in some behavior pattern.

FLASH CARD — A card on which a word or phrase is exposed for perception for only a very brief period (a second or less).

FREE-ASSOCIATIVE RESPONSES — Responses to whatever comes to mind, rather than to the goals, controls, and conditions of a problem.

FRUSTRATION — Experience of emotional tension from being blocked in motive satisfaction or goal-directed activity.

FRUSTRATION TOLERANCE — Ability to stand blocked motives without loss of efficiency or disorganization of behavior.

FUNCTIONAL — Pertaining to knowledge and skills learned in situations in which they are needed and used, and which are readily available for use in meaningful applications.

GALVANIC SKIN RESPONSE — Electrical reactions on the skin detected by a sensitive galvanometer, which vary with the individual's emotional activity.

GENERALIZATION — Application in different specific situations of a general concept or principle derived from various specific observations or experiments.

GESTALT — A structure of configurations or integrated patterns of elements which possess characteristics beyond those inherent in the elements; the system of psychology which emphasizes the unique properties of wholes and is critical of attempts to understand them by analyzing them into parts, and which considers the achievement of insights the central feature of learning.

GIFTED CHILDREN — Usually, the highest 1 or 2 per cent of the population according to intelligence, having IQs of over 130 or 140; also, children with special talents in specific fields, such as art, music, or mathematics.

GOAL-DIRECTED — Referring to problem-solving behavior guided by tentative concepts of how the goal striven for is to be attained; oriented toward the goal in learning.

GRADE EQUIVALENTS — The grade levels which correspond to the mean scores on standardized tests of representative children at each grade level at each month throughout the usual nine-month school year. For example, a grade equivalent of

4.2 means achievement equal to the average of children in the second month of the fourth grade.

GRADE PLACEMENT (OF CURRICULUM CONTENT) — The grade level in which curriculum content is located to match the maturity and experience background of children.

HETEROGENEITY — Differences in a trait or traits among the members of a population. For example, an unselected class of children are classified heterogeneously with respect to intelligence.

HIERARCHICAL — Referring to an ordered arrangement of processes or things according to degree of importance or dominance.

HOMEOSTATIC NEEDS — Physiological processes which regulate and maintain optimum body states with respect to such conditions as temperature, air, sugar, salt, and many other body conditions.

HOMOGENEOUS — Uniform; similar. For example, school children grouped homogeneously fall within a relatively narrow range of intelligence.

HYPERTENSION — Excessive tension; overactivity; inclination to uncontrollable, restless activity.

HYPOTHESIS — A tentatively predicted solution to a problem; a hunch; a provisional assumption; a supposition.

HYPOTHESIS-GUIDED — Pertaining to responses guided or goal-directed by tentative assumptions as to outcomes.

HYPOTHESIZE — To formulate a hypothesis; to predict a result on the basis of some assumption or inferred relationship between conditions or events.

HYSTERIC — Unconsciously simulating some disability or weakness which excuses one from meeting an ego-threatening challenge.

IDENTICAL ELEMENTS — The specific elements into which larger patterns of behavior can be analyzed. Patterns of behavior are considered to be alike in so far as they have identical elements in common.

IMPLICIT — Not directly given or observable; only implied. Thought processes are implicit, inferred from outcomes or from other behavior.

IMPULSE — A tendency to motive-satisfying action.

INCENTIVE — The object, goal, or situation which an individual has learned will satisfy a motive; as, food is an incentive for a person motivated by hunger.

INCIDENTAL PRACTICE — Practice of a skill only as it is needed in carrying on some other related activity, such as learning spelling from reading and writing.

INCIPIENT — Commencing; beginning; not yet fully developed.

INCREMENTS — Gains; increases.

INDIVIDUAL DIFFERENCE — Deviation of one individual from another or from the average.

INDIVIDUALIZED INSTRUCTION — Teaching adjusted to each child's abilities, interests, and needs.

INDUCTIVE — Generalizing; discovering from varied experience a common feature or principle, such as discovering that "band," "land," and "sand" are alike except for the initial consonant.

INFLECT (the form of words) — To change or vary the form of a word to indicate number, tense, person, etc.

INHERENT — Belonging to an object or process as an integral part of it.

INITIAL — First in a series.

INNATE — Inborn; inherited.

INSIGHT — Understanding; seeing through a problem, so that the organization and interrelations of the significant parts are comprehended.

INTEGRATION — A combination of parts organized to achieve a unified, coherent whole.

INTELLECTUAL EFFICIENCY — The quality of an individual's work methods and problem-solving approach; refers to the efficiency with which the individual uses his intelligence rather than to his intellectual capacity.

INTELLIGENCE — General capacity for learning and problem solving; more specifically, capacity for comprehending and dealing effectively with symbols in abstract relationships.

INTEREST — A conditioned response of pleasure or satisfaction which accompanies intellectual consideration of some thing or idea, or participation in some activity.

INTERMEDIATE PERIOD — The school years from grade 4 through grade 6.

INTERPERSONAL RELATIONS — Relations between people.

INTERPOLATED — Inserted or placed between other parts or events.

INTERVENING — Occurring in time between other events; sometimes applied to the inferred events of the central nervous system which occur between stimulation and response.

INTRA — Within. For example, intraindividual differences are trait variations within the individual; intragroup refers to differences within rather than between groups; and intraclass grouping is subdivision into small groups within a class.

INTRINSIC — Inherent; belonging. Intrinsic interest, for example, is motive satisfaction in an activity itself, apart from ulterior or extrinsic rewards.

INVENTORIED — Listed, itemized, or summed, as objects, events, or personal traits.

INVOLUNTARY — Without intent, conscious purpose, or control.

IQ (INTELLIGENCE QUOTIENT) — The ratio of a child's mental age to his chronological age, indicative of his rate of mental development and relative brightness $(IQ = MA/CA)$.

ISOLATE — In a sociogram, an individual who is not chosen by any member of his group.

JOB ANALYSIS — Analysis of a learning process or problem-solving approach to find the most efficient mode of attack.

KINESTHETIC — Referring to self-perception of movement from senses in the muscles, tendons, and joints.

LEARNING CURVE — A graphic representation of progress from successive practice trials.

MALADJUSTMENT — Poor adjustment; lack of harmony with one's environment, especially in respect to interpersonal relations; failure to achieve personal and social efficiency and happiness.

MANUSCRIPT WRITING — Letters in words written separately as in print, as contrasted with cursive writing, in which the letters in a word are joined.

MASSED PRACTICE — All the practice required for mastering a skill concentrated in one long practice period, or into a few relatively long practice periods.

MATURATION — Development resulting from growth of the nervous system and other biological structures upon which capacity for increasingly complex learning and performance are dependent.

MEAN — The measure of the central tendency of a distribution of scores, obtained by summing the scores and dividing by the total number; the point in the distribution at which the sums of the deviations above and below it are equal.

MEASUREMENT — Determination on a quantitative scale by measuring the amount, quality, or efficiency of performance, or the quality of results.

MEDIA — The substances on which something is registered, or the processes through which something is accomplished.

MEDIAN — The measure of the central tendency in a distribution of scores representing the point above and below which there are equal numbers of scores.

MEDIATING — Going between; connecting; establishing a relation between things or events.

MENTAL AGE — An index of mental maturity. The mental age unit score on a developmental-intelligence scale, which is assigned as equivalent to the mean score of representative children at each age for which the scale is standardized. For example, if an eight-year-old should earn the mean score of representative ten-year-olds, he would be assigned a mental age of 10.

MENTAL HEALTH — Personally and socially efficient and satisfying adjustment; more positively, constructive and satisfying use of the individual's resources and talents.

MENTALLY RETARDED CHILDREN — Children whose mental growth is so slow that they are significantly handicapped in school progress. Mentally retarded children requiring "special-class" instruction range in IQ from 50 to 70 or 75.

METABOLIC — Pertaining to the biological processes of building up and destroying protoplasm incidental to growing and deteriorating and to assimilating and discharging energy.

METAMORPHOSIS — Change or transformation of form or structure.

MOBILIZED — Activated, assembled, or energized, as resources readied for use.

MODES OF ATTACK — The specific approaches to or methods of finding solutions to problems and learning tasks.

MOTIVE — An internal condition of the individual which arouses, sustains, directs, determines the intensity of effort, as well as defining the consequences of goal-directed behavior; roughly synonymous with "drive," "need," "desire," and "aspiration."

MOTIVE-SATISFYING — Providing satisfaction of motives; rewarding.

MOTOR SKILLS — Skills involving body movements and manipulation of body parts.

NARCISSISTIC — Concerned with personal self-gratifications; self-centered.

NEGATIVE — Opposite to "positive"; backward rather than forward; unfavorable rather than favorable.

NEGATIVE TRANSFER — An inappropriate generalization or incorrect application of prior learning, such as spelling "recite" with an *s* instead of a *c*.

NEGATIVISM — Persistent resistance toward complying with requests and directions of other people, especially of parents and teachers.

NEUROTIC — Emotionally maladjusted; characterized by personally and socially ineffective reactions to frustration.

NORM — The mean or median scores of representative populations on standardized tests, by comparison with which individual test scores can be interpreted.

NUANCE — A fine, precise difference or gradation in a color, form, sound, etc.

OBJECTIVE TEST QUESTIONS — Test items for which answers are indicated simply by a word or number, or by + or − for "true" or "false."

OVERINTELLECTUALIZING — Avoidance of dealing directly with problems by excessive talking about them; compensating for feeling inferior by showing off with superficial knowledge.

OVERLEARNING — Practicing memorized content or a skill beyond the point of initial mastery.

OVERT — Apparent; manifest; observable.

PARENT-TEACHER CONFERENCE — An interview between a parent and teacher of a child in which each contributes information about the child from his unique sources, resulting in a cooperative plan for desirable experiences for the child.

PARTICIPATION CHART — A chart expressing the quantity and quality of each individual's contributions to a group discussion.

PATTERN OF ABILITIES — The variation among an individual's different abilities, such as relatively little competence in verbal reasoning, average in drawing ability, and high in ability to assemble mechanical gadgets.

PERCEIVE — To interpret or comprehend through the senses a stimulus object or process.

PERCENTILE SCORES — Test scores, arranged from zero to 100, in which any score indicates the percentage of individuals in the distribution below this score.

PERCEPT — Awareness, attachment of meaning to, or interpretation of a stimulus object.

PERCEPTION OF EFFECTS — A process of checking goal-directed, provisional trials to ascertain if the performance has been correct or incorrect or to determine how nearly the goal has been attained.

PEER — An equal. Peer groups or peer friendships refer to a child's associates of his own age.

PERFORMANCE SCALE (INTELLIGENCE PERFORMANCE SCALE) — An intelligence scale comprised largely of nonlanguage items, such as assembling picture puzzles or making designs with blocks.

PERFORMANCE TEST — A test for measuring overt behavior, skill, or proficiency directly, rather than inferring proficiency of performance from measures of knowledge.

PERFUNCTORY — Done indifferently, mechanically, carelessly, or without care or close attention.

PERMISSIVENESS — That attribute of a secure teacher-child or parent-child relationship by which the child feels free to express both negative and positive feelings without guilt or expectation of criticism.

PERSEVERATION — Persistence in naively giving as a solution to a new problem a solution found acceptable in a previous problem, rather than attacking a new problem by creative problem solving.

PHANTASY — Achievement in imagination only of goals about which the individual often feels frustrated in actual life.

PHENOMENON — An observable, recognizable experience.

PHONICS — A procedure for learning to read or spell in which words are systematically analyzed and then pronounced as a combination of sound (phonetic) elements.

PHONOGRAM — A phonetic combination of letters representative of a word, syllable, or single speech sound, such as *am*, *ane*, or *ee*.

PICTORIAL REPRESENTATION — Representation by drawing a picture of a visually conceived object, idea, or feeling.

PLATEAU — A flat segment in a learning or maturation curve indicating a temporary period of no apparent progress.

PLAY THERAPY — Treatment of a child's emotional and social maladjustment in which the child comes to express himself freely in play and to work through his problems with an accepting, permissive, understanding, and friendly therapist.

POTENTIALITIES — Talents, proficiencies, and other constructive or creative traits whose emergence, though not yet manifest, are possible with maturation, education, and other opportunities.

PRACTICE — Repeated goal-directed efforts to improve performance of learning tasks.

PRAGMATIC — Judging a process in terms of practical values, consequences, or outcomes.

PREADOLESCENCE — An approximate two-year period just prior to attainment of sexual maturity in which growth is especially rapid and often uneven.

PREPOTENT — Referring to a strongly motivated response which predominates or wins expression in competition with other responses.

PRIMARY MENTAL ABILITIES — Relatively independent, differentiated abilities, such as verbal reasoning, facility with numbers, speed of perception, etc.

PRIMARY PERIOD — The school years from kindergarten through grade 3.

PRINCIPLE — A comprehensive generalization, law, or rule applicable to a class or variety of specific situations.

PROACTIVE INHIBITION — The intrusion of earlier learned content to interfere with accurate recall of later learned content.

PROBLEM SOLVING — Adjustment to a situation by learning, through trial-and-error efforts, new modes of response.

PROFICIENCY — Acquired or learned skill, understanding, or expertness in some performance.

PROFILE — A graphic representation of the variations in comparable scores of a single person on tests of different abilities or areas of achievement.

PROVISIONAL TRIAL — A method of testing a tentative hypothesis by trying it; a "try-and-see" attitude toward goal-directed learning trials.

QUASIGENERAL — Seemingly general; approaching generality.

QUESTIONNAIRE — A set of questions on some topic or aspect of personality for gathering information or opinions from a group of individuals.

RATING SCALE — An appraisal device in which a rater is guided in judging the degree to which an individual exhibits certain defined traits, such as "work habits," which may range from "very effective" to "very ineffective."

RATIONALIZING — Defending oneself by irrational excuse making; finding "good" reasons for guilt-producing actions.

READINESS FOR LEARNING — Sufficient mental and experience maturity for successfully beginning or taking a "next step" in some learning activity.

RECIPROCAL — Mutual; interacting; complementary.

RECRIMINATION — Counter-blaming; accusing an accuser.

REFRACTION — The deflection from a straight path of a ray of light as it passes from one medium into another, as from air into water.

REGRESSION — A return or reversion to a simpler and developmentally earlier level of behavior when frustrated or threatened with failure on a more mature level.

REINFORCEMENT — The reward or motive satisfaction attending a learned response.

REJECTION — Condition of being not wanted, avoided, disliked, or denied acceptance in social relationships.

RELIABILITY — The degree to which measuring instruments yield self-consistent scores on repeated measurements, usually indicated by intercorrelations between scores on different forms, parts, or repeated applications of the same test.

REMEDIAL TEACHING — Teaching directed toward overcoming diagnosed, specific learning difficulties.

REMINISCENCE — A tendency to recall, with the passage of time, more rather than less of something memorized.

REPRESSION — A defense mechanism of unconsciously keeping out of mind or inhibiting anxiety- and guilt-provoking impulses and ideas.

RESPONSE — A reaction such as doing something, talking, thinking, or feeling. The reaction or act may result from external or internal stimulation, or be a product of central-nervous-system activity.

RESPONSE SETS — Variable attitudes which, as an uncontrolled factor, cause individuals to differ in their performances in learning, problem solving, and test taking—such as deciding on an arithmetic test either to make sure every answer is correct or to do the problems as quickly as possible.

RETARDATION — Failure to keep pace in mental growth or in school achievement with one's agemates.

RETENTION — As used here, remembering.

RETROACTIVE INHIBITION — The interaction and interference of later learned content or behavior patterns with accurate recall of earlier learned material.

SCHEMATA — An outline, formulation, or classification for interpreting experience.

SELF-ACTUALIZATION — Development of one's resources and talents; use of one's potentialities for personal satisfaction and constructive social contributions.

SELF-CONCEPT — An individual's awareness and appraisal of himself—his physique, abilities, social roles, and worth.

SELF-DEFEATING — Referring to anxiety-motivated behavior which handicaps the individual in attaining more important motive satisfactions and goals, such as being overcritical of other people whose esteem is needed, or not trying at all because of fear of failing.

SELF-DISCOVERY (in learning) — Learning concepts, improved skills, or solutions from one's self-initiated (or teacher-encouraged) trial-and-error, exploratory, and problem-solving efforts.

SELF-ENHANCEMENT — An increment to self-evaluation as compared to the previous status of the self-concept, from development or more constructive use of the individual's talents and resources.

SELF-IDENTIFICATION — Projection of oneself into the role of another person or persons; playing as if one were the other (often loved and admired) person.

SELF-INVENTORIES — Classified lists of questions, answers to which are indicative of relative status in areas of interest, personality traits, attitudes, or emotional and social adjustment.

SELF-PERSPECTIVE — An adequate, unambiguous, and sufficiently distant view of oneself.

SELF-REALIZATION — (See SELF-ACTUALIZATION.)

SELF-RECITATION — A memorizing and study technique in which the learner actively and creatively strives for independent performance of the task in advance of complete mastery (contrasted with passive reading and rereading, or "absorption," of the content to be learned).

SEPARATE-SUBJECT TEST — A test designed to measure achievement in a single subject, such as reading or arithmetic.

SET (as in "set to learn") — A preparatory, goal-directed orientation or expectation.

SHADING (in drawing) — Representing depth, roundness, or differences in elevations of objects by variations in lightness and darkness.

SIBLING — A brother or a sister.

SIGHT VOCABULARY — Words immediately recognized in reading.

SOCIALIZATION — The social learning processes by which a child acquires his social techniques, understandings, personal and social attitudes, and social roles for relating himself to other people.

SOCIALIZED PROJECTS — Curriculum activities characterized by considerable pupil initiative, interaction, and cooperation.

SOCIOGRAM — A diagrammatic representation of the friendship or other interpersonal relationships among the members of a group.

SOCIOMETRIC — Measuring interpersonal relations, such as the pattern of friendship relationships within a group of school children.

SPECIAL CLASS — A class with a modified curriculum and methods of teaching, adapted especially to the needs of mentally retarded children whose IQs usually range from 50 to 70 or 75.

SPLIT-HALF RELIABILITY — An estimate of the reliability of a whole test from the correlation between the sums of scores on two separate halves of it—usually on the odd- and even-numbered items summed separately.

SPURIOUS — Deceptively distorted. A correlation between intelligence and achievement, for example, may be spuriously high because of irrelevant factors, such as marked age differences in the population on which the correlation is based.

STANDARD DEVIATION (SD, σ) — A measure of the spread or deviations of scores about the mean of a distribution. It is the root of the average of the sum of the squared deviations. In a normal distribution about two-thirds of the cases fall within the limits of one SD above or below the mean.

STANDARD ERROR OF MEASUREMENT — The extent to which test scores may be expected to vary on retests because of some unreliability of the measuring instrument. Approximately two-thirds of retested children whose initial IQs are all 100, for example, may be expected to vary between 95 and 105.

STANDARDIZATION — The establishment of uniform methods of administering, scoring, and interpreting tests, and the collection of representative norms with which individual scores can be compared for interpretation.

STANDARD SCORE — A derived score in standard-deviation units for making scores from different tests comparable. The standard deviations from different tests may be arbitrarily set equal to any constant value, such as 1, 10, or 20; and in terms of this value, the deviation of an individual's scores from the mean (also arbitrarily set at 0, 50, or 100) may be expressed.

STATISTICAL SIGNIFICANCE — Referring to estimates of the probability that limited experimental results can be trusted to be representative of *general* or entire populations. (See, for example, *t* RATIO or CRITICAL RATIO.)

STEREOTYPED — Mechanically, repetitively executed, without variation or originality.

STIMULUS — Any object, event, or energy change either outside or within the individual which excites a response.

STIMULUS-RESPONSE PATTERN — A connection between a given stimulus and a given response such that the first consistently elicits the second.

STRATIFIED SAMPLE — A population sampled according to a criterion, such as socioeconomic levels.

STRUCTURAL ANALYSIS (of words) — The analysis of words into meaning and pronunciation elements, such as finding the prefix, root, and suffix in "re-fill-ing."

STRUCTURE — The pattern, arrangement, or organization of the parts in a whole; used in a figurative sense when referring to mental processes.

STRUCTURED — Organized; configured; arranged in a pattern.

SUBJECTIVE — Dependent on an individual's internal processes; not open to observation or verification by other people.

SUBSTRATE — An underlying substance or structure, as the organic substrate of a trace; the nervous system in which experience is registered.

SURVEY TESTS OF ACHIEVEMENT — Tests which measure and yield comparable scores for several curriculum areas, such as reading, language, arithmetic, social studies, and science.

SYLLABICATION — Division of words into syllables to aid in reading or spelling.

SYMBOL — A word, number, diagram, or mental process which represents something else from an individual's experience, such as a picture or image which may stand for an object or a concept.

SYMBOLIC ACTIVITIES — Vicarious activities carried on in terms of symbols, such as remembering, reasoning, or imagining.

SYMPATHETICISM — A defense for feelings of inadequacy involving excessive appeal to sympathy; excusing independent effort on the basis of claimed handicaps.

SYNDROME — A set or combination of signs or symptoms which characteristically occur together and as a pattern are indicative of a certain illness or condition.

SYNTHESIZING — Combining or putting together elements or components into an integrated whole.

SYSTEMATIC PRACTICE — Periodically scheduled, teacher-guided, goal-directed practice.

SYSTEMATIC TEACHER-GUIDANCE — A method of teaching children a uniform, specific, and efficient way of performing a learning task.

TABOO — Strongly disapproved; forbidden by tradition or social usage.

TEACHER-GUIDANCE — Guidance of children in approaching learning problems by explaining, demonstrating, correcting provisional trials, or leading questions and arrangements for self-discovery experiences.

TELESCOPED — Shortened and simplified by combining discrete elements so as to create a smoothly functioning pattern.

THERAPEUTIC — Curative; tending to alleviate illness or maladjustment.

THERAPY — Treatment of an illness; psychological treatment of emotional and social maladjustment, often involving counseling.

TRACE (MEMORY TRACE) — A hypothetical residual pattern left in the nervous system as a result of learning or experience, and because of which behavior is subsequently altered.

TRAIT — A differentiated and relatively enduring characteristic of personality, such as verbal reasoning ability, interest in art, emotional control, or love for other people, which can be appraised in degree and compared from one individual to another.

TRANSFER OF TRAINING — The application to new learning tasks or problems of concepts, skills, or principles learned previously in different situations.

t RATIO — The ratio of an obtained experimental difference on some measure to the variations to be expected from errors of sampling and measurement. For small samples, the "t" value needs to exceed 1.96 and 2.58 to be significant at the 5 and 1 per cent levels, respectively.

TRIAL — One of a series of attempts to solve a problem or to improve an individual's skill by learning.

TRIAL-AND-ERROR — Referring to the various efforts or alternative attempts to find a solution in problem-solving learning tasks.

TRIDIMENSIONALITY — Condition of appearing to have three dimensions in space.

TUITION — Instruction or teacher-guidance; explanations, demonstrations, and other ways of showing a learner how to approach his task.

TWO-FACTOR THEORY — A comprehensive theory integrating the theories of learning by conditioning and learning by trial-and-error problem solving.

UNIFIED CURRICULUM — As contrasted with a curriculum of separate, unrelated subjects, the organization of several subjects and other curriculum experiences around a central unifying idea, such as "pioneer life in the West," which may involve social studies, reading, language, arithmetic, art, and other phases of the curriculum.

UNIFYING — Combining according to common or complementary features otherwise diverse elements into an organized whole.

UNIT — A segment of the curriculum in which a subject or several subjects are related in a functional way to children's interests in their own activities or in their community. An example might be "Where we get our food."

UNSELECTED — A representative, randomly chosen sample of a population, as unselected children.

VALIDITY — The extent to which a test actually measures the traits for which it was designed; usually indicated by correlations between scores on the test and other accepted criteria of validity, such as school achievement in the case of intelligence tests.

VARIATIONS — Individual differences in traits, both interindividual and intraindividual.

VERBALIZATION — Expression of an idea orally.

VERBAL SCALE (VERBAL INTELLIGENCE SCALE) — An intelligence scale comprised largely of language items, such as vocabulary, range of information, reasoning with language symbols, etc.

VICARIOUS — Substituting for; taking the place of, as substituting imagination for real action.

WORD IDENTIFICATION — The process in reading of determining the meaning of an unfamiliar word—from the context, by pronouncing it phonetically, from visual analysis, or from other clues.

WORD RECOGNITION — The process in reading of recognizing a word for which the pronunciation and meaning have been previously identified.

WORK SAMPLE — A test of an individual's aptitude or proficiency for learning or work in some area made by appraising an actual sample of performance in the area, as in appraising from a sample of a child's drawing or handwriting proficiency.

Name Index

Subject Index